# The Subtlety of Emotions

# The Subtlety of Emotions

*Aaron Ben-Ze'ev*

A Bradford Book
The MIT Press
Cambridge, Massachusetts
London, England

This book was set in Palatino by Best-set Typesetter Ltd., Hong Kong.

Printed and bound in the United States of America.

Library of Congress Cataloging-in-Publication Data

Ben-Ze'ev, Aaron.

    The subtlety of emotions / Aaron Ben-Ze'ev.

      p.  cm.

    "A Bradford book."

    Includes bibliographical references and index.

    ISBN 0-262-02463-2 (alk. paper)

    1. Emotions.  2. Affect (Psychology)  3. Mood (Psychology)

  I. Title.

  BF531.B43  2000

  152.4—dc21                 99-23903

                                CIP

*This book is dedicated to*
*my parents, Haika and Israel;*
*my brothers, Yehuda and Avinoam;*
*my wife, Ruth;*
*and my sons, Dean and Adam.*

# Contents

# Acknowledgments

The study of emotions has been at the center of my research over the last decade. During this time, I have met with many people who have helped to shape my views on emotions: these include my colleagues, students, and many others. I cannot, of course, mention everyone, but I am deeply grateful to all those who have contributed to the development of my perspectives.

The University of Haifa has always been a warm and supportive home for me. Although it is hard to feel grateful to an institution such as a university (as I indicate in this book, gratitude, like other emotions, is typically directed at people), I want to thank the many people at the University of Haifa who are responsible for the supportive atmosphere which I have enjoyed while writing this book.

A book that comes straight from the heart owes many emotional debts to those people who have shaped my heart. Since I am not able to mention all of them, I will focus on the most important ones. These include my late mother, Haika, and my father, Israel; more than any others, both are responsible for my emotional education. This education was transmitted not through learned lectures but through their example of sensitive moral behavior. My late brother, Yehuda, who was killed during the Six-Day War, and my brother Avinoam, have also deeply influenced my beliefs and behavior. Their unique moral sensitivity is a moral compass for me. I met my beloved wife, Ruth, after my emotional character had already been shaped; nevertheless, her wisdom and sensitivity have greatly influenced me. My two sons, Dean and Adam, who frequently touch the deepest parts of my heart, have also enriched my understanding of emotions, and I have learned much from them. The time I have spent on my research may be time away from these dear people, but my family has never wavered in their emotional support during the process of writing this book, and I thank them for their understanding.

I would like to thank Glendyr Sacks for the excellent and engaged editorial work she has done. I also thank the people from MIT Press for their wonderful editorial work: Amy Brand, Katherine Almeida, and G. W. Helfrich.

Many of the ideas in this book first took shape in my earlier articles. I wish to thank the following for permission to use materials from these articles. "Why did Psammenitus not pity his son?" *Analysis, 50* (1990), 118–126; "Describing the emotions," *Philosophical Psychology*, 3 (1990), 305–317; "Envy and jealousy," *Canadian Journal of Philosophy*, 20 (1990), 487–516; "Pleasure-in-others'-misfortune," *Iyyun*, 41 (1992), 41–61; "Emotional and moral evaluation," *Metaphilosophy*, 23 (1992), 214–229; "Anger and hate," *Journal of Social Philosophy*, 23 (1992), 85–110; "Envy and inequality," *Journal of Philosophy*, 89 (1992), 551–581; "Another look at pleasure-in-others'-misfortune," *Iyyun*, 42 (1993), 431–440; "You always hurt the one you love," *The Journal of Value Inquiry*, 27 (1993), 487–495; "Envy and pity," *International Philosophical Quarterly*, 30 (1993), 3–19; "The virtue of modesty," *American Philosophical Quarterly*, 33 (1993), 235–246; "The vindication of gossip," in R. Goodman and A. Ben-Ze'ev (Eds.), *Good gossip* (Lawrence: University Press of Kansas, 1994), 11–24; "Typical emotions," in W. O'Donohue and R. Kitchener (Eds.), *Philosophy of psychology* (London: Sage, 1996), 228–243; "Emotional intensity," *Theory and Psychology*, 6 (1996), 509–532; "The intentional and social nature of human emotions: Reconsideration of the distinction between basic and non-basic emotions," *Journal for the Theory of Social Behaviour*, 26 (1996), 81–94 (written with Keith Oatley); "Appraisal theories of emotions," *Journal of Philosophical Research*, 22 (1997), 129–143; "Romantic love and sexual attraction," *Philosophia*, 25 (1997), 3–32; "Emotions and morality," *The Journal of Value Inquiry*, 31 (1997), 195–212; "The affective realm," *New Ideas in Psychology*, 15 (1997), 247–259.

# Introduction

When God measures a person he puts the tape around his heart, not his head.
—Unknown

Emotions play a central role in our lives and are of interest to everyone. Every-day conversation, beginning in the third year of life, is full of emotion-laden language. Talking to laypeople about emotions is instructive: ordinary people are highly curious and knowledgeable about emotional phenomena. Common sense, poems, novels, movies, historical accounts, psychological studies, and philosophical discussions supply us with a host of information about emotions. Love, for instance, is most widely discussed. The vast majority of popular music themes, movies, and other art forms deal with love. In dictionaries of quotations, *love* is one of the most frequently cited words.[1]

Although emotions punctuate almost all the significant events in our lives, the nature, causes, and consequences of the emotions are among the least understood aspects of human experience. It is easier to express emotions than to describe them and harder, again, to analyze them. Despite their apparent familiarity, emotions are an extremely subtle and complex topic, one that has been neglected by many social scientists and philosophers.[2] It is, perhaps, the complexity of emotions that has deterred many social scientists from dealing with this subject. It is not easy to have precise quantitative measures of various emotional features. Despite the growing scientific interest in the study of emotions, robust empirical findings still cover only a small portion of emotional phenomena and our intuitive knowledge of most emotional phenomena is not yet backed by scientific findings. The study of emotions has not been a central issue in philosophical discussions, possibly because of the practical and personal nature of emotions, which differs from the theoretical and general nature of many philosophical discussions. No wonder, then, that the best descriptions of emotions have been provided so far by artists rather than psychologists or philosophers.

Further progress in understanding emotions requires an interdisciplinary approach that combines a philosophical perspective with other types of scientific research (especially psychology), as well as with insights from other sources, such as folk wisdom and art.

The complexity of emotions and the current level of scientific knowledge of emotions have direct implications for the nature of the discussions in this book. Although the claims presented here are often supported by reference to empirical research, others are nevertheless speculative, based mainly on introspection, folk wisdom, and casual observation—offered for want of more solid knowledge and for the sake of a fuller picture. Discussing all sorts of claims, without limiting ourselves to those confirmed by empirical studies, paves the way for a better and more comprehensive understanding of emotions.

The topic of the emotions, René Descartes said, does not seem to be one of the more difficult to investigate since everyone feels emotions and so has no need to look elsewhere for observations to establish their nature. Nevertheless, previous writings about this topic were so confused that Descartes decided not to rely on them and to write as if he were examining a topic that no one had dealt with before.[3] I agree that people are knowledgeable about emotions; indeed, in writing this book I have benefited from various commonsense sources, ranging from conversations with laypeople, listening to popular songs, and reading and watching various films or programs which were not created for the purpose of investigating or understanding the emotions. Accordingly, I often refer to such everyday sources throughout the book. Such references are not intended to provide any conclusive proof for the suggested arguments. They are important, however, as an indication of the way people think about emotions. And even if such lay beliefs are often imprecise or partly mistaken, they do tell us something about emotions and the way we treat them. Thus, when a popular love song declares that "you are everything and everything is you," this should not be understood to imply that in romantic love only the beloved carries emotional significance. This is, no doubt, lyric exaggeration. However, such exaggeration expresses the focus (though not the exclusive focus) typical of love; it also indicates a prevailing myth in our culture about romantic love. Revealing the focus and the myth helps us to understand better the emotion we call romantic love.

When writing about other issues relating to the philosophy of mind, such as perception, memory, and the mind-body problem, similar everyday resources were not available. But the difficulties in studying emotions begin when we try to organize our commonsense knowledge into a comprehensive conceptual framework. The enormous complexity and diversity of emotions make such a construction quite difficult. This is, of course, no reason for not trying to provide such a framework, but it imposes constraints on the optimal way of doing so.

Unlike Descartes, who claimed that he was going to write about emotions as if no one had approached the subject before, my own discussion has gained a great deal from earlier writings. In this regard I adopt the attitude expressed by the German psychologist Carl Stumpf, who claimed that being influenced by previous thinkers may reduce the surprise value of our own theory, but absolute originality in matters that are open to introspection at all times may be a recommendation of the author's inventiveness, but not of his or her case.[4] It is beyond the scope of this book to discuss previous writings critically. Such a discussion, although important in itself, may distract from the goal of presenting a comprehensive framework for the understanding of emotions. I refer to these writings when I believe that such a reference can throw light on some aspect under discussion or when they support my theses or present an interesting alternative to them.

The book is divided into two major parts: the first presents an overall conceptual framework for understanding emotions, the second discusses individual emotions toward others. Part I provides an answer to the question: "What is an emotion?" It does so by analyzing the typical characteristics and components of emotions, distinguishing emotions from related affective phenomena, classifying the emotions, and discussing major relevant issues such as emotional intensity, functionality and rationality, emotions and imagination, regulating the emotions, and emotions and morality. The principal emotions discussed in part II are envy, jealousy, pity, compassion, pleasure-in-others'-misfortune, anger, hate, disgust, love, sexual desire, happiness, sadness, pride, regret, pridefulness and shame.

# Part I

# The Nature of Emotions

Say I'm weary, say I'm sad,
Say that health and wealth have miss'd me,
Say I'm growing old, but add,
Jenny kiss'd me.
—Leigh Hunt

# Chapter 1

## The Complexity of Emotions

For every complex problem, there is a solution that is simple, neat, and wrong.
—H. L. Mencken

Emotions are highly complex and subtle phenomena whose explanation requires careful and systematic analysis of their multiple characteristics and components. Before embarking on such a task, I would like to address the reasons for this complexity of emotions and to explain accordingly the methods I use when analyzing them.

### Reasons for the Complexity of Emotions

If we only wanted to be happy it would be easy; but we want to be happier than other people, which is almost always difficult, since we think them happier than they are.
—Montesquieu

The major reason for the complexity of emotions is their *great sensitivity to personal and contextual circumstances*. The manner in which we conceive of a certain context or a certain person plays a crucial role in the generation of our emotions. The emotional susceptibility to contextual and personal attributes makes it difficult to define the characteristics common to all emotions; hence, no single essence is necessary and sufficient for all emotions. Classic definitions in terms of sufficient and necessary conditions are not very useful in the study of emotions.

The sensitivity of emotions to personal and contextual circumstances is nicely illustrated by the example of an artist's model who is suddenly made to feel ashamed of her nudity because she realizes that the artist for whom she is posing no longer regards her as a mere model but is thinking of her as a woman. The shift in the artist's attitude has changed from an initially detached, impersonal relationship into a close, personal one. Since only the latter relationship is typical of emotions, the model begins to feel shame at her nakedness.[1] Another example in kind would be that of a man whose wife is a top executive in a large company and who does not normally experience jealousy. One day he reads in the newspaper about another female top executive who had an affair with her employee and suddenly he begins to feel jealous. In both examples, emotions are generated without apparent difference in "objective" circumstances; the change is in one's subjective evaluation of the other's subjective attitude.

In other cases, an emotion may be generated in one situation but not generated in another situation that is identical to the first apart from one aspect: it is not experienced for the first time. Macbeth is horrified the first time he commits murder, but grows increasingly immune to emotional response in his subsequent murders. Similarly, a prostitute may feel shame with her first client, but not with her client number five thousand two hundred two. After participating in an orgy and being invited back the very next night, Voltaire declined with the following explanation: "Once, a philosopher, twice, a pervert!"

Looking simply at the "objective" nature of the situation is not sufficient for predicting the generation of emotions. Such prediction is much more complex and should refer to other personal and contextual features.

Another example of the sensitivity of emotions to personal and contextual circumstances is the pathological case, reported in the psychological literature, of a woman whose prerequisite for falling in love with a man is that he be a widower still in mourning for his deceased wife. Limitations of this kind are, in varying degree, characteristic of emotions in normal cases as well. Thus, something that normally arouses curiosity may inspire fear in an unfamiliar context. Similarly, a dollar attained because of good luck could elicit surprise; a dollar earned by hard work might produce pride; and a dollar received from a friend when in need is likely to beget gratitude.[2]

Other mental capacities are also sensitive to personal and contextual circumstances but not to the extent that emotions are. Seeing my neighbor remains more or less the same in diverse contexts and is fairly, though not entirely, independent of my personality. My memory of and thoughts about this person are also sensitive to contextual and personal circumstances, but not in the way emotions are.

Another major reason for the complexity of emotions is that *they often consist of a cluster of emotions and not merely a single one*. Thus, grief may involve anger, guilt, and shame; guilt may be associated with fear; love may incorporate jealousy, hope, and admiration; and hate may be connected with fear, envy, and contempt. These connections are not accidental; rather they express the fact that the emotional situation is unstable and that our emotions are directed at imaginary and not merely actual situations. Hence, great love and joy are associated with jealousy and fear which stem from the possibility of losing the beloved.

The complexity of emotions is further compounded when we consider that each separate emotion appears in a variety of forms with great differences between them. There are many types of love, sadness, fear, and other emotions; these types express the variety of emotional circumstances. An emotional term usually refers to a highly complex and interactive cluster of emotional states rather than to a single and isolated entity. An emotion involves an ongoing activity in which we are constantly evaluating new information and acting accordingly. Being in love or being angry is not an isolated internal entity; rather, it is a continuous state of the person as a whole. Emotions should not be described as pictures inside our heads, but as ongoing dynamic experiences that spread over time and may be modified during the course of that time.

An emotion has public aspects, expressed in our behavior, as well as private or unique aspects, for example, a certain feeling. Such public aspects of fear as trembling, perspiring, and feeling weak-kneed cannot, of course, be regarded as internal entities. But neither should the private features of the emotions be thus regarded. Private is something restricted to an individual or a group; it is not necessarily something internal to the individual. The existence of emotions, like that of other mental states, is relational: it presupposes the existence of someone who feels the emotion. There is no love without lovers, and no fear without a frightened agent.

In light of the complexity of emotions, everyday language in this regard is not clear either. The characterization of the term "emotion" is disputable and accordingly different lists of emotions have been suggested. It is commonly accepted that fear, anger, and jealousy are emotions, but it is arguable whether surprise, loneliness, or aesthetic experiences are emotions. The everyday broad usage of "emotion" often refers to situations that are actually not at all related to emotional states. For example, the statement "I am afraid I can't give you the job" does not refer to fear. People use "emotion" with different connotations, and the meanings of emotional terms differ from one language to another. Different languages have a different vocabulary for emotions. For instance, many languages make no distinction between "jealousy" and "envy", and have no special word for the emotion termed in German *Schadenfreude* (pleasure-in-others'-misfortune). The linguistic diversity is not accidental but expresses the centrality of emotions in our life and the difficulties inherent in defining emotions. Such diversity makes it difficult to identify and understand emotional phenomena.

## Explaining Emotions

Mistrust the person who finds everything good; the person who finds everything evil; and still more the person who is indifferent to everything.
—Johann Kaspar Lavater

The diversity and complexity of emotional phenomena have led people to doubt the explanatory value of the general concept of emotions.[3] I believe that although the concept of emotions is indeed quite general and diverse, we nevertheless can make plausible generalizations about emotions. This is precisely what I intend to do in this book.

Explaining emotions despite their complexity requires us, however, to adopt certain conceptual tools. Three such tools are the following:

1. prototype categories;
2. various levels of description and various cognitive perspectives;
3. classifying the emotions into general categories.

These conceptual tools are valuable for many, if not most, phenomena. I believe that the combination of all three of them is of particular importance in explaining emotional phenomena. I turn now to a brief description of the relevance of each of these tools in explaining emotions.

*The Prototype Analysis*
Few things are harder to put up with than a good example.
—Mark Twain


A distinction can be made between two major types of cognitive categories: "binary" and "prototypical." *Binary categories* provide a clear criterion that constitutes the sufficient and necessary conditions for membership. It is usually an all-or-nothing category ("love me or leave me," as Elvis Presley said) with two basic attributes: (1) clear-cut boundaries within which the criterion's conditions are met, and (2) an equal degree of membership for all items. There are no varying degrees of membership in this category because meeting the criterion is not a matter of degree; it is either met or not met. War veterans, eligible voters, only children, and pregnant women are examples of binary categories. One cannot be a partial veteran, a semieligible voter, almost an only child, or a little bit pregnant.

Membership in a *prototypical category*, on the other hand, is determined by an item's degree of similarity to the best example in the category: the greater the similarity, the higher the degree of membership. The prototypical category has neither clear-cut boundaries nor an equal degree of membership. Some items are so similar to or so different from the prototype that we have no doubt about their inclusion or exclusion; with other items the degree of similarity makes it difficult or impossible to say for sure whether they belong or not. Many of our everyday categories are prototypical, for example, weapons, clothes, birds, and furniture. Prototypical categories are generally more appropriate to the psychological realm which is complex and has no clear-cut boundaries.[4]

Emotions in general, as well as each particular emotion separately, constitute prototypical categories. Inclusion is determined by *the degree of similarity to the most typical case.* Hence, there is no single essence which is a necessary and sufficient condition for all emotions, and no simple definition of emotions or even of one type of emotion exists. Membership in the general category of emotions, as well as membership in the general category of a particular emotion, is a matter of degree rather than an all-or-nothing affair. Accordingly, each category has a certain internal structure, and no sharp boundary separates members from nonmembers. Thus, the boundaries between romantic love, liking, and friendship are fuzzy, as are those between envy and jealousy. Different phenomena can be reliably ordered from better to poorer examples of the general category of emotions or of categories of particular emotions. The typical aspects of emotional experiences are fully manifest in prototypical examples; in less typical examples, these characteristics occur in a less developed form and some may even be absent.[5]

Within the prototype framework, emotions are analyzed *as if* they were context-free. For example, the characterization of typical envy is supposed to be valid for all instances of envy. Indeed, in psychological experiments when subjects are asked to describe prototypical categories of emotions, they are left to imagine whatever contexts they like. The sensitivity of emotions to a particular context is not to be found in different characterizations of typical envy, each suitable to a different context, but rather in the flexibility of a single characterization of typical envy. Not all instances of envy have all features of typical envy, nor do they possess these features in the same intensity. Each person may have a somewhat different version of typical envy; the membership of the particular instance in the category of envy is determined by its similarity to the typical case. This manner of analysis can provide general characteristics common to the diverse instances of emotions, while preserving their contextual sensitivity.

I would like now to briefly discuss some of the *difficulties* in using the prototype analysis. A major difficulty in this regard is to define clearly the central notion of "typical." There are various senses which are not always compatible with each other.[6] For our purpose, it is important not to confuse descriptive terms, such as "common" and "frequent," with normative terms, such as "typical" and "extreme." In the terminology used here, "common" and "frequent" are descriptive terms, referring to the distribution of different items. Common cases are the most frequent and widespread cases of a certain category. "Typical" and "extreme" are terms referring to the structure of a category. Typical cases are those exhibiting significant characteristics of a category. An instance is typical of a category if it has the essential features that are shared by members of that category and does not have many distinctive features that are not shared by category members.[7] Extreme cases are those having an excessive measure of a property which is by and large diagnostic of the category, but usually appears in a much more moderate form. Generally, typical cases are more common than extreme cases, and common cases are more typical than extreme ones. Common cases are not disproportionate, like extreme cases, but are sometimes not as complex as the typical ones.

Typicality tends to covary with frequency; common instances are generally more typical than unusual instances. A warm and sunny day is both typical and frequent in the summer. Similarly, the typical and common American family has two children. There are, however, circumstances in which typicality is at variance with frequency. This occurs if an attribute is typical of a class when it is highly diagnostic, that is, when the relative frequency of this attribute is much higher in that class than in a relevant reference class. For example, in one experiment most people stated that it is more typical (or, rather, representative) for a Hollywood actress "to be divorced more than four times," than "to vote Democrat." However, most people from another group stated that, among Hollywood actresses, there are more "women who vote Democrat" than "women who are divorced more than four times." Multiple divorce is diagnostic of Hollywood actresses, but having so many divorces is neither typical nor common among them. That X is diagnostic of a category does not mean that an excessive measure of X is diagnostic, typical, or common.[8]

Quite often, extreme cases constitute the public image of the category and are mistakenly *perceived* to be both typical and frequent because, like other abnormalities, they are more noticeable than the typical or the common. Indeed, the media are more interested in unique, abnormal cases than in common, normal ones; only the former are exciting to most people. Take, for example, jealousy. The public image of male jealousy invokes the picture of a husband killing his wife because of her infidelity. Yet it is obvious that murder is neither the common nor the typical behavior found in jealousy. Far less than 0.01% of the U.S. male population commits murder in response to adultery.[9] The typical case of jealousy includes some kind of revenge, or at least a desire for revenge; however, this does not usually take the extreme form of murder. Jealousy encompasses a host of other kinds of more moderate attitudes and activities. The common case of jealousy may not include all components present in typical cases, but includes many of them, and these are not present in a disproportionate amount. Despite the widespread belief that jealousy is a destructive, unacceptable emotion in close relationships, empirical findings indicate that in general, couples both understand and forgive each other's occasional jealousy. Similarly, perceived typical anger is more violent than the actual common and typical anger. Typical cases are often perceived to be more intense than they actually are.[10]

The confusion between extreme, typical, and common cases of a mental category confounds not only the public image of these categories but also the public image of psychologists whose patients represent extreme, pathological cases. Indeed, much of the research on emotions has focused on their extreme manifestations, in particular on depressed individuals.[11] The tendency to confuse extreme with typical attitudes is greater with regard to perceived morally negative attitudes, such as hate, anger, pleasure-in-others'-misfortune, jealousy, gossip, or revenge, than with perceived positive attitudes, such as happiness, gratitude, or friendship. The reason may be that an excess of negative attitudes is more threatening to the individual and society than an excess of positive attitudes; hence, it is more noticeable. Although there are circumstances in which negative attitudes are valuable, their absence in these circumstances is less damaging than the presence of their excessive forms in other circumstances.[12] The confusion between extreme and typical also prevails regarding attitudes whose definition includes a subtle equilibrium between various factors; this equilibrium can easily be distorted, turning the typical attitude into an extreme one. As we shall see, this is particularly true concerning gossip and pleasure-in-others'-misfortune, but it is true of all emotions in general.

A typical case is, then, one that exhibits the significant features of the given emotional category and has but a few distinctive features that are not shared by category members. How can we determine what those significant and distinctive features are? One way is to ask people to describe typical cases. Another way is to discover by conceptual analysis the significant features that are related or unrelated to a certain emotional attitude. The first method is common among psychologists, while the second prevails among philosophers. In this work, I use both methods since I consider them complementary. The description of typical cases by laypersons gives us an initial and broad outline of such cases. This outline should, then, be supplemented by a more precise and detailed analysis discerning some underlying characteristics and relationships. Using both methods may prevent confusing a distorted public image with a typical case; it may also ascertain that typical cases are usually common.

The use of prototypical categories may draw the criticism that there can be no counterexamples to the prototypical characterization, since any such example may be regarded as atypical. It is true that confirmation and falsification of a prototypical category are more complex than those of the ordinary binary (all-or-nothing) category, but so is their characterization. Working with categories which have clear-cut and definite boundaries is easier, but they do not adequately represent reality. Since in reality there are usually no such clear boundaries, working with prototypical categories is often more to the point. In light of the prototypical nature of emotions, we should frequently use terms such as "usually," "typically," and "often" while characterizing emotions. Although employing such terms will make it harder to refute the suggested claims, it is implied by the use of a prototypical category. Various instances of emotions are not as nicely divided and clearly arranged as we would like them to be. The refutation of the suggested characterization is still possible, but it cannot consist of describing one isolated case which seems to be an exception; it would have to show that most phenomena are different from the suggested characterization or that the conceptual analysis is inconsistent.[13]

*Levels of Description*
We don't see things as they are, we see things as we are.
—Anaïs Nin


Any given event may be described by referring to various levels of description. Aristotle argues that anger can be described on two major levels. A scientist may describe anger as a boiling of the blood and the presence of heat around the heart, and a philosopher may describe anger as the desire to retaliate by returning evil for evil.[14] The desire to retaliate cannot be found in the boiling blood, which is, however, a necessary supporting basis for that desire. To explain the desire we have to refer to the evil that was inflicted and not to the boiling blood. We cannot understand the nature of higher-level phenomena—for instance, the emergence of social movements—by merely studying discrete lower-level entities, such as individual persons; nevertheless, understanding the latter may be relevant to understanding the former. A clear distinction between the various levels of descriptions is essential to dealing with complex phenomena in general and with the emotions in particular.

An emotion is a complex phenomenon describable on different levels, for example, physiological, biological, psychological, sociological, or philosophical. The physiological level, for instance, consists of neurotransmitters and autonomic and somatic activities of the nervous system involving changes that are primarily associated with the flow of adrenaline, blood pressure, blood circulation, heart rate, respiration, muscular tension, gastrointestinal activity, bodily temperature, secretions, and facial coloring. On the psychological level, an emotion consists of feeling, cognition, evaluation, and motivation. For example, fear is associated with the feeling of dread, some information about the situation, the evaluation of the situation as dangerous, and the desire to avoid the peril. The philosophical level of description considers issues such as emotions and morality and the rationality of emotions.[15] My discussion focuses on the psychological and philosophical levels. This, of course, does not imply that the other levels are of less importance; it merely means that discussing other levels is beyond the scope of this book.

Although each level of description provides us with a unique cognitive perspective, we can also use several cognitive perspectives within the same level of description. Thus, the psychological and philosophical levels can utilize many nonscientific and nonphilosophical sources. Commonsense knowledge, works of art, and other nonscientific sources are quite useful in understanding emotions. There are no robust scientific findings concerning the explanation of most emotional phenomena and general philosophical discussions may not be relevant. The mixture of sources is therefore not indicative of methodological confusion but rather expresses a firm attitude concerning the value of these sources.

### Systematic Classifications
When women hold off from marrying men, we call it independence. When men hold off from marrying women, we call it fear of commitment.
—Warren Farrell

The complexity of emotions require us to be highly systematic when describing and classifying the emotions—otherwise, we may become lost in this complexity.

Discussions of emotions are often reduced to either a collection of interesting stories about emotions or a general, vague discourse about some essence of emotions. Neither is satisfactory. The former approach ignores general aspects of emotions, leaving us with some interesting trees but no wood. The latter ignores significant particulars, leaving us with vague general formulas and very little knowledge about actual emotional phenomena. What is needed is a systematic search for general patterns throughout the primeval jungle of emotions. One of the challenges of studying emotions is to formulate a comprehensive conceptual framework that can adequately explain the subtlety of emotional phenomena in all their enormous complexity. I hope that this book will provide an adequate explanation of specific emotional phenomena without obscuring the overall general regularity that is typical of the emotional realm.

All approaches to the classification or analysis of emotions strive *to reduce complexity and heterogeneity*. This simplification has been organized in two major ways: (1) all emotions are classified by referring to elements that are not themselves emotions—for instance, aspects of the feeling dimension or intentional components; (2) all emotions are classified by reference to a few simple emotions which are considered to be basic. Although I believe that the first approach is more useful, the second has an explanatory value as well. The use of different types of classification is not problematic as long as the perspective of each classification is distinguished from the others.

In this book I classify and explain in a systematic manner many aspects of the emotional realm; for example, the characteristics and components of emotions, the affective phenomena related to emotions, the types of emotions, the intensity variables, and the ways of regulating emotions. Such a systematic explanation will help us to better understand the complex emotional realm.

## Summary

The truth is rarely pure, and never simple.
—Oscar Wilde


Describing the emotions is a very complex task. Emotions are something people think they can recognize when they see them, yet it is difficult to define them unambiguously. Emotional complexity stems from the fact that emotions are highly sensitive to contextual and personal factors; emotions do not appear in isolation, but in a cluster of emotional attitudes; and the linguistic use of emotional terms is confusing.

In light of this complexity, it is useful to describe emotions by using prototypical categories in which membership is determined by the degree of similarity of an item to the best example in each category. These categories have neither clear-cut boundaries nor is the degree of membership equal. Each emotion can be analyzed on some level of description, for example, physiological, biological, psychological, or sociological. This book concentrates on the philosophical and psychological levels. Another way of dealing with the complexity of emotions is to use various systematic classifications of different emotional aspects and components. Such systematic classifications facilitate the understanding of emotional regularities.

Due to the diverse linguistic usage surrounding the emotions, any discussion of them calls for an explanation of the way the author uses the term "emotion." Since I believe that emotions constitute a prototypical category, it is not necessary to present a precise definition of emotions, but only a characterization of typical cases. Such a characterization, which is presented in the next chapter, may yield an approximation of what an emotion is. Finer distinctions are provided in the following chapters.

# Chapter 2

# What Is an Emotion?

Love me or hate me, but spare me your indifference.
—Libbie Fudim

This chapter provides an initial characterization of typical emotions. It will be suggested that the typical cause of emotions is a perceived significant change in our situation, the typical emotional concern is a comparative concern, and the typical emotional object is a human being. Typical emotions are considered to have a few basic characteristics: instability, great intensity, a partial perspective, and relative brevity.

## The Typical Cause of Emotion: A Perceived Significant Change

Experience is in the fingers and head. The heart is inexperienced.
—Henry David Thoreau

Between two evils, I always pick the one I never tried before.
—Mae West

Emotions typically occur when *we perceive positive or negative significant changes in our personal situation*—or in that of those related to us. A positive or negative significant change is that which significantly interrupts or improves a smoothly flowing situation relevant to our concerns. Like burglar alarms going off when an intruder appears, emotions signal that something needs attention. When no attention is needed, the signaling system can be switched off. We respond to the unusual by paying attention to it. The extraordinary is perceived as significant—it does not permit us to shrug it off and walk away. In contrast, the usual is taken for granted, safe, almost invisible. Emotions are generated when we deviate from the level of stimulation we have experienced for long enough to get accustomed to it. The change, rather than the general level, is of emotional significance. Accordingly, loss of satisfaction does not produce a neutral state, but misery; loss of misery does not produce a neutral state either, but happiness. Hence, continued pleasures wear off; continued hardships lose their poignancy.[1]

The importance of personal changes in generating emotions is evident from many everyday phenomena, as well as scientific findings. People are very excited when facing changes in their lives: the birth of a child, marriage, divorce, entering school for the first time, going to an interview that can significantly alter the course of one's life, and so on. Likewise, almost all young children react with an acute emotion of mild fear for several minutes upon encountering a large group of unfamiliar children. A certain kind of change is also required for happiness. This may explain boredom in marriage and the excitement of love affairs. It may also explain why rich people who seem to have everything are not necessarily happy—after a while they get used to having everything, and only changes make them happy.[2]

There is also a considerable amount of evidence indicating that sexual response to a familiar partner is less intense than to a novel partner. Consequently, frequency of sexual activity with one's partner declines steadily as the relationship lengthens, reaching roughly half the frequency after one year of marriage compared to the first month of marriage, and declining more gradually thereafter. Decline has also been found in cohabiting heterosexual couples and in gay and lesbian couples.[3] This may be a regrettable fact, but nevertheless it expresses the structure of our emotional system.

Baruch Spinoza most strongly emphasizes the importance of changes in our situation for producing emotions. He claims each individual strives to maintain its existence. When we undergo great change, we pass to a greater or lesser perfection, and these changes are expressed in emotions. As we change for the better, we are happy, and for the worse, unhappy.[4]

The *evolutionary rationale* for the important role that changes play in emotions is similar: for survival purposes it is crucial that the organism pay special attention to significant changes which may increase or decrease the chance of survival. Being emotional, which is the opposite of being indifferent, forces the organism to pay such special attention. Responding primarily to changes is a highly economical and efficient way of using limited resources. From an evolutionary point of view, it is advantageous for us to focus our attention on changes rather than on stationary stimuli. Changes indicate that our situation is unstable, and awareness of this is important for survival. When we are accustomed to the change, mental activity decreases, as there is no sense in wasting time and energy on something to which we have already adapted. When we are already familiar with certain items, their mere repetition yields no new information and we can ignore them. Indeed, information theory measures the amount of information content by the extent of change brought about by a given operation. A change includes more information than repetition and as such is more exciting. Repetition reduces excitement and may have a relaxing function; no new activity is required, thereby resulting in an absence of consciousness. This is what people mean when they refer to a state of being "on automatic pilot."

Not only emotions but consciousness in general is strongly activated when the organism is confronted with changes. This is true, for example, of sensory sensitivity. Thus, if we were to suffer all our life from a toothache in a way that no change in our environment could alter the ache, then we would be unaware of it so that, in effect, we would have no pain. Without enough variety, the pleasure system tends to become satiated and our awareness decreases accordingly. We get bored when doing the same thing over and over, even if that activity was initially pleasant. Perceptual awareness is also connected with changes. Under normal conditions, we are unaware of air pressure even though it affects us constantly. We only perceive it when the level of air pressure changes, as when we take off or land in an airplane. The same applies to the visual system. The lack of relational properties, such as motion and change, results in the disappearance of perception. For instance, when a uniform color fills our field of vision, the color vanishes, to be replaced by a dark gray.[5] Higher systems of consciousness, too, such as focusing attention, come into play when a sudden change takes place in our circumstances. We can drive a car without paying particular attention to the sidewalk; however, if a child playing with a ball on the sidewalk should suddenly come into view, we take notice. The sort of consciousness connected with thinking is also activated when the agent is confronted with new problems.

This decrease in awareness may be viewed as constituting a process of *adaptation*. In this process, which expresses the system's return to its homeostatic state, the threshold of awareness keeps rising as long as stimulus intensity remains constant, so that the organism increasingly withdraws its consciousness from more and more events. This is how our awareness decreases when we are driving along a uniform stretch of road. The opposite process is *facilitation*, when the threshold of awareness diminishes and consciousness focuses on an increasing number of events. This occurs when new stimuli are encountered.

The importance of changes to consciousness in general and emotions in particular may be connected to our learning system, which must have a protective schema to prevent it from becoming trapped into endlessly repeating the same activity.[6]

An important difference between the changes associated with consciousness in general and those associated with emotions is that emotional changes are of *highly personal significance*. Our attention may be directed to any type of change, but in order for the change to generate emotions, it must be perceived as having significant implications for us or those related to us. The mere presence of change does not guarantee the generation of emotions. An emotional change is always related to a certain personal frame of reference against which its significance is evaluated. For example, when a certain team wins the championship for the first time, this change generates intense emotions in the team's fans, who consider the change as significant, while other people, who do not perceive the change as important, are left feeling completely indifferent. We feel no emotion in response to change which we perceive as unimportant or unrelated; we simply do not care. Emotions arise only when we care. They express our attitude toward unstable significant objects which are somehow related to us.

The change relevant to the generation of emotions is a *perceived change whose significance is determined by us*. A significant emotional change may involve perception of changes that have actually taken place, or imagined changes. Although the perceived change may be considered as more objective than the imagined change, it is also essentially a subjective change. It is the subject who perceives the change and accordingly considers it more or less significant. A distinction can be made between the (objective) size of the change and its (subjective) significance. We construct a psychological reality in which despite the apparent great "objective" weight of some changes, they may not be emotionally significant and hence are perceived as smaller. Moreover, changes associated with emotions may not merely refer to the subject, but also to those constituting the subject's environment. Again, it is the subject who determines which people belong to this environment. The subject not only determines the significance of the change but also its *scope*.

The significance of the change is determined by factors associated with the event's impact, for example, the event's strength, reality, and relevance, and factors related to the subject's background circumstances, for instance, controllability of the eliciting event, readiness for such an event, and deservingness of it. These factors are the main determinants of emotional intensity and are be discussed in chapter 5. It can be noted that since these factors can be expressed to different degrees, there are no clear-cut boundaries between significant and insignificant events, but there are various degrees of significance. Below a certain degree of perceived significance, the event does not generate an emotional reaction; above a different degree, our reaction will clearly be emotional; in between, the classification is not clear.

So far I have discussed specific changes which generate everyday emotions. In addition to these changes, our affective reactions are related to a more profound type of change connected with our contingent existence. Our possible death is always in the background of our existence: it reminds us of our profound vulnerability. This type of change expresses *our profound vulnerability* and dependence on external factors which we do not control.[7] Certain affective disorders, in particular anxiety and depression, are often related to such existential issues. Emotions themselves are typically concerned with more specific issues; the profound existential issues function as an important background framework influencing our specific emotional reactions. These differences are expressed, for instance, in the difference between the emotion of fear and the more general affective attitude of anguish.

Our ability to face the two types of changes constitutes human sensitivity. Those believing their well-being to be immune to such changes may not be as emotional on an everyday basis. For example, people believing in life after death will probably be less sensitive to death and usually also to specific everyday changes, as they attach less significance to them. Those accepting the inevitability of death are also less sensitive than those dwelling on death or other fundamental existential issues. It is interesting to note that there is an alteration in the emotional sensitivity of people who are faced with a severe threat, a loss, or the prospect of death. Victimizing events often prompt people to reorder their priorities, giving low value to such mundane concerns as housework, petty quarrels, or involvement in other people's trivial problems, and high priority to relationships with relatives, personal projects, or just enjoying life. The latter begin to be perceived as the essence of life.

Emotions may be viewed not merely as an expression of our profound vulnerability but also as *a way to cope* with it. By attaching significance to specific, local changes in our current situation, we ignore, in a way, the more profound type of change underlying our vulnerability; this is a type of self-deception. A certain measure of such self-deception is highly advantageous from an evolutionary point of view, as it enables us to protect our positive self-image and mobilize the required resources for facing daily changes. We deal with such changes as if our profound vulnerability is insignificant. This may seemingly reduce our vulnerability, but it does not significantly change it. The ninety-year-old woman who is enthusiastically studying for her graduate degree in history is enriching her life in a way that seems to reduce the vulnerability of her age, but her basic vulnerability, expressed in the nearness of death, remains unchanged. She is studying as if her near death is a factor which should hardly be considered. Indeed, the fact that in the long run all of us will die does not imply that in the short run we should attach no significance to specific changes. Similarly, a person who is dying from cancer, but is still careful not to waste electricity and goes around the house turning off lights, is behaving as "business as usual," and as if his death is not imminent. This is in accordance with Spinoza's claim that "a free man thinks of nothing less than of death, and his wisdom is a meditation on life, not on death."[8]

Evaluating changes may be done from different perspectives. When looking at the profound change associated with our very existence, namely, death, we may negatively evaluate such a change. In this sense, we normally strive, as Spinoza contends, to persevere in our being.[9] However, specific everyday changes are typically not concerned with profound issues such as the termination of our life, but rather with the personal significance of specific events in our life. From this perspective changes are essential to an exciting and meaningful life. Concerning specific changes, I would disagree with the saying, "Only a wet baby likes change"; rather, I would agree with the saying, "If our days were all alike, then we would have little need to live more than one of them."

The role that changes play in the generation of emotions indicates the dynamic and complex nature of our emotional life. A change is not any event; it is an event which is measured against a complex personal and dynamic framework. The analysis of emotions must take into account this comparative nature.

### The Typical Emotional Concern: A Comparative Personal Concern

Have you ever noticed? Anybody going slower than you is an idiot, and anyone going faster than you is a maniac.
—George Carlin

Emotions occur when a change is appraised as relevant to our personal concerns. Concerns are our short- or long-term dispositions to prefer particular states of the world or of the self. Emotions serve to monitor and safeguard our personal concerns; they give the eliciting event its significance. Emotional meaning is mainly comparative.[10]

The typical emotional concern will be described by referring to the following aspects: the comparative concern; the availability of an alternative; social comparison; and group membership.

### The Comparative Concern
Lots of people know a good thing the minute the other fellow sees it first.
—Job E. Hedges

Nobody goes there anymore; it's too crowded.
—Yogi Berra, declining an invitation to a certain restaurant

Significance, or meaning, is by nature relational; it presupposes *order and relations.* To have meaningful information about something is to apprehend some relations in which it can be found. To know Barbara's personality is to apprehend her relations with her family, friends, enemies, strangers, and so on. Something which is in complete isolation, that is, has no relations whatsoever to anything else, cannot be known. Relations are to meaning as colors are to vision: a necessary condition, but not its whole content. Meaning is closely analogous to a point in space: the meaning of a point is constituted by its relation to other points; its very essence is relational. The set of relations in which something stands constitutes its meaning. Attributing meaning is the setting of bounds and establishing of connections; what does not affect relation has no handle by which the mind can take hold of it.[11]

The relational nature of meaning implies its *comparative nature* as well. Being in a certain relation means not being in a different relation. Understanding something implies grasping, to a certain degree, its alternative. We can understand what love is only if love can be compared to different states. Being in the water all the time makes it hard for the fish to grasp the meaning of water. Likewise, a person who had spent her whole life doing nothing but seeing a single shade of blue, would really never have seen that shade at all. Only on returning to it from a different experience would she say: "Now for the first time I see the color for which I never had eyes before."[12]

Various philosophers have indicated the connection between reasoning and comparison. David Hume, for example, claimed that "all kinds of reasoning consist in nothing but a *comparison*, and a discovery of those relations, either constant or inconstant, which two or more objects bear to each other."[13] I would like to argue that not only intellectual reasoning but also emotions are comparative. The emotional environment contains not only what is, and what will be, experienced but also all that could be, or that one desires to be, experienced; for the emotional system, all such possibilities are posited as simultaneously there and are compared with each other.[14] However, whereas intellectual thinking expresses a detached and objective manner of comparison, the emotional comparison is done from a personal and interested perspective; intellectual thinking may be characterized as an attempt to overcome the personal, emotional perspective.

The importance of comparative concern in emotions is also connected with the central role of changes in generating emotions. An event can be perceived as a significant change only when *compared against a certain background framework*. If emotions occur when we confront a significant change in our situation, our concern is mainly comparative, referring to a situation different from the novel one.

The background framework against which emotional events are compared may be described as a personal baseline. We envy those whose standing is evaluated to be higher than our current baseline. We pity or have contempt for those who are significantly below our current baseline. We are ashamed when our behavior is well below the standards perceived to be part of the state in which we ought to be, and are proud when it is well above these standards. We feel gratitude when the gift received exceeds the one expected, and we feel anger when others' behavior deviates from what we consider as a behavior others ought to take toward us.

The personal baseline, which actually expresses our values and attitudes, depends on many biological, social, personal, and contextual features; it is not a rigid entity, but a flexible framework enabling us to match it with our experiences. Such flexibility, however, is limited since our ability to change our values and attitudes is limited. The possibility of varying baselines is one reason why the same event occurring at different times may be associated with different emotional reactions.

The comparative perspective of emotions is then *personal*: we compare our personal situation with other situations. As Immanuel Kant suggested, it is not things themselves that affect us, but things in their relation to ourselves. The personal baseline determines the way in which we perceive our current, previous, ideal, and "ought" states, as well as these states in other people. We can compare our current, novel situation to a different situation we have been in or to that of significant others, such as parents, siblings, spouse, friends, or outstanding figures. This different state can be a previous actual state, an ideal state in which we desire to be, or a state in which others think we ought to be. The different state of others can also be an actual state, an ideal state, or a state in which we think they ought to be. Emotions are generated whenever a significant discrepancy between our current personal state, or that of significant others, has occurred.[15]

The comparison of our current novel state with a previous actual state of ours may induce emotions such as sadness and happiness; the comparison with an ideal state is associated with disappointment, hope, fear, love, hate, sexual desire, and disgust; the comparison with current states of others may generate emotions such as envy, jealousy, pity, compassion, happy-for (namely, happiness for others), and pleasure-in-others'-misfortune; the comparison with normative states is connected with pride, shame, guilt, and regret. Some emotions are related to several types of discrepancies at the same time. For example, anger and gratitude often involve a comparison with a previous state and with an "ought" state (namely, the situation in which we think we *ought* to be).

The exact division of the possible types of discrepancies and the emotions associated with them is of less importance for our present purposes than the realization that discrepancies, and hence the comparative concern, are crucial for the generation of emotions.

The importance of the comparative concern is illustrated by the story of the man who was upset because he had no shoes—until he met a man who had no feet. One person's ceiling is another person's floor. Satisfaction and happiness depend on comparative measures related, among other things, to our expectations and the fortune of relevant others. Thus, someone who receives a 5 percent raise might be happier than someone who receives an 8 percent increase if the former expected less than the latter. Similarly, a 5 percent raise can be quite exhilarating until one learns that the person down the hall received an 8 percent increase. In the same vein, people assess their own lives more positively if a disabled person is present in the room when the question is put to them.[16] Accordingly, if I consider myself to be worth less than you are, I may frequently think of myself as worthless. From an emotional viewpoint, comparative evaluations often override evaluations concerning our absolute position.

The comparative nature of emotional meaning implies that emotions go beyond the information given; hence, it involves an imaginary aspect. A perceived change may be *actual or imaginary*. Both types include a certain comparison and are present in typical emotional states. Perceiving the significance of an actual change involves its comparison with some imagined alternatives; and imagining an alternative involves a comparison with our present situation. Perceiving actual changes entails a comparison of our current situation with our normal, baseline situation: the more significant the change is perceived to be, the more intense the emotion. The actual and imaginary types of change may be in conflict, as when we are satisfied with having won a small prize, but unsatisfied since we perceive ourselves as having just missed a much larger prize. Similarly, we would feel extremely lucky to have escaped from a car crash with only minor injuries, as it is easy to imagine far worse outcomes.

Actual and imaginary changes are present in all emotions, but their relative importance varies. In negative emotions, where our evaluation of the situation is negative, the imaginative type is usually more dominant since the preferred reality is imagined. However, imagination is also present in positive emotions, where our evaluation of the situation is positive. For example, it is dominant in hope and in sexual desire.[17]

Whereas emotions in animals involve mainly, though not merely, the actual type of change, complex emotions of the imaginative type are more typical of human beings. Humans do not live exclusively in the immediate present. Through our mental capacities, we imagine what is likely to happen, what already happened, or what might happen.

*The Availability of an Alternative*
I almost had to wait.
—Louis XIV, when his carriage pulled up just as he stepped out the door

No one has ever bet enough on a winning horse.
—Richard Sasuly

The comparison underlying emotional significance encompasses the mental construction of *an alternative situation*. The more available the alternative, namely, the closer the imagined alternative is to reality, the more intense the emotion. A crucial element in emotions is, indeed, the imagined condition of "it could have been otherwise."

The importance of the availability of an alternative is well illustrated in a study where participants were asked to contemplate the reactions of two travelers who both missed their scheduled flights, one by five minutes and the other by thirty minutes. The factual outcome is the same—both will have to wait for the next flight—but since it is easier to imagine a counterfactual reality in which the first traveler arrives on time, this traveler will count as the more disappointed. Disappointment is stronger when one can imagine oneself within close reach of the desired emotional object.[18] Another illuminating example comes from research on singles bars: as closing time approached, men and women viewed the opposite sex as increasingly attractive. The looming alternative—the likelihood of going home alone—increased the value of those still available.[19]

The notion of the availability of alternatives may explain many seemingly puzzling situations, such as people who remain in unfulfilling marriages or jobs. Although their satisfaction is low, these people perceive other available alternatives to be even worse.[20] There is much evidence indicating the tendency of people to react more strongly to those events for which it is easy to imagine a different outcome occurring. Therefore, the fate of someone who dies in an airplane crash after switching flights evokes a stronger reaction than that of a fellow traveler who was booked on the flight all along. The emotional amplification associated with a greater availability of an alternative underlies a favorite technique of film directors. Whenever a character in an action film announces that "This is my last mission," we know that the character is unlikely to survive to the final scene. The death of such a character evokes particularly strong emotions because he "almost" made it out of harm's way.[21]

Considering the importance that the availability of the alternative thus attains, "almost situations" or "near misses" come to have intense emotional effects. If we happen to hold number 55555 in a lottery and learn that the winning number is 55554, this near success is more difficult to bear than if the winning number had been nowhere near our own. The objective outcome would of course have been precisely the same, whether we held number 55555 or any other number. The difference lies only in the imagined reality we constructed after our failure. In certain situations it is easier to imagine that failure could have been avoided. The American basketball star, Magic Johnson, who is infected with the AIDS virus, explains that it is particularly hard for him to accept the disease since "I could have easily avoided being infected at all. All I had to do was wear condoms."[22]

A near success is more frustrating than an outright failure for all-or-nothing goals, such as winning a game, but not necessarily for partially attainable goals, like marks in an examination, in which doing less than perfect is better than outright failure. A very close loss in a game usually generates greater sadness when the two teams are perceived to be more or less equal. When one team is clearly perceived to be inferior, a close loss may generate pride in this team's fans—this is especially true not during the game, but a while afterward when we try to cope with the loss by reducing our disappointment. It should be noted that sometimes outright failure may lead to depression since we cannot even imagine a better alternative: we are deep in the mud and are unable to see any way out of it.

Availability of an alternative is determined by how likely it is to occur. The closer a certain alternative is, the more other possibilities are eliminated; it becomes more real and hence more emotionally significant. For instance, regardless of the quality of their marriage, people who consider that "not being married" is a highly available alternative to their present marriage are more likely to experience jealousy, since the idea of not being married at all then becomes a real possibility.[23] The situation in which no particular alternative is more likely to occur than others is also emotionally significant, since it increases uncertainty, which is a variable of emotional intensity. For example, people who undergo medical tests are usually more fearful before the outcome of the tests than after, because once the results are known their uncertainty concerning the many possible alternatives will have been eliminated. Even when the imagined worst alternative—

emotionally the most significant one—is confirmed by the tests, it means that the person involved now knows what to expect and can start adapting her behavior accordingly, consequently reducing the fear of the unknown.[24]

The notion of the availability of an alternative is connected with that of *abnormality*: an abnormal event is one that has highly available alternatives. Since an emotional change is a change departing significantly from our normal situation, abnormal or exceptional events are surprising and often generate intense emotions. On the other hand, an unanticipated event will be judged as normal if it fails to evoke strong alternatives. Exceptional events are emotionally more significant than normal ones since they are infrequent or unusual, and hence more salient than routine or familiar events. The more exceptional the situation, the more available the normal alternative and the more intense the emotion.[25]

Given the importance in emotions of comparison to a normal framework, a crucial feature of many emotions is the experience of feeling lucky or unlucky rather than merely feeling good or bad about something. Luck typically refers to what is perceived as exceptional, or at least uncommon, circumstances. The experience of luck is linked to comparison with a highly available alternative rather than with characteristics of actual events. So, the statement, "I am lucky to be healthy" is clearly seen as expressing more intense gratitude than "It is good I am healthy." The comparison with an alternative is more evident in the former sentence and is expressed, for instance, in cases where one recovers from a long or serious illness or escapes an epidemic threatening the community.[26] (The relationship between emotions and luck is discussed in chapter 7.)

*Social Comparison*
I have noticed that the people who are late are often so much jollier than the people who have to wait for them.
—E. V. Lucas

Always go to other people's funerals, otherwise they won't come to yours.
—Yogi Berra


In chapter 4 I will argue that whereas the initial evolutionary and personal stages of emotional development are mainly concerned with actual and existential issues, the developed emotional environment of humans is more complex: the imaginary and social aspects are by far more dominant. Now I would like to briefly describe the social concern in emotions.

Among humans, the social world is a principal theater of emotions since other people are most important for our well-being. Emotions are a very important glue that links us to others, and the links to others are important determinants for the generation of emotions. Our emotional environment is mainly social and our social environment is highly emotional—it typically involves positive rather than negative emotions. Thus, when people have more social contact, they are happier and healthier, both physically and mentally.[27]

Social comparison is not exercised indiscriminately; it typically refers to people and domains currently perceived to be relevant to our well-being or predominant in our concerns. We neither compare ourselves with everyone nor do we compare every aspect of ourselves. Although social comparison typically occurs with those close to us, it can also occur upon a merely casual contact with another person.

In its broader sense, social comparison does not merely compare our current state to that of other people, but also to our own previous, ideal, or "ought" states. Our perception of these states—especially of the ideal and "ought" states—are heavily dependent on social norms and the way others perceive them. Social comparison is important in determining our values and hence our emotions; it reduces uncertainty about ourselves and is helpful in maintaining or enhancing self-esteem. Accordingly, social comparison presents a potential source of personal instability, particularly regarding self-esteem. Thus, the presence of a person perceived to have highly desirable characteristics produces a decrease in our self-esteem and consequently generates negative emotions. It was further found that the mere presence of others around us facilitates simple tasks and impairs our performance on complex ones. Similarly, the mere belonging to a group tends to alter—in various directions—our performance.[28]

The crucial role of social comparison is evident in many emotions; for example, in envy, jealousy, pleasure-in-others'-misfortune, pity, gratitude, hate, anger, embarrassment, pride, and shame. In other emotions, such as fear and hope, which are concerned with more existential issues, the importance of social comparison is less obvious. Fear of death and hope for better health are such cases in which the concern for our existence is so dominant that social comparison is less significant. In other cases of fear and hope, social comparison may be significant.

Emotions are to a large extent social not only because social concerns are crucial elements in emotional concerns but also because emotions are typically socially infectious. When people who are socially related to us are sad, we are saddened as well, and when they are happy our own happiness is increased. As Van Morrison sang, "I'm in heaven when you smile." Similarly, when some people (mainly men) see erotic pictures, they are erotically aroused. This may explain why it is easier for both men and women to achieve sexual orgasm when they know that their partner is enjoying the sexual interaction. Moreover, there is empirical evidence that when partners empathize, their own body mimics their partner's body. Thus, if the heart rate of the partner in a videotape goes up or down, so does the heart rate of the empathic spouse.[29]

Social concerns may be expressed in various relationships. Major social relationships in the emotional domain include rivalry and cooperation, conformity and deviation. Whereas rivalry and cooperation are characteristic of relations between individuals, conformity and deviation are measured in relation to certain values. The emotional significance of these relationships is evident in light of the importance of people and values for the generation of emotions. Rivalry prevails in emotions, such as envy and pleasure-in-others'-misfortune, where satisfaction or dissatisfaction depends on our relative superiority in comparison with others. By contrast, cooperation occurs in emotions such as compassion and love, where our satisfaction or dissatisfaction depends on whether both we and others do well. Conformity and deviation prevail in emotions such as guilt, regret, gratitude, anger, hate, pride, and shame, which are concerned with whether our behavior, or that of others, is in accordance with certain norms.

A common form of *rivalry* is direct competition. However, rivalry may be more subtle. Without any competition or rivalry over public positions, Keith can relish the misfortune of the Conservative ministers of Great Britain, who, after preaching the importance of family values, are exposed in sex scandals. However, Keith probably opposed the views of the Conservative Party in the first place; hence, his attitude toward them may be described as a kind of rivalry. If sex scandals were uncovered among the leaders of the party he favors, he might be frustrated or sad, but probably would not take pleasure in their misfortunes. The competitive form of rivalry makes emotions more intense than in a distant rivalry, since a competitive rivalry is more personal and relevant to our self-esteem: another person's gain is interpreted as our loss in that it changes our comparative stands. Accordingly, we often identify worse situations with bad situations. Moreover, in most competitions there are many losers for every winner.

The competitive nature of social comparison generates a negative attitude toward other people who are perceived as an obstacle to our success. This can explain Montaigne's claim that there is no other creature who is so unsociable and yet so sociable as a human being. Human society is essential to our existence and well-being; but our desire to improve our relative position—even if by a very small measure—may significantly hurt this society.

In *cooperative situations*, rewards are allocated on the basis of joint excellence. Where rivalry is absent, the other's comparative gain need not necessarily lead to an actual change in our situation. Similarly, improvement in our comparative stand need not necessarily lead to improvement in our situation. A competition for a better comparative stand often does not lead to a greater level of satisfaction. Competitive comparison is not the sole source of satisfaction; indeed cooperation may prove to be satisfying in many situations. In cooperation, the diversity is viewed favorably, and the participants equally. In rivalry, the diversity is viewed favorably, but the participants are considered to be unequal.

*Conformity and deviation* refer to attitudes and behavior relative to some standards. Since emotions are typically generated in the presence of significant changes, deviation, rather than conformity, is more significant in emotions. Conformity expresses acceptance of the current situation and there is therefore no reason to mobilize our resources, which is one of the functions of emotions.

A different type of distinction between the social relations which underlie emotions is that between relationships seeking *intimacy* and those seeking *independence.* Deborah Tannen suggests that intimacy is key in a world of connection where individuals negotiate complex networks of friendship, minimize differences, try to reach consensus, and avoid the appearance of superiority, which would highlight differences. In a world of status, independence is key, because a primary means of establishing status is to tell others what to do, and taking orders is a marker of low status. In intimacy people are the same, feeling equally close to each other. Intimacy says, "We're close and the same," and independence says, "We're separate and different." Tannen argues that although all humans need both intimacy and independence, women tend to focus on the first and men on the second.[30] Intimacy is related to the cooperative relation, and independence to the competitive one; conformity is found in both. The comparative concern is more dominant in a world of status.

## Group Membership
You white people are so strange. We think it is very primitive for a child to have only two parents.
—Australian Aboriginal elder

Group membership is one of the most powerful factors in our emotional lives: the mere act of assigning people to different groups tends to accentuate the perceived cognitive and evaluative differences between them.

Similarity between persons permits categorization, that is, their subsumption under the same abstract concept. However, similarity can refer to many aspects—some of which are of marginal importance. Hence, categorization based merely on similarity may be of no importance. Thus, one can find similarity between any two persons in the world, and although such similarity permits us to classify them in the same group, this does not indicate the presence of meaningful relationships between them. A husband, a wife, and a baby are in many respects less similar to each other than the baby is to other babies, or the husband to other men, or the wife to other women; nevertheless, they form a natural and meaningful group.

Group membership requires more than similarity: it requires significant interdependence between its members. This interdependence with respect to various matters of great importance implies that the members share norms about something. Conformity to such norms is an important measure in evaluating each individual and hence in determining one's self-esteem. A group, then, is a structured collection of individuals who share certain norms and have relations to one another that make them interdependent to some significant degree. Group membership, rather than mere similarity, is thus more crucial in affecting the individual's goals, self-esteem, and well-being. Group members are connected to one another with definite role expectations involving status differentiation and task differentiation among them.[31]

In the same way that similarity can be determined by referring to various aspects, so there are various aspects in light of which group membership can be determined. For instance, a person may be a member of her small family, a larger family group, an economic class, an ethnic group, a religious group, a political party, a group within her workplace, and a group consisting of the parents of her child's class. However, the different groups to which a person belongs are not all equally important at a given moment.[32] The importance of a group at a certain moment depends on various considerations, some of which are of a more permanent nature and some of which are more transitory. Thus, belonging to a small family group has a high degree of importance most of the time, whereas belonging to a political party gains more importance in periods of political uncertainties, such as election time.

The formation of groups is of great significance in the emotional domain. Emotions are concerned with issues of survival and social status, both of which are highly dependent on the formation of groups. I believe that in the emotional domain two major types of groups are of particular importance: social groups and reference groups.

Our *social group* consists of those with whom we have frequent social contacts, that is, in essence, those to whom we are socially close. An important function of our social group is to provide the individual members with mutual support and intimate social ties. Our *reference group* typically includes those who are comparable to us and hence are most relevant to the achievement of our goals or our self-esteem. Our social group consists of people with whom we have actual relationships; our reference group also includes people who do not know about our existence and with whom we have merely imagined relationships.

Our social group is less structured and less binding than our reference group; it may consist, at least in part, of people with whom we do not have hierarchical relationships. Our reference group has a far greater role in defining the attitudes we uphold and cherish and the norms and rules that we consider binding for regulating our behavior. The reference group is the group with which the individual identifies or to which he aspires to belong. Whereas our reference group defines our goals and self-esteem, our social group helps us to cope with the tension and frustration associated with achieving and maintaining such goals and esteem. Our status within our reference group may change quite significantly, whereas our social group provides us with more stable and secure social ties. Our social group prevents a state of social isolation which, for the individual, is unbearable as a permanent state; our reference group prevents a state of normlessness which may result in loss of personal identity.[33]

Our social group is usually larger than our reference group, but our social group does not necessarily include all members of our reference group: there are some people who are relevant to our self-esteem, but with whom we have no social contacts. Typically, those who are socially close to us are also those who are most relevant to our self-esteem; nevertheless, the other direction is valid as well—those who are most relevant to our self-esteem are also those with whom we would like to have social contacts. A social group that is different from our reference group broadens our perspectives; since such a broad perspective is contrary to the partial and focused nature of emotions, emotional intensity is usually decreased in these circumstances. Limiting our social group by reducing it to the size of our reference group involves narrowing down our perspective and typically results in intensifying the given emotion. By focusing our mental resources on limited objects, these objects become more significant to us. Hence, when our social group is limited to our reference group, we are more likely to experience intense emotions.

The size of the social group may have different effects upon emotional intensity. The more people with whom we have frequent social contacts, the more events around us are likely to have emotional significance. However, there is a certain quantity—which may differ from one person to another—above which it is difficult to conduct an intense emotional relationship with each person. A smaller quantity may sometimes mean a higher quality of relationship and hence greater emotional intensity.

Our reference and social groups are associated with different emotions. Our reference group is obviously related to emotions in which rivalry and self-esteem are prominent, for example, envy, pleasure-in-others'-misfortune, hate, shame, and pride. In our social group the relative status of each member is of less concern than in the reference group; the actual situation of each member is of greater significance. Prevailing emotions in this group are therefore emotions such as compassion, happy-for, fear, hope, and love. Some emotions are typical of both groups as they involve concern for our self-esteem within our social group; anger and gratitude are typical emotions of this sort.

The borderlines of our reference group and social group are to a certain extent flexible, depending upon the way we view our relationships with the people around us. Including or excluding someone from this group may significantly change the nature and intensity of our emotional attitudes toward this person. We may increase the impact of a positive event by including people associated with this event within our group; similarly, a decrease of a negative impact can be achieved by excluding those associated with it from our group. Changing the boundaries of the social group is easier than changing those of the reference group. It is more up to us to determine with whom we have social contacts than to determine who is significant within the areas of importance to us. Thus, it is relatively easy to choose the people in our neighborhood with whom we have social contacts. Such a choice is more difficult in the case of our reference group; for example, it is difficult to avoid comparing our professional status and achievements with a colleague who is superior to us. It should be noted, however, that sometimes we change the borderlines of our reference group as a result of our personal development or to protect ourselves from frustration and other negative emotions.

The social group of children is usually identical to their reference group. This is so since children's self-esteem has not yet been fully shaped, so every child in a social relationship with another child is also part of her reference group. Moreover, most of the friends of a given child are children who study with her and are, therefore, part of her reference group. A child's lack of distinction between these two groups is one reason why emotional intensity in children is higher than in adults. Indeed, one way of decreasing emotional intensity is to broaden the scope of the social group and limit the scope of the reference group.

The importance of inclusion within a certain group is evident in other psychological realms as well. In perception, for example, equal-sized physical differences between stimuli are perceived as smaller or larger depending on whether the stimuli are or are not in the same category. Two different shades of green look more like each other than like any shade of yellow, even when there is no greater difference in wavelength between the yellow and one of the greens than between the two shades of green.[34] In perceiving colors, inclusion in the same category reduces subjective significance—hence a given distance within the category is less significant than the same distance between a member of the category and a nonmember. On the other hand, in emotions such as envy, such inclusion increases subjective significance—hence a given distance within the category is more significant than the same distance between a member and a nonmember. Thus, we are more likely to envy those who are within our reference group. This difference between perception and emotions is compatible with the claim that emotions are involved and interested states concerning those who are related to us.

### The Typical Emotional Object: A Human Being

If we were not all so interested in ourselves, life would be so uninteresting that none of us would be able to endure it.
—Arthur Schopenhauer

The typical emotional object is either the person experiencing the emotion or another person. People are more interesting to people than anything else. The things that people do and say, including the things that we ourselves do and say, are the things that affect us most. Accordingly, Spinoza claims that nothing is more useful to a person than a person. And Thomas Reid characterizes emotions as "principles of actions in man, which have persons for their immediate object, and imply, in their very nature, our being well or ill affected to some person, or, at least, to some animated being."[35]

Although emotions are typically directed at a particular agent, they may sometimes be generalized and appear to be directed at a whole group of agents. We may hate people belonging to a particular ethnic group, be attracted to people with a specific physical appearance, or fear rodents. In these cases, when an emotion is generated, it is directed at a particular agent; however, any agent belonging to this general group can induce that emotion.

The human nature of emotions is illustrated by the fact that we are almost indifferent to the collapse of big companies, but can be very upset about the financial disaster of a particular person we have known personally or with whom we can identify ourselves. Similarly, people are seldom sorry when they cheat a large corporation but do not feel the same when cheating a person known to them.

Emotions are typically directed toward agents who are capable of enjoyment and suffering. We can identify ourselves with other agents who are enjoying or suffering and this induces emotions. Given the great similarity of other human beings to us, we can most easily identify ourselves with them and therefore their enjoyment and suffering have great impact upon us. Cruel behavior toward people often assumes that the other people do not fall within the category of humanity and hence do not merit considerate treatment. Such an attitude may overcome emotional resistance to cruelty. Furthermore, our moral attitudes are directed only at those who are capable of enjoyment and suffering. Our attitude toward a stone, for example, is neither moral nor immoral—it is a nonmoral attitude as the stone cannot be a moral object. This overlap between emotional and moral objects indicates the importance of emotions in morality (see chapter 9).

Emotions may be directed at living creatures such as dogs, cats, or birds. The more the creature is perceived to be similar to human beings, the greater is the emotional intensity toward it. It is evident that the closer the animal is to us, the more intense our emotions will be toward it. Accordingly, an injury to my cat may sadden me more than the injury to a stranger which I read about in the newspaper. However, when all relevant factors concerning my relationship with a certain person and a cat are similar, my emotions toward the person will be more intense.

Emotions may also be directed at objects which are actually not agents but have some properties resembling agents or at least are construed to have such properties. Thus, we may feel anger toward our car, envy the power of a mountain, or have compassion for an old house due for demolition. For example, it was recently reported that a man in Issaquah, Washington, apparently became frustrated with his personal computer, pulled out a gun, and shot it; the computer, located in the man's home office, had four bullet holes in its hard drive and one in the monitor. Reid explains that "When we speak of affection to a house, or to any inanimate thing, the word has a different meaning; for that which has no capacity of enjoyment or of suffering, may be an object of liking or disgust, but cannot possibly be an object either of benevolent or malevolent affection." Take, for example, anger. Since an inanimate thing is incapable either of intending to hurt or of being punished there is no sense of being angry with it: "For what can be more absurd than to be angry with the knife for cutting me, or with the weight for falling upon my toes?" Only if we ascribe some life or feeling to the inanimate thing, as does a little girl to her doll, can we have emotions toward it.[36]

A related phenomenon is that of emotions directed at dead people or fictitious objects. Thus, we may be jealous of previous lovers of our mate, who may even be dead by now. In this case, we construe the dead person as having some properties of a real agent, and indeed the dead lover may have such properties in the imagination of our mate. A very favorable attitude of our mate toward this person may seem to be threatening the exclusivity of our present relationship; hence, this jealousy assumes the nature of a typical jealousy.

Although the typical emotional object is a human being or a living creature, in cases that are not typical the object can be more general; thus, we may be excited by a beautiful view, enjoy a piece of art, or love an idea. Usually we would not characterize these cases as emotions but rather as moods or other related phenomena.

## Cause, Concern, and Object

Gravitation cannot be held responsible for people falling in love.
—Albert Einstein

After describing the typical cause of emotion, the typical emotional concern, and the typical emotional object, I will briefly discuss the relationships among these factors.

The *emotional object* is the focus of our attention; it is the *cognitive object*. The *focus of emotional concern* is the *evaluative object*; it is the basis for our evaluative stand. The agent who feels the emotion is the emotional object of embarrassment, but the focus of concern of this emotion is the way others evaluate this person. Sometimes the emotional object and the focus of concern are directed at the same person: in compassion, the person who suffers is both the emotional object and the focus of concern and this is so, too, in some cases of fear and other emotions. In romantic love, the other person is the emotional object and the focus of concern also includes our relationship with that person.

The focus of concern is sometimes unknown to us, not being the focus of our attention. For example, when we feel resentment, the focus of attention is the other's improper activity, but the focus of concern may be its implication for our own status and self-image; such implications are not always obvious to us as we want to believe that the other's activity is also the focus of our concern.

The focus of concern usually refers to our personal situation in a certain group. In envy, the emotional object is the person having something that we would like to have, and the focus of concern is our undeserved inferiority. The focus of concern in each emotional experience can be translated into a *core evaluative theme*. Thus, if the focus of concern in envy is our undeserved inferiority, then the core evaluative theme is a negative evaluation of our undeserved inferiority. Similarly, if the focus of concern in anger is a specific demeaning offense against us, then the core evaluative theme of anger is a specific negative evaluation of someone considered to have inflicted a demeaning offense against us.

There are many disputes concerning mental causality, and the notion of "causality" is complex. I do not intend to discuss this issue here, but merely to mention that in speaking about the *emotional cause* we may broadly refer to all relevant circumstances present prior to a certain emotional attitude. In such a broad sense the cause is general and consists of many factors. The object of Bertrand's love may be Evelyn; however the cause does not consist merely of Evelyn but also of his background, taste in women, standards of beauty, ethical norms, and so on. The cause is much more complex than the object and often belongs to a different ontological category, in which case the object of an emotion cannot be its cause.[37]

In this discussion I use "cause" in a narrower sense referring to the specific event eliciting the emotional attitude. The emotional cause is usually connected with the emotional object. Mice are both the cause and object of our fear; and someone's misfortune is both the cause and the object of our pleasure. In other instances, the object is hardly related to the cause. A man may be angry at his wife, although the real cause of his anger is having been insulted by his boss; the wife may touch on a sensitive spot or evoke unpleasant memories of his boss, but her behavior is not the real cause of his intense emotion.

The emotional cause often precedes the emotion and is separate from it. The focus of concern and the emotional object are constitutive parts of the emotional experience.

### Typical Characteristics: Instability, Intensity, Partiality, and Brevity

In times of war the heart of a nation rises high and beats in the breast of each one of her citizens.
—Omar Bradley

I suggest that instability, great intensity, a partial perspective, and relative brevity be considered as the basic characteristics of typical emotions. This characterization refers to "hot emotions," which are the typical intense emotions. The more moderate emotions lack some of the characteristics associated with typical emotions. Hot emotions, or, simply, emotions, should be distinguished from other affective experiences such as moods, affective disorders, and sentiments. The differences between these affective experiences are discussed in chapter 4.

### Instability
I feel the earth move under my feet,
I feel the sky tumbling down,
I feel my heart start to trembling,
Whenever you're around.
—Carole King

In light of the crucial role that changes play in generating emotions, instability of the mental (as well as the physiological) system is a basic characteristic of emotions. Emotions indicate a transition in which the preceding context has changed, but no new context has yet stabilized. Emotions are like a storm: as unstable states which signify some agitation, they are intense, occasional, and of limited duration. Another popular metaphor compares emotions to a fire.[38]

The instability associated with intense emotions is revealed by their interference with activities requiring a high degree of coordination or control. One cannot easily thread a needle while trembling with fear or seething with anger. When we are in the grip of a strong emotion, our intellectual faculties no longer function normally, with the result that we "lose our heads" and act in ways which differ from our norm. Consider the following lines of the Greek poet Sappho:

> When I see you, my voice fails
> my tongue is paralyzed,
> a fiery fever runs through my whole body
> my eyes are swimming,
> and can see nothing
> my ears are filled with a throbbing din
> I am shivering all over . . .[39]

The opposite of being emotional is being *indifferent*, namely, being apathetic. Contrary to emotional people, indifferent people are unresponsive to and detached from changes in their situation; they remain stable in the face of such changes. The life of people low in emotional intensity is characterized by endurance, evenness, and lack of fluctuation. The life of people high in emotional intensity is characterized by abruptness, changeableness, and volatility.[40]

Emotional instability is applicable not only to the personal domain but also to the *sociological* arena: emotions are more intense in unstable societies where, for example, the regime can rapidly change or people's personal status is subject to fluctuations. In stable, or static, societies, the availability of alternatives hardly exists, and hence emotional intensity is reduced. Envy, for instance, is less intense in such a society. Similarly, citizens living under historically corrupt political rule tend to characterize the abuse of fellow citizens as the result of agitation on the part of the victim rather than the political system. Thus, a failure to appreciate the possible variability of governmental behavior means that less blame is attributed to it.[41] The greater availability of alternatives in unstable societies also indicates greater individual insecurity, thereby intensifying most emotions.

One may argue that people in unstable societies may learn to adjust to instability and become accustomed to change. For people in stable societies, a small alteration in their condition may be perceived as a huge change. In response to this argument it should be noted that we are speaking here about *perceived* instability; those who are accustomed to change perceive their society as stable. Similarly, the society which seems from an "objective" perspective to be stable, but in which small alterations are perceived as huge changes, is not stable from an emotional point of view.

Some emotions may seem to be stronger in static societies. For example, people who consider the stable social order as humiliating and unjust may experience hate and despair more intensely. However, we must remember that if these people consider the present social order as humiliating and unjust, then they already have some notion of an alternative society which is, in their opinion, more just. Their inability to change the "abnormal" present social order to the more "normal" justified order is the source of their intense emotions. The alternative seems close in the sense that it is perceived to be more normal; it is remote in the sense that it is not feasible in the near future.

## Intensity

Many waters cannot quench love, neither can the floods drown it.
—Song of Solomon, 8:7

One of the typical characteristics of emotions is their relative great intensity. Emotions are intense reactions. In emotions the mental system has not yet adapted to the given change, and owing to its significance the change requires the mobilization of many resources. No wonder that emotions are associated with urgency and heat. One basic evolutionary function of emotions is indeed that of immediate mobilization. This function enables us to regulate the timing and locus of investment in the sense of allocating resources away from situations where they would be wasted, and toward those where investment will yield a significant payoff.[42]

Low intensity of the feeling dimension, as well as of other mental components, usually expresses neutral or indifferent states of the mental system. Emotions are the opposite of such states. Accordingly, it is preferable to consider low-intensity states as nonemotional or nontypical. Although it is impossible to delineate the precise borderlines of emotional intensity, we can say that typical emotions have such an intensity which influences our normal functioning but not in a way that disables us completely—as is the case in affective disorders.

In the emotional domain there is no such thing as a minor concern; if the concern is minor, it is not emotional. A typical characteristic of emotions is their magnifying nature: everything looms larger when we are emotional. The fact that our colleague earns 2 percent more than we do is not a minor issue in the eyes of envious people: it is perceived to reflect the undeserved inferior position in which we are now situated. Similarly, the slightly smaller size of a woman's breast is not considered a minor imperfection by the many women who undergo breast implants. Every emotional concern is perceived to be a profound one.

The above considerations may explain why it is easy to evoke emotions although they express our most profound values. We do not need a profound argument to generate emotions; on the contrary, what seem to be very superficial matters easily induce emotional reactions. An external observer may evaluate such matters to be superficial, but for the person experiencing the emotions, these matters are perceived to be very profound, hence eliciting an intense emotional reaction. Another reason for the ease of evoking emotions is that because of their depth, emotional values are comprehensive and relate to many events in our life.

Typical emotions, characterized as possessing relatively great intensity, should be distinguished from extreme manifestations of affective disorders such as severe anxiety or depression which is the focus of a great deal of psychological research on pathological states.

If indeed perceiving significant changes determines emotional intensity, then we should indicate what makes us perceive—or rather evaluate—one change as significant and another as insignificant. Chapter 5 addresses this issue.

*Partiality*
I live one day at a time.
—Willie Nelson

I know nothing about sex, because I was always married.
—Zsa Zsa Gabor

Emotions are partial in two basic senses: they are focused on a *narrow* target, as on one person or a very few people; and they express a *personal* and interested perspective. Emotions direct and color our attention by selecting what attracts and holds our attention; they make us preoccupied with some things and oblivious to others. Emotions are not detached theoretical states; they address a practical concern from a personal perspective. This perspective may also include considerations of those related to us. These people are like extensions of our egos, even though their emotional weight is typically of a lesser degree than the weight of personal considerations having direct bearing upon our own lives.

Not everyone and not everything are of emotional significance to us. We cannot assume an emotional state toward everyone or those with whom we have no relation whatsoever. The intensity of emotions is achieved by their focus upon a limited group of objects. Emotions express our values and preferences; hence, they cannot be indiscriminate. Being indiscriminate is tantamount to having no preferences and values; in other words, it is a state of nonemotion.

Take, for instance, romantic love. We cannot be indiscriminate in whom we love. We cannot love everyone; our romantic love must be directed at a few people. For most of us, having one romantic partner is more than enough as the partner exhausts all our mental (not to say, financial!) resources. More energetic people may have two, three, or even five romantic partners; but even those talented people cannot have a thousand romantic partners. Since romantic love, like other emotions, necessitates limiting parameters such as time and attention, the number of its objects must be limited as well. We have greater resources to offer when we limit the number of emotional objects to which we are committed. So there is some sense in Whitney Houston's line, "I'm saving all my love for you." The beloved has emotional significance that no other person has; the beloved fills much of our emotional environment. A police officer in Israel was once asked in which direction the police were focusing their investigations; the officer replied: "We are focusing in all possible directions." This reply involves a conceptual mistake as we cannot focus in all directions. Similarly, we cannot focus our emotions on all human beings.

This limitation in the number of possible emotional objects forces us to focus upon those who are close to us. When we hear of the death of thousands of people in an earthquake occurring in a remote (that is, from our vantage point) part of the world, our emotional response comes nowhere near the intensity of our grief at the death of someone close to us, nor does it even approach the level of feeling we experience in watching the suffering of a single victim of that same earthquake on television (thereby establishing some affinity with that particular victim). Television news coverage maintains our emotional interest by describing global situations in terms of particular stories about individual people or families. As Stalin argued: "One death is a tragedy; a million is a statistic." Similarly, when UNICEF campaigns for donations to help disadvantaged children, it does not supply us with statistics about these children, but indicates that by donating thirty-two cents, we can provide a vial of penicillin to treat a particular child's infection. Emotions express what may be termed "the hammer point of view": When you have a hammer in your hand, the whole world looks like a nail. When Bob Dylan started his career, he wrote about depressed people suffering daily crises. After a few years, when his income had risen to eight figures, he started to write only about happy, cheerful people. When asked about the change, he is reported to have said: "It's hard to be a bitter millionaire."[43]

In intense emotional states, we are somewhat similar to children. A young child will promise to jump off a tower tomorrow if you give her a cake today, not only because the child does not understand the concepts of tomorrow and promise but because the child's interest is mainly focused on the immediate partial situation. Therefore, young children have difficulties in working out that someone watching a scene from a different vantage point may not be able to see all they see. Like children, our emotional perspectives are highly partial and involved. Our immediate situation, no matter how grave or insignificant it is, is the only thing that concerns us when we are in intense emotional states. We may believe that the world is pointing its fingers at a pimple on our nose. No intellectual explanations concerning broader perspectives are relevant in these circumstances.

In intense emotional states, we resemble children insofar as we have trouble distinguishing fantasy from reality. Commercials, which are particularly influential among young children who confuse ads and programs, can also easily influence adults who are induced into an emotional state. Due to their more partial perspective, children experience emotional states more often and for a shorter time than adults. For example, children laugh much more than adults; some estimate that whereas a child at the kindergarten age laughs about 300 times a day, an adult laughs only seventeen times a day. Generally, children's behavior is more emotional than adult behavior: children have fewer defense mechanisms which inhibit spontaneous behavior; such behavior is typical of emotions.[44]

The partiality of emotions is demonstrated by their cognitive, evaluative, and motivational components. The *cognitive* field of emotions does not offer varied and broad perspectives of our surroundings; it narrows and fragments our perspective. Selective abstraction, in which the focus of attention is on specific aspects, and overgeneralization, which is the construing of a single event as representative of the whole situation, are frequently associated with emotions. Thus, sexual desire and envy considerably limit our focus of attention. The *evaluative* perspective of emotions is partial due to its highly polarized nature and its concern with very few objects. In comparison with other people, a typical emotional object is evaluated as being either highly positive or highly negative; it is also evaluated to be highly relevant to our well-being. Highly emotional people overestimate the degree to which events are related to them and are excessively absorbed in the event's personal meaning. The *motivational* field is narrow in the sense that the desired activity is often clearly preferred to any alternative. Even in emotions such as love, in which the range of activities concerning the beloved is wide, these are clearly preferred to other activities unrelated to the beloved; the latter are hardly considered at all.[45]

The partial nature of emotions influences other mental capacities involved in the emotional experience. Take, for example, memory. Since emotions narrow attention to a few stimuli, the recall of these stimuli is facilitated by greater emotional intensity. However, emotional intensity decreases recall for non-emotion-inducing stimuli because the attention-narrowing process screens such stimuli out. Thus, it was found that great emotional intensity experienced while watching the Super Bowl on television reduced recall for advertisements broadcast during the game.[46]

In light of the partial nature of emotions, we may reduce emotional intensity by broadening our scope, and increase the intensity by further limiting it. Counting to ten before venting our anger enables us to adopt a broader perspective that may reduce anger. A broader perspective is typical of people who can calmly consider multiple aspects of a situation; it is obviously not typical of people who experience an intense emotional reaction to the situation.

Pathological cases are often characterized by the lack of a broad perspective or the adoption of a peculiar perspective. Consider, for example, the following case of a schizophrenic patient who had a love affair during which his girlfriend slept with him in his apartment for three weeks. He angrily terminated this relation abruptly when one night his girlfriend went to the kitchen and took some soda from his refrigerator. He considered her behavior as an "intolerable intrusion in his privacy."[47] This person adopts a peculiar and narrow perspective: it is normally considered that sharing a bed for three weeks attests to a greater degree of intimacy than taking something out of a refrigerator; in any case, when considering other events in our life, taking some soda from the refrigerator is not such a severe offense.

Although emotional partiality may sometimes lead to distorted proportions, it is not necessarily so. Finding the right proportion between the partial emotional perspective and more general perspectives is difficult, but nevertheless the presence of both is crucial for human life.

Much of television's power lies in its capacity to strike personal emotional chords in viewers without requiring them to invest much in the way of mental resources or complex skills. Triggering emotional states is done by increasing the viewers' identification with characters and deepening their personal involvement in the television experience. Examples of such methods include escape from the constraints of routine ("the show helps me escape from the boredom of everyday life"), emotional release ("the show makes me want to cry"), companionship ("the characters in the show have become like close friends to me"), personal reference ("the show sometimes brings back memories of certain people I used to know"), and value reinforcement ("it is nice to know there are still families around like the one in the show").[48]

The personal nature of emotions is not in conflict with the characteristic of social comparison. Emotional social concerns are part of a personal perspective. We compare the situation of other people with that of ourselves. Personal situations of other people, rather than social ideas, are of great emotional significance to us. Although emotions are personal, others are not necessarily considered as mere tools for our own satisfaction. They may be invested with intrinsic value and regarded as constitutive rather than instrumental parts of our flourishing. The personal perspective is evident in the fact that we attach to those close to us greater emotional value than to those completely unrelated. The continuation of the connection with those related to us is of emotional significance, but this connection does not have to be in one direction concerning merely our own well-being. My love for my two sons is expressed in my wish for them to flourish no matter what my fate is; I want them, however, to be close to me all the time. Similarly, although my grief over the death of my brother contains the sad realization that we will never be together again, my grief stems less from concern for my future well-being, but more from sadness that this young person will not be able to fulfill his wishes and be with those who love him.

The partiality typical of emotions is less dominant in other mental capacities, such as perception, memory, and thinking: these capacities are usually directed at more objects and they typically include a less personal perspective. For example, although perception is limited in its scope to events and objects currently confronting us, we are able to perceive many things simultaneously. Similarly, memory may be limited to things we have experienced or learned in the past, but in a brief period we can remember quite a few people. Contrary to the partial nature of emotions, intellectual reasoning is not partial: it is focused on a broad, rather than narrow, target, and it is not done from a personal and interested perspective. Intellectual reasoning is a detached state: it looks at all implications of a current state; it takes us far beyond the current situation. Intellectual reasoning is committed to formal logical rules of valid arguments, but it has no commitment to values; it is value-free. In intellectual reasoning we are supposed to consider all available alternatives and then choose the best one. Unlike the case in emotions, the present situation has no privileged status in intellectual reasoning; on the contrary, we are required not to be influenced by that situation, but to consider all other possible situations in an objective manner.

Humor is similar to emotions in having a strong element of incongruity or change. Both emotions and humor combine two perspectives—the expected and the unexpected. However, whereas in emotions the simultaneous presence of incongruent perspectives is problematic, and hence requires immediate practical action, in humor the incongruity is enjoyable and requires no action. The ability to entertain several different perspectives is typical of humor and moderate positions, and is contrary to the partial nature of emotions. A sense of humor is thus often incompatible with an extreme emotional state. The ability to entertain several alternatives is also a sign of mental health. For example, a person who suffers from paranoia denies that alternatives to his position are possible.[49]

The mental capacities involved in emotions can in principle refer to other objects besides the emotional object, but they typically do not do so and are limited to our immediate environment. Moreover, our interest can hardly change perceptual content, but it often changes emotional states. This partiality is typical of all emotions, though varying in degree. It is more evident in negative emotions, where the immediate situation is of great concern to us.

Emotional partiality does not diminish emotional complexity and diversity; a focused and partial attitude may express complex phenomena and be conveyed in multiple forms.

Emotional partiality is related to the other major characteristics of typical emotions, namely, instability, great intensity, and brief duration. A partial perspective is less stable than an impartial one. Since a partial perspective does not take into account many circumstances, there are more circumstances which represent significant changes for it and thereby upset the system's stable equilibrium. Partiality is also correlated with great intensity. In light of their intense nature, emotions require resources such as time and attention. Since these resources are finite, emotions must be partial and discriminative. Focusing upon fewer objects increases the resources available for each and hence increases emotional intensity. It is like a laser beam which focuses upon a very narrow area and consequently achieves high intensity at that point. In the words of Robert Southey: "If you would be pungent, be brief; for it is with words as with sunbeams—the more they are condensed, the deeper they burn." A partial perspective—focusing our entire set of resources on a few personal objects—must also be transient in duration, because it may be harmful to neglect other objects for too long.

*Brevity*
In Hollywood a marriage is a success if it outlasts milk.
—Rita Rudner


Typical emotions are essentially transient states. An emotional event may be compared to a large rock being thrown into a pool of still water: for a short time, emotional chaos reigns before calm gradually returns.[50]

The mobilization of all resources to focus on one event cannot last forever. A system cannot be unstable for a long period and still function normally; it may explode due to continuous increase in emotional intensity. A change cannot persist for a very long time; after a while, the system construes the change as a normal and stable situation. The association of emotional intensity with change causes the intensity to decrease steadily due to the transient nature of changes. This association is a natural mechanism enabling the system to return within a relatively short period to normal functioning—which may be somewhat different from the previous normal functioning. If emotions were to endure for a long time regardless of what was occurring in our environment, then they would not have an adaptive value.

The exact duration of emotions is a matter for dispute. Paul Ekman believes that emotions are typically a matter of seconds, not minutes, hours, or days. His view is based, among other things, on the duration of both expressive and physiological changes; thus, most adult facial expressions last from approximately half a second to four seconds. He argues that when people report experiencing an emotion for longer periods, they summate in their report what was actually a series of repeated but discrete emotion episodes.[51] Other studies, as well as common sense, indicate that emotions last longer. A cross-cultural study found that fear rarely lasted longer than an hour, and in many cases less than five minutes. Anger usually lasted for more than a few minutes, but rarely more than a few hours. Sadness and happiness lasted over one hour in many cases; in fact, sadness lasted even longer than a day in more than half of the cases studied. Emotions such as love and jealousy can last longer. Some emotions have concrete, usually negative, specifications with respect to their duration. An attitude cannot be regarded as grief or love if it lasts for only five seconds; nor can anything lasting for years count as pleasure-in-others'-misfortune or relief. Other emotions, however, do not have such temporal specifications and can last for different periods of time.[52]

The transient nature of emotions does not imply that emotions must last no more than a few seconds: sometimes the transition from one stabilized state to another takes longer. Such a transition is not just a switch from one state to another; it involves profound changes in our plans and concerns and, as such, it may occupy us for some time. The typical temporal structure of an emotional response involves a swift rise-time, taking less than half a minute in most cases, followed by a relatively slow decay. After an emotional response reaches its peak, it can take hours, or even days, to get back to the stable, normal state again.[53] Consequently, the dispute concerning the duration of emotions can be settled by claiming that all typical and diagnostic features of emotions are indeed present for a very short time—typically a matter of seconds. The longer an emotion lasts, the more such features drop away.

The fact that emotions are transient states does not imply that their impact is merely transient—a brief emotional state can have profound and long-lasting behavioral implications. Moreover, our emotional values have a persistent impact on what we do and what we do not do.

### Difficulties and Objections

The human race is faced with a cruel choice: work or daytime television.
—Unknown

A brief discussion of some of the possible difficulties of and objections to the proposed characterization of emotions may be useful here. As this book is not polemic in nature, the critical discussion is brief. Its purpose is not to discuss all possible difficulties and objections or to prove them to be wrong, but to indicate the ways in which my view can deal with various types of criticism.

### A Perceived Significant Change

Any idiot can face a crisis; it is this day-to-day living that wears you out.
—Anton Chekhov

The hypothesis that emotions occur when we perceive a significant change in our situation can be challenged by claiming that (a) it is unclear what a significant change is; (b) the significance of the change is important only in some emotions; (c) changes are not essential to emotions; and (d) changes are essential not only to emotions but to all mental states—as such, they cannot be used to distinguish emotions from nonemotions.

It can be argued that a detailed a priori description of what constitutes a significant change is impossible, since such changes are highly sensitive to personal and contextual factors. This genuine difficulty complicates, but does not preempt, the description of typical emotions. After all, many mental states are highly sensitive to personal and contextual attributes, but we are not ready to dismiss the usefulness of psychological research concerning them. I have suggested that one way of confronting emotional complexity is through the use of various conceptual tools.

A more specific manner of dealing with the sensitivity of significant changes to personal and contextual factors is to characterize a significant change as exceptional, namely, as departing significantly from a person's normal situation.[54] Although the concept of "normal" has its own hurdles, it is an intelligible concept used in many scientific and nonscientific contexts. Abnormal or exceptional events have indeed greater emotional significance than normal ones.

Even if the intelligibility of the notion of "a significant change" is admitted, it may still be claimed that its usefulness is limited, as the significance of the change is a crucial component only in some emotions. For example, this component is evident in grief, but not in anger, when subjective elements, rather than significant changes, are dominant. In response, I would point out that any type of significance is basically subjective; significance is determined by our *perception* of its importance for our well-being. Perceiving an event to be significant depends, among other things, on our personal makeup and the nature of the given event. In some emotions, the role played by the event in determining its (subjective) significance is far greater than in others. The death of a friend usually generates grief regardless of our personality, whereas anger depends, to a large extent, on our personality and the given context. Although the factors constituting the event's significance vary, emotional significance is typically related to a perceived change.

Whereas the first two difficulties refer to the element of significance in the claim that emotions occur when we perceive a significant change, the next two difficulties refer to the element of change. The first of these difficulties involves the claim that changes are inessential to emotions, and the second refers to the claim that changes are essential to all mental states and not merely to emotions.

The claim that changes are inessential to emotions can be based either on the claim that familiarity, rather than change, is crucial for emotions in general, or on the claim that changes are not crucial for affective phenomena, such as long-term sentiments, despair, and frustration. Here, changes seem to be absent. One can argue that without a familiar background, an event cannot be regarded as a significant change, and hence familiarity rather than change is crucial for emotions.

I have already acknowledged the crucial role that the framework of one's personal background plays in emotions. To give one more example, it has been found that campaign commercials conveying new information are not as effective as those appealing to an idea that is already accepted by voters. Familiarity is indeed important in generating emotional significance. However, excess of familiarity produces boredom. Accordingly, campaign commercials do not merely repeat well-known facts. Likewise, the success of a television program usually lies in the grafting of the novel onto the familiar.[55]

Neither repetition nor change alone can guarantee an increase in emotional intensity; such an increase is generated by a significant change, namely, a change related to a familiar framework which is relatively stable.[56] We may distinguish between relative (or localized) novelty and absolute (or global) novelty. Relative novelty implies a difference within a familiar framework, whereas in absolute novelty the framework itself changes. A significant emotional change does not necessarily imply absolute novelty. On the contrary, since absolute novelty is something quite alien to us, it often does not have emotional significance; when it does, the emotions generated are frequently negative.

The second claim dismissing the suggested essential role of changes in emotions refers to sentiments and specific emotions such as despair and frustration in which changes seem to be absent. In analyzing sentiments (enduring emotions), we should bear in mind the distinction between a change within a familiar framework and a change of the framework as a whole. For example, enduring love is intensified in the presence of specific changes, such as the beloved's temporary departure or return, or a certain unusual achievement or misfortune of the beloved. Love can also be intensified in the presence of fundamental changes, such as a threat to the whole relationship by the beloved's serious illness. I admit that in regard to sentiments, perceiving changes has a relatively smaller weight, and familiarity a relatively greater weight. For example, perceiving a change is quite significant in sexual desire, while it is less significant in romantic love and even less so in parental love. Familiarity plays a greater role in parental love. Such a negative correlation between the length of the emotional relationship and the role of change in it is compatible with the transient nature of emotions. Strong interest in something or strong ideological commitments are similar to sentiments. The intensity of both is mainly associated with specific changes, as when a significant challenge is presented in our discipline; their intensity may also be connected with fundamental changes threatening the very existence of the underlying framework.

Despair and frustration are different examples of emotions in which changes are claimed to be absent. Indeed, stability and lack of any perceivable alternative seem to be essential to them. Explaining these emotions should refer to our personal baseline and in particular to our expectations. In terms of the personal baseline typical of despair and frustration, the relevant change is a change in our expectations. We view our expectations of a change in an unpleasant situation as normal. The fact that these expectations are not fulfilled, and the situation remains as bad as it was, can be considered as a significant change in our situation; hence the emergence of despair and frustration. If we could become accustomed to our bad situation and accept it as normal, then despair and frustration would not occur.

One may argue that changes are essential not only to emotions but to all mental states—as such, they cannot be used to distinguish emotions from nonemotions. I have indicated that paying attention to changes has adaptive value for the mental system, and hence all mental capacities are indeed sensitive to changes. However, emotions are further characterized as being generated by the perception of a *significant* change *in our situation*. Unlike other mental changes, the change associated with emotions must have significant implications for our personal situation. Although an emotional change has this unique character, the distinction between emotions and nonemotions is based not merely on the different types of change associated with both, but, as mentioned, on other characteristics.

### The Comparative Personal Concern
Always remember that you are unique. Just like everyone else.
—Unknown

The centrality of the comparative concern does not imply that before the generation of each emotion, we are busy comparing various sorts of events. As I indicate in the next chapter, comparison is not incompatible with the spontaneous nature of emotions. The event responsible for the emotional experience activates an evaluative pattern (schema, structure) which is comparative in nature; however, the activation itself is not initiated by a deliberative process of comparison. Consider, for instance, the situation in which Robert hears that his wife is having an affair with a colleague of his. This event has an immediate emotional impact on Robert, who begins to be jealous. The basic evaluative pattern of jealousy is comparative: it compares our present situation to an alternative situation in which we lose our mate, and it compares our present standing to that of our rival. Hearing about his wife's affair immediately induces Robert's jealousy, as it is immediately perceived as threatening to his marriage and social standing. It is typically the case that only after the emotion is generated do deliberative thinking processes take place which usually further intensify the emotion. No doubt, the comparative concern in emotions is often addressed by deliberative, conscious thinking. However, since a major function of emotions is to provide an immediate response to a significant change, it should be possible for emotions to emerge without such a lengthy and mediate process.

### Human Beings as Emotional Objects
Politicians are interested in people. Not that this is always a virtue. Fleas are interested in dogs.
—James Baldwin

Although I have proposed that typical emotions are directed at agents and in particular at human agents, there are occasions when inanimate objects seem to be the object of emotions. These cases do not counter the assumption that emotions are typically directed at human agents. For one, by employing the term "typically," the presence of exceptions is assumed. But more to the point, a closer look reveals that most of these apparently exceptional cases are in fact not directed at inanimate objects.

The most common case of such seeming exceptions is that in which inanimate objects are construed as agents or at least as having some properties of such agents. Since emotions are described in terms of prototypical categories, certain similarities of an inanimate object to the typical human agent can generate an emotion, even though that emotion may not be the typical one. If a man is jealous of his wife's devotion to her work, the work itself is not an agent which is the typical object of jealousy. However, since the work has some representative properties of the typical rival—namely, that it attracts much of the wife's attention—then it can also arouse some sort of jealousy.

A similar analysis may apply to emotions such as those expressed in the statements "I hate wars," or "I love cereal." Wars and cereal have some properties which function in a similar way to those of agents that are the objects of hate and love. These expressions may also refer to the general attitudes of dislike or fondness, rather than to the emotions of hate and love as experienced when directed at particular agents. Similarly, love for a work of art lacks many features typical of loving a person, including the wish to be approved of and cared for by the beloved, benefiting the beloved, wishing for the beloved's further development, and the like.

In some other cases in which the emotional object seems to be an inanimate thing, the actual emotional object is the agent having the emotion. Thus, when we say that one is afraid of a bridge, we mean that one is afraid of walking or riding across a bridge, and this fear is directed at oneself. Similar situations are those in which we say that we love the thought of having a love affair, hate to be angry, or are ashamed of our pridefulness. These emotions are directed at oneself and not at some inanimate object.

*Typical Characteristics*
A ship in the harbor is safe, but that's not what ships are built for.
—Unknown

The suggested use of "emotion" (or, more precisely, "typical emotion" or "emotion in the full sense") is more restricted than the common usage of the term. This difference may be dismissed as merely terminological, thereby allowing that another term could be chosen to describe the states being discussed. The choice, however, is not entirely arbitrary. The definition of "emotion" in the *Oxford English Dictionary* is: "any agitation or disturbance of mind, feeling or passion; any vehement or excited mental state." Likewise, the definition in *Webster's New Collegiate Dictionary* incorporates basic elements of the suggested characterization: an emotion is "a psychic and physical reaction subjectively experienced as strong feeling and physiologically involving changes that prepare the body for immediate vigorous action." My restricted use of "emotion" is also compatible with prevailing practice in psychology and philosophy. Thus, in his *Dictionary of Psychology*, Drever argues that all psychologists are in agreement about emotion as a complex state of "excitement or perturbation, marked by strong feeling, and usually an impulse toward a definite form of behavior."[57]

Some objections to the suggested characterization of emotions may indicate that (a) the suggested characteristic is also associated with nonemotional states, or (b) this characteristic is not associated with all emotions. For example, it may be argued that *instability* is also characteristic of nonemotional states and that stability is characteristic of some emotions. My reply to the first type of objection is to note that the characteristic in question—for instance, instability—is not the sole characteristic of emotions. There are quite a few such characteristics, and only their unique equilibrium characterizes emotions. The second type of objection can be addressed by noting that these characteristics admit different degrees and that typical, though not necessarily all, emotions possess each of these characteristics. Thus, instability is a matter of degree. Very low levels of instability may not differ much from normal situations and hence are not associated with emotions. Very high levels of instability may also not accord with typical emotions. We cannot draw precise borderlines of emotional instability, as it depends on various personal and contextual factors. Nevertheless, we can characterize emotions as involving a significant level of instability.

In the same vein, I would argue that states of extreme *intensity*, such as those associated with affective disorders, are not necessarily emotions, as they lack the other characteristics typical of emotions. Again, it is the unique combination of all the characteristics which distinguishes emotions from nonemotions. Likewise, states having a very low level of intensity are not emotional—they express indifference rather than emotional sensitivity. As with other suggested characteristics, the great intensity of emotions should be understood in relative terms. I would deal in a similar manner with objections concerning the ascription of partiality and of brevity to typical emotions.

Along these lines, my contention that emotions are associated with a strong feeling component can be contested by claiming that all normal experiences have a feeling component and hence are emotional. According to this view, emotionless experiences are pathological. Thus, most schools of psychoanalysis take affectlessness in general or in specific areas of life as a sign of serious psychological disorder.[58] I agree that a feeling component is typically part of our mental state; hence, it may be argued that we always have a certain feeling. In my view, however, such a background feeling does not constitute the more complex emotional experience. By describing all experiences as "emotional," the term loses its specific meaning; in that case, I would have to look for another term denoting what I mean by "emotional." The dispute may thus be merely terminological. It may, however, also express the belief that the phenomena I characterize as emotional do not have enough interesting properties to be categorized separately. The many fruitful discussions of emotions—in the more limited sense suggested here—prove this belief to be false.

Objections to my suggested characterization of emotions can also refer to the more specific nature of the connection between emotions and a given characteristic. I will briefly refer to such objections concerning instability and emotional duration.

It may be argued that *calmness*, rather than *instability*, is the essential characteristic of certain emotions, such as hope, happiness, and cases of stable love. In response, I would first point out that such calmness is not the same as indifference: it expresses a higher level of emotional equilibrium. This equilibrium is unstable in the sense that it is fragile and transient. When such equilibrium is maintained for long periods it becomes a sentiment, which is a state different from that of emotions described here (see chapter 4 for a detailed discussion of this difference). In any case, most emotions involve a high degree of arousal on the arousal-calmness continuum.

Turning to the complex issue of *emotional duration*, the claim that emotions are typically transient and brief states seems to conflict with the ongoing nature of emotions. Emotions are not isolated entities, but are rather dynamic states. The emotional system may be considered as a self-organizing system having an ongoing positive feedback loop.[59] It is often the case that once we are in an emotional state, we focus our attention on the emotional object; consequently, the object becomes even more significant to us, and our emotion intensifies. When the emotion is intensified, we devote even more resources to the object, and the object becomes in turn more significant, and so on. In this manner, the positive feedback of the emotion keeps its intensity level high and sometimes even increases it.

A particularly important thought process in this regard is rumination, namely, unbidden thoughts which come to people's minds frequently. Ruminative thoughts, generated by significant events, are expressed in repetitive, intrusive thoughts. Rumination connected with negative events may cause people to polarize the negative feelings they associate with their failure to attain their goals. It has been shown that the more people think about something toward which they initially had a slightly favorable or slightly negative attitude, the more extreme their attitudes become. Indeed, it has been suggested that women, who are more emotionally sensitive than men, tend toward rumination to a greater extent than men, whose response is more behavioral.[60]

Emotions, then, are ongoing states which, because of their positive feedback loop, tend to be perpetuated as long as no external negative constraints are introduced. This does not, as it would appear, contradict the suggested brief nature of emotions: If the external negative constraints are frequent and powerful enough, then focusing all our resources on a particular event must be limited to a short period, since other events require our resources as well. The brief nature of emotions is mainly due to the diverse nature of the environment in which the emotional system operates. When new events in the external environment are of little significance, the emotional state lasts longer. This is, for instance, the situation in affective disorders, such as depression, elation, and anxiety, or in sentiments such as grief stemming from the death of someone very close to us. The duration of an emotion is thus determined by two conflicting features: (1) the perpetuating nature of emotions, and (2) external constraints forcing the system to diffuse its resources. The relative weight of each feature is crucial in determining the length of any given emotional state.

## Summary

Emotion is not something shameful, subordinate, second-rate; it is a supremely valid phase of humanity at its noblest and most mature.
—Joshua Loth Liebman

The classic question of "What is an emotion?" has been partially answered by describing typical emotions. It has been suggested that the typical cause of emotions is the perception of a significant change in our situation; the change may be either actual or imaginary. The typical emotional concern is a comparative concern in which our present situation is compared with an imaginary alternative. The comparisons involved in emotions are usually social: they refer to significant other people and to previous, ideal, or "ought" states of ourselves. In light of their social nature, emotions are typically directed at human beings—ourselves or other people. The basic characteristics of typical emotions are instability, great intensity, a partial perspective, and brevity of duration. In the next chapter, another level of describing typical emotions will be added: I will argue that the basic components of emotions are cognition, evaluation, motivation, and feeling.[61]

The suggested characterization is not arbitrary; it intended to be helpful in understanding emotions and is compatible with "common sense" as well as with more scientific approaches. There are, however, states which are somewhat different from the typical ones but still are considered as emotions. Although the states termed "typical emotions" do not constitute a natural kind, they have many interesting distinguishing features that justify combining them into a separate category. Henceforth, by "emotions" I mean typical emotions in the sense suggested here.

# Chapter 3

# Basic Components

It isn't necessary to be rich and famous to be happy; it's only necessary to be rich.
—Alan Alda

In addition to the typical characteristics discussed in the previous chapter, that is, instability, intensity, partiality, and brevity, there are other relevant features of emotions which might help us to understand them. One such feature is the division of emotions into four basic components, namely, cognition, evaluation, motivation, and feeling. The difference between typical characteristics and basic components is that characteristics are properties of the whole emotional experience, whereas components express a conceptual division of the elements of this experience. It is arguable that one could perhaps find a few relevant characteristics other than those I have discussed; however, the conceptual division of emotions into four components is more comprehensive and is supposed to cover all possible components.

## Intentionality and Feeling

Most people are willing to change not because they see the light, but because they feel the heat.
—Unknown

I consider intentionality and feeling to be the two basic mental dimensions.[1] Intentionality refers to a subject-object relation, whereas feeling expresses the subject's own state of mind. When a person is in love, the feeling dimension surfaces in a particular feeling, say a thrill, that is experienced when the lovers are together; the intentional dimension is expressed in the person's knowledge of her beloved, her evaluation of his attributes, and her desires toward him.

Intentionality is the relation of "being about something." It involves our cognitive ability to separate ourselves from the surrounding stimuli in order to create a meaningful subject-object relation. The intentional object is something about which the person has some information. This object does not have to be a person or a certain thing; it can be a general situation or even an abstract concept. The intentional dimension includes several references to objects, such as those involved in perception, memory, thoughts, dreams, imagination, desires, and emotions.

The feeling dimension is a primitive mode of consciousness associated with our own state. It is the lowest level of consciousness; unlike higher levels of awareness, such as those found in perception, memory, and thinking, the feeling dimension has no meaningful cognitive content. It expresses our own state, but is not in itself directed at this state or at any other object. Since this dimension is a mode of consciousness, one cannot be unconscious of it; there are no unfelt feelings. In the intentional domain we play a more active role; feelings, on the other hand, just seem to surface, and can overcome us when they are intense.

The intentional dimension in emotions can be divided into three components: cognitive, evaluative, and motivational. The cognitive component consists of information about the given circumstances; the evaluative component assesses the personal significance of this information; the motivational component addresses our desires, or readiness to act, in these circumstances. When John envies Adam for having better grades, John has some information about Adam's grades, evaluates his own inferior position negatively, and wishes to abolish this inferiority.

Neither these three intentional components nor the feeling dimension is a separate entity or state. Emotions do not entail the separate performance of four varieties of activity: knowing, evaluating, desiring, and feeling. All four are distinct aspects of a typical emotional experience. It is possible that some of these aspects existed as separate states prior to the appearance of the emotion, that they were among the reasons for its generation and subsequently became part of the complex emotional attitude. Thus, Nancy might have known for some time that there were mice in her room, but her fear of mice emerged only after her parents told her that these were harmful and evil creatures; only then did the knowledge of their presence become part of her fear.

Typical mental states in human beings consist of both intentional and feeling dimensions. Thus, seeing something often evokes pleasant or unpleasant feelings relating to the content of what we see. The relationships between the two dimensions vary in type and degree for different mental states. Whereas in emotions both dimensions are central, in most mental states only one of these is dominant. For example, the feeling dimension is dominant in painful experiences, thirst or hunger, and in affective disorders. The intentional dimension dominates the cognitive capacities of perception, memory, and thinking. To a greater extent than other mental states, emotions include diverse components within their scope, ranging from intense and primitive feelings to complex, intellectual evaluations. The more fruitful approach to emotions, therefore, is to treat them as unique combinations of the entire range of mental components, rather than to account for them by referring merely to a single basic component.

The intentional and feeling dimensions are, to a certain extent, dependent upon each other. When one of them is predominant, the other often recedes to become hardly noticeable. It is known, for example, that seriously wounded soldiers frequently feel almost no pain while on the battlefield; they only begin to experience severe pain from their wounds when they are evacuated.[2] While in combat they were focused on the enemy, which is their intentional object, since this is most useful for survival; in these circumstances, the feeling dimension was pushed into the background. Once danger recedes and the intentional object is not someone else, they become more aware of their own situation and feelings become central again. Feelings of pain or hunger may also diminish when one is deeply immersed in an intellectual activity. Likewise, diverting attention away from pain and focusing on other things instead may be expressed in reduction or even elimination of the pain altogether. The placebo effect may also be interpreted as an instance when the intentional dimension overrides the feeling dimension.

The inverse relation between the complexity of the intentional dimension and the intensity of the feeling dimension is typical of cases in which the activity level of the mental system remains constant. When the level changes, as is the case in old age or situations of intense agitation, both dimensions often change in the same direction.

Intentionality and feeling are not two separate mental entities but rather distinct dimensions of a mental state. The typical relation between these dimensions is not that of *causality*—which prevails between separate entities—but that of accompanying or *complementing* each other.[3] Since the two dimensions are distinct aspects of the same state, it is conceptually confusing to speaking about a causal relation between them within this particular state.

I believe that we could characterize the *mental-physical relationship* in a similar manner. Discussing this relationship is beyond the scope of this book. However, I do wish briefly to state my general view.[4] Two prevailing descriptions of the mental-physical relationship are (1) a relation of *causality* in which neurophysiological states precede mental ones; and (2) a *complementary* relation of support or correlation in which the two states constitute different aspects of the same event. The latter relationship seems more appropriate with regard to emotions. It is impossible to arrange the multiple neurophysiological and mental properties involved in emotions in a single linear causal chain. In the making of an emotion, some events are, of course, the cause of and hence precede them. However, once the emotion is fully manifest, these factors usually surface simultaneously. Increases in adrenaline output, blood flow, and respiration rate do not produce a mental entity, such as fear, and then disappear. Such physiological changes exist concurrently with the mental state of fear, and function as a supportive basis for it as long as it persists. Since emotions are ongoing states, it is less plausible to conceive of them as isolated products of a preceding physiological process; rather, they are supported by, or realized in, such processes. A related issue in this regard is whether emotions can be distinguished by reference to physiological changes alone. My view of the mental-physical relationship implies that in principle this should be possible, but we still have to wait for further evidence to confirm this claim.[5]

Since I concern myself in this book with the description of the mental level, the mental-physical problem is not crucial here. This does not mean that I am assuming a clear-cut dichotomy between the physical and mental realms. On the contrary, emotions furnish an example which invalidates such a dichotomy. It is difficult to classify the whole of an emotional state as being either purely mental or purely physical. An emotion expresses the state of a whole organism; only an abstract analysis can break it down into properties that are ordinarily identified with either the mental or the physical realm. In any case, most claims made in this book can be examined without assuming a particular position concerning the mental-physical relationship.

### The Cognitive Component

When your heart is on fire you must realize, smoke gets in your eyes.
—The Platters

The cognitive component supplies the required information about a given situation. No emotional attitude toward something can emerge without some information about it—whether veridical or distorted. The fear of riding a motorcycle requires some knowledge about the dangers of motorcycles. Similarly, being in love with someone involves entertaining certain beliefs concerning the beloved's virtues. Whereas the cognitive component describes the object, the evaluative component addresses a certain assessment of the same.[6]

Given our personal makeup, the cognitive component is in many cases the reason for the generation or termination of emotions. Ludwig's belief that Gilbert stole his book may be the reason he is angry with him; once it is revealed that Gilbert did not actually steal the book, he is no longer angry. Jean's fear of being seriously ill may be laid to rest when she gets the results of her medical tests and finds them to be negative; yet, her fear may not be so significantly reduced if she knows the limitations of these tests. Sometimes, the converse may take place as well: certain beliefs can be shaped by emotions. In such situations, a change in these beliefs may not change the emotional attitude. For example, Dean's love for Jessica determines to some extent what he believes her personal qualities to be. Dean's love may not be changed although he has come to realize that Jessica is not quite as intelligent as he had thought when he fell in love with her. His love may now be based on another belief, for instance, that she is quite wealthy. The above examples illustrate the complexity of the relationship between our beliefs and emotions.

The cognitive aspect in emotions is often *distorted*. This is due to several related features typical of emotions: (a) partiality, (b) closeness, and (c) an intense feeling dimension.

Emotional *partiality* contradicts the broad and impartial perspective involved in intellectual and scientific knowledge. When one does not see the whole picture, distorted claims may be adopted. Aristotle compares emotions such as anger to hasty servants who run out before they have heard the whole of what one says, and then muddle the order, and to dogs who bark if there is but a knock at the door, before looking to see if it is a friend. And Malebranche argues that "the senses and passions must be silent if one wishes to hear the word of truth."[7]

The partial nature of emotions is compatible with great *closeness*, which in turn further distorts the cognitive content in emotions. When we look at someone from a short distance, our vision is fragmented and often distorted. In the extreme case where there is no distance at all, namely, when we place the object right next to the eye itself, we do not see it for what it actually is at all. We need some distance to achieve a perspective that encompasses multiple aspects of the object and thereby makes the perspective less fragmented. However, keeping a distance is contrary to the involved and intimate perspective typical of emotions.

The *intense feeling* dimension in emotions often tends to override our ability to make sound cognitive assessments. When we are in the grip of intense feelings, some of our intellectual faculties no longer function normally. The more intense the emotional state, the easier it is for cognitive distortions to occur. Accordingly, it has been claimed that emotions are blind; they do not look beyond immediate gratification.[8]

All the above may function as obstacles to adequate knowledge of our emotional context; however, the unique nature of emotions has also some cognitive advantages. The Spanish thinker Salvador de Madariaga asks: "If our eyes had X-ray vision, would the information about reality they presented to us be more objective, more accurate, more complete, more penetrating?" He then answers: "Yes and no. A beautiful young woman would look like a walking skeleton to us. We would receive some information which our eyes hide from us—information about her bones—but we would never know what her face, her legs, her hands, her breasts, or the color of her eyes are like. If our eyes had X-ray vision, we would describe a tree as a vertical liquid stream that springs from the ground and which, if approached, causes one to receive an awful bump on the head."[9] X-ray vision, which lacks emotional significance, presents a dull world which can hardly motivate us to act and understand our environment. Unlike the gray, flat surfaces presented by X-ray vision, emotional vision provides an exciting colorful view of mountains and valleys. It is not merely more interesting to walk in the latter scenery, but often the emotional aspect facilitates our understanding of the environment.

There are indeed several indications of the importance of emotions in cognitive processes. A person who is prejudiced against a certain ethnic group, and hence typically has a distorted emotional view of that group, is nevertheless often better than most other people in identifying members of this group. Partisans on both sides of a rough football game tend disproportionately to notice penalties committed by the opposing team. Although when in emotional states we focus on a limited area, the knowledge of at least some aspects of that area may be better than that gained by a detached perspective. A person living in a ghetto may see her deprivations more accurately through indignation and anger than a person who does not live in a ghetto and looks at it from a detached and "objective" perspective. There are other cognitive advantages to emotions. Thus, emotional arousal increases *attentional capacity*. Accordingly, emotions typically increase memory. We remember events better when they are emotionally significant.[10]

The seemingly contradictory aspects of the cognitive component in emotions, namely, its distorting yet reliable nature, can be reconciled by realizing the kind of *environment* in which emotions function. This is our immediate environment, which includes those who are close to us. Emotions are central cognitive means for knowing this environment—or at least important aspects of it. Here the reliability of the emotional cognitive component is high. Regarding more distant objects, the emotional perspective is often distorted. Likewise, perception is a useful cognitive tool for our immediate present environment; for more distant objects in space and time, thinking, memory, and imagination are more useful. Similar conclusions can be drawn concerning the evaluative component in emotions. As will be further discussed in chapter 9, partial emotional evaluations are very important in our relationships with those near and dear; concerning strangers, impartial evaluations are usually more valuable from a moral point of view. It should also be mentioned that the extent of cognitive distortion or reliability may differ from one emotion to another; for example, fear may have the worst cognitive distortion, while sadness often leads to reliable cognition.

The cognitive component in emotions may refer to the three factors of emotional experience discussed in chapter 2: the emotional cause, the emotional object, and the focus of concern. We are typically, but not always, aware of all three factors.

The *emotional cause* is usually known to us, as its perception indicates a significant change in our situation. However, we may notice the change in our situation and still attribute it to something other than the real cause. Because the emotional cause precedes the emotional experience and is quite complex, this factor is the most likely to be misidentified.

It is usual, too, for the agent who is experiencing the emotion to be aware of the emotional object, and this agent often has a privileged epistemological position in this regard. However, such a position can be in error. A privileged epistemological position is one that is unique or private in that it is not shared by anyone; nevertheless, such a position can lead to mistakes. Indeed, the emotional object is sometimes illusory. We may fear or be jealous of someone who does not actually exist. Similarly, Dean at first may believe he loves Nancy but may later realize that it is really Patricia, her sister, whom he loves. Conversely, someone may know she is angry without precisely recognizing the object of her anger. In these cases, the emotional object, but not the nature of the emotion itself, is illusory.

Awareness of the nature of our emotions involves *identifying the focus of concern*. This type of awareness is possible since the feeling component is always conscious—there are no unfelt feelings—and the motivational and cognitive components are typically easy to notice. We are also generally aware whether our basic evaluative stand has a positive or negative attitude. There are, however, two major considerations which could make it difficult to be fully aware of our focus of concern and hence the precise nature of the given emotion: (1) our cognitive resources are directed at the object and not at the state itself; (2) admitting the existence of the emotion in question may not be in our interest.

The first consideration suggests that since our attention is often focused on the emotional object, we may at times have difficulty in identifying our own emotions. We may be jealous, angry, afraid, or in love, without realizing the precise nature of our emotional state. Some people know they are in love only because they experience jealousy. People say, "I only thought I was happy, but I wasn't really"; or, "He was jealous of her, but didn't realize it."

The second consideration indicates our unwillingness to admit, both to others and to ourselves, the presence of some emotions. Indeed, self-deception is frequent in connection with emotions. We might not wish to admit to ourselves that we are jealous, angry, resentful, or in love, because it violates our cherished view of who we are. The longer an emotion lasts and the greater its intensity, the more easily it is identified.

The possibility of erroneously identifying an emotion may help to explain a difficulty inherent in the notion of "unconscious emotions." Like other notions referring to the unconscious realm, this notion is also problematic since it is unclear to what mental experience it refers. Take, for example, a case in which we hate someone without being aware of our hate. One may interpret this situation as referring to an unconscious emotion having all four basic components of which we are not aware. In that case, we should assume the existence of unconscious feeling, in other words, of "unfelt feeling." This is an obvious absurdity. A more plausible explanation is that in the so-called unconscious emotions, not every component is unconscious. What is unconscious, or rather unknown, not realized, or mistakenly identified, is the nature of the emotional state, that is, our basic evaluative stand expressing our focus of concern. An unconscious emotion, then, is an emotion whose nature is unclear, while some of its components are known.[11]

Emotions having a unique feeling dimension are easier to identify; indeed the subject is likely to be the first, and sometimes even the only one, to do so. It is meaningless to say that we are unaware of our feelings. As Gilbert Ryle notes, it would be absurd to say, "I feel a tickle but maybe I haven't one." However, it makes sense to say, "I feel as if I am in love but maybe I am not."[12] Love is more complex than the mere awareness typical of feelings; the presence or absence of love may therefore be wrongly indicated. Given that we are sincere, the mere presence of a feeling cannot be wrongly indicated because feeling is a mode of awareness. However, we may wrongly identify the kind of feeling we are experiencing. Identification of this sort is a cognitive activity which often involves perception, memory, imagination, and thought; such activity may result in error. The feeling dimension places us in a better position than anyone else to identify our emotions; the intentional components sometimes make it easier for other people to identify this state.

### The Evaluative Component

People are not moved by things but the views which they take of them.
—Epictetus

The evaluative component is extremely important in emotions. Every emotion entails a certain evaluation. Hate implies the negative evaluation of a certain person, pridefulness indicates a positive evaluation of oneself, and regret involves evaluating what one has done as being wrong. Evaluating something to be dangerous underlies the emotion of fear; a highly positive evaluation of someone underlies the emotions of love and admiration. In a state devoid of an evaluative component, or one in which its weight is marginal, we are indifferent. In emotions we are neither neutral nor indifferent, but have a significant personal stake. The evaluative component appraises the "cold" information presented by the cognitive component, in terms of its implications for personal well-being.

The presence of an evaluative component is what distinguishes the emotion of hope from that of expectation: we do not hope for something unless we evaluate it as being somehow favorable; whereas our expectation of something entails no comparable evaluation. For similar reasons, surprise, when considered merely as a cognitive state, is not an emotion.[13] The distinction between cognition and evaluation should not, however, be overstated. Quite often we are unable to separate the cognitive and evaluative components from a certain belief, for example, from the belief that the situation is dangerous for us. Nevertheless, the distinction itself is important for certain explanatory purposes. As I argue below, the evaluative component is the factor which distinguishes one emotion from another.

The *evaluative component* intrinsic to a certain emotional state should not be confused with *moral evaluation of the entire state*. Thus, pleasure-in-others'-misfortune involves a positive evaluation of the misfortune of others, and hence its feeling component is agreeable. However, this emotion is often evaluated as negative from a moral viewpoint. Similarly, pity involves a negative evaluation of others' misfortune, and hence its feeling component is disagreeable, even though it is often considered to be morally positive.[14]

We are often *unable to describe the exact details of our evaluative stand*; however, we usually know the type of evaluation involved, at least whether it is positive or negative. Although a nestling cannot tell us what constitutes a menacing situation for it, it can certainly identify many such threats and is visibly afraid in their presence. The baby bird does not know what eagles are, but it promptly responds with alarm and by hiding its head when wide-winged objects fly overhead at a certain speed.[15] Similarly, we may be unable to describe the exact circumstances in which embarrassment is aroused, although the evaluative pattern causing us to become embarrassed is there. Emotions are usually easily identified, even though their precise evaluative nature may be hard to describe.

Emotions often include mixed, namely, positive and negative, evaluations; hence, they are often associated with both pleasure and pain. For example, my anger includes a negative evaluation of the other who insulted me and a positive evaluation which arises from the expectation of revenge. Similarly, my love contains admiration of the beloved and a fear that I might lose her. Despite the presence of contrary evaluations, typical emotions have an overall positive or negative value. However, some emotional states have no clear overall value, and hence it is unclear whether they are pleasant or painful. This does not mean, of course, that such an emotional state is neutral, or that we are indifferent while being in that state. We do not know what to do, but we are not indifferent.[16]

Emotions, then, presuppose cognitive and evaluative capacities. Some emotions require *more developed capacities* than others. Animals and human infants may be capable of anger and fear, but probably not of remorse, embarrassment, or pleasure-in-others'-misfortune. They may also experience sadness in the same way as adult human beings; but they do not experience regret because they lack the complex degree of intentionality required for conceiving what could be or might have been. Human infants and animals can remember events, but cannot experience guilt, which requires more developed mental capacities. Moreover, although some emotions occur in animals, their counterpart human emotions are much more complex. The objects of human emotions may also be different from those of animals; for instance, only humans make their own emotions the object of their emotions. Thus, only humans are capable of being ashamed of their sexual desire or being fearful of their anger. (This issue of emotion's in human and animals is further discussed in chapter 4 when analyzing the notion of basic emotions.)

*Deliberative and Schematic Evaluations*
An intellectual is a person who's found one thing that's more interesting than sex.
—Aldous Huxley

A distinction can be made between two major types of evaluations: deliberative and schematic. Deliberative evaluations are present, for example, when we ruminate about a certain event and as result begin to feel angry. An example of a schematic evaluation is love at first sight. *Deliberative evaluations* typically involve slow and conscious processes, which are largely under voluntary control. Such processes usually function on verbally accessible, semantic information and they operate in a largely linear, serial mode. *Schematic evaluations* involve spontaneous responses depending on a more tacit and elementary evaluative system. Schematic activity is typically fast, automatic, and with little awareness. It is based upon readymade structures or schemes of appraisal which have already been set during evolution and personal development; in this sense, history is embodied in these structures. Since the evaluative patterns are part of our psychological constitution, we do not need time to create them; we just need the right circumstances to activate them. Schematic activity largely occurs outside of focal awareness, can occur using minimal attentional resources, and is not wholly dependent on verbal information.[17]

The two types of evaluations may clash. Thus, we may persist in being afraid even when our conscious and deliberative judgment reveals that we are no longer in any peril. We can explain such cases by assuming that certain schematic evaluations become constitutive to a degree where no intellectual deliberation can change them. This corresponds to situations in which intellectual knowledge fails to influence illusory perceptual contents. Spontaneous evaluations are similar to perceptual discriminations in being immediate, meaningful responses. They entail no deliberative mediating processes, merely appearing as if they were products of such processes.

The schematic nature of typical emotional evaluations enables us to consider emotions not as an isolated result of a cognitive inference, but as part of ongoing interaction. Deliberative evaluation is a preparatory process that precedes and is separate from its product. A schema is an active principle of organization which is constitutive in nature; it is not separate from the organized state, but part of it.

Complex deliberative evaluations are a more recent evolutionary phenomenon: they entail conscious deliberation, characteristic mostly of human beings. The presence of emotions in some higher animals and the existence of conflicts between emotional evaluations and deliberative thinking indicates that many emotions involve schematic rather than deliberative evaluations.

An interesting question is whether all emotions involve schematic evaluations or some are the result of deliberative processes alone. A key consideration in this respect is that emotions are typically generated when we confront a sudden and significant change. In light of the sudden generation of emotions, it is reasonable to suppose that most of them involve schematic evaluations which do not require a lengthy process of deliberation. This, however, does not imply that deliberative thinking has no role in the generation of emotions. We may think about death and become frightened, or think about our mates and become jealous. Thoughts also have an effect on moods, and moods influence our thoughts. Typically, negative thoughts are related to negative moods, and positive thoughts are related to positive moods; thoughts and moods are usually congruent.[18]

Deliberative thinking, however, has a preparatory, rather than a constitutive role in emotions. Thinking may prepare the system for the activation of schematic evaluations: it brings us closer to the conditions under which evaluative patterns are spontaneously activated. Such thinking may be the immediate stimulus for the activation of an evaluative pattern, but the emotional evaluation itself is non-deliberative. This gives the emotional system the ability to react almost instantaneously to significant events, and yet to draw fully upon the power and flexibility of complex cognitive and evaluative capacities, such as theoretical thinking.[19]

The biological function of emotions provides a clear explanation for the development of an automatic appraisal mechanism: to provide a quick response to urgent situations. The great role of personal and social circumstances in generating emotions does not change the spontaneous and unreflective nature of emotions. Such circumstances mold our character so that some of our spontaneous and natural emotional responses assume a certain form. Here we may speak of "learned spontaneity"; this spontaneity is an immediate response, but has been shaped by our personal and social history.[20]

## The Computational Approach to the Mind

I refuse to admit that I am more than fifty-two, even if that does make my sons illegitimate.
—Lady Astor

The dispute concerning the conceptual or schematic nature of emotional evaluations is related to a more general dispute concerning the computational nature of the mind. The prevailing view, which is often termed "cognitivism" or the "computational approach," considers mental states to be products of conceptual or reasoning processes such as computations, inferences, interpretations, and decoding. Historically, the computational approach is derived from the Cartesian view that considers thinking to be the essence of the mental realm. In accordance with this view, several authors have also considered the emotional system to be a basically computational system. My critical attitude toward the computational approach in general has been presented elsewhere.[21] I will not repeat it here but rather briefly indicate some of the implications of this criticism for the emotional system.

People often confuse two different senses of "computation": (1) a simple transition from one state to another, and (2) a deliberative process having a meaningful content. I have no objection to describing emotional evaluations as computational in the first sense; I would just doubt the adequacy of the term "computation" in this connection. I agree that emotions are a transition from one state to another, but so are many other nonmental states. Using "computation" in this sense is not very informative and can be incorporated within opposing views of emotions.

The second sense of computation, namely, a deliberative process having a meaningful content, is more controversial and is directly relevant to various theoretical discussions concerning the nature of emotions. The computational (in the second sense, which is the one I refer to from now on) approach considers the creation of emotions to be a production process in which the *emotional end products are separate from the physiological and cognitive processes preceding them.* Deliberative processes, such as computations and inferences, resemble production processes in that they precede their conclusions and are separate from them. The fundamental cognitive system in this approach is an intellectual, conceptual system; its essential activity consists of unconscious deliberative processes which are similar to those typical of the conscious realm.

Several *difficulties* are associated with the computational approach. I will briefly mention two of them. The first difficulty concerns the attempt made by the computational approach to explain emotions by duplicating in the unconscious realm reasoning processes typical of the conscious realm. In this approach we should imagine the presence of a little man in the brain (homunculus) who perceives the incoming data, then, through consulting various personal characteristics, evaluates them, and decides upon the appropriate emotion. However, duplicating a system does not explain the system, it only shifts the problems to different arenas: now there is the need to explain the homunculus' evaluation and an endless computational regression is created. Another difficulty of the computational approach is that emotions are explained by postulating reasoning processes typical of thinking. In this view we first think and then emote. However, according to the evidence of evolution, these thinking processes evolved only later and are absent in many animals that do experience emotions.[22]

The presence of deliberative processing in emotional evaluations does not imply advocating a computational approach to emotions. My proposed characterization of emotional evaluations differs in several crucial aspects from the one assumed by the computational approach. First, emotional evaluations are the product of schematic rather than deliberative activity. The presence of deliberative processes preceding emotional experiences is not the typical situation. Second, deliberative processing in the emotional realm usually serves the function of bringing us closer to conditions under which schematic activity is triggered. Third, deliberative processing in emotional evaluations is typically conscious, whereas in the computational approach these processes are basically unconscious.

In short, we can assume the presence of evaluations in the emotional process and even the presence of deliberative evaluations without subscribing to a model of the mind in which thinking underlies all mental states.

### The Motivational Component

Only dead fish swim with the stream.
—Unknown

The motivational component refers to the desire or readiness to maintain or change present, past, or future circumstances. In the case of "passionate" emotions, such as anger and sexual desire, the desire is typically manifested in overt behavior; in "dispassionate" emotions, such as envy and hope, the behavioral element is less in evidence and appears merely as a desire. The importance of the motivational component is suggested by the etymological link between "emotion," "motion," and "motives," in that "emotion" was originally a term used to express a kind of motion. Another indication of the importance of the motivational component is that numerous neurophysiological and hormonal systems involved in the experience of emotion also participate in arousing the organism to activity.[23]

Emotions are not theoretical states; they involve a practical concern, associated with a *readiness to act*. Since emotions are evaluative attitudes, involving a positive or a negative stance toward the object, they also entail either taking action or being disposed to act in a manner compatible with the evaluation. For example, a positive emotional evaluation of someone is often correlated with a readiness to be with that person. The readiness to act in emotions is not neutral, but is a sort of desire expressing our favorable attitude toward this course of action. When we are indifferent to someone, we experience no emotion and no tendency to do something for or against that person. Consider the following description of beauty by a modeling agent: "It's when someone walks in the door and you almost can't breathe . . . I mean someone you literally can't walk past in the street."[24] Emotional states, such as those generated when we meet a beautiful person, cannot leave us indifferent. They make us literally stop doing whatever we are doing and focus our activities and resources upon the emotional concern.

Emotions typically express our most profound values and attitudes; as such, they often express not merely superficial involvement but deep commitment. The difference between involvement and commitment may be illustrated by the bacon and eggs people eat for breakfast. The chicken's attitude is that of involvement, the pig's attitude is that of commitment. The deep commitment associated with emotions is expressed in a strong motivational component. Unlike emotional states in which the evaluative concern is very profound, nonemotional evaluations may not involve a motivational component.

The evaluative component in emotions is connected to a certain type of motivation rather than to a certain type of behavior.[25] The motivational component can be connected to actual behavior in different ways: (a) a full-fledged desire, which is expressed in actual behavior; (b) a desire or want, which is not expressed in actual behavior because of external constraints; (c) a mere wish, which is not intended to be translated into actual behavior.

Love is a typical emotion which includes full-fledged desires expressed in certain characteristic activities: caressing and cuddling, attentiveness to the needs and wishes of the beloved, and so on. Not all of these have to be manifest at all times and in every instance of love; however, the total absence of such behavior all the time may suggest that love is absent as well. Furthermore, the presence of other modes of behavior may also suggest the absence of love. So, someone might say, "If you really loved me you wouldn't behave that way." The complex nature of love and the varieties of behavior that are associated with it, make the claim "I love someone" less of a specific description than "I kissed someone."

Despite the close connection of emotions and motivation, we cannot say that each emotion is associated with a specific behavior. Some emotions are more closely connected with specific behaviors than others. For example, the behaviors typical of fear are easier to specify than those typical of envy or joy, which are more open-ended. Yet, even the connection between fear and a specific behavior, such as flight, is not as predictable as, say, the connection between hunger and eating.[26] Moreover, it has been suggested that the great evolutionary advantage of emotion was to allow a stimulus to be registered and reacted to without committing the organism to an overreaction; this allows behavior to be contingent on a stimulus, but not dictated by it.[27]

Sometimes the motivational component is expressed in desires or wants which are not translated into actual behavior because of various constraints. The behavioral manifestation of any emotion varies according to circumstances and is sometimes absent—being either suppressed or merely imagined. Someone who is suffering from total paralysis may have emotions, although these are unaccompanied by any muscular activity. But even in such cases the action tendency is present. Although flight is a behavior characteristic of fear, and aggression is typically associated with anger, there are instances of fear and anger when these modes of action do not occur for various reasons; for example, such modes of action may hurt us in the long run. All the same, the readiness to act in these modes is still there. In such cases, translating the motivational component into action depends on *external constraints*, such as prudential considerations or other desires we have. Hence, the absence of appropriate behavior does not necessarily imply the absence of a motivational component.

The weakest connection between the motivational component and actual behavior is that in which we have a mere wish. Unlike a nonpractical want, which is not translated into actual behavior because of external constraints, a mere wish is not manifested because of the nature of the wish itself. Thus, someone's wish to meet again with her deceased beloved cannot be translated into behavior because it is directed at past events and is therefore impossible to realize. Similarly, one's momentary wish to kill a successful colleague is not translated into reality because of the moral repugnancy of killing. In both nonpractical wants and mere wishes, the emotional tendency toward action is expressed only in *mental motions*, that is, we go through the motions in our mind. But whereas in wants these motions are intended to be executed, in mere wishes such intent is absent. In any case, the motivational component of emotions is more strictly related to *action tendency* than to actual behavior.

The close connection between emotions and action tendency makes emotions a useful tool for persuading people to take a certain course of action. Aristotle argued that people are persuaded to do something when their emotions are stirred; accordingly, his main discussion of emotions can be found in his book *Rhetoric*. Indeed, we often explain and justify our actions by reference to emotions. No wonder that politicians persuade us to vote for them by appealing primarily to the emotional domain. An efficient way to provoke positive or negative feelings in voters is to use emotional issues, such as abortion or civil rights. Rather than intellectual discussions about the issues, emotional slogans and pictures are at the heart of most political campaigns.

*Emotional persuasion* is not totally devoid of any type of information, but in accordance with the nature of the cognitive component in emotions, this information is often partial and superficial. The persuasive force of political advertisements, as of other commercials, is facilitated by the use of half-truths and fallacious logic which makes us think that we are responding on the basis of profound information rather than emotional images. The length of these ads is one indication of their partial and superficial nature. The most dominant time frame for American presidential ads is the thirty-second spot. Research on product commercials has demonstrated that thirty-second spots are just as effective as sixty-second spots in getting the message across, that is to say, in their ability to trigger an emotional state. No wonder that over 80 percent of the information retained about television commercials is visual.[28]

Commercial ads are also directed essentially at playing on our emotions. Their primary goal is not necessarily direct persuasion, but emotional impact whereby the viewers are made aware of the product and associate it with something desirable, such as sex appeal, that consequently triggers positive emotions. An advertisement can induce a happy mood and at the same time not give people too much time to think; it can incline a person favorably toward the product, independent of its merit or usefulness. Indeed, commercial ads often lack "hard" product information, such as material, price, or performance, and rely instead on techniques that emphasize stylistic features such as action, appearance, fun, or novelty. The seductiveness of advertising is evidenced by the fact that background music and the character of the person delivering the commercial message can significantly affect the viewer's evaluation of the product, by making us experience certain emotions.[29]

The importance of action readiness in emotions is emphasized when we compare them to *humor*. In contrast to the practical orientation of emotions, humor involves a more abstract and less purposeful activity. Thus, in the case of fear or anger, we prepare ourselves, both physiologically and mentally, to flee or to fight; but when we laugh at something amusing, we are not preparing for action of any kind. Indeed, at the moment of laughter, we are temporarily disabled.[30] We often use humor to block emotions such as fear, anger, or sorrow, or to resolve tensions. Humor is not a joke for nature. Its survival value consists, at least in part, in its functioning as a counterweight to the strong influence exerted by emotions and moods on our behavior. In this sense humor is also similar to art; both draw attention away from the self and its desires, thereby enabling us to look at reality from a safe and somewhat different perspective. This makes it possible for us to relax and cope better with reality. Like laughter, weeping would appear to be a mode of behavior that has the function of interrupting other behavior. Weeping, however, is associated with helplessness, whereas laughter is linked to the resolution of tensions or other problematic situations. Incidentally, the facial features assume similar configurations when we laugh or cry.[31]

### The Feeling Component

Love is not a feeling. Love is put to the test, pain not. One does not say: "That was not true pain, or it would not have gone off so quickly."
—Ludwig Wittgenstein

The term "feeling" has several meanings: awareness of tactile qualities, bodily sensations, emotions, moods, awareness in general, and so forth. In this discussion, the term is confined to modes of awareness which express our own state and are not directed at a certain object.[32] In light of its importance in identifying our own state, it is plausible that mental life begins—from both an evolutionary and a personal viewpoint—with states of feeling; life at this stage is a succession of agreeable and disagreeable sensations. Later on, when the intentional capacities have developed, the feeling dimension usually becomes part of a complex mental state which also includes the intentional dimension. Indeed, human mental states with a single basic dimension, that is, states of pure feeling or pure intentionality, occur rarely, if at all. Actual mental states are complex experiences which typically entail both feeling and intentionality.

The homogeneous and basic nature of feelings makes it difficult, though perhaps not impossible, to describe them. Indeed, there are few words for feelings, and we often have to resort to metaphors and other figures of speech in referring to them. Many feelings have only an "as if" recognizability ("It feels as if it is a lemon"; "It feels as if a knife stabbed me").[33]

It is not easy to identify the varying characteristics of the feeling component. No doubt feelings have intensity, duration, and some have location as well, but what about other qualities? The qualities of being painful or pleasurable are obvious. Some level of pleasantness or unpleasantness, albeit often of low intensity, is experienced by most people most of the time. In addition to pleasure and displeasure, the continuum of arousal may be a common aspect of the feeling dimension.[34]

Feelings are frequently described as emotions, and emotions are often defined by reference to feelings. In everyday speech, we tend to say that we feel an emotion ("I feel ashamed/embarrassed/jealous"). In the terminology suggested here, this use of "feeling" is figurative rather than literal. In fact, we feel a certain feeling; we do not feel an emotion, which is a complex state including other components besides feelings. (However, as a matter of convenience, I sometimes use the term "feeling" in this figurative manner.) In popular locutions, such as "I feel she is right," the word "feel" conveys a general attitude rather than a specific feeling. Specific feeling terms are also ambiguous. "Pleasure" may refer, among other things, to a raw feeling contrasted with pain, or to a complex emotional state opposed to sorrow. "Pain" can also refer to a raw feeling in contrast to a pleasant one, or to a complex experience involving this feeling and a second-order awareness of this and other elements. Despite the linguistic ambiguity in using these terms, the meaning is usually clear in the given context.[35]

The closeness of feelings to emotions in everyday language is an indication of the important role of feelings in emotions. Feelings are more noticeable and intense in emotions than in most other mental states due to the urgency and exceptional nature of emotional situations. Since it is an advantage to be aware of the sudden changes associated with emotions, feelings have a crucial role in this regard.

Despite the importance of feelings in emotions, equating the two is incorrect since emotions have intentional components in addition to the feeling component. Take, for example, the distinction between sexual pleasure and sexual desire. Sexual pleasure is basically a feeling which indicates our pleasant situation while having sex, imagining having sex, or artificially stimulating the physiological basis underlying sexual activity. Sexual desire is a complex emotion having intentional components directed at a certain object. Unlike the complex experience of emotions, mere feelings are more localized in space and time and are not intentional. Mere feelings are more passive states than emotions. Moreover, people can experience and identify feelings typical of a certain emotion without experiencing the emotion itself.[36]

Sometimes two different emotions, such as grief and pride, can be distinguished by virtue of the feeling component bound up with them. In other instances, the feeling component may be inadequate in this respect. The same emotion, such as love, may share a variety of feelings, and the same feeling may be shared by different emotions, like shame, remorse, regret, and guilt. Although many emotions embrace a variety of feelings within their scope, their range is generally restricted to a particular set of characteristic feelings; in any case, not every feeling can be linked with every emotion.

Feelings are often described as having an evaluative component, with pain involving a negative evaluation and pleasure, a positive evaluation. We should distinguish between the complex pain or pleasure experience and a felt quality which is one component of this experience. Experiences of pain, for instance, incorporate affective attitudes, such as fear, anxiety, and hostility, which are intentional as they involve a certain evaluation. Feelings themselves are not intentional: they do not have cognitive content describing a certain state; they are merely an initial expression of our current state. Pain or pleasure is an inherent property of feeling. However, the painful sensation of toothache does not mean that toothache is an intentional state evaluating the condition of the tooth. It is rather our self-perception of the condition of the tooth which includes a negative evaluation of the situation. Although feeling is perceived as value-laden, it is not an intentional state, inherent in which is a certain evaluation.

Masochists and people who prefer not to enjoy themselves exemplify the difference between the mere feeling component and our intentional self-perception of this feeling. Masochists desire and even seek out *painful feelings*. Both the masochist and nonmasochist are made uncomfortable by pain. If those who inflict pain on themselves found the feeling to be as agreeable as pleasure, they would not be masochists; the difference is in the evaluative attitude. Creatures who are capable of feeling both pleasure and pain but are devoid of evaluative attitudes cannot be masochistic. Similarly, normal people may have different evaluative attitudes toward the same feeling: circumstances determine whether we like or dislike being tickled. The characteristic negative way of evaluating pain is more natural, since the unpleasant feelings induced by pain are generally connected with physical injury. Avoidance of pain has adaptive advantages, because ordinary activities that enhance the chances for survival are not easily carried out when we are in pain.

The attitude toward *pleasurable feelings* is more complex, as the correlation between an agreeable feeling and a positive adaptive value is flexible in human beings. Sometimes we may even find an inverse correlation; for example, when we indulge our appetite for cake, chocolate, or alcohol. In animals the positive correlation is stricter, so that emotions are usually not harmful to them. These differences may be explained in the following manner. Pain and pleasure are indicative of changes in our situation. Radical changes are often harmful, since they can destroy the biological and sometimes mental equilibrium essential to our existence. Similarly, even though a certain amount of illumination is necessary for vision, excessive light can destroy the visual system. While excessive pain prevents us from functioning normally and compels us to address the injurious situation, an excess of pleasure hardly imposes any practical limits on our behavior. Yet, artificially induced pleasure in excessive amounts can be harmful to animals, just as it is often harmful to human beings. In a well-known experiment, a group of rats learned to stimulate the part of their brain controlling enjoyable sensations by depressing a pedal; it was found that the rats depressed the pedal nonstop until they died from exhaustion.[37] Since excessive pleasure is not a natural phenomenon, evolution provided no mechanism to curb it. The artificial circumstances typical of excessive pleasure are usually present only in the newly created human environment which is rapidly changing. Accordingly, the negative survival value of pleasure is usually typical only in humans and not in animals.

Another indicator of the absence of the evaluative component in feelings is that we cannot speak of our *reasons* or grounds for experiencing a feeling, as we can in the case of emotions. There is no point in asking people about their reasons for having a toothache, although it does make sense to ask about the causes of such feelings. It is therefore futile to try to justify or criticize feelings in the same way as we do with emotions. We cannot reason people out of their toothache as we might reason them out of their hatred. Unlike emotions, feelings are not subject to normative appraisal. In the same vein, feelings do not encompass the intentional motivational component. Although feelings are an important factor in determining our behavior, feelings themselves are neither modes of behavior nor tendencies to behave in certain ways. As John Dewey remarks, "I should not fear a man who had simply the 'feel' of anger," for "anger means a tendency to explode in a sudden attack, not a mere state of feeling."[38]

## Comparing the Different Components

My husband and I are either going to buy a dog or have a child. We can't decide whether to ruin our carpet or ruin our lives.
—Rita Rudner

Cognition, which contains descriptive information about the object, logically comes prior to the evaluation of this object, namely, to a normative appraisal of its value. Hence, there can be cognition without evaluation. Evaluation presupposes a certain degree of cognition; we cannot evaluate something without having some information about it. Evaluation typically occurs prior to motivation; motivation usually implies evaluation. In having desires one makes certain evaluations, but (as Aristotle contends) one can evaluate something as good without being thereby motivated to pursue it. The pursuit involves practical considerations which may result in different types of desires. However, when the evaluation is highly positive or negative, it is likely to be expressed by a certain motivation. The feeling component has no logical connection with the intentional components, but is associated with them in typical emotions.

The actual link between the cognitive and other components is contingent: the same cognitive content may give rise to different evaluations, motivations, and feelings. The link between the evaluative and the motivational and feeling components is more rigid: all these components are correlated with the positive or negative nature of the emotion. For example, anger includes a negative evaluation of the other's action, negative types of actions toward this person, and unpleasant feelings. The link between these components has obvious evolutionary advantages: pleasant feelings are an important motivating force for doing things we positively evaluate. Take, for instance, sex. Sex, after all, is time-consuming, messy, and dangerous. Nevertheless, we often indulge in sex which is positively evaluated in light of considerations referring to reproduction and increasing emotional closeness. Pleasure makes sex worthwhile; it provides the benefit needed to offset the sizable costs associated with intercourse.[39]

Despite the logical priority of the cognitive component over the evaluative component, the evaluative component is the most important component in emotions: emotions are basically evaluative attitudes rather than cognitive states. Perception, on the other hand, is essentially a *cognitive state*. Accordingly, an emotion may be described as reasonable or justified, but not as true or false; whereas a perceptual state may be described as true or false, but not as reasonable or justified. To perceive something is to be aware of a particular content. Although an emotion involves some type of awareness, it is not merely a mode of awareness in the same way as perception.

The emphasis upon the evaluative component suggested here is not a new explanatory direction. It can be found in the writings of ancient and contemporary philosophers and psychologists.[40] Indeed, today, evaluative theories are the foremost approach to emotions in philosophy and psychology. The general assumption underlying these theories is that evaluations (appraisals) are the most crucial factor in emotions. This assumption may imply at least two different claims: (1) evaluative patterns distinguish one emotion from another; (2) evaluative patterns distinguish emotions from nonemotions. These claims, which are not clearly distinguished by appraisal theorists, are not necessarily related. Accepting one of them does not necessarily imply acceptance of the other. I believe that whereas a simplistic formulation of (2) is false, (1) is basically true.

Which component is the *distinguishing, or individualizing, component of emotions*? It is clearly not the *cognitive* component, since a similar cognitive content can generate multiple, even opposing, emotions. For example, information about the appearance of someone may result in love, sexual desire, admiration, or envy. Emotions are not generated in the presence of every event; they emerge in the presence of significant changes. Determining the significance of a change is basically an evaluative rather than a cognitive task. Hence, reference to the cognitive content is not sufficient for the distinction between different emotions. Accordingly, Descartes argues that "the objects that stimulate the senses do not excite different passions in us because of the differences in the objects, but only because of the various ways in which they may harm or benefit us, or in general have importance for us."[41]

The *motivational and feeling* components show a higher degree of correlation with the nature of the emotion in the sense that they can indicate its positive or negative character. Essentially, positive emotions incorporate a positive evaluation, pleasant feelings, and the desire to maintain the situation; negative emotions incorporate a negative evaluation, unpleasant feelings, and the desire to change the situation. This global correlation is due to the centrality of the evaluative component. Distinctions in the motivational domain typically mirror distinctions in the evaluative domain. Distinctions in the feeling domain can be more arbitrary, but some general correlation with the evaluative domain can be found.

Motivational and feeling components may serve to distinguish between some emotions. For example, the motivational component is crucial in distinguishing between pity and compassion: readiness to assist the object is much more evident in compassion. The difference in the motivational component also surfaces in the evaluative component. Thus, pity involves evaluating the object to be inferior to us, whereas compassion entails a more egalitarian evaluation.

Some people argue that the nature of emotions, as well as their intensity, can be determined by the two major aspects of the feeling dimension: *pleasantness-unpleasantness* and *arousal-calmness*. According to one view, the nature of an emotion depends on the proportion of pleasure-displeasure and arousal that is experienced, whereas its intensity is determined by the absolute values of pleasure-displeasure and arousal. Empirical studies, some of which were done by the proponents of this view, indicate that reliable discrimination between the emotions merely on the basis of these aspects of the feeling dimension is impossible. For example, in one study disappointment, envy, and shame had similar proportions of pleasure and arousal, but yet they are clearly different emotions.[42] I believe that basing the classification of emotions on the motivational component alone will also fail to distinguish clearly between all emotions.

The motivational and feeling components may distinguish among some emotions, but not all emotions can be distinguished on the basis of their motivational or feeling component. For example, shame and embarrassment may often have a similar motivational component. Likewise, many different emotions—and perhaps also nonemotional states—may have a similar feeling component.

Distinguishing one emotion from another is best done by referring to the evaluative component. In most cases, the *cognitive* component allows for the greatest variation concerning the nature of the given emotion, as the same piece of information can evoke different emotions. The *motivational* and *feeling* components can specify the positive or negative nature of a given emotion better than the cognitive component, but frequently they cannot further specify the unique nature of the given emotion. The *evaluative* component is the most reliable means to distinguish between different types of emotion. Although there are some elements of similarity in different emotional evaluations, for example, concerning their positive or negative nature, the uniqueness of each emotion is determined by a specific evaluative theme. The evaluative component allows for the least variation in specifying the nature of a given emotion. Regarding the other three components, even their most detailed specification will not preclude the possibility of two different emotion types possessing this specific component. It may be the case that finer distinctions between certain types of emotion require a reference to some other components besides evaluation. Still, this component remains by far the best means of differentiating between emotions.

Are there any cases involving an emotional but not an evaluative change? Consider, for example, the case in which a woman's love for her husband has changed into dislike, even though her appraisal of his character seems to be unaltered, as she may have become bored with him for displaying the same familiar characteristics. Such cases should not be interpreted as lacking an evaluative change.

Although the change in her attitude from love to dislike may not involve a change in evaluating some of his traits, say, his wit and good looks, it involves an essential change in evaluating his whole personality and in particular his ability to be a pleasant companion. A basic change in our emotional state requires a change in the evaluative component.[43]

*Do evaluative patterns distinguish emotions from nonemotions?* The distinguishing nature of the evaluative component does not mean that it necessarily constitutes a sufficient condition for the generation of emotions, namely, it is not the sole criterion *distinguishing emotion from nonemotion.* Evaluating the death of someone as bad is far from experiencing the emotion of grief. The two states may share an identical cognitive and a similar evaluative component, but they often differ in their feeling and motivational components. There are many situations in which we evaluate something as good or bad without being emotionally affected by it. This is often the case when the eliciting event is not strong enough, does not seem real, or is irrelevant and remote from us. For instance, one may harbor a negative evaluation of the good fortunes of others, but if this evaluation is not part of a more complex state comprising motivational features and a certain type of feeling, then the resulting state will not be that of envy. I may wish to be in the position of King Solomon who had a thousand wives, but my attitude toward him is unlikely to be envy, as he is not in my reference group.

In arguing that emotions can be distinguished by their evaluative component, I am not attempting to reduce emotions to this component. Emotions are complex states drawing upon a subtle equilibrium of diverse components; the presence alone of the evaluative component—or for that matter any other component—is not sufficient for the generation of emotions. But when the presence of an emotional state is not in question, but rather the identification of its nature, then reference to the evaluative component becomes significant.

I have indicated that a similar evaluative pattern—for example, a negative evaluation of the misfortune suffered by another person—can be a component of both an emotion and a nonemotional state; accordingly, we cannot discern the two phenomena on the basis of the pattern alone. However, when we consider the whole evaluative component—which includes, in addition to the conceptual pattern, also the depth and particular perspective of the given evaluation—discerning the two phenomena becomes possible. I can negatively evaluate the death of Martha's mother, but Martha's evaluation is more profound, involving a more personal perspective, a greater commitment and attachment; accordingly, only Martha, as the daughter, will experience grief. A sufficient condition for grief, then, is not merely a negative evaluation of someone's death, but also a very profound type of evaluation indicating that life has considerably changed. When taking into account the nature of the evaluation in question, and in particular its depth, we may be able to distinguish emotions from nonemotions.[44]

The presence of the four basic components—cognition, evaluation, motivation, and feeling—is a necessary, but not sufficient condition for generating emotions.

A typical emotion must include each of these components. However, a situation can arise in which all four components are present but no emotion is generated since these components are not of the required intensity, or other characteristics of emotions are absent.

An interesting question is what makes us evaluate one thing in an emotional manner and something else in a nonemotional manner: that is, what determines the emotional significance of the eliciting event? This issue is discussed in chapter 5 where I describe the evaluating factors which determine emotional intensity. Among such factors, which I term "intensity variables," are the event's strength, reality, and relevance, and background circumstances such as controllability, readiness, and deservingness.

It should be noted that by making the strength, or the depth, of the emotional evaluation a criterion for distinguishing emotions from nonemotions, we admit that there is no clear-cut borderline between them, as strength and depth are a function of degree. There is an obvious difference between typical emotional and nonemotional states, but there is also a large gray area whose classification is, to a certain extent, arbitrary. Because of the prototypical nature of emotions, a precise distinction between these and other states is not feasible, nor has it significant implications. Assuming that there is a continuum of evaluative depth is also important for distinguishing different degrees of emotional intensity. I may sincerely grieve upon hearing about the death of a friend, but my grief is not as intense as it was upon hearing that my brother had been killed in a war.

Granting that the evaluative component in its broad sense can distinguish one emotion from another, and an emotion from a nonemotion, does not imply the identity of emotion with such evaluation. The evaluative judgment "the most beautiful person in the world" may distinguish Claudia Shiffer from other people in the world, but it is not identical with Claudia Shiffer herself. Similarly, an emotion is a much more complex state than a mere evaluation; it includes a subtle equilibrium of other components and characteristics. Each emotional factor may be described as having a certain weight. A significant increase in the weight of one factor may reduce the weight of other factors and thus disturb the subtle emotional equilibrium. For instance, too much weight on the feeling component may reduce the role of the intentional dimension in a way which is not typical of emotions. The difference between anger and a negative nonemotional evaluation of a particular act may be expressed by the fact that the latter lacks the minimal intensity of the feeling and motivational components which are typical of emotions.

The presence of a *global correlation* between evaluation, motivation, and feelings is not always obvious. One reason is the compound and diverse nature of emotions. Thus, since emotional objects are complex, we may evaluate some of their aspects positively and others negatively; hence, emotions may have both positive and negative components. For example, a mother may have mixed feelings at her daughter's wedding; she is glad at her daughter's happiness, but sad at losing her. Love is not always pleasant, as it may involve fear of losing the beloved; no wonder that Eros is described as "bittersweet." Similarly, hate does not always involve pain alone, as it may provide us with the opportunity to unload negative emotions.[45]

A complex emotional attitude includes both positive and negative elements of the evaluative, motivational, and feeling components. Hence, there are situations in which a global correlation between all positive and all negative components of a given emotion seems to be absent. There may be a situation in which a negative evaluation may seem to be correlated with a positive component of motivation and pleasurable feelings. In such situations the general correlation does exist but the various components are wrongly connected: actually all positive components are correlated with each other and so are the negative components. If we positively evaluate a beloved, then this evaluation is connected with pleasant feelings and the wish to be with that person. We may also negatively evaluate the possibility of losing the beloved; this evaluation is connected with an unpleasant feeling and a different type of motivational attitude. Both types of evaluation are part of the complex emotion of love, and in both the general correlation pertains. When we say that love is basically a positive emotion, we mean that the positive evaluation and its associated positive motivational component and pleasant feelings are more essential in love than are the negative elements. Despite the frequent presence of conflicting elements in complex emotions, we can nevertheless characterize their typical cases as either positive or negative.[46]

The view suggested here may be considered as an evaluative view, or an *appraisal theory* of emotions. We may distinguish two types of appraisal theory: constitutive and causal. In the *constitutive* type, which is a weaker version of appraisal theory, appraisals (or evaluations) are necessary constituents in the emotional state; in the *causal* type, appraisals are necessary constituents not only in the emotional state but in its cause as well. Take, for example, joy. The constitutive view claims that joy must include a certain evaluation, for instance, a positive evaluation of my present situation. The causal view agrees with this claim but also adds that such evaluation is included in the cause of this emotion—that is, I had evaluated the eliciting positively prior to the emergence of joy.[47]

I believe that although in typical emotions appraisals are a constitutive element in both the cause and the experience of the emotion, this is not necessarily so. There may be emotional states whose generation does not involve evaluations; they are generated by merely having the suitable facial or physiological features. Thus, there is some evidence that joy can be induced by merely changing the facial configurations in a way typical of a smile.[48] In such a case, we should not say that we smile because we are happy, but that we are happy because we smile. These cases are problematic only for the causal type of appraisal theories but not for the constitutive type which is adopted here—while remembering that in typical cases the causal view is valid as well. Many heated disputes concerning the role of appraisals in emotions could be settled by clarifying the distinction between these two types of appraisal theories; as yet, little attention has been paid to such a distinction.[49]

Admitting that appraisals are typically present in both the emotional cause and the emotional experience may give rise to the problem of self-causation: that is, how can an event be a cause of another event of which it is a part? If an appraisal is both the cause and the essence of an emotion, we must assume self-causation, namely, that a certain event precedes another event and is its cause but at the same time is the caused event itself. To overcome this problem, we should take into account that both the emotional cause and the emotional experience are complex events which include other elements besides appraisals; an appraisal is part of both the cause and the experience. It is not the case, for example, that appraising someone as beautiful causes a different appraisal and is also part of this appraisal. Rather, appraising someone as beautiful is a component of two mental states: that of looking at a person one finds attractive and that of having sexual desire toward this person. The two states are complex experiences having other components besides this common component of positive evaluation. The problem of self-causation arises only when the cause and its result are the very same event; this problem does not arise when a certain element is present in both the cause and its result.[50]

## Difficulties and Objections

Too bad the only people who know how to run the country are busy driving cabs and cutting hair.
—George Burns

Many theories of emotion attempt to reduce emotions to one basic component or to exclude a certain component from the essential nature of emotions. Such attempts can be found regarding each of the four suggested basic components of emotions, namely: cognition, evaluation, motivation, and feeling.

Feeling and cognition are often described as two basic components of emotions. A major dispute in this respect concerns the question of which component is more essential in the sense of being the necessary and sufficient condition for emotions. This dispute is simplistic for two major reasons. One reason is that neither component is the necessary and sufficient condition for the generation of emotions; however, as suggested above, the evaluative component may serve to distinguish between diverse emotions. The other reason is that in addition to the cognitive component, the intentional dimension includes evaluative and motivational components. (It must be noted that many psychologists use "cognitive" broadly, thereby incorporating other intentional components, including the evaluative component.)

Some people suggest that the motivational component is the most important, or even the defining component of emotions.[51] However, despite the importance of readiness for action to emotions, they should not be reduced to such a behavioral or quasi-behavioral level. One difficulty of such a reduction is that in some emotional experiences, for example, aesthetic experiences and backward-looking emotions, the role of the motivational component is not at all evident.

*Aesthetic experiences*, such as listening to music or looking at a painting, are not so much about the work of art as they are an expression of our own state. The intentionality of the cognitive and evaluative components in aesthetic experiences is similar in its generality to that of moods; however, unlike moods, the motivational component in aesthetic experiences is often absent or at least not dominant. The aesthetic experience has indeed been described as apprehension without interest. Although some kind of motivational component—for example, the wish to preserve a current situation—may be present in many aesthetic experiences, it is far from being essential. Aesthetic experiences are also not typical emotions in the sense that they are usually not directed at people.

The identification of the motivational component is also problematic in *backward-looking emotions* directed at people or general concerns from the past, for example, hatred of Hitler, admiration of Aristotle, or nostalgia in general. In these examples, the practical aspect is not obvious. Unlike aesthetic experiences, the above emotions do not lack a motivational component, but rather this component seems to lack immediate practical implications since it pertains to an imaginary realm. However, my admiration of Aristotle or hatred of Hitler entails diverse types of behavior in the constructed imaginary situation in which I meet them. It may also have some implications for my present behavior; for example, my wish to imitate Aristotle or to behave in ways that are as far as possible from Hitler's behavior.

Emotions toward the *past* are in this sense similar to emotions toward fictional figures. In both cases, the motivational component is present but it is basically focused on our imaginary behavior. In comparison with forward-looking emotions which contain the element of wanting, backward-looking emotions contain the element of wishing. As William Lyons suggests, one might wish that the dead person could be brought to life, but such wishful thinking does not issue into impulses to action. This wish may be futile, but it is not necessarily illogical.[52]

In contrast to those who consider motivation as the defining emotional component, others claim that motivation is not essential to emotions.[53] The above description of the motivational component is contrary to this claim. As suggested, although emotions are not always accompanied by a full-fledged desire which is expressed in actual behavior, they nevertheless involve a desire, want, or a wish which may not be expressed in actual behavior or may not even be intended to be translated into actual behavior. In any case, some kind of motivational component is always present in emotions.

A *desire* in itself is not an emotion, but rather a motivational component of a complex emotional state.[54] Emotions include such a component, but desires also take part in nonemotional states. The desire to go to sleep is neither an emotion nor a component of an emotion. Desires can be devoid of the feeling dimension; typical emotions are not. Accordingly, there are unfelt desires but not unfelt emotions. I can desire to eat when I do not feel hungry—as when I do not expect to have a chance of eating for quite a while—or to go to sleep when I do not feel sleepy, as when I know I must wake up in the early morning hours to catch a plane. Emotions are complex states including many other components besides desire.

One popular view among psychologists reduces emotions to both *feelings and behavior*. According to this view, emotions are (a) nothing but bodily feelings, and (b) the result of some behavior. Following William James, the proponents of this view argue that happiness is nothing but a certain feeling and that we smile not because we are happy, but we are happy because we smile.[55]

The two basic assumptions of this view appear to be quite misguided. We have seen that emotions are much more complex than simple bodily feelings. The assumption that feelings are the result of emotional behavior appears to be mistaken as well. For one, we can adopt a certain emotional behavior, for example, a smile, without having the emotional experience of happiness. (This is a general objection against behaviorism.) Many people—such as receptionists, flight attendants, social workers, and so on—must behave in a way which is incompatible with what they feel. Likewise, there are cases of having a certain emotional experience, for example, fear, without the typical behavior associated with it, namely, flight. (This is another general objection against behaviorism.) The essential role played by the intentional components in emotions further indicates why we should reject identifying emotions with feelings which are not intentional.

By behaving in a way typical of a certain emotion, we may experience the corresponding emotion, but this is not necessarily the case. When smiling we may feel joy, but then again, we may not. Feelings are not necessarily connected to our behavior, but rather to the underlying physiological states. Both are different levels of describing the same event. If indeed a smile is necessarily correlated with the physiological state underlying happiness—a quite dubious proposal—then we do not smile because we are happy, nor are we happy because we smile; rather, happiness and smiling are two expressions of the same event.

Alongside the philosophical and psychological traditions identifying the emotions with feelings, there are also scholars who argue that feelings are not essentially involved in the concept of emotion.[56] Their argument relies on the assumption that it is possible and indeed quite common for us to have emotions without experiencing any feelings at all. The cases in which emotions seem to lack the feeling component can be divided into three major groups: (1) enduring emotions; (2) calm emotions; and (3) unconscious emotions. In order to defend the assumption that feelings are in fact essential to emotions, it needs to be shown either that these phenomena are not emotions or that they do not lack the feeling dimension.

*Enduring emotions* (*sentiments*) are those lasting for a long period of time. (A detailed discussion of sentiments is found in the next chapter.) While we do speak about experiencing an emotion over a long period of time, we do not assume that we actually feel the emotion over the whole of that time span. Similarly, when we say that Susan is kind, we do not say that she is continuously occupied with helpful activities. She may watch television, work in a factory, and do a variety of other things that have nothing to do with her kindness. Despite the absence of helpful activities, we can still say that Susan has an enduring personality trait of kindness. However, we will not conclude from this that helpful activities are not essentially connected with kindness. Likewise, a witty person does not have to amuse other people continuously in order to be regarded as witty. However, being amusing is essentially connected with being witty. In the same vein, a man's enduring love of his wife does not have to involve continuous intense feeling, but this does not mean that his feelings are not essentially bound up with a constant, enduring emotion of love.

*Calm emotions*, such as hope and gratitude, also seem sometimes to lack the feeling component; while it can be acknowledged that there are emotions in which the feeling component is less dominant than in others, this does not mean that they lack any kind of feeling. The feeling component in hope and gratitude may be less significant than in anger and fear, but it is present in both cases. As we saw earlier, the feeling dimension is composed of at least two continuums: pleasantness-unpleasantness and arousal-calmness. Emotions are typically characterized by their extreme positions on each continuum. This is obvious insofar as the pleasantness-unpleasantness continuum is concerned. Most emotions also involve a high degree of arousal; however, in some situations, emotions may entail a high degree of calmness.

The last group of emotions, which seems to contradict the essential tie between emotions and feelings, consists of the so-called unconscious emotions. I have suggested that the so-called unconscious emotions actually refer to emotions whose nature is unclear, while many of their components are known. "Unconscious emotions" do not refer to an experience in which we are not aware of all four basic components of emotions, but rather to a situation in which what seems to be unconscious is better described as referring to the unknown, not realized, or mistakenly identified nature of the given emotion. In this case, we do not have to assume the existence of an emotion which has no feeling component.

In the same way that the identification of emotions with feelings should be rejected, the attempt to detract from the importance of the feeling dimension in emotion should be rejected. Feelings are more than a frequent accompaniment of emotions; they are a constitutive element, as they play a crucial role in expressing the urgency of emotional situations.

*Some Conceptual Aspects*

Emotion is the shortest distance between two people.
—Unknown

In the preceding two chapters I have described various characteristics and components of emotions; these offer a general picture of a typical emotion. However, this picture does not answer more general conceptual questions:

1. Is an emotion a mental capacity, as are perception, memory, imagination, and thought?
2. Is an emotion a mental mode of reference, such as cognition, evaluation, and motivation?
3. Is an emotion an action or a passion?

Let me summarize my position on these issues.

1. Traditional descriptions of mental phenomena suggest the presence of a few mental capacities (faculties)—for example, sensation (or feeling), perception, memory, imagination, thought, and the will. It is doubtful whether each of these capacities can be described as a single, unitary capacity. Thus, it has been suggested that memory is not a single capacity, but that what we call memory actually consists of various learning systems. Without entering into this debate, it seems that an emotion is not a single, unitary capacity. While experiencing an emotion, some of the above mental capacities, and often of all of them, are activated. Nevertheless, an emotion is not on the same conceptual level as each of them: an emotion involves, for example, perception and imagination, but it is not a type of perception and imagination; an emotion is a general term referring to a certain combination of such capacities.

2. In addition to the above mental capacities, we may discern a few mental modes of reference: cognition, evaluation, and motivation. Not all mental capacities involve these modes. Sensation, which is the most primitive mental capacity, lacks any of these modes of intentional reference. The more complex mental capacities, such as perception and memory, have the cognitive mode of reference. The will utilizes the motivational mode, while imagination and thought may include all modes. These types of intentional references are essential components of emotions, but an emotion is not identical to any of them. Again, they belong to a different conceptual level from that of an emotion.

3. The description of mental states as divided into actions and passions is based on the issue of choice: actions, but not passions, are subject to our free choice. Thinking, remembering, and imagining are actions, while feeling is passion. In light of this division, an emotion is passion as we cannot choose our emotions: we do not willingly create the emotional state, but find ourselves in it. However, an emotion is a dynamic state including many actions.

We can see that traditional descriptions of mental phenomena are not suitable for describing the emotions because of their greater complexity. An emotion is, then, neither a mental capacity nor a particular mode of reference. An emotion is a complex system consisting of various mental capacities, modes of reference, attitudes, activities, and states. Accordingly, it is preferable to replace the substantial notion of emotion with a functional concept. For the purpose of an initial explanation we may consider an emotion to be an entity, but when a more scientific explanation is required, a functional explanation is in order.[57]

## Summary

We can do no great things; only small things with great love.
—Mother Teresa

Four basic components of emotions can be discerned: cognition, evaluation, motivation, and feeling. All four components are present in typical emotions, and emotions cannot be reduced to one of them. Among these components, the evaluative component is the one through which one emotion is distinguished from another. A detailed specification of the unique nature of each emotion should refer to the evaluative patterns underlying this emotion. The distinguishing nature of the evaluative component does not imply that it is the sole criterion distinguishing emotion from nonemotion. Such a criterion is much more complex, referring to other components as well as to other characteristics of typical emotions.

# Chapter 4

# The Affective Realm

I'd like to meet the person who invented sex and see what he's working on now.
—Unknown

The previous chapters provide an initial characterization of emotion. In addition
to emotions, the affective realm includes other phenomena such as sentiments,
moods, affective disorders, and affective traits. The first sections of this chapter
are devoted to clarification of the differences among affective phenomena. Then
a detailed classification of emotions is offered. The chapter ends by discussing a
few other suggested classifications of emotions and in particular that of basic and
nonbasic emotions.

## Typical Cases of Affective Phenomena

They were doing a full back shot of me in a swimsuit and I thought, Oh my God,
I have to be so brave. See, every woman hates herself from behind.
—Cindy Crawford

I have suggested that we consider intentionality and feeling as the two basic
mental dimensions. In characterizing the mental aspects of the affective realm, a
reference to these basic dimensions is in order. Accordingly, I characterize an affective phenomenon as having an inherent positive or negative evaluation (this is the
typical intentional feature) and a significant feeling component. The combination
of a valenced aspect, namely, an inherent evaluation, with a significant feeling
component is what distinguishes affective phenomena from nonaffective ones.
A mere positive or negative evaluation, as is expressed for example in verbal
praise, is not an affective attitude; similarly, a mere feeling, such as a tickle, which
is devoid of an inherent type of evaluation, is not included within the affective
spectrum.

The two suggested characteristics, namely, inherent evaluation and a significant
feeling component, may serve not only to distinguish affective from nonaffective

phenomena but also to discern the various phenomena within the affective realm. Accordingly, I suggest that we characterize the differences between the major types of affective phenomena by referring to (a) the specific or general type of evaluation involved, and (b) the occurrent or dispositional nature of the given phenomenon.

An evaluation is an intentional state; one difference between various evaluations concerns the degree of specificity of their intentional object. Some evaluations may focus on a specific object, and others may be more diffuse, having quite a general intentional object. We can distinguish affective phenomena, then, on the basis of the degree of specificity of their intentional object.

The distinction between *occurrent* (*actual*) and *dispositional* (*potential*) properties is crucial for describing mental states. Many mental features are not actualized at any given moment. These features are often described as unconscious. Without entering into a critical discussion concerning the nature of unconsciousness,[1] I would like to note that these features can also be described as dispositional. Dispositions are not hidden occurrences; rather, they represent tendencies to become occurrent states of a certain kind in given circumstances. In describing dispositions we have to refer to the potential realm: if a particular set of circumstances materializes, the dispositional state is actualized. And when mental dispositions are not actualized, they nevertheless have an actual supportive neural basis. The disposition may also be expressed in actual mental features—although the presence of these features does not as yet constitute the actualized state pertaining to this disposition. Thus, the behavior of a jovial person may be different from that of someone disposed to be solemn, even when the former is not being overtly cheerful.

Intentional states, such as beliefs and desires, can be dispositional in the sense that even if at the moment I do not attend to this belief or desire, I can still be described as having it. This is not the case concerning feelings. I do not have feelings which at the moment I do not feel; feelings do not have such a dispositional nature. When describing certain attitudes—for example, sentiments or affective traits—as dispositional, I mean the following: a certain person may have the sentiment of (say) love when she does not actually have an occurrent state of love; if she tends to experience it quite frequently, and when she actually experiences it, the typical feeling associated with love is present as well. In such dispositional attitudes, we are easily disposed to reach an attitude with an occurrent feeling dimension.

The two suggested criteria for distinguishing the various affective phenomena (i.e., the intentional nature of the evaluative stand, and the occurrent or dispositional nature of the given phenomenon) form four possible combinations which can be considered as the basic types of affective phenomena:

1. specific intentionality, occurrent state—emotions, such as envy, anger, guilt, and sexual desire;

2. specific intentionality, dispositional state—sentiments, such as enduring love or grief;

3. general intentionality, occurrent state—moods, such as being cheerful, satisfied, "blue," and gloomy;

4. general intentionality, dispositional state—affective traits, such as shyness and enviousness.

Emotions and sentiments have a specific intentional object, whereas the intentional object of moods, affective disorders, and affective traits is general and diffuse. Emotions and moods are essentially occurrent states; sentiments and affective traits are dispositional in nature. These differences are expressed in temporal differences. Emotions and moods, which are occurrent states, are relatively short, whereas sentiments and affective traits, which are essentially dispositional, last for a longer period. Emotions typically last between a few minutes and a few hours, although in some cases they can also be described as lasting seconds or days. Moods usually last for hours, days, weeks, and sometimes even for months. Sentiments last for weeks, months, or even many years. Affective traits can last a lifetime.[2]

The above types of affective phenomena represent major paradigmatic cases; there are various phenomena which are borderline cases. This should be expected in light of the fact that one of the defining criteria of affective phenomena, namely, the specificity of the intentional object, admits various degrees.

In the above description of typical affective phenomena, two groups, which are often considered to be affective, are missing: feelings and affective disorders.

Feelings, such as a toothache, feeling cold and enjoying icecream, are often described as having an evaluative component. In light of such description, feelings should be regarded as affective phenomena. The situation, however, is more complicated. As I have explained, pain and pleasure are inherent properties of feeling, but they are not intentional states evaluating the condition of our body. Hence, strictly speaking, feelings are components in affective attitudes; they are not such attitudes in themselves.

Affective disorders, such as depression and anxiety, do not clearly fit in either group of affective phenomena; their intentionality is not as specific as that of emotions, nor as general as that of moods. Furthermore, with regard to the dispositional and occurrent nature, affective disorders are in an intermediate position between emotions and moods on the one hand, and sentiments and affective traits on the other hand. I suggest that we explain affective disorders as extreme, or pathological, instances of the above typical cases. For example, when fear takes a very extreme form, it may turn into anxiety and in a similar vein, sadness may turn into depression.

I turn now to discuss in more detail the differences among paradigmatic affective cases. Since emotions and feelings were discussed in previous chapters, the discussion here will focus on the other affective phenomena.

*Emotions and Sentiments*

Sentiment is intellectualized emotion; emotion precipitated, as it were, in pretty crystals by the fancy.
—James Russell Lowell

I have already described the specific intentionality and occurrent (actual) nature of emotions. We have seen that emotions are partial in the sense that they are focused on specific objects, typically one person or a very few people. Emotions are also occurrent states; their feeling dimension is intense and acute. Low intensity of the feeling dimension usually expresses neutral or indifferent states, which are the opposite of emotional states.

In light of their specific intentionality and their intense nature, emotions typically last for a brief period. The intense focus on one specific object cannot last forever. Although typical emotions are brief, transient states, 50 percent of reported emotional incidents were described as having lasted for longer than one hour, and 22 percent for longer than twenty-four hours.[3] Emotions are ongoing states and not isolated entities. An emotion can be enduring if all major components are present for a certain period. In this straightforward sense, all emotions are enduring states; they differ, however, in length of duration. In this regard, we may distinguish between emotions and emotion episodes.

Emotion episodes last longer than emotions. They are similar to emotions in their intentionality and occurrent nature since they consist of an emotion that is described as lasting intermittently for an extended period of time, say, over an hour. The successive phases are felt to belong together to the same emotion and not to a succession of individual emotions. Even though the emotion episode may last for a few days, people describe all successive occurrences as belonging to one emotion. Overall intensity fluctuates over the episode, and the nature of the emotion involved may be changed. Although the incidents were reported as exemplars of a given emotion (say, anger, fear, or joy), they were described as sequences in which one emotion followed another; for example, annoyance followed by anger, followed by disgust, followed by upset and indignation.[4]

Extended emotion episodes become sentiments. The longstanding love for your partner, parents' grief for their son, and a child's longstanding hostility to her parents are sentiments. The difference between emotions and sentiments mainly concern their dispositional nature. Humans possess dispositions to respond affectively. Unlike affective traits, which are general dispositions having usually some innate basis, sentiments have more specific dispositions; their generation and continued existence is related to a specific object or event. Sentiments, which are more stable states than emotions, are related more to ongoing processes than to specific, transient events. In this sense, their intentional object is somewhat more general than that of their corresponding emotion.

The differences between affective traits, sentiments, and emotions are expressed in the differences between a tendency to anger, hostility toward someone, and a state of anger. A tendency to anger, which is an affective trait, is the disposition to get angry irrespective of the situation. Hostility toward someone, which is a sentiment, is the disposition to get angry with this person whether or not we are provoked by an offensive action. Anger at someone who hurts us is an example of an emotion. We may always be hostile toward that person, but we only get angry when provoked. The differences in their dispositional nature are expressed in the different duration of these phenomena: sentiments are enduring emotions which last longer than typical emotions, but are shorter than affective traits.

A sentiment is not pure potentiality; it affects occurrent attitudes and behavior. Having a sentiment does not merely result in repeating a given emotion in the future; it also shapes or colors our present attitudes and behavior. A man's long-standing love of his wife may not involve continuous, occurrent feelings, but it influences his attitudes and behavior toward her and other people. For example, it influences his interest in what she does, the things he does in her company, his desires toward her and other women, and so on. Similarly, a mother can grieve for a lost child for a very long period during which she often feels intense sadness and inability to concentrate on any complex activity. It may be the case that some intense sentiments, such as grief, are also similar to moods in providing a background framework of feeling.

Emotions differ in their tendency to become sentiments. Emotions involving a more specific attitude, for instance, sexual desire, embarrassment, disgust, and pleasure-in-others'-misfortune, are less likely to become sentiments. Their very limited focus and the dominant position of their feeling component make it hard to conceive of them as extending over a long period of time. Some specific emotions, such as anger and gratitude, are typically hot emotions; however, in some cases, they may take the more general and stable form typical of sentiments. Many emotions may take the form of long-term sentiments. This is true, for instance, of love, regret, envy, hate, compassion, hope, happiness, sadness, grief, pride, shame, and guilt. The concern of these emotions can also have general and stable features which enable the transformation of the emotion into a sentiment.

To illustrate the difference between emotions and sentiments, consider the case of love. Love as an emotion is aroused in particular circumstances, whereas love as a sentiment is the disposition to experience the emotion of love and is characterized by a long-term favorable attitude toward someone. Whereas the emotion of love, is unstable, intense, expresses a very partial attitude, and is relatively brief, the sentiment of love is more stable, less intense, more general, and lasts longer. The emotion is typical of the period which may be termed "falling in love," while the sentiment is associated with the period of "being in love" or "staying in love."

The long-term sentiment is often punctuated by outbursts of short-term emotions. For example, loving one's mate for twenty years consists of brief outbursts of passionate love and long periods in which love is mainly dispositional. Some sentiments may lack any outburst of their corresponding emotion. Thus, the sentiment of wistful regret may lack outbursts of the emotion of regret. In any case, sentiments should not be characterized as merely aggregates of emotions. They have their own character which differs from both their corresponding emotion and a nonemotional state.

I have suggested that we consider perception of a significant change in our situation as the typical *cause* of emotions. Such perceptions may equally lie at the root of sentiments, but since sentiments last longer, their continuing presence does not stand in need of reiterated significant change. In addition to the everyday changes that generate specific emotions, there is a more profound type of change, rooted in our awareness of the contingency of our own existence, that can evoke emotional reactions. A stark reminder of our own vulnerability, death is always in the background of our existence. This type of change expresses our ineluctable dependence on external factors over which we have no control. Although the affective reactions to such types of change can be emotions, they are often sentiments and affective disorders.

I have argued that the *focus of concern* of emotions is the comparative concern and that the imagined and social aspects are most dominant in this regard. In sentiments, the comparative concern is of somewhat less importance, as is the relative weight of the imagined and social aspects. This is so since sentiments, which are of longer duration, are concerned with more profound, existential issues; transient, specific events are often of no relevance to sentiments. The comparison to another agent is often of limited effect and hence is of lesser influence on sentiments.

When it comes to *object*, there is no significant difference between emotions and sentiments; in both cases, a human being—or more generally, a living creature—is the typical object. The characterization of the intentional object constitutes the main difference between emotions and moods.

Emotions, as we saw, have unique *characteristics* through which we distinguish them from other mental states. Do sentiments have such unique characteristics? Sentiments retain some of the characteristics typical of emotion, while others are expressed, if at all, in a more moderate manner. In sentiments, the system is less *stable* than an indifferent state; it is more stable than in emotions. Similarly, sentiments are more *intense* than an indifferent state, but less intense than emotions. They are also more *general* than emotions and *last* longer. The stability of the system in sentiments is a dynamic one, associated with greater intensity than in a nonemotional attitude.

A person may be described as having a sentiment if all *intentional components* of the corresponding emotion, namely, cognition, evaluation, and motivation, are present, but the feeling component is not. Anti-Semites can be characterized as hating Jews in this sense even while they do not actively think about Jews. They may experience no emotion of hate, but their persisting attitude includes intentional components typical of hate. Moreover, asked if they hate Jews, they will answer in the affirmative. Although love and grief may persist for a long time—suggesting that time neither heals all wounds nor suppresses all types of excitement—the feelings typical of these emotions are not present at every moment of that time span. In describing sentiments, we assume their continuous existence, not merely their frequent occurrence, although frequent occurrence of the corresponding acute emotion is typical of sentiments. Getting angry at our children a few times a week does not necessarily imply the sentiment of hostility toward them; rather, it may reflect the affective traits of nervousness or caring for them.

The basic evaluative pattern underlying a certain emotion remains in the corresponding sentiment, but the more specific evaluation may be changed. For example, the basic evaluative pattern underlying love is that of a positive, global evaluation of the object. This pattern is common to both the emotion of love (typical of falling in love) and the sentiment of love (typical of staying in love). The more specific evaluations constituting this pattern may differ: in the emotion, the evaluation of the object as appealing is typically more dominant; in the sentiment, the evaluation of the object's action and character as good is more typical.

Contrary to my depiction of emotions as having a brief duration, people sometimes describe some of their emotions—such as love, grief, or regret—as growing more intense as time goes by. It should be mentioned that these people refer to sentiments rather than acute emotions. Several reasons may explain this phenomenon: (a) familiarity increases the intensity of some sentiments; (b) changes in our situation generate in us a different evaluative perspective; (c) the emotional object can gain different meaning. In any case, the increase in the intensity of a certain sentiment is not contrary to the brief nature of emotions.

When we speak about a sensitive person we may refer to two types: (1) emotional, and (2) sentimental. An emotional person is one who frequently experiences intense emotions. This person's sensitivity is focused on our immediate environment: everything in that environment is perceived as very urgent. The sentimental person may be more calm in the short run, but her emotional ties are deeper.

General attitudes, such as hope for peace, love of country, or respect for the law, which are described in emotional terms, are more similar to sentiments in often being dispositional. However, even when actualized, their feeling component is not normally evident; accordingly, these are not typical affective states.

At the basis of our responses to ongoing situations of long duration there is usually a mechanism which makes our emotional evaluations less extreme. An example of such moderation concerns the aesthetic impressions we have when meeting a new person. Such impressions are often extreme: the new person is viewed as either quite beautiful or quite ugly. After a while our impressions begin to be more moderate: the beautiful person is typically perceived as less beautiful and the ugly one as less ugly. Time is a thief not only of beauty but of ugliness as well. As the English novelist Ouida indicated: "Familiarity is a magician that is cruel to beauty but kind to ugliness." Extreme impressions, which are associated with intense emotional reactions, enable the formation of a quick response toward the unfamiliar person. When we get used to a person, there is no longer any need to maintain our extreme response. On the contrary, there is a need to perceive this person in a moderate manner which will enable smooth communication.

When the negative or positive situations we encounter are in essence of long duration, we cope with them by moderating our evaluations. This is especially evident in the case of negative situations: in such situations we try to reduce their negative nature and even emphasize their positive aspects. One example in this regard is physical exercise. Although physical exercise is not a pleasant activity (at least not when one begins), those who exercise a lot hardly see its negative aspects and considerably overrate its positive ones. In this way it is easier for us to cope with unpleasant, but still necessary, activities.

The distinction between emotions and sentiments is not always clear-cut; nevertheless, considering such a distinction is valuable for understanding emotional experiences. Generally speaking, whereas emotions are a response to temporary situations, sentiments respond to situations of long duration. Temporary situations generate strong emotions which help us to mobilize our resources quickly and hence cope with them successfully. When the situations are of long duration, short-term, intense emotions are not suitable responses; different responses are required. Such responses can be either responses that are not affective at all or affective responses that are not emotional, such as sentiments.

## Moods and Affective Traits

So of cheerfulness, or a good temper . . . the more it is spent, the more it remains.
—Ralph Waldo Emerson

The term "mood" refers to diverse experiences having no clear borderlines between them. In everyday life, "mood" has a broad meaning, referring to the entire feeling continuum. According to this usage, we are always in some kind of a mood. Examples of such moods are being cheerful, contented, happy, pleased, satisfied, warm-hearted, blue, depressed, downhearted, gloomy, lonely, sad, and unhappy. In another common usage the term "mood" is used in a narrower sense, referring to experiences such as anxiety, apathy, depression, and euphoria; it indicates an intense and pervasive frame of feelings which is not frequent. This narrow sense of "mood" is termed in psychological literature "emotional disorder." (In light of the analysis offered here, the term "affective disorder" is more proper.) Sometimes "mood" is used in neither of these senses, but rather as a kind of inclination. Thus, we speak of someone being in the mood to make love or to take a walk.

The sense that is used here is close to the everyday, broad meaning: moods are general background frameworks of the feeling dimension. Unlike feelings such as headaches and toothaches, which are localized but not intentional, moods are intentional but not localized. However, the intentionality of moods is not as complex and specific as that of emotions. It is a more primitive type in which the intentional object is diffuse and difficult to specify—quite often moods seem to be objectless.

In light of their primitive intentionality, it is a matter of dispute whether to classify moods as either intentional emotions or nonintentional feelings. Those who treat moods as emotions have suggested a number of ways to account for this difference: (a) Moods lack a particular object; they are generalized emotions directed at the world at large. (b) Moods are emotions in search of an object, or emotions with alternating objects; moods are general frames of mind that focus on a wide variety of loosely affiliated objects.[5] Moods may also be regarded as nonintentional and therefore as representing varieties of feeling rather than varieties of emotions. According to this view, moods are not directed at anything in particular, but merely reflect our own situation at any given point in time.

I believe that the best way to describe moods is not by reducing them either to emotions or feelings. Although the intentional dimension is more diffuse in moods than in emotions, some degree of intentionality exists in moods which is absent from feelings.[6]

In analyzing the typical characteristics of moods, the two basic continuums typical of the feeling dimension, namely, the arousal continuum and the pleasantness continuum, seem to be most relevant.

Robert Thayer suggests dividing the arousal continuum into two types: one that ranges from energy to tiredness and one from tense to calm. Hence, we have four basic mood states: calm-energy, calm-tiredness, tense-energy, and tense-tiredness. Each of these states can be associated with a certain state on the pleasantness continuum. Thus, Thayer considers the state of calm-energy to be the most pleasant state, whereas tense-tiredness is the most unpleasant one.[7] The evaluative component, which leads us to regard the situation as good or bad, is present then in moods too; as mentioned, the presence of this component is an important property of affective attitudes. In this regard we should not confuse "calmness" with "indifference." Whereas the first refers to absence of arousal, the second denotes the absence of evaluative preference.[8]

Although moods have a certain degree of intentionality, they essentially express the subject's own situation; in this sense they are similar to feelings. The subject-object relationship, which is the major concern in emotions, is of less importance in moods.

In light of their less specific nature, moods are relatively longer, and typically milder in intensity than emotions. Their less specific nature may also indicate that moods have to do with larger, longer-lasting, issues about the person's life as compared with the more specific events generating emotions. Such larger issues are not perceived as effecting a significant change in our situation, and hence they do not generate intense emotions. This difference may also be expressed in the fact that while many of the emotions have unique facial expression, moods do not have a particular facial expression, at least none that is universal and none that has signal value. Emotional expressions provide information to other agents about antecedent events, concomitant responses, and probable next behavior; such a signal value is absent in moods.[9]

The diffuse nature of the *intentional object* in moods is related to another difference between them and the emotions: the nature of the *affective cause*. The typical cause of emotion is a specific change which is usually unexpected and urgent; the typical causes of moods are less specific and urgent, occurring over a slower time course. Thus, weather can often affect mood: a dreary, rainy day can produce a depressed mood, while a bright, warm sunny day can engender a positive mood. Moods can also be generated in a cumulative fashion over time; small doses of mild negative interactions might cumulatively produce a negative mood over the course of a day. Often there is not an obvious cause-and-effect relationship between our moods and events.[10]

Hunger and thirst, which some consider to be emotions, resemble moods in some respects. Their feeling dimension is prominent and their intentional status is not entirely clear. Some regard hunger and thirst as intentional states directed at eating and drinking. However, it is more accurate to describe these as frameworks of feelings expressing states of deprivation. They are not about eating and drinking, but rather associated with them: by eating and drinking, we put an end to being in a state of hunger and thirst. Intense hunger and thirst are similar to intense moods and affective disorders in that they are pervasive and not amenable to being evaluated as reasonable or unreasonable. The role of belief and imagination in generating hunger and thirst is significantly smaller than in emotions. We can easily eat without any contribution from the imagination, but it is much harder to have sexual intercourse without imagination. Accordingly, sexual desires, but not hunger, can be satisfied by a substitution. It is said that Diogenes the Cynic was found masturbating in the public square. When reproached for his behavior, he explained: "I wish I could rub my stomach to satisfy its hunger."[11]

Affective traits are aspects of personality which can last a lifetime; they express a tendency to behave in an affective manner. Thus, shyness implies a tendency to social anxiety or fear, enviousness expresses a tendency to be unhappy with others' good fortune, and an individual's susceptibility to embarrassment is another type of consistent affective trait. Although most personality traits are affective in nature, there may be some which are not: for example, achievement striving, self-discipline, and dutifulness. Hence, I do not use the more common term of "personality trait" but prefer the more precise term of "affective trait."

As in the case of negative emotions, negative affective traits, such as hostility and aggression, are usually associated with a more intense feeling dimension than positive affective traits, such as benevolence. This is possibly so because of their prehistoric origin in situations where the agent's survival was endangered.

Major dimensions of affective traits suggested by modern personality theories are neuroticism, extroversion, openness, and agreeableness. Unlike emotions, but similar to moods, affective traits are not so responsive to contextual features; they last longer than any other affective phenomenon. Affective traits differ from moods and affective disorders in being largely dispositional; they are also less intense and pervasive than affective disorders. The differences between emotions and affective traits are evident when we compare, say, pride as an emotion and pride as an affective trait. As an affective trait, pride (or pridefulness) may be regarded as an ignoble general attitude, while as an emotion it is a specific short-term state which often has positive value. The same applies to shyness and embarrassment. Shyness is an affective trait primarily related to a fear of strangers and associated with a negative evaluation. Embarrassment is a specific short-term emotion which derives from our belief that we are in a specific social situation that is incompatible with our character.[12]

## Affective Disorders

Depression is a period during which we have to get along without the things our grandparents never dreamed about.
—Unknown

I have suggested considering affective disorders, such as depression, mania, and anxiety, as extreme, or even pathological, instances of the four basic types of affective phenomena. In many cases they take an intermediate place concerning the two major criteria of affective phenomena: intentionality and the occurrent or dispositional nature of the given phenomenon. Affective disorders typically have less specific intentionality than emotions, but are more specific than moods. They are less dispositional than sentiments and affective traits, but more dispositional than emotions and moods.

It should be noted that when we describe people as feeling depressed about their financial situation, or anxious about the welfare of their children, we are not necessarily referring to affective disorders, but rather to negative moods or to emotions such as fear or worry.

Affective disorders seem to be closer to moods than to any other affective phenomenon. The major difference between them is that affective disorders last longer and are much more intense and pervasive. Whereas moods provide the affective background or tone of experiences which remain relatively stable, affective disorders are at the very center of the affective experience. Affective disorders are also more intense than emotions. This does not imply that the intensity peak is always higher in affective disorders than in emotions; however, since affective disorders last longer, their overall magnitude is considerably higher. Whereas in emotions there is some balance between the intentional and feeling dimension, in affective disorders the feeling dimension is by far the more dominant. In fact, the feeling dimension in affective disorders is so dominant that it significantly reduces the scope and complexity of intentional components.

Affective disorders are pervasive in the sense that they have profound and far-reaching effects on our conditions. Emotions also affect our conditions, but generally not for so long as affective disorders or to the same degree of intensity. Emotions are typically short-term states expressing some instability of the mental system. Affective disorders, which are of longer duration, express higher stability of the system; however, this stability is pathological since it involves a highly intense and pervasive feeling component. Unlike emotions, which are associated with changes and interruptions, affective disorders are usually longer-lasting affective attitudes resisting further changes and interruptions. Accordingly, affective disorders can be maintained over a longer period without apparent connection to external events.[13]

Concerning their adaptive function, affective disorders may be considered as (1) exaggerations of normal affective responses such as emotions or moods, (2) subspecialized adaptations, or (3) pathological states unrelated to normal emotions. All three possibilities may have some explanatory value in different cases. Moderate affective disorders may be regarded as *exaggerations of normal affective responses*, fulfilling a subspecialized adaptive function in some situations. Because of their long duration and great intensity, affective disorders often have a *negative adaptive value*. The more exaggerated the response, the more pathological is the state. An intense feeling component or an excessive focus on one issue, which is typical of emotional disorders, impedes normal functioning. The *pathological* nature of affective disorders surfaces in the fact that the feeling component is not only more pervasive and often more intense than in emotions but also of longer duration. Accordingly, it is especially difficult to function normally while experiencing an affective disorder.

The intense and pervasive nature of affective disorders underscores the more extreme nature of the threats to coping potential that accompany the emergence of many affective disorders. Negative events that are perceived as threatening produce a depressed affective disorder when one perceives that resources are inadequate to cope. If we anticipate sufficient resources which can easily cope with the event, then positive emotions or positive affective disorders, such as euphoria, may emerge.[14] Both emotions and affective disorders contain a reference to external events and our potential to cope with them. The emphasis, however, is different: in emotions it is on the way in which events influence us, and in affective disorders it is on the way in which we cope with such events. For example, the emphasis in the emotion of fear is on the threatening aspects of the event, whereas in the affective disorder of anxiety, it is on our inability to cope with this event. Similarly, sadness is an emotion generated by loss, and depression is an affective disorder generated by the perception that we cannot cope with the loss. The concern about the self is more dominant in affective disorders.

It is useful to mention that coping is not merely concerned with negative but also with positive events. Since emotions are generated when we are confronted with changes which destabilize our situation, emotional coping may be characterized as our ability to restore our stable situation. This is true of both negative and positive emotions. Nevertheless, coping ability is more important in negative situations, which present a greater threat to our existence.

In light of their primitive intentional nature, the explanation of affective disorders is different from that of emotions and mere feelings. A mere feeling, say a sensation of cold in one's hands, is usually explained by referring to a physiological mechanism. Intentional components, such as beliefs and desires, need hardly be taken into account, if at all. However, these components are of great importance in accounting for emotions. The primitive intentionality of moods and affective disorders reduces, but does not entirely eliminate, the value of explaining their generation, or of treating them by referring to intentional components. *Physiological factors* are crucial in dealing with simple feelings, and *intentional components* in dealing with emotions. Moods and affective disorders may be treated either way. In the case of severe affective disorders, however, it is quite likely that an approach focusing on intentionality would be less effective.[15]

The primitive intentionality typical of moods and affective disorders is also the reason for the different role of moods and affective disorders on the one hand and emotions on the other in explaining individual behavior: emotions are usually offered as *reasons* for one's behavior, whereas moods and affective disorders are like feelings in being regarded as *causes*. Little Johnny's fear of dogs may be cited as the reason for his having kicked a dog. But if we say that Johnny kicked the dog because he was depressed or in a bad mood, we seem to be giving a cause rather than a reason for his action. Unlike emotions, but similar to feelings and moods, affective disorders are typically not evaluated in terms of the reasonable-unreasonable or justifiable-unjustifiable dimension. Accordingly, in the explanation of many affective disorders, the reference to mental processes is less crucial than in explaining emotions.[16]

The perceived degree of our responsibility for the affective attitudes depends on our ability to control their causes. When the physiological causes are hard to control, as in the case of affective disorders, we do not consider ourselves to be responsible for them. The physiological causes of moods are perceived to be easier to control and hence we consider ourselves to be more responsible for them. The degree of responsibility for our moods is often even higher than for our emotions, since emotions are perceived to be more connected with external causes.

The above discussion of affective disorders mainly refers to neuroses such as depression and anxiety; their pervasive feeling component make them obvious examples of affective disorders. Psychoses, such as schizophrenia and paranoia, are certainly mental disorders; they can also be considered as affective disorders if their impairment involves a problematic feeling component or a distorted evaluation. Most psychoses do indeed exhibit these attributes and hence can also be regarded as affective disorders.

To sum up, we may say that the *cause* of affective disorders is less associated with specific changes than the cause of emotions. The *focus of concern* in affective disorders is less comparative and social; it refers more to personal, existential issues. The *object* of affective disorders is more problematic to define as their intentional dimension is more diffuse. Affective disorders are more stable, more intense, more general, and of longer duration than emotions. In affective disorders the *feeling component* is by far more dominant than the *intentional* one; in emotions, both types of components are quite dominant.

Given the two basic mental dimensions, all mental states and attitudes may be arranged along a continuum whose opposite poles are pure feeling and pure intentionality. Although mental states can probably be ordered in accordance with their distance from these hypothetical poles, it is doubtful whether actual mental states are ever located at the extreme poles of the continuum. A toothache is closer to the pure feeling pole, and abstract thinking to the pure intentional pole. There are no definite boundaries along the continuum, as mental states constitute prototypical categories which usually have no such boundaries. Emotions occupy a middle position on the continuum, since both the intentional and the feeling dimensions are strongly manifest in them. In most other states, only one of these is clearly dominant.[17]

The above differences among the various affective phenomena should enable us to distinguish most instances of them. However, since they largely differ in degree, there may be instances in which the identification is not self-evident. For example, when the feeling component in the emotion of sorrow or fear is highly pervasive and persists for a long time, these emotions may turn into a long-term sentiment of sadness or the affective disorder of depression or anxiety. It is thus difficult to distinguish between intense sadness and nonsevere depression, although normal depression is quite different from normal sadness.

### Classifying the Emotions

It seemed the world was divided into good and bad people. The good ones slept better . . . while the bad ones seemed to enjoy the waking hours much more.
—Woody Allen

Emotions are complicated, seemingly heterogeneous, states or processes that have been described in many ways. As in other fields of inquiry, taxonomies are required as steps toward insightful theory; that is to say, emotions require classification to reduce their variety. Such classifications depend for their value on their success in clarifying the nature of each emotion and its relationship to others. In this section an overall classification of emotions is suggested. The classification provides a comprehensive picture of the different emotions and indicates some important relationships among them.

Emotions can be classified by referring either to (a) our *own* state, or (b) the emotional object. In the former case, the classification is typically made in terms of the feeling dimension. For example, one may classify emotions by virtue of their being species of joy or sorrow (as Spinoza suggests), by dividing them into calm and violent emotions (as Hume suggests), or by the proportion they contain of the two main aspects of the feeling dimension, namely, pleasure-displeasure and arousal-calmness (as some psychologists suggest).[18] As indicated in the previous chapter, more detailed classification of emotions would have to account for their intentional dimension.

Several classifications of emotions which refer to the emotional object, and hence are categorized in terms of the intentional components of emotions, have been suggested. One such classification uses the categories of "backward-looking" and "forward-looking" emotions. Most emotions are backward-looking in that the eliciting event has already occurred; examples are anger and shame. Forward-looking emotions, such as fear and hope, focus on a future event. Some emotions, such as love and sexual desire, are, however, hard to classify in this scheme as they contain elements of both groups. Accordingly, sometimes this classification is formulated as one that includes retrospective, immediate, and prospective emotions. The usefulness of this classification is limited because the temporal criterion is not central to emotional experience; the eliciting event has current significance, often regardless of whether it concerns the past, present, or future. Another suggested classification is that between emotions directed toward *animate* or toward *inanimate* objects. In light of the social nature of emotions, this classification is also of little value.[19] Yet another classification which refers to the type of the emotional object is that between *factive* emotions toward something that is, or is believed to be, the case, and *epistemic* emotions toward something that might be the case. This classification is also of limited value in light of the great role imagination plays in generating emotions.[20] Another type of classification uses various criteria at once. For example, in one such classification, the suggested criteria are that it is social, involves judgements of deservingness, and is certain or uncertain.[21] The problem with such classification is that the various criteria often overlap: thus, envy is both social and constituted by the issue of deservingness.

I would like to describe my own classification, which utilizes features referring to both our own state and the emotional object. This classification is based on what I consider to be the distinguishing component of emotions, namely, the evaluative component (figure 1). The proposed classification uses two distinguishing features of emotional evaluations: (1) their positive or negative nature, and (2) their object. The first feature expresses the evaluation of our own state and the second describes different types of emotional objects.

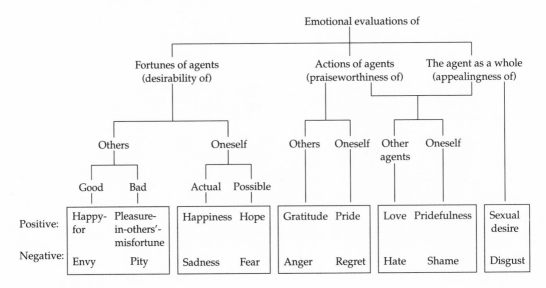

Figure 1
The classification of emotions.

In emotions we are not indifferent, but very much involved in what is going on. Accordingly, emotions cannot be neutral; they must be either *positive* or *negative*. Being neutral is being nonemotional. The positive-negative division expresses our basic attitude in evaluating a given situation. Positive emotions express a favorable evaluation, a positive desire, and an agreeable feeling, while negative emotions are the opposite, expressing an unfavorable attitude, a negative motivation, and a disagreeable feeling. Hence, all emotions can be described as a kind of liking or disliking of something.[22]

Given the positive-negative division of emotions, two major generalizations have been suggested: (1) positive emotions are species of joy, and negative emotions of sorrow; (2) positive emotions are species of love, and negative emotions of hate. The first position, which is advocated by Spinoza, emphasizes the role of emotions within our own selves, and the second position, advocated by Franz Brentano, stresses the importance of our relation to others.[23]

Characterizing emotions as a kind of liking or disliking, may seem to be closer to Brentano's position, which emphasizes more the role of the evaluative component in emotions. However, in light of the general correlation between the evaluative and feeling components, we can say that each positive emotion includes an agreeable feeling which may be considered as a type of joy, and each negative emotion includes a disagreeable feeling which may be considered as a type of sorrow. Moreover, if there is a common element among all positive or negative emotions, it would be joy or sorrow rather than love or hate; love and hate have a more specific definition than sorrow and joy and hence are less suitable candidates for being a common element in all positive or negative emotions. In this sense my position is closer to that of Spinoza.

I have indicated that Spinoza considers all negative emotions to be species of sorrow and all positive emotions to be species of joy. I believe that this is certainly true with regard to many types of negative emotions: those toward the good and bad fortune of others (namely, envy, pity, compassion, and sympathy); those toward our own actual bad fortune (sorrow and sadness); and also those toward our actions (regret and guilt) and probably our personality in general (shame). However, sorrow is not necessarily part of our negative emotion toward a potential state (fear), another agent's action (anger), and of our global negative emotion toward another person (hate) or object (disgust). It may be the case that more positive emotions could be regarded as species of joy, but even here, this may be problematic for the identification of some emotions. Thus, it is not entirely clear whether sexual desire or gratitude can be regarded as species of joy.

Despite the positive-negative polarity of emotional states, the pairs described in the figure do not constitute diametrical opposites. Anger is not simply the opposite of gratitude, nor is pity merely the opposite of pleasure-in-others'-misfortune. This is so because of the great complexity of each emotion and the presence of nonevaluative components, namely, cognition, motivation, and feeling, which do not necessarily have such a polar nature. Furthermore, the examples of emotions given in the figure are the most *typical* emotions in the given group; they are not necessarily the most *general* ones. Each group of negative emotions has a diametrically opposed group of positive emotions, but the examples of typical emotions do not constitute diametrical opposites. The group of positive emotions toward the good fortune of others is diametrically opposed to that of negative emotions toward the good fortune of others; however, happy-for, which is the typical example of the former, is not diametrically opposed to envy, the typical example of the latter. Love and hate are closer to being such opposites. It should be emphasized once again that the proposed division of emotions into positive and negative is determined merely by the basic evaluation underlying the emotion; this division is not necessarily connected with the division of emotions according to their functional or moral value.

The proposed classification is not only determined by our positive or negative attitude but also by the *multiple types of objects* characteristic of emotional evaluations. The typical emotional object is a certain actual or fictional *agent* who may be another person (or another living creature in general), or the person experiencing the emotion. Emotions can be directed at different situations of agents: events involving agents (a woman can be overjoyed at the return of her son from war, or fear that the war endangers her life and that of those related to her); states of persons (a woman can be worried about her husband's illness); attributes of people (a person can be envious of someone's beauty); relationships (a man can be jealous of his wife's friendship with another man); behavior (a man can be ashamed of the way he treated his parents); and so on.[24] In claiming that agents are the typical emotional objects, it is not assumed that emotions cannot be directed at nonagent, namely, inanimate objects. However, such emotions are either not typical or they are concerned with the effects of such objects on agents. There is no doubt that agents are of greater emotional concern than inanimate things.

If agents are the typical emotional objects, then emotions may be sorted into *three groups* according to (1) fortunes of agents, (2) actions of agents, and (3) the agent as a whole. Each group can be further divided into emotions directed at *other agents* and at *oneself*. These groups express *three basic patterns* involved in evaluating agents: (1) desirability of the agent's situation; (2) praiseworthiness of the agent's specific actions; (3) appealingness of the agent.[25] Although each of the three evaluative patterns is indeed the basic pattern in the corresponding group of emotions, the other two basic patterns may be present as well. Thus, although the basic evaluation involved in envy concerns the desirability of the other's situation, the praiseworthiness of the other's actions and the appeal of the other are also important evaluative patterns in envy. The three evaluative patterns are sometimes interdependent. Thus, desirability often depends on praiseworthiness and appealingness; appealingness sometimes depends on desirability.

The evaluative component in each emotion is far more complex than the mere basic patterns. In addition to the basic pattern, each emotion may involve more specific evaluations. Moreover, the determination of the basic evaluative pattern depends on specific evaluations. Consider, for instance, sexual desire, which is essentially based on the seemingly simple pattern of the other's appealingness. This pattern may be influenced by other factors, for example, class, race, odor, looks, height, accent (at least in England!), power, resemblance to past lovers, intellect, history of Pavlovian conditioning, risk of AIDS, current mood, and so on. Such multiplicity expresses the complexity of emotional evaluations: the more complex the emotion is, the greater weight these personal and contextual factors have in generating the emotion.

The three basic evaluative patterns determine not only the *nature* of the emotion in question but also its *intensity*. Greater similarity to the prototype of each evaluative pattern means greater emotional intensity. Thus, the more desirable the other's position, the more intense is our envy. Similarly, the more we condemn the other's action, the angrier we feel; the more appealing the other person seems, the more intense is our love or sexual desire. The event's strength is determined by how a given event matches one of these evaluative patterns.

A major division within each group of emotions is into those directed at *others* and those directed at *oneself*. This division, which expresses the social nature of emotions, reflects two central social concerns: the manner in which we view others and the manner in which others view us. Our relationship with others is indeed central to emotions. Although in emotions directed at ourselves, we are both the subject and the object, our concern is focused on the manner in which others evaluate and treat us.

In the group of emotions directed at the *fortune of agents*, the major evaluative pattern is the desirability of the given situation. This group is not only divided into emotions directed at others and those directed at oneself, like other subgroups, but it encompasses a further division: those directed at the *bad or good* fortune of others, and those directed at *actual or possible* fortunes for ourselves. The different criteria for these divisions are not accidental; they represent a different concern in each case. Emotions toward the fortune of others encompass an important comparative concern, relating the desirability of the others' situation to that of our own. We experience intense emotions toward the fortune of others mainly because it has great significance in determining our own fortune. Accordingly, emotions toward the fortune of others involve two basic types of evaluation: (1) the value of the others' fortune for us; (2) the value of the others' fortune for themselves. Sometimes the two types of evaluation are not correlated, as in the case of envy, jealousy, and pleasure-in-others'-misfortune; sometimes they are, as in the case of compassion and happy-for. Accordingly, the comparative concern becomes a competitive one when there is a conflict between the two types of evaluation. However, in emotions where evaluating others' fortune is correlated with evaluating our own fortune, the comparative concern does not become competitive but, rather, turns into a cooperative concern.

In the group of emotions directed at our own fortune, there is a positive correlation between the positive (or negative) evaluation of the fortune and whether it is good (or bad) for us. Accordingly, there is no reason to divide the group further into good and bad fortune. In this sense, emotions toward others are more complex. However, emotions toward oneself are more complex in a different sense: whether our good and bad fortunes are actual aspects of our (present or past) situation or are merely possible future aspects. Regarding other agents, the actual-potential dimension is less significant, as the main concern focuses on the actual situation. Sometimes the actual-potential distinction also collapses in emotions toward oneself. Many people "live the future in the present" and experience, for instance, an anticipated loss as actual; in this case, sadness is likely to occur concerning future and not merely present loss. Similarly, anticipation of future pleasure may lead to immediate pleasure.[26]

The positive emotion toward the good fortune of others is happy-for and toward the bad fortune of others, pleasure-in-others'-misfortune. The negative evaluation of others who are experiencing good fortune underlies the emotions of envy and jealousy, and that of bad fortune underlies the emotions of pity and compassion.

The division within the group of emotions directed at *our own fortune* is as follows: the basic positive emotion toward our potential fortune is hope, and the basic negative one is fear. The positive emotion toward our actual fortune is happiness, and the negative one is sadness. Since these emotions are directed at our own actual fortune, they are the most profound expression of our emotional situation.

In the second group of emotions, which are directed at *specific actions of agents*, the major evaluative pattern deals with the approval or disapproval (praiseworthiness) of these actions. The typical positive emotion approving the actions of another agent is gratitude; the typical negative emotion disapproving the actions of another agent is anger. Similarly, pride expresses our approval of our own actions, while regret and guilt express our disapproval of our actions.

In the third group of emotions, which are directed at *the agent as a whole*, the major evaluative pattern is the appeal of the agent, namely, its attractiveness or repulsiveness. These emotions include comprehensive evaluations of the agent. Here we may again distinguish between emotions directed at other agents and at oneself. Major examples of emotions directed at other agents are love and hate; those directed at oneself are pridefulness and shame. I use the term "pride" to refer to the emotion involving a positive evaluation of one's own action, and "pridefulness" to refer to the emotion involving an evaluation of oneself as a good person.[27] The term "pridefulness" may also be understood to refer to an affective trait, but in this book I use it mainly in the sense indicated above.

Another subgroup of emotions directed at the agent as a whole are more primitive emotions, such as mere attraction and repulsion. Those emotions, which may also be directed at nonagents, may have a similar feeling dimension to that of emotions directed at agents, but their intentional dimension is much simpler. Typical emotions in this group are disgust and sexual desire.

The pattern underlying *the evaluation of the whole agent* is complex, as it consists of considerations concerning both attraction (or repulsion) of the agent, and approval (or disapproval) of the agent's actions. Although hate involves a kind of repulsion, it also entails a negative moral evaluation of the agent's basic traits and actions. Love also involves more than a simple form of attraction, and to a lesser extent, this is true of sexual desire. Since people are perceived to be responsible for their actions, those actions are important in evaluating their whole personality. In fact, the agent's actions are what emotionally distinguishes agents from nonagents. In light of their more complex nature, it is plausible that emotions toward the agent as a whole, such as hate and love, develop after mere repulsion and attraction and after emotions toward the agent's actions, such as anger and gratitude. A mere attraction toward or repulsion by the whole agent may exist before the emotions evaluating the agent's actions appear.

The classification presented here depicts *conceptual relationships among the emotions*. Accordingly, the basic evaluative patterns on the basis of which the classification has been made are universal. Less basic patterns may depend on the specific culture or context. Thus, the consideration of romantic love as an expression of a global positive attitude which combines both the patterns of praiseworthiness and appealingness, is a conceptual claim that is not culture-dependent. In comparison, the issue of mutuality is culture-dependent. It has been claimed that whereas this issue is central in the modern notion of romantic love, it does not appear in the notion which prevailed in ancient Greek culture.[28]

A related issue, which is not represented in the proposed classification, is the salience of each emotion within a certain person or in a particular society. Although the description of this factor may add another dimension, it will not change the proposed conceptual relationships. Personal and cultural factors do not influence the basic characteristics of each emotion, but rather the type and frequency of the circumstances giving rise to the different emotions. Describing personal and cultural factors needs a reference to each individual and society, and as such is beyond the scope of this book, which attempts to provide a general understanding of emotions. Personal and cultural factors are nevertheless mentioned throughout the forthcoming discussion.

*Positive and Negative Emotions*

There can be no rainbow without a cloud and a storm.
—John H. Vincent

The division of emotions into positive and negative ones is a basic division expressing the centrality of the evaluative component in emotions: an emotional evaluation can be either positive or negative. Although in the proposed classification, every negative emotion has a corresponding positive emotion, negative emotions are more differentiated than positive emotions. A linguistic indication for this is that there are considerably more ways to describe negative emotional experiences than positive ones. Thus, although English contains more words with positive than negative connotations, the reverse is true of emotion words. Indeed, we do not have satisfactory terms for all positive emotions. It seems that we are more aware of negative emotions, which are more differentiated than positive emotions. The love-hate pair seems to be an exception: love is more common and noticeable than hate, and there are indeed more types of love than of hate.[29]

Another difference between positive and negative emotions, which makes the latter more noticeable, concerns their *temporal* character: the duration and the amount of rumination associated with negative events are usually far greater. People ruminate about events inducing strong negative emotions five times as long as they do about events inducing strong positive ones. Hence, it is no wonder that people tend to recall negative experiences more readily than positive ones.[30]

A major reason for the more noticeable role of negative emotions is that they possess greater *functional value*. The risks of responding inappropriately to negative events are greater than the risks of responding inappropriately to positive events; thus, as Fredrickson notes, "the cost of failure to respond appropriately to a life threat could be death, whereas the cost of failure to respond appropriately to a life opportunity is not likely to be so dire." Sudden changes for the worse are usually more significant than sudden improvements in terms of the resources required to respond appropriately. A greater variety of response options is needed to cope with potential harm than is needed to "cope" with potential good. In a sense, one does not need to "cope" with good fortune. Moreover, there are more ways in which a situation can be unpleasant than in which it can be pleasant, and there are more ways to ruin something than to build it. Further, individuals governed by the seeking of pleasure more than by the avoidance of pain could not survive. Another relevant consideration in this regard is that negative emotions are often experienced when a goal is blocked; this requires the construction of new plans to attain the blocked goal, or the formation of a new goal to compensate for the lost one. In contrast, positive emotions are usually experienced when a goal is achieved. Accordingly, negative emotions require more cognitive resources to be allocated for dealing with the given situation.[31]

These considerations are compatible with the findings that people who are depressed are more realistic than those who are optimistic, and those who are perceptive are more likely to be pessimistic and depressed because they have a more accurate picture of life and its troubles. Nevertheless, most people appreciate optimism more than pessimism.[32] In Shakespeare's *Love's Labour's Lost*, the Princess of France says: "A heavy heart bears not a humble tongue." In light of the above findings, we could say too that the heavy heart bears not a deceptive eye. However, we should recognize that negative moods have cognitive disadvantages also. There is some evidence indicating that negative moods may impede various types of cognitive capacities, whereas positive moods may enhance our ability to perform well. Thus, as with positive moods, negative moods may also induce biased evaluative judgments and impede normal functioning.[33]

The more noticeable nature of negative emotions may also be connected to the functional value of positive illusions. As I indicate below (see chapters 7 and 15), the majority of people see themselves as above average where most of their qualities are concerned and rate their happiness as more than one-third above the middle of the scale. This means that our baseline is above the average in the positive realm, a location that has several advantages. For example, it allows threatening events to be noticed quickly; it has motivational value, which is important in coping with our surroundings; and it produces a strong immune response to infections.[34]

The more noticeable nature of negative emotions does not imply that their impact on our life is greater. This issue is connected to our general view of human beings, and conflicting views in this regard can be found. Thus, Spinoza argues: "A desire that arises from joy is stronger, other things equal, than one that arises from sadness." Spinoza connects this contention to the claim that the very essence of a person is a striving to persevere in his being. Similarly, while Adam Ferguson claims that "pain, by its intenseness, its duration, or frequency, is greatly predominant," he thinks that "love and compassion are the most powerful principles in the human breast." Ferguson believes that positive emotions are more compatible with our basic positive disposition toward others. Descartes' view is different: "Sadness is in some way primary and more necessary than joy, and hatred more necessary than love."[35] Whereas an empirical investigation can determine whether negative emotions are more noticeable, it is more difficult to verify empirically which type of emotion has a greater impact on our life.

The above differences between negative and positive emotions may indicate that, in general, negative emotions are closer to the prototype of emotions than are positive emotions. It has even been suggested that the two groups may be explained by different explanatory models. Two proposed differences in this regard are that unlike negative emotions, positive emotions (1) are not necessarily connected to specific action tendencies, and (2) they broaden, rather than narrow, the agent's perspective.[36]

Although I agree that, generally speaking, negative emotions are closer to the prototype of emotions than positive emotions, I believe that the view suggested here can explain both types of emotions. Concerning the first claim, I think that the difference here is more a matter of degree. There are positive emotions, such as sexual desire, gratitude, and romantic love, whose motivational component is quite specific; the motivational component of other positive emotions, such as happiness and pridefulness, is less specific. Generally speaking, because of the specific threat involved in many negative emotions, the linkage to a particular mode of behavior is indeed stronger in negative than in positive emotions.

The second claim states that positive emotions are not partial in the sense that they do not focus our attention on a limited number of objects, but rather broaden our attention. This is so since in positive emotions we do not have a threatening stimulus which forces us to mobilize all our resources and focus them on the stimulus. Our contented state in positive emotions enables us to express more openness. I believe that although this claim is not entirely misleading, the situation is more complex.

To begin with, we should distinguish between positive moods and positive emotions. As indicated, the intentionality of moods is not as complex and specific as that of emotions: the intentional object of moods is diffuse and difficult to specify. In comparing the cognitive value of positive and negative moods we may say that whereas negative moods provide us with a more precise picture of our surroundings, positive moods broaden our perspective (which is also valuable from a cognitive point of view). In neither negative moods nor positive ones do we focus our attention on a specific event, but our general contented state in positive moods enables us to be more open to other people.

The impact of positive as well as negative moods on helpfulness has been abundantly researched in psychology. The research indicates that positive moods are usually accompanied by an increased inclination toward helpful behavior. For example, people who had just found a dime in a public telephone booth were more likely to help a stranger who had dropped some papers. A major reason for such increased helpfulness is that a person who feels good seeks to maintain this feeling by eliminating unpleasant or discomforting stimuli, including the suffering of others. Indeed, many findings suggest a positive association between the pleasure gained through helpfulness and the likelihood of helping when feeling good.[37] It seems, then, that positive moods involve less concern about our immediate situation and hence we can afford greater openness.

Negative moods are likely to be related to an increase in helpfulness only when helping is the most effective means either to achieve a positive mood or to terminate the negative stimulus. Typically, negative moods are not likely to increase helpfulness and may even result in a decrease. With regard, for example, to aggressive behavior, the emotion of anger usually evokes aggressive motivation toward the thwarting agent, but negative moods can lead to reduced action, including reduced aggression.[38]

Like positive moods, positive emotions also involve less concern regarding the immediate situation than is typical of negative emotions; can we conclude that they also involve greater openness? If they do, how can we distinguish between positive emotions and positive moods?

It is obvious that positive emotions are focused in a way in which positive moods are not. Thus, it has been found that although programs which induce moderate pleasure facilitate advertising recall, positive emotional intensity usually reduces recall, as in such a state we are much more focused on our own situation.[39] The focused nature of positive emotions is clearly expressed in romantic love. Love limits our range of interest, focusing almost exclusively on the beloved and our relationship with this person. As the popular song has it, "millions of people go by, but they all disappear from view—because I only have eyes for you." Similarly, Marcel Proust claims, "When we are in love, we no longer love anyone else." Accordingly, when a person has many lovers we do not consider this person to be intense in love—since such behavior has a greater degree of openness. On the contrary, such a degree of openness can be taken to indicate that there is no genuine love here. Genuine love, we assume, should be partial. A major criticism of promiscuity is its indiscriminate nature.

In analyzing positive emotions we should distinguish between various types of positive emotions. One such distinction is between positive emotions toward oneself, such as pride, pridefulness, and happiness, and positive emotions toward others, such as love, sexual desire, and gratitude. Some positive emotions toward oneself—for instance, pride and pridefulness—are not characterized by greater openness than negative emotions: they are focused on oneself. Happiness, which refers to a larger group of emotional states, may in some cases involve greater openness; in other cases the partial attitude is evident. There is evidence that in certain situations, happy people may be less likely to help others because they wish to protect their own agreeable emotional state and hence are less likely to take risks. Thus, when people have to make judgments in a situation involving equity, being happy themselves may make them less fair, since maintenance of their own happiness is their central concern.[40]

Another relevant distinction in this regard is the aforementioned distinction between affective attitudes which are positive or negative from (a) a psychological viewpoint, and (b) a moral viewpoint. From a psychological viewpoint, a positive emotion is one which involves a positive evaluation of the object, a positive type of motivation, and an agreeable feeling. From a moral viewpoint, a positive emotion is one which is positively evaluated in light of moral values. The two perspectives may conflict: for example, pleasure-in-others'-misfortune is a positive emotion from a psychological viewpoint, but negative from a moral one; compassion is a negative emotion from a psychological viewpoint, but positive from a moral one. The openness ascribed to positive emotions actually refers to the moral viewpoint since compassion, which is a negative emotion from a psychological viewpoint, is as broad as love. It is unclear whether psychologically positive and morally negative emotions, such as pleasure-in-others'-misfortune, are similarly broad.

The above distinctions indicate that what seems to be a broad perspective of positive emotions is not common to all positive emotions and is not limited to positive emotions; hence, it is not a characteristic of positive emotions. I would further claim that this seemingly broad perspective is not as broad as it may appear. I propose to term this perspective "focused openness."

Focused openness is, for example, the perspective typical of romantic love and compassion. Like other emotions, these emotions are focused on one or very few objects. However, they are open in the sense that the subject may want to be integrated with the object; the limits of the self broaden to include the object within these limits.

It seems then that the broad perspective ascribed to positive emotions is actually a property of positive moods; this property is due to a lesser concern for our immediate situation. In emotions, both negative and positive, the concern for our situation (or for that of those related to us) is greater; hence, our focus is mainly upon our situation (or upon the situation of those related to us). This focus may be somewhat broadened if there is no conflict of interest between us and those around us—as in the case of love and compassion, but not in the case of pridefulness and pleasure-in-others'-misfortune. Thus, it seems that grief, which is an intense negative emotion, may also involve a greater openness toward the needs of other people; grief sensitizes us to the value of fellow human (or living) creatures. One effect of grief may be the realization of the fragility of our life and the importance of valuing the life of every human being.

Explaining positive emotions does not require, then, a different model than that used for explaining negative emotions—it just requires particular attention to the unique circumstances in which they are generated.

*Basic and Nonbasic Emotions**

Sex is hereditary. If your parents never had it, chances are you won't either.
—Joseph Fischer

Though several other classifications of emotions have been suggested, classification into basic and nonbasic emotions has a continuing fascination, and is seen as central by many theorists. Above all, "basic" means simple, as opposed to complex. Accordingly, any emotion is a simple irreducible emotion, or it can be analyzed as a simple emotion plus x, where x is either another emotion or some nonemotional element. Hence, embarrassment might be analyzed as fear plus anger or, alternatively, fear plus the self-evaluation of being the object of unwanted attention. Criteria for simple or basic emotions vary from one theory to another, however, and such differences may cast doubt on the existence of basic emotions.[41]

The following list shows representative criteria for considering some emotions as basic:

- *development*—early emergence in human evolutionary or individual development;
- *function*—possession of functional value related to basic forms of action tendencies in individual and reproductive survival;
- *universality*—universality among humans;
- *prevalence*—most frequent occurrence as compared to other emotions;
- *uniqueness*—possession of unique features of physiology, expression, phenomenology;
- *intentionality*—occurrence without specific intentional objects.

In light of the *developmental* criterion, emotions clearly did not develop all at once; therefore, the suggestion has been made that basic emotions appeared before nonbasic ones. As the result of evolution, a variety of creatures have emerged, ranging from those with hardly more than sensitivity to pleasurable and painful elicitors to those with several basic emotions, such as enjoyment, sadness, anger, fear, and disgust, as well as (in mammals) the emotions of attachment. In social primates, some nonbasic emotional attitudes, such as depression from bereavement and vengefulness toward individuals, also exist.[42] In adult humans, an even wider range of nonbasic emotions is present. In individual human development, too, there is a comparable progression: at birth, an infant shows an emotional life marked by general distress and general pleasure (though disgust can also be demonstrated in the first few days of life). Sadness emerges by the age of three months. Later, anger and fear emerge. The first nonbasic emotions—embarrassment, envy, and empathy—only emerge in the latter half of the second year of life.[43]

---

* Parts of this section were written together with Keith Oatley.

Empirically, there has been some difficulty in determining at what point in early infancy certain basic emotions occur, as compared with merely generalized pleasure and distress. The absence of a precise developmental borderline between basic and nonbasic emotions is problematic for those who want to present a clearcut distinction between the two types of emotions.

In offering a developmental account, one does not have to assume that ontogeny recapitulates phylogeny. Thus, although sex is more ancient than language, we talk before we have sex. Some similarity between evolutionary and individual development may nevertheless be detected. The relationship between sex and talk is an interesting topic on its own. Thus, it sometimes seems that there is more talk about sex than there is sex itself.[44] Several factors may explain this interesting phenomenon: (1) our society overrates sex; (2) there are many sexual relationships in which we would like to be involved but because of various constraints (moral, social, and other types) we are unable to pursue these desires and so merely talk about sex; (3) the commitment and resources invested in talking about sex are significantly lower than those required in actual sexual relationships. The prevalence of discussion about sex is related to the important role imagination plays in emotions.

The developmental criterion of basic emotions is closely related to the *functional* one: basic emotions developed first in evolution, the argument goes, because they express basic action tendencies in response to important and recurring situational demands. Many situations can be thought of as positive or negative; accordingly, emotions could be distinguished as positive or negative. Some scholars assume that this distinction is the only basic characteristic of emotions. Certainly, for some purposes this distinction is sufficient. From the functional perspective, however, further differentiation is needed.

The following is a suggested list of situational changes and their correlated emotions:

*Positive changes*
1. actual improvement of the situation—happiness;
2. possible improvement of the situation:
   - someone to approach—love/desire (attachment, caregiving love, sexual desire);

*Negative changes*
1. actual deterioration of the situation—sadness;
2. possible deterioration of the situation:
   - something or someone to avoid—fear;
   - someone to counter—anger;
   - something or someone to reject—disgust, contempt.

The differentiation in the negative realm is more detailed because sudden changes for the worse are usually more demanding than sudden changes for the better, and different courses of action are implied by different kinds of negative situations. In light of this list, our emotional reaction to *actual change* in our situation is expressed in a basic emotion in both the positive and negative realms—in both happiness and sadness. The emotional reaction to possible changes is more differentiated in the negative realm. In both realms, we find a basic emotion referring to the possibility of approaching the object (love) or avoiding it (fear). Some emotions of love are distinguished by having different objects, such as attachment figures, offspring, and sexual partners. Basic negative emotions expressing possible deterioration of the situation are further differentiated by anger, disgust, and (possibly) contempt. The positive correlates of these emotions appear to be nonbasic. For instance, an inverse correlate of anger is gratitude. Although gratitude is seen in chimpanzees,[45] its complexity makes it an unlikely candidate for a basic emotion. The positive correlates of the emotions of rejection (of possible deterioration) are attraction and admiration. Although some forms of these emotions (e.g., sexual desire) may be regarded as basic in light of some of the above criteria for basic emotions, they are less compatible with these criteria than their negative correlates.

In light of the *universality* criterion, basic emotions are present in all humans. This is explained in light of their highly functional value.

The *prevalence* criterion reflects the assumption that basic emotions occur most frequently, as compared with other emotions. At the early stages of development, basic emotions are almost the only emotional reactions, and as such, they are the most frequent ones as well. Concerning more developed creatures, which also have nonbasic emotions, basic emotions are not necessarily the most frequent ones—though in light of their functional value, they occur quite frequently.

The *uniqueness* criterion of basic emotions indicates that these emotions have unique manifestations in several realms: for example, physiology, facial expression, and phenomenology. It is reasonable that primitive emotional reactions to specific emotional requirements are hard-wired and expressed in some unique manifestations. The main function of these reactions is to provide a quick response to certain situations; the speed is achieved by having a somewhat rigid response. Basic emotions have a simpler structure which is expressed in a more rigid pairing of a specific stimulus with a specific response. More complex emotions, which developed later, express a more flexible and, accordingly, a less rigid emotional response.

A less frequently discussed, but also important, criterion of basic emotions is the idea that emotions can have more or less of an elaborate *intentional* structure. Intentionality involves the ability of a cognitive agent to separate itself from immediate stimuli and to create a meaningful subject-object relation. Complex forms of intentionality, such as thinking and complex types of imagination, are absent in animals and at birth. Hence, complex intentionality is only typical of nonbasic emotions; basic emotions may have more primitive forms of intentionality. Accordingly, it has also been suggested that emotional development proceeds from a state of general excitement to one of more specific emotions. At birth most affective attitudes are undifferentiated; the process of differentiation and integration takes place gradually.[46] Accordingly, one suggested criterion for an emotion being basic is that some emotions can occur without intentional content—for instance, one can be sad without any object of sadness—and that these emotions are also the basis for moods which often lack a specific intentional object. Thus, happiness, sadness, anger, and fear can each occur in this objectless way, and each has a corresponding mood: enjoyment, melancholy, irritability, and anxiety.[47] By contrast, complex emotions, such as envy and pleasure-in-others'-misfortune, are always intentional, being based on complex social comparisons, and developed more recently in evolutionary terms.

Relationships among the criteria of basic emotions listed above are not logically necessary: an emotion that emerged first in evolution does not necessarily emerge first in individual development, and is not necessarily the most functional, the most frequent, and so on. Nevertheless, postulating such criteria is compatible with some empirical findings and is open to further empirical test. Anyway, it seems that at least a few of the criteria of basic emotions are graded, rather than all-or-nothing, indicating that the borderlines of the category of basic emotions are not clear-cut.

My major concern here is not to argue for the existence of basic emotions. Instead, I propose a different argument about intentionality and its importance for the social world. I do, however, first assume the possibility of basic emotions, defined in terms of being simple, and perhaps with some other characteristics listed above. Then we can inquire into the relationships of basic to nonbasic emotions. The argument will then enable us to reconsider the necessity of postulating basic emotions.

If we assume that basic emotions emerged first in evolution or individual development, what about nonbasic emotions associated with *intentional capacities* that enable us to refer to remote situations and to possible states of ourselves and others? First, I argue that having the possibility of an imagination to give intentional content to our emotions enables a whole new range of emotions to occur that are not available to other animals. Second, I claim that in our human adaptation, the most frequent emotions are social ones. As it turns out, these two properties are closely connected.

A complex social environment is perhaps one of the most species-typical of all human characteristics. So I suggest that the development of nonbasic emotions is associated with the development of human intentional capacities as applied to this social world. The *ability to imagine* others as having intentional states comparable to our own, and the ability to imagine ourselves as having intentional states different from our current one, are crucial for the development of complex social relationships and for a moral standpoint. Morality is inconceivable without the idea of choice among imagined alternative actions, and we cannot consider others to have moral rights and responsibilities if we cannot imagine them as having experiences such as suffering and joy that we ourselves know.

The development of second-order intentionality expresses concerns about our own and others' attitudes, not merely about behavior. An agent's attitudes, including intentions, wishes, desires, beliefs, and so on, are important for social and moral relationships. In the nonhuman social environments of primates, we can postulate that actions are almost the sole concern, although some intended actions can be recognized in emotional expressions.[48]

We should distinguish between information available to an agent about its own intentional relations (first-person information), which differs from the information available to that agent about other agents' intentional relations (third-person information). The integration of the two types of information is crucial for complex social understanding. Most animals cannot integrate the first- and third-person sources of information. Among nonhuman species, the great apes exhibit social understanding that integrates these sources of information, and one can postulate that they have uniform representations of intentional relations. But, it seems, only humans can represent intentional relations to imaginary objects. Through a common intentional schema, comparative concerns have become the crucial element in the consideration of complex emotions. It becomes possible to see differences and similarities between our own perspectives and those of others, and between our own perspective in the present and those of the past or future. These different perspectives become the bases for our own morality, as well as for making moral judgments about others.[49]

When perceiving the other's situation we should distinguish between imagining how the other feels in a certain situation and how I would feel in it. Although both types of perspectives increase sympathy toward the agent who is actually in this situation, the first perspective consists of relatively pure empathy, whereas the second is contaminated by personal concerns as well. Hence, while imagining how the other feels typically leads to relatively pure altruistic motivation, imagining how I would feel in that situation typically leads to a mix of altruistic and egoistic motivation.[50] This emphasizes once again the importance of the personal concern in generating emotions.

When the whole self becomes an emotional object, social comparison becomes the basis for a sense of personal worth, as we compare our current self to our expectations for ourselves, and to what we imagine others expect of us (where "self" is best thought of as a representation of "self-with-other"[51]). Thus in emotions of shame and pridefulness, we compare our current self to an ideal of our own or of society; in emotions of regret, guilt, and pride, we compare our current self to one we had in the past or to an ideal one. In emotions such as hope and social anxiety, we compare our current self to possible selves in the future. In emotions of envy, pleasure-in-others'-misfortune, pity, and compassion, we compare our current self to the selves of others.

In making the distinction between evolutionarily earlier, less social, environments and our more social human environments, I do not imply that social environments have no biological foundations, or that earlier environments lacked social relationships. Indeed, as recent ethological studies have shown, most primates are intensely social and have social emotions concerning dominance hier-archies, issues of sexual life, and rearing of their young.[52]

A critical incident concerning the borderline between humans and other pri-mates was described by Barbara Smuts: it was a case of putative jealousy.[53] Gen-erally when observing in the wild, one ethologist concentrates on one animal. In this incident, however, Smuts was observing olive baboons while another ethol-ogist was also observing; they were talking with each other about what they saw. Smuts' colleague was observing a particular male animal who suddenly became tense and threatening as he looked toward another animal. He mentioned this to Smuts. At the same moment, she was observing a female friend of this same male animal, the object of the male animal's gaze, many yards away. This friend had just come close to a rival male who was showing interest in her, and as she moved on, the male animal relaxed again. Jealousy can be inferred—but when the imme-diate danger from the rival was past, so too was the jealousy. How unlike the life of humans in which a continuing sense of self in relation to a wayward other can be threatened over a long period as jealousy lingers and imagined possibilities multiply.

It is ironic to note that some people have connected differences in complexity of imagination to class differences. Thus, the Kinsey Report published in 1948 assumed that the lower classes have no complex imagination and cannot tell the difference between plain and "fancy" sex. This claim is compatible with the assumption of dominant groups that lower classes and other races are relatively insensitive; accordingly, those in subservient positions do not suffer or feel pain as keenly, so they can be abused or exploited without guilt and with impunity. A similar bigotry has been extended to the presence of emotions in women, the poor, the foreign, those raised in impoverished or "unenlightened" cultures, and in chil-dren.[54] The absurdity of these claims should not lead us to the opposite extreme of assuming that there are no emotional differences between humans and animals; we should not deny the emotional lives of animals, but we should not assume that they are as complex as those of humans.

What I am arguing is that the evolutionary niche of humans is not just social—an attribute also of baboons, chimpanzees, and many other primates—but that it is overwhelmingly social and interdependent: humankind is that vertebrate species in which individuals accomplish together what they cannot achieve alone. And, because of the demands of creating and maintaining a self that is sufficiently robust for the vicissitudes of cooperation and competition, I suggest that this self is very frequently compared with other selves, both imaginary and real. The devel-opment of nonbasic emotions is thus related to developing intentional capacities that include second-order intentionality, enabling us to imagine an intentional state different from the current one. Complex social and imaginative relationships are at the very center of the human emotional environment.

The classification into basic and nonbasic emotions is useful for characterizing the evolutionary and personal development of emotions and possibly for indi-cating some of their functions. It does not describe the various emotional attitudes humans can take toward objects in their environment. In order to provide such a description, we must refer to what distinguishes one emotion from another. I have suggested that such a distinguishing feature is the evaluative component. Accordingly, the conceptual classification describing the various possible emotional attitudes should refer to the evaluative component.

We have seen that the emergence of a complex social environment is associated with the generation of nonbasic emotions. Let us examine the relationship between basic and nonbasic emotions in light of the proposed classification of emotions.

Those emotions I have considered above to be basic belong to the following groups: (a) fortunes of oneself—happiness, sadness, and fear; (b) actions of other agents—anger; and (c) another agent as a whole—repulsion and the different types of love. Basic emotions do not refer at all to the following groups: (a) fortunes of other agents—for example, envy, pleasure-in-others'-misfortune, and pity; (b) actions of oneself—for example, regret, guilt, and embarrassment; and (c) oneself as a whole—for example, shame and pridefulness. Nonbasic emotions are complex emotions which require second-order intentionality. They depend on reference to a conception of the self and a social comparison of the present situation of the self with imagined alternatives of the self or others.

Emotions toward the *fortunes of others* are based on a comparative concern relating the desirability of the others' situations to that of ourselves. These emotions contain two kinds of evaluation: the value of the others' fortune for us, and the value of the others' fortune for them. As mentioned, in some cases the two types of evaluation coincide, as in the case of compassion and being happy for someone we care about; and in other cases they are in opposition, as in the case of envy and pleasure-in-others'-misfortune. We experience emotions toward the fortune of others when we can imagine a first-person experience of others. We typically do not experience compassion unless we imagine that others have a worse first-person experience than our own.

Among animals, only chimpanzees, and maybe some other kinds of higher animals, can clearly be said to show compassion. The less complex affective attitude of empathy, namely, merely responding to another's perceived affective attitude by experiencing feelings of a similar sort, has been found in human neonates and in lower animals such as rats and guinea pigs. All of them respond empathically to the perceived sufferings of their peers. However, the more complex emotional state of compassion in which we also try to do something to bring comfort to the other is found only in humans older than eighteen months and higher animals. Chimpanzees, for example, will sacrifice eating opportunities to rescue other chimps in distress. This occurs even in instances where no kind of prior relationship exists, and in which the "altruist" chimp is hungry.[55] Similarly, we do not experience envy unless we imagine that others have a better first-person experience than we do. As indicated previously, we may also assume that forms of envy or jealousy exist among baboons and chimpanzees. In these animals, however, it seems that such emotions refer to perceptions of the current situation of the other agent; in humans these emotions are, as suggested above, directed at imaginative situations of others who need not be present.

Emotions directed at *our own fortune*—happiness, sadness, hope, and fear—are most often basic; only hope is not considered as basic. These emotions express the most profound self-preservative concerns, and for the most part require less complex intentional capacities. The emotions of this group can be directed merely at our current situation, and, in any case, they do not require the complex intentional ability of imagining others having a first-person experience. (Hope and complex fears occur with possible, rather than actual, improvement or deterioration of our situation.) No wonder that emotions from this group are usually regarded as basic emotions.

Among emotions directed at *actions of agents*, the typical positive emotion approving the actions of another agent is gratitude; the typical negative emotion disapproving the actions of another agent is anger. Similarly, satisfaction expresses our approval of our own actions, and regret or guilt expresses our disapproval of our actions. The negative emotion toward others' actions, namely, anger, is generally thought to be a basic emotion; the positive emotion toward others' action, namely, gratitude, is generally not. On the basis of primate evidence we may, however, suppose that gratitude developed well before the human and ape lines diverged.[56] Emotions directed toward our own actions require a yet more complex social comparison, involving a sense of self and counterfactual thinking which involves mentally undoing the past. We cannot experience regret or guilt unless we are able to imagine undoing our past actions, and a self different from the current one.

The group of emotions directed toward *the agent as a whole* involve comprehensive evaluation of the object. The comprehensive emotions toward oneself, namely, shame and pridefulness, require social comparison between the standards and achievements of oneself and those of others, and they also involve imagining others' first-person experiences toward oneself. Examples of emotions directed toward the other agent as a whole are attraction, love, disgust, and contempt, which have often been considered as basic emotions.

The centrality of social life for the human species makes the content of most emotions social, and makes social comparison frequent. The social environment has generated not only new emotions, but also changes in basic emotions themselves, so that social comparison has become central to them too. The social nature of emotions may be more evident in positive than negative emotions because changes for the worse are more closely related to survival issues.[57] Nevertheless, most emotions are social in that they involve comparing our present situation with that of others or with that of ourselves in different circumstances.

In modern society, happiness, sadness, anger, fear, and disgust are mainly associated with social issues. For instance, typical anger in Western society is usually caused by people we know and like—parents, children, spouses, and friends—

having done something that damages our sense of ourselves as persons. Being angry about something that hurts or even threatens us is rare. Indeed, one study showed that in 63 precent of angry incidents, the motive of the angry person was to assert authority or independence, or to improve self-image.[58] The social nature of anger was so obvious to Aristotle that he characterized it as a reaction to an unjust insult, suggesting that it is a response to a lack of respect.[59]

In happiness, social elements related to marriage, family, friends, and children seem to predominate. These have been found to be more significant than economic elements such as income. For instance, married people tend to be happier than single people, regardless of their economic situation. Similarly, it was found that people who could list five or more close friends with whom they discussed important matters over the past six months were 55 percent more likely to feel "very happy" than those who could not name any.[60] The same holds for joy or amusement. It was found that children who watched humorous films alone laughed less than those watching in pairs, who in turn laughed less than children in groups of four or more. Moreover, children watching humorous material with a friend showed more amusement than those watching with a child they did not know well.[61]

Human disgust has become another socially directed emotion, often concerned with social or immoral activities, such as incest and other types of "abnormal" sexual behavior. This kind of extension of disgust from its original function, protecting the body against disease, now enables this emotion to express protective feelings against more symbolic contamination.[62]

Sadness and negative affective disorders such as depression were found to be connected to social factors. Social support, for example, is quite important in this regard. Thus, it was found that the effects of negative life events were less for those people who had a close relationship with a confidant such as their spouse or partner. People around us can in some cases soften the blow and in others highlight the positive aspects. To give one example: one study found that the state of "being married and being unable to talk to one's spouse" was associated with a massive twenty-five-fold increase in the odds of being depressed.[63]

As a consequence of the increasing elaboration of basic emotions, when they occurr in humans they are sometimes as complex as nonbasic emotions. The difference is that basic emotions may occasionally show a more primitive form of intentionality. As suggested, happiness, sadness, anger, and fear may occur as moods, and in very few cases they may even occur without the subject knowing why.[64] Such cases may be reminiscent of the primitive origin of these emotions.

The emergence of social concern is a crucial determinant of our values and is associated with the emergence of the moral world—that is to say, a world in which it is understood that performance in roles, specific actions, and even attitudes is open to approving or disapproving social commentary. Hence, social comparison becomes pervasive. There is no morality without a conception of the current self and its comparison with other agents. Basic emotions in more primitive forms are not connected with moral behavior; instead, ethologists have tended to trace the basic concerns to those of existence or reproduction. However, when basic emotions acquire social content, then both these and such nonbasic emotions as shame, remorse, guilt, compassion, empathy, and pity become raw ingredients of morality.

Despite the importance of the social concern in emotions, we should be careful not to see everything in emotions as social. Emotions were developed as a response to biological needs, and those needs are still in evidence today. Hence, we may find in emotions some universal features which do not depend on social constructs and whose function is not essentially a communicative one. Thus, the basic regularity of some intensity variables, to be presented in the next chapter, will be formulated without specifying social constraints. For example, in describing the intensity variable of the event's strength, the following regularity is suggested: A positive correlation exists between the strength of the event as we perceive it and emotional intensity; the stronger the event is, the more intense is the emotion. This correlation, if true, is valid regardless of social or personal constraints.

We have seen that nonbasic emotions differ from more primitive forms of basic emotions in that they are always intentional and are based on social comparison. In many other respects, the two types of emotions are similar since they are generated in similar circumstances and have similar types of functions. In both cases, emotions typically occur when we perceive highly significant changes in situations that affect our goals and self-esteem, interrupting or substantially improving a smoothly flowing pattern of life. A major functional value of both basic and nonbasic emotions is to switch resources from one concern to another, to organize the system into a configuration broadly appropriate to the event that has occurred. Emotions enable the system to function in unstable situations in which such disturbances are liable to occur.

In light of their similar eliciting circumstances and functions, we can postulate that both basic and nonbasic emotions are made of similar psychological components, including cognition, evaluation, motivation, and feelings. The characteristics of both groups include instability of the system, substantial intensity, a partial perspective, and relative brevity. If the psychological aspects of basic and nonbasic emotions were more clearly differentiated, then it would be easier to distinguish between them. The fact that there are many disputes concerning the identification of basic emotions suggests that differences in the psychological aspects of emotions are subtle.

The classic dispute about basic emotions can be formulated in terms of the possibility of reducing nonbasic emotions to basic emotions. Those favoring such a reduction of more complex to simple emotions suppose that basic emotions express reactions to basic types of emotional situations, but that nonbasic emotions are reactions to situations that maintain some similarity with these basic types. Those opposing the notion of basic emotions argue against this reduction.

They argue that in the course of evolutionary and individual development, the environment has changed and brought about entirely new emotional situations, especially complex social ones. In this new emotional environment, social comparative concerns become as crucial as the self-preservative biological concerns and cannot be reduced to them.

The dispute concerning reduction of nonbasic emotions to basic ones may be less important than questions of how intentional capacities and social concerns have developed. The development of our intentional capacities has allowed the emergence of the concept of self and hence social and moral concerns. Arguably, second-order intentionality—the ability to imagine ourselves acting differently or to imagine another agent having a first-person experience—which is absent in simple forms of basic emotions, is a new development unique to humans. Yet, the evolutionary recent and intensely social quality of human life seems to have made even the so-called basic emotions occur most frequently in relation to other people. In other words, most basic emotions typically also have objects which are social, and in this way they are similar to complex social emotions. In this sense, a major evolution in human emotions is this development of basic emotions, thus bringing them closer to nonbasic emotions.

Emotions are concerned with self-preservative, reproductive, and social issues. We fear dying, we fear for our children, and we also fear humiliation. Sexual desire is concerned with both reproductive purposes and pleasurable social relationships. The notion of "basic emotions" is useful for certain explanatory tasks—mainly for developmental explanations—but it may not be sufficient for explaining all emotional phenomena. In light of the complexity of the human social environment, our investigations should not be limited to attempts to reduce it to the predominantly biological or physical environments of the past. Such reductions may have interesting developmental implications, but they may divert attention from yet more central issues: the intentional, social, personal, imaginative, and moral aspects of human emotions.

## Summary

For every minute you are angry you lose sixty seconds of happiness.
—Ralph Waldo Emerson

The affective realm may be described as consisting of four basic prototypes: emotions, moods, sentiments, and affective traits. These phenomena can be discerned by referring to two criteria: the specific or general type of evaluation involved and the occurrent or dispositional nature of the given phenomenon. In light of such distinction, affective disorders are explained as extreme, or pathological, instances of the above typical cases. Affective phenomena also differ in their temporal dimension. Of all phenomena in the affective realm, emotions typically have the shortest duration, usually lasting minutes or hours; affective traits have the longest duration and can last for a lifetime.

The typical cause of emotions is a perceived specific change in our situation. Specific changes become less important in sentiments, moods, and affective disorders. The typical concern of emotions is a comparative concern where the imaginative and social aspects are quite dominant, whereas in sentiments, moods, and affective disorders, existential, personal issues are of greater concern. The typical object in both emotions and sentiments is a human being; the object in moods and affective disorders is more diffuse.

The four characteristics of emotions, namely, instability, great intensity, partiality, and brief duration, are not all manifest to the same extent in sentiments, moods, affective disorders, and affective traits. Sentiments and moods are more stable, less intense, more general, and of longer duration than emotions. Affective disorders are more intense, more general, and of longer duration than emotions; such disorders may be regarded as more stable in the short run, but this stability is a fragile one. Affective traits are dispositional in nature. In emotions, both intentional components (cognition, evaluation, and motivation) and the feeling component are strongly manifest; in sentiments it is the intentional dimension that dominates; in moods and affective disorders, the feeling dimension.

A comprehensive classification of emotions has been suggested. The proposed classification is based on two evaluative characteristics: (1) the positive or negative nature of the state, and (2) the object at which the state is directed. Concerning their object, emotions have been divided into three basic groups: (1) fortunes of agents, (2) actions of agents, and (3) the agent as a whole. Each group is further divided into emotions directed at others and at oneself. Various issues related to the suggested conceptual framework should be determined by further empirical investigations. Among these is the prevalence of particular emotions in a specific individual or in a specific society, as well as the developmental order and functional value of various emotions.

The distinction between basic and nonbasic emotions is at the center of current disputes over the psychology and philosophy of emotions. It has been suggested that the notion of basic emotions is valuable for certain explanatory purposes—especially those referring to the development of emotions. The development of complex social environments has generated novel emotions which do not seem to derive from basic emotions. Moreover, the major concerns of basic emotions have become social as well.

The emotional realm has been frequently explained by reducing emotions either to their components, such as feeling, cognition, evaluation, and motivation, or to basic emotions, such as anger, sadness, fear, and happiness. The two explanations are not contradictory in that they refer to different aspects of emotions; as such, they both have some explanatory value. However, a simple reduction to either one component or to one or a few basic emotions ignores other interesting aspects of emotions. The complexity of the emotional realm is unlikely to be compatible with any kind of simple reduction. The value of classifying emotions in light of their evaluative component and of explaining the evolutionary development of emotions in light of their division into basic and nonbasic emotions does not imply that understanding emotions can be achieved merely by referring to these factors. Other components and other emotions are equally important for such an understanding.

# Chapter 5

# When Feelings Overflow—Emotional Intensity

When two people are under the influence of the most violent, most insane, most delusive, and most transient of passions, they are required to swear that they will remain in that excited, abnormal, and exhausting condition continuously until death do them part.
—George Bernard Shaw

People often talk about the intensity of their emotions: they tell us that their anger is overwhelming, that they feel extremely sad, or that they are madly in love. Despite the common usage of terms which measure emotional intensity, the notion of "emotional intensity" is far from clear. In this chapter I first clarify this complex notion and then discuss the circumstances in which emotions become intensified.

*The Complexity of Emotional Intensity*

Half of the people in the world are below average.
—Unknown

The concept of "emotional intensity" is complex; it applies to different phenomena, not all of which are correlated. When Paul says to Karola that he loves her now more than he has ever loved any other woman, what does he mean by this? He may mean several different things, such as (a) his feeling toward her is the strongest he has ever experienced, (b) his love toward her has lasted longer than any other love of his; (c) he keeps thinking about her all the time; (d) he believes she is the most wonderful person in the world; (e) he is ready to do more for her than he has ever been ready to do for any other woman. Analyzing emotional intensity should take into account all such diverse features.

The diverse features of emotional intensity are expressed in two basic aspects: magnitude (*peak intensity*) and temporal structure (mainly, *duration*). If Adam's feeling component is very strong at this moment, but it lasts only a few minutes, we may say that his love is weaker than love of a similar magnitude lasting for a few hours. Similarly, if thinking about her occupies him most of the time, this is indeed intense love; when this preoccupation lasts several weeks, the love is more intense than if it lasts several days. Duration can vary dramatically with comparable levels of peak intensity. In one study, participants rated the positive emotion associated with having "someone you find attractive suggest you meet for coffee" as almost as high as the emotion experienced after "saving your neighbor's child from a car accident." However, the average estimated duration associated with the former was twenty minutes, whereas for the latter it was more than five hours. Similarly, respondents estimated that they would stop ruminating about the coffee suggestion after about two hours, whereas the experience of the car accident would lead to rumination for about a week.[1]

The two basic aspects of emotional intensity, namely, peak intensity and duration, are expressed in each of the four basic emotional components: feeling, motivation, evaluation, and cognition. We may speak about the peak intensity and duration of a certain feeling, urge to act, extremity of evaluation, and cognitive preoccupation. Highly significant emotional events are expressed by the two aspects of all four components.

From a psychological point of view, then, an emotional state of great intensity is a state in which the two aspects of the basic four components, or a certain combined measure of them, have high values. From a physiological point of view, an emotion of great intensity has different measures referring to the strength of various physiological activities. In both perspectives, emotional intensity is a property of the agent experiencing the emotion and not of the event giving rise to the emotion.

The aspects of peak intensity and duration are typically related to the *partiality* of emotions. Emotions with a more partial focus are usually associated with greater peak intensity and shorter duration than more general emotions. Anger and sexual desire, which express a more partial concern than hate and love, usually have a stronger momentary magnitude but are of a shorter duration. The feeling component in sexual desire usually consists of short outbursts of intense feelings, whereas in love the peak intensity of the feeling may be lower, but it may last for a longer period of time. Likewise, short-term urges are more dominant in those emotions which have a more specific focus, whereas more general emotions have a more enduring impact on our conduct of life. The intensity of anger, for example, is more evident in the urge to act, whereas grief may have little impact on our immediate conduct even though it "colors" our behavior for a longer period of time.

Various difficulties in *determining the intensity* of different emotions exist. The central ones concern the relative weight of the various aspects and components of emotional intensity.

One obvious difficulty in determining emotional intensity is that of the *relative weight of the two basic aspects*, namely, peak intensity and duration. It is obvious that if two emotional states have a similar peak intensity but one of them lasts longer, then this is the more intense one. Comparing emotional intensity is more complex if one emotion has a higher peak intensity but lasts for a shorter period. Can we say that a brief outburst of strong sexual desire is stronger than a long-term romantic love whose peak intensity does not come close to that of the sexual desire? This is comparable to the difference, for example, between moving 100 lb of books all at once, or one book at a time.

Another difficulty in determining emotional intensity concerns the *relative weight of the various components of the temporal aspect*. Measuring the peak intensity is relatively simple, as it can refer to various measures at a given moment. Thus, it may refer to physiological measures or to self-reports of the peak intensity of the feeling component. Measuring the temporal aspect of emotional intensity is more problematic, as it does not necessarily refer to a steady persistence of a certain magnitude, but typically consists of frequent appearances of different magnitudes. Consider, for example, a man's longstanding love for his wife. This love does not consist of one emotional state lasting for years; rather, it consists of frequent appearances of strong and relatively brief emotional states. How can we measure this aspect of frequency? It is obvious that the more frequent the emotional state appears, the more intense is the emotion. But what about the comparison between frequent appearances which do not last for a long period of time and less frequent appearances which last longer?

The relationship between the different emotional components poses another difficulty for determining emotional intensity: it is not clear whether the degree of strength of the various components can be combined on a *common scale*. Can we say that the degree of positive evaluation in love ("she is the most heavenly person on earth") is always of the same measure as the strength of the urge to act ("I want to run out and buy her a diamond ring")? Some emotions have an intense feeling component, but the evaluative component does not express extreme (negative or positive) evaluation. Thus, it has been claimed that embarrassment is "slightly negative, but intense."[2] In some cases it is difficult to determine the value of even a single component. Thus, it is not obvious whether the value of the motivational component should be determined by referring to the desire or to the action which arises from that desire.[3] Even if a common scale for all four components were to be found, we would still have the problem of determining the *relative weight of each*. This is very difficult since such weight depends on personal characteristics, contextual features, and the type of emotion. Thus, it may be that in some emotions, such as love and compassion, the weight of the motivational component is far greater than in others, such as grief.

A positive correlation usually prevails between all expressions of emotional magnitude, and the same kind of correlation generally prevails between all expressions of emotional duration. But there is often no correlation between magnitude and duration. Thus, a high feeling magnitude may be associated with an intense urge to act, intense preoccupation with the emotional object, and extreme evaluation, but those usually last for a very brief period. A feeling that lasts longer may be correlated with long-term expressions, such as an enduring impact on the agent's way of life, lasting preoccupation with the emotional object, and enduring evaluation, but those are usually of lower magnitude. A high magnitude of the peak intensity is often negatively correlated with long-term components, such as enduring behavioral impact. When the peak is lower, we may not feel the need to unburden the system by taking action; hence the impact of the event may not be so evident in our immediate behavior even though it may affect our behavior in the long run.[4]

In addition to the above difficulties in measuring emotional intensity, there are further difficulties concerning the *accuracy of such measurements*. For example, emotional memories are often inaccurate. Moreover, conscious reflection upon previous emotions, or for that matter even upon ongoing emotions, may have a distorting influence.[5]

Even if we overcome the above difficulties and arrive at some quantity representing emotional intensity, the result will be comparative by nature, that is, the scale will be merely ordinal. We will be able to say that 20 is more intense than 10, and 10 more intense than 2, but we will not be able to claim that 20 is twice as intense as 10 or that 10 is five times as intense as two. This is because of the different scales used in measuring emotional intensity and because each determination of emotional intensity is comparative by nature.

Despite the enormous difficulties in measuring emotional intensity, ordinary people can and do measure such intensity. In speaking of emotional intensity, we all resort to quantitative language. We speak of "more" or "less" emotional intensity, and quite often correctly estimate the intensity of the emotions of others and ourselves in our everyday behavior. Thus, self-reports of happiness are surprisingly valid. Moreover, even four-year-old children can predict experiencing one emotion of varying intensity in a situation, and around age eight they can also predict multiple emotions of varying intensity and opposite valence.[6] Accordingly, psychologists have developed a variety of means and scales for measuring emotional intensity in general, as well as the intensity of particular emotions. There is a scale for almost every major emotion. In addition to such psychological measures, emotional intensity is often estimated in scientific experiments by measuring the underlying physiological components, which indeed renders reliable results.

The concept of "emotional intensity" denotes a complex construct whose components seem to be incommensurable; nevertheless, the intensity of the whole emotional state can be estimated by comparison with similar states.[7] Our ability to compare various emotional intensities is based on finding a *certain feature* whose changes are typically correlated with intensity changes of the whole state. Instability may be such a feature, as it is a basic characteristic of emotions, and it is easy to make a comparative estimate of its value. Greater instability manifests itself in many obvious physiological and psychological aspects. Another factor like this may be overall felt intensity.[8] Referring merely to one feature to get a rough approximation of emotional intensity represents a psychological abbreviation of complex mathematical formulas. These useful devices are quite common. Birds do not actually solve the complex mathematical formulas underlying their flight, and spiders do not solve such formulas when building their webs. They do it by using simpler biological devices. Similarly, human beings use a simple psychological device, rather than complex mathematical formulas, when they evaluate the personalities of people they have just met.

If our estimate of emotional intensity is comparative, then it does not require determination of the exact value of each emotional component. The *more similar* the two situations, the easier is the comparison, since we can more easily treat "emotional intensity" as if it were a unitary notion. If we were angry with the same person twice within one hour, it would be easy for us to determine the comparative strength of each experience. In many such situations, instability and other emotional components are easily compared. For example, the overall felt intensity and the strength of the urge to act are easily compared in two similar situations.

Determination of emotional intensity is more problematic, but still possible, in situations of *reduced similarity*, as when long periods separate the two emotions, when two different emotions are concerned, or when the emotions in question involve different agents. Nevertheless, we do compare the intensity of the same emotion experienced at different times and directed at two different people ("I love you more than I have loved any other woman before"), or the same emotion that other people have felt at different times ("You used to love me more than you do now"). We may also compare the intensity of different emotions in the same person ("Because of my great love for you, I manage to control my anger") or the same emotion in different people ("This person is more fearful than his wife"). A more difficult endeavor is to compare the intensity of different emotions in different people; nevertheless, people sometimes make such comparisons ("My hope is greater than my partner's fear"). Emotional intensity is not measured in all cases in the same manner. Thus, reference to the feeling dimension is important in measuring the intensity of our own emotions, but not that of others. In the latter case, behavioral manifestations are the most important.

An interesting case is that in which we have to determine the intensity of two *conflicting emotions* we are experiencing at the same time—for example, a woman who is sexually attracted to a man but fears the consequences an affair with him may have on her relationship with her husband. One may say that the two emotions, sexual desire and fear, are incommensurable and hence their intensity cannot be compared. However, this woman can compare the strength of the two emotions and indeed behave accordingly (assuming that external, for instance, moral, considerations are excluded).

A somewhat similar situation is that of *moral dilemmas* in which we have two conflicting values that seem to be incommensurable, but nevertheless we are able to determine the comparative weight of each value and to choose between them. An example of such a case would be the discovery of some criminal activity of a good friend and the ensuing decision about whether to report the case to the police. The two conflicting values here are loyalty to a friend and acting in accordance with the law. As in the emotional domain, comparing the two alternatives may be done by referring to a third feature: for example, we may choose the alternative which causes us the least moral discomfort. The view suggested here assumes that commonsense perceptions of instability and discomfort are in some cases adequate measures of intensity in the emotional and moral domains.

Dealing with the problem of incommensurability in the cognitive realm may be similar. The presuppositions of two conflicting scientific paradigms, for example, that which prevailed in ancient Greek physics and that prevailing in modern physics, may be incommensurable, but we may find a third feature, such as predictability, which is usually correlated with truth, and may lead us to a cognitive comparison between them. It may also be the case that the two paradigms have some common elements whose adequacy can be compared.

Although the concept of emotional intensity is quite complex, emotional intensity is often measured and compared in everyday life as well as in scientific experiments. This enables us to proceed with our discussion of the circumstances which determine emotional intensity even if the concept itself may not be entirely clear from a theoretical point of view.

### Intensity Variables

If only God would give me some clear sign! Like making a large deposit in my name in a Swiss bank.
—Woody Allen

Emotional intensity depends on the way in which we evaluate the *significance of events*. Although emotions arises from an immediate eliciting event, their intensity depends on broader sets of circumstances that circumscribe our sensitivity to such an event. Since the typical emotional cause is a perceived significant change in our situation, the circumstances influencing emotional sensitivity determine which of the multiple changes we continuously undergo are perceived as significant. The significance of a change is not an intensity variable, but the way in which we evaluate the situation on the basis of the different intensity variables.

The various intensity variables may be divided into two major groups, one referring to the perceived *impact of the event* eliciting the emotional state and the other to the *background circumstances of the agents* involved in the emotional state. The major variables constituting the event's impact are the strength, reality, and relevance of the event; the major variables constituting the background circumstances are accountability, readiness, and deservingness.[9] The suggested classification is not arbitrary; it expresses two major aspects of the emotional situation: the impact of the eliciting event, and the subjective background circumstances preceding it. The first group is crucial for determining our current situation; the importance of the second group is in realizing whether the situation could have been prevented and whether we deserve to be in such a situation.

The first group of variables may be considered as addressing *primary appraisals*, since they are directly relevant to our current situation. The second group addresses *secondary appraisals* in the sense that they refer to background circumstances that are not directly relevant to our current situation. Emotional intensity may be high even if the variables constituting the background circumstances are absent. A snake may arouse fear, irrespective of background variables such as our personal accountability, readiness, or deservingness. On the other hand, the absence of the variables constituting the event's impact precludes the possibility of an emotion: if the event has no impact, then no emotion will be generated. Similarly, when primary variables are very strong, the weight of secondary variables may be significantly reduced. When one's daughter is killed in an accident, the issue of whether the daughter or someone else was responsible for the accident is in many cases of little significance to the intensity of grief. This issue acquires greater importance as time goes by and one's attention can be more easily diverted from the event itself to its background circumstances. Although the reference to the background circumstances may seem to be redundant in our current situation, it has a great functional value in preventing or encouraging future similar experiences.

The general primacy of the primary variables does not mean that in each case a consideration related to these variables has greater weight than one belonging to secondary variables. Take, for example, the relationship between temporal closeness, which is a primary variable, and controllability (or accountability), which is a secondary one. In a series of independent events, later events, which are closer to us, are typically of greater emotional significance than are earlier ones. Thus, when two people lost the opportunity to win $1000 because they failed to match coin tosses, it was easier to imagine the outcome of the second toss as different; hence the person who tossed second was predicted to experience the greater guilt and receive the greater blame. In this case, temporal closeness has greater weight than accountability. However, in a causal chain of events, the initial event triggering the whole chain, although more remote from us than a later event in the chain, is of greater significance, as controllable events are more significant than uncontrollable ones.[10] If, for example, Neil puts poison in a drink and hands it to Oscar, who, without knowing about the poison, gives it to George, our negative emotions, which are generated by George's death, are directed toward Neil, who is responsible for the initial event, and not toward Oscar, who took part in the last event. In this case, accountability is of greater importance than temporal closeness.

The intensity variables determine not only the intensity of an emotional state but also its nature. When describing the nature of a particular emotion, we should not merely point out the general relationship among the factors constituting its basic evaluative pattern but also specify the quantitative relationship among them. Pity, for example, involves a negative evaluation of another person's misfortune, but it refers to grave misfortune only; when the misfortune is minor, pleasure-in-others'-misfortune is often the typical emotion. The intensity variable of the event's strength determines not merely the intensity of pity but also whether the given emotion will be pity or a different one entirely. There may be factors which determine the nature of an emotion, but which are not intensity variables. For example, evaluating a certain person as a friend or an enemy determines the nature of the emotional attitude, but not its intensity.[11]

Each emotion is typically *associated with a certain range of intensity variables*. The function depicting the relationship between a certain intensity variable and the intensity of a given emotion is valid only within that range which defines the emotion in question. Thus, if pity is characterized as positively correlated with the event's strength, then within a certain range typical of pity, an increase in the event's strength will increase the intensity of pity. As to events whose strength is outside that range—for example, when the other's misfortune is too weak to induce in us the emotion of pity—this correlation is irrelevant, since we are no longer dealing with pity.

*The Event's Impact*
Smoking kills. If you're killed, you've lost a very important part of your life.
—Brooke Shields

The variables constituting the event's impact may be divided into three: (1) the strength of the event, (2) the event's degree of reality, and (3) the event's relevance. It should be noted once again that we are speaking here about the event's perceived impact; hence, we refer to the perceived strength, reality, and relevance of the event.

*STRENGTH*
I have been poor and I have been rich and rich is better.
—Bessie Smith

The event's strength is a major factor in determining the intensity of the emotional encounter. It refers, for example, to the extent of the misfortune in pity, the extent of our inferiority in envy, the level of damage we suffer in anger, or the extent of beauty of the beloved. A positive correlation usually exists between the strength of the event as we perceive it and emotional intensity: the stronger the event is, the more intense is the emotion. Though positive, the correlation is not always linear: a stronger event may result in a more intense emotion, but the increase in intensity is not always proportional to the increase in the event's strength. In very strong events, an additional increase in their strength will hardly increase emotional intensity, which anyway is quite high and almost at its peak. This kind of correlation is also typical of other variables. The typical curve of emotional intensity rises to a point with increases in the given variable; from this point on, emotional intensity hardly changes with an increase in the given variable.

Television, movies, and novels have a strong emotional impact, since they depict extreme situations and their characters have great compatibility with basic prototypical evaluative patterns. In the words of Barbara Cartland, an author of romantic novels, "All my heroines are good, pure and very, very womanly, tender and sweet. All my heroes are sporting and very, very dominating, but honorable, because that is what a woman wants."[12] Since televised displays of emotions are more expressive than real-world displays, frequent viewers may adopt a more highly expressive style. I once met a young Japanese man who told me about his first kiss. He was 23 years old and had just arrived in Germany without knowing German. He invited a girl he met to his hotel room. After a while he began to kiss her. Since this was his first kiss, he tried to imitate what he had seen in movies and on television. There, he told me, they kiss very forcefully and with much enthusiasm. He imitated this, causing his German companion to shout, "It's painful!" My friend thought she was saying "stronger," so he kissed her more forcefully. She ran away.

Indeed, television has often been criticized for portraying the world unrealistically, in either overly positive ways or in excessively negative and stereotypical ways. Extreme situations are more unstable and hence more emotionally loaded. This is one reason why television overrepresents the extreme, scandalous aspects of society. Action series, dramas, soap operas, and movies are all founded on violence, criminality, deviance, pathological behavior, abnormal sexuality, and the like.[13] Similarly, sexual imagination, inherent in masturbation and other sexual activities, can achieve sexual satisfaction since it provides more extreme stimuli, namely, more perfect partners than the real world supplies. This may explain why so many people masturbate, although they often feel guilty about it (in one extensive study, 60 percent of men and 40 percent of women said that they had masturbated in the past year) and why people living with a sexual partner masturbate more than people living alone.[14] It seems then that the function of masturbation is not merely that of providing an imaginary stimulus when a real one is absent, but of amplifying a present stimulus.

In most emotions, evaluating the event's strength is simple, as it mainly refers to apparent properties of the event. In typical cases, hate is more intense, the more evil the other person is; hope is more intense, the more promising the future seems; and fear is more intense, the graver the danger appears to be. Describing what constitutes the event's strength may not be easy in some emotions, but nevertheless it is clearly perceived by us. We may not know for sure what constitutes the ideal person in our mind, but our love is stronger when we meet a person who is closer to such an ideal.

In some emotions, the event's strength can be specified between lower and upper limits. Thus, pleasure-in-others'-misfortune presupposes a certain degree of the other's misfortune; when this misfortune becomes very severe, it may exceed the upper limit typical of this emotion, and our emotion then turns into pity. Similarly, another person's improved fortune can make us happy up to the point where this person's fortune is so good that our emotion of happy-for turns into envy. There is also an upper limit of strength in events which cause embarrassment; beyond this limit, embarrassment may turn into shame. The positive correlation between the event's strength and emotional intensity is typically kept within specified limits.

*REALITY*
I love Mickey Mouse more than any woman I have ever known.
—Walt Disney

The second major variable constituting the event's impact is its degree of reality: the more we believe the situation to be real, the more intense the emotion. This variable is particularly important in forward-looking emotions, such as hope and fear[15]; it is, however, significant in other emotions as well. The importance of the degree of reality in inducing powerful emotions is illustrated by the fact that a very strong event, which may be quite relevant to our well-being, may not provoke excitement if we succeed in considering it as fantasy: the emotional intensity decreases accordingly. Thus, despite the horrifying impact of a potential nuclear holocaust, many people do not allow this to upset them, since they do not consider the event to be a real possibility.[16] A good friend of mine is so fearful of a nuclear war that he stocks water and food in his house for just such an emergency. (When we go on trips, he brings along the food that is near to the expiration date.) My friend and I differ not so much in our estimation of the impact or devastation of a nuclear war, but purely in our estimation of its impending reality. I believe that there are more real threats to my life than nuclear war. We may also say that an event which has seemingly no relevant impact may evoke strong emotions if we succeed in considering it to be real. Thus, although events in a fictional movie may have no relevant impact upon us, we may nevertheless become very emotionally involved, as we choose to believe in the possible reality of the events in the movie. Indeed, works of art are quite successful in inducing emotions.

In analyzing the notion of "emotional reality" two major senses should be discerned: (1) the *ontological*, and (2) the *epistemological*. The first sense refers to whether the event actually exists or is merely imaginary. The second sense is concerned with relationships of the event to other events. The first sense expresses the "correspondence criterion" of truth where a claim is seen as true if its content corresponds to an existing event in the world. The second sense is related to the "coherence criterion" of truth in which truth is determined in light of whether the given claim is coherent with other claims we hold.

The ontological sense is often understood to imply physical existence; indeed, in modern discussions "real" is often identified with "physical" (or "material") and "unreal" with "mental" (or "spiritual"). Such identification is unwarranted even in the ontological sense of reality: we should assume the actual existence of mental states. When I say that a certain person is jealous or in love, this claim can be true in the first sense of reality, although it refers to mental states.

The epistemological sense of reality allows for a greater variety of real entities. In this sense, "real" and "unreal" are context-dependent attributes: something may be real in one context and unreal in another. Something is real in a certain context if it has relations to other things in that context. In the context of physical reality, moral values and feeling pleasure over the misfortune of others are not real. However, they are real at the psychological level of describing human experience since they directly influence such an experience. In the perceptual context, colors and sounds are real, whereas wavelengths and photons are not. There is also a context where dreams are real: they are real experiences of the dreamer. In dreams physical laws become unreal since they are constantly violated.[17]

In analyzing the perceived reality associated with our emotional experiences, the two senses of reality are relevant as well. The ontological sense is expressed in the actual existence of the emotional object, and the epistemological sense is typically expressed in its vividness. The degree of reality is highest *when the object is real in both senses*. Interesting cases are those with a conflict between the two senses, for example, when a fictional character is more vivid than a person we have just met. Both persons are real for us, and it is not obvious as to who may induce greater emotional intensity.

Referring to the *ontological* sense of reality, we may say that emotions aroused by imaginary objects are less intense than those elicited by actually existing objects. When we know that the danger actually exists, we are more frightened than when we suspect that the danger is illusory. Likewise, we are less envious of a successful person in a movie than of an actually existing successful person. Indeed, viewers watching a film of a bloody operation, who repeatedly told themselves that this was a staged event, showed a decreased emotional response.[18] Similarly, campaign commercials often use man-in-the-street ads in which real people say positive things about one candidate or nasty things about the opponent. By using real people, the ads acquire a quality of believability, despite the fact that viewers know this is mere performance. In the same vein, we are influenced by advertising even though we know that it is not reliable.[19]

The *epistemological* sense of emotional reality relies on the vividness of the object. We receive information from various sources and with varying degrees of vividness. Pictures are most vivid due to the vast amount of information supplied by vision; hence, their importance in our everyday life. A picture, or better still, a film clip, of one wounded child has usually more emotional impact than reports about thousands killed. This vividness may account for the weakness of intellectual reasoning when opposed to the strength of emotions. Intellectual deliberations typically refer to something that is far away while emotions refer to what is present in the here-and-now. One important function of emotional imagination is to transform abstract general information into concrete partial information; consequently, a strong evaluative tone is attached to the given information and the readiness to act is greater.[20]

In light of the *crucial role imagination plays in emotions*, the importance of the degree of reality may be questioned. Thus, although works of art are understood to describe imaginary characters, they easily induce intense emotions. Art may in fact quite often induce more intense emotions than those we have toward real people, for example, starving people in a (from our point of view) remote place in the world, about whose fate we read in the newspaper or hear on the radio. Many people are much sadder when their favorite star, or even a cartoon character, gets hurt in a movie than when they read about a few hundred people killed in a remote place in the world. When the dog Lassie died in the popular TV series, millions of viewers, not all of them children, grieved. Except for the youngest, the mourners knew that Lassie didn't really exist. In view of the widespread grief, evidenced by some people wanting to know where to send flowers, the screenwriters thought it best to rewrite the story.[21]

Responding to this difficulty requires taking account of both senses of reality. Works of art are obviously real in the epistemological sense of being vivid. They provide us with more vivid information than that reported about actual existing events. The degree of vividness is clearly different when reading a newspaper and watching a movie are compared. The detailed and concrete description we have of the life of a fictional character in a movie makes this character more vivid and closer to us than an actual existing person reported in a newspaper.

Works of art are less real in the sense of actual existence. We have some background knowledge about the imaginary nature of the emotional object—this is what distinguishes emotional and aesthetic imagination from hallucination, psychotic fantasy, or dreams. Despite this knowledge, we attribute to the object some kind of existence. It is as if we put in brackets its imaginary existence. We are, therefore, irritated by someone who jokes during a movie, reminding us of its fictional character. We know that we are watching a movie or reading fiction; yet, by concentrating on the picture or the story, we behave as if it were real to a certain extent. Thus, we may wish that the death of the hero could be avoided, even though we have already seen the movie or read the book. In reading a novel or viewing a movie, we do not perceive unreality, but we knowingly abandon the actual realm to an imaginary one in which we accept the events as if they are real. This entails a suspension of disbelief.[21] This may explain the results of a recent poll which found that 87 percent of Americans think they will go to heaven, even though only 67 percent believe heaven exists at all.

We are moved by a book or movie despite, and not because of, its being imaginary: its higher degree of reality in the sense of its being vivid generates intense emotions despite its low degree of reality in the sense of its actual existence.

Indeed, various studies have suggested that the influence of television is greater when the characters are perceived to be more real. Such an influence is particularly significant in the case of young viewers who cannot easily make distinctions between reality and fantasy.[23]

The attribution of reality to works of art is enhanced by several factors. First, although works of art deal with imaginary characters, they bring to mind real people in real situations. By allowing this play with reality, works of art may offer us the opportunity to rehearse our emotional lives in situations we may have the opportunity to experience. In this way, we bring our own emotional reality to bear on fictional situations, which allows us to empathize with characters in the fiction. Second, works of art involve looking at things from another's point of view; they enable people to follow the event from within, to become part of it. By seeing life through the eyes of those directly involved, we adopt their perspective and feel emotionally close to them; consequently, intense emotions are easily generated. Third, works of art, and imagination in general, introduce various alternatives to our situation. They do not necessarily describe how people behave in reality but how they could behave. This opens the door to alternatives we did not think existed. Encountering such new alternatives excites us. In any case, flight into fictional fantasy is not so much a denial of reality as a form of play with it.[24]

Some artistic works may have a very low degree of reality, but are nevertheless quite emotional. In these cases, other intensity variables are strong. For example, great emotional intensity of novels and movies may occur as a result of the extreme or idealized circumstances they depict. These situations are far from representing real situations, but their unusual nature considerably increases the variable of the event's strength and the resulting emotional intensity.

A crucial difference between an emotion generated by actually existing objects and that generated by images concerns the activity associated with each; for example, we will run away from a live lion but not from one in a movie. The different actions address different beliefs and desires.

The degree of similarity of an emotion experienced through art to the one elicited in everyday life may differ in different emotions. I would speculate, for example, that while watching a movie such similarity is less for fear and hate than for sadness and sexual desire. An important factor in determining the similarity is the role of imagination and actual behavior in maintaining the given emotion. The role of imagination in fear and hate is not as crucial as in many other emotions since fear and hate involve concrete existential threats which should be addressed by an immediate, real activity. The role of imagination in sadness and sexual desire is greater and its correlation to an immediate, real activity is weaker.

The importance of the degree of reality should not diminish *the importance of imagination* in emotions. Imagining an alternative to current circumstances is a crucial factor in the emergence of emotions. However, the imagined alternative should be perceived as real as possible to have emotional impact. Awareness of the imaginary nature of an emotional object need not eliminate the emotional state, though it may weaken it. The more we tend to accept the reality of images, the more intense our emotions are. Taking account of this variable may explain why sometimes there is a time lag between the experience of some highly positive or negative situation and the experience of the related emotion. In such situations, for instance, when the loss of a loved one is involved, people are simply unable or unwilling to believe in the reality of what has happened.[25]

The more we know about a certain object, the more real (in both senses) it is typically perceived to be. An object perceived by sight, hearing, and smell is usually considered to be more real than that perceived by sight alone—other things being equal. More detailed knowledge about someone's life makes this person more real to us than someone we hardly know about.

It may be argued that in contrast to the suggested positive correlation between degree of reality and emotional intensity, there are cases in which the very possibility of a given emotion may depend on our thinking the object fictitious: for example, relish at the imaginary death of a rival. If such an event came to pass, it would not make us at all happy. So too, sometimes the possible-but-uncertain is more terrifying than its real occurrence. Further, some people who have strong, sexually excited emotional reactions to imagined seductions are left cold or are consumed by fear of "real" possibilities: for instance, the fantasizing seducer whose fantasized object, noticing his apparent interest, propositions him. In the same vein, a half-naked woman may induce greater sexual desire than a fully naked woman. Similarly, erotic talk over the phone may stimulate greater sexual desire than talking erotically to someone who is actually present.

The confusion concerning the positive correlation between the degree of reality and emotional intensity occurs when we compare events that also differ in other significant intensity variables. In all the above examples, the two compared objects are not identical: the imaginary object is different from the observed one. Imagination involves abstraction or selective attention more than ordinary perception. For example, when people fantasize about the gruesome death of their rival, the emotional object of such imaginings is not identical to the emotional object, should a death actually occur. In the fantasy, the object is abstracted from all the gruesome details which are unavoidable in reality. Accordingly, only when the actual event occurs are we forced into empathy with the sufferer, and are disturbed by self-blame and other negative moral emotions.

A similar explanation is adequate for the examples of sexual desire, fear, and related cases. The real and imagined situations in these examples are different not only concerning their degree of reality; they differ in other significant intensity variables. The same holds for the comparison between the half-naked and the fully naked woman. A half-naked woman may in some cases be more exciting than a fully dressed or a stark naked woman, since looking at her excites a man while leaving enough room for fantasy, which is also significant in sexual desire. The nakedness increases the arousal level and its partiality sustains the fantasy of a woman who is more attractive than the real one. Here men do not compare two identical objects in which the imagined object arouses a stronger emotion. Rather, the two objects are different: the half-naked woman is imagined to have other properties—which are typically more attractive—than those of the real one. (It is interesting that men find women in revealing clothing more attractive than fully clothed women as sex partners, but not as marriage partners.[26] Sexual desire is apparently not necessarily the most important factor in marriage partners.)

Our problem is not whether imagination influences emotional intensity, but whether there is a *positive correlation between the degree of reality and emotional intensity*. In order to examine this, we should examine whether all other intensity variables are equal in the two compared events. The positive correlation between the degree of reality (or any other intensity variable) and emotional intensity is valid only when other variables remain constant. Refuting the suggested correlation requires a comparison of two identical events whose only difference is that one is real and the other imaginary, and the latter induces stronger emotions. Isolating the degree of reality while keeping other variables constant is not easy, but whenever it succeeds the positive correlation of the degree of reality with emotional intensity is evident. If, for example, people see two identical movies whose only difference is that the first one is described as having been based on an actual case, this movie will generate more intense emotions than the other movie.

*RELEVANCE*
Never go to a doctor whose office plants have died.
—Erma Bombeck

No matter how great your triumphs or how tragic your defeats—approximately one billion Chinese couldn't care less.
—Unknown

The third major variable constituting the event's impact is its relevance: the more relevant the event, the greater the emotional significance and hence intensity. Relevance is of utmost importance in determining the significance of an emotional encounter. What is irrelevant to us cannot be emotionally significant for us.

Emotional relevance typically refers either (a) to the achievement of our goals, or (b) to our self-esteem. Goal relevance measures the extent to which a given change promotes or hinders our performance or the attainment of specific significant goals. Changes which promote our goals are associated with positive emotions, and those which hinder these goals are associated with negative emotions. An enjoyable event may be negatively evaluated if it impedes the attainment of a particular goal. In light of the social nature of emotions, our self-esteem is an important emotional issue. We do not envy trees their height or lions their strength, since these are irrelevant to our personal self-esteem. The relevance component restricts the emotional impact to areas of particular significance to us.

The two related aspects of relevance are associated with all emotions, but to varying degrees. The aspect regarding goal achievement is more dominant in fear, hope, regret, and hate, whereas the aspect concerning our self-esteem is usually more evident in emotions such as envy, jealousy, shame, and pridefulness. Sometimes greater relevance changes the nature of a given emotion. If someone is better than us in an area that is of little relevance to our self-evaluation, then our attitude toward this person may often be admiration. However, in a case of high relevance, other things being equal, the attitude is more likely to be envy.

Emotional relevance is closely related to *emotional closeness*. Events close to us in time, space, or effect are usually emotionally relevant and significant. Characterizing the relationship between relevance and closeness is not a straightforward task. Some may perceive them as different headings for the same thing. Others may conceive either relevance or closeness to be the basic factor. I believe that relevance is more directly connected with emotional significance than is closeness. *Relevance* is defined as "having significant and demonstrable bearing upon the matter at hand"; *closeness* is defined as "being near in time, space, effect, or degree."[27] A close object is usually emotionally significant because it is often relevant to our well-being. However, not everyone who lives in our neighborhood is of great emotional significance to us. Spatial proximity does not always lead to emotional significance.

The two major comparative emotional groups, namely, reference and social groups, are associated with relevance and closeness. Our reference group is associated more with relevance than with closeness, whereas our social group is associated more with closeness than with relevance. Nevertheless, relevance is also a major factor in determining our social group and closeness often determines our reference group. Events close to us in time, space, effect, or degree are usually relevant to the achievement of our goals and to our self-esteem; and events relevant to us are typically close to us as well. In light of such affinity, the boundary between our reference group and our social group is not always clear.

*Closeness* is a crucial element in determining emotional relevance. Greater closeness typically implies greater significance and greater emotional intensity. Closeness sets the conditions for meaningful relationships and comparisons. When someone is too detached from us, we are unlikely to have any emotional attitude toward her. Closeness may be broken down into two factors: (1) similarity in background, for example, biological background, place of birth, education, significant experiences, and opportunities; and (2) proximity in current situation, for example, proximity in time, space, age, status, salary, or possession of a certain object.[28]

*Similarity in background* provides the appropriate circumstances for comparison which is essential to emotions. Thus, we often envy or are proud of those who were born in the city of our birth, or we typically fall in love with a person who is similar to us or reminds us of someone from our past. Likewise, it has been suggested that after the death of a child, parental grief intensity is correlated with the child's similarity to the parent. Similarly, adoptions are more successful where parents perceive the child to be similar to themselves.[29] Like memory, which improves when we are in circumstances similar to those of the original event, emotions also intensify when we confront circumstances which remind us of highly emotional events: for example, in a cemetery, a place where two lovers first met, or the site of a battlefield.

Similarity can refer to diverse aspects, and it is up to us to choose the aspect according to which the similarity is determined. In this sense, similarity in background has a strongly subjective and sometimes peculiar character. Thus, it is not entirely clear why one should be proud of being born in the same town as a famous politician. (I even know of someone who took pride in telling everyone that once he and the defense minister had urinated at the same time in a public toilet.) Although there are various ways to find similarities between any two people, and these ways may have varying weight in different emotions, the establishment of similarity is important in creating emotional relationships between people. Similarity in background is of particular importance in forming our social group; we tend to include in our social group those who have a background similar to ours—for instance, those with a similar place of birth, education, and significant experience.

The second component of closeness is *proximity in current situation*. We compare ourselves with people who are close to us in time and space and those we consider to occupy an approximately similar position or possess a similar ability. We tend to exclude from our reference group people who appear definitely superior or inferior to us, as well as those belonging to irrelevant domains. Accordingly, a greater subject-object gap does not necessarily imply greater emotional intensity; it may also change the nature of the given emotion. A typical difference between envy and admiration is that in envy the gap is much smaller. A small gap is also typical of pleasure-in-others'-misfortune and, in general, of emotions in which rivalry is central. Our superior or inferior position is important when the gap is not wide and there is still a chance of changing our current position. When the gap is wide, we often take it as a given, thereby experiencing no rivalry and hence no emotion. Wide gaps are typical of pity, gratitude, and other emotions in which rivalry is not a central concern and we are not expected to try and overcome the gap.

Research concerning levels of aspiration confirms the prominence of the proximity variable. It has been shown that in most situations, our level of aspiration is placed slightly above our current performance. This is in accordance with the tendency of the level of aspiration to be absent from situations that are too difficult or too easy. It is also in accordance with our wish to be slightly better than those with whom we compare ourselves.[30] Various studies asked people with different salaries how much of a raise they required in order to live comfortably. In all studies most people, in all salary ranges, indicated a fixed percentage of increase. To put it crudely, this percentage usually represents the range of our envy. The more money we make, the more expenses we have and the harder it is to be satisfied. After getting a raise, and adapting to the higher level, the extra money is no longer "extra" and again one becomes dissatisfied with the current situation. This phenomenon is also related to achievement, whereby we are not satisfied with our situation despite having achieved something we desired.[31]

I would guess that in societies where the availability of alternatives is more significant, the percentage of additional income which is perceived to be required for living comfortably, will be considerably higher and hence the envy in such societies will increase. It is probable, therefore, that in our dynamic modern Western society, where new opportunities are constantly generated, the problem of envy will increase rather than disappear (see also chapter 10).

Proximity in time and space is an important factor in determining emotional intensity. The smaller the distance in time and space an event is from us, the more intense our emotions are; great distances often reduce emotional intensity. Hence, sometimes time can heal a wounded heart.

An interesting question concerning the temporal distance refers to the situation in which the distance is zero, namely, the event is occurring at the present moment. Spinoza, like Bacon and other philosophers, argues that "an affect towards a future or past thing is milder, other things equal, than an affect towards a present thing." Pascal, on the other hand, claims that our strongest passions are directed not so much to the present moment as to the near future and near past.[32] Without entering into a philosophical discussion concerning the status of the present as a line separating the past and the future, it seems that both philosophers may be right in different circumstances. Spinoza is right concerning very powerful events which we actually witness—for example, if we witness a murder or the adultery of our partner. However, in most other circumstances what generates our emotions is not a present event, but an event which has just happened or is likely to happen. This is true concerning not only fear and hope but also other emotions in which our imagination plays a major role.

Changes in the degree of closeness are quite important in managing emotional intensity. Take, for example, emotions induced by television. Closeness and familiarity are important in making the fictional environment more real. Accordingly, most TV shows are set in the present or in a time within the memory of the viewers. Most characters are supposed to be types with whom we are familiar. Such closeness and familiarity make it easier for us to perceive the imaginary story to be a real one. In other circumstances, such as when violence is shown on TV, the closeness variable is used to reduce emotional intensity. Television entertainment tends to place social problems involving violence in another time and place, letting us watch those fictionalized characters search for solutions to our problems in settings safely removed from our own. When violence occurs in a contemporary setting, it is generally the product of the interaction of police and criminals—again, it is removed from the lives of good citizenry.[33]

The correlation between relevance and emotional intensity is positive: greater relevance leads to greater emotional intensity. Things become more complex if we discuss the constituents of emotional relevance, namely, goal relevance, relevance to self-image, similarity in background, and proximity in current situation. This becomes particularly complex when these constituents are dependent on each other; for instance, when an increase in one constituent causes a decrease in another. Thus, if two siblings, having a high degree of background similarity, want to remain emotionally close, they must reduce the relevance of each other's deeds to their own self-image; otherwise, envy will prevail and their relationship will be damaged.[34]

As in other variables, relevance influences not merely the intensity of a given emotional state but its nature as well. Thus, when our fortune is worse than that of another person our emotional attitude can be that of envy or happy-for. Relevance is an important factor determining which of these attitudes we may have: in the case of high relevance envy is more likely to emerge and in the case of low relevance happy-for is more likely to be our emotional attitude.

*Background Circumstances*
For of all sad words of tongue or pen, the saddest are these: "It might have been!"
—John Greenleaf Whittier


This group of variables refers to background circumstances of the agents involved in the emotional encounter. The major aspects of these circumstances are accountability, readiness, and deservingness. Accountability refers to the descriptive issue of who was responsible for the emotional change; readiness refers to the agent's preparedness for the change; deservingness refers to the normative issue of whether the agent has deserved the specific emotional change.

*ACCOUNTABILITY*
I want to have children and I know my time is running out: I want to have them while my parents are still young enough to take care of them.
—Rita Rudner


Accountability refers to the nature of the agency generating the emotional encounter. Generally, the more responsible we are for the given change (e.g., by having some control over the situation or by investing effort to bring it about), the more available is the alternative and hence the more intense the emotion. The major issues relevant in this regard are: (a) degree of controllability, (b) invested effort, and (c) intent. I will focus my discussion on the issue of controllability.

*CONTROLLABILITY*
Misfortunes one can endure—they come from outside, they are accidents. But to suffer for one's own faults—Ah! there is the sting of life.
—Oscar Wilde

The various types of controllability may be divided into two major groups: (1) personal controllability, and (2) external controllability. Each group may be further divided into two subgroups. In the first group we can distinguish between events due to (1a) our deliberative behavior, (1b) behavior stemming from our character and habits, and (1a) our nondeliberative behavior. The second group may be divided into events due to (2a) others' deliberative behavior, (2b) others' nondeliberative behavior, and (2c) impersonal circumstances. The order of controllability is as follows: (1a), (1b), (1c), (2a), (2b), and (2c). It can be noted that the division of personal controllability is more specified than that referring to the controllability of others: personal controllability refers to deliberative behavior, behavior stemming from our character and habits and nondeliberative behavior; others' controllability refers merely to deliberative and nondeliberative behavior. This difference stems from the fact that the varieties of our own accountability are of greater emotional concern than those of others. In any case, although classifications can be useful, we should not attach too much importance to these categories.

The order of emotional intensity is similar: events due to our deliberative behavior have the greatest emotional impact and those due to impersonal circumstances, the least. The dependence of emotional intensity on the variable of controllability can be demonstrated by many everyday phenomena and empirical studies. People feel more entitled to (or frustrated by) an outcome they have helped to bring about than to (or by) an outcome resulting from the whim of fate or other powerful agents. Envy increases if our inferior position is due to our own failure, and frustration intensifies if the failure is attributed to us. It should be noted that quite often a greater degree of accountability does not merely increase emotional intensity but also increases the complexity of emotions because other emotions, such as guilt or regret, also become part of the emotional state.[35]

In one study, people were given the following scenario:

> Tom and Jim were both eliminated from a tennis tournament, both on a tiebreaker. Tom lost when his opponent served an ace. Jim lost on his own unforced error. Who will feel worse about the match?

All respondents said that Jim will feel worse. The greater controllability of Jim increases the availability of the alternative, namely, winning the game; hence, the situation is more frustrating. Indeed, a major means by which imagination influences emotional intensity is by changing the perceived control of either the subject or the object.[36] Accordingly, another study found that offering simple choices—such as giving people in a nursing home a choice of two kinds of juice for breakfast—leaves people feeling better than if they had no choice.[37]

In the movie *Sophie's Choice*, a Nazi officer demands that a Jewish mother choose which of her two small children will be sent to the gas chamber and which child will be allowed to live. The mother begs the Nazi to choose the child himself and thus to eliminate her control over the choice. The Nazi's cruelty is expressed, among other things, in his refusal to do so. By forcing the mother to choose which child will die, he creates one of the cruelest events for any parent: the death of her child which is perceived to be due to the parent's behavior.

The variable of controllability may also distinguish between different emotions. Whereas remorse and guilt typically involve a state of affairs for which we had some measure of personal responsibility or control, regret may also be directed at circumstances beyond our control.

In accordance with the suggested positive correlation between emotional intensity and controllability, it has been found that we tend to overestimate our degree of control over positive outcomes and underestimate our control over negative outcomes; we also underestimate the degree of control of others over positive outcomes and overestimate their control over negative outcomes. Similarly, we attribute others' negative emotions equally to situational factors and to their personal dispositions, whereas our own negative emotions are attributed to the situation more than to personal dispositions. This helps us to maintain a positive self-image and prevent unflattering comparisons.[38]

These considerations can explain why errors typically cause emotions. Errors do not merely involve an unexpected change but also a change that was to a certain extent under our control.[39]

In accordance with the suggested role of controllability in emotions, it can be predicated that we will be more envious of a colleague who wins a professional prize than one who wins a lottery. Winning a lottery is a random event due to impersonal circumstances beyond the control of any agent. Winning a professional prize is not random, as it is due to a decision controlled by other agents. Although in both cases we do not have full control of the eliciting event, in the prize situation our responsibility for the loss is greater.

The situation is somewhat more complex when we compare the case in which we win a professional prize to one in which we win a lottery. Here also our accountability is by far greater in the case of winning the prize and from this perspective this case will induce more intense emotions. However, we may have some expectations of winning a professional prize and hence the variable of readiness is stronger and since this variable has a negative correlation with emotional intensity, emotions will be less intense in this case. Although I believe that in most circumstances the accountability variable will have a greater weight, and hence winning the prize will be more exciting, this may not be true of all circumstances— for example, when one is certain of winning the prize.

In some cases people tend to take more personal responsibility for negative events. Thus, victims of wrongdoing often search for ways in which they are responsible for the wrong done to them. By doing this they avoid admitting that someone else has greater control over their lives. They trade the status of "victim" for that of "guilty agent" in order to retain a positive self-image, which entails having control over one's life. For similar considerations, women are often insulted when their spouses explain their seemingly aggressive behavior as due to their monthly period. They prefer to be seen as culpable rather than as having no control over their behavior.

In characterizing controllability, we should distinguish between situations due to our *character and habits* and those due to our *accidental or deliberative behavior*. The former are harder to modify and control; hence their alternative is less available and emotions associated with them are less intense. Consider the following examples suggested by Daniel Kahneman:

> Mr. Adams is very absent-minded. He accidentally destroyed an envelope which contained $300. Mr. Bender is very tidy and well-organized. He accidentally destroyed an envelope which contained $300. Who will be more upset?

Mr. Bender will be more upset since he has more personal control and takes greater responsibility for things. On the other hand, losing money seems natural for Mr. Adams in light of his character; the alternative is quite far from reality. The next example is similar but it refers to our habits rather than our character. Although our personal responsibility for habits is greater than for personality traits and can be changed more easily, they function like a second nature.

> Mr. Jones almost never takes hitchhikers in his car. Yesterday he gave a man a ride and was robbed. Mr. Smith frequently takes hitchhikers in his car. Yesterday he gave a man a ride and was robbed. Who will experience greater regret over the episode?

Mr. Jones is likely to experience more regret, since the alternative to his misfortune is more available.[40]

There are various phenomena which *seem to contradict* the suggested positive correlation between controllability and emotional intensity. I believe that in all such cases, the correlation is absent because other variables besides controllability have also changed and these are responsible for the apparent exception to the general correlation.

Consider, for example, the strong tendency of both men and women to claim responsibility for initiating a breakup, regardless of who actually initiated it. In this case, controllability of the eliciting event decreases the intensity of the sadness and shame associated with a breakup. It is easier to accept and cope with the breakup if one views it as a controllable, desired outcome than one imposed against one's wish.[41] Although this case may appear to be an exception to the general positive correlation between controllability and emotional intensity, its explanation is actually different: it relates to a different emotional variable, namely, relevance. Claiming greater responsibility for the breakup reduces the relevance to our self-image, and hence the emotional impact of the breakup decreases. A related situation is that in which, for example, someone wants to end a romantic relationship but she is worried that her partner will be hurt; to reduce his hurt, she leads him to believe that the breakup is actually his own decision, made for his own well-being. In such a case, the woman's concern for her partner's self-image causes her to exaggerate his accountability and hence to decrease the event's relevance to his self-image. Both situations do not express exceptions to the general positive correlation between accountability and emotional intensity.

Other such apparent exceptions are cases in which controllability itself is negatively or positively evaluated. For example, in pleasure-in-others'-misfortune, we are not willing to be personally involved in causing the other's misfortune. Accordingly, pleasure-in-others'-misfortune is more pleasant if the failure of the other person is not due to some wicked behavior on our part, but just happens to occur. The explanation of such cases also involves references to other intensity variables. The negative evaluation of our controllability reduces the other's deservingness of the misfortune, thereby reducing the intensity of pleasure-in-others'-misfortune.

The complexity of determining the role of controllability in generating emotional intensity can be illustrated by examining excuse-making. An obvious function of excuses is to reduce threats by shifting causal attributions for negative outcomes from personal to situational sources. This function is compatible with the general correlation between controllability and emotional intensity. When we attribute the outcome to external situations, we have less control over it and hence the intensity of our negative emotions is reduced. In many cases, however, we cannot entirely externalize the locus of causality; hence, we wish to give the impression that we are not fully responsible for the bad act. Thus, you might not have reported all the income you received from tips in your job as a waiter to the IRS. After having done this "bad" thing, you can reduce your guilt by saying that "everyone does it."[42] One's personal control is reduced when everyone does it; accordingly, the negative aspects of the deed are less significant from an emotional point of view. It should be noted, however, that in making excuses we do not completely remove the blame from ourselves but merely reduce its weight. Thus, in excusing ourselves we implicitly accuse ourselves.

By making excuses, an attempt is made to shift the attribution from a more to a less threatening (or damaging) aspect. It is usually the case that the less central the aspect is, the lesser the threat it poses to our self-image. For instance, it is less threatening to say that we failed the exam because we did not study than because we are stupid.[43] The tendency to attribute negative outcomes to less central aspects seems to be incompatible with the suggested correlation between controllability and emotional intensity; although the less central aspects are those which are more under our control—it would be easier to succeed in the exam if the failure were due to our decision not to study than if it were because of our stupidity—they produce less intense negative emotions. I believe that here also the change in emotional intensity is not due to changes in controllability variables, but rather in other variables—mainly relevance. When the outcome is due to a less central aspect of our personality, it is less relevant to our self-image and hence emotional intensity decreases.

The variable of controllability, referring to our past control over the circumstances that generated the given emotion, should not be confused with our present control of the emotional circumstances. Whereas a positive correlation exists between emotional intensity and past control, the correlation between emotional intensity and present control is negative. When an event is perceived to be under our personal control, it does not produce as much stress as one perceived to be uncontrollable.[44] A threatening event is perceived to be stronger when we are unable to control its course. The relevant intensity variable here is not controllability, which refers to background circumstances, but the event's strength, which refers to the present impact of the event upon us.

When discussing the passivity of emotions, we are usually not referring to the controllability of the eliciting event, but to our inability to control the emotional circumstances.

We should also distinguish between our past control over the event which induces the emotion and self-control while experiencing the emotion. Again, the correlation between emotional intensity and past control is positive, whereas the one between emotional intensity and self-control is negative. Self-control indicates stability of a system, and this is contrary to the circumstances typical of intense emotions.

We should distinguish between the subject's and the object's control over the circumstances in which the emotional change was generated. The variable of controllability discussed here refers to the former. The object's control over the eliciting event is also positively correlated with emotional intensity. We are angrier at someone who hurts us deliberately than at one who hurts us accidentally. Similarly, we are more grateful to those whose help was under their control than to those who were forced to do so.

In some cases, however, the object's control seems to have a negative correlation with emotional intensity. Although controllable causes lead to greater anger, uncontrollable causes lead to greater pity. Thus, individuals responded with anger to a request by another person to borrow their class notes when the need for the notes arose because the borrower went to the beach rather than to class on a particular day. These individuals responded with pity to the same request when it arose because the person suffered from an eye problem. Similarly, greater control of the person involved in a car accident will lead to a lesser pity.[45] Explaining these cases, along the view suggested here, can be done by arguing that in these cases other variables besides controllability, in particular the variable of deservingness, have changed. The person's greater control in bringing about the unfortunate event makes us perceive the person as more "deserving" of the misfortune, thereby decreasing emotional intensity. If we could eliminate changes in deservingness, the usual correlation between controllability and intensity would remain unchanged. Consider, for example, the following case: Tom and David are poor and must work many hours to support their large families. One night they are involved in two separate car accidents and seriously wounded. Both were very tired while driving their cars, but only David's accident was due to his tiredness; Tom's accident occurred when a rock fell on his car. I believe that pity will not be less and may even be somewhat stronger toward David, even though his accident was more under his control and could have been more easily avoided. In this example, because of David's unique situation, his control over the eliciting event does not lead us to perceive him as deserving his misfortune; therefore, the variable of deservingness does not influence the intensity of pity and the usual correlation prevails. (I discuss this issue further in chapter 11.)

*EFFORT*
There has never yet been a man in our history who led a life of ease whose name is worth remembering.
—Theodore Roosevelt


Effort is an additional factor constituting the variable of accountability. Like controllability, effort describes the extent of our involvement in the generation of emotions. Effort should be understood as including physical and mental effort, as well as investment of all types of resources. Generally, the more effort we invest in something, the more significant it becomes and the more intense is the emotion surrounding it. As the saying goes: the more you pay, the more it is worth. The converse is, of course, also true: when the stakes are greater, we invest more effort.[46]

Effort is closely related to the variables which signify the impact of the event, especially that of relevance. Thus, we invest more effort in something that is relevant and hence significant to us; conversely, something we invest more effort in becomes more relevant and significant. The saying "easy come, easy goes" expresses situations in which something we have gained without much invested effort is less significant to us and hence we may lose it quite equably.

The connection between effort and the event's significance is expressed not only in our attitude toward our success and failure but also in the attitude toward the success and failure of other people. When effort is invested, we perceive ourselves and others to be more deserving of success, and less deserving of failure. Accordingly, when great effort is perceived to be the cause of another's success, our emotional attitude is more positive than if great ability is the cause. Similarly, lack of effort is perceived more negatively than low ability. The strongest emotional reaction is when high effort is accompanied by low ability and success—consider reactions toward a handicapped person who exerts great effort and succeeds. Conversely, low effort accompanied by high ability and failure elicits the greatest negative reaction.[47] The greater emotional significance of effort over ability stems from the greater availability of the alternative in the case of effort. We are perceived to be more personally responsible for the amount of invested effort than for the level of ability; hence, we are more able to control a situation that is associated with invested effort.

As with other variables, effort may determine not only the intensity of a given emotional state but also its nature. Kant noted that everyone at a meal might enjoy the food, but only the cook of that meal could experience pride. Similarly, the amount of effort we could have invested but did not is important for generating guilt: when we attribute our failures to a lack of sufficient effort on our part, we feel guilty. We feel guilty because we believe that succeeding was within our control, but that we missed the opportunity.[48]

As with controllability, we should distinguish between the degree of effort involved in generating a particular emotional state and the degree of effort involved while experiencing the emotion. The variable of effort discussed here refers to the former; the latter belongs to an analysis of each emotion. Thus, whereas the intensity of both anger and hope is a function of, among other things, the effort invested, anger usually requires a higher level of effort than hope while experiencing the emotion.

One important factor determining the level of effort is the difficulty of the task. In positive backward-looking emotions, such as pride and joy, where we accomplished a certain task successfully, a positive correlation exists between the difficulty of the task and emotional intensity; in negative backward-looking emotions, such as shame and sadness, the correlation is negative. Since a difficult task is characterized as that in which the probability of failure is high, namely, the alternative of failure is more available, then accomplishing a difficult task is a greater reason for excitement than failing such a task. Moreover, in the former case, our personal involvement is magnified, whereas in the latter it is usually perceived as marginal and the main blame is placed on the difficulty of the task. The situation is more complex in forward-looking emotions, such as hope and fear, where the difficult task has not yet been confronted. In very easy or very difficult tasks, our involvement may be perceived by us as marginal and hence emotional intensity is lower. When the difficulty of the task is not extreme, emotional intensity is greatest. In this case, the availability of an alternative is greatest since it is not clear whether we will succeed in accomplishing the task.[49]

*INTENT*

When a man says he approves of something in principle, it means he hasn't the slightest intention of putting it into practice.
—Otto von Bismarck

The President has kept all of the promises he intended to keep.
—Clinton aide George Stephanopolous

Intent is another factor constituting our accountability. If we intended to do something, then our involvement and responsibility will typically be greater than when the event happened without our prior intention. Accordingly, the emotional intensity is typically greater. Thus, our anger will be more intense if we believe that the other person intended to hurt us, and our shame will be more intense if we intended to act in the abysmal way we did.

Intent and controllability generally have a high covariance: people intend to do what is controllable, and can control what is intended. But there are instances where intent and control do not coincide. For example, an overachiever might intend to take some time off from work, but cannot control her working habits. The differentiation between intent and control lies at the heart of the distinction between murder and manslaughter: both involve control, but only murder is associated with intent as well.[50]

*READINESS*

Blessed is he who expects nothing, for he shall never be disappointed.
—Jonathan Swift

I never expected to fall in love with the President. I was surprised that I did.
—Monica Lewinsky

The variable of readiness measures the cognitive change in our mind; major factors in this variable are unexpectedness (or anticipation) and uncertainty.

*Unexpectedness*, which may be measured by how surprised one is by the situation, is widely recognized as central in emotions. Since emotions are generated at the time of sudden change, unexpectedness is typical of emotions and is usually positively correlated with their intensity, at least up to a certain point. We are more angry if we happen to be expecting a contrary result, just as the quite unexpected fulfillment of our wishes is especially sweet. Unexpectedness may be characterized as expressing the gap between the actual situation and the imagined alternative expected by us. When the actual situation is better, pleasant surprise occurs; when it is worse, disappointment or remorse occurs.[51]

In light of the importance of unexpectedness in determining emotional intensity, one way to decrease negative emotional impact is to lower our expectations.

In doing so, we will be less frustrated by negative, and more surprised by positive, events. People who expect nothing will never be disappointed. However, their positive emotions will be limited as well, since no event will be perceived as a significant change—to perceive an event as a significant change implies expectations of the normal situation from which the given event significantly deviates. The emotional sensitivity of those who expect nothing is low and this is true of both positive and negative emotions.

The suggested negative correlation between expectedness and emotional intensity can be challenged. It may be argued that expectation of significant events, such as a difficult examination or a desired sexual encounter, often increases emotional intensity. It was found, for instance, that people who worry about what may happen suffer more from information about surgical operations or about their children's illnesses than "avoiders" do.[52] As in other cases of apparent exceptions, we do not actually have here counterexamples to the suggested general correlation, but rather circumstances in which other variables, for example, relevance and the event's strength, have changed. The more important the anticipated event is, the longer we think about it and the stronger and more relevant it becomes; hence, the greater emotional impact.

There is an interesting study exploring the impact which the discovery of deception by a partner has upon emotional intensity. It was found that the degree of suspicion before the discovery, namely, the degree of expectation, was not directly correlated to emotional intensity. Suspicion decreased emotional intensity when deception was perceived as relatively inconsequential. When deception was perceived as important, suspicion actually seemed to enhance emotional intensity.[53] Explaining these findings requires taking into account the variable of relevance to our self-image. When deception was perceived as relatively inconsequential, the variable of relevance played no role in determining emotional intensity and the general positive correlation between unexpectedness and emotional intensity was maintained. When deception was perceived as important, the variable of relevance was significant and it is this variable which determines emotional intensity. In this case, the general positive correlation between relevance and emotional intensity remains: when relevance is greater, emotional intensity is greater as well. When the influence of the relevance variables, and other variables, is eliminated, the general correlation between unexpectedness and emotional intensity remains valid.

An apparent exception to the general positive correlation between emotional intensity and the variables of unexpectedness and controllability are cases in which we are passively awaiting negative outcomes; such passive anticipation, which expresses a great degree of uncontrollability and expectedness, is intolerable and often leads to intense fear and sadness or even to affective disorders such as anxiety or depression. This is, for instance, the case with women whose husbands repeatedly beat them. Although the violence is expected, their anxiety is not reduced, since they are concerned with a negative event which they cannot prevent. Another example is the great anxiety experienced by people in Israel during the Gulf War when, not able to take action to intervene in the situation, they were forced to wait passively for the next missile attack. Similarly, during wars people at home feel helpless and are often more anxious than their relatives in the battlefield. In laboratory experiments, stress was reduced when people were led to believe that they had control, whether or not they did.[54]

Again, these examples are not genuine exceptions to the general positive correlation between emotional intensity and the variables of controllability and unexpectedness, since they involve changes in other intensity variables. Expectedness usually increases coping ability and hence decreases emotional intensity. Thus, if we know in advance the questions on our examination paper, we will be better able to cope with the situation, and our fear will be less intense. However, there are cases in which expectedness does not change our coping ability because of their great adversity or unpredictability. In such cases, expectedness usually increases emotional intensity, since the anticipated event becomes more central and relevant; thus, we keep thinking about it constantly. For similar reasons, expectation of a positive event enhances emotional intensity. When the media describe an upcoming sport competition, the competition increases in significance for us. Here, emotional intensity is enhanced since the greater degree of expectation does not improve our ability to predict the results and the competition becomes more central for us.

Families of missing soldiers typically suffer greater emotional stress than do those who discover their beloved's fate. Uncertainty hinders stabilization of the mental system. An Israeli submarine, lost at sea over thirty years ago, was recently found, thereby confirming the death of all on board. A family member said: "The day my brother was found was the happiest day of my life." Confirmation of his death was preferable to the uncertainty of speculating about his fate.

A factor related to, but not identical with, unexpectedness is *uncertainty*. We can expect some event to happen but may not be certain of its actual likelihood. Uncertainty is positively correlated with emotional intensity. The more we are certain that the eliciting event will occur, the less we are surprised at its actual occurrence and the less the emotional intensity accompanying it. In situations of certainty, the alternative to the situation is perceived as less available and hence emotions are less intense. Spinoza emphasizes this variable, arguing that the wise man "who rightly knows that all things follow from the necessity of the divine nature, and happen according to the eternal laws and rules of nature, will surely find nothing worthy of hate, mockery or disdain, nor anyone whom he will pity."[55]

An apparent exception to the positive correlation between uncertainty and emotional intensity is the fear of death. The intensity of this fear seems not to be diminished, and perhaps is even increased, by the certainty of our inevitable death. The explanation of this phenomenon is bound up with the event's highly negative impact on us. Such a significant impact reduces, if not eliminates, the weight of other variables. As suggested above, when knowledge of an expected negative event does not enable us to increase our coping ability, the event becomes more central, namely, more real and more relevant, and hence its emotional impact increases. In accordance with these considerations, it has been found that certainty of negative outcomes sometimes increases negative emotions.[56] If we could give less weight to the negative impact of death and concentrate only on its inevitability, then the fear of death may be reduced. Thus, Seneca argued that we may relieve ourselves of the fear of death by meditating regularly on its inevitability.[57] Indeed our sadness concerning the death of others is reduced when we keep thinking about its inevitability or when we have expected the death for quite a while, for example, because of a long illness. If death were not inevitable, our emotions concerning everything that could prevent death would be even more intense.

As with the other variables, we must distinguish our certainty before and after the occurrence of the eliciting event. The uncertainty variable, expressing our readiness for the eliciting event, refers to our state before its occurrence. When we speak about our certainty that the eliciting event actually occurred, this is a backward-looking attitude which actually refers to the reality variable. This explains the finding which suggests that fear and hope are associated with uncertainty, and anger with certainty.[58] In fear and hope, which are forward-looking emotions, our certainty refers to the upcoming eliciting event, and therefore the correlation is in accordance with the general positive correlation between uncertainty and emotional intensity. In anger, which is a backward-looking emotion, our certainty refers to the reality of the eliciting event. Hence, the more we are certain of the occurrence of a given event, the greater the degree of reality we attach to it, and the more intense is the anger.

### DESERVINGNESS
It never occurs to fools that merit and good fortune are closely united.
—Johann Wolfgang von Goethe

The perceived deservingness (equity, fairness) of our situation or that of others is of great importance in determining the nature and intensity of emotions. No one wants to be treated unjustly, or receive what is contrary to one's wish. Even though people disagree about what is just and unjust, most people would like the world to be just. Most people believe, explicitly or implicitly, that the world is a benevolent and meaningful place and that the self is a worthwhile person.[59]

Accordingly, the feeling of injustice is hard to bear—sometimes even more so than the actual hardship caused. When we perceive ourselves to be treated unjustly, or when the world in general is perceived to be unjust, this is perceived as a deviation and generates emotional reactions. The more exceptional the situation, namely, the more the situation deviates from our baseline, the more we consider the negative situation to be unfair or the positive situation to be lucky. In such circumstances, the issue of deservingness is crucial and emotions are intense. In some emotions, such as pity and envy, the variable of deservingness is very important; in others, such as fear, its role is less significant.

The characterization of deservingness is complex due to its similarity to, yet difference from, *moral entitlement*. Claims of desert, such as "I deserve to win the lottery," are based on our sense of the value of our attributes and actions; claims based on moral right, such as "she is entitled to receive a raise in her salary," often refer to obligations constitutive of the relationships with other agents. Claims of desert are not necessarily grounded in anyone's obligations, but rather in the value persons perceive themselves to deserve. In an interesting study, people were asked to participate in an interview with a psychologist. During the interview, the psychologist was interrupted by a colleague and excused herself. Attractive people waited three minutes and twenty seconds on average before demanding attention. Less attractive people waited an average of nine minutes. There was no difference in how the two groups rated their own assertiveness. Attractive people merely felt that they deserved better treatment.[60] The value attractive people perceive themselves to have induces the difference in claims of desert.

A major reason for the partial and often private nature of claims of desert is that they are often based on personal desires. It is not the case that there are certain objective situations upon which we either do or do not bestow emotional value. Rather, emotional value, and hence what we perceive as deserved, depends on personal attitudes and desire. We do not always desire something that is good in itself; in many circumstances, what we desire becomes good. Something that would not otherwise have much value to us becomes emotionally valuable because we want it. We often make people important to us, and hence perceive them to deserve more from us, simply by caring about them. A crucial reason why my children are important to me is that I love them. This is sufficient for substantiating my belief that they deserve more from me than do other children.[61] This character of deservingness makes it quite difficult to provide an objective description of claims of desert.

Claims based on moral right refer to some mode of *treatment* by other persons, whereas claims of desert also refer to the *fairness* of the situation. When we perceive our situation to be undeserved, we do not necessarily accuse someone else of criminal or immoral behavior; we assume, however, that for us to be in such a situation is in some sense unfair. Similar considerations apply to circumstances in which we perceive our situation to be deserved.

In typical claims based on moral right the agent is a person with some responsibility, whereas in claims of desert an impersonal cause can also be an agent. Heavy rain may be the cause of undeserved but not of immoral circumstances. Similarly, whereas claims based on moral right are directed at humans and sometimes at other living creatures, claims of desert may also be directed at inanimate objects. One can say that "Cleveland deserves better publicity, since it is an interesting city."[62]

Claims of desert are based on *perceived* undeserved or deserved situations that are not necessarily undeserved or deserved in a more objective sense. Perceived undeserved situations may be due to impersonal, arbitrary circumstances. Being unlucky may not involve any criminal or immoral deeds or attitudes of a particular agent, but the unlucky person may still be right to regard it as undeserved. It is not immoral for a rich person to win a big prize in the lottery or to marry another rich person; nevertheless, many poor people may consider it to be undeserved. Being born with a handicap may be considered unfair in the sense that no one deserves such a misfortune, but it does not entail a criminal or immoral deed. Similarly, when we say that hard workers deserve to succeed, we seldom imply that other people are morally obligated to help them succeed.

Claims of desert are different from claims based on right, even when both refer to a mode of treatment of other persons. Entitlement requires *eligibility* and satisfying some *general* rules, whereas deservingness requires satisfying certain conditions of *personal worthiness* which are not written down in any legal or official regulation. Sometimes claims based on entitlement are also claims of desert, for example, when the winning presidential candidate is the best-qualified person. The two types of claims may conflict if a person is entitled to something she does not deserve, or deserves something to which she is not entitled. An informer who betrays his brother is entitled to the advertised reward, but he does not deserve it; conversely, a defeated presidential candidate who is the best-qualified person deserves to be the president, but is not entitled to it. It is obvious that claims based on right do not exhaust the normative terrain of fairness.[63]

Although emotions may sometimes involve claims based on moral right, claims of desert are more typical. Claims of desert typical of emotions are personal and are only rarely directly relevant to moral actions. Such claims are often not considered as serious moral claims; dismissing many of them as morally irrelevant may be considered an appropriate moral response. Moreover, in most cases there is no one to whom to address claims of desert, and anyhow these claims cannot be fulfilled in light of practical considerations. When David envies Adam's beauty, his envy involves a claim of desert but not a serious moral claim. Telling David that he should be satisfied with his own good fortune in other domains is in this case a proper moral response. There is no one to blame for Adam's beauty, and it is impractical to try and change the situation by doing plastic surgery on David and all other people who are not as beautiful as Adam.

A distinction can be made between *wishing* and *deserving*. When we express our wish to have something, we do not necessarily imply that our lack of this thing involves unfairness or injustice. In claiming that we deserve something, we do suggest that there is something unfair in the fact that we do not have this thing. Envy involves not merely a wish claim but a desert claim as well. People in an emotional state usually overlook this distinction and consider their wishes to imply their desert and even their moral entitlement. The borderline between typical claims based on moral right and claims of desert is not clear-cut, and people tend to consider personal claims of desert as claims concerning their moral rights. For example, envious people often describe the unfairness of their situation as unjust in terms of their moral rights; thus, they attempt to legitimize their envy and present it as resentment based on moral norms of justice.

Different emotions are associated with different normative claims. When someone has committed a severe moral offense, such as a criminal act, our typical emotions are those of rage, disgust, and hate. The emotions toward less severe moral offenses are often those of resentment, indignation, and anger. We would not say that we resent a brutal murderer, but rather that we hate or are enraged or disgusted by this person. On the other hand, we do not hate or feel rage or disgust when our friends do not listen to our complaints on a particular occasion. Envy, pleasure-in-others'-misfortune, happy-for, and pity are examples of emotions that are often associated with the domain of desert, whereas resentment and guilt are more readily associated with the moral domain.

The relationship between *emotional intensity* and *deservingness* is quite complex due to the personal nature of deservingness. In describing this relationship, we should distinguish between the subject's and the object's deservingness, as well as between good and bad situations. The general positive correlation typical of the relationship between emotional intensity and other variables is also present between emotional intensity and undeservingness of the subject's bad situation. Thus, envy, jealousy, anger, and hate are stronger the more we consider ourselves as undeserving of our current bad situation. The same holds for the object's bad situation which we evaluate negatively. For example, pity is stronger, the less the object is considered as deserving the misfortune. In these situations, the subject's and the object's evaluations of the situation are similar, and therefore the correlation between the subject's bad situation and emotional intensity prevails here as well. When the subject's and the object's evaluations of the situation are different, the correlation is determined by the subject's evaluation. For instance, pleasure-in-others'-misfortune is stronger the more we believe that the object deserves her misfortune—even if the object believes otherwise.

Generally, undeserved situations are perceived to be less *normal*; hence the availability of an alternative is stronger and consequently emotional intensity is also stronger. Therefore, in many popular television series (such as *Murder She Wrote*), in which each episode involves the act of committing a murder, the person who is murdered has usually behaved immorally so in a certain sense seems to deserve punishment. Such deservingness decreases the intensity of the negative emotions we have while seeing the murder; it also allows us actively to enjoy the positive emotions we have when the murder is being committed, without feeling guilt.

In good situations, a positive correlation between the deservingness of the person (the subject or the object) enjoying the good fortune and emotional intensity prevails. It is as if the good guys win. Thus, we are usually more proud about truly deserved praises. Similarly, we are happier with the success of a deserving friend than with that of an undeserving one.[64] It can also happen that we enjoy our undeserved good fortune more since we are more surprised at receiving it. In such circumstances, the variable of readiness is different and therefore the general correlation is not maintained.

The complex, personal considerations underlying deservingness often change not merely the intensity but also the nature of the emotional attitude. Considering the other's superiority to be undeserved may change the emotion from envy to resentment or anger. On the other hand, considering their superiority to be deserved may change the emotion from envy to admiration. Considerations of deservingness are crucial in determining whether our emotion toward the other's success is positive, negative, or a nonemotional attitude of indifference.

*Personal Makeup*

Jacob served seven years for Rachel; and they seemed unto him but a few days, for the love he had to her.
—*Genesis* 29: 20

In assessing the significance of an emotional change, our personal makeup should be taken into consideration. Factors such as personality traits, world views, cultural background, and current personal situation are crucial for determining the emotional significance of given events. Differences in personal makeup may result in assigning different *significance* to given events, but they *do not undermine general regularities* concerning a certain intensity variable and emotional intensity. For example, different people may evaluate differently the reality of a given event: some consider the event to pose a real threat to their self-image, while others consider it to be imaginary. Thus, trivial social conversations between married women and other men may be perceived differently by their husbands depending on their personalities and cultural backgrounds. One man may perceive the situation as posing a real threat to him, while another will consider it as posing no threat at all. The differences in attached significance will result in differences in the intensity of jealousy. However, in both cases the general correlation between the degree of reality and emotional intensity is maintained; the more real the event is perceived to be, the greater the emotional intensity it provokes.

The same holds for bodily skills and other physiological differences. These are not intensity variables, but personal factors constituting our ability to express and cope with the emotional situation.

In the same vein, the influence of culture is mainly in the perception and interpretation of the significance of events and not in shaping general appraisal regularities. Thus, cultural differences may determine differently the relevance to our well-being of a certain event, or the degree of accountability others have for their behavior, but these differences do not affect the general positive correlation between emotional intensity and the event's relevance or between emotional intensity and accountability. In one study, positive and negative events were more readily assessed as being relevant to social prestige and to that of one's family and one's group by Surinamese and Turkish respondents than by Dutch respondents. Similarly, the Surinamese and Turkish groups attributed more intent to people who had hurt them and more often assumed that those people intended to benefit themselves. The differences in emotional intensity between the two groups should be attributed to these differences in interpreting the significance of the events and not to differences in emotional appraisal regularities. Although the emotional events that elicit emotions and the significance of emotions may differ appreciably from one culture to another, the dimensions of appraisal, the major patterns of appraisal, and the regularities of intensity variables are highly similar.[65]

When we describe someone as emotional we refer, among other things, to the great sensitivity of the person: emotional reactions are easily invoked in the person. Highly emotional people perceive the events of their daily lives as being more significant than do those with less emotional sensitivity. The world of highly emotional people is a place where many events assume great significance. These people do not go out seeking emotionally charged situations, but react more strongly to everyday situations that are perceived by them as more significant. Highly emotional men would be more easily drawn to attractive women and more easily repelled by unattractive women than would men with a lower level of arousal. People of low emotional sensitivity have to look for unique events, or even create unique events (e.g., a mountain climbing expedition), in order to be confronted with such significant events.[66]

Differences in personal makeup, then, are not variables of emotional intensity, but factors determining the significance of given events. Such differences alter the significance of each variable in terms of the function describing the relationship between a certain emotional variable and emotional intensity, but basically they do not change the shape of the function. Since my main concern here is understanding general relationships constituting emotional intensity, personal and cultural differences are not the focus of my discussion.

Personal makeup can be divided into two parts: (1) personality, and (2) personal current situation. Variables of the first group are relatively stable and include, for example, personality type (e.g., nervous or calm), sensitivity to other people, fundamental beliefs (e.g., moral and religious beliefs), gender, age, and cultural background. Variables constituting our current situation are more transient and include, for instance, our moods, attitudes, and personal resources.[67]

*Personality*
An ideal wife is one who remains faithful to you but tries to be just as charming as if she weren't.
—Sacha Guitry

Research has consistently demonstrated the existence of stable individual differences in the intensity with which people typically experience their emotions. Those of high emotional sensitivity are typically more sensitive to both negative and positive situations; accordingly, their sadness and happiness are more intense. People who become extremely overjoyed when good things happen are more likely to experience an equally strong negative impact when bad things happen. Great emotional intensity remains fairly stable across a life span. Although emotional intensity is usually unrelated to the nature of the given emotion, some personality traits may influence one type of emotion, but not another.[68]

Various divisions of personality dimensions have been suggested. The most common division is into five dimensions: extroversion, neuroticism, agreeableness, conscientiousness, and openness to experience. Extroverts tend to experience positive affective attitudes, to behave in a more dominant and active way, and to be socially active. Neurotics tend to experience negative affective attitudes, especially anxiety, and are more unstable. Agreeableness refers to cooperation, trust, and altruism, and is related to activities such as nurturing, caring, and providing emotional support. Conscientiousness encompasses organization, dependability, achievement motivation, and prudence. The openness dimension is seen as a broad dimension of intellect, aesthetic sensitivity, curiosity, and so on.[69]

These types of personality dimensions are the basis for further divisions. Consider, for example, the following division of temperament types suggested by Melvyn Kinder.[70] Kinder defines temperament according to two major aspects: *arousal* and *action tendency*, that is, the predisposition to express arousal in a particular way. Arousal is divided into high and low arousal, and action tendency into introversion and extroversion, that is, whether the person is inward-oriented or outward-oriented. Following Kinder, we can discern four main temperament types using these two scales:

1. *Sensor*: high arousal and introvert. Sensors are easily aroused and tend to discharge their tension inwardly. They try to avoid external stimuli as much as possible; hence, they are inclined to feel nervous or anxious about such stimuli.

2. *Discharger*: high arousal and extrovert. Dischargers are easily aroused and tend to discharge their tension outward. They try to seek out activities in which they can unload their emotional tension; hence, they are prone to anger and hostility.

3. *Focuser*: low arousal and introvert. Focusers are typically underaroused and tend to turn inward and ruminate on their feelings and actions. This self-focusing increases their arousal. Focusers are prone to melancholy and depression.

4. *Seeker*: low arousal and extrovert. Seekers are typically underaroused and tend to turn outward to seek out sensations and high-risk activities that will arouse them. Their seeking may result in impulsive, self-destructive behavior or in hedonistic behavior.

Another personality factor which I will briefly discuss is *gender difference*. In accordance with common ideas in popular culture and fiction, numerous empirical findings indicate the greater emotional sensitivity of women. This gender difference, which in many circumstances is not significant, is expressed in both positive and negative emotions, as well as in affective disorders, such as depression and anxiety, which are nearly twice as common in women as in men. The greater emotional sensitivity of women may be associated with their greater focus on close interpersonal relationships; emotions are most typical in such relationships. Women are more concerned with establishing close relationships than men and also better at doing so. These relationships have a higher relevance for women with regard to self-esteem. In one study, men were found to be more likely than women to attribute the cause of feeling depressed to academic concerns, while women were more likely than men to attribute the cause to problems in interpersonal relationships.[71]

Other findings indicate that emotional items constitute the key components of identification with the feminine and not with the masculine sex role. The belief that females are more emotional than males is one of the most consistent findings in research on gender stereotypes. Most people believe that the labels "very emotional" and "very aware of the feeling of others" are more characteristic of females. One study suggests that more than 80 percent of males and females name a female target when asked to name the most emotional person they know. Popular psychology books on relationships are read almost exclusively by women. The assumption that women are responsible for maintaining intimate relationships is suggested by the perennial popularity of articles in women's magazines on how to maintain a good relationship. On the other hand, the best-selling men's magazines focus on sexual fantasies, heroism, and athletic, financial, or military achievements.[72]

The above considerations are compatible with the findings that women smile and cry more often than men. This is not due to differences in status but various other factors such as greater involvement in social relations. The emotions of happiness, shame, guilt, and fear, as well as the attitudes of caring and warmth, are more intense in women, whereas anger, pride, sexual desire, and contempt are more intense in men. The former are related to affiliation, vulnerability, women's lower social status and power, and their traditional gender roles, while the latter are consistent with male roles of differentiation from and competition with others. In accordance with these considerations, it was found that mothers and fathers who interacted more with their children reported higher levels of stereotypical feminine emotional attitudes than those who interacted less.[73]

A major dispute concerning gender differences in emotionality is whether they measure emotional experiences or their expressivity. Some believe that these differences measure the intensity of *emotional experiences themselves*. Others emphasize the social nature of these differences, arguing that gender differences in emotionality are due to self-presentational conformity with prescribed sex roles:

women and men reporting on their tendency to be generally emotional may be reporting their beliefs regarding appropriate or expected gender-linked behavior.[74] Thus, in a study on regret, women had a more positive attitude toward regret and believed that they expressed more regret than the men, but in fact there was no gender difference in measurement intended to reflect the actual experience of regret.[75]

In a certain sense, both views are right. No doubt, sociological and cultural standards influence emotional expressivity. However, expressivity is often a kind of self-fulfilling prophecy: greater expressivity may increase the intensity of the emotional experience. It is not my concern at the moment to determine whether the source of gender differences is biological or sociological; it may be both. Even if the source is merely sociological, the difference sometimes surfaces in the emotional experience itself.

Another type of personal characteristic influencing emotional intensity is *age*. There is evidence for clear age differences in emotional intensity: younger subjects appear to be more emotionally intense. These differences are easier to explain in that as people grow older, they are likely to have encountered more events; accordingly, there are fewer events they would consider as novel and significant changes. I would speculate, however, that in old age people may again become quite emotional, since their biological system is highly unstable and they increasingly interpret events as being relevant to their own death. Indeed, soap operas, which are loaded with highly emotional issues, such as intimate relationships and the emotions that other people experience, appeal more to women and to the elderly. There are some emotions, such as long-term regret, which are obviously stronger among older people. Long-term regret seems to be more common in older age, since there are more events to regret and fewer or no opportunities to undo the damage.[76]

As an example of cultural characteristics, I would like briefly to discuss the issue of the relationship between religion and emotional intensity. This is a complex issue as religion influences various intensity variables and the influence may be in opposing directions. There is also variation among the religious beliefs themselves (hence, in this discussion I refer only to the belief in one God, as expressed, for example, in Judaism, Christianity, and Islam). Despite the complexity of this issue, and at the risk of being somewhat simplistic, I would like briefly to discuss three important factors in this regard: (1) meaningfulness of events, (2) deservingness, and (3) controllability.

*Meaningfulness of events.* An important factor in comparing the emotional intensity of religious and nonreligious people is the degree of meaningfulness we attach to various events; it should be remembered that emotional events are those which are meaningful for us. For most people, everyday events are meaningful since they believe that the world is a meaningful place and that the self is a worthwhile person. However, everyday events are usually more meaningful for religious people who perceive them to express God's will and intention. The belief that God directs all our everyday events makes them much more meaningful and hence the emotional reaction toward them is more intense. In this sense, the variable of relevance is stronger for religious people as each event may be interpreted as God's message to the given person. Victims of adverse events cope with their situation by finding meaning in these events. Victims ask, "Why me?" and may come to see the event as symbolic, a warning to them that the course of their life must change if it is to be a long and rewarding one. Thus, a heart attack can be reinterpreted as a benign, cautionary warning, designed to protect the sufferer by forcing him to change his lifestyle.[77] For the nonreligious person, significant adverse events are the major events which prompt a search for meaning; for the religious person, this search is much more common and is prompted by more types of events.

We may assume that in comparison with nonreligious people, religious people are usually less sensitive to existential issues—since they believe in life after death—and are more sensitive to specific, everyday events. This is in accordance with some findings indicating that religiousness is correlated with lower depression—and depression is often associated with existential issues.[78]

*Deservingness.* Issues related to deservingness are more central for religious people and this increases their emotional intensity. However, at the basis of religious considerations concerning deservingness lies the belief that all events express God's intention and will, and hence there is some acceptance of and justification for such events. A horrible accident in which many people are killed can be perceived by religious people as expressing God's will, however mysterious, and will ultimately be beneficial to the human race and to each individual. Nonreligious people consider many events as unjust and undeserved. Since deservingness is typically negatively correlated with emotional intensity, this variable usually increases emotional intensity in nonreligious people.

For religious people, the variable of deservingness has, then, two opposing types of influence: (1) the issue of deservingness is more significant and this increases emotional intensity, and (2) there is acceptance and justification of the situation and this decreases emotional intensity. It is difficult to determine generally which type of influence is stronger; any such determination should take into account personal and contextual features.

*Controllability.* Religious people believe that God controls and directs everyday events; hence, they believe that they have a lower degree of control over daily events than is believed by nonreligious people. Since controllability is positively correlated with emotional intensity, the emotional intensity of religious people would be less than that of nonreligious people if this consideration were the only relevant one. However, the issue is much more complex. Many of our everyday events are not within our own control: this is true, for example, of accidents, illness, other people's success, and global events such as war, as well as certain economic trends. Nonreligious people consider these events to be instances of luck and to be beyond their own control, possibly even beyond the control of other people. In events that are perceived to be lucky, the degree of control appears to be very low—if it exists at all. But religious people perceive these events not as instances of luck but as an expression of God's control. Consequently, in these events, the degree of controllability appears to be higher for religious people and hence their emotional intensity should be enhanced.

Concerning controllability, there are also two opposing factors which influence the emotional intensity of religious people: (1) since events in the world are subject to the control of God, the degree of controllability of an individual human being is less than that assumed by nonreligious people; (2) since God directs events in the world in light of people's conduct, such conduct has a certain influence on all events in the world—including those which seem to be random and the result of pure luck. These opposing factors prevent a general determination of whether controllability increases or decreases the emotional intensity of religious people.

To sum up our findings concerning the three factors we have discussed: the degree of meaningfulness is higher in religious people and this increases their emotional intensity; the issue of deservingness is also more significant and hence more emotional for religious people, but religious people are more ready to accept and justify the situation and this decreases emotional intensity; concerning controllability, opposing types of influence can also be found. We have seen that even when we limit our discussion to three factors—and there is no doubt that there are other relevant factors—the comparison between the emotional intensity of religious and nonreligious people is still a complex issue and it is difficult to draw general conclusions without examining the given context.

The great complexity of emotional phenomena is expressed in the influence of various factors on them. Emotional phenomena are influenced not merely by the general characteristics of emotions, such as a significant change in our situation, the comparative concern, and the different intensity variables, but also by more personal characteristics, such as unique personal traits, values, and cultural habits. Take, for example, the findings suggesting that the single best predictor of extramarital sex is premarital sexual permissiveness—people who have many sexual partners before marriage are more unfaithful than those who have few sexual partners before marriage.[79] We may explain these findings by referring to the importance of change and comparison in emotions. It is not the case that we have a certain magical number of sexual partners after which we can relax with a single partner. The excitement of having many partners is often the baseline against which our present excitement is compared. Another explanation, which may add to the previous one and not necessarily contradict it, may refer to personality traits: people with a great sexual appetite will have many sexual partners regardless of their being married or unmarried. Still another explanation may indicate the great importance in this regard of moral values and cultural habits which forbid having sexual relationships before marriage, and which forbid sexual relationships with anyone except one's spouse after marriage.

I will not discuss personal and cultural factors further, as my focus here is on a comprehensive framework relevant to all emotional phenomena. After such a framework is provided, it will be appropriate to examine the significance of personal and cultural details.

*Current Situation*
Everyone should have enough money for plastic surgery.
—Beverly Johnson

In addition to personality traits, our personal makeup also includes short-term personal features representing our current situation; moods, attitudes, and personal resources are major features composing this group.

Everyday experience leaves little doubt that moods influence emotional states. The typical influence is that positive moods and affective disorders are more likely to lead to positive emotions, and negative moods and affective disorders to negative emotions. For example, depression will increase the likelihood of negative emotions. The emergence of moods themselves depends on many features related to our current situation. Thus, the type of mood we experience as a response to the same problem depends, among other things, on the time of day. The same problem is rated as more serious in the afternoon than in the late morning. Hence, negative moods and emotions are more likely to emerge in the afternoon. Other examples of such features of current situation are exercise, diet, health, and sleep.[80]

The attitudes we assume also have a significant influence on emotional intensity. Thus, the positive or negative attitude we have toward someone influences the type and intensity of the emotion we feel toward that person. For example, an attitude of settling for less may significantly reduce envy and increase happiness. The attitude of competitiveness may have different effects. Similarly, when people are looking for adventure, craving to leave home, and passing into a new stage of life, they become more susceptible to falling in love. As with other emotions, timing also plays an important role in love.[81] In addition to moods and attitudes, personal resources are crucial in determining our coping potential and, as such, can significantly influence emotional intensity.

Our knowledge of the emotional situation is another aspect of our current situation. This knowledge is not directly connected to emotional intensity; instead it changes the magnitude of a certain emotional variable, and accordingly changes emotional intensity. The change, however, can be in various directions. Thus, there is not a definite relationship between knowledge and closeness, for example. Further knowledge of someone usually makes this person closer to us. But newly gained information may reveal aspects which decrease emotional closeness. Similarly, further knowledge about a certain event may reveal that it is actually stronger or weaker than we had previously thought, and may consequently generate different effects on emotional intensity. Knowledge, then, affects emotional intensity through its impact on various intensity variables; since knowledge can affect each variable in different directions, no definite correlation between knowledge and emotional intensity is to be found.

Personal variables are of particular importance regarding our coping potential. A certain change can be quite relevant to our well-being, but if we can cope with this change in a way that does not significantly change our well-being, it will not generate great emotional intensity or it may shift the nature of the emerging emotion from negative to positive. Thus, if we feel confident of our ability to cope with or repel the threat, then fear is minimized. Perceiving our personal resources to be inadequate with regard to the perceived change increases emotional intensity; in cases of such great gaps, crisis situations can develop.

A detailed description of personality and personal current situation is very useful in the analysis of particular individuals and predicting the significance they will attach to various events. However, this is a very complex and individualistic task and is not appropriate for our purpose, which is to uncover the more general circumstances influencing emotional sensitivity. In the same way that the enormous difficulties in measuring emotional intensity do not prevent people from assessing it, the enormous complexities of describing the influence of personal and cultural factors on emotional significance should not prevent us from utilizing a general framework which can contribute to explaining emotions and predicting emotional intensity.

## Summary

Too much of a good thing is wonderful.
—Mae West

The notion of "emotional intensity" has been found to be an extremely complex notion. Nevertheless, emotional intensity can be described and predicted. This chapter has described six basic variables of emotional intensity: the strength of the event generating the emotion, the reality of the event, the relevance of the event, our accountability for the event, our readiness for the event, and our deservingness of our present situation.

I have proposed a clear correlation between each variable and emotional intensity. A significant issue in describing the correlation between each variable and emotional intensity is that of the seeming exceptions to the general correlation. It may be argued that dealing with such exceptions requires assigning a negative sign to the variable in the exceptional situations. I have suggested leaving the value of the specific variable intact, but changing the values of other variables. The so-called exceptions are exceptions only from a local and partial perspective; from a general perspective, they tally with the overall function.

One way of examining the validity of my proposed framework is to construct a computer simulation of the suggested list of variables and their relationships. Although this may be a very complex task, it can be done, at least in principle.[82] An interesting issue in such a simulation is that of the default value of intensity variables. This value expresses the system's presuppositions; it is the value the system presupposes in normal circumstances. Assigning a certain default value may reveal the way in which the emotional system works, as these values express the state of each variable when no information about it is given. The ranges given for each variable describe the values assigned to the variable in typical emotional situations. Although the assignment of the possible range of each variable and its default value cannot be precise, describing them may give us an initial approximation of the nature of the given variable and its role in the whole emotional experience.

The intensity variables are global in the sense that they are related to all emotions. This does not mean that they are necessarily prominent in every emotional situation. For instance, the issue of readiness may not be significant in sexual desire, but it is not entirely irrelevant to this emotion either—in some cases, readiness greatly influences the intensity of sexual desire. Generally, the more complex the emotion, the more variables of emotional intensity are likely to be associated with its emergence. In addition to global variables associated with all emotions, there may be also local variables which derive from the particular nature of the given emotion.

Determining the influence of a certain variable should be limited to comparisons within a given emotion. Thus, it is misleading to say that anger, which is typically characterized as having a low degree of controllability, since it is primarily caused by others, would always be a less intense emotion than shame, which is characterized as having a high degree of controllability. The positive correlation between controllability and emotional intensity is maintained in both anger and shame: a greater degree of controllability will result in more intense anger and in more intense shame. Although the correlation between each intensity variable and emotional intensity is positive in all emotions, the specific curve depicting the details of this correlation may vary from one emotion to another.

An important task for future research is that of determining the adequacy of the suggested correlations in specific emotions. There may be emotions in which the general curve is somewhat modified or may not apply at all. I do believe that the general correlations attributed to the relationships between emotional intensity and each variable are valid for all types of emotions, but this belief should be examined in more detailed empirical research.

The proposed framework for characterizing emotional intensity has important implications for understanding the emotional process and for emotional management. Regulating emotional experiences should refer, among other things, to the intensity variables. This is the topic of chapter 8.

# Chapter 6

# Rationality and Functionality

Periods of tranquillity are seldom prolific of creative achievement. Mankind has to be stirred up.
—Alfred North Whitehead

The rationality and functionality of emotions have often been regarded in negative terms: because of their assumed irrational nature, emotions were perceived as disrupting optimal functioning. I believe that this contention is wrong. Emotions are not irrational in the sense of preventing optimal functioning; on the contrary, they serve important functions in everyday life. Even emotional pretense is often functional. This chapter concludes with a discussion of the relationship between emotions and gossip which seem to have several similar functions.

## The Rationality of Emotions

The heart has its reasons which reason does not understand.
—Blaise Pascal

My heart has a mind of its own.
—Connie Francis

Emotionally, you're an idiot.
—Renee, in *Ally McBeal*

There is a long tradition criticizing the rationality and functionality of emotions. In this tradition, which pervades much of current culture, emotions are regarded as an impediment to rational reasoning and hence as an obstacle to normal functioning. This tradition typically combines several assumptions which are not necessarily consistent with each other:

    a. intellectual thinking is the essence of the mental realm;
    b. emotions are nonrational in the sense that they are not the product of intellectual thinking;

    c. emotions are irrational in a normative sense; for example, they are dys-
    functional, or they lead us to distorted conclusions.

The first two assumptions are descriptive; the last one is normative. While accepting (b), I wish to refute (a), and (c).

I have criticized the first assumption elsewhere,[1] and I will not pursue it further.
I would only like to mention briefly a major shortcoming of this view which is
relevant to the issue of the rationality of emotions.

Intellectual thinking is considered by evolutionary evidence and common sense
to be the most developed mental capacity typical only of the most advanced living
creatures, namely, human beings. In this view, other living creatures have more
primitive mental capacities. Assuming intellectual thinking to be the essence of
the mental realm undermines this diversity and assumes the uniform nature of
the mental realm. This uniformity may be expressed in two different positions: (1)
excluding all living creatures except human beings from the mental realm; (2)
assuming that intellectual thinking is present in all living creatures having mental
capacities.

Descartes adopts the first option, whereas the current computational approach
to the mind favors the second. Both options have obvious difficulties stemming
from the failure to realize the complexity and variety of the mental realm. Neither
conceptual reasons nor empirical evidence compels us to deny the evolutionary
nature of mental capacities. On the contrary, such nature is consistent with our
current knowledge.

Concerning the emotions, the intellectualist tradition is faced with several
positions:

    a. emotions are present only in human beings;
    b. emotions are present in all living things;
    c. emotional capacities are present in different degrees of development in
    different living creatures.

The first position is assumed by Descartes and is refuted by ethological research
as well as by commonsense observations (at least by those who have animals
around them). The second position is hard to defend in light of the great complexity of emotions which requires various mental capacities not found in lower
living organisms. The third option is the most plausible one. Its adoption by the
intellectualist tradition creates, however, an odd situation: the most developed
mental capacity, namely, intellectual thinking, is present in all living creatures,
while the more primitive emotional capacities are developed gradually and are
present therefore only in more developed animals. I believe that the evolutionary
approach should be used to explain the development of both emotional and intellectual capacities. In this case, we cannot assume that intellectual thinking is the
essence of the mental realm.[2]

Emotions may be regarded as rational or nonrational in the descriptive sense
which refers to whether they are the product of intellectual thinking. In accor-

dance with my opposition to the view characterizing intellectual thinking as the essence of the mental realm, I believe that emotions are not necessarily the product of intellectual thinking.

Contrary to the view assuming that emotions are not necessarily the product of rational thinking, one may argue that the presence of emotional regularities, and the centrality of the comparative concern in emotions, imply the participation of intellectual calculations in the process of generating emotions. Such calculations are not always simple and often involve multiple factors of different relative weight.

Dealing with this objection requires the distinction between rule-following behavior and rule-described behavior, that is, behavior that follows rules and behavior that is in accordance with the rules. The difference is between being guided by a known rule and simply being in accordance with a rule, or between intentional rule-following and nonintentional forms of mere lawful connection. Relevant to this idea is Kant's distinction between doing what reason dictates because reason dictates it (acting on a given rule), and merely doing what reason dictates (acting in accordance with a given rule). This is the difference between having the power to be affected by reason, and just happening to do a reasonable deed. Only in the first case do we appreciate the relevant data and regularity involved before rationally deciding to act accordingly. The phenomenon of under-standing, so typical of intelligent behavior, may be entirely absent when one merely behaves in accordance with rules. "To be intelligent," Ryle tells us, "is not merely to satisfy criteria, but to apply them; to regulate one's actions and not merely to be well-regulated."[3] Describable regularity need not imply actual intel-lectual calculation. Although a bird's flight and the spider's behavior in making webs can be described by complex, abstract mathematical formulas, neither birds nor spiders follow rules or make intellectual calculations.

The same holds true for the emotional system. The regularities typical of emo-tions should be described as assumptions structured into our personality, not as intellectual calculations carried out inside our heads. The emotional agent is not necessarily aware of premises and does not therefore necessarily infer conclusions from them. Instead of assuming an intelligent agent who makes explicit intellec-tual calculations, we should assume a well-designed and somewhat inflexible system, thus providing a more economical explanatory mechanism. Indeed, simple mechanisms often underlie what seems overwhelmingly complicated when described by formal idioms.

Our emotional behavior is clearly not rule-following behavior. When we fall in love or become angry, we do not calculate our emotional response; in most cases the relevant data and the general principles of calculation are simply unknown to us. Although we do not actually make intellectual calculations, the emotional response, being in accordance with such calculations, may be perceived *as if* it were the result of such calculations. When one is angry with the right person to the proper extent at the right time, one acts in accordance with what reason dictates, but not because of it. Here anger speaks with the same voice as reason, but this does not mean that we employ reason through deliberative, intellectual processes.[4] We do not need such processes here; we simply act in accordance with our character.

If we are less conscientious, acting according to character may not be in accordance with what moral reason dictates, but it can still be an immediate response. We should distinguish between the descriptive issue concerning the psychological nature of the emotional response, that is, whether it is an immediate or a mediated response, and the normative issue of whether this response accords with what reason prescribes. The emotional response can be immediate (or spontaneous), that is, not preceded by mediating intellectual processes, but it may still accord with such processes.

It should be noted that when I assume that we are acting in accordance with our character, I do not claim that emotional regularities are necessarily unique; in the same way that there are similarities and differences in personality types, there are similarities and differences in emotional regularities.

In light of the above distinctions, we may say that emotions can be immediate but still be influenced by our personal characteristics. I have argued elsewhere for the direct and meaningful nature of perceptual experiences[5]; similar considerations are valid in the case of emotions. Emotional experiences are impure and direct: they are influenced by our personal makeup, but they are not mediated by intellectual deliberations. The influence of personal characteristics is expressed by the responsiveness or sensitivity of the system.

The adaptive value of emotions is to be found in the way emotional patterns have evolved. The burden of explaining emotions should shift from reasoning to developmental processes. Evaluative emotional patterns have emerged and have been modified throughout the evolution of the species and personal development of the individual agent. Explaining emotional phenomena cannot be limited to the fractions of seconds in which we are supposed to make the various intellectual calculations, but has to account for many evolutionary and personal factors. We need not undergo the whole process of evolutionary and personal development each time we have an emotional encounter. This process has modified, or tuned, our emotional system in such a way that our surroundings immediately become emotionally significant.

Generating emotions consists mainly of activating basic evaluative patterns rather than a process of intellectual persuasion. This explains why, from an emotional point of view, it is true that "one picture speaks louder than a thousand words." The emotional system is more easily activated by visual than by verbal stimuli, whereas the intellect is more susceptible to verbal stimuli. Poetry, so successful in inducing emotions, is, of course verbal, but it affects us in the way that pictures do: it does not present long intellectual descriptions, but rather excites points of sensitivity which activate the emotional system. This process is also one of the ways in which music induces emotions.

Commenting on La Rochefoucauld's maxim that "The head is always fooled by the heart," Jon Elster asks: Why should the heart bother to fool the head? Can't it just get on with it and do whatever it wants? The answer he suggests is that it is an important part of our self-image that we believe ourselves to be swayed by reason rather than by passion. Elster terms this tendency "addiction to reason" and rightly claims that it makes those who are so addicted irrational rather than rational. A rational person would know that under certain conditions it is better to follow emotional tendencies than to use more elaborate intellectual procedures.[6] Sometimes the opposite tendency is evident as well: people present their calculated actions as if they were contrary to intellectual reasoning but in accordance with the moral commands of their hearts, because it puts them in a better light. Politicians, who often behave in a calculated and immoral manner, typically use this tactic.

### The Functionality of Emotions

The passions are like fire, useful in a thousand ways and dangerous only in one, through their excess.
—Christian Nestell Bovee

An emotion is a prostrating disease caused by a determination of the heart to the head. It is sometimes accompanied by a copious discharge of hydrated chloride of sodium from the eyes.
—Ambrose Bierce

Along with the tradition which considers emotions to be irrational, there is a tradition considering emotions as disorganized interruptions of mental activity and as impediments to normal functioning. Some even consider emotions to be a kind of disease that we need to cure, since to neglect these illnesses would be little short of suicidal. It has been claimed that grief represents a marked deviation from the state of well-being and should therefore be regarded as a pathological condition, to be treated and cured. Fear also has been considered as a disease. Even positive emotions such as love, whose adaptive value seems to be evident, have been regarded as signs of inadequacy. Many poets and authors have described love as a sort of illness; such love—especially unrequited love—may wound and even kill the lover. Since emotions are considered to be disruptive, they must be eliminated or controlled. Thus, Plato thinks that emotions are to be distrusted, the Stoics advise the wise man to rid himself of emotions, and Augustine argues that God and the angels have no emotions.[7]

The identification of emotions with illness often depends on external considerations not related to the psychological nature of emotions. Thus, in the United States and other countries, emotional problems have been regarded as illnesses for financial reasons: medical insurance will not cover psychotherapy that is not considered as medical treatment for a specific illness. Since most people cannot afford to pay the entire cost of psychotherapy out of their own pocket, excluding emotional problems from mental illness would mean bankruptcy for most therapists. Opposing financial considerations lead medical insurance companies to exclude emotional problems from the definition of illness in the regular medical sense.[8]

In light of the claim that emotions essentially lack functional value, it has been assumed that in realms where our mere self-interests are concerned, emotional behavior should be excluded. One example of such a realm is the economic one. It has been suggested that the market community is based on entirely impersonal relations which undermine and exclude emotions. Purely economic relationships are essentially emotionless. The monetary economy and the dominance of the intellect dispelled emotions from socioeconomic relationships and limited them to the exclusive province of personal experiences. Thus, to be professional at work is to be fully rational and hence emotionless.[9]

I believe that the above criticism is unfounded and is often based on the failure to distinguish between two senses according to which emotions can be considered rational: (1) a descriptive sense, in that the generation of emotions involves intellectual calculations, and (2) a normative sense, in that emotions may express an appropriate response in the given circumstances.

The two senses are not interdependent; emotions can be rational or nonrational in each sense or in both. Emotions are essentially nonrational in the descriptive sense, since they are typically not the result of deliberative, intellectual calculations. Emotions are often rational in the normative sense: frequently, they are the optimal response. In many cases, emotions, rather than deliberative, intellectual calculations, offer the best means to achieve our optimal response. This may be true from a cognitive point of view—that is, emotions may supply the most reliable information in the given circumstances; from a moral point of view—that is, the emotional response is the best moral response in the given circumstances; or from a functional point of view—that is, emotions constitute the most efficient response in the given circumstances. In such cases, it is rational (in the normative sense) to behave nonrationally (in the descriptive sense). The failure to distinguish between these two senses of rationality underlies much of the heated dispute about the rationality of emotions.[10]

Emotions are the optimal response in many circumstances associated with their generation, namely, when we face a sudden significant change in our situation but have limited and imperfect resources to cope with it. In these circumstances the emotional response is often optimal, because optimal conditions for the normal functioning of the intellectual system are absent. For example, in circumstances when much of the relevant data are missing but speed may be more important than accuracy, our decision making must be done in a more or less predetermined form without having to think about what to do exactly. Fire drills are meant to help us acquire such forms of behavior. Emotions express these forms without undergoing such "drills"—those were done, so to speak, during our evolutionary and personal development. Deliberative calculations are not required for the emotional system to behave rationally in the functional sense: reason in emotions is not simply a matter of calculation but first of all a matter of sensibility. Moreover, in many situations the calculated pursuit of self-interest is incompatible with its attainment. In light of its evolutionary origin, behaving emotionally may in many cases promote our own interest.[11]

The functional value of emotions does not imply that emotions are beneficial in all circumstances. Emotions are quite often rational in the normative sense of being an appropriate response. This kind of rationality may be characterized as local, since it does not take into account global implications, but only those limited to the local present situation.[12]

There may be situations in which the emotional response is not merely the optimal response in the immediate circumstances, but in other circumstances as well; that is, we would choose the emotional response even after profound intellectual consideration. Love at first sight expresses an emotional response which is made instantly and on the basis of partial information. If this love continued for a long time, then the first emotional response would be the best response not only in terms of the partial information present at the first date, but also considering other types of information and considerations that were not available at the first date.[13]

As suggested, emotions typically occur in significant, changing, and often unusual circumstances. Emotions are indicative of a transition in which the preceding context has changed, but no new context has yet been established. Because of the unique nature of their generation and their partiality, emotions are quite intense and hence readily lend themselves to excesses and distortions.[14] This, however, does not mean that emotions are disorganized phenomena we should get rid of. The fact that emotions often occur in what we perceive as abnormal circumstances does not imply that emotions are abnormal responses having no functional value. In the same way that it is not advisable to cut off your head to get rid of headaches, it is not advisable to eliminate our emotions to get rid of the difficulties associated with them.[15]

Emotions constitute an adaptive mechanism in the sense that they are flexible, immediate responses to changing stimuli. They are useful urgent responses to emergencies; indeed, emotions are often the most practical and useful states that we can assume. Grief over the death of a person is of value; it is a natural evaluative response conveying our appreciation of the worth of a fellow human being and is important for the development of moral behavior. Likewise, love is of value in helping us to establish a more intimate and stronger bond with other people, and fear is an alerting mechanism, important in ensuring self-preservation. Strong emotions also rouse us to perform in ways that might otherwise be beyond our capability. Thus, fear spurs humans and animals to run faster and longer than they ordinarily can. Emotions discontinue normal functioning either by disrupting it or by significantly strengthening it. Both cases have an adaptive function.

The functional value of emotions can be clarified by considering three basic constraints imposed upon human activities:

1. human beings often encounter uncertain circumstances in which they must make immediate decisions;
2. human beings have limited resources and multiple goals;
3. human beings need other humans to achieve their goals.

In light of these constraints, emotions may be described as having three basic evolutionary functions:

1. an initial indication of the proper manner in which to respond;
2. quick mobilization of resources;
3. a means of social communication.

Emotions function within individuals to indicate and regulate priorities, and between individuals to communicate intentions. Since emotions are generated when we perceive a significant change in our situation, their purposes must be related to our ability to function in these circumstances. This is clearly expressed in the first two functions. The *indicative* function is required to give us an initial indication of how to cope with the uncertain circumstances we are facing. The *mobilizing* function is needed to regulate the locus of investment, that is, away from situations where resources would be wasted, and toward those urgent circumstances where investment will yield a significant payoff. The *communicative* function is used to reveal our evaluative stand and thereby elicit aid from others and insist upon social status. The cognitive component is essential to the indicative function, the motivational component to the mobilizing function, and the evaluative component is quite significant for the communicative function. All functions are particularly important when urgency is in evidence.[16]

The *indicative* function of emotions is to point out the positive or negative nature of the uncertain circumstances we face and to help us choose the initial course of action accordingly. Due to the uncertainty and urgency of the situation, a decision must be made quickly; however, it is not necessary that the decision be detailed in the very first moment. Emotional responses indicate the general direction of our actions by presenting us with an immediate evaluation of the positive or negative nature of the situation. Indeed, emotions often amplify, or even provide, the first indication that something has changed and in particular that something has gone wrong. As Elster indicates, there are occasions when gathering too much information is dangerous: if a doctor makes too many tests before deciding on treatment, the patient may die under his hands. In this sense, emotions enable us to avoid procrastination. Elster further argues that emotions may help us make decisions by acting as tiebreakers in situations of indeterminacy, and, more generally, they improve the quality of decision making by enabling us to focus on salient features of the situation.[17] The indicative function is fulfilled not by presenting a convincing argument but by inducing certain feelings.

The neurologist Antonio Damasio provides some evidence for the neurological basis of the indicative function of emotions. He speaks about somatic markers which highlight the negative or positive nature of each option. For example, when a bad outcome connected with a given response option comes to mind, we experience an unpleasant gut feeling. The somatic marker forces attention on the negative outcome of a given option and functions as an automated alarm signal which warns us of the danger ahead.[18] The intellectualist tradition argues that in order to obtain the best results from a logical decision-making process, emotions should be factored out. In light of the indicative function of emotions, this contention is plainly incorrect. Damasio even describes cases in which a decline in rationality is accompanied by diminution or absence of feeling. Emotions assist "cool" reason by reducing the number of possible options to be considered and directing reason to the more advantageous options.

Emotions may not only attribute an initial positive or negative value to each option but also some preference order for choosing among them. Emotions make the cognitive landscape uneven, that is, with more or less salient and valuable contents. This may explain why the emotional defect in Damasio's patients is also connected to the way in which they consider future prospects: they appear to be insensitive to the future. The defect in these patients is not cognitive, but evaluative: they are aware of future options, but attach no value to them. Accordingly, they have no emotions toward these options.

A major function of the perceptual system is to bestow upon the physical world initial *cognitive* meanings which are useful for survival. Thus, instead of finding our ways in a physical world populated by atoms moving in the void, we live in a perceptual environment populated by different types of objects and events which can be easily discerned by their shape, size, colors, smells, and other perceptual qualities. In this context, the psychologist James Gibson introduces the notion of "affordances." Affordances are properties of the perceptual environment that are meaningful in reference to an individual; affordances are what the environment offers the individual, what it provides or furnishes the individual. Thus, the presence of a supporting surface at approximately the height of an individual's knees affords being sat upon. Perceptual affordances are then crucial for guiding our activities.[19]

In a similar vein, a major function of the emotional system is to bestow upon the perceptual environment initial *evaluative* meanings expressing our personal values and attitudes. These evaluative meanings are directly relevant to our personal well-being. Although perceptual meanings are essentially cognitive, they do not entirely lack an evaluative aspect. We do not merely perceive people around us as having a certain height, weight, and skin color, but also as being attractive or dangerous. Perceptual meanings become emotional when the personal evaluative aspect becomes central. Perceptual evaluative meanings can arise when I see at a distance an attractive person or a dangerous animal; emotional evaluative meanings will be generated when I consider myself (or those meaningful to me) as being with this person or near that animal. In the latter circumstances some urgent actions are required and we cannot remain indifferent; the emotional system provides us with some initial guidelines for behaving in such circumstances. Unlike the perceptual environment which mainly *affords* various activities, the emotional environment *seduces* us into behaving in certain ways. The emotional environment is more action-oriented than the perceptual one since it is more directly relevant to our personal well-being.

The emotional function of bestowing personal evaluative meanings upon objects and events in our personal surroundings is quite useful from another perspective: our brief and temporary existence. As indicated, our imminent death is always in the background of our life. Taking death seriously, we may avoid bestowing much value on our minute everyday failures and successes. These events are not significant at all when compared with our imminent death. Why should I feel happy that my son has improved his grade in biology if I know that not too long from now I will be dead? Indeed, many people who are seriously ill and can foresee their imminent death become indifferent to their surroundings. A major function of emotions is to put death in brackets, that is, to bestow significant personal meaning on the events in our transient surroundings although the weight of such events is considerably reduced, if not completely eliminated, when compared with the profound event of our death. When people want to concentrate on the deeper meaning of life, they indeed retreat from everyday activities.

A person totally without emotions has no guidance and warning system, that is, no immediate evaluative guidelines determining relevance and importance. In a world without emotions, a young man, when meeting a young woman, may be able to see her, touch her, and think to himself: "This is someone with whom I could get along well." However, without emotions, the young man will not be excited by her presence and will not be attracted to her. Lacking emotional sensitivity is not human. Those for whom nothing is pleasant or painful and one thing does not differ from another in this respect can hardly be regarded as human; such sensitivity is essential even for higher animals.[20]

It is often the case that our emotional system fulfills its task of bestowing personal evaluative meaning on what may be regarded as minor and insignificant matters: we often bestow too much value on these issues. Accordingly, it is common knowledge that too much emotion can impair reasoning in general and decision making in particular. Indeed, emotional regulation intended to reduce emotional intensity seems to be the prevailing form of emotional regulation. However, the evidence described above, and other types of recent scientific evidence, suggest that too little emotion can also impair reasoning and decision making.[21] Hence, it is likely that our emotional regulation may also be concerned with increasing emotional sensitivity.

The *mobilizing* function of emotions is evident in light of the urgency of the situation: there is an urgent need to respond quickly and with all our resources to an event which can significantly change our situation. Since it is quick and intense, the emotional response is less accurate and more partial. By being partial, emotions focus our limited resources on those events that are of particular importance, thereby increasing the resources allocated for these events. Because of our limited resources and multiple goals, we need a system that is able to switch our resources quickly from one event to another. Emotions constitute such a system, and serve to switch our resources in order to discontinue a certain smooth operation and jolt the system into a more helpful frame. Emotions enable the system to function in such a state of instability. Once the initial switch is made, and the mental system has been shifted toward a more or less suitable frame, then finer tuning of the system to its environment must follow. This process of fine tuning is no longer emotional; it expresses the eclipse of emotions.

In some cases, however, emotions seem to be too slow from a practical point of view. Sometimes emotions surface after the significant change has already disappeared. For example, when we are driving a car and nearly miss causing an accident, the intense fear that emerges comes too late to have an effect on the behavior that got us into the situation in the first place. In such situations, the functional value of emotions lies not in providing an immediate response to a sudden change, but in realizing the significance of this change and appreciating its usefulness for the future in preventing or facilitating the circumstances that led to its happening.

There are many cases in which the emotional response seems to be quite slow, but nevertheless has important adaptive value. Examples of such circumstances are those in which a soldier is wounded in a battlefield but does not feel the pain until he is evacuated to the hospital, a policeman who dismantles a bomb and begins to feel fear only after completing his mission and realizing how dangerous it was, and a physician who conducts a complex operation and becomes excited only after the operation is completed. In all these specific circumstances, the successful completion of the task depends, among other things, on nonemotional behavior. Only after the task is completed does the mental system allow for an outburst of emotions.

Incidentally, being in an emotional state already may either slow down or accelerate the next emotional response. Thus, sadness slows the agent down, while fear usually has the opposite effect.

In light of the essentially social nature of the emotional environment, the *communicative* function of emotions is quite important. The unique social sensitivity typical of emotions ensures that the situation of others is taken into account by us and that our situation is taken into account by others. Our limited resources and multiple goals force us to make constant choices in our daily life—we cannot do or attain everything we want. Such choices must consider the ability and needs of others, and these are fraught with uncertainty. Our emotional response must adequately communicate our attitude and must take into account the attitudes of others. Quite often, emotions may express our profound attitudes better than words. People who do not know the language or customs of a foreign country may still know how to flirt with locals. They use emotional communication, which is largely universal. When emotional communication fails, serious adverse consequences may follow.

There is no doubt that emotions genuinely express our present attitude. An interesting question is whether they also express our more stable and general attitudes; in other words, is emotional communication valid only in the short term or also in the long term? Take, for example, anger. Does anger express (a) a temporary outburst which involves losing control over our behavior and saying and doing things with which we do not really agree, or (b) what we really think about the other person? The first possibility is represented in a few common sayings such as, "Don't judge a person when he is angry" and, "Hate drives one insane." The second possibility is expressed by Henry Ward Beecher: "Never forget what a man says to you when he is angry." The first possibility is explained by the fact that, like other emotions, anger expresses our current attitude toward a sudden change in our situation. In an intense emotional state, we are not stable and since we focus on what is right in front of us, we may overrate it and describe it in a manner that is incompatible with our long-term, stable attitudes. The second possibility is based on the fact that emotions express our basic values and attitudes and hence are sincere. It seems that both options are possible: it is true that emotional communication basically expresses our temporary and partial attitude, but this attitude is based on our more profound attitudes and values. We must analyze the given context to determine the depth of the temporary emotional attitude.

There is various physiological evidence for the functionality of emotions. It is well-known that the emotional fight-or-flight response, generated when something threatens us, is associated with physiological changes—such as an adrenaline rush, pupil dilation, and faster heart rate—that prompt us to run away or fight. Another finding concerns the immune system. It has been found that during intense emotional states, there is an increase in the number of natural killer cells. These cells are able to kill cells that have been infected with viruses, and, potentially, they are also able to kill tumor cells. The increase in killer cells, which is associated with both positive and negative emotions, is quite brief, lasting no more than twenty minutes. Other findings suggest that group therapy in which individuals experience feelings more freely also has a positive impact on the immune system. Thus, there may be some truth in the American cure-all that "a smile a day keeps the doctor away." Conversely, there is also evidence that prolonged stress weakens the ability of the immune system to fight infection. For example, it has been shown that lonely students have a poorer immune response to infection than do those who are not lonely. It has also been suggested that anger is a factor in the cause of heart disease.[22]

The functional role of emotions and feelings in general is evident in cases where they are absent. Consider the following description of a patient who suffered the loss of several feelings and emotions as an aftereffect of illness:

This patient possessed no sense of time or duration, no feeling of hunger nor any of sympathy for her own children. She had to look at the clock to distinguish five minutes from two hours. She had to eat according to the clock since neither hunger nor appetite guided her. She even had to go to sleep according to the clock, and so on. With regard to her children, she could manage only the *judgment* that these were her children, which could move her to act dutifully toward them as sympathy could not.[23]

There is no doubt that lack of feelings and emotions is a severe handicap. A similar case is that of a schoolteacher who, as a result of injury in the right hemisphere of her brain, was rendered incapable of expressive intonation in speech. She despaired of keeping order in class, because she had completely lost the ability to sound angry. This made it impossible for the children to take her efforts to discipline them seriously.[24]

In this context, it is relevant to mention the example of Mr. Spock from the science fiction series, *Star Trek*.[25] Spock is not a human being but a creature from another planet whose members are solely logical beings; they are incapable of feeling emotions. He starts out in the series as a paragon of the purely intellectual being, a perfect example of what has been advocated through the ages, of what men should strive for. The producers of the series, however, recognized early on that if Spock were to remain a purely intellectual, unemotional being, communication between him and the crew would be almost impossible. So, they gave him an earth mother thus allowing him to show an occasional "lapse" at the human level.

Not only the existence of emotions but also our awareness of their existence is important. There is a phenomenon termed "alexithymia," which refers to people with emotional blankness. These people seem to lack feelings and emotions altogether, although this may actually be because of their inability to describe emotions—their own or anyone else's—and a sharply limited emotional vocabulary. It is difficult for these people to discern their own feelings and emotions and to communicate with people around them. There are other types of less severe emotional deafness.[26]

Emotions may be harmful in two major situations: (1) when they are applied in circumstances that are not suited to the given emotion, and (2) when they are excessive.

In animals, emotions operate within a much more limited set of circumstances. In these circumstances, emotional instincts are highly functional as they serve an ongoing sense of survival. Accordingly, in most, but not all, circumstances, emotions are not harmful to animals.[27] In humans there are more circumstances in which emotions are not adaptive. This is because human beings alter their (essentially social) environment more rapidly than adaptive changes may take place in their emotional system. Moreover, in addition to their spontaneous emotional system, humans have a deliberative intellectual system to guide their life. There are many circumstances in which the intellectual system is more adequate for responding; even so, emotions may override the intellectual system owing to their intense nature. This may have harmful consequences.

Emotions may also be harmful when they are excessive. Emotional excess is harmful for the same reasons that other kinds of excess are harmful. It is true of many circumstances, and not merely emotional ones, that too much of something tends to spoil it. Those considering emotions in a highly negative manner concentrate on extreme rather than typical emotions. The occurrence of emotional excess does not turn every emotion into a disease. In Aristotle's view, a person is bad by virtue of pursuing excess, not by virtue of pursuing necessary pleasures such as dainty foods and wines and sexual intercourse. The excess rather than the emotion itself may be harmful from survival and moral perspectives. It should be remembered that not only is emotional excess harmful but so is emotional depletion. The ideal situation is that of emotional balance. Whether an emotion promotes or disrupts the performance of a task depends on a number of factors: the nature of the task, the type and intensity of the emotion, and the specific character of the person.[28]

Most emotions are associated with behavior which clearly expresses the functional role of this emotion. Thus, fear is associated with flight which takes us away from the danger, and love is connected with behavior which brings us closer to the beloved. In some other emotions, the functional role of their typical behavior is not immediately clear. For example, when one feels joy, one may jump in the air, even though the functional value of this action is unclear. However, a detailed analysis of such behavior usually reveals its functional role. It may be argued, for instance, that feeling joy enables us to be more active and powerful, and jumping in the air is simply an expression of such abilities.

The unique functional value of emotions can be clarified when compared to lower and higher mental systems. We may compare the adaptive function of emotions to that of reflexes and physiological drives.[29] Reflexes enable organisms to interact with their environments in highly stereotyped ways. However, their simplicity—the rigid pairing of a specific stimulus with a specific response—has high costs, particularly in complicated interactions. With increasing complexity, there is increasing selective pressure to surmount this behavioral rigidity. Physiological drives, such as hunger and thirst, evolved in the service of particular internal, homeostatic needs. These drives remain stimulus-specific even in the most complicated species. They are distinguished from reflexes by being somewhat more flexible. This flexibility, which enables some adjustment to environmental contingencies, must be supplemented with something that guides the organism toward specific appropriate behaviors. Hence, drives depend upon learning.

Emotions differ from both reflexes and drives in flexibility, variability, richness, and dependence on mental capacities. Emotions are more flexible; they lack stimulus-specificity since they need to be responsive to a wide variety of circumstances associated with an agent-environment relationship. The increasing variability and complexity of the environmental input requires the involvement of higher mental capacities such as imagination and thought. However, the urgency of some situations may require an immediate response; this immediacy can be achieved by relying on a schematic, nondeliberative capacity.

In order to account for the great environmental variability, emotions need to be flexible, and in order to respond rapidly to the demands of an urgent situation, they need to be rigid as well. Flexibility is expressed in the involvement of different mental capacities which can refer to all environmental aspects. Rigidity is manifested in the activation of already set evaluative patterns. These patterns can be changed by past experience or learning and, in some situations, even by deliberative means such as thought. However, at any specific moment these patterns are set, and their activation may generate an emotional response. There is no rigid relationship between the stimulus and the emotion or between the emotion and its behavioral manifestation. A given stimulus can elicit many emotions, and no stimulus will always elicit the same emotion. The relationship between emotion and its behavioral manifestation is somewhat more rigid, but still quite flexible. In this context we should distinguish between action readiness and behavioral manifestation. The former is more closely related to the nature of the emotion in question, whereas the latter can also represent irrelevant factors such as practical considerations or the wish to deceive other people.

*Emotional Intelligence*

I never hated a man enough to give him his diamonds back.
—Zsa Zsa Gabor

The concept of "emotional intelligence" is recent in psychology. The reason for the late development of this concept is that integrating the emotional and intellectual systems, which is the essence of emotional intelligence, was considered to be a contradiction in terms. In this section, I first discuss the more general and philosophical issue of the possibility of integrating the two systems; then I indicate the psychological implications of such integration.

The evaluative systems underlying emotions and intellectual thinking can be discerned on the basis of their mechanism and content. I have described two basic mechanisms: (1) the schematic mechanism, and (2) the deliberative mechanism. Concerning the content, we may distinguish between (a) narrow (or partial) validity, and (b) broad validity of its content. Whereas the emotional system typically uses a schematic, or spontaneous mechanism and the validity of its content is partial, the intellectual system is typically deliberative and has a broader validity.

These two basic differences are not unrelated: the spontaneous, schematic mechanism deals with local stimuli which require immediate attention; deliberative considerations require more time but they are able to refer to much broader and general circumstances. Emotional attitudes focus upon rather narrow informational content and the content's validity is limited to these cases only. Intellectual attitudes refer to a much broader informational content and accordingly the content is valid concerning many more circumstances. The intellect is concerned with the general and the stable, whereas emotions are engaged with the particular and the volatile. The aim of the intellect is to see a specific event as a specific case of general regularities; the foundations of intellectual thinking are features common to individual cases. Emotions prevail as long as a specific event can be seen as mutable and unique. Accordingly, the intellect has difficulties in understanding change and movement, whereas emotions have difficulty in prevailing under stable and universal conditions.

These substantial differences cast doubt on whether the emotional and intellectual systems can ever be integrated into one system that may be characterized as having a high degree of emotional intelligence. Hence, the two systems are usually described as contradictory and the dispute focuses on which of the two we should prefer.

A prevailing tradition has seen these differences as an indication of the shortcomings of the emotional system and hence drawn the conclusion that the intellectual system is the true essence of the mental realm. Plato, Descartes, and Kant are prominent representatives of this tradition which considers thinking to be the essence of the mental realm. In a modern formulation of this view, the mind is an intellectual processor of knowledge which sorts out information in a relatively unbiased manner and emerges with carefully drawn conclusions and well-considered decisions. From this perspective, the mind is envisaged as a sober little creature seeking the most intellectual answers. This attitude is still common in philosophy and psychology. It is clearly expressed in the computational approach to the mind which constitutes the prevailing view in the fields of the philosophy of mind and cognitive psychology.

The opposite view, represented by David Hume and Henri Bergson, considers the emotional system to be of greater cognitive value. Hume believes that emotions are extremely useful and that we should prefer their guidance over that of intellectual reasoning. Similarly, Bergson disputes the tradition that assumes intellectual reasoning to be superior, and he challenges the notion that rational thinking is the only—or primary—means to comprehend reality. For Bergson, the ultimate cognitive tool is instinct, which shares many characteristics with emotions. Bergson's criticism of intellectual reasoning is based on its reliance on the stable and unchangeable, whereas reality encompasses exactly the opposite attributes: instability and change are its central characteristics.[30]

I believe that the differences between the emotional and intellectual systems are genuine; nevertheless, I think that integration between the two is still possible. My starting point for describing this possibility may seem surprising: Spinoza's view of the different levels of cognition.[31]

Most people consider Spinoza to belong to the intellectualist tradition; I believe that Spinoza actually presents a view different from the two outlined above. He believes that the ultimate cognitive tool combines both the emotion and the intellect. Spinoza distinguishes between three different levels of cognition (or knowledge). Cognition stemming from singular (or unique) things, and which is based on the senses and imagination, is considered to be confused and false. Cognition based on common and universal notions is considered as necessarily true. However, according to Spinoza, the highest form of cognition is not intellectual knowledge, but a kind of combination of the two types. It is an intuitive knowledge which combines elements from the other two types: it proceeds from singular things but expresses universal knowledge concerning the essence of things. For Spinoza this kind of cognition is related to an emotional attitude: the intellectual love of God.[32]

In the terms suggested above, we may say that Spinoza's first level of cognition, namely, emotional cognition, uses the spontaneous mechanism, whereas the second level, namely, intellectual cognition, uses the deliberative mechanism. The content of the first level is partial and that of the second level general. The third level of cognition is similar to emotional knowledge concerning its mechanism—it is a type of a schematic mechanism; it is similar to intellectual cognition in the sense that its content has a broad validity as it refers to many circumstances.

We may identify the third level of knowledge as a kind of intuition. Intuition may be characterized as expressing a claim whose content is correct but seems to be unfounded. The spontaneous mechanism underlying the intuitive claims seems to be insufficient for substantiating these claims; this mechanism refers to limited data which have no necessary connections to the broader content implied in intuitive claims. Such lack of foundation can lead to many errors and distortions— and indeed this is a common situation concerning emotional claims. How can we explain that a type of cognition, which is basically unfounded, is considered to be the highest type of cognition? How can we distinguish between the lowest and highest type of cognition?

The psychological model which may explain intuitive knowledge is that which refers to expert knowledge. Like emotional knowledge, expert knowledge is intuitive in the sense that it is not based upon a careful intellectual analysis of the given data, but rather on activating cognitive structures such as schemata. Because of the urgency associated with emotional situations, the cognitive activities associated with emotions are typically those which do not require a lot of time and processing, as do intellectual deliberations, but rather immediate responses based on existing cognitive structures. Acquiring cognitive schemata is like acquiring skills. Before acquiring the cognitive schema associated with riding a bicycle, riding is a controlled thoughtful activity done in stages; the transition from one stage to another is usually accompanied by conscious deliberations. Once the schema is acquired, the mediating stages disappear along with the reasoning processes. These learned activities can then be performed automatically since the intellectual rules have became part of the agent's cognitive structure. In these circumstances, the cognitive effort is mostly restricted to a trigger function. Take, for example, wine experts. These people have developed perceptual sensitivity which enables them to discern perceptually different types of wine without using mediating intellectual deliberations. Other evidence suggests that people can sense intuitively in the first thirty seconds of an encounter what basic impression they will have of the other person after fifteen minutes—or even after six months.[33]

The famous American architect, Frank Lloyd Wright, argued that "an expert is one who does not have to think; he knows." Expert knowledge, which is a type of intuitive knowledge, expresses the highest form of knowledge. Emotions also typically involve such type of intuitive or immediate knowledge, but this is so because of the urgency of the situation and not necessarily because we are experts in the matter of emotions. This may lead to many distortions which indeed are associated with partial emotional attitudes. It is interesting to note that the cognitive mechanism of the highest form of knowledge, namely, expert knowledge, is similar to that of knowledge that is frequently distorted, namely, emotional knowledge.[34]

The intuitive mechanism is not a mysterious entity which necessarily contradicts the results of intellectual deliberations. A person using the intuitive mechanism does not use the deliberative one because the latter necessarily leads to false claims, but because in these particular circumstances this person does need it. The deliberative mechanism may be used in similar circumstances by other people or in other circumstances by the same person.

The possibility of acquiring cognitive schemata which make us experts indicates that emotional intelligence, which is a kind of expert knowledge, can be learned. It can be learned to a greater degree than intellectual intelligence. Unlike intellectual intelligence, which hardly changes after our teenage years, emotional intelligence continues to develop. In fact, it appears that as we mature, we acquire a greater degree of emotional intelligence.[35]

The dispute concerning the cognitive value of the emotional system is much like the dispute concerning "knowing" God and other religious beliefs. One view claims that God can be known only by the heart. A second view insists that God can be known by intellectual reasoning. A third view places a high value on intellectual reasoning in arriving at religious truths, yet also believes that a properly disposed heart is needed to see the force of religious truths. The relevance of the heart to the perception of certain claims is explained by assuming that perceiving the value of something is similar to adopting certain attitudes toward it. When someone is of a defective moral nature, this person will not be able to perceive the truth of a moral claim. Concerning certain objects, one has to be akin to them in order to perceive them. If God is goodness itself, then is not surprising that properly ordered affections are needed to grasp truths about God. Accordingly, in some circumstances proper emotional states are necessary for using our cognitive capacities correctly.[36]

Emotional intelligence may be characterized as sensitivity to certain types of higher-level stimuli. Like other types of intelligence, emotional intelligence expresses our ability to understand or to deal with complex situations; unlike the intellectual intelligence, this ability involves a unique type of sensitivity rather than intellectual deliberations. This sensitivity is beneficial in our everyday life as it integrates in an optimal manner the emotional and intellectual systems. In light of the integral role of emotional sensitivity in intelligence, it has been claimed that if we want computers to be genuinely intelligent, then they will need to have emotional intelligence.[37]

When discussing the place of emotions in morality (see chapter 9), I claim that also optimal moral behavior is that which combines emotions and intellectual reasoning. Such an integration, which is required in complex moral situations, is not simple; small wonder, then, that it requires high emotional intelligence.

Some aspects of the above emotional sensitivity may be innate, while others are acquired through engaging in various activities—usually both emotional and intellectual—until general rules and past experience are embodied in our mental system, thus sensitizing this system to more complex and general circumstances and regularities. The great value of integrating emotional responses with intellectual deliberations and thus creating a system with high emotional intelligence does not mean that we should try to achieve such integration in all circumstances. There are certain circumstances in which the emotional system is optimal; in other circumstances, intellectual deliberations are more proper. Only in some circumstances can we combine the two and reach the third level typical of emotional intelligence.

Emotional intelligence can be characterized as the capacity to process emotional information accurately and efficiently, and accordingly to regulate the emotions in an optimal manner. We may speak about two domains of emotional intelligence:

1. recognizing emotions, in ourselves and others;
2. regulating the emotions, in ourselves and others.

Emotional intelligence consists of recognizing and regulating emotions in an optimal manner. It is not obvious whether it is easier to apply these strategies when it comes to our own emotions or those of others. Thus, recognizing our own emotions seems to be easier than recognizing the emotions of others; however, this may be only true concerning positive emotions since in negative emotions the mechanisms of denial and repression are common and hinder our ability to recognize our own emotions. Similarly, the capacity to regulate the emotions of others seems to be more indicative of emotional intelligence since such regulation requires a more complex understanding of circumstances; however, in some cases, it is easier for us to give advice to others rather than to ourselves.

A person who can easily recognize and regulate her emotions, or those of others, is emotionally intelligent. Someone who knows that anger is destructive or useless in a particular situation and who repeatedly behaves angrily in spite of such knowledge, may be considered emotionally unintelligent. This person may either misidentify her anger or may identify it correctly, but while angry, evaluate it positively. Emotional intelligence expresses the skills, rather than knowledge per se, that an individual can attain in order to function adequately from an emotional point of view.[38]

Our ability to be accurate in identifying our emotions and those of other people is not merely a cognitive ability, but also an evaluative ability which largely depends upon our emotional sensitivity. Identifying emotions in other people requires emotional closeness to them, just as the ability to perceive a certain value, like the normative belief in the goodness of God, requires the adoption of certain values. As I have indicated, proper emotional attitudes are sometimes necessary for proper cognition. Emotional intelligence is not merely intelligent; it is emotional as well.

I have suggested that emotional intelligence expresses the integration of intellectual and emotional abilities. Recognizing and regulating the emotions requires both emotional self-awareness and empathy; but it also requires an intellectual ability which can calculate the various implications of different alternatives. For example, to know how and why I, or other people, feel, requires not merely emotional acquaintance but intellectual reasoning as well. We cannot adequately recognize and regulate emotions without some intellectual ability. Small wonder that emotional intelligence was found to be more important in contributing to excellence than pure intellect[39]; emotional intelligence includes intellectual capacities plus other capacities.

There is evidence that the ability to resist emotional temptation occasionally, and the capacity to postpone emotional gratification in particular, is an important indicator of success in life. In a well-known experiment, four-years-olds were offered the following proposal: If you can wait until I return, you can have two marshmallows for a treat; if you can't wait until then, you can have only one—but you can have it right now. In this experiment, resisting present emotional temptation affords better results in the future. Twelve to fourteen years later, these same children were traced and it was found that those who were able to postpone gratification when they were four were now, as adolescents, more socially competent and could better cope with difficulties and challenges.[40]

No doubt, the ability to manage our emotions plays a key role in improving our well-being. However, we must remember that such ability should not be understood as implying that we should disregard our emotional tendencies; this may prevent us from enjoying the many advantages of the emotional system. The popular advice to count to ten before expressing our anger—and to count to one hundred when very angry—reflects an awareness of the risks of an immediate emotional response. Such advice, however, does not completely dismiss the functional value of emotional responses: it does not go so far as to count to a thousand. Similarly, being professional is not synonymous with being emotionless; professionalism is simply not associated with excessive emotional intensity, which prevents normal functioning. In many circumstances, professional work needs to be emotional. Accordingly, Betty Bender is right in arguing that "when people go to work, they shouldn't have to leave their hearts at home." In light of the rapid changes in the types of work and the structure of organizations, emotional intelligence is highly important for various types of work.[41]

How is emotional intelligence related to emotional intensity? Is there a correlation between the two in the sense that a person with high emotional intelligence is also a highly emotional person? The connection between the two is complex. Emotional intelligence may influence emotional intensity in various manners. On the one hand, emotional intelligence includes the capacity to identify emotions easily—our own and other people's emotions—and this capacity is usually related to high emotional sensitivity. On the other hand, emotional intelligence includes the capacity to regulate and utilize emotions and this capacity involves a certain type of indifference and detachment which is not typical of emotional people. Emotional intelligence involves flexibility and comfortable relationships—these are not typical of very intense emotions. Also the ability to stop something we have started and found to be harmful, which is typical of emotional intelligence, is not typical of highly emotional people. Accordingly, we may assume that emotional intelligence will not be very high both among indifferent people, whose distance from the emotional circumstances will make it hard for them to identify such circumstances, and very sensitive people, whose tremendous emotional involvement will make it hard for them to keep the distance required for emotional regulation. I would speculate, therefore, that people with high emotional intelligence will have moderate emotional intensity; people at the extremes will have low emotional intelligence.

Ernest Hemingway once said that "happiness in intelligent people is the rarest thing I know." He might be right if by intelligence he meant merely intellectual intelligence. Such intelligence in itself may reduce or even eliminate many types of emotion, in particular happiness, which, as we shall see, takes sometimes an illusory perspective. However, emotionally intelligent people are precisely those who are from time to time able to be happy despite everyday hardship. In emotionally intelligent people happiness is not rare.

*Emotions and Communication*

If other people are going to talk, conversation becomes impossible.
—James McNeill Whistler

I have indicated that emotions play a crucial role in personal and social communication. Emotions sincerely express our profound attitudes and detecting such attitudes is crucial for survival and well-being. The role of emotions in communication will be further evident when discussing specific emotions in the second part of the book. In this section I briefly discuss two phenomena which are prominent in personal and social communication, namely, pretense and gossip. I indicate their relationship to emotions and suggest that they are compatible with the characterization of emotions and their functionality suggested here.

### Emotional Pretense

If you haven't seen your wife smile at a traffic cop, you haven't seen her smile her prettiest.
—Kin Hubbard

Despite the crucial role of emotions in sincere communication, there are circumstances in which deceptive emotional messages are conveyed. Obvious examples of emotional pretense can be found in romantic relationships, for example, using the tactics of "hard to get" or "easy to get": in both cases, the emotional message is somewhat deceptive, and the receiver is not supposed to take it at face value. In playing hard to get, the other person is encouraged to continue sustained efforts to interest the player despite apparent evidence of disinterest; in playing easy to get, the other person is encouraged to engage in sexual courtship while the player does not always intend to engage in sexual activity. In playing hard to get, an emotional "yes" is replaced by a verbal "maybe," and in playing easy to get, an emotional "maybe" is replaced by a verbal "yes" (see also chapter 14).

Emotional pretense can take two basic forms: veil and mask, that is, hiding an emotion one feels and showing an emotion one does not feel.[42] The veil and the mask can be effective in different circumstances and the ease of using them may differ in various situations and emotions. It seems, for example, that in "cool" emotions, such as envy and hope, putting on a veil is usually both more effective and easier to use than putting on a mask. In emotions such as fear and anger the opposite is usually true. Both veils and masks are less effective and harder to use in sentiments such as long-term love or grief.[43]

Emotional pretense can be useful in several circumstances: (a) to gain some personal benefits, for example, by faking affection for the boss in order to get a promotion, faking anger or sadness in order to get attention, and faking remorse in order to escape punishment; (b) to avoid hurting other people, for instance, by choosing not to express our sadness while standing near the bed of our dying friend; and (c) to protect our privacy, for example, by concealing our envy or sexual desire.

Emotional pretense that is intended to achieve personal benefits is no different from other types of deliberative lies. In all these cases people take advantage of other people to gain personal benefits. In light of the typically sincere nature of emotional expressions, successful pretense of emotions is usually more effective than other types of deception.

The second type of emotional pretense, that which is intended to avoid hurting other people, is similar to the first one in that it aims to make other people think we are experiencing a certain emotional attitude that is quite different from the one we are actually experiencing. However, the motive in the two cases is completely different: in the first, it is egoistic and in the second, altruistic. Furthermore, this type of pretense does not stem from the unique nature of emotions, but rather from the unique nature of morality which requires that we do not hurt others.

The third type of emotional pretense, which aims to protect our privacy, is the one which provides the strongest defense of emotional pretense, as it is mostly related to the very nature of emotions. As indicated, emotions express our most profound values and attitudes; revealing them may disclose our innermost, private emotions, thereby making us more vulnerable. Those who know all our emotional intimate details are in a better position to hurt us, if they chose to do so. Privacy is an essential characteristic of human existence and relinquishing it can be dangerous. We are not supposed to expose ourselves to everyone and to the same extent; the degree of exposure depends on the degree of closeness in our relationship. Full and limitless exposure is dangerous not merely to our physical well-being but also, or even mainly, to our mental safety. Despite the great authenticity of emotional states, expressing them constantly and publicly may be harmful insofar as our private self becomes part of the public domain. The demand for a total mental exposure is typical of totalitarian systems in which privacy endangers the very existence of the system.

The problematic nature of total emotional exposure can be illustrated in the context of romantic relationships. Romantic relationships are constant sources of threat to our self-esteem as they are perceived to express the other's profound evaluation of us. Another's reluctance to enter a romantic relationship with us hurts our self-esteem. Emotional pretense in romantic relationships not only increases uncertainty and mystery, which usually magnify emotional intensity, but also facilitates positive illusions concerning ourselves, which typically also have adaptive value (see chapter 7). When a man propositions a woman and she responds with "maybe," rather than "yes," it allows her to cope with any future disappointment should the man be unwilling to develop a genuine romantic relationship later on. Another problem concerning exposing ourselves in romantic relationships is that such exposure may have the unwanted effect of erasing mystery and imagination from romantic relationships. In light of the crucial role of imagination in emotions, it is doubtful whether romantic love could survive such a loss.

It may be argued that defense of privacy may just be as applicable to beliefs as to emotions and hence emotional pretense is no more justifiable than false beliefs. It should be noted, however, that (a) we have far more types of beliefs than types of emotions, and (b) most of our beliefs—for example, that the sun is bigger than the moon or that five is greater than four—are not personal. All emotions are, by definition, personal and quite often they express our profound values and attitudes. Hence, revealing our emotional attitudes is more problematic for the purpose of defending our privacy than revealing (at least most of) our beliefs.

It is obvious that emotional pretense has not merely advantages but also shortcomings stemming from misinterpreting emotional messages. I would like to discuss in some detail such a danger in the romantic realm, namely, sexual harassment.

Confusing the real and the deceptive message may lead to the of charge of sexual harassment. Thus, it has been suggested that sexually aggressive men use a suspicion schema when interpreting the way women communicate their (lack of) sexual interest: such men assume that women do not tell the truth when it comes to sex. The consequences of misinterpretation of women's emotional communication may result in sexually aggressive behavior such as assault or even rape.[44] Ironically, deceptive strategies are also required to prevent sexual harassment. People are required to hide their sexual interest. For example, it was reported that the city of Minneapolis ordered its male workers not to stare at women, since this is considered an unwanted sexual advance and, as such, constitutes an offensive act of sexual harassment.

It is obvious that emotional pretense does not justify what is regarded to be clear cases of sexual harassment, such as unwanted sexual relations. However, the nature and extent of sexual harassment is disputable and accordingly there are circumstances in which the connection between emotional pretense and sexual harassment is more complex. Thus, emotional pretense attempts to increase the other's attention; hence, greater attention cannot be regarded as sexual harassment. Accordingly, it is not obvious that looking at women in public constitutes sexual harassment. It seems that there is no simple general solution to these complexities, which should be dealt with on a more individual level.

The confusion concerning the authenticity of emotional messages can be reduced by eliminating the use of deceptive tactics or, for that matter, any type of pretense. But such reduction has its own shortcomings. Guarding our privacy, as well as avoiding hurting other people, requires the use of some deceptive measures. We should, however, limit their use in the establishment of sincere relationships.

*Emotions and Gossip*
The nice thing about egotists is that they don't talk about other people.
—Lucille S. Harper

There isn't much to be seen in a little town, but what you hear makes up for it.
—Kin Hubbard


Like emotions, gossip has a central function in personal and social communication. Although it is hard to imagine a human society which lacks either emotions or gossip, the functionality of both is doubted and consequently they are often negatively evaluated from a moral point of view. This is not an accident, but rather reflects misunderstanding, and perhaps also normative dispute, concerning the nature and functions of both emotions and gossip.

Typical gossip is an idle, relaxing activity whose value lies in the activity itself and not the achievement of external ends.[45] This does not imply that gossip has no consequences, but those are mostly byproducts, not ends in themselves. Typical gossip is relaxing and effortless and, like games, often relieves people of daily tensions. One reason for the relaxing nature of gossip is being able to talk about what is really on our minds. People indulging in gossip do not want to ponder deeply the content or consequences of what they say. Sometimes gossip seems to be talk for the sake of talking. When people are involved in serious, practical, and purposive talk, they are not gossiping, since gossip is idle frivolous talk. When two psychiatrists discuss my neighbor's love affair, their discussion is not gossip; however, when my wife and I discuss the same situation, it does constitute gossip.

It is important to distinguish between gossip and spreading unsubstantiated rumors. When recounting a personal affair that one has witnessed, one is engaged in gossip, but the information conveyed is substantiated. Since the typical content of gossip is usually behind-the-scenes, intimate information, it is indeed hard to verify and hence is often unsubstantiated. Lack of substantiation is not, however, an essential element of gossip, but a byproduct of the confidential nature of the information conveyed. This unsubstantiated characteristic is more typical of rumor; indeed, it forms part of its definition. Moreover, unlike gossip, spreading rumors is essentially a purposive activity having mainly an extrinsic value. The derogatory connotation of gossip is by and large due to the failure to distinguish gossiping from the spreading of rumors.

Like emotions, gossip is a sort of sincere communication all people share. Both cases do not require intellectual knowledge of the abstract, but awareness of the specific. The specific and the concrete are quite meaningful in both emotions and gossip. Informal talk about trivial and particular issues furnishes an alternative perspective which may in fact shed light on matters that are sometimes misunderstood in serious, abstract discussions. Similarly, emotional knowledge provides us with an understanding often missing from intellectual thinking. Yet, unlike gossip, emotions are directed at issues that are perceived by us to be quite significant.

Gossip satisfies the basic need to acquire information about the personal and intimate aspects of other people's lives. Such information is very interesting and gives rise to emotional attitudes, and there are a very few other ways to satisfy this need. Although intimacy plays an important role in our lives, we remain quite ignorant about how it works in other people's lives. Candid and open self-description is rare and limited to a very few close friends. Gossip is an enjoyable way to gather information that is otherwise hard to obtain, and it satisfies a personal curiosity concerning people who are of particular interest to us. In the same way that emotional attitudes reveal more about the personalities of other people than does their public behavior, so the intimate and personal aspects described in gossip reveal more than their public behavior.

Group membership is important for the emergence of both emotions (as we have seen) and gossip. Indeed, gossip satisfies a tribal need, namely, the need to belong to and be accepted by a unique group. (One meaning of "gossip" is indeed "being a friend of.") The sharing of intimate and personal information and the intimate manner of conveying this information contribute to the formation of an exclusive group with intimate and emotional ties between its members. Most people like to gossip now and then: it is a form of enjoyable social communication that usually revolves around information not yet widely known and therefore intriguing. The information, which is sometimes negative, generally concerns people who are not there to hear it and includes both a description and an evaluation of their behavior. (As George, in the television series *Seinfeld* said: "I'm much more comfortable criticizing people behind their backs.") Participants appear to share the same standards of right and wrong. Although adherence to such standards is often superficial, even the mere appearance of common moral standards establishes intimacy among the participants.

Both emotions and gossip express a personal concern toward other people. Emotions and gossip are concerned with people who are of interest to us, namely, those who are psychologically close to us and those who may be in somewhat unusual circumstances. Both emotions and gossip express our interest and involvement in the lives of other people, albeit in a more profound way in the case of emotions. In the same way that abolishing emotions means abolishing both negative and positive emotions, abolishing gossip would mean abolishing all types of conversations about other people. Emotions and gossip express our sensitivity toward other people; abolishing them would lead to our indifference toward other people. I would rather live in a society whose members have positive and negative attitudes toward me than in a society whose members are indifferent to me. Caring about someone does not always mean showing a positive attitude toward that person's deeds.

The enjoyable and interesting elements in gossip stem not merely from acquiring novel information, but also from the content of this information. Like emotions and jokes, gossip often includes unexpected features. Thus, the sexual life of a priest, or even of our next-door neighbor, makes for juicier gossip and more intense emotions than the exploits of a prostitute. Likewise, the romance between a very old woman and a very young man is more likely to arouse interest and emotion than that between two people of a similar age. This gap between reputation or conventional behavior and actual behavior is what makes gossip interesting.

One important difference between emotions and gossip concerns the practical nature of emotions and the nonpractical nature of gossip. Gossip is typically relaxing and effortless, since it relieves us of daily tensions; emotions are typically tense and require most of our resources, since they deal with changes we are not sure how to cope with. Owing to their intense nature, emotions are relatively brief, whereas gossip is a relaxing activity that can go on for quite a while.

Do women gossip more than men? Research indicates that contrary to a popular stereotype suggesting that women talk too much, both women and men spend a similar amount of time in idle conversations; however, their topics differ: women tend to talk more about other people, whereas men dwell on sports, politics, and the weather. In this sense, women more often discuss topics typical of gossip and of emotional concern. This difference may be explained by traditional cultural expectations: feminine activities were supposed to be confined to family and friendship networks, whereas masculine activities were supposed to involve more worldly concerns. Traditionally, many men "have little use for small talk, since they believe talk is designed to convey information" and hence should have "significant content, be interesting and meaningful."[46] Men were supposed to maintain their manhood by keeping their distance and not getting too involved in the close relations typical of gossip and emotions. Thus, males report greater satisfaction with their dating relationship when the exchange is perceived to have followed sex-typed norms, that is, with the male disclosing less about himself relative to his female partner.[47] Just as "real" men should not cry and should be reticent about their emotions, "real" men should not concentrate unduly on their personal and sentimental affairs.

I have indeed indicated that women are more emotional than men. Influenced by this traditional image, men often doubt that they too can benefit from a candid discussion with their peers; hence, the topics of their relaxing, enjoyable conversations are less personal and less emotional. Nevertheless, these idle conversations provide the benefits typical of gossip: they are relaxing, enjoyable activities that express a form of friendship. Perhaps the gender difference in topics of idle conversation, like that in emotional sensitivity, stems not from men's lack of interest in these personal matters but from the pressure on them to eschew such matters. After all, gossiping about the intimate and personal matters of other people can easily lead to discussing these issues in one's own life—a situation most men would rather avoid. One indication of the importance of gossip to both sexes is that children gossip practically from the time they learn to talk and can recognize other people.[48]

Gossip is engaged in for pleasure, not for hurting someone, and though gossip may inflict some damage, it is usually minor. Many people would not really enjoy themselves by gossiping if they thought that their activity could be significantly harmful to others. As I indicate below, pleasure-in-other's-misfortune is also concerned with minor misfortune. When gossip does inflict significant damage on other people, the gossips themselves do not usually consider the damage to be significant. The idle nature of gossip implies not merely the absence of declared purpose but the lack of concern for such a purpose. Typical gossip is not talking-against, but rather talking-about. Nor is it true that the information conveyed in gossip is totally negative. One study suggests an even distribution of negative and positive information in gossip, and almost half of the information was found to be neither clearly negative nor clearly positive. Furthermore, when the information was negative, it often concerned minor misfortunes.[49]

Contrary to its popular reputation, gossip is not basically concerned with detraction, slander, or character assassination. Negative information may be better remembered, and hence the illusory impression of its dominance. In some cases, gossip may indeed involve exaggerated or distorted information, but usually the gossip does not deliberately convey false information. Sometimes gossip is the only way to acquire accurate information, and often gossip is more accurate and more complete than "official" information. Gossip is not essentially an activity of telling lies, and there is no reason that it should be morally condemned on these grounds. If indeed gossip mainly conveyed false information, most people would not find it interesting. Gossip may also have some positive byproducts. It may help to sustain values of a community in which people fear becoming a target for gossip. This is especially true of small communities or of famous people. Gossip may also provide people with an acceptable outlet for frustration and anger.[50]

No doubt, gossip and emotions have a bad reputation. I believe, however, that this reputation is more in the nature of an unsubstantiated, and even malicious, rumor than of reliable judgment. Although the moral condemnation of gossip is not entirely groundless, it applies primarily to nontypical extreme cases of gossip and is not justified with respect to typical gossip, which is largely harmless. Aristotle's emphasis on the right proportions is relevant here. Distorting the subtle equilibrium of typical gossip and emotions may indeed be harmful if excessive. Such distortion is not rare in both cases. With emotions this distortion may be caused by their great intensity. In the case of gossip, it is due to the lack of a clear borderline between a harmless event, minor harm, and substantial harm; such a borderline may depend on contextual factors that are not known to us while in the act of gossiping. This may require taking extra steps of precaution while engaged in gossiping. However, the fact that excessive and distorted cases are harmful does not establish the intrinsic malicious nature of typical gossip or the dysfunctionality of emotions, just as the fact that excessive eating is harmful does not imply an intrinsic evil in eating. Much of the negative press that gossip and emotions have received stems from the confusion of extreme and excessive instances with typical and common instances. The extreme case, which many people take to be the prototype of gossip and emotions, is neither essential nor common to either.

If my claim that typical gossip satisfies basic human needs and is mostly harmless is correct, then gossip cannot be reprehensible from a moral viewpoint. It may even have some positive moral values. Indeed, the exchange of relatively insignificant details about daily life sends a message of caring. The noticing of details, so typical of gossip and emotions, shows caring and creates involvement. Unlike emotions, gossip usually does not express a genuine concern for other people's problems. The focus is on the interesting, superficial aspects of other people's lives. Emotions express a much more profound interest. Gossip is not a virtuous activity; yet, it is not vicious either.

*Summary*

Emotions have taught mankind to reason.
—Marquis de Vauvenargues

There is a long tradition that criticizes emotions as being irrational and nonfunctional. I have suggested that this tradition is fundamentally wrong. Emotions are rational in the normative sense of being an appropriate response in the given circumstances. This does not imply that emotions are rational in a descriptive sense, referring to the presence of intellectual deliberations in the process of generating emotions. We can behave rationally without constantly thinking about our behavior. Although emotions are not functional in all circumstances, they are tremendously important when facing urgent situations involving a significant change. In these situations, emotions are the optimal response. Three major functions of emotions are an initial indication of the proper direction in which to respond, quick mobilization of resources, and social communication. Emotional excess may have harmful consequences, but so may all types of excess. We should neither suppress our emotions nor have them in excess; our goal should be emotional balance.

Emotional intelligence is the optimal integration of the emotional and intellectual systems; it consists of recognizing and regulating emotions in an optimal manner. In light of the differences between the two systems, we may speak of emotional reasoning as different from intellectual reasoning. Neither type violates the rules of formal logic, such as the rules of contradiction and identity, but they do follow different principles from the point of view of their content. (This distinction is in a certain sense similar to Kant's distinction between formal and transcendental logic.) To give one example: A basic principle of emotional reasoning is that those who are close to us are more precious; an alternative principle, more typical of intellectual thinking, states that our distance from an object does not change its value. There are certain everyday and moral circumstances in which following the emotional principle is more appropriate and hence taking the emotional avenue is more rational. The differences between the two types of reasoning suggest that integrating them is not going to be an easy task.

The chapter ends with a brief discussion of two phenomena related to the communicative function of emotions: pretense and gossip. Although pretense is contrary to the sincere nature of emotions, it has an important function of reducing the possible harm which may be the consequence of a sincere emotional communication. This is especially true concerning maintaining our privacy. The comparison of emotions to gossip indicates certain similarities between them and suggests the importance of both in social relations and personal communication.

# Chapter 7

# Emotions and Imagination

---

I can't sleep. There is a woman stuck between my eyelids. I would tell her to get
out if I could. But there is a woman stuck in my throat.
—Eduardo Galeano

I have already suggested that imagining an alternative to a present situation is
crucial for the generation of emotions. This chapter discusses in more detail the
nature of imagination, its various types, and its role in generating emotions. The
discussion focuses on one type of imagination, which is crucial for the generation
of emotions, namely, counterfactual imagination. The discussion concludes with
an examination of three issues related to the role of imagination in emotions: positive illusions, the role of emotions in the future modern world, and the relationship between emotional experience and the experience of being lucky.

*The Role of Imagination in Emotions*

You cannot depend on your eyes when your imagination is out of focus.
—Mark Twain

I'll see you in my dreams.
—The Mills Brothers

The ability to imagine situations that are different from those presented to the
senses is an essential feature of human consciousness in general and of emotions
in particular. People envy others when they can easily imagine themselves in the
others' place—others who are somewhat like themselves. Fear and hope entail
imagining a future alternative to the present one. Anger implies imagining what
should have been done but was not. Gratitude and pride involve the realization
that the current situation is superior to its alternative.

How significant imagination is in our emotional life can be gauged from the
success the various forms of art have in inducing emotions. Art is not bound by

any fixed logic, and the imaginative alternatives it can create are almost limitless. Through art we can mimic our experience of childhood and of dreaming where the boundaries are not rigid and instability is high.

The importance of imagination in emotions comes clearly to the fore in cases where imagination is sufficiently powerful to make those who are objectively worse off feel happier than those in a better position. An illuminating example in this regard comes from a study which found that bronze medalists in the Olympic games tend to be happier than silver medalists.[1] The suggested explanation for this surprising result is that the most compelling alternative for the silver medalists is winning gold, whereas for the bronze medalists it is finishing without any medal at all. The silver medalists focused on having almost won gold because there is a qualitative difference between coming in first and any other outcome, and this exalted status had been only one small step away. The silver medalists also finished only one step from winning bronze, but such a downward comparison does not involve much of a change in status. In contrast, bronze medalists are likely to focus their imagination downward, as there is a categorical difference between finishing third and finishing fourth. The situation of the silver medalists is similar to that of a person who misses out on the jackpot, but wins a modest sum for coming close. The prize provides some enjoyment, but the knowledge of having just missed the jackpot is bound to come up from time to time and ruin otherwise blissful moments. That finishing second can be a mixed blessing is shown by the amazing example of Abel Kiviat, the 1500-meter silver medalist in the 1912 Olympics in Stockholm who had the race won until Arnold Jackson "came from nowhere" to beat him by a mere one-tenth of a second. About 70 years later, at age 91, Kiviat admitted in an interview: "I wake up sometimes and say, 'What the heck happened to me?' It's like a nightmare." Thus, a certain imagination may come back and plague us for a very long time.[2]

The close connection between imagination and emotions may also explain the immense role television has come to play in our social life. Since in the average American home TV sets are switched on for more than six hours a day, we may speak of a new kind of imaginary environment. To give just one example, a survey showed that over 50 percent of Americans knew who Judge Joseph Wapner of *The People's Court* was, as compared with only 12 percent who knew who Chief Justice William Rehnquist of the Supreme Court was. For our social relationships, or for culture in general, we no longer need to leave the house but can take part in this imaginary environment at home. We can leave the frustrations of our everyday world behind and enter a world that is far more pleasant and less difficult to cope with—the world of television. By the time American children reach the age of eighteen, they will have spent an estimated 18,000 hours in front of the tube, as compared with 11,000 hours in the classroom.[3] No wonder that Bart Simpson (in the TV series *The Simpsons*) can say to his dad, Homer: "It's just hard not to listen to TV—it's spent so much more time raising us than you have."

The highly attractive women we see on TV and in movies or magazines do not represent typical women in our actual social environment: they are imaginary symbols. Most people are aware that their appearance has been artificially enhanced by various means: they become what ethologists call "supernormal stimuli." Incapable of changing our own social relationships, we find ourselves emotionally preoccupied with this imaginary environment.

Despite its success in inducing moderate emotional states, television does not require much personal investment, since the viewers are involved in imaginary relationships. When viewing television, people report feeling more passive and less challenged and alert, as well as concentrating less and using fewer skills than in almost any other daily activity except resting and "doing nothing."[4] Because of its imaginary and superficial nature, television succeeds in stimulating moderate emotional states without inflicting upon us the great costs associated with intense emotions. Hence, television viewing can be simultaneously a passive, relaxing, low-concentration activity and an emotional experience.

Although imagination describes events which do not obey all normal regularities and are not constrained by the laws of nature, this does not mean that it knows no regularity or constraints at all. On the contrary, unlike free-form fantasy, emotional imagination is often strongly constrained by various factors. In order for such imagination to be effective, it is important that it be perceived as real, namely, as resembling reality in some sense.

Consider the following description of a prostitute who used to work for the Hollywood madam, Heidi Fleiss: "Heidi gave me an outline on the client. Some were turned on by sexy lingerie, others by dirty talk; some wanted hard-to-get, others, bad girls; some preferred a natural look, others requested lots of makeup and big hair. It was my job to flesh out the small details, make the fantasy real."[5] No doubt, fantasies were most important in generating male sexual desire in the above cases, but the prostitute's job was to guarantee that these fantasies would look very real. Accordingly, Olivia St. Clair offers her readers who are ready to "unleash their sex goddess" to make their fantasies as real as possible by adding a dash of tactile reality, for example, a filmy scarf for their harem sojourn or juicy fruits for their fantasy love with Tom Jones: Your fantasies "become much more erotically solid when draped with the stuff of reality."[6] Similarly, works of art provide us with imaginary situations, but their authors make us believe in their reality by referring to real everyday events.

### Types of Imagination

Last time I tried to make love to my wife nothing was happening, so I said to her, "What's the matter, you can't think of anybody either?"
—Rodney Dangerfield

In this section, I clarify the nature of imagination by distinguishing various types of imagination. I begin by briefly indicating the way in which mental capacities have developed.

Sensation may be considered as the most primitive form of mental capacity. In sensation we are only aware of changes in our own body. Sensation may be characterized as a sign, rather than a cognitive description: it does not describe the changes we are undergoing but merely indicates their presence. Despite the primitive nature of sensation, its survival value is enormous. Sensory awareness of changes in our body is crucial for survival as it forces us not to be indifferent to changes. Indeed, those very few people who because of illness lack sensation are in real danger every moment of their lives.

Sensation is not an intentional capacity as it is not directed at some object and has no cognitive content. Intentional capacities emerged later when the organism was able to be aware not only of changes in its own body but also of the circumstances responsible for these changes. The first intentional capacities to emerge are perceptual abilities in which we separate the stimuli impinging on our sensory receptors and create a perceptual environment as a mental object. While possessing merely perceptual capacities we are restricted to our immediate environment. The development of further intentional capacities, such as memory, imagination, and thought, enables us to be aware of things that are not present and to consider factors beyond our immediate environment. The more complex our intentional capacities, the less trapped we are in the present. Indeed, paying attention exclusively to what is present before us is not easy for most humans. Thus, during routine activities our minds often wander off into various imaginary situations.

Intentionality expresses the establishment of a subject-object relation. The subject goes beyond its limited boundaries and becomes aware of other objects and other aspects of reality. Complex intentional capacities, which go beyond the environment present to the senses, require some kind of self-awareness: we have to realize the limits of our environment, as well as the fact that we are deviating from it. Indeed, complex intentional capacities, such as imagination and abstract thinking, are associated with complex self-awareness. Complex intentional capacities also enable us to carry out more complex types of activity, especially purposeful activity which pertains to future goals. We engage in such activity not for its own sake but because we want to fulfill some future plan. The reference beyond present circumstances is also an essential feature of moral deeds and aesthetic experiences. Deprived of the ability to make such a reference, human beings would remain enslaved to the present.

The evolutionary advantages of being able to respond to imaginary events are obvious. For example, it enables us to avoid dangers rather than merely reacting to their effects upon us and to pursue positive goals rather than passively sitting back and waiting for things to happen. As suggested above, the development of imagination indicates a significant evolutionary step. Although animals can refer to something beyond their immediate environment, they do so in a less complex manner than humans.

Imagination, which is an intentional capacity, may be broadly characterized as a capacity enabling us to refer to what *is not actually present to the senses*. This capacity can refer to past, present, future, or possible circumstances. In such a broad characterization, which is epistemological in nature, memory and thought are types of imagination, as in both of them we refer to what is not actually present to the senses.

In addition to the imaginative capacity, thought also possesses the ability to conceptualize, namely, to discern abstract and general relationships. Whereas in imagination we are aware of a content which may or may not correspond to a content in reality, in conceptualization the issue of correspondence is of no importance, while the issue of coherence is most crucial.

As it progresses, scientific thinking goes further beyond the information present to the senses. Science describes reality which not only is not present to the senses, but is not perceptually available at all. For example, physicists speak about ten-dimensional space and make various calculations which describe its properties. However, we are unable to see, and even to have visual imagination of such a space. Reaching the ultimate scientific reality may mean relinquishing the reality presented to our senses. It is simply an alternative type of reality, different from the perceptual environment toward which our senses are directed. Such a reality can only be described by conceptual analysis.

A narrower characterization of imagination, which facilitates distinctions between imagination and capacities such as memory and thought, adds an ontological criterion to imagination: imagination is an intentional capacity referring to *nonexisting objects*.

In light of this narrow characterization, recalling the face of John F. Kennedy is an act of memory, but imagining myself speaking with Kennedy is a matter of imagination—since such a conversation did not take place. Similarly, when I think about my son at school, this is a type of ordinary thinking; if I think of him on the moon, this is a type of imagination. When the intentional content refers to future circumstances, the distinction between thinking and imagination is finer, but still possible. In this case, the probability of the event's actualization is the factor distinguishing thinking from imagination. If I now think about tomorrow's sunrise, this is a type of ordinary thinking. But if I consider myself as the King of England, this is imagination. Likewise, a person who buys a lottery ticket and begins to consider how best to spend the money is engaging in a flight of imagination, since the chances of winning the lottery are very low. If, however, this person won, the distinction between thinking and imagination would have had no clear-cut boundary.

In the narrow, ontological sense of imagination, imagination refers to an object that is not present to the senses and which has never existed or which, on the basis of our current knowledge, has very little chance of existing. This type of imagination can be further divided into two kinds: (1) the subject *does not know* about the falsity of the imagined content, and (2) the subject *knows* about the falsity of the imagined content. The first type includes cases of hallucinations, illusions, and simple mistakes. The second type may be termed "counterfactual imagination"; the content of counterfactual imagination is false and is known to be so.

For the purpose of understanding emotions, counterfactual imagination has great relevance. It goes some way toward explaining why we think about something we know to be false and how such fantasy can affect us. Accordingly, in the next section, I examine counterfactual imagination in more detail and discuss its complexity. Although such imagination is common in emotions, its psychological mechanism and functional value are not obvious.

### Counterfactual Imagination

Evils which are patiently endured when they seem inevitable become intolerable when once the idea of escape from them is suggested.
—Alexis de Tocqueville

The different types of counterfactual imagination can be divided according to the following factors: (1) whether the imagined situation occurred in the *past*, exists in the *present*, or will be in the *future*; (2) whether the imagined situation is *better* or *worse* than the actual one; (3) whether generating it involves *adding* something to or *subtracting* something from reality; and (4) whether generating it involves changing our *own* actions or those of *others*.[7]

(1) Counterfactual imagination may refer to *past, present, and future* situations. Undoing the past is expressed, for instance, in regret, relief, or disappointment when we imagine ourselves having done something else than what we actually did. An example of counterfactual imagination undoing the present is when people fantasize about other people while making love with their partner. It has been suggested that 40 percent of men have such fantasies while making love with their partners (in Britain many men appear to be fantasizing about the pop star and actress Madonna).[8] Similarly, Johnny Carson proposed that when turkeys mate they think of swans.

The notion of counterfactual imagination referring to future situations is more problematic as it is not obvious what the meaning is of undoing the future. Nevertheless, we may use this notion when it is clear that on the basis of current knowledge, there is hardly any chance of this imaginary situation becoming reality. In future counterfactual imagination we undo the expected, normal situations. Needless to mention that the borderline between future imagination and future counterfactual imagination is not as defined as that between past imagination and past counterfactual imagination. Thus, if a simple worker in Britain imagines himself in the future in the arms of Madonna, although this event is unlikely to happen, nevertheless it is not absolutely false. On the other hand, when we undo the past, we refer to a situation which is clearly counterfactual.

(2) Counterfactual imagination can refer to better or worse alternatives. The comparison with a more attractive alternative is termed *upward comparison* and that with a less attractive alternative, *downward comparison*. Imagining ourselves

to be with another sexual partner than the one we are with now—what may be termed, the "Madonna effect"—illustrates upward counterfactuals. Downward counterfactuals may be found, for instance, in patients with severe, chronic handicaps who often turn such counterfactuals into a coping strategy to help them avoid hopelessness and depression. Similar downward comparisons are expressed in the comfort that rape victims sometimes seem to draw from the thought that they could have been injured more seriously or even been killed, and in the solace that cancer patients may generate by reasoning that their illness could have been more severe. In the same vein, rapists try to escape their guilt by comparing themselves to murders. Whereas people can make themselves feel better by comparing their present situation to either a better or a worse alternative, it is the optimists and individuals with high self-esteem who are more likely to engage in downward comparison than in upward comparison.[9]

(3) Counterfactual imagination can undo a given situation. This can be accomplished by either *adding* something to reality (e.g., "If only I were at home more, my wife would not have started this affair"), or by *subtracting* something from reality (e.g., "If only we had not gone to that party, my husband would not have this affair"). Additive counterfactuals are generated more frequently following failure than success outcomes. Sometimes there is no additive or subtractive imaginary process at the center of counterfactuals, but simply the realization of how close at hand the alternative has been. This is, for example, the case when a basketball game is lost by just one point or one's lottery ticket is one number away from the winning number.

(4) Counterfactual imagination may focus on our *own actions* or those of *others*. Persons with high self-esteem following failure tend to generate counterfactuals blaming others and following success, counterfactuals where the credit goes to themselves. Persons with low self-esteem are more likely to undo their own actions following failure, whereas persons with high self-esteem are more likely to undo other people's actions following failure.[10]

All types of counterfactual imagination are concerned with imaginary events. Nevertheless, the generation of such imaginary events is not arbitrary; there are various constraints in light of which counterfactual imagination is generated. I will now briefly describe these constraints.

Three major categories of constraints on counterfactual generation have been suggested: (1) natural law constraints, (2) availability constraints, and (3) purpose constraints.[11]

Counterfactual imagination is strongly constrained by people's knowledge of the *laws of nature*. Concepts such as gravity and the direction of time are generally considered to be constants in the universe and are therefore left unchanged in most of the counterfactual alternatives that people construct. Accordingly, no one reverses a plane crash by saying, "If only the plane had fallen upward," and they are more likely to focus on such causal factors as human or mechanical error. Their implicit knowledge of constant factors limits the nature of the counterfactuals people generate. If they already mentally mutate natural laws, they are unlikely to do so when other alternatives are available.[12]

*Availability* constraints specify to what extent the alternative to the present situation is available. As indicated throughout this book, the more available the alternative, the more emotional significance it will have.

The third category of counterfactual constraints is that of *purpose* constraints: different purposes of generating the imaginative reality may lead to different counterfactuals, as when assigning blame and consoling others. For example, a person who is trying to determine who was at fault for an accident will consider how the accident might have been avoided, that is, will imagine ways in which things could have turned out for the better. If this person is trying to console someone, the more natural counterfactuals will be those in which things could have turned out for the worse. A person's reason for generating counterfactuals may serve to eliminate entire sets of alternatives that, in the given particular context, are inappropriate.[13]

The three categories of counterfactual constraints do not constitute rigid regularities which are never violated. Violations of each category occur depending on how spontaneous the process is that generates them and how rational its imagined content. Thus, violations of natural law constraints, for instance, imagining objects falling upward instead of downward or effects preceding causes, typically require conscious deliberation, and their imagined content is hardly rational. Even so, such counterfactual constraints impose certain regularities and an internal structure on the counterfactual reality.[14]

Counterfactual imagination (in the sense used here) involves the falsity of its antecedent: it specifies a prior or current event that has not occurred. Since we are aware of this falsity, counterfactual imagination involves some kind of self-deception: we deceive ourselves into believing that reality is, or was, different from what we know it to be. However, while counterfactual imagination involves a subjective, mental simulation of reality, this simulation is experienced as an act of observation, not as an act of construction, enabling us to attribute some sort of objectivity to the imaginary content.[15]

Another interesting assumption underlying counterfactual imagination is that the perceived world is not deterministic: possibilities and alternative states of affairs are real from a psychological point of view. Determinism is the view which assumes that for everything that happens there are conditions such that given them, nothing else could have happened. The crucial place of counterfactuals in emotions suggests that in such a deterministic view most emotions would not appear. This is Spinoza's view which emphasizes the deterministic nature of the world and the importance of imagination in arousing our emotions. Spinoza argues that the more a person grasps the fully deterministic nature of the world, the wiser he will be, and the less likely to experience emotions. No one pities an infant because it cannot speak, walk, or reason; but if most people were born fully grown and only some occasionally as an infant, everyone would pity infants.[16] When everything is known to be fully determined, there is no place for luck and for imagining counterfactual alternatives; hence, no emotions are likely to be generated. Misfortune appears less distressing when it is thought of as inescapable than when it is seen as something that could have been prevented.

I have characterized counterfactual imagination as awareness of information which (a) is not present to the senses, (b) is false, and (c) is known to be false. Those studying counterfactual imagination tend to identify it with two other features: mutability and surprise. I would like briefly to examine these identifications.

Mutability is characterized by the ease of undoing the content of our awareness. The more mutable the situation is, the easier it is to undo it, the more likely we are to engage in counterfactual imagination. Highly probable situations, in which an alternative is highly available, are therefore natural candidates for counterfactual imagination. Mutability is not a defining characteristic of counterfactual imagination, but a characteristic that is typically associated with counterfactual imagination. One can counterfactually imagine something that is not easily mutable, if at all; for example, the prevention of the death of a parent who died at an old age. From a psychological point of view, it is hard to imagine an alternative to a situation that is not easily mutable, but from a conceptual point of view, this can be done and actually is done in everyday life.

Surprise is another phenomenon that is typically, but not always, associated with counterfactual imagination. Surprise refers to characteristics of the subject: it is a state of the subject whose intentional content differs from what the subject has expected. Counterfactual imagination refers to characteristics of the imaginary content: it is an awareness of something that is not present to the senses and is known to be false. Given the differences in the characterization of surprise and counterfactual imagination, I believe that each of these two phenomena does not necessarily imply the other, although they often do.

There is no doubt in my mind that counterfactual imagination does not necessarily imply surprise; that is, it can be directed at something we expect. Take, for example, a basketball game in which I expect my team to lose, and indeed the team does lose, but only by one point. Although the result comes as no surprise to me, my awareness of its mutability is likely to generate counterfactual imagination.

Substantiating the claim that surprise does not necessarily imply counterfactual imagination is less straightforward. Since surprise implies the absence of a state which we expected, it is plausible that this state will have been the subject of counterfactual imagination. However, the fact that I did not expect the presence of a certain state does not necessarily imply that I imagine alternative states once this state has occurred. For example, I may not expect anyone to visit me on a certain evening, but nevertheless a friend arrives and surprises me; I focus my attention on my friend, and generate no counterfactual imagination at our meeting. In this case, surprise is present without counterfactual imagination.

We have seen, then, that although counterfactual imagination is closely connected with mutability and surprise, they are not identical. I now examine the functionality of counterfactual imagination.

*The Functionality of Counterfactual Imagination*
It's not a lie if you believe it.
—George Costanza


Since counterfactual imagination involves some distortion of reality, it may appear to be dysfunctional. A closer look indicates that it has at least two important functions: (1) a *cognitive* function, in that it helps us to understand our environment better, and (2) an *affective* function, in that it enables us to call up desired emotions and moods.

Imagining future possibilities has an important *preparatory, cognitive function*: it helps us to understand why something happened and accordingly prepares us to function more effectively in our environment. In other words, imagination helps us to understand, predict, and control our environment. However, while this seems quite obvious, a great deal of emotional imagination is directed not toward future possibilities but to counterfactual situations, namely, to creating alternative versions of past or present situations. Still, the cognitive function is certainly at play here: by trying to imaginatively change the past or the present, we may be better able to understand our environment. Indeed, the ability to reason counterfactually and to deal with imaginary possibilities is an important component of intelligence. Running a counterfactual simulation in one's head may be compared to a proxy experiment.[17] Although counterfactual imagination cannot alter reality as it is, it can have a profound effect on how we interpret and react to reality. Our emotional preoccupation with the causes of events enables us to realize the preparatory function of counterfactual imagination.

It should be obvious that the cognitive function of the imagination can be negative as well, that is, imagination can distort reality. Imagination often helps us to deny reality and to construct a false picture of the world.

There are situations in which the preparatory, cognitive function of imagination is clearly absent. In what sense do we prepare ourselves better by fantasizing about another person while making love to our partner? It seems that such counterfactual imagination has hardly anything to do with our future behavior or with a better understanding of our situation. Rather, it is a self-deceptive method intended to make us feel better. Indeed, the other major function of counterfactual imagination is the *affective* function of making us feel the way we want. Sometimes a too precise knowledge of reality is hurtful to the point that it prevents us from functioning properly; counterfactual imagination allows us to make life more tolerable and less stressful. In such cases, the content of our imagination expresses more our own nature than that of the object.[18]

The affective function of counterfactual imagination is central to sexual fantasies. We cannot have sex with everyone we would wish to and in every way we desire. Among the many constraints upon our sexual activities are moral, social, and personal ones, as well as constraints of feasibility. Some of these we want to remove, but cannot; others we can remove but do not want to; and others we neither want to nor can remove. Sexual fantasies offer an effective way of coping with these constraints. An imaginary sexual reality can be constructed as the ideal environment in which the negative aspects of breaching the constraints are no longer present, and only the positive aspects are there to be enjoyed. One can always fantasize the most outrageous encounters done in exactly the way one wants and with precisely those whom one most desires. As Olivia St. Claire vividly describes it: You may imagine "having wild sex with Bjorn Borg on Wimbledon's center court as thousands of horny onlookers applaud—while still keeping your marriage, your self-esteem, your emotions, and your pocket-book intact. What a divine luxury." No wonder that many women say they can achieve orgasm by fantasy alone, with no physical stimulation at all. Indeed, recent surveys indicate that only about 30 percent of women have orgasms through intercourse alone, but over 80 percent can achieve climax with masturbation; over 60 percent of women who easily had orgasm could do it through sexual fantasies and dreams with no physical contact.[19] Woody Allen's reply, when questioned about his obsession with masturbation, was, "At least this way I can have sex with someone I really love."

Sometimes counterfactual imagination may actually make us feel worse. In the case of negative situations, imagining that things could have turned out better may be upsetting because it makes the present undesirable state of affairs even more salient. On a more positive note, it may guide our future actions in the sense that we will avoid repeating these negative circumstances. Such comparisons may be explained through the preparatory, rather than the affective function of counterfactual imagination. There are also situations in which the affective function leads to unpleasant emotions such as sadness or fear. We go to a thriller or a sad movie in the full knowledge that fear and sadness will be generated; still, we enjoy such movies. This may be because seeking short-term unpleasant emotions has its affective benefits, such as allowing us to unload our emotional tension and feel better about our current situation, or its preparatory reasons, such as enabling us to look in a safe manner at the dangerous aspects of life and thereby understand ourselves better. By experiencing negative situations for a short period of time, we can in a way become somewhat immune to them. In all these cases, we resort to an illusory means of improving our situation.

Counterfactual imagination can be harmful insofar as it ignores actual circumstances. An endless replaying of past failures may lead to depression; conversely, constantly imagining positive situations may induce an unrealistic degree of optimism. Such harmful consequences are expressed in the following lines by Otomo No Yakamochi:

Better never to have met you
In my dream
Than to wake and reach
For hands that are not there.

Like other useful mechanisms, the ability to imagine alternatives to our present situation becomes harmful when used excessively and when it is not kept within the bounds of particular circumstances. Generally, if something beneficial can be done, but the illusory nature of counterfactual imagination prevents it from being done, such a strategy of coping is clearly not productive and may even be harmful. However, in a situation where nothing much can actually be done, counterfactual thinking can help us feel better at no serious cost. For example, although denial is life-endangering when someone is trying to respond to what appears to be clear symptoms of an oncoming heart attack, during the recovery period in the hospital denial may very well be useful in calming excessive anxiety. Similarly, women who discover breast lumps and deny the potential of cancer are risking their lives, but patients who deny the risks involved in their impending minor surgery are found to show lower levels of anxiety, and to have a more rapid recovery than those who are fully aware of the dangers and apprehensive about the upcoming surgery.[20]

Emotional imagination may be compared to receiving a salary without earning it. Emotional imagination enables us to acquire various affective benefits, such as feeling better, without carrying out the relevant tasks required for obtaining such benefits. For example, in sexual fantasies one may simulate the pleasure of intercourse with an attractive person without building an actual relationship and carrying the burden associated with this. It is obvious that there is no free lunch; the grass of your neighbor is greener since her water bill is bigger. Accordingly, we have to pay a price for this unearned emotional salary. The cost will be high if we repeatedly use tactics such as gaining emotional benefits from imaginary relationships; we may, for example, increase the risk of distorting reality to the extent that coping with it becomes not easier, but harder.[21]

An example of such a price comes from a study in which two groups of men were asked to look at photographs either of highly attractive women or of women of average attractiveness. Men who had been shown the pictures of the highly attractive women were thereafter found to judge their own partners as less attractive than did the men who had been given the pictures of average-looking women. Beyond that, those who had viewed the more attractive women subsequently rated themselves as less committed, less satisfied, less serious, and less close to their partners.[22]

The strength of sexual imagination is clearly illustrated by the vast popularity of sexual sites on the Internet. Although these sites mostly attract men, many women visit them as well. Like other types of addiction, the addition to electronic sex involves an element of self-destruction. Thus, one woman reported that she spent sixteen hours a day visiting sex sites on the Internet, which resulted in her marriage breaking down. There is a significant increase in the number of people who cite, as grounds for divorce, their partner's neglect due to hours spent visiting sexual sites on the Web. The use of sexual imagination is also evident in the many virtual love affairs conducted on the Internet. These imagined relationships may also cause damage. One such an example is that of a man who sought to divorce his wife on grounds of virtual adultery: she had an electronic affair over the Internet with someone she had never met. No wonder that Olivia St. Claire, who strongly encourages women to indulge in sexual fantasies, advises them not to share their fantasies with their mate.

The extensive use of emotional imagination raises interesting moral questions. These questions concern the assumed reality of the imaginative environment. If that environment were in no sense real for us, it would be of less relevance to moral discussions. But emotional imagination has such a powerful impact precisely because it is considered to be in some sense real.

Take, for example, the issue of masturbation. Although masturbation seems to involve mere imagination and to do no harm to other people, it has been the subject of considerable moral criticism. For example, the Jewish book Zohar identifies masturbation as the most abhorrent of the sins recorded in the scriptures, and St. Thomas Aquinas suggested that after the sin of homicide, masturbation takes next place.[23] Masturbation may be harmful to three types of people: (1) the next generation, (2) people in the close circle of the person who is masturbating, and (3) the person who is masturbating. Whereas the first type of harm concerns direct harm to the potential next generation, the harm inflicted on the next two groups is indirect and depends on belief in the reality of the imaginative environment.

The issue of virtual affairs, and in particular the question of whether they should be regarded as adultery, is also related to the degree of reality we attach to the imaginative environment. As long as the virtual affair has no bearing upon reality, it should not be regarded as adultery. However, the issue is more complex as the virtual affair can be highly significant for the participants. Thus, if in a virtual affair two people reveal to each other sexual fantasies or sexual secrets that they do not reveal to their actual partners, it is not clear which sexual intimacy is greater. Such emotional imagination is not typically subject to moral criticism and guilt feelings—at least not to the extent that actual behavior is—but it is not completely immune to negative attitudes, as it has concrete implications for our actual behavior. Moreover, moral obligations are not concerned merely with actual behavior, but also with emotional attitudes and values. Traditional wedding vows include a commitment "to love and to cherish" which refers to recommended emotional attitudes; marriage vows are not limited to types of behavior only. Virtual affairs are incompatible with such a commitment and hence can be regarded, in some sense, as adultery. However, avoiding imaginative affairs is almost impossible. Thus, even Jimmy Carter admitted that although he was very religious, he had lusted after a woman in his heart. Hence, there are many circumstances in which adultery of the imagination seems to do less harm and hence may be preferable given that the alternative is much worse.

Like most other capacities, the ability to fantasize improves with practice; but the more we use it, the more we risk becoming enslaved to it, making coping with everyday reality harder. Too much sexual imagination may make actual sexual activity a rarity and this can be harmful in many respects.

## Positive Illusions

Better a dish of illusion and a hearty appetite for life, than a feast of reality and indigestion therewith.
—Harry A. Overstreet

Nothing makes a woman more beautiful than the belief that she is beautiful.
—Sophia Loren

The affective function of imagination involves what may be characterized as positive illusions, namely, illusions that are beneficial for us. Shelley Taylor, who presents an excellent account of this phenomenon, indicates that psychologists have typically assumed that contact with reality is a hallmark of mental health: "The well-adjusted person is thought to have a clear perception of reality, whereas someone whose vision is clouded by illusion is regarded as vulnerable to, if not already a victim of, mental illness."[24] Recognizing reality is clearly important: believing incorrectly that one can swim can lead to drowning. Nevertheless, Taylor convincingly shows that the above intellectualist view of mental health is wrong.

Taylor suggests three major aspects in which people are positively biased: (1) their assessment of themselves, (2) their assessment of their ability to control what goes on around them, and (3) their assessment of the future.[25]

(1) Most adults and children hold very positive views of themselves. When asked to describe themselves, most people mention many positive qualities and few, if any, negative ones. Most people see themselves as better than others and as above average in the majority of their qualities. (This is in accordance with the claim that "the average person thinks he isn't.") Thus, most people believe that they drive better than others, irrespective of their accident records. Similarly, husbands' and wives' estimates of their contribution to housework produce a total that greatly exceeds 100 percent. As a friend of mine said, when combining the 80 percent that he believes he contributes to housework with the 95 percent his wife believes she contributes, he began to doubt some basic axioms of mathematics. Even when we admit our weaknesses we do it in such a way as to round out a positive human portrait. A woman may be more likely to admit to others that she is hopeless at math than to confess that she sometimes cheats on her husband. Similarly, people typically take credit for good things that happen and deny responsibility for unfortunate events. This tendency is stronger among men who are more likely to blame others for their failures and reward themselves for their

successes. Thus, although girls, on average, do better in elementary school than boys do, girls are more likely to attribute failure to their general lack of ability.[26]

(2) Most people believe that the world is inherently controllable and that their own ability to control events around them is exceptional. Experienced crapshooters engage in a variety of behaviors which imply a belief that they can control what numbers turn up on the dice. Virtually everyone is subject to the same illusion of control as these gamblers. Consequently people prefer to choose their own lottery ticket, rather than have it chosen for them; they believe that their choice increases their chances of winning.

(3) People are characteristically hopeful and confident that things will improve; they are unrealistically optimistic about the future. Human beings tend to see themselves as having improved even when no actual progress has been made. This may be one reason why the initially hard-to-get girlfriend or boyfriend may be more highly valued than an old faithful partner who has always been responsive; only the former case represents an improvement in our situation.

Taylor argues that the widespread existence of these kinds of positive illusions indicates that the normal human mind is far from being a sober, intellectual agent that perceives an unbiased picture of reality. The normal human mind is positively biased. Moreover, she argues that these illusions are not only normal but actually adaptive, promoting rather than undermining mental health. Psychologically healthy people are not those who see things as they are but those who see things as they would like them to be. Other findings suggest that positive illusions even contribute to physical health.

Although there are disputes concerning the precise definition of mental health, most experts agree that the ability to be happy, or at least relatively contented, is a major hallmark of mental health and well-being. Positive illusions about one's personal qualities, degree of control, and likely future in fact promote happiness. Those who have high self-esteem consider themselves to be happier than other people. Such high self-esteem is also important in preventing high suicide rates. Those who believe that they have a lot of control in their lives and who believe that the future will bring them even more happiness are, by their own reports, happier than people who lack these perceptions. The prevalence of positive illusions is in accordance with the fact that most people say they are happy most of the time.[27]

Positive illusions also promote another important aspect of mental health, namely, better social relationships. Thus, there is evidence that people with positive self-esteem have higher regard for others and are better liked by others than people with low self-esteem. Positive illusions, and optimism in particular, may make it easier for people to make certain sacrifices on behalf of others. Accordingly, the belief that one's own children are talented, attractive, and generally appealing facilitates parents' willingness to sustain sacrifices so that these remarkable offspring can realize their potential. Positive illusions are also helpful to the readjustment process following devastating victimizing events such as a severe threat, a loss, or the prospect of imminent death.[28]

Positive illusions also lead to higher motivation, greater persistence at tasks, more effective performance, and ultimately, greater success. Thus, a positive view of the self typically leads a person to work harder and longer on tasks. The same goes for optimism, including unrealistic optimism, which is often a self-fulfilling prophecy. Another advantage of positive illusions is the promotion of intellectual ability, that is, the ability to be more creative or cleverer in one's work. Thus, there is evidence suggesting that people recall information more easily and quickly when they are in a good mood than when they are in a bad mood; good moods also speed up mental processing. An important skill symptomatic of mental health is that of postponing gratification. This skill is especially important for achieving long-term significant goals. There is indeed evidence that positive moods help children and adults to tolerate frustration better and to postpone gratification.[29] The advice to "look on the bright side of life" is basically offering us a good strategy. Hellen Keller, who was deaf and blind, clearly illustrated this strategy when she said: "So much has been given me, I have no time to ponder over that which has been denied." However, we should not do it all the time—sometimes looking on the dark side of life also has some advantages.

Positive illusions may also be associated with evaluative advantages. Spinoza, who was not a religious person, urged his maid to go to church every Sunday. He thought that for people like her, whose intellectual capacities were not as developed as his, church attendance and the (illusory) belief in God, might help them behave in a more moral manner. Similarly, positive illusions concerning the moral behavior of other people may help us to behave more morally.

The many advantages of positive illusions should not lead to the impression that they offer only positive aspects. Illusions, whether positive or negative, involve distorting reality and this can be harmful in certain circumstances. Establishing the adaptive value of positive illusions should take into account two aspects: (1) a qualitative aspect referring to the difference between adaptive and maladaptive illusions, and (2) a quantitative aspect referring to the right proportion in using such illusions.

Concerning the qualitative aspect, Shelley Taylor suggests a distinction between positive illusions and repression or denial. She argues that whereas repression and denial alter reality, positive illusions simply interpret it in the best possible light. Repression and denial distort threatening information by pushing it beyond awareness, and hence lead people to distort reality. In contrast, positive illusions enable people to make the most of bad situations by adopting a positive perspective. The following study is instructive in this regard. Shoppers in a mall were given a free gift and then later interviewed for a consumer survey which asked them and also people who had not received a free gift how their cars, televisions, washers, and dryers functioned. Those who received the free gift reported that they were happier with their cars and other appliances than the people who had not received gifts.[30] Being in a positive mood helps us to see the positive aspects of reality and to ignore, or at least to diminish, the negative aspects.

Positive illusions represent a distortion of statistical reality and not of actual facts. While holding positive illusions people hold beliefs that are more positive than reality can sustain; however, hoping for the best, believing you can beat the odds, and thinking very well of yourself do not represent misconstructions of the facts. Take, for example, our social environment. People construct their social environment in such a way that they will receive primarily positive self-assessments and avoid negative ones. We select as our friends those who value our positive qualities, are aware of our shortcomings, and love us despite our faults. Such a social environment is not an adequate statistical sample of the people in the world, but it does not misconstrue the facts; it merely chooses those we prefer. Selective attention and selective memory are similar filters for screening out negative information and thereby creating a better environment. Even if positive illusions are in many cases instances of self-deception, they still have adaptive value. There are some findings suggesting that people who are self-deceptive are in some respects mentally healthier than those who are not.[31]

I am not sure that the suggested distinction between positive illusions and repression or denial is as qualitatively clear as Taylor presents it. The distinction between altering reality and interpreting it is not so clear; it should also be mentioned that repression and denial are sometimes adaptive too. The distinction between positive illusions and repression is nevertheless valuable for depicting different emphases in our perception of reality.

Another aspect establishing the adaptive value of positive illusions is a quantitative one which takes into account an appropriate proportion in the use of such illusions. As indicated, an excessive use of positive illusions may be harmful, distorting the facts rather than merely interpreting them positively. Large doses of positive illusions may cross the borderline between them and repression or denial. A quantitative difference may easily becomes a qualitative one.

I have suggested above that our immediate environment is the one which suffers most from our emotional imagination; those close to us pay the price for the emotional return we gain without investing any actual resources. It is similarly true that our positive illusions are most likely to cause hurt to those around us. When someone has positive illusions concerning her worth or her ability to control what goes on around her, she is likely to pay less attention to those close to her; after all, she believes that she knows better than they do what should be done. It is not pleasant to be in the company of such a person. In many cases, positive illusions, especially those concerning our own worth and our ability to control the events around us, are useful for the agent but harmful to those around her.

To sum up, there are many circumstances in which positive illusions are beneficial; in others they are harmful. Generally speaking, it seems that a moderate dose of positive illusions, namely, of self-deception, is usually helpful in coping with everyday life and achieving our goals. Knowing the precise nature of all the negative details of our life is not always advantageous. As with other illusions, positive illusions also have harmful consequences.

### Emotions in the Future World

The trouble with our times is that the future is not what it used to be.
—Paul Valery

We live in an age when pizza gets to your home before the police.
—Jeff Marder


I have suggested that modern communication actually increases the role of imagination in emotions. I turn now to briefly discuss the influence of tomorrow's computerized world on our emotional experiences. Such an influence may be expressed in the following three major views:

1. the future world will be emotionless;
2. the future world will be emotional, but different types of emotions will populate it;
3. the future world will be emotional, but emotions will be generated differently.

I believe that the first view is inadequate: tomorrow's world is bound to be emotional, as the basic reasons for generating emotions do not disappear with the advance of the computerized world. Existential and social changes, which underlie the generation of emotions, will also be present in the future world; the changes may be even more pronounced, and so emotions are likely to be more intense.

The second view may be partially true in the very distant future. In that future we may witness the emergence of new emotions; however, those will be added to the current ones. Similarly, the evolution from nonhuman animals to humans was characterized by adding new types of emotions and making animals' emotions more complex; yet, in this evolutionary process, no animal's emotion has completely disappeared (see chapter 4). It would be an interesting task to predict the types of new emotions which may be generated, but this is beyond the scope of this book.

The most feasible possibility is expressed in the third view: the main difference between today's world and the computerized world of tomorrow will be in the way that emotions are generated. A major difference in this regard is the greater role that imagination will play in generating emotions. As indicated, this kind of development is also typical of the development from animals' emotions to human emotions: in humans, the imagination plays a far greater role.

In the future world, we may be even more physically isolated than we are now—we shall have less actual, face-to-face human contact. Nevertheless, we shall have more connections with other human beings. We shall use our imagination more and may become more creative. This development does not make us less human; on the contrary, the development of complex imaginary capacities is unique to the human race.

Television and computer communication have created the so-called global village. However, they separate us from actual experiences of the world; they create an environment in which images are substituted for reality. This environment does not have many of the constraints that the actual world has, and hence it may be a safe, moral, and clean environment. However, it can also distort reality to the extent that it is more difficult for us to cope with the actual world. Hence, more and more people will try to transfer into actual reality the distorted imaginative environment provided by modern communication. There are indeed more and more horrible crimes that are heavily influenced by such communication.

We can also expect to find in the future more psychological problems stemming from the inability to distinguish imagination from reality. Indeed, some evidence suggests that the present generation of children are more emotionally troubled than the last; these children appear to have a lower degree of emotional intelligence. On average, the present generation of children seem more liable to be lonely and impulsive, more nervous, depressed, and angry.[32]

Emily Dickinson wrote, "The soul selects her own society." So in Western societies where isolation becomes more and more common, and Western cultures urge us toward autonomy, the sociality of our life does not diminish; rather, many actual social relations are replaced by imaginary ones. We feel emotions which have as their objects what we imagine people feel toward us, rather than merely what they are doing with us. Dreams are no longer the major tool for imagining a better situation; modern communication becomes more efficient for such a purpose. Complex imaginative relationships will be at the very center of tomorrow's world. We shall select our own society. The sociality of our life will not diminish; rather, many actual social relations will be replaced by imaginary ones. As suggested, the price of constructing a new imaginary society is that of having difficulties in coping with our actual society. Indeed, a recent study suggests that greater use of the Internet was associated with declines in participants' communication with family members in the household, declines in the size of their social circle, and increases in their depression and loneliness.[33] In order to avoid some of the harmful consequences of such a development, it is advisable to moderate the use of such imaginative mechanisms.

It should also be noted that the use of chemical means to change our emotions or moods may be considerably more widespread and efficient in the future. Although such use will make it easier for us to regulate our affective attitudes, it will increase the negative consequences associated with excessive use of emotional imagination.

*Emotions and Luck*

Being deeply learned and skilled; being well-trained and using well-spoken words—this is the best good luck. To support mother and father, to cherish wife and child and to have a simple livelihood—this is the best good luck.
—Buddha

Imagination plays a significant role not only in emotional experiences but also in the experience of being lucky (or unlucky). The experience of being lucky is typically an emotional experience; however, not every emotional experience involves the sense of being lucky. In this section I discuss the relationships between emotions and luck. I begin by clarifying the notion of luck.

*Different Types of Luck*
Luck never gives; it only lends.
—Swedish Proverb

It is bad luck to be superstitious.
—Andrew Mathis

Different classifications of lucky events may be suggested. Those are formulated in terms of different issues:

1. *The nature of lucky events.* Describing a certain event as lucky may refer to several meanings: (a) the event is *uncaused*, (b) the event is due to a *random* state of affairs, (c) the event is beyond our *control*, and (d) the event has a highly *available alternative*. All these meanings indicate that as far as the person affected is concerned, the lucky event came about by accident; as such, these meanings represent different degrees of opposition to a scientific picture of a causal, predictable, and controllable world.

The first meaning of luck refers to the *uncaused* nature of lucky events and suggests that there are in the world events with no cause. This meaning contradicts the causal, and hence the predictable and controllable, nature of the world. Hence, no wonder that Kant argued that science cannot refer to such events.

The second meaning, referring to the *randomness* of luck, is not necessarily in opposition to the causal nature of the world, but only to its predictable and controllable nature. If everything were random, then science would be impossible as well. If only some events in the world were random, then science would still be possible, but its predictions would be of a limited scope. Uncaused events cannot be part of a scientific explanation, whereas random events can—although their presence limits the scope of lawful regularities typical of such explanations.

The third meaning of lucky events refers to the *lack of our control* over them; in this sense, whatever "just happens" to us is luck. This meaning opposes neither the causal nor the predictable nature of the world; it is merely incompatible with our ability to change the world.

The fourth meaning of luck refers to the *availability of an alternative* situation to the present one: a lucky event is one which could easily be replaced by a different event. Hence, the saying: "An unlucky man breaks his neck on a straw."

The four meanings are related in the sense that an uncaused event is also random, uncontrolled, and has an easily imagined alternative. However, an event which has a greatly available alternative is not necessarily uncaused, random, or uncontrolled. The difference between being uncaused and being random or uncontrolled is of significance for ontological and epistemological considerations. However, from the point of view of the person experiencing the lucky event, this difference is of no importance. From this point of view, a typical lucky event can be described as the product of chance, one beyond our control, and something that could easily have been different.

Rational thinking in general, and "hard" science in particular, can be described as an attempt to reduce the role of luck in our explanations and behavior. They spring from our desire to reduce the uncertainties of a seemingly chaotic world. To omniscience there could be no luck; to advancing knowledge there is less luck. Rational thinking is perceived as being incompatible with the belief in luck and with attaching a significant role to emotions in our life. A professional intellectual behavior is an emotionless behavior which attaches no importance to luck. In light of such a view, education should eliminate, or at least significantly reduce, the influence of both luck and emotions.

Although intellectual, scientific thinking has indeed reduced uncertainties in human life and brought about tremendous practical and intellectual advantages, it is not necessarily the case that a complete success in this endeavor, namely, a complete reduction of uncertainties, would be advantageous as well. Luckily, our generation, and those in the foreseeable future, do not have to worry about this. It seems, however, that if such a success were to be achieved, it would completely change the nature of human beings, making them more intellectual and less emotional. Such a luck-less world, in which everything could be planned and nothing unexpected ever happened, would be a very dull place to live in.[34]

2. *The source of lucky events.* The division of luck according to the source of lucky events may be formulated in terms of circumstantial and resultant luck.

*Circumstantial* luck refers to our luck in being in certain circumstances; for example, being born into a certain family, being in the office when the house was burglarized, attending a certain school, or being stuck in an elevator during a power failure. This refers to the proverbial luck of being "in the wrong place at the wrong time." Circumstantial luck can be either *constitutive* or *occasional*. The *constitutive* sense refers to factors constituting our relatively stable personal makeup: the genetic structure determining our health, gender, intelligence, and physical appearance, and the environmental circumstances of our personal development and current situation, such as the political and educational systems under which we have been raised. The *occasional* sense refers to specific events we encounter in everyday life; for instance, the type of people we meet, occasional opportunities, accidents, the fortune or misfortune of other people, and so forth. The constitutive sense of circumstantial luck is more likely to be associated with long-term affective phenomena such as sentiments and affective disorders, and occasional luck is typically connected with short-term affective phenomena such as emotions and moods.

*Resultant* luck refers to our luck in doing something which turned out to be either a success or a failure; for example, buying the right stocks, choosing the right partner, or avoiding a disastrous trip. Resultant luck is typically occasional: it refers to specific, occasional actions of ours. Whereas circumstantial luck is due to external circumstances having hardly anything to do with our personal choice, resultant luck is due to chosen actions.

The concept of circumstantial luck raises many interesting *moral issues* concerning the alleged impartial nature of morality. The basic issue is whether and to what extent circumstantial luck (and especially the constitutive part of it) should be taken into account in our moral attitude toward other people. It is hard to doubt that circumstantial luck, which determines to a large extent our personal makeup and current personal situation, should be taken into account. The moral behavior toward disadvantaged, retarded, or mentally disturbed people should be different from that directed toward other people. The problem is what are the circumstantial factors which are relevant to moral behavior. The discussion about affirmative action is one concrete example of such a problem. It seems that no clear criterion for determining such relevance exists, and therefore the moral discussion should take into account many particular features.[35]

3. *The status of luck.* Luck may also be divided in light of its epistemological or ontological status, namely, whether it refers to the way we know the events in the world or whether it refers to an entity which actually exists in the world. In the first sense, luck refers to the limitations of our cognitive capacities which can perceive many events in the world as random or uncontrollable; in the second sense, luck is a causal agent.

It is tempting to move from the epistemological to the ontological concept and consider luck as a *personified power* whose favor can be cultivated or lost. This move is expressed in the belief in Lady Luck (the ancient goddess Fortuna), an unlucky day (Friday the 13th), a luck-controlling force (one's lucky star or, conversely, the evil eye), and one's lucky charm (a four-leaf clover, a rabbit's foot). Indeed, many sayings express the ontological status of luck. For instance, "If my father had made me a hatter, folk would have been born without heads"; "Luck was always with me"; "Luck may visit the fool, but does not sit down with him." In this view, we may know something about luck and have a certain degree of control over it.

Consider the popular belief connecting sneezing to a certain type of luck. This belief is still expressed today when we say "God bless you" after someone sneezes, as if to prevent bad luck. Our blessing expresses our partial control of luck. The same holds for the belief, which once prevailed in Germany, that if a man sneezes on arising he should lie down again for three hours; otherwise he will have the bad luck of having his wife be his master for a week. In this belief, sneezing begins a chain of events that is beyond our control and finally results in a most unfortunate consequence. Averting the above unlucky consequence is, to a certain extent, under our control, as we may not sneeze in the morning or we may lie down again for three hours. Hence, we do have a certain limited control over the lucky chain of events. Similarly, in Russia, the peasants considered it unlucky on leaving the house to meet a priest, but they could avert the bad luck by throwing a pin at him in the case of women or spitting on his beard in the case of men. Other more modern-day instances include such adages as "Sing before breakfast, cry before night." In the same vein, it is considered unlucky to live on the thirteenth floor or to do anything dangerous on Friday the 13th. Likewise, if a black cat crosses in front of someone or if someone mistakenly walks under a ladder, this is taken as a sign of bad luck to come. On the more positive side, finding a "lucky penny" can only mean that good fortune lies ahead.

Considering luck to be a personified agent is mistaken. It is almost a matter of definition that *luck cannot be an agency* which controls the chance element in human affairs. When we characterize an occurrence as lucky, this is a description of our *perception* of a certain state of affairs; "luck" is not an external, independent entity. From our perspective a certain state of affairs may appear to be random and to have a highly available alternative, but this does not mean that there is someone who designs things to be perceived by us as random. Irregularities need not imply an actual agency controlling these irregularities. We have a tendency to explain regularities or irregularities by assuming the existence of a personified agency regulating them; for example, people explain mental regularities or irregularities by assuming the presence of a homunculus, namely, a little man living inside our head. A chain of lucky or unlucky events sometimes makes people believe in the existence of Lady Luck, which regulates this orderly chain of irregularities. But if luck is regulated by a certain agency, then its basic characteristics are absent: it is caused, and therefore is not random, nor is it beyond the control of a personified agent, and its alternative is not highly available.[36]

*The Relationship between Luck and Emotions*
We must believe in luck. For how else can we explain the success of those we don't like?
—Jean Cocteau


The scientific human endeavor to *eliminate luck* and to have greater control over our lives seems contrary to another fundamental characteristic of human life: having emotions and hence an exciting life. Full knowledge and calculated intellectual behavior would seem to eliminate the role of both luck and emotions from our lives. Combining luck and emotions to oppose the scientific picture of the world seems odd if we restrict luck to the meanings of chance and uncontrollability. In light of these meanings, luck is something which should reduce or even eliminate emotions. For the experiencing person, something that is perceived as random or uncontrollable is as inevitable as the events in the causal world. In both cases, there is nothing to do or change and hence there is no reason to be emotionally excited.

Emotions are not typical of environments perceived to be *fully ordered* or *fully chaotic*. Intense experiences of luck and emotions typically require conditions of limited knowledge and controllability. In a fully known and controlled environment or a fully unknown and uncontrolled environment, emotional and lucky experiences are not intense. God is sometimes characterized as emotionless, since his infinite knowledge allows him to perceive the world as fully ordered. Very low animals, to whom no form of knowledge or expectation can be attributed, have sensation but no emotions. Their world is fully chaotic. Human beings are somewhere in between: they do have knowledge and expectations, but those are not complete; accordingly, humans are essentially emotional beings. Similarly, in a world whose events are perceived to occur completely independent of the influence of human beings—either because they follow the eternal laws of nature or because they are random and uncontrolled—indifference rather than emotional excitement would be the prevailing mood. In such a world, neither human success nor human failure would be possible; nor would there be motivation or aspirations. Human beings, in the form we know them today, would not be able to live in this world.

The environment we encounter in everyday life is different from both a fully known *causal* world or a fully *random* and uncontrolled world. Our everyday environment contains elements from both worlds. We know in advance the inevitable consequences of some events and can accordingly choose to generate or avoid them; some other events are not known to us and are perceived as random and beyond our control. Emotions are generated in an environment where an alternative to the current situation can be imagined. This situation may be the result of (a) lucky events perceived to be random or uncontrolled, or (b) accountable events in which we have invested effort and for which we feel responsible.

To feel lucky is to have a certain emotional experience; to have a certain emotional experience does not always imply the sense of being lucky. In emotions generated by perceived lucky events, the intensity variable of readiness, which includes unexpectedness and uncertainties, is quite dominant. Many emotions may be generated in such a manner, for example, envy, pity, and disappointment. The emotions in which luck is not dominant are the result of what we perceive to be accountable events; in these emotions the intensity variable of accountability, which includes controllability, effort, and intention, is quite dominant. Pride and guilt are examples of such emotions. A positive correlation between emotional intensity and luck is present only in the first type of emotions.

Like emotional experiences, lucky experiences involve the *perception of significant changes* deviating from the expected, normal course of events. As in emotions, perceiving something to be lucky or unlucky depends on the availability of an alternative: lucky experiences are based on a close avoidance of something worse, and unlucky experiences are based on a close miss of something better. Perceiving the significance of every event may be described as implicitly involving comparison with some alternative. The experience of luck is linked to comparison with an imagined alternative rather than with characteristics of the actual events.

Lucky events are those in which the alternative is very close and hence easily imagined. This is clearly evident when reading or watching interviews with victims of life-threatening attacks, illnesses, or natural disasters. Such interviews give the impression that each survivor is lucky. Victims commonly feel lucky because they could have been more severely victimized. Thus, one crime victim said that "We were very lucky. He took only the stereo and the TV. It could have been a lot worse." Similarly, instead of bemoaning the loss of her home and car, the tornado victim is relieved, even jubilant, that she and her family so narrowly escaped death. Likewise, the victim of fire expresses gratitude that her life was spared. When the alternative is immediate, highly possible, and significant, it makes us evaluate our present situation differently.[37]

Luck is positively correlated with unexpectedness and uncertainty. A lucky event is exceptional or out of the ordinary; hence, it is unexpected and uncertain. In the case of an unexpected and uncertain event, the normal and common alternative is easily imagined, due to its being readily available. As indicated, imagining an alternative is even more important for luck than for emotions, since luck depends more on the unexpected or exceptional nature of the event in question.

Luck plays a role also in *sentiments* such as long-term love and grief. In such sentiments the change is typically not a specific, transient change, but a more profound type of change related to our contingent existence. In grief we often think how unlucky the person we are grieving over was; and in long-term romantic love, we believe that we are very lucky to have met our partner. Everyday specific events may remind us of how lucky or unlucky we are, but they do not have significant impact on the more profound belief in our being lucky or unlucky.

In an impressive set of studies, Karl Teigen clearly shows the importance of the *availability of an alternative* to the experience of luck.[38] He shows, for example, the presence of a high positive correlation between ratings of luck and ratings of how "easily" the situation could have led to a different outcome. Perceiving ourselves as lucky or unlucky is heavily dependent upon comparison of the actual event with an alternative one. People feel extremely lucky to escape from a car crash with only minor injuries, because a far worse outcome is possible, or even probable. Louisa Bohm, a woman who lost her husband and three children in a car accident, said eight years later that she considers herself to be lucky since she was able to go on living, remarry, and have more children. Pain and sorrow are part and parcel of every day of her life, but she still feels lucky.

A lucky person is typically only millimeters or seconds away from disaster or misfortune. Consider the following example:

> At 4:29 P.M., a customer runs out of breath into the local liquor store, his first question being: "When is closing time?" "4:30." "Then I was lucky."

Teigen rightly suggests that "For this customer it was not enough to observe that he had reached his goal in time. To feel lucky, he needed another piece of information, namely how close he was to have had the door shut in his face. He was not lucky just because he made it, he was lucky because he *just* made it."[39]

If the availability of a good alternative makes us feel unlucky, then making this alternative less available would reduce the bad feeling. In this sense, an added barrier to an attractive alternative may make a person feel less unlucky because it makes the alternative seem further away. This point is illustrated in the following example.

> A person had to cancel his trip to Africa since the vaccination he had made him sick. While lying in bed, he heard that the trip had been canceled because of an airline strike.

This person would feel luckier upon hearing about the strike, as it would make the attractive alternative of going to Africa more remote and would thereby make the feeling of being unlucky less intense.[40]

In both luck and the emotions in which the availability of an alternative is particularly important, the current situation is perceived to be *exceptional*: the emotional change and the event eliciting the lucky experience are surprising in light of the expected normal circumstances. This can explain why regularities in gambling situations are ascribed to luck, whereas in other situations luck is associated with variability of outcomes. In gambling situations, the normal circumstances are those expressing variability of outcomes; hence, regularities are perceived as exceptional and attributed to luck.

The experience of being lucky or unlucky, rather than merely feeling good or bad about something, is crucial for many emotions. The comparison to an imagined alternative is more natural and much easier in the former case. Thus, the statement, "I am lucky to have such a good wife" is clearly seen as expressing more intense gratitude than the sentence "It is good I have a good wife." The significance of the former sentence is more closely related to a comparison with an imagined alternative.[41]

Imagining an alternative is important not only for perceiving occasional luck but for perceiving constitutive luck as well. Teigen has shown that in terms of more permanent conditions, like having a talent, good health, or a family, the idea that something could have been different is most important.[42] This may be reflected in the popular notion of "the luck of the Irish," represented by leprechauns and four-leaf clovers.

*Luck and Emotional Intensity*
I'm a great believer in luck, and I find the harder I work the more I have of it.
—Thomas Jefferson


Does perceiving an event as lucky (or unlucky) increase or decrease the emotional impact of that event? Two opposing considerations can be presented: (1) perceiving an event as lucky may indicate high availability of an alternative and this increases emotional intensity, and (2) perceiving an event as lucky suggests lack of our control in the event and this decreases emotional intensity. Emotional intensity will be determined in light of the relative weight of each factor.

If an event is perceived as lucky mainly because we lack control over it, this event will not generate intense emotions. In such cases, lucky events will be perceived as inevitable, deterministic events, and since here there is no available alternative, there is nothing to get excited about. The experiences of emotions and luck do not prevail in a fully random and uncontrolled environment for which we are not responsible. As mentioned, we are usually happier after winning a certain amount of money on account of our professional achievements than winning the same amount of money in a lottery (in both cases all other relevant factors, including the number of people we are competing with, are the same). The variable of accountability (and hence deservingness as well), which is absent from a limited notion of luck, is responsible for the lack of emotional intensity.

In other lucky events the factor of the availability of an alternative has more weight and therefore it increases the emotional impact. Consider the following example.

> Whoever goes to Africa should be vaccinated against yellow fever. There are two types of vaccine, A and B. About 5 percent of the population are allergic to type A and another 5 percent are allergic to type B—nobody is allergic to more than one type. Where Arne lives, only type A vaccine is available; Arne had an allergic reaction, became ill, and had to cancel the trip. Where Bjorn lives, the two types are available; he had the choice between the two vaccines. He chose A, became ill, and had to cancel the trip. Who was the unluckier one?

Most people say that Bjorn is unluckier than Arne. The existence of choice seems to have added to the amount of bad luck, even if it also makes the person more responsible for the outcome.[43] Indeed, we feel luckier if our success comes as a result of voluntary choice than when no choice is possible.

The difficulty in determining the emotional intensity of lucky events stems from the presence of two different features of luck, namely, great availability of an alternative and lack of controllability, which exert opposing influences on emotional intensity. This difficulty is reduced when we recognize that lucky events are not perceived to be completely uncontrolled. Controllability is present in at least two senses: (1) we are responsible for initiating the causal chain which finally resulted in the lucky event; and (2) other agents are somehow responsible for the lucky event. Although lucky events are not perceived as being under our control, they are at the same time not believed to be completely beyond our control. Our responsibility over lucky events is expressed in our readiness to meet the opportunities we encountered. Edward Filene (who was described as the "distinguished merchant-philosopher") argues that "Luck is chance. Chance comes to everybody. When it comes to the man who is ready, he is lucky."[44]

Nicholas Rescher claims that "chance favors the prepared—those who are so situated as to be in a position to seize opportunities created by chance." In this sense, luck is perceived as the residue of design. Rescher indicates that we can have no control concerning whether we will be lucky or unlucky, but we can influence the scope of luck's effect on our lives. The student who works hard does not rely on luck to pass the examination. Generally, Rescher indicates the presence of three major ways in which we can influence the element of luck in our lives: (1) risk avoidance—people who do not court danger need not count on luck to pull them through; (2) insurance—people who make proper provision against unforeseeable difficulties by way of insurance need not rely on luck alone as a safeguard against disaster; (3) probabilistic calculation—people who try to keep the odds on their side can thereby diminish the extent to which they become victims of misfortune. By thoughtful planning, we can reduce the role of luck—and emotions as well—in our lives.[45]

In addition to the direct responsibility we bear for being prepared or unprepared, we often feel responsible for choosing an action which unknowingly started a lucky or unlucky chain of events. We may not have known which chain of events would lead to a better or worse fortune, but we had some influence on the choice of the *initial event* in the chain. Consider the following example. One day someone decided to go to work earlier and via a different route; on her way to work, another driver did not stop at a red light and consequently collided with her car, killing her husband. Although her choice of a different route and time was arbitrary regarding the safety of the ride, it initiated a chain of events causing her husband's death; accordingly, she may feel responsible for indirectly causing her own misfortune. This kind of indirect, causal responsibility is of emotional significance as well.

*Effort* is an additional variable included in the group of variables constituting our accountability. Great personal involvement, which is expressed in our effort, is in opposition to the random and uncontrolled nature of the limited concept of luck. Effortless consequences are typically considered as luckier, but they induce less intense emotions. Therefore, we consider Alf, who won a competition without investing much training and effort, as luckier than Ulf, who won due to his persistent effort. Yet we consider Ulf to be happier.[46] Alf's constitutive luck is by far greater than Ulf's. Ulf's persistent effort makes him less lucky, as effort is negatively correlated with luck, but happier, as effort is positively correlated with emotional intensity, including happiness (see chapter 5). Like emotions, lucky experiences involve comparison with alternative situations. However, luck entails the presence of very close alternatives, whereas emotions can refer to more remote ones. Hence, the experience of being lucky is typically emotional, but not every emotional experience entails the sense of being lucky.

The phrase "lucky at cards—unlucky in love" describes the fact that many persons are notably lucky in some ways and unlucky in others. This phrase may also indicate that we can always consider ourselves lucky from a certain viewpoint. Thus, Socrates said that having a wife is always good: if you find a good wife, you will be happy; if not, you will become a philosopher. This attitude may be described as alert optimism.

Perceiving ourselves as lucky is important for the generation of emotions and hence for an exciting human life. Luck and emotions should, however, have a *limited* role in our lives if we are to fulfill our potential and achieve our goals. Long-term happiness cannot be achieved by being emotionless or by not considering ourselves to be in some sense lucky. However, such happiness also requires us to partly disregard the influence of specific emotions and the role of luck in our lives.

## Summary

Often it is just lack of imagination that keeps a man from suffering very much.
—Marcel Proust

Imagination has a crucial role in generating emotions. This role has to do with the comparative nature of emotions: emotional comparison involves reference to a situation that is different from the present one. Emotional imagination does not merely refer to situations that are not present to our senses, but also to situations that do not exist at the moment—most of which will never exist at all. An important type of emotional imagination is counterfactual imagination, namely, imagination whose content is incompatible with reality.

The reference to imaginary situations has important cognitive and affective functions: (a) it helps us to understand our environment and prepare ourselves for future situations, and (b) it improves our affective attitudes. Although emotional imagination is frequently connected to illusions and self-deception, it is often advantageous as it helps us cope with the harsh reality around us. The escape into emotional imagination may be more pronounced in modern society. Although television and computer communication create some links between people, they also separate us from actual experiences of the world by creating an environment in which images are substituted for reality.

## Chapter 8

## Everything Is Not under Control—Regulating the Emotions

The Stoical scheme of supplying our wants by lopping off our desires, is like cutting off our feet when we want shoes.
—Jonathan Swift

Having described the circumstances in which emotions are generated and terminated, we are ready to discuss the means of regulating, and hence of coping with, emotions. Being aware of these means is of the utmost importance if we are to use them beneficially. Emotional regulation, or management, refers to any initiative we take to influence which emotions we have, when we have them, and how we experience and express these emotions.[1]

We have many strategies for regulating emotions: averting our gaze from a frightening sight, whistling a cheerful tune when afraid, concentrating on happy thoughts when we are sad, removing ourselves from a person who makes us nervous, reducing our attachment to other people, distracting ourselves, and so on. Many types of service work, such as those performed by lawyers, physicians, nurses, therapists, teachers, hairdressers, police, waiters, and prostitutes, require some kind of regulating of the emotions. In light of such variety, there is no doubt that we can regulate our emotions to a certain extent; the remaining issue of interest is how we manage to do it.

Although emotional regulation may increase with age, children readily learn diverse strategies to regulate their emotions, such as self-gratification, cognitive distraction, withdrawal, nurturing social interaction, and taking corrective action. Younger children (under five years old) have no more difficulty in finding means to regulate their emotions than older ones (eight years old and above), but they prefer behavioral means, whereas older children opt for cognitive interventions.[2]

The factors responsible for increasing emotional intensity are the same factors that we have to deal with to reduce emotional intensity. Thus, if the factors increasing anger are perceptions that an offense is intentional, malicious, and unjustified, then the factors reducing anger will be perceptions of the offense as accidental, well-intended, or justified.[3] If emotions occur when we face significant changes in our situation, then preventing such changes or perceiving them as not meaningful are basic methods for preventing emotional experiences. Whereas a profound manner of increasing emotional intensity is to become more involved and sensitive to the events around us, making those events seem less significant can be accomplished by becoming less involved and more detached.

We should distinguish between regulating emotions and regulating the manifestations of emotions. The latter, which is easier to achieve, often requires useful pretense. Thus, calm people who want other people to take them seriously have sometimes to pretend that they are angry. The ability to induce anger is also useful for bill collectors, among other professions. Accordingly, the Dale Carnegie Institute for improving social communication teaches students how to induce anger in themselves by exhibiting behavior typical of anger. Sometimes it is difficult to separate the regulation of an emotion from the regulation of its manifestation because pretense can easily turn into the real emotion. Indeed, when people are induced to behave as if they feel an emotion, they often report actually feeling it. As Jean-Paul Sartre observed, the best way to fall asleep is to pretend you are asleep. Similarly, controlling the manifestations of a given emotion usually changes its intensity.

An interesting issue in this regard is whether the expression of emotions reduces or increases our overall emotional intensity. The Greek physician Galen claimed that controlling the manifestation of emotions may reduce their intensity, and that it is easier to control the manifestations than the emotion itself. Indeed, in many cases, if the manifestations are controlled, the emotions too begin to wither gradually.[4] However, the situation is more complex. In some cases, repressing the manifestation of a given emotion will result in greater intensity later on. In other cases, expressing a certain emotion reinforces it by developing the habit of that emotion.[5]

### Possible Divisions of Regulating Means

I cannot control the direction of the winds, but I can always adjust my sails to reach my destination.
—Unknown

Various divisions of regulating means are possible. The first division of regulating means refers to the extent of the regulating means, namely, whether they refer to factors influencing our *emotional sensitivity in general* or only to factors influencing our *specific emotional reactions*. Changing the nature of our emotional sensitivity, which is a function of our personal makeup, is often not possible and, in any case, is much harder to achieve than changing our specific emotional reactions. However, once a change in emotional sensitivity is achieved, it has profound implications for our specific reactions.

The second division of regulating means refers to the *focus* of these means—problem-focused, person-focused, intensity variables, and so on. We can discern here regulating means by which we try to rectify a situation and solve its under-lying *problem*, and regulating means directed at our own *responses* to the emotional situation. The regulating means can also be focused on each *intensity variable* or other factors such as increasing or decreasing emotional intensity or focusing on negative or positive emotions.

The third division of regulating means is related to the three intentional aspects of emotions: motivation, cognition, and evaluation. Accordingly, emotions can be regulated by using *behavioral*, *cognitive*, and *evaluative* means. Behavioral means facilitate or prevent certain types of changes, thereby regulat-ing emotional intensity. Cognitive interpretations can focus not merely on the presence or absence of the changes themselves but on the manipulation of their significance. The evaluative method of regulating emotions focuses on changing our evaluative structure rather than on the interpretation of particular circumstances.

The suggested divisions of regulatory means are complementary; each means can be characterized in light of each of the three divisions: it can either refer to our emotional sensitivity in general or to our specific emotional reactions; it can either focus on the emotional situation or on our own attitude; it can use behavioral, cognitive, or evaluative means; and it can refer to each of the inten-sity variables. Thus, keeping ourselves busy at work as a response to some problem in our family is a behavioral means which aims to regulate our specific emotional reactions by avoiding the problematic situation; by using this means, we decrease the relevancy of the problem. The attitude of settling for less by not assuming that we deserve to have everything other people have is an evalu-ative regulatory means which refers to our overall emotional sensitivity and focuses on our own attitude; this means is concerned with the intensity variable of deservingness.

Some combinations of the above means may be more common than others. Thus, whereas evaluative means are typically profound means of changing our emotional sensitivity in general and not merely our specific emotional reactions, behavioral means are more specific. Although some combinations are more common than others, it seems that all combinations are possible in principle.

The distinctions between the various means of regulating emotions are not always clear-cut; some means are hard to classify into a specific group, as they contain elements of a few groups. For example, the evaluative means of settling for less focuses mainly on our own attitude rather than on the emotional situa-tion, but adopting such a profound attitude may result in changing the nature of the emotional situation with which we are confronted, and in this sense it is also a problem-focused means. Despite such overlaps, the division into the three groups has some explanatory value.

In what follows, I briefly discuss the first two groups of regulating means. Then I provide a more detailed discussion of the third group, which relates to behavioral, cognitive, and evaluative means, for the discussion of these means is closely related to the other issues discussed so far.

*The Extent of Regulating Means*
It is foolish to tear one's hair in grief, as though sorrow would be made less by baldness.
—Cicero

The regulating means can either influence the nature of our *emotional sensitivity* or our *specific emotional reactions*. The first type of influence is more difficult to achieve, but if it is done it has more profound effects.

A radical example of a change in emotional sensitivity is adopting the attitude of complete detachment. The Buddhist state of neutral feeling, which is an attitude of even-mindedness and impartiality toward all conditioned things, is an instance of such an attitude. The Buddhist peaceful and emotionless state of *nirvana* is characterized as not belonging to the realm of the "changeable"[6]; hence, it is devoid of emotional sensitivity. This approach to reducing emotional sensitivity may be highly effective, but is extremely difficult to achieve, not least because it requires complete detachment from normal everyday life. A significant reduction in emotional sensitivity may be harmful, as emotions fulfill important functions in our lives. Accordingly, we should not attempt to eradicate emotional sensitivity, but rather to moderate its intensity. A less radical example of changing emotional sensitivity is decreasing the weight of the comparative concern, which is so central to emotions. Such a decrease would have the effect of reducing emotional sensitivity insofar as it makes us less sensitive to the discrepancy between our current state and our other past or possible states, or those of other people.

Reducing our specific emotional reactions can be accomplished by reducing the weight of each *intensity variable*. By reducing the strength and reality of the specific eliciting event, the event would induce less intense emotions. If we were able to evaluate the events around us as less strong and real, our emotional reactions would be weaker. Similarly, by reducing closeness with other people, namely, by decreasing the number and quality of our relationships with others, fewer people would be of emotional significance to us. Reducing emotional intensity can also be done by referring to background circumstances. People who believe that nothing is within their own control—since, for example, blind fate determines the course of events in the world—are less subject to emotions. Likewise, decreasing our expectations regarding a particular event, or being less firm in our belief that we deserve a certain outcome, will weaken our specific emotional reactions toward such an event.

The difference between the means of regulating our emotional sensitivity in general and those regulating our specific emotional reactions is a difference in degree which concerns the extent of the influence of the regulating means. Hence, it is obvious that there are no precise borderlines between the two types of regulating means. Take, for example, the important means regulating the lowering of our expectations. It has been said that expectation is a great enemy of happiness, as those who do not expect are not disappointed. However, expectation does not entail merely sadness or happiness in general, but being prone to specific emotional reactions. We can lower our expectations in response to a specific event or many events. When many events are concerned, this means is closer to becoming a general means, which regulates our emotional sensitivity in general.

### The Focus of Regulating Means
Never lend your car to anyone to whom you have given birth.
—Erma Bombeck

The focus of regulating means can vary and accordingly various classifications are possible in this regard. One important classification concerns whether these means focus on the event generating the emotion or the person experiencing it. The means focusing on the event may be regarded as direct means and those on the person as indirect ones. Evaluating or analyzing the emotional situation to determine its cause is an example of the first group, while listening to music or exercising is an example of the second group. To give another example, if someone has insulted me and made me angry, I may either directly clarify the issue with this person, or avoid confrontation by changing my emotional attitude. Whereas in direct, problem-focused means we try to change reality, in indirect, person-focused means we try to change our attitude toward reality. Changing our attitude can be done, for example, by avoiding the emotional situation through distancing ourselves from it or denying its very existence.

Other possible classifications of the focus of regulating means concern (a) whether the regulating means focus on increasing or decreasing emotional intensity, and (b) whether the regulating means focus on negative or positive emotional states.

Most regulating means focus on increasing or maintaining the intensity of positive emotional states and decreasing or eliminating negative emotional states. This is self-evident in Spinoza's view which, as mentioned, assumes that each individual strives to maintain his or her existence and that positive emotions express a person's passage from a lesser to a greater perfection, while negative emotions express a person's passage from a greater to a lesser perfection. From an evolutionary perspective as well, positive emotions are elicited by situations that are beneficial to us and negative emotions by harmful situations.

There are, however, situations in which we seek to increase negative emotions. For example, we watch sad movies or deliberately take various actions which increase our anger or hate toward someone. As mentioned above, in these cases the increase of negative emotions in the short run may have a beneficial outcome in the long run. Thus, the sad movie may prepare us emotionally for sad events in real life. Similarly, increasing our anger or hate toward someone may save us a lot of trouble in the future. Increasing our anger toward someone may also be a substitute for increasing our envy toward this person. Since envy has greater negative implications for our personality, substituting anger for envy may be beneficial in the larger context.

Concerning moods, we can distinguish in a similar manner between regulating means which aim to raise our energy level, thereby making us feel better, and those which attempt to reduce our tension, thereby making us feel less bad. Many means combine both aims. The most common means of increasing energy or alertness are rest, taking a shower or splashing water on the face, getting some fresh air, keeping busy, drinking a caffeinated beverage, listening to music, and eating something. The most common means of reducing tension are being with someone, controlling our thoughts, listening to music, exercising, using a relaxation technique, resting, engaging in nervous behavior (e.g., pacing, biting nails, biting a pencil), and engaging in stress management activities (e.g., organizing oneself, planning ahead, making lists). Both the above groups of means are presented in order of their frequency of usage in everyday life.[7]

Another classification of the focus of regulating means refers to the six intensity variables, namely, the event's strength, reality, and relevancy, and background circumstances referring to our accountability, readiness, and deservingness. A different perception of one of these variables may increase or decrease emotional intensity.

To illustrate the ways in which regulating means refer to intensity variables, consider the means by which Janet's jealousy can be reduced despite rumors suggesting that her husband Ed is having an affair. Janet can undermine the *event's strength* by believing that this is not a real affair, but merely a few kisses and hugs. She may also dismiss the *reality of the event* by choosing not to believe in its occurrence and endorsing Ed's denial of the affair. Another way to reduce the negative impact of the event is to assume that its occurrence has no *relevance* to her self-image or her relationship with Ed. This can be done, for example, by remembering that Ed was a womanizer long before he met her and that he attaches no significance to his extramarital affairs; he regards these as vitamins he needs to take from time to time. Janet can also assume that the initiation of the affair was beyond Ed's control and that he was, in a sense, forced into the affair, thus reducing his *accountability*. Janet's jealousy would also be reduced if she *expected* such affairs. She can say to herself that her husband is so handsome and famous that women will naturally try to have an affair with him, and some of them will finally succeed. Janet can also reduce her jealousy by thinking that in light of Ed's strong sexual drive and her own weak sexual drive, he *deserves* to be with other women. These affairs may also compensate him for the great effort he is investing in his work. The above means of reducing jealousy can be used with respect to behavioral, cognitive, and evaluative means. For example, Janet can dismiss the reality of her husband's love affairs by avoiding stories about them, not paying attention to them, or adopting the evaluative attitude of having an unshakable, strong belief in her husband's honesty.

Sometimes, a specific manner of regulating emotions influences a few intensity variables simultaneously. When horrible atrocities occur in a remote country and many people (as well as the media) do not seek details of these deeds, the negative impact is reduced by making the event both less real and less close to us.

To further illustrate the ways in which regulating means use the various intensity variables, let us consider the reasons people give for refusing dates. These reasons are primarily impersonal, uncontrollable, and unstable, even though the true reasons may be quite different.[8] A major reason for such white lies is concern about the rejectee's possible emotional reaction. People are less distressed by rejection when it is due to impersonal reasons ("I'm going out of town") than when it is due to their own characteristics ("You're a boring person"). A common excuse in this regard is "You are too good for me." Impersonal reasons reduce the relevance of the event to the rejectee's self-image and hence reduce the event's strength. People are also less distressed by uncontrollable reasons (the rejector has to study that night) than controllable ones (the rejector does not want to go to a movie that night). Reducing controllability here reduces emotional intensity. Also, unstable, temporary reasons (the rejector is ill) are less depressing than more stable, permanent reasons (the rejector is engaged to be married). Unstable, temporary reasons reduce somewhat the reality of the rejection and hence emotional intensity.

The phenomenon of refusing dates by offering reasons which reduce the hurt to the other person is so common by now that it is no longer so effective. In the television series *Seinfeld*, a woman who wants to stop dating George explains: "It's not you [who is to be blamed for this], it's me." This hurts George, mostly because he claims that no one else should be entitled to use this line, which he believes he invented and has often used. Indeed, in another episode, George, in an attempt to get rid of his current girlfriend, says: "You can do better than me. You could throw a dart out the window and hit someone better than me. I'm no good!"

Although we are willing to reduce the pain of the person from whom we wish to separate, there are some limits to what we are prepared to do for other people. For example, a man may plan to offer several reasons for reducing the personal liability of the woman from whom he wants to separate, but at their next meeting she anticipates him and suggests the value of such a separation, while, of course, trying to reduce his personal liability. Such a situation is bound to hurt the man. It is true that there is now no danger that the woman will be hurt by the separation (and this was his primary purpose), but preventing the hurt was not achieved by a generous (though superficial) sacrifice on his behalf, but in a manner which places him as the inferior—after all, he knows that the reasons given are merely an attempt to reduce his pain and are not genuine.

## The Nature of Regulating Means

### Behavioral Means

The only cure for grief is action.
—George Henry Lewes

When women are depressed, they eat or go shopping. Men invade another country. It's a whole different way of thinking.
—Elayne Boosler

Behavioral means of regulating emotions are common and involve popular activities, such as exercising, reading, working, listening to music, watching TV, going for a walk, being with people, eating, and shopping. Most of the behavioral means are indirect strategies for avoiding the circumstances that intensify the given emotion or for pursuing circumstances that generate other emotions. Thus, to avoid fear, we shut our eyes or change the channel when a frightening scene is about to be shown on television; to avoid fear of heights, we do not climb mountains; to avoid romantic love, monks do not meet women; to induce happiness, we dwell on positive memories. Similarly, some parents try to prevent their children from witnessing negative events that provoke emotions like sadness or anger. Consider the following advice, suggested by Kant, for reducing anger:

> When an angry man comes up to you in a room, to say harsh words to you in intense indignation, try politely to make him sit down; if you succeed, his reproaches already become milder, since the comfort of sitting is [a form] of relaxation, which is incompatible with the threatening gestures and shouting one can use when standing.[9]

Here, the mere change in one's posture is of emotional significance, as it prevents the posture typical of anger.

Although behavioral means are mainly distracting mechanisms, some of them may be considered as direct mechanisms which attempt to rectify a situation. For example, by adopting the practice of moderation in action, we can directly change our emotional behavior and even our whole emotional responsiveness. Preserving moderation while feeling angry may replace anger with another nonemotional state. Common affiliative-communicative activities, such as phoning, talking to, or simply being with someone, usually involve indirect strategies for controlling emotions. By being with other people, we divert some attention from our own situation to that of others and thereby reduce emotional tension. However, such social activities can also deal directly with our emotional concerns. Thus, talking to people who hurt and engaging in activities with them may directly rectify the situation by giving rise to other emotions.

Behavioral means are readily available, and their impact is immediate. Indeed, these means are quite common and effective. Thus, exercise appears to be the most effective mood-regulating behavior. Other useful behavioral means (listed in the order of their effectiveness) are listening to music; phoning, talking to, or simply being with someone; tending to chores; resting, napping, or sleeping; avoiding the person causing the mood; and being alone. Generally, active means are more successful in changing unhappy emotional states than are passive means. Most distraction activities, such as chores, hobbies, fun activities, shopping, reading, and writing, are considered by people to be successful means of changing negative emotional states. A notable exception is watching TV, whose success rate in changing negative emotional states is apparently low. Nevertheless, more Americans reported getting pleasure from television than from sex, food, hobbies, religion, marriage, money, or sports.[10]

Behavioral means are usually of use in regulating specific emotional reactions, rather than in regulating emotional sensitivity in general. Behavioral escape is limited in its usefulness, since this means usually modifies our encounter with reality, but changes neither our personality nor reality. There is always the possibility that we will have to face the reality at some future time, and the accompanying emotional intensity may then be increased. Many behavioral means are types of escape devices which can be compared to taking aspirin: they fail to cure the illness, but they help us to cope better with its symptoms. Nevertheless, behavioral means are generally adaptive because they are readily available and have immediate results. As in other cases, excessive use of behavioral means can be maladaptive since such use may ignore crucial information about reality.[11]

Behavioral means, either direct or indirect, are often not specific to each intensity variable, but rather affect global factors such as our overall mood or the focus of our attention. Listening to music in order to reduce anger does not affect specific variables of the anger, but instead changes our global mood by diverting our attention to something pleasant. On the other hand, speaking to a friend about the inevitability of the event which generated the anger may reduce the weight of the specific variable of controllability.

*Cognitive Means*
Glory is fleeting, but obscurity is forever.
—Napoleon Bonaparte

The streets are safe in Philadelphia. It's only the people who make them unsafe.
—Frank Rizzo, ex-police chief and mayor of Philadelphia

Cognitive means of regulating emotions are very popular and can be found quite early in our development. Examples of such means include diverting our attention, thinking positively, giving ourselves a pep talk, and interpreting the situation in a way which avoids unpleasant implications.

Cognitive means can be in the form of attention deployment or manipulating the emotional content. When we use the means of attention deployment, we divert our attention from the emotional concern to something else. Thus, it is often better to ignore an insult than to respond to it. Such means are similar to behavioral escape devices in that they use indirect strategies. Whereas behavioral means refer to the situations themselves, cognitive means refer to our cognitive content. In using behavioral means, we approach or avoid certain people, places, or objects in order to regulate our emotions; in using cognitive means, we distract our attention from or concentrate on certain descriptions of people, places, or objects. Cognitive means reduce emotional intensity by avoiding thinking about certain emotional circumstances, rather than by escapist behavior that actually removes us from these circumstances. Such means are valuable in that they require less investing of resources than does escapist behavior. However, in cases where physical proximity to the emotional event may prevent us from ignoring it, the usefulness of cognitive means is limited, and they may need to be supplemented by behavioral means.

Cognitive means can also involve direct strategies in which we manipulate the significance of the given emotional circumstances. We can interpret an event in a way that changes its emotional significance and hence regulates emotional intensity or even alters the nature of the given emotion. For example, we can interpret a situation in such a way that our inferiority seems slighter or less relevant, thereby reducing or avoiding envy. Similarly, we may interpret a mate's extramarital relationship as due to "sexual curiosity" rather than preference for the rival. There is a story which tells of a husband who, when asked whether he cares that his wife is having an affair, answered: "I'd rather have 50 percent of the shares of a good business, than 100 percent of a poor one."

The choice of a different emotional perspective makes the whole difference. Flight attendants use a broad array of techniques to avert anger toward obnoxious passengers. A common tactic is to conceive of such a passenger as suffering, thus deserving of pity rather than anger. They focus on what the other person might be thinking and feeling, that is, they imagine a reason that excuses his behavior, such as fear of flying. The method of changing our perspective has been found to be most useful in treatment programs for sexual offenders. The offenders were asked to imagine what the victim felt, and went through a simulated reenactment of the crime, this time playing the role of the victim. Sex offenders who have been through the program had only half the rate of subsequent offenses after release compared with those who had no such treatment.[12]

Cognitive interpretations of emotional situations are often expressed in our tendency to view the current situation in a way that minimizes negative emotional load and maximizes emotional gain. Denial and depersonalization are instances of the former, and anticipation of positive events exemplifies the latter.[13]

In light of the partial nature of emotions, a common cognitive manner of regulating emotions is changing, and in particular broadening, our perspective. Emotions are partial in the sense that they are directed at very few people—mainly those included in our reference and social groups. The people within these groups are most relevant to the achievement of our goals and to our self-esteem. As suggested, the borderlines of these groups are to a certain extent flexible; hence, including or excluding someone from these groups can change our emotions toward this person. Since one is always better off than someone else, provided one picks the right dimension for evaluation, determining the borderlines of our reference and social groups is of immense emotional significance. In one study of breast cancer patients, lumpectomy patients compared themselves favorably to mastectomy patients, but mastectomy patients never evaluated themselves against lumpectomy patients. Older women diagnosed with cancer considered themselves to be more fortunate than younger women diagnosed with cancer since they had contracted the disease at a later stage in life. The women with the poorest prognoses consoled themselves with the fact they were not in pain or not yet dying. Dying people often focus on the fact that they have achieved spiritual peace or lived a long and full life, compared with people who might never experience these things. Evaluating oneself favorably against others who are worse off can be a successful way of coping with stressful events and restoring self-esteem.[14]

Changing the scope of our reference and social groups can also be accomplished via both behavioral and evaluative means. A useful behavioral means in this regard is that of enlarging our social group in such a manner that it will consist of many people who are not very relevant to our self-esteem. Such a diversification of our social group usually broadens our perspective and hence often reduces emotional intensity. An evaluative means of achieving such a decrease would be, for example, if we changed the value that we attach to people within our reference group.

Narrowing down our perspective typically results in intensifying the given emotion. By focusing our cognitive resources on limited objects, these objects become more significant for us. Focusing our attention on the possibility of our mate having an affair increases jealousy, and constantly thinking about a forthcoming positive event intensifies our hope. Broadening our perspective typically has the effect of reducing emotional intensity. As the proverb goes, "company in distress makes sorrow less." Comparing our misfortune with those of others makes our misfortune seem less grave—hence the reduction in emotional intensity. Similar considerations underlie the following practical advice: "Remember that whatever misfortune may be your lot, it could only be worse in Cleveland." Broadening our perspective creates a certain detachment which is not typical of emotions.[15]

There are, however, situations in which broadening our perspective may intensify emotions. In these situations we are usually concerned with strong events having wide implications for our life; understanding these implications may indicate that we are actually confronted with an event that is much stronger than that perceived through a narrow perspective. Thus, the grief of a teenage boy on the death of his father may be more intense than that of his little brother, since the brother cannot yet comprehend all the terrible implications of the father's death.

To illustrate how a change in perspective can reduce emotional intensity, consider, for instance, envy. Envy, which involves feeling inferior to someone from our reference group, may be reduced by either (a) limiting the group's scope in a way that excludes this person from the group, or (b) broadening the group's scope in a way that includes other attributes besides the one which makes us feel inferior.

Let us see how Robert, an average philosopher, reduces or even avoids feeling envy by limiting the scope of his reference group. He may consider a well-established philosopher as being outside his reference group since she is at a level far above him. Similarly, Robert, who deals with the philosophy of mind, does not regard a somewhat better philosopher who works on Greek philosophy as being superior to him; Greek philosophy, he contends, is not real philosophy, and anyway is not as complex as the philosophy of mind. Then Robert may hear of another more successful philosopher who also works in the field of the philosophy of mind. Robert excludes this person from his reference group since, while Robert examines the complex issue of emotions, this person discusses the old and redundant mind-body problem. Robert then discovers an even better philosopher who deals with emotions; he avoids envying this person by assuring himself that, in the important field of the philosophy of envy, he is still one of the best. In these instances, uncomfortable comparisons are avoided by the potentially envied people being seen as not comparable, that is, as not belonging to the same reference group. William James once said that he would feel mortified if he met someone who was a better psychologist than he, but would not feel at all threatened in the presence of an eminent scholar of Ancient Greek.

Envy may also be reduced if the scope of the reference group is enlarged in such a way that it includes other attributes besides the one to which we are inferior. Thus, a perspective that does not merely focus on the other's superior position but also on that person's character may reduce envy. An envious person may think that although her colleague surpasses her on the professional level, she has such an obnoxious husband no one would wish to be in her situation. Likewise, reducing our envy of a beautiful person may consist of diverting our attention to other attributes of this person. Accordingly, Elster notes that the stereotype that beautiful blonds are dumb may be due to other women's envy rather than to male chauvinism. Indeed, it was found that good-looking women have difficulty in forming friendships with other women; they are less liked by other women, including other good-looking women. This hostile attitude expresses the wish to exclude the good-looking women from other women's reference groups. As Nancy Etcoff notes, since we try to control our social environment to make ourselves look good, we do not want our own light dimmed by having a beacon next to us.[16] Similarly, if the envied person is kind and modest, envy may decrease since it can be assumed that this person respects us. Isocrates, the ancient Athenian orator, said that we envy those who surpass us in intelligence or in any other respect, unless we are won over by their daily kindness.[17] The absence of envy in such a case may be due to our interpretation that these people deserve their good fortune or that their kindness implies respect for others rather than a feeling of superiority.

Envy may also decrease if the object of our envy is mean, since the negative evaluation of his character will outbalance his superiority; accordingly, it has been claimed that "only the shameless envy the wicked." What matters in reducing envy in these cases is not so much how we evaluate the object, but that we do so from a broader perspective which refers to many aspects of the person. The broader the perspective, the lesser is the weight of the particular inferiority that generates the envy. We may also broaden our perspective by looking beyond the given circumstances. For example, we can assume that our inferiority is temporary, either because our genuine value is soon to be revealed or other fundamental factors are about to change the situation.

Envy may also be reduced by using behavioral and evaluative means. A behavioral approach would be one in which we do not choose those obviously superior to us as friends and acquaintances. Evaluative means may devalue the desired end by claiming, for instance, that the other's achievement is not worth the sacrifice it required. As mentioned, we can also devalue the envied person by broadening our perspective to include domains in which the other is inferior to us.

The partial nature of emotions does not mean that the fewer people we are associated with, the more intense our emotions are. What is important is the type of relationship we have with other people and in particular the relation between our social group and our reference group. The size of the social group may have different effects upon emotional intensity. A smaller quantity may sometimes means a higher quality of relationship. Nevertheless, there is a certain quantity—which may differ from one person to another—above which it is difficult to conduct an intense emotional relationship with each person. However, the more people with whom we have social contacts, the more events around us are likely to have emotional significance.

It may be argued that we actually regulate all of our emotions, as the generation of emotions depends on our cognitive interpretation of the situation, and we interpret the situation in the way we wish. At the basis of this argument is the contention that there is no difference between cognitive interpretation and cognitive manipulation. This contention also underlies the claim that there is no truth, since any claim to truth depends on our cognitive capacities. I agree that such dependence is present in both cognitive interpretation and manipulation, but this does not eliminate the difference between them. Cognitive interpretation is person-dependent but is not arbitrary or illusory in the same way as cognitive manipulation; it takes full account of environmental properties.

It must be admitted, however, that it is sometimes hard to distinguish between cognitive interpretation and cognitive manipulation. Consider, for instance, the cognitive activity of flight attendants aiming to avert their anger toward obnoxious passengers, and the cognitive activity of nurses aimed at facilitating compassion toward their patients. Both the flight attendants and nurses try to interpret the behavior of obnoxious people in a way which will lessen clients' responsibility for their obnoxious behavior. This kind of interpretation makes it easier for them to give their clients good service and treatment. Although both flight attendants and nurses use similar cognitive means, we usually evaluate their activities differently: the means used by flight attendants are considered as cognitive manipulation, whereas those used by nurses are considered as cognitive interpretation. This is so since we perceive the obnoxious patient as deserving of compassion and his suffering as substantial. On the other hand, the obnoxious passenger is perceived as deserving of anger and his misfortune as insubstantial. When nurses use regulating means to prevent their anger, we perceive this as a correct cognitive interpretation, whereas the means used by flight attendants is perceived as cognitive manipulation intended to keep the company's clients happy.

Unlike escape devices, cognitive interpretations do not necessarily avoid reality; nevertheless, they are likely to be illusory when used excessively. For example, when people deny or imagine the presence of an emotion, such denial is essentially an illusory remedy, often with harmful consequences. Cognitive manipulations are frequently a kind of wishful thinking rather than objective cognition. However, when the imaginative projection has some basis in reality, these procedures can be valuable and indeed are commonly used.

*Evaluative Means*
The best way out is always through.
—Robert Frost

Evaluative means are the most profound and difficult means of regulating emotions, as they often involve modification of specific norms and personal architecture. Whereas cognitive means are mainly concerned with changing our interpretation of the emotional object, evaluative means are concerned with changing our attitudes toward the emotional object. The cognitive interpretation may turn out to be inadequate to our surroundings; for an evaluative change, the requirement for some correspondence with reality is less relevant.

Evaluative means of regulating emotions can refer to *specific* evaluations underlying specific emotions, as well as to *profound* evaluative patterns underlying our emotional sensitivity.

Consider, for example, jealousy, which may be generated when seeing our spouse speaking intimately to another person. A behavioral method of decreasing our jealousy would be to avoid looking at them, and a cognitive method would be to interpret their conversation as limited to business matters. A specific evaluative manner would be to evaluate this intimate conversation as meaningless for the spouse. The more profound evaluative change which modifies the evaluative patterns of jealousy is expressed, for example, by changing our self-evaluation in a way that increases our confidence, or by attaching less weight to the exclusive nature of the relationship with our spouse or to our spouse's behavior with other people.

Another example of a specific evaluative change is found in studies showing that encouraging subjects to reappraise negatively valenced films resulted in decreased negative emotional experience—at least when these films were not extremely disgusting.[18] An evaluative change may also occur when adopting a modest perspective which recognizes that limitations are part and parcel of the human condition. Recognition of our inevitable limitations can assuage the negative emotions, such as envy and sadness, which often accompany our knowledge of personal flaws and failures.[19]

Since emotional evaluations are essentially spontaneous, that is, activated by existing evaluative patterns, then profound modification of these patterns is more useful than specific attempts to alter a particular evaluative response. In many cases, however, this is not possible.

Profound evaluative means do not merely involve surface behavior, where we try to change our outward appearance, but a deep change in which we alter ourselves and spontaneously express a real emotion that has been self-induced. In surface behavior we may deceive others about our real emotions, but we do not deceive ourselves. Such a separation of display and emotion is hard to sustain. With a profound change, however, our behavior is a natural consequence of that change, and feigning is unnecessary.[20]

Sometimes emotional changes occur when one pretends to feel a certain emotion, but such deception directed at others frequently becomes self-deception. Since it is hard to maintain a separation between an emotion and its display for a long time, one needs to reduce the strain by altering either the display or the emotion. If, for professional reasons, the display is important, then the best way to reduce the strain is to assume the required emotion. Take, for example, social workers who need to exhibit positive emotional attitudes toward their clients. If someone tends to find needy people irritating, then this person is not suited to be a social worker, as the role will demand a continual discrepancy between emotional experience and emotional display. Adopting a basically favorable tendency toward the needy may avoid the discrepancy, but since this would involve a change in attitude, it would be difficult to achieve. On the other hand, it may be the case that a certain social worker possesses a basic positive tendency, but because of temporary circumstances, such as a bad mood, finds it difficult to exhibit the necessary positive attitude. In this situation, behavioral and cognitive means of regulating emotions are the most appropriate.

Exhibiting a positive attitude is also required in commercial sex. Thus, prostitutes report that their clients seem to want reassurance of their prowess sometimes even more than they want sex. Similarly, a survey of women's sexual behavior indicates that enjoyment of intercourse for a large majority of women depends on their belief in their partners' honesty in expressing affection. Another survey indicates that both women and men care for the sexual satisfaction of their partners.[21] In the case of commercial sex, reducing the discrepancy between surface and deep attitudes would be impossible—no change in evaluative patterns could enable prostitutes to enjoy sex with anyone at any time. Using behavioral and cognitive means may be more efficient in producing the appropriate display, but their success in eliminating the emotional discrepancy is limited.

The evaluative manner of regulating emotions does not change their spontaneous nature; the basic evaluative patterns may have changed, but their spontaneous activation remains the same. Also, the behavioral and cognitive means do not essentially influence the spontaneous nature of emotions, but rather select the desired emotional responses by facilitating the appropriate circumstances, and thereby encouraging or postponing the activation of the emotional state. Experiencing an emotion is not a matter of a voluntary, deliberative decision, but of the system being in the appropriate conditions. Sometimes placing the system in such conditions is a matter of a few, simple actions, and sometimes it requires lengthy and profound alterations.

### Combining All Means

You can get more with a kind word and a gun than you can with a kind word alone.
—Al Capone

In light of the fact that there are many means of regulating emotions, a useful way of succeeding in such regulation is to combine several means at the same time.

To illustrate the presence of the three basic means of regulating emotions, consider how these can prevent us from loving a particular person. Behavioral means would make us avoid seeing the person with whom we wish not to fall in love or with whom we are already in love—according to the tradition of "out of sight, out of mind." In the cognitive realm, we may focus our attention on the person's unlikable attributes; we can also interpret as unlikable some attributes which, under normal circumstances, would be considered otherwise. As for the evaluative domain, we can decrease or even eliminate our love toward a particular person by altering some of our evaluative norms of the ideal mate. Thus, we may start to consider kindness, rather than external appearance, as the most important trait in a partner.

We should distinguish in this connection between self-persuasion and persuasion by other people. Thus, a woman told me that someone tried to persuade her to have sex with him by saying that "beauty is of no importance for me." Such a claim is important for the self-regulation of this man's emotions, but it is of negative value in regulating the other's emotions. (Just for the historical record, the two did not have a sexual relationship—at least, this is what I was told.)

In comparison with love, sexual desire is easier to provoke or terminate; provoking such a desire can be bought and sold. (Although commercial sex is quite successful, it has its own emotional limitations; prostitutes offer no money-back guarantees.) Behavioral means of provoking sexual desire usually alter the circumstances in which sexual activity takes place; for example, changing time and location, changing partners, or watching pornographic movies. The cognitive means of provoking sexual desire make extensive use of imagination, such as imagining that we are with someone other than the person we are actually with, or imagining the person we are with to be more attractive than he actually is. The evaluative patterns underlying sexual desire are harder to change. Nevertheless, some such changes are available as well. Thus, a profound religious belief may decrease sexual desire for anyone other than one's mate.

In the same vein, we can increase our compassion toward a disadvantaged person by frequent association with this person, by focusing on this person's qualities and the things we have in common, and by making our basic evaluative framework more egalitarian and less achievement-oriented. In another example, the behavioral means of dealing with envy may be to avoid seeing or being with the successful person. The cognitive procedures may include different interpretations of our own deeds and those of others. We can also change our evaluative patterns in such a manner that another person's success will not be considered our own failure, or by convincing ourselves that the other person's success is actually not relevant to our self-esteem. When someone says that he would not accept the top job even if it were offered to him on a gold plate, this person has adjusted (or at least want us to believe that he has adjusted) his evaluative patterns in such a way that it would not hurt his self-esteem if he were not offered the job. When the fox kept away from the grapes and declared the grapes to be sour, he did not change his basic values: he did not deny the value of sweetness. He simply interpreted the situation as one in which these particular grapes were below his accepted standard. A fox desiring a more profound evaluative change would have said: I really do not care for sweet things; only children enjoy such things.[22]

The means of regulating emotions differ, both in our ability to achieve them and in their prospects of success. The change in evaluative patterns is the hardest to achieve, since some of these patterns are set in early years and become increasingly inflexible. By the time we reach adulthood, most of these patterns are already part of our well-established nature, and changing them requires a radical change in our character and lifestyle. A profound change in our evaluative patterns may also require reflective critical examination. Although our ability to change our evaluative patterns is limited, such changes do promise better and more permanent results.

A change in our evaluative patterns may reduce one type of discrepancy between our present state and another compared state, but at the same time it may enlarge another kind of discrepancy. For example, changing our evaluative patterns by settling for less may reduce the discrepancy between our current state and the ideal one, but may increase the discrepancy between our current state and the state in which significant others, such as spouse, parents, or friends, believe we ought to be. Consideration of social norms and opinions of other people further limit the possible range of evaluative changes.[23]

Behavioral and cognitive means of regulating emotions are easier to achieve but are sometimes illusory. They are useful in helping us to avoid or create circumstances in which emotions are likely to appear, or to reduce the intensity of a given emotion. They are less effective in preventing the appearance of emotions in unavoidable circumstances. Moreover, when we consider the central role of imagination in emotions, the limited efficacy of various escape means becomes clear. Even if we refrain from meeting our beloved, the beloved may still be in our mind. Escape devices, which fail to change our situation in a profound way, are often a short-lived illusory remedy.

There are many circumstances in which behavioral escape devices are not available and evaluative means are hard to achieve—thus leaving cognitive means as the most feasible ones. In modern service work, one cannot use behavioral escape devices such as avoiding clients, and it is unlikely that workers could change their evaluative patterns in a short period of time. When flight attendants are required not only to appear happy but to be happy, and bill collectors are expected to be angry, the most efficient way to fulfill their work requirements is to use cognitive means. Accordingly, they might reinterpret the situation by adopting another perspective—usually that of the client or employer. This practice may, in the end, facilitate an evaluative change.

There are individual differences in the use of emotion-regulating means. One difference is age. Young people are more likely to listen to music or engage in pleasant activities to change their negative affective attitudes. Older people are more likely to tend to chores or engage in religious or spiritual activities for this purpose. Overweight people reported a greater likelihood of eating when they are in a negative affective attitude.

Another individual difference is gender. Women are more likely to use cognitive means such as rumination, whereas men are more likely to use distracting behavioral means. When using behavioral means, women tend to seek social interaction more. In response to stress and depression, women are more likely than men to use food, and men are more likely than women to use alcohol and drugs. Shopping helps many women, but not most men, to change their bad moods. Women tend more to adopt passive, rather than active, means of dealing with their emotions than do men.[24]

Individual differences are also expressed in different emotional comfort zones. An *emotional comfort zone* is the range of emotional arousal in which the individual has comfortable feelings. Too high a level of arousal leads to discomfort, but too low a level results in boredom. Pleasure is the experience of a change from either too much or too little arousal back to a level of optimal comfort.[25] The *core* of the comfort zone is that range within which the individual actively experiences enjoyable feelings; the rest of the comfort zone consists of the area which lacks adverse feelings. The comfort zone is not merely defined by a certain degree of arousal, but also by the nature of this arousal, that is, whether it includes enjoyable or adverse feelings. In regulating emotional sensitivity, we try to expand the comfort zone; in regulating specific emotional reactions, we attempt to include as many events as possible within the core of the comfort zone. By expanding our comfort zone, we are expanding our life experiences and hence living in a more fulfilling manner. When we drift out of our comfort zone, we instinctively obey homeostatic laws and try to return to our comfort zone, and in particular to its core.[26]

The value of regulating our emotions has been often doubted on the basis that sincere emotional experiences are important for our well-being. Of course, I agree that emotions have an important functional role in our life and we should not try to eliminate them. However, emotional regulation should not be perceived as attempting to eliminate emotional sensitivity but rather as trying to guide the emotions—that is, to foster certain emotional states and weaken others. In particular, such regulation reduces the intensity of excessive emotional states, which hinder our normal activities, and increases the intensity of certain positive emotional states. Emotional regulation can indeed have positive implications for various aspects of our life such as mental health, social relationships, and greater success in work. This does not mean, of course, that the more we regulate our emotions, the healthier and better we are. Regulation has a positive value when it is done moderately and only in certain circumstances; in other circumstances, emotional regulation may be harmful.[27]

Regulating our emotions should not be done only when we are in the midst of stormy negative emotional states we do not know how to cope with. It can and should be done in a way which will increase the relative weight of positive emotions in our life. It is common to speak favorably about people after their death. Such descriptions reveal to us high-quality characteristics we all admire. Why were such descriptions absent when these people were alive? I would argue that we should adopt more often the perspective people take toward their dead acquaintances. Taking such a perspective will give us an opportunity to better see the positive aspects of other people and hence considerably increase the frequency and intensity of positive emotions.

Regulating emotions is not only the private business of the individual but is also practiced by society and other institutions. Various means of social education can be seen as ways to modify our evaluative patterns. However, these are largely means that we do not consciously choose to employ. There are some kinds of social education whose initiation depends on our will. Thus, by reading certain writers, watching certain movies, or engaging in actions that are typically associated with certain emotions, we can, to a certain extent, deliberately mold our emotional capacities. Society and various institutions also employ behavioral and cognitive procedures to regulate emotions. Social rules and institutions limiting our behavior and views often regulate our emotions. A teaching hospital, for example, prepares the environment for medical students facing their first autopsy in order to reduce the emotional impact of the event. Similarly, by preventing children from going to nightclubs or watching certain movies, we regulate their emotions to a certain extent. In light of such social procedures to regulate emotions, it is plausible that certain social groups, especially those that are historically disadvantaged, are to a greater extent subject to emotional regulation than are other groups. Thus, there is evidence that women do more emotion-regulating than men, especially with regard to activities that affirm, enhance, and celebrate the well-being and status of others. This runs counter to the traditional image of women as more prone to uncontrolled emotions.[28]

Awareness of the nature of our emotional (or more generally, affective) state is fundamental to regulating emotions. However, it is not clear what type of influence such an awareness may have on emotional intensity.[29]

Awareness of the nature of an emotion may have different effects on that emotion. Concerning many emotions, in particular negative ones like envy and anger, such self-awareness typically reduces their intensity and may even eliminate them altogether. This is so because awareness requires some detachment from the emotional situation, which clashes with the subject-object closeness typical of emotions. Concerning other emotions, in particular positive emotions such as love, the opposite is true: awareness of being in love usually intensifies love. Love, as well as some other positive emotions, has the nature of a self-fulfilling prophecy: when we believe we are in love, we behave in ways that are likely to reinforce love. Thus, being an optimist often increases people's success, which in turn enhances optimism.

The situation, however, is more complex, since there are additional relevant considerations. For example, awareness of the nature of romantic love may have different effects upon the intensity of our love. If we find out that love is based on aspects which we consider as insignificant—for instance, the financial resources of the beloved's family—then its intensity will decrease; when those aspects are significant for us, love will intensify. Our determination of what is significant and what is insignificant can sometimes be revised; however, in some cases significance depends on basic values, which are not easily altered. Similarly, Elster argues that awareness of one's anger may either dampen or consolidate the emotion: it would be dampened if the awareness induces shame, guilt, or prudence, which urges me to control my anger, or it could be consolidated if the realization that I have no good reason to be angry induces me to find one.[30]

Such complexities prevent us from predicting the exact impact that self-awareness will have on emotional intensity. However, it is clear that self-awareness is crucial for coping with emotions as it allows us to exercise some self-control.

Is there a difference in our ability to rid ourselves of an unwanted emotion and our ability to provoke an emotion in ourselves? The answer to this question may differ from one individual to another and from one emotion to another, but nevertheless a few global considerations can be indicated. Generally, it is more difficult to get rid of an unwanted specific emotion, or reduce its intensity, than to induce in ourselves a specific emotion, or to increase its intensity.[31] In light of the intense and partial nature of emotions, our degree of freedom while subject to an intense emotion is quite limited. Take, for example, the cognitive method of attention. Not paying attention to the emotional object is a useful means of reducing emotional intensity. However, in intense emotions it is typically difficult to avoid paying attention to the emotional object, as that object is constantly occupying our mind. As time goes by and the emotion becomes less intense, it is easier to apply the various means of emotional regulation. The above considerations are valid concerning short-term acute emotions, but not necessarily regarding long-term sentiments. Provoking in ourselves a profound sentiment such as love usually takes time and involves building a profound relationship. Often, building such a relationship can be more difficult than destroying it.

*Summary*

Be grateful for luck. Pay the thunder no mind—listen to the birds. And don't hate nobody.
—Eubie Blake

Regulating emotions is quite common in our everyday life. Nevertheless, reaching an optimal level of regulation usually requires long practice. There are many kinds of regulating means; they can be classified in light of their extent, focus, nature, and content. I have focused on the division which refers to the nature of the regulating means and which divides such means into behavioral, cognitive, and evaluative means. I have suggested that whereas behavioral and cognitive means are easier to apply, evaluative means have a more profound impact. Since regulating emotions can be accomplished in many different ways, it is useful to be aware of these ways so that we may utilize them in our daily life.

# Chapter 9

# Emotions and Morality

What is moral is what you feel good after and what is immoral is what you feel bad after.
—Ernest Hemingway

The long tradition that criticizes emotions as being irrational and nonfunctional also considers emotions to be essentially immoral. Having shown that emotions are functional and in a sense also rational, I can now demonstrate their importance in the moral domain. The difficulties in attaching to emotions a significant moral value stem from two basic characteristics of emotions: (1) the lack of intellectual deliberation, and (2) their partial nature. The first characteristic seems to contradict the possibility of assigning moral responsibility to emotions and the second characteristic would appear to contradict the general and egalitarian nature of many moral evaluations. I will argue that these characteristics eliminate neither emotional responsibility nor the role of emotions in morality; they do, however, introduce certain constraints in this regard.

## Emotions and Moral Responsibility

Vices are often habits rather than passions.
—Antoine Rivarol

The hottest places in Hell are reserved for those who in time of great moral crises maintain their neutrality.
—Dante Alighieri

Any discussion concerning the role of emotions in morality should address the issue of whether we can attribute responsibility to emotional behavior. Without such responsibility, the role of emotions in the moral domain cannot be significant. Indeed, the spontaneous nature of emotions leads people to argue that we are not responsible for them; hence, emotions are irrelevant to the moral domain. The major problem in this respect concerns the allegedly necessary presence of intellectual deliberations in behavior for which we are responsible. The problem may be formulated as follows:

1. Responsibility entails free choice; if we are not free to behave in a certain manner, then we are not responsible for this behavior.
2. Free choice entails an intellectual deliberation in which alternatives are considered and the best one is chosen. Without such consideration, we cannot clearly understand the possible alternatives and are not responsible for preferring one of them.
3. Since intellectual deliberations are absent from emotions, we cannot be responsible for our emotions.

Remarks such as, "I couldn't help it, I was madly in love with her," or "Ignore his action, he was overcome with anger," indicate that we sometimes do not attribute responsibility (or at least, full responsibility) to agents having certain emotions or acting emotionally. However, it is obvious that there are many circumstances in which we do impute individual responsibility for emotions. We praise and criticize people for their emotions; we speak of appropriate reasons for being afraid, or inappropriate grounds for hating someone. We often advise others to forbear from some emotions as when we say: "You have no reason to be angry." We may also urge them to adopt emotions as with the injunction: "Love your wife." The problem we face, then, is not whether we ascribe responsibility to persons for their emotions, but how such ascription is justified and what kind of responsibility is ascribed.

The major flaw in the argument denying responsibility for our emotions is that it presupposes a too simplistic picture of responsibility and emotions. I turn now to a more detailed discussion of this flaw.

Responsibility may be described as having two major aspects: causality and praiseworthiness (which also includes blameworthiness). In terms of causality, P is causally responsible for X if P is the cause of X. Thus, if P gives a glass containing poison to X and consequently X dies, then although P is causally responsible for X's death, P cannot be blamed if P did not know that the glass contained poison. Moral responsibility is not concerned with causal responsibility but with responsibility related to praise or blame.

Moral responsibility concerning praiseworthiness can be divided into direct and indirect responsibility.

Paradigmatic cases of direct responsibility encompass (a) intending to do and doing X freely, (b) the ability to avoid X, and (c) the ability to foresee the consequences of X. These factors are important in describing the ideal situation for complete and direct personal responsibility. It is hard to see how we can be directly responsible for something that we did not intend to do, were forced to do, were not able to avoid, or whose consequences we could not predict. However, the ideal situation in which all three factors are fully present is rare. There are different degrees of these factors, and it is impossible to find the highest degree in any given situation. Nevertheless, we often assign direct personal responsibility even if the ideal situation is not fully present.[1]

Personal responsibility is also assigned when these three factors are clearly absent at the time we perform the particular deed, but were present at some time in the past. Here we assign indirect responsibility. A drunken driver who causes a fatal accident and a drug-addicted person who steals to obtain money for drugs are examples of such cases. Indirect responsibility is assigned when we are responsible for cultivating the circumstances which gave rise to the blameworthy deed or attitude.

In addition to indirect responsibility, legal and moral systems recognize partial responsibility. For example, provocation is understood as a partial defense of murder, since it is seen as reducing the agent's responsibility: a successful provocation plea involves a concession of partial responsibility—hence the manslaughter conviction—but a denial of full responsibility.[2]

Our responsibility for our emotions is perceived to be less than our responsibility for our intellectual, calculated actions. This difference in responsibility is related to the different punishments we receive for emotional or intellectual actions. Emotional actions are punished less severely because we are perceived to be less able to avoid them. There are hardly any legal sanctions against having certain emotions, while nonlegal punishments for having particular emotions are more common. Thus, we may not want to live with someone who is jealous or angers easily. This sort of punishment is indirect in the sense that it is not a localized response to a particular emotion, but one factor in the negative assessment of a whole person. It is thus often the case that although people are perceived to be somehow responsible for their emotions, they are hardly punished for having them. A major reason for this is that we have merely an indirect and partial control over our emotions.

The personal responsibility we bear for our emotions is, by and large, indirect and partial. In this regard there is a legal distinction between responsibility for the emotions we experience and for the behavior stemming from such emotions. Thus, typically there are laws not against hating someone, but against some of the actions associated with hate. Similarly, we may not persecute a person for ceasing to love someone, but we may persecute someone for failing at the last moment to show up at his wedding ceremony. This distinction is based on the (justified) assumption that concerning such actions, our responsibility is often direct and of high degree, whereas concerning the emotional experience itself, it is usually indirect and partial.

The view that denies our responsibility for emotions often encompasses not just a narrow notion of responsibility but also a narrow picture of emotions. Emotions are reduced to fleeting, unreliable feelings over which we have little control and no responsibility. In the same way that we do not choose to be hungry, and accordingly are not responsible for it, it is assumed that we do not choose our emotions and are not responsible for them.[3]

Contrary to this view, emotions are obviously more complex than fleeting feelings. The presence of intentional components enable us to impute responsibility for emotions and consequently to criticize or praise them. Indeed, emotions may be criticized or praised with regard to their three intentional components: the cognition of the situation may be flawed, false, or partial; the evaluation of the situation may be flawed or inappropriate, as when based on unfounded, vague, or immoral grounds; and the motivational components of desires and conduct may, for instance, be self-defeating, excessive, socially destructive, or only of short-term value.

The whole emotional attitude may also be regarded as appropriate or inappropriate to the given circumstances. Thus, we may criticize ourselves for grieving too much or too little. Emotions may also be experienced as inadequate with regard to their timing. It is disputable whether all emotions, in particular love and grief, can be criticized in light of the above considerations, but it is clear that we do criticize or applaud people for having certain emotions.[4]

Typically, we cannot immediately induce ourselves or others to assume a certain emotion. We do not usually invoke emotions by a deliberate decision. We cannot experience, or stop experiencing, an emotion by simply deciding to do so. This, however, does not imply that there are no voluntary elements in experiencing emotions, or that we are incapable of regulating our emotions. Such regulation is, however, basically indirect. As indicated above, this can be accomplished by changing ourselves or our environment. We can cultivate or habituate emotions by attaching more or less value to certain things. For example, attaching much importance to the boss's opinion may increase vulnerability to fear and disappointment. Since emotions express our profound values, cultivating values may also be the cultivation of emotions. Furthermore, we can create or avoid the circumstances generating emotions. We may indirectly, but intentionally, make ourselves angry, sad, or envious by imagining that the circumstances typical of such emotions are indeed present. How we feel is less a matter of choice at the moment than a product of choice over time in which we habituate certain dispositions.[5]

The view of emotional responsibility suggested here is basically Aristotelian. For Aristotle, virtuous people have the kind of character that leads them to experience emotion in a proper way, as well as lead them to act in a proper way. Similarly, to display vice is to depart from the proper response; it is to show either excess or deficiency in our emotional and behavioral responses. To shape our character properly is partially our responsibility, but is neither entirely nor directly under our control. As we are responsible for our affective traits, so are we responsible for our emotions; the responsibility for our emotions may be even greater, since it is easier to manage them. Emotions and affective traits are not raw impulses, but rather socialized modes of response.[6]

Like other types of habituation, emotional habituation can be more successful if started at an early age. Accordingly, we have responsibility to educate our off-spring to generate the proper emotions in the proper circumstances. We teach our children "not just to avoid fire but to fear it, not just to consort with others but to love them, not just to repair wrongdoing but to suffer remorse and shame for its execution."[7] Habituating emotional dispositions is also possible with adults, but it is more difficult and limited.

There are different degrees to our flexibility, and hence different degrees of responsibility regarding our various affective attitudes. We have least responsi-bility for our affective traits since those were mainly shaped by genetic factors and early environmental factors. Nevertheless, affective traits can be modified to a certain degree: we can change our profound evaluative attitudes to some extent and in this way we may shape our affective traits.

Responsibility for our specific emotions is also of a lower degree since emotions are typically spontaneous reactions which are activated when certain circum-stances are present. However, in many situations we are able to take steps which can prevent us from entering into the emotional mode, or at least entering without great intensity. We are often responsible for being in circumstances which are espe-cially susceptible to the generation of certain emotions. Thus, if I know that every time I see a certain politician on television I become angry, and this is then expressed in my behavior toward my wife and children, then I have the moral obligation to avoid those circumstances, for instance, by turning off the television or going to the toilet. If I have already listened to this person for a few minutes, I will be in a situation similar to that of a drunken driver who is no longer able to control the wheel. My responsibility regarding this anger refers to my failure to avoid the circumstances which generate it.

Responsibility for our moods is of a greater degree since there are various manners of avoiding or regulating moods. The fact that moods last for a longer period of time enables us to use various means for regulating them. The greatest responsibility seems to be in regard to our sentiments. Sentiments are neither the product of genetic structure nor a spontaneous response of our emotional system. We have more time and more resources for modifying them—or even for pre-venting them from developing in the first place. Thus, we are the least responsi-ble for our personal tendency to anger, we are more responsible for getting angry in a certain situation, and even more responsible for being in a certain aggressive mood for a long time; the greatest responsibility concerns our ongoing hostility toward someone.

Our partial and indirect responsibility for our affective attitudes are expressed in two major ways: (1) responsibility for the nature of our affective attitudes, and (2) responsibility for being in circumstances which typically lead to such states. In both cases, our responsibility concerns not so much the particular activation of the affective response, but rather the creation of the mechanism underlying that response.

The view defended here, which ascribes a certain type and degree of responsibility to our affective attitudes, avoids two extreme positions: that affective attitudes are always manifestations of freedom, and that people can never be responsible for their affective attitudes.[8]

### Emotional and Moral Evaluations

The most important thing a father can do for his children is love their mother.
—Theodore M. Hesburgh, C.S.C.

I turn now to examine the second difficulty in attaching to emotions a significant moral role, namely, the incompatibility between the discriminative, partial nature of emotions and the egalitarian and impartial nature of intellectual moral rules. Those who consider this difficulty to be unresolvable believe that emotions impede moral behavior. The functional role of emotions in our everyday life does not necessarily imply a moral role as well. It can be argued that although emotions have practical value in terms of leading a more enjoyable life, they have nothing to do with leading a more moral life. The difference between practical and moral values is clearly expressed in the phrase "the prosperity of the wicked and the suffering of the righteous."

I will begin to discuss the incompatibility of partial emotional attitudes and egalitarian intellectual norms by comparing emotional and moral evaluations. The comparison will confirm that many moral evaluations are more general and egalitarian than typical emotional evaluations. Then I will proceed to show that there are moral circumstances which require partial emotional evaluations.

In evaluating other people, we can refer to various domains, such as moral, aesthetic, and commercial domains. For instance, we can evaluate a person as an honest, ugly, and wealthy person. In this chapter, I focus on moral evaluations and consider whether emotional evaluations are part of them or whether the two are contradictory and moral evaluations consist of merely intellectual evaluations.

Many moral evaluations seem to be more general than emotional evaluations. Specifying the exact nature of that difference is difficult for several reasons. First, there is no consensus concerning the generality of either type of evaluation. Thus, it has been claimed that there are no general moral principles and that our ethical decisions are made case by case. On the other hand, it has been argued that emotional evaluations are general in the sense of being objective and rational.[9] Second, there are several aspects of generality, and it is not clear whether emotional evaluations differ from moral ones in all aspects. Third, there are numerous types of emotional and moral evaluations. The distinction between them requires a subtle, and sometimes tedious, description.

Doing justice to all these complexities is far beyond the scope of this work; however, they will be mentioned briefly. My comparison of emotional and moral evaluations will focus on their generality. In particular, I will refer to the two basic senses of emotional partiality: their narrow and personal perspectives.

*Narrow Perspective*
Ask her to wait a moment—I am almost done.
—Carl Friedrich Gauss, when informed that his wife was dying

Emotions are partial in the sense that they are narrowly focused; they are hardly relevant beyond their specific object. It is clear that there are moral attitudes which are not limited in this sense. Morality is basically concerned not only with a particular person but with general relations among many people. It presupposes that other people—or creatures in general—have moral rights we should respect. Considering the impact of our actions upon other people is essential to morality. The difficult task of moral theory is not to determine whether moral evaluations entail considerations beyond a particular case, but rather to pinpoint the nature of such considerations. Owing to this general nature, moral principles have commonly been associated with intellectual principles.

One intellectual principle expressing the general nature of morality is that of universality: *If, in a particular case, something is judged to have a certain value, then this and other similar things will be judged to have the same value in similar cases.* In one sense, this formulation is trivially true: for identical situations, there must be identical evaluations. The trouble is that there are no two identical situations, but rather only situations similar in some respects and different in others. Hence, the moral task is to determine which differences are morally relevant.

There is no precise general theory of moral relevance, and probably such a theory is impossible. However, some criteria of relevance are implied in our moral behavior, even if we cannot specify them. We know, for example, that a difference in hair color is not relevant to evaluating the moral behavior of two murderers. On the other hand, the issue of self-defense is relevant to evaluating the moral behavior of someone who killed a burglar. Although determining moral relevance is often difficult, moral evaluations should address the possible implications for other creatures who may be influenced by the result of such an evaluation. An extreme formulation of this type of generality is found in Kant's view, which demands that our moral rules be as general as possible: It should be possible for the moral precept underlying any particular action to become a universal law, governing the actions of all people in similar circumstances. I am duty-bound to perform an action only if it is also possible for all other people to act on the same precept. One need not adopt such an extreme intellectual formulation, but since morality entails respect for the moral rights of other people, the need for considerations beyond a particular case is obvious.

Emotional evaluations are not repeatable in the strong Kantian sense of universalization. Thus, because my beloved happens to be tall, blond, and has blue eyes, it is not therefore a universal law of my behavior to fall in love with every tall, blond, blue-eyed woman I happen to meet. For it is in the nature of romantic love that it cannot be universally applied. If I knew of ten women identical to my beloved, my love for her might be affected. But if I knew ten people who behaved in an identical manner—who, for example, beat their children—my moral attitude toward all of them is likely to be no different from my attitude toward only one of them. Similarly, if I could turn the clock back thirty years, I might behave morally in exactly the same way that I did in the past, but I may choose to experience different emotional situations. Repetition does not reduce the value of moral behavior, but it may reduce emotional excitement.

Emotional evaluations also have an impact beyond the particular case that they address. Thus, Karen's love for Adam has implications beyond those concerning Karen and Adam alone. Her love may affect the life of her husband, their children, their friends, and so on. However, taking account of such general implications is basically a practical or a moral task rather than an emotional one. If Karen decides not to pursue her love for Adam, then her decision will be based primarily not upon emotional considerations concerning love but upon other considerations, for instance, practical, moral, or economic ones. The considerations involved in emotions themselves are usually limited to the people with whom we have contact. Morality commits us also to general considerations extending beyond the participants or those in their immediate circle.

The greater partiality of emotions is related to their greater sensitivity to personal and contextual attributes. This does not imply that emotions are sensitive to every change in such attributes. There are different degrees and types of emotional sensitivity. Love may continue despite contextual changes, including changes in the beloved, and grief arises in most cases where people close to us die despite the different contexts in which these deaths occur.

Moral evaluations are also sensitive to context, but to a lesser degree. Many contextual attributes are relevant to the emotional, but not the moral, domain. Whereas all, or at least most, moral evaluations are not sensitive to, for example, the hair color of a person, many emotional evaluations may be sensitive to such contextual features. Our emotional evaluations are typically directed at a particular person and concerned with our relationship with this person. Moral evaluations are also typically directed at a particular person; however, they are often not merely concerned with our relationship with this person but also with standards relevant to other people as well. Accordingly, the weight of reference to other cases has greater consideration in moral evaluations, and they are therefore less sensitive to personal and contextual attributes. All types of evaluations are dependent on context, but the scope and significance of relevant contexts differ.

One can argue that from a strictly logical point of view, emotional evaluations are also general in some sense of universalizability. If a certain event has emotional significance, then this and other similar events would have the same emotional significance in similar cases. Again, this may be true in the trivial sense that two identical situations are also identical in their emotional aspects. However, since emotional evaluations are very sensitive to contextual attributes, there are many attributes whose presence makes two situations dissimilar from an emotional viewpoint. Accordingly, even if the universalizability principle is adequate, it has little significance for the emotional domain. Consider again the case of the blonde woman. If the present circumstances were similar in relevant respects to those prevailing at the time I met this woman, then I may indeed fall in love with every similar woman that I meet. But the circumstances are not similar in the relevant respects because my own situation has changed; for example, I am in love now and have an intimate history with this woman that was absent before.

The more general nature of moral attitudes is expressed not merely in their reference to a greater number of people but also in the way we should treat those people. Moral attitudes encompass a strong egalitarian element. Although in some moral theories the egalitarian element is more important than in others, every moral theory presupposes some kind of egalitarian principle. The fact that morality deals with actions directed toward other people suggests that those people have certain moral rights. The very notion of morality implies concern for others having certain moral rights. Each society may ascribe different rights to different people (or creatures), but some basic rights are common to all those constituting the moral domain. It is hard to imagine a moral framework that accords moral rights only to one person. Even extreme positions, like ethical egoism, need to assume the existence of some moral principles referring to other people.

In light of the partial nature of emotions, emotional evaluations are basically discriminative and nonegalitarian. An emotional evaluation is concerned with a few people, and the perspective is very personal: we neither love everyone, nor are envious of all of them. The emotional object has an emotional significance that no other person has. Whereas in the moral domain an egalitarian principle makes sense but its scope is disputable, in the emotional domain it hardly makes sense. Hence, there is no room for a general theory of egalitarian emotions; it is hard to conceive of a theory of emotions in which all people have equal significance.

Some moral theories recommend the adoption of emotional attitudes which seem to be general and egalitarian. For example, the moral norm which recommends that we love everyone implies that this kind of love is nonspecific and egalitarian. It is obvious, however, that such an attitude is different from a typical emotion. This type of love is significantly different from romantic love, which is discriminative. Egalitarian love is therefore a general moral attitude, but it is not an emotion, or at least not a typical emotion. General and egalitarian attitudes are profoundly different from the partial and discriminative emotional attitudes.

I have suggested that many moral evaluations are more general than emotional evaluations in the sense that they refer to more people and are more egalitarian. Still another sense of generality is concerned with whether a particular evaluation should be compatible with a general normative framework to be considered a certain type of evaluation. Only moral evaluations are general in this normative sense.

There are moral, immoral, and nonmoral evaluations; there are, however, only emotional and nonemotional evaluations. There is no emotional category corresponding to that of immoral evaluations. Not every evaluation concerning moral issues is a moral evaluation; some are immoral. Praising the torture of a baby for the fun of it pertains to the moral realm, but it involves an immoral evaluation. Being glad about such an act entails an emotional evaluation. There is no emotional norm that requires being sad about every unjustified murder, but there is a moral norm that requires condemning each unjustified murder. Likewise, being angry with our spouse while knowing that the anger stems from having been insulted by our boss is unjustified, but nonetheless real, anger. Although we may criticize emotional states, in so doing we do not deny their reality as emotions, whereas when we morally criticize a certain behavior, we do deny its moral status. (I argue below that there are moral norms requiring us to experience certain emotions in some circumstances. For example, morality requires me to be sad and furious when I hear of someone hurting a child deliberately. However, morality does not require me to be sad upon hearing about the untimely death of each and every person on earth—it merely requires me to evaluate these deaths negatively.)

With regard to emotional evaluations, the attitude of "I can't help it" is both common and acceptable. With moral evaluations—in contrast to moral behavior—such an attitude is neither common nor acceptable. We may not actually be able to change an immoral situation, but this does not mean that we should positively evaluate it. The normative aspect of moral evaluations is also reflected in the fact that when we believe that our moral evaluation is wrong, we will quickly change it. However, in the emotional domain, this is not necessarily the case. Many moral evaluations have a general normative aspect that is largely absent from emotional evaluations. There are many moral imperatives, but very few emotional imperatives. Nevertheless, we do have some normative responsibilities for our emotions. The partiality of emotions does not imply their arbitrariness. If emotions can be rationally criticized or justified, then they cannot be completely arbitrary, and we do indeed justify or criticize our emotions.

*Personal Perspective*
Whenever I date a guy, I think, is this the man I want my children to spend their weekends with?
—Rita Rudner

The second sense of partiality refers to the interested and personal perspective expressed by the emotional agent. In other words, it refers to whether our closeness to, or personal involvement with, a certain person should play any role in forming our attitude toward this person. Denying such a role constitutes generality with regard to impartiality. When our closeness to someone does not form part of our perspective, we consider ourselves to be impartial.

A principle of impartiality may be formulated as a normative requirement for moral evaluations: *Our closeness to a certain person should play no role in our evaluation of the actions of that person.* Formulated in this way, the principle of impartiality seems to be adequate from a moral point of view: my closeness to, or historical association with, a criminal should not change my negative moral evaluation of this person's activities. The issue of our future behavior toward this person (to be discussed below) is separate from the issue of our moral evaluation of this person's behavior (discussed here). Consider the following example: A crime is committed by two people whose background and current situation are identical except for the fact that one of them is my friend. Although my behavior toward the two may be different, my moral evaluation of their crime should be similar. My evaluation may be somewhat different if the crime is committed against me, for instance, in the case of stealing from my house. Here the moral evaluation will still be negative toward both, but it may be even more severe toward my friend. The reason is not that the principle of impartiality is being violated, but that we are dealing with two different crimes. The crime of my friend involves not merely stealing but betraying my trust as well. Adhering to the principle of impartiality may be psychologically difficult, but it is essential to many moral evaluations. This is why an affinity between a defendant and a judge is a good reason for replacing the judge. The aspect of "for old times' sake" is normally morally irrelevant to the formation of many moral evaluations, but carries with it great emotional relevance. A partial evaluation made by a judge is an immoral one, but it can be an emotional evaluation. Whereas emotional evaluations are those made by a partial agent, many moral evaluations are those made by an impartial one.

Since emotions are directed at those who are close to us, the principle of impartiality is not applicable to the emotional domain. Not everyone and not everything is of emotional significance to us. Emotions are of a discriminative and partial nature.

The principle of impartiality can also be formulated as a normative requirement of our behavior: *Our closeness to a certain person should play no role in our behavior toward that person.* It is clear that this formulation does not apply to emotions, since it entails a stronger requirement than that which merely concerns our evaluations, and even the latter formulation is not applicable to emotions. Our closeness to a certain person is crucial in determining our emotional behavior. I believe that, by and large, this formulation is not applicable to moral behavior either. It is not feasible to require a completely equal distribution of one's limited resources. Thus, I devote more resources to my son than to other people's children without necessarily assuming that he is in greater need than they are. Nor does this formulation have any moral justification. Moral behavior presupposes that people have moral responsibility toward each other, but one cannot be expected to take on the same degree of moral responsibility, or moral commitment, for everybody. Responsibility requires resources, and if one's limited resources were to be equally divided among all people, then there would be no room for genuine profound responsibility. Like other kinds of responsibility, moral responsibility is limited by its nature.

The alternatives we face are not whether to be responsible for all people, not to mention other living creatures, or merely for some people, but rather whether to be responsible for some people or for none. Some people may still consider this normative formulation of the principle of impartiality, or some modified version of it, as a kind of ideal to which we should aspire in order to enlarge the group of people for whom we feel responsible. I have no objection to such an ideal as long as we bear in mind its practical limitations.

The more general nature of many moral evaluations can be illustrated by the following example. Susan's father is in a coma, and her husband Tom assumes the moral responsibility for taking care of his needs. Now suppose that Paul is Tom's identical twin. Paul is identical to Tom in all respects except Tom's history. Should Susan let Paul take moral responsibility for her father (if Tom is away for a week)? Should Susan let Paul make love to her (if Tom is away for a week)? Because of the difference between moral and emotional attitudes in terms of their generality, the answer is not identical in the two cases. As long as Paul's moral stance is indistinguishable from Tom's, then Susan—as well as Tom—should not object to the idea that Paul will take care of her father. However, Susan's emotional attitude toward Paul is different from that toward Tom. Here the particular features associated only with Tom, such as their shared history, can make a difference, and Susan may not wish to make love with Paul. Tom may also reject the idea that his brother be allowed to make love to his wife, or at least he may be jealous. Since emotions are discriminative in their nature, the shared history and other personal attributes may form the basis for such discrimination.

A similar situation is described in Greek mythology. Alcmene was the faithful wife of Amphitryon whom Zeus was able to seduce only by taking the form of her husband. The problem is: When Alcmene discovers the real identity of her seducer, should she mind?[10] A real-life example is that of a man who deceptively introduced himself as a physician, pilot, professor, and so forth. Many women were deceived by his charm and had sexual relationships with him. Once the deceit was revealed, some women sued him (and won the case). Without discussing the legal aspects of such a case, the deception here is significant both from a moral viewpoint (since the man lied) and from an emotional viewpoint (since falling in love with someone is also related to this person's character).

The situation is less clear regarding the decision of the mayor of Rome to replace hundreds of original statues in the streets of Rome with copies in order to protect the originals from damage or theft. The copies are of high quality so it is very difficult to distinguish them from the originals—one indication of this is that people have stolen the copies, as well. The problem in this case is not moral—as there is no harm to a moral agent—but emotional: should the mere historical difference between the two types of statues have an impact on our aesthetic emotions? Although the two types are similar in their external appearance, the substitution has emotional significance for some people, who have claimed that their aesthetic enjoyment has been reduced as a result of the substitution. A similar problem exists in the context of forged paintings. There are some imitations which are so good that only a complex laboratory examination can distinguish them from the originals. Although from an aesthetic point of view, the two paintings are identical, when the counterfeit is revealed, the commercial and emotional values of the forgeries are almost eliminated. The past is of great emotional significance, as our emotional tendencies were shaped in the past; we anticipate the future, but we have been molded by the past.

The above examples indicate the importance of the unique history of, and the personal relationship with, the emotional object; taking account of this expresses emotional partiality. I may not care who fixes my car, as long as this person does it competently. I do, however, care about the history and the nature of the person with whom I am in a personal relationship. Impartiality is not typical of personal relationship.[11]

In accordance with their more general nature, it is more natural to speak about consistent moral evaluations than about consistent emotional evaluations since consistency is a type of general behavior. In the emotional domain, consistency is basically limited to one particular case, whereas moral consistency can refer to either simultaneous or successive evaluations.

The difference between emotional and moral evaluations concerns two paradigmatic cases rather than two clear-cut categories. These evaluations range from highly particularistic emotional evaluations to universalistic moral evaluations with differing degrees of generality in between.

In light of the foregoing comparison, extreme moral particularism that denies the existence of general moral evaluations is an inadequate position. This is so for the simple reason that many moral evaluations are more general than emotional evaluations. Extreme emotional particularism, which denies the existence of general emotional evaluations altogether, cannot be entirely adequate either, though it is closer to the truth than extreme moral particularism. We have seen that there are several types and degrees of generality among emotional evaluations. Furthermore, extreme moral universalism, which assumes that morality consists of the application of general principles, is also inadequate. Although most moral evaluations are more closely bound up with general principles than are most emotional evaluations, they are not completely insensitive to personal and contextual attributes either.

I have admitted in this section that many moral evaluations have general aspects that are absent in typical emotional evaluations. However, this does not mean that emotional attitudes have no role in moral behavior; it just means that such attitudes are suitable in only certain types of moral circumstances. In the next section I show that there are indeed important moral circumstances in which partial emotional attitudes play a central role.

### Emotional Partiality and Morality

A morality based entirely on general rules and principles is tyrannical and disproportionate.
—Stephen Toulmin

The profound nature of emotions and their natural emergence toward those who are close to us is related to their central moral characterization: with regard to our intimates, preferential emotional treatment is morally required and justified. We ought to treat our intimates with special emotional preference since our commitments toward them are much richer and deeper. The intensity and intimacy of the relationships we develop with those close to us generate profound and wide obligations which are not typical of our relationships with strangers. General moral rules cannot cover the whole range of activities and attitudes required for personal emotional relationships. General intellectual rules and preferential emotional attitudes are related to two basic types of moral behavior: one toward strangers and the other toward our intimates. Whereas the former type is based upon impartial intellectual principles, the latter requires partial emotional attitudes.

Henry Sidgwick justifies special care toward friends insofar as humans are psychologically so constituted that we are capable of affection for only a limited number of people; furthermore, most of us are not in a position to do much good to more than a very small number of persons. Part of our commonsense understanding of friendship is that we are often morally required to promote our friends' well-being to a greater extent than we promote the well-being of strangers.[12] A friend is a person with whom one has a shared history of mutual special concern. Emotions, which express a special concern, take account of a shared history. History and special relations matter because they shape our emotional structure.

Stephen Toulmin argues that in dealing with our families, intimates, and immediate neighbors or associates, "we both expect to—and are expected to—make allowances for their individual personalities and tastes, and we do our best to time our actions according to our perception of their current moods and plans." In dealing with complete strangers, our moral obligations are limited and chiefly negative—for example, to avoid acting violently. In dealing with intimates, our moral obligations are profound and chiefly positive—for example, to help them develop their capacities and fulfill their wishes. In the ethics of strangers, Toulmin claims, respect for general rules and absolute impartiality may be a prime moral demand, but among intimates the relevance of strict rules is minimal, and a certain discreet partiality is, surely, only equitable, and certainly not unethical.[13] We need to recognize, Toulmin says, that "a morality based entirely on general rules and principles is tyrannical and disproportionate, and that only those who make equitable allowances for subtle individual differences have a proper feeling for the deeper demands of ethics."[14]

The moral difficulty of ignoring subtle individual differences is highlighted by Anatole France's remark that "the law, in its majestic equality, forbids all men to sleep under bridges, to beg in the streets, and to steal bread—the rich as well as the poor." Being moral is not necessarily being alienated; abiding by morality need not alienate us from the particular commitments that make life worthwhile. In the moral context, the personal emotional perspective addresses, among other things, the concern for the well-being of others. The personal concern should not be excluded from morality. Personal relationships are central for moral behavior and such relationships "are partial to the core: they are always focused on one single person."[15] The personal concern should, however, be molded into morality in such a way that considerations about the well-being of others are not excluded either. The concern that people have for the well-being of others is an important element in their own well-being. Accordingly, people often sacrifice their own well-being for the well-being of those they care about.[16]

The morality of caring suggested by some feminists attempts to incorporate personal concerns typical of the emotional domain into the general moral domain. In this approach, the particularized self is of no lesser moral significance than the abstract general self assumed by some impartialist approaches to morality; sensitivity to particular differences and care and concern for individual persons are as central to morality as general principles.[17]

Legislation and contracts may reduce the risk of harmful discrimination in our behavior toward various persons, but they cannot replace care and individual emotional attitudes. Whereas in personal relationships care is the essential feature, more distant relationships are based on contract. We should avoid the tendency, prevailing in modern society, to base all relationships on formal contracts.

There is some psychological evidence indicating the presence of two major principles of behavior which are related to the distinction suggested here between behavior toward our intimates and behavior toward strangers. The psychologist Tory Higgins distinguishes between promotion-focus behavior, which is concerned with strong ideals related to attaining accomplishments or fulfilling hopes, and prevention-focus behavior, which is concerned with strong oughts related to protection, safety, and responsibility. This is a distinction between nurturance-related behavior and security-related behavior. The promotion mode focuses upon the presence or absence of positive outcomes, whereas the prevention mode focuses upon the presence or absence of negative outcomes. In the prevention mode, interactions between people occur only when something is going wrong—when some oughts are violated. The promotion mode is characterized by ongoing activities related to the creation of optimal conditions for fulfilling the other's strong ideals. In the prevention mode, the behavioral categories are minimal and binary; there is no sense of progress. In the promotion mode the categories are prototypical and there is a sense of progress toward fulfilling the ideal.[18]

I believe that whereas the moral requirements of our behavior toward strangers are primarily those of the prevention mode, the requirements of our behavior toward our intimates also include the promotion mode. We are required not merely to be concerned with the safety of our intimates—that is, to prevent negative events befalling them—but also with fulfilling their hopes and ideals, by actively promoting positive outcomes. One indication of how the promotion mode dominates interactions among intimates is that salespeople imitate a promotional attitude in order to create an illusion of closeness between their clients and them.

The distinction between intimates and strangers is obviously not clear-cut. In addition to personal relationships with our intimates, and nonpersonal relationships with strangers, there are other types of relationships in between. Thus, although my relationship with my dentist is not as personal as that with my children, the dentist is not a complete stranger to me (although I may sometimes wish he were). We may say that close relationships are characterized by the lack of rigid rules and the greater importance of individual considerations. This does not mean that relationships with our intimates lack any kind of generality. However, such general rules are not constitutive of the relationships and in any case should not override individual considerations, especially when grave matters are involved. In relationships with strangers, general rules are constitutive factors, whereas in close relationships, they are merely practical guidelines.

Our behavior toward those who are close to us is less restrained and more sincere than toward strangers. For instance, we can fall asleep while watching TV together, express our opinions more freely, and be less careful in our efforts not to insult other people. Indeed, calculated, impartial behavior is often taken to indicate the lack of an intimate, close relationship. As James Grunebaum suggests, "once friends begin to keep a credit-debit accounting of their relationship (making sure that they are not giving more than they receive or that they have not incurred too great a debt of gratitude), the beginning of the end of the friendship is close at hand."[19]

There are circumstances in which partial emotional attitudes should be applied to strangers, and impartial attitudes to our intimates. Some situations, such as those in which a stranger suffers a great misfortune, call for our compassion. Because of the huge resources demanded by compassion, such an attitude cannot be applied to more than a few strangers, making each previous stranger closer to us. Likewise, there are situations in which the attitude toward our intimates should be impartial and nonemotional, such as when partial behavior would hurt the basic rights of strangers. Thus, when serving as judges, referees, or teachers, we should not favor our children over strangers. Since not doing that is difficult, it is preferable to avoid such circumstances in the first place if at all possible. In these circumstances, we are required to regard our intimates as strangers, hence justifying the impartial behavior.

Emotional and moral attitudes are not contradictory. We can have close emotional ties with our intimates and still exhibit moral behavior toward strangers. There may be cases in which the two attitudes clash, but in most cases the conflict is not inherently unresolvable and a sensible compromise is often available.

Take, for example, loyalty, whose diverse types to our family, friends, community, and nation usually involve some conflict between a partial emotional state and a more general and impartial moral attitude. Thus, patriotism involves a partial preference for the well-being of our country, which may be in conflict with a more universal concern for the well-being of all humanity. The moral difficulty of patriotism is clearly expressed by George Bernard Shaw who said that "Patriotism is your conviction that this country is superior to all others because you were born in it." Patriotism, or at least a moderate form of it, can be defended by indicating the importance of reference groups in our social and emotional life. A morally acceptable form of patriotism is similar to the morally acceptable form of love or family loyalty.

We really should care more about those near and dear to us than we care about strangers, but this should not be an exclusive concern that violates the rights of strangers. Our love should not submerge us in one person to the exclusion of worldly responsibilities. Likewise, our partial attitude toward our nation is morally recommended, so long as it is curbed by other moral attitudes and principles. Our loyalty to our nation should not lead us to disregard our moral obligations toward larger and more remote groups, such as other nations, and toward smaller and more intimate groups, such as family and friends. E. M. Forster once said that if he were ever called on to choose between a friend and his country, he hoped that he would have the courage to choose his friend. Indeed, I believe that in many circumstances such a choice may well be the moral one.[20]

In order to avoid misunderstanding, I would like to emphasize that the approach suggested here does not call for indifference toward strangers; strangers are moral objects who deserve caring and moral treatment. I have just indicated that in many circumstances such caring and moral treatment cannot be identical to that which we typically offer our intimates. One may claim that caring about our intimates is easy and natural so that our major moral task is to increase our sensitivity toward strangers. I agree that conceiving the stranger as a human being having similar moral rights to those close to us is a crucial moral task. Indeed, many atrocities would be prevented if we were not so detached from other people. One horrific example in this regard concerns Nazi Germany. Germans hardly protested against the Nazi mass destruction of Jews, but when Hitler decided to kill Germans who were mentally ill or physically handicapped, intense public protest forced Hitler to stop these killings, at least partially. These protests arose because Germans, not Jews, were being murdered. The ability to detach ourselves from other people—and hence to consider them as less human than we are—

enables mass destruction and other types of atrocities all over the world even today. Less major moral misdeeds, which do not kill others but "merely" ignore some of their moral and human rights, are possible because we lack sufficient emotional sensitivity to strangers.

The fact that increasing our sensitivity toward strangers is one of our central moral tasks does not imply that the conceptual analysis offered here is incorrect. Although my obligations toward my intimates are by far greater than those toward strangers, I have serious moral obligations toward strangers as well. I must consider strangers as human beings with full moral rights which should be protected; hence, I should fight for the fulfillment of those rights. Moreover, as Hugh Lafollette rightly argues, those who are deeply involved in a caring, personal relationship, are better equipped to recognize the needs of strangers. There is a strong correlation between the extent of our involvement in close relationships and the extent of our ability and motivation to care for strangers. He claims that a person needs some exposure to personal relationships to acquire the knowledge and motivation to act morally toward strangers as well.[21]

The moral rights of strangers do not abolish the moral difference between intimates and strangers. Moral differences should not imply the exclusion of others from the moral domain; they merely mean that in some circumstances, moral obligations toward the two groups are different. The view presented here is certainly more complex than the view which claims that there is no difference in our moral obligations toward our intimates and strangers, or the one claiming that we have moral obligations only toward our intimates. There are different types of moral obligations, some of them—such as our duty not to hurt other people and to prevent such hurt by other people—are common to both our intimates and strangers; other obligations—such as those referring to the time we should spend with other people—are concerned, in most circumstances, only with our intimates.

As indicated, the personal, emotional care, which sometimes is part of our moral obligation toward our intimates, is by nature limited; it cannot be directed toward everyone. The moral ideal may be to enlarge the circle of people who enjoy our personal, emotional care. Consider the following Stoic metaphor of moral development. Imagine that each of us lives at the center of a set of concentric circles, the nearest being our own self, the furthest being the entire universe of living creatures. The task of our moral development is to move the circles progressively closer to the center, so that we regard our parents and children like ourselves, our other relatives like our parents, and strangers like our relatives.[22]

This metaphor is apt for describing our ideal moral development, as long as it is remembered that the process of drawing the circles closer to the center can never be completed and should not result in their elimination. The differences between the various circles need to be maintained as they express the very foundations of our social and emotional structure: we will always belong to some types of groups and our emotions will always be more intense toward people included in the closest group. We must realize the inevitable presence of emotional groups and, accordingly, our partial emotional perspectives.

It may be argued that we can adopt a general moral principle demanding that each person develop a greater emotional commitment toward her intimates. I am ready to adopt this principle, but we must remember that such a principle is not sufficient for supplying detailed moral prescriptions. It cannot, for example, indicate the degree and circumstances in which a partial attitude is required. It goes without saying, also, that the general principle recommending the integration of emotional and intellectual perspectives cannot supply detailed moral prescriptions. This is exactly my claim concerning the limitation of general principles and the need to integrate them with emotional sensitivity.

To sum up, I have shown that although emotional attitudes are partial and discriminative, they play important roles in moral behavior; these roles, however, are limited to certain circumstances. These happen to be very significant moral circumstances. We still have to face the problem of integrating into the moral decision-making mechanism the emotional partial perspective with the other major mental perspective, namely, the general intellectual perspective. Before discussing this problem, I would like to describe further advantages of integrating emotions into the moral domain.

*Further Moral Advantage of Emotions*

Two things are bad for the heart—running up stairs and running down people.
—Bernard M. Baruch

In the last section I indicated the crucial importance of emotions in our relationships with those with whom we have the deepest emotional commitments, namely, our intimates. I will indicate now other factors which strengthen the importance of emotions in moral behavior in general and not only in the behavior toward our intimates.

The moral value of emotions may also be established by showing that partial emotional concern is not so egoistic, as it often addresses the well-being of others too, and that it is extremely valuable in some moral circumstances. The inadequacy of identifying emotional, personal concern with immoral, egoistic concern is evident from the fact that helping other people may be as emotionally exciting as if we were gaining something for ourselves; similarly, hurting others may be as emotionally distressing as if we were being hurt ourselves. As indicated, positive emotional states usually increase inclinations toward helping. The reverse direction is also common: helping other people may increase our happiness, and perceiving injustice can also provoke negative emotions which may lead to the elimination of the injustice. If benevolence is as essential to our constitution as personal gratification, then helping others may be an important constituent of our happiness.[23]

Emotions which in themselves can be regarded as morally negative may have instrumental moral value in the sense that they may lead to positive moral consequences. Jealousy is morally valuable in protecting unique relationships; envy may encourage improvement of our situation and that of other people; and anger may be useful in maintaining our values and self-respect. Along these lines, Adam Ferguson argues that, "As jealousy is often the most watchful guardian of chastity, so malice is often the quickest to spy the failings of our neighbour. . . . the worst principles of our nature may be at the bottom of our pretended zeal for morality."[24] It is often the case that pursuing our own egoistic happiness may increase the happiness of other people as well. Adam Smith's view of economic benefits is similar: by pursuing our own private economic benefits, we contribute to the well-being of other people. Only excessive intensity of negative emotions is morally harmful; moderate forms of negative emotions are typically morally beneficial since they prevent indifferent attitudes toward others. Society would be less humane if we were not immediately irritated by the presence of evil or ashamed of our misdeeds.

Another advantage of negative moral emotions is their necessary coupling with positive moral emotions. (In a somewhat similar manner, it has been claimed that one advantage of living in Philadelphia is that you can always see the lights of Camden, New Jersey.) Emotions express our sensitivity to what is going on around us. Elimination of negative moral emotions would require eliminating our sensitivity, and hence also eliminating positive moral emotions. Elimination of the capacity for jealousy and pleasure-in-others'-misfortune would require elimination of love and happiness-for-the-fortune-of-others. The elimination of the capacity for anger and regret would require the elimination of gratitude and pride. Where there is no pain, there is no gain.

The coupling of negative and positive emotions in the moral domain or elsewhere is compatible with the view which assumes that an emotional state tends to generate an opposite emotional state. Thus, interruption of a pleasurable sexual experience tends to create acute disappointment and irritation before a return to a neutral state. This pairing is also compatible with the commonsense idea that we cannot have emotional highs without exposing ourselves to emotional lows. It also fits in with some Stoic views and the Buddhist notion that the proper object of character planning is to get rid of all emotions, not just the unpleasant ones, since that is not feasible.

The choice we face is not that of having positive emotions or a mix of positive and negative emotions, but rather that of having close emotional ties, or living in an isolated environment. Whereas having close emotional ties includes many emotional benefits and risks, living in isolation has few. People with no strong emotional attachments have only their own health and success to worry about, but they are also deprived of the joy of being with family and the pleasure in the misfortune of others. Nancy Sherman rightly argues that by letting emotions play an important role in our lives, we assent to being passive in a certain sense; we give up control in order to be able to live emotionally. Yet this is precisely what our friends may value in our relationship with them—that we show a willingness to be emotionally drawn, to be vulnerable to emotional losses and gains resulting from our close relationship with them.[25]

The great personal involvement implicit in an emotional relationship has not merely advantages, but risks as well. Those who are close to us can easily hurt us and we can easily hurt them—as the popular song (discussed in chapter 15) puts it: "You always hurt the one you love." Telling our secrets to someone may establish a friendship relationship, but it also exposes our vulnerability.[26] Some people actually avoid having friendships for this reason. I once lived in an apartment building of low-income families. Being acquainted with my new neighbors was mostly a sad experience, as many of them had very difficult economic and social situations. I noticed that members of one family on my floor avoided making social contacts; later on I realized that they did that in order to avoid being exposed to the sad emotional experiences associated with these families.[27] Kant clearly realizes the immoral nature of such behavior: "It is a duty not to avoid places where the poor, who lack the most necessary things, are to be found; instead, it is a duty to seek them out. It is a duty not to shun sickrooms or prisons and so on in order to avoid the pain of pity, which one may not be able to resist."[28]

The value of emotions is also expressed in the fact that feeling a certain emotion in certain circumstances is morally valuable. From a moral viewpoint, we care not only about how people act but also about how they feel. This is so since emotions are genuine expressions of our basic attitudes and enduring values. When we really value something, our evaluation is often accompanied by a certain emotion. Holding a certain value emotionally is necessary if that value is to become central to us.[29] Accordingly, an important advantage of incorporating emotions into the moral domain is the greater role of sincerity in our behavior. A system based on intellectual calculations can more successfully hide our real attitudes. Children, whose behavior is based more on spontaneous emotional evaluations, are more sincere than adults. Knowing how to hide our emotions is a personal discovery. Teaching children good manners is teaching them, among other things, to hide their real emotions. At least in this sense politicians are well educated.

Unlike emotions, good manners often express superficial attitudes, which are more typical of our behavior toward strangers. Take, for example, the following response of Miss Manners to a question by a professional woman in business who is wondering about the proper way for a man to shake a woman's hand: "Gentlemen were taught to shake ladies' hands lightly because ladies, but not gentlemen, often wear diamond rings on their right hands. . . . Other reasons for light shaking include arthritis, sweaty palms, and a hand frozen onto a cocktail glass."[30] In light of their superficial nature, good manners can be deceptive insofar as they do not necessarily express our genuine profound attitude.

Another reason for the moral value of emotions is that they serve as a kind of moral compass. Emotions often provide moral barriers to many types of immoral behavior.[31] Some of the most horrible crimes have been committed on the basis of cool intellectual calculation. Rudolph Hoess, the commandant of Auschwitz for three years, who supervised the murders of more than 2 million people, can be regarded as a thoroughly intellectual man. Even while awaiting execution for his crimes, Hoess defended these killings as just and rational. Hoess excoriated both those Nazis who had sadistically enjoyed brutalizing their victims, and those who had been unable to control their good nature and kind heart. He wanted his men to be thoroughly intellectual and not to show the slightest trace of emotion.[32]

What sometimes prevents a person from committing a crime is emotional resistance. Miquel de Unamuno, the Spanish thinker, declared that "confession is very useful because it allows one to sin again more comfortably."[33] A major function of confession is that of reducing negative emotional intensity, like that of guilt or shame, stemming from immoral behavior. Hence, neglecting the emotional perspective may lead to immoral behavior. In one trial of white-collar workers in the United States, forty-five executives were convicted of secretly fixing consumer prices for electricity. One senior executive conceded in the trial that in retrospect, he seemed to "intellectually believe" that what he was doing was wrong, but he avoided emotional recognition and heartfelt conviction about his wrongdoing.[34]

Sometimes we must violate one moral duty in order to fulfill another, as in cases of "dirty hands" in which an agent must harm one to help the other. In these situations, our moral character is expressed in the negative emotional experiences, like sadness and regret, that are associated with them.[35] Our moral strength is often measured by the types of emotional resistance we have against wrongdoing. A person who behaves exclusively in accordance with the intellectual system may easily become indifferent to other people, since emotions express sensitivity toward other people. Moral behavior comes harder for people who lack feelings and emotions. Such people cannot have any feeling toward their children or others; they have to convince themselves or remind themselves to behave morally, as they cannot do so out of compassion or friendship. The role of sympathy is crucial in this regard. It is hard to conceive of a moral agent who completely lacks sympathy. Sympathy enables us to come closer to other people and better understand their needs. Sympathy, which appears quite early in our development, is essential to social and moral relationships.[36]

The importance of emotions in leading a social and moral life does not imply that immoral behavior cannot stem from emotions. Violence is often associated not with anger but with joy. Perfectly normal people can be cruel and be so enthusiastically, without having any sympathy. Despite its enormous importance, sympathy is easily overcome by nonsympathetic emotions. Hence, the moral conflict between sympathetic and nonsympathetic emotions is as central as the conflict between emotions and the intellect.[37] The first conflict expresses the differences between two major emotional concerns: personal and social. The emotional concern is first of all personal: the existence and well-being of the agent. However, the fulfillment of this concern is closely related to a social concern regarding the existence and well-being of others. Other people are extremely important for our own existence and well-being: sometimes they enhance and sometimes they diminish our well-being; hence, the presence of sympathetic and nonsympathetic emotions. Since emotions stem from a personal concern, sympathetic emotions may be easily overcome by nonsympathetic ones.

The general functions of emotions are also evident in the moral domain. I have suggested three major functions of emotions: (1) an initial indication of the proper direction in which to respond; (2) a quick mobilization of resources; and (3) a means of social communication. The corresponding moral functions are:

> 1. Emotions have a *cognitive and evaluative* role of initially indicating moral salience and hence the general moral response. Emotional sensitivity helps us to distinguish the moral features of a given situation and as such it serves as an initial moral guide.
> 2. Emotions have a *motivating* role of supporting moral behavior and opposing immoral behavior. In accordance with their general mobilizing role, emotions help us to mobilize the resources needed for moral behavior, which is often not the most convenient course of action.
> 3. Emotions have a *communicative* role of revealing our moral values to others and to ourselves. Since emotions express our profound values, emotional experiences can reveal these values. Taking care of another person with sympathy and compassion can reveal how much we value this person. Sometimes we do not know how much we care for someone until emotions such as jealousy, fear, or compassion are generated.[38]

*Integrating Emotions into Moral Decisions*

When the passions attain due measure and degree, this is known as the state of harmony.
—Mencius

The previous sections have demonstrated how important emotions are for moral behavior. I now turn to examine whether we should attempt to retain the seemingly opposing emotional and intellectual perspectives in our morality. After indicating the advantages of such integration, I examine the more difficult issue of how to accomplish this.

*The Importance of Integrating the Emotional and the Intellectual Perspectives*
God gave us a penis and a brain, but not enough blood to use both at the same time.
—Robin Williams

A spontaneous, emotional system and a deliberative, intellectual system are both important for conducting a moral life. The presence of several systems in the moral domain is as valuable as the presence of several powers in the political domain. For example, in a modern democracy it is important to have legislative, executive, and judicial systems, as well as national and local powers, to balance each other. The different systems often express opposing tendencies and competing interests, and each system retains a somewhat independent voice and influence. It is as important for an individual as it is for a state to have potential sources of dissent from within. The possibility of internal conflict is sometimes a wellspring of vitality and sensitivity, and a check against one-sidedness and fanaticism.[39] If our moral decisions were reached only through intellectual deliberations, then our decisions would often be morally distorted insofar as they would be one-sided, neglecting important aspects of our lives. The presence of conflict between the intellectual and emotional systems is frequently useful from a moral viewpoint, since it indicates a moral predicament to which we should pay attention.

Since preferential emotional commitments readily lend themselves to excesses, they should be combined with a more general and impartial perspective for strengthening their moral value. Partial emotional attitudes and impartial intellectual attitudes represent complementary perspectives for the evaluation of human beings and their activities. A healthy human society needs all these perspectives. Utilizing such different perspectives is not only natural but morally recommended.[40]

Emotions should not be overlooked, but often their weight should be limited. Neglecting the role of intellectual deliberations in morality is as dangerous as neglecting the role of emotions. Although emotions serve as our moral compass, the compass may in some cases provide inadequate directions. In oppressive societies, ranging from regimes such as Nazi Germany to many examples of male chauvinist societies, inappropriate emotions have been cultivated. There, the emotional compass becomes largely immoral, generating inappropriate emotions, and requiring intellectual deliberations to reveal its deficiencies. An important task of intellectual deliberations in such societies is that of correcting the emotional compass. Otherwise, the intellectual objections will scarcely be expressed in actual behavior, as they will not be absorbed into the basic evaluative system. In communist regimes, too, inappropriate emotions were cultivated and the emotional compass was distorted to the extent that it was unable to provide adequate moral direction. But in contrast to Nazi Germany or male chauvinist societies, communist societies were based on proper moral values and the moral distortion was due to inappropriate intellectual considerations concerning the application of these values. Emotional resistance to communism played an important role in overthrowing these regimes.

The intellectualist approach, which recommends that we treat critically the obvious, namely, the emotional natural, is of great value for approaching truth and justice. This does not imply that we should or could eliminate the emotional natural, which is the product of long evolutionary and personal development. Such elimination involves an intellectual vanity which assumes that the intellect alone can uncover truth and justice. This approach ignores human limitations: it is irrational to ignore such limitations since these are part and parcel of human existence.

In addition to the emotional system, which in some primitive form is shared by both animals and people, people also possess an intellectual system. It is implausible to suppose that it is not involved in determining our moral behavior. If it were not, we would be like nonhuman animals. But it is morally dangerous to determine our moral behavior by referring to the intellectual system alone. Some scholars argue that God acts in this way: in a cold and calculated manner, unfeelingly, and only as intellectual reasoning directs.[41] Contrary to animals and God, the moral behavior of people should be determined by both systems. Virtuous people should not attempt to imitate the behavior of animals or God; they should combine the two systems. Virtuous people are not calm and unfeeling, but they are also not people dominated by passion. Combining the two systems is complex and difficult, and one of the attributes of virtuous people is that they accomplish this smoothly. Virtuous people are not angels; their advantage over most of us is that in their case combining the two systems is not a source of conflict, but a valuable means to a moral and happy life.

Both intellectual reasoning and emotional reasoning are necessary for moral behavior; alone, neither of them is sufficient. Cases in which intellectual reasoning conflicts morally with emotions pose a real moral predicament. The question of which system should be dominant in such cases has been usually answered by a firm commitment to the intellectual system. In Plato's metaphor, intellectual reasoning is the shepherd and emotions are the dogs; in Kant's view, also, such reasoning clearly has the dominant role. Hume, on the other hand, argued that "reason is, and ought only to be the slave of the passions."[42] I believe that in different situations different types of dominance should prevail. The complexity of human life stems from, among other things, the lack of a golden rule telling us whether, in a particular situation, intellectual reasoning or emotions should be dominant. Understanding the nature of emotions, and the differences between them and intellectual reasoning, can be helpful in drawing this distinction more clearly.

*Virtuous People and Heroes*
None of us can boast about the morality of our ancestors. The records do not show that Adam and Eve were married.
—E. W. Howe

Ninety percent of the politicians give the other ten percent a bad name.
—Henry Kissinger

Aristotle introduces a distinction between the "continent" or "self-controlled" type of person and the one who is fully virtuous. The continent person is the one who, typically, knowing what she should do, does it, *contrary* to her desires. The fully virtuous person is the one who, typically, knowing what she should do, does it, *in accordance* with her desires. The desires of the fully virtuous person are in complete harmony with her intellect; she gladly acts morally. In Aristotle's view, the fully virtuous person is morally superior to the merely self-controlled one. Kant seems to draw the same distinction as Aristotle, but weights it the other way—the self-controlled agent is considered to be morally superior, for she acts without any emotional inclination, but for the sake of duty alone. Kant indicates that there are people who find satisfaction in helping others and making them happy, without any motive of vanity or self-interest; in Kant's view, the activities of these people have no true moral worth. Helping other people has such moral worth when it is done not out emotional inclination, but from duty perceived by our reason.[43]

At the core of the dispute concerning the role of emotions in morality lies this dispute between Aristotle and Kant: Is moral behavior contrary to or in accordance with our emotional inclinations? Can moral behavior give us pleasure or should it be a dutiful experience in which we overcome our desires?

For Aristotle a virtuous person is one who not only acts virtuously but also has the appropriate emotional dispositions and affective traits to do so. Not having the proper emotion is as significant as not acting in accordance with it. As Robert Ewin claims, those who are unmoved by the sufferings of others are failing morally even if they act to relieve the sufferings of others for different reasons. Similarly, Elster argues: "To want to be immoral *is* to be immoral. A person willing to take the guilt-erasing pill would not need it." The virtuous, good-tempered person is first of all a sensitive person who cares about other people. This person is not only someone who acts angrily against the right person, to the right degree, at the right time, for the right purpose, and in the right way, but someone who also feels anger in these circumstances. The virtuous person is pleased when she helps other people: she feels joy over their joy and sorrow over their sorrow. A central feature of the virtuous person is the harmony between her emotional attitudes and moral norms. If such harmony is achieved, one can follow Augustine's famous instruction, "Love, and do what you will." In Confucianism, also, the ideal is to achieve a state of harmony with one's self, with others, and with nature. Confucius said that only at seventy "I could follow the dictates of my own heart; for what I desired no longer overstepped the boundaries of right."[44]

The moral person in the Kantian sense is one who is struggling all the time to overcome her emotional tendencies and is successful in this struggle. Moral norms are important for this person and she is ready to pay a heavy price for behaving according to them. Intellectual reasoning points out the importance of moral norms and this is sufficient for this person to sacrifice her personal desires.

The actor Dustin Hoffman may be considered to be a virtuous person in the Aristotelian sense, since he claims that after meeting his wife, he felt no passion toward other women. There is no infidelity in the behavior and heart of such a true lover, since the emotions and values are not in conflict. Most other people are less fortunate, and overcoming such a conflict is a major step toward behaving morally. This is obviously the case with certain American presidents, such as John Kennedy and Bill Clinton. If we believe Bill Clinton and assume that in his last year of presidency he did not have sexual relationships—at least not full sexual relationships—with anyone but his wife, then Clinton can be regarded as a virtuous person in the Kantian sense. Despite his emotional tendencies and many temptations, Clinton has managed to behave morally; the heavy emotional price paid for this did not deter this virtuous person from moral behavior.

I believe we should distinguish here between a virtuous person and a hero. There is a Talmudic saying: "Who is a hero? He who conquers his desire." The virtuous person is not a hero since he does not need to conquer his desires: his desires are in harmony with moral norms and there is no need to conquer them. Conquest of desire is not a natural state and therefore cannot be the basis for moral harmony. When Clinton refrains from adultery he is a heroic, but not a virtuous person. The virtuous person is also not a monk who seeks solitude in order to conquer his emotional tendencies. The virtuous person is the one who finds harmony while engaging in pleasant activities with other people; in his quest for harmony, the hero is busily engaged in a struggle to overcome his desires.

An essential moral difference between virtuous people and ordinary people is in their sensitivity. Virtuous people are less sensitive to immoral temptations and are more sensitive to moral wrongdoing. They cannot be characterized merely by their insensitivity to sinful temptations; they should also be characterized by their sensitivity to the suffering of other people. In order to be a really virtuous person, it is not enough that a faithful husband desires no woman other than his wife; he should also care for other women and men. On the opposite side, one may describe Don Juan as a kind person, since he has a very positive attitude toward every woman. Even if some womanizers are indeed kind in nature, I would not describe them as virtuous people, since they are not insensitive to certain temptations.

A faithful husband and Don Juan may be taken to represent two types of sensitivity: discriminate and indiscriminate. The indiscriminate sensitivity refers to all persons in an equal manner: all persons are entitled to receive from me the same moral behavior. Hence, all women are perceived by Don Juan as deserving a loving attitude. The discriminate sensitivity distinguishes differences among various individuals and hence adopts a different emotional attitude toward them.

The call for emotions to play a larger role in our moral life is generally understood as a demand for greater sensitivity toward other people, since emotions express our sensitivity toward other people. However, this is not a call for indiscriminate moral sensitivity, but for greater sensitivity within structured boundaries. Moral sensitivity without boundaries may be seen as expressing greater sensitivity, but such sensitivity can be harmful because it lacks any order of moral priorities, hence implying an inability to distinguish between significant and insignificant moral issues. Although increasing moral sensitivity is a central moral task—as most people do not have the optimal level of moral sensitivity—there are better and worse ways of increasing moral sensitivity; a greater quantity in this regard does not always imply improvement in moral behavior.[45]

It seems that common sense provides many examples supporting Aristotle's, rather than Kant's, position in the dispute concerning the character of a moral agent. Thus, with reference purely to their sexual behavior with women, a faithful husband is closer to the ideal of a virtuous person than Don Juan is. Similarly, it is implausible to claim that the person who visits her friend in the hospital "because she is her friend" is morally inferior to the one who visits her "out of a sense of duty." Nevertheless, Aristotle's victory in this debate is not so clear-cut for two major reasons. First, the combination of the intellect and the emotions, which is typical of the Aristotelian virtuous person, makes the two positions closer to each other; second, we are not in the ideal situation in which our emotional tendencies are in harmony with moral norms. The Aristotelian approach may be seen as a kind of preventive medicine; the Kantian approach is more appropriate when the disease has already spread. In this sense, both approaches are important, but as in medicine, the preventive approach is often the more efficient.

In discussing emotional cognition, I mentioned Spinoza's view of the three different levels of knowledge: emotional knowledge stemming from unique things is considered to be confused and false; intellectual knowledge is considered as true; and knowledge combining emotions and thinking is regarded to be of highest cognitive value. It seems that also in the moral domain we can speak about three levels of moral behavior: (1) behaving exclusively according to our emotions may often lead us to immoral behavior; (2) behaving exclusively according to intellectual dictates may bring us closer to moral behavior, but may still lead to immoral behavior as well; and (3) combining emotional and intellectual perspectives is the ideal moral behavior, but is extremely difficult to achieve. The virtuous person is the "moral expert" who can combine the two perspectives by abolishing the conflict between them.

The emotional sensitivity of virtuous people is accompanied by a more acute moral perception. Virtuous people can better perceive the moral features of the various situations they encounter. In the cognitive realm, we have similar phenomena. Thus, people who are sensitive to tea can better perceive various features of tea. It was also found that anti-Semites can identify Jews better than other people. (Needless to mention there is no correlation between having acute moral perception and having acute cognitive perception!) Moral perception in itself does not necessarily lead to moral behavior. We can imagine a person who clearly perceives other people's suffering but is totally unmoved by it—the person simply does not care.[46] Although moral perception includes both the cognitive and evaluative components associated with certain emotions, these emotions may not emerge if the situation lacks those circumstances related to the various intensity variables; for example, the situation may be perceived as irrelevant to our well-being or as not under our control. Virtuous people not only possess better moral perception but also have the appropriate emotional sensitivity.

It should be obvious that the ideal of a fully virtuous person whose emotional tendencies are identical to her impartial moral norms is very hard, if at all possible, to achieve. We are condemned to experience continuous conflict between our emotional tendencies and our impartial moral norms—no wonder there are so few virtuous people these days. This may explain the following seemingly paradoxical saying of Abraham Lincoln: "It has been my experience that folks who have no vices have very few virtues." If we are not speaking about fully virtuous persons, then such lack of vices is due to insensitivity to other people; sensitivity to other people underlies moral behavior.

*How Can We Integrate Emotional and Intellectual Perspectives?*
Everything in excess is opposed to nature.
—Hippocrates

Better bend than break.
—Scottish proverb

Having discussed the importance of integrating emotional and intellectual perspectives into the moral domain, and indicating that fully virtuous people are those who have achieved such an integration, I turn now to the difficult issue of how this can be attained. In dealing with this issue, we should be especially concerned with showing how the gap between partial emotional attitudes and impartial intellectual attitudes can be reduced. I would like to point out a few possible routes to achieving this: (a) shaping our emotional tendencies in a way that they will be compatible with general intellectual norms that are accepted as moral norms as well; (b) imposing certain constraints on emotional responses; (c) seeking a common evaluative component in both our emotional and intellectual attitudes; and (d) being acquainted with many partial emotional perspectives.

Emotional and moral education should strive to shape our emotional tendencies in a way which will make them more compatible with moral intellectual norms. Such a proposed type of emotional and moral education was indeed recommended in Greek thinking. Thus, Plato suggested that a sound education consists in training people to find pleasure and pain in the right objects. Aristotle also argued that, to a certain degree, moral dispositions or habits can be acquired by action. If, indeed, emotional education is one of our major moral responsibilities, then the state should also contribute to the improvement of people's characters; the state should not remain neutral when it comes to normative considerations.[47]

Some emotions, such as grief, parental love, compassion, hope, and regret, are easier to experience in accordance with our moral standards than are others, such as envy and sexual desire. (Needless to say, the last emotion is notoriously difficult to regulate in such a manner.) We should attempt to reduce this gap in all types of emotions.

The behavior of virtuous people is in accordance with the dictates of reason, but it is not generated by intellectual deliberations; it is rule-described behavior rather than rule-following behavior. The role of moral education is to develop in us emotional dispositions that are in accordance with moral standards adopted by both emotional and intellectual perspectives. In this manner, the conflict between emotional and intellectual moral norms will be reduced to a certain extent, as people will come closer to a situation where they enjoy moral deeds and experience negative emotions when committing a moral sin.

Emotional responses are often expressed in extreme behavior and it is this type of behavior whose moral consequences are most harmful. Accordingly, intellectual reasoning may allow emotions to direct our moral conduct as long as these are, for example, moderate; when the responses tend to become extreme, we should in most cases consult the intellect before behaving in light of them. In this sense, the intellect allows certain degrees of freedom to the emotions, but this is not a complete freedom. For example, I have suggested that in the case of anger, which is quite an aggressive emotion, intellectual reasoning recommends that we refrain from behaving in light of our initial intense response and instead count to ten; after that, the emotional response will be more moderate.

We may say that in order for emotional behavior to be regarded as moral it should typically have an evaluative component similar to that of a correlated intellectual reasoning. The emotional perspective should somehow be in line with the general moral perspective. The two cannot be merged into one unitary perspective, but they can share the crucial moral element, namely, the evaluative component. Without reducing the partial emotional language to the impartial intellectual one, the two may nevertheless denote the same thing. This affinity is achieved not after the emotional perspective has taken a general intellectual perspective, nor as a result of the exercise of intellectual capacities, but once the two perspectives share a common normative element.[48]

Take, for example, the situation in which I hear about the death of my neighbor in a car accident and the death of a stranger in a different car accident. In both cases, I will negatively evaluate the accident, but only in the case of my neighbor will grief be generated and I may be motivated to offer substantial help to his family. The two different responses I have are both morally justified, as there is a general evaluative component that is common to all such situations. I cannot and should not grieve over the death of every innocent person in the world—otherwise, I will spend every minute of my life doing nothing but grieving. Grief requires resources whose allocation cannot be general and egalitarian; negative moral evaluation of the death of innocent people does not require allocation of various resources and therefore should be general and egalitarian. When people do not feel some grief on hearing of the death of their neighbor, it may mean either that their relationship was not sufficiently close or that their emotional values are distorted. When people are close to us, we must be moved by their untimely death.

In the above example, both the partial emotional perspective and the impartial intellectual perspective operate within the moral domain. The stranger is devoid of the profound emotional attitude, not because of moral considerations referring to her deeds or personality, but because of practical considerations concerning our limited resources and the (morally and practically) optimal way of distributing them. In principle, an emotional attitude can be directed toward a stranger, should circumstances permit or require this. The recommended moral attitude here is one that everyone can share, but it is not the completely impartial view "from nowhere."[49] It is a view from somewhere, but it can be adopted by anyone. In this sense, each one of us may be regarded as both a citizen of the world and a citizen of our family.

Another way of dealing with the shortcomings of emotional partiality is to be acquainted with many partial emotional perspectives. Learning to appreciate the diversity of partial human perspectives is crucial for giving our own perspective its proportionate weight.[50]

The position I am advocating provides guiding principles—such as "drive safely"—rather than specific rules—like "don't exceed sixty miles per hour." What constitutes safe driving may vary considerably, depending on several factors, such as the competence of the driver, the conditions of the road, and the driving of other people.[51] Similarly, moral behavior, which combines both emotional sensitivity and general intellectual rules, may vary considerably, depending on several personal and contextual features. We may provide some specific rules which may help us achieve moral behavior, but at the end of the day personal and contextual features will have a crucial role in determining our moral behavior.

The integration suggested here between emotion and thinking is not easy to attain. On the contrary, it is extremely difficult as there are no clear directions or rules for attaining it successfully.

*Emotions and Tolerance*

I am extraordinarily patient provided I get my own way in the end.
—Margaret Thatcher

Morality is concerned with taking care of others' needs. Hence, tolerance, which may be characterized as the disposition to be patient with the opinions or practices of others which deviate from a standard, is central to morality. But how can we be patient with something we are convinced is not moral? Is it moral to disregard something which in light of our principles is perceived to be a sin? As Herbert Samuel noted, "It is easy to be tolerant of the principles of other people if you have none of your own."

Following Peter Nicholson, a few major characteristics of typical tolerance may be discerned:

1. *Deviance*: what is tolerated deviates from what the tolerator believes should be done.
2. *Disapproval*: the tolerator disapproves morally of the deviation.
3. *Importance*: the deviation is not trivial.
4. *Power*: the tolerator has the power to try to suppress what is tolerated (a powerless person can be tolerant only in a dispositional way).
5. *Nonrejection*: the tolerator does not exercise his power, thereby allowing the deviation to continue.
6. *Goodness*: the tolerator believes that toleration is right.[52]

The deviation toward which we are supposed to be tolerant should be significant; there is no sense in speaking about toleration concerning insignificant matters. The moral deviation should be in substantial conflict with our values in order to create the moral dilemma underlying tolerance. It should also be remembered that tolerance is no longer a virtue when the deviation is very severe. Thus, it is not moral to be tolerant toward murders. The deviation we should tolerate is located then within a lower and an upper limit.

Tolerance includes the belief that freedom of speech and actions is of important moral value; hence, we should try to have such a freedom even if it means the presence of opinions and deeds that we believe are morally wrong. Tolerance is not recommended when it is in conflict with basic values whose importance is greater than that of such a freedom. All of us have a hierarchy of values; tolerance is typically quite high in this hierarchy, but it usually does not occupy the highest position. Thus, saving human life has usually greater moral value than maintaining the freedom of certain people. Therefore, we should not be tolerant toward murders.

The reference to an evaluative hierarchy may solve the theoretical problem of why we are tolerant of deeds we believe are immoral. The value of freedom of speech and actions is higher than the negative value we attach to their content. The moral problem of tolerance remains in the practical domain: how could we know when the value of such a freedom, and hence tolerance, is higher than the negative value of the consequences of such a freedom? To this problem there is no definite answer and the matter should be examined in the different contexts in which such a freedom is required.

When comparing emotional and tolerant attitudes, we can notice that in both cases the object deviates from a standard held by the subject and the deviation is of some importance. Emotions are not generated in the presence of insignificant changes, and there is no room for tolerance if the disputed matter is of little significance. The difference in this regard between emotional and tolerant attitudes is that emotional attitudes take the deviance to be temporal: we should either overcome the change or become accustomed to it. The emotional system does not necessarily assume that the deviance is harmful or morally wrong. It rather assumes that if the person decides to maintain the deviance, this given event must change its status from a deviance to that of a normal and stable feature of our life. When such a change in status takes place, this event will not be the responsibility of the emotional system, but of another one. Unlike the situation in emotional attitudes, in the attitude of tolerance there is the belief that the deviance could stay for a long time and that tolerating the deviance is good.

A related difference between emotional and tolerant attitudes seems to be the one concerning emotional partiality, namely, the narrow and involved nature of emotional attitudes. Unlike the emotional perspective, and like the intellectual one, tolerance is characterized by a broad perspective. George Eliot said: "The responsibility of tolerance lies in those who have the wider vision." Tolerance requires holding a few perspectives at once and making room for all such perspectives. In emotions such a coexistence is impossible: in an emotional state we clearly prefer one narrow perspective over other perspectives.

Tolerance is closer to intellectual reasoning than to emotions, not only in its broader perspective but also in its less involved nature. A broader perspective typically reduces the involved and intense nature of our attitude. In accordance with its broad perspective and less involved nature, people often identify tolerance with neutrality between competing perspectives of the good. Thus, Somerset Maugham claimed: "Tolerance is another word for indifference." If we are deeply committed to a certain value, how can we be tolerant of a behavior expressing an opposing value? The neutral, and sometimes even indifferent, attitude typical of tolerance raises the specter of losing our own identity. Will Rogers indicated that "broad-minded is just another way of saying a fellow's too lazy to form an opinion."

In light of the above considerations, our emotional preferences seem to be irrelevant to tolerance. Indeed, it has been argued that "toleration is a matter of moral choice, and our tastes or inclinations are irrelevant."[53] One may further claim that emotions are obstacles to tolerance: tolerance is an attitude in which intellectual reasoning overcomes emotional values, although the tolerator still believes in the truth of those values. Toleration may be characterized as doing what you do not want to, namely, allowing wrong opinions and actions to continue.

The assumption that tolerance is a state in which we overcome emotional attitudes conflicts with the notion of tolerance as a neutral attitude. We allow the expression of some opinions and actions with which we do not agree because we believe that intolerance may have worse consequences. Accordingly, tolerance may be described as the ordering of priorities done by a prudential intellectual calculation.[54] Tolerance is then not a neutral stand, but a stand having priorities which override specific personal values or beliefs.

Solving the above conflict concerning the neutrality of tolerance requires, I believe, a distinction between the intellectual and emotional aspects of tolerance. When describing tolerance as an attitude in which intellectual reasoning overcomes or neglects emotional values, there is in tolerance an emotional neutrality, but not an intellectual one. In this notion of intellectual tolerance, emotions are an obstacle to tolerance as they prevent us from seeing the other's perspective. I agree that this notion of intellectual tolerance is valid for many circumstances. I believe, however, that there is also a notion of emotional tolerance. In that notion, emotions can overcome intellectual beliefs and this accordingly involves an intellectual neutrality, but not an emotional one.

If indeed there are different principles at the basis of our moral behavior toward our intimates and toward strangers, we should expect to find different types of tolerance in the two situations: intellectual and emotional. In the intellectual type, which is typical of our relationship with strangers, a broad, impartial, and indifferent perspective is essential. This type of tolerance is obviously not adequate in our relationship with our intimates: an impartial and indifferent perspective cannot be the main perspective in such a relationship. The intellectual type of tolerance is compatible with the dictionary characterization of tolerance as the disposition to be patient with the opinions or practices of others which deviate from a standard; this type of tolerance is limited and chiefly negative—it mainly consists of prohibitions against interfering with the opinions or practices of other people. Emotional tolerance is a more profound type of tolerance; it involves providing other people with the necessary means for expressing their opinions and exercising their practices, although those may be incompatible with our own values. Similarly, one aspect of morality is not to hurt other people, but a more profound aspect is that of extensively helping others by devoting to them many resources such as time, attention, and money.

If, for example, Aaron's wife likes fashionable clothes and his son is enthusiastic about football, while Aaron himself believes that investing money in those things is of no value whatsoever, Aaron's tolerance should not merely be expressed by his lack of objections to their pursuing their interests. Real tolerance implies that he should actively assist them, even if this means sacrificing resources that he believes would be better devoted to more valuable activities. Here, there are no emotional difficulties to overcome, as Aaron loves his wife and son, but there are intellectual beliefs to overcome: the assumption that our resources should be invested in more valuable things in life.

Devoting our personal resources requires personal sacrifice and to do this we need to have strong emotional ties to those for whom we sacrifice our resources. The greater the sacrifice, the more emotional involvement needed. Tolerance presupposes taking the other's perspective. In the case of intellectual tolerance this can be done by merely being aware of other people's perspectives. However, when tolerance requires significant sacrifice, taking the other's perspective means more than being aware of it; it implies identifying oneself with the other's perspective. In this case, we should assume an emotional attitude similar or close to that of the other person.

We readily make significant personal sacrifices toward our intimates not because we believe in the equality of all human beings—such a belief is sufficient merely for intellectual tolerance—but because we love them very much. For those near and dear to us tolerance is not something required of us; it is an attitude we want to have, and we are emotionally convinced of its value.

I have suggested that whereas intellectual tolerance requires overcoming emotional attitudes, emotional tolerance requires overcoming intellectual beliefs. Although we may believe that spoiling our children may have negative consequences, we sometimes overcome this intellectual belief and run family affairs not from the adult's perspective but from that of the children. When we surrender to the unique, and sometimes even intellectually bizarre requirements of our intimates, we exhibit emotional tolerance which overcomes intellectual beliefs. In such behavior, we express intellectual neutrality, or even indifference, but clear emotional preferences.

Despite the differences between the two types of tolerance, there are some elements common to them. In both types we tolerate behavior which is to some degree objectionable to us. Moreover, although in an important sense intellectual tolerance should overcome emotional tendencies, it also includes, in another sense, emotional approval. Similarly, although emotional tolerance should overcome some intellectual beliefs, in another respect it also agrees with them. Intellectual tolerance overcomes our immediate emotional tendencies, but overcoming these tendencies requires some kind of empathy toward others. Others are perceived to be human beings toward whom we have emotional affinity. They are not complete strangers; they are human beings who have beliefs, wishes, and desires the way we have. In the same vein, emotional tolerance overcomes some intellectual beliefs concerning the negative value of what others are doing, but it also contains the intellectual belief that in some sense it is important to let other people do what they want to do.

Tolerance is then an attitude toward the deviant which from at least one perspective is negatively evaluated; nevertheless, there is another perspective in light of which it is positively evaluated. Quite often the two different perspectives are the intellectual and emotional ones. The intellectual perspective, and hence intellectual tolerance, is more dominant in our behavior toward strangers; in these circumstances emotions are irrelevant and often even an obstacle. The emotional perspective, and hence emotional tolerance, is more dominant in considering our behavior toward our intimates; in this perspective, which constitutes the main bulk of our everyday behavior, emotions are crucial in generating and maintaining tolerant behavior.

*Summary*

I love thee for a heart that's kind—Not for the knowledge in thy mind.
W. H. Davies


The role of emotions in the moral domain has frequently been disputed. The partial nature of emotions seems to contradict the more general and egalitarian nature of many moral evaluations. Although the difference in generality between emotional attitudes and many moral rules is indeed evident, emotions are nevertheless morally valuable. They are especially important in our relationships with those near and dear to us. In such circumstances, which constitute the bulk of our everyday behavior, partial emotional attitudes are not only possible but morally commendable. Sincerity and particular attention to specific needs, both typical of emotional attitudes, are of crucial importance. Emotional attitudes are also a moral barrier against many crimes. Emotional evaluations have emerged through a long process of evolutionary and personal moral development. Accordingly, they are significant in expressing some of our deepest values and commitments and in providing basic guidelines for moral behavior. However, the crucial role of emotions in moral life does not imply their exclusivity; the intellectual capacity is important as well.

We can consider as moral a person who possesses an emotional disposition which fits our moral values, as well as an intellectual reasoning which can direct our moral behavior when there is no secure emotional direction or when the emotional direction is obviously morally distorted. Accordingly, our moral education should aim at increasing the correlation between emotional dispositions and moral values, as well as developing the capacity for critical intellectual reasoning which can examine our emotional behavior from a broader perspective.

# Part II

# Analyzing Emotions

How far you go in life depends on your being tender with the young, compassionate with the aged, sympathetic with the striving and tolerant of the weak and strong. Because someday in your life you will have been all of these.
—George Washington Carver

After providing a general framework for understanding emotions, we turn now to apply this framework to individual emotions. The analysis of particular emotions is made by comparing at least two emotions. Such a comparison will demonstrate the different relationships between emotions, thereby improving our understanding of each. A somewhat rigid form of discussion was chosen in order to emphasize similarities and differences among the different emotions. Such a systematic discussion is quite useful owing to the complex and diverse perspectives of the relevant phenomena. Without a systematic discussion we may uncover some interesting emotional phenomena, but would not understand the realm as a whole.

The discussion of each emotion begins with describing its general characteristics to be followed by an analysis of its relationship with other emotions. Then, an examination of the intensity variables influencing the emotion is presented. A discussion of the moral value of the emotion ends each discussion.

# Chapter 10

# Why Do We Feel Bad When You Feel Good?
# —Envy and Jealousy

I have never been envious. Not even when my dad finished fifth grade a year before I did.
—Jeff Foxworthy

Emotions toward the fortune of others constitute a common group whose prevalence is related to the importance we attach to the comparison with others in assessing our own value and happiness. This group is divided according to others' good or bad fortune. The major items in the group of negative emotions toward the good fortune of others are envy and jealousy; the major emotions in the parallel group directed at the bad fortune of others are pity and compassion. Positive evaluation of the good fortune of others underlies the emotion of happy-for, and positive evaluation of the bad fortune of others underlies pleasure-in-others'-misfortune. The major emotions discussed in this chapter are envy and jealousy.

Envy involves a negative evaluation of our undeserved inferiority, whereas jealousy involves a negative evaluation of the possibility of losing something—typically, a favorable human relationship—to someone else. Envy and jealousy would seem to address a similar emotional attitude. Both are concerned with a change in what one has: either the wish to obtain or the fear of loss. The wish in envy is for something one does not have, while in jealousy it is something one fears losing. This distinction is not negligible: the wish to obtain something is notably different from the wish not to lose it. Another difference is that jealousy is typically associated with exclusive human relationships. Envy has no such restrictions. The focus of concern in envy is our undeserved inferiority. Because inferiority can stem from a variety of factors, envy may be born of any or all of them and not merely from the threatened loss of some human relationships. While in principle jealousy may also refer to the possible loss of something other than exclusive human relationships, typical jealousy is concerned with a most painful loss: that of an exclusive relationship in which our mate, or anyone who is closely associated with us, prefers someone else.[1]

The meaning of the terms "envy" and "jealousy" overlap; some languages do not even have two separate names for these emotions. What causes conflation of envy and jealousy are the frequency of their co-occurrence and the discomfort with envy's moral connotations. In English, for example, "jealousy" has a broad meaning which may denote either the sense of jealousy described here or envy. The word "envy," on the other hand, will almost always have the specific meaning mentioned here. The lexical meanings of emotional terms and their everyday use are not of major concern here, but rather the distinct nature of emotional states. Nevertheless, I hope that the analysis provided in this chapter preserves some of the central meanings of these terms. Thus, in accordance with their usage in English, the attitude described here as envy may easily occur without jealousy, but jealousy is often accompanied by envy.[2]

*General Characteristics*

*Envy*
Where there is no comparison, no envy; and therefore kings are not envied but by kings.
—Francis Bacon

Envy is typically directed at human beings. We do not envy a mountain of gold, but the person who has more gold than we. In some atypical cases, envy may be directed at animals or inanimate objects. The person we envy has personal attributes (such as beauty, patience, or intelligence), possessions (such as a car), or positions (being the boss) that we lack but desire. We envy both what other people are and what they have.

The things associated with the people we envy may be transferable or nontransferable. Knowledge is an example of the former, beauty of the latter. In envy we are primarily concerned with our comparative position and not with the intrinsic value of the goods in question; hence, what is crucial is that someone owns the desired object. Because the envious person lacks the desired item, this person has not yet developed a personal attitude toward it and will therefore be satisfied to attain something similar. If Tom envies Dean for having a beautiful wife, Tom does not necessarily want Dean's wife; some other beautiful woman will suffice. Although we may envy the particular characteristics, possessions, or status someone has, we would usually prefer to acquire what we envy in a somewhat different form. In this respect envy is general. Quite often, the envier does not envy one particular person, but many people. A woman whose complexion has been seriously damaged may envy every smooth-skinned woman; a father of daughters may envy everyone who has sons. Yet, while envy is general in this sense, its generation is often associated with a particular event. Thus, the father of daughters may feel a more intense envy when a baby boy is born to his friend.

Two major issues appear to be prominent in explaining envy: (1) inferiority, (2) desert. Taking each issue as a central concern of envy results in the formulation of two major approaches: (1) envy is concerned with *our inferiority*; (2) envy is concerned with someone's *undeserved good fortune*. The first approach assumes others to be entitled to their superiority; in this view, envy does not express moral protest. In the second approach envy might be basically considered a justified, moral emotion since others are unworthy of their good situation. Following Aristotle, Adam Smith adopts the first approach: "Envy is that passion which views with malignant dislike the superiority of those who are really entitled to all the superiority they possess."[3] In accordance with the second approach, Descartes emphasizes the unwarranted position of others: in envy "we judge the others unworthy of their good." This difference is reflected in the way envy is related to resentment which supposedly expresses a moral protest. The first approach clearly distinguishes the two emotions; in the second, envy is perceived as a type of resentment. Thus, for Aristotle both envy and resentment involve pain caused by the sight of other people's good fortune; but whereas resentment is concerned with undeserved good fortune, envy is concerned merely with others having something that we want. In contrast, Ortony and his colleagues regard undeservingness as the central concern of envy and classify envy as a specific example of resentment: resentment involves a concern for the undeservingness of the other person enjoying the benefit; envy adds to this concern our desire to obtain the benefit.[4]

The assumption that moral concern is central to envy is fraught with difficulties. To begin with, envy is often directed at people who are lucky, but being lucky is not immoral. Moreover, envy addresses a partial concern rather than a moral concern: it entails the desire to improve our personal lot, not the desire to improve the well-being of other people. This is in accordance with the discriminative and partial nature of emotions in general. Furthermore, sometimes the envious person wishes to deprive others of their greater benefits, even if this means depriving oneself of some benefits as well. There can hardly be moral justification for such a desire; it would make sense only if our comparative inferiority were of crucial importance. The readiness to suffer in order to make the other person suffer more is illustrated in the story about the angel who came to earth and promised a farmer the fulfillment of any wish, though on one condition: his neighbor would receive twice as much of the same. In that case, said the farmer, please remove one of my eyes.

If moral concern is not essential to envy, its classification as a particular example of resentment is inadequate. Resentment may be characterized as an emotional protest against what is perceived as morally unjust. Accordingly, it is closer to anger than to envy. Although resentment is sometimes directed at the superiority of others, it focuses on some injustice rather than on superiority itself. We may distinguish between discontent, envy, and resentment. Discontent arises when we believe that something is wrong, namely, a better alternative is available. Envy occurs when the wrongness is related to our inferior situation; resentment occurs when wrongdoing is perceived: it conveys an implicit accusation. When unjust treatment, but not inferiority, is perceived, anger and resentment are more dominant than envy. Envious people often like to emphasize their concern for moral justice, thus attempting to justify it. Accordingly, they tend to describe their attitude as resentment rather than envy. It is clear, however, that this is often a kind of rationalization of their negative attitude to being inferior.

If desert is not the central concern of envy, the natural candidate for such concern is inferiority. The importance of the inferiority concern in envy conveys the weight we attach to our comparative stand. People compare themselves with others to reduce uncertainty about themselves and maintain or enhance self-esteem. An unfavorable comparison often leads to envy. Social comparison appears in many forms; an obvious form typical of envy is competitiveness. Our inferiority displeases us since it is perceived as reflecting some loss in a certain ongoing competition. The differences among different people are often perceived as reflecting different positions in an underlying competition. As Kohn argues:

> Competition creates a prized status where none existed before, thereby giving us something to desire. Then it insures that not everyone can get it. Finally, competition requires that those who obtain the reward can do so only by defeating everyone else. Both the objective and subjective conditions for envy are established, in other words: restricted access to something desired and a (quite accurate) belief that someone else has got it at one's own expense.[5]

Envy presupposes a certain social comparison, but not necessarily—though typically—competition. Competition is one form of social comparison. My wish to be as wealthy as Bill Gates involves social comparison, but not competition. I cannot conceive of myself as competing with Bill Gates in this regard.

It is our relative deprivation, rather than all types of deprivation, which bothers us in envy. A rich person can be envious of another having a bit more; a beautiful movie star can be envious of another star's beauty. As Samuel Johnson remarks: "Our desires always increase with our possessions. The knowledge that something remains yet unenjoyed impairs our enjoyment of the good before us." Enviers want to be better more than they want to be better-off. Hence, "kings may seem to have almost everything good a person could have, but they may envy if there is anything good they yet lack and if they think that other kings have some advantage over them."[6] The notion of relative deprivation implies a distinction between the objective and subjective well-being of the subject, and the claim that the two are not isomorphically related; sometimes the better-off from an "objective" viewpoint feels subjectively worse-off. Thus, a survey revealed that first-line supervisors earning between $12,000 and $15,000 a year were more satisfied with their salaries than company presidents earning about $40,000 a year. It is often true that those who are the most deprived in an objective sense are not the ones most likely to experience deprivation.[7] The fact that envy involves relative deprivation emphasizes the importance of the inferiority concern in envy. It may also explain why what seems to be most envied is glory.[8]

It may be argued that envy is generated not only when social comparison indicates our inferiority but whenever we desire something that we lack: for example, when we are tired or wish to have more money. I believe, however, that such cases represent discontent or covetousness rather than envy. In discontent and covetousness social comparison is not as essential as in envy. Unlike covetousness and discontent, which are merely concerned with gaining something or achieving a certain state, envy is mainly concerned with someone else who has something or is in a certain state. I covet money and am discontented with my financial situation, but I envy the rich. Since inferiority is comparative in nature—to be inferior is to be situated lower than someone else—its central place in envy also indicates the comparative nature of envy. It is not actual, but comparative absence of something which concerns us in envy.

We usually do not envy dead people and can afford to be generous to them because we usually do not compete with them. Following Thomas Hobbes, we may even say that praise of dead figures frequently proceeds from envy of the living with whom we compete rather than from reverence of the dead. When we consider ourselves as competing with the dead, as when we want to outstrip their achievements, we may envy or be bitter toward them. Aristotle argues that the lack of competition is also the reason why we do not envy those not yet born.[9] It seems, however, that we envy future more than past generations. One reason is the constant improvement in the quality of life. Since such rapid improvement was less typical in ancient times—it was even assumed that the golden age was over—this factor has less weight in Aristotle's view. Another reason is rooted in the fact that it is easier for us to imagine a past world without us than a future world in which we do not exist.

It is quite clear that the central element of envy is not a moral concern but perceived inferiority. If inferiority were the only concern in envy, we should expect a positive correlation between the intensity of envy and our inferiority. However, before adopting this conclusion we should examine whether inferiority is the only concern in envy and whether envy involves all kinds of inferiority.

Like other emotions, envy is partial; it typically addresses people who belong to our emotional environment, that is, those of emotional significance for us. The inferiority concern in envy is partial in referring to specific people in specific domains. We neither compare ourselves with everyone nor do we compare everything. We do not envy those who succeed in areas insignificant to us. As indicated, our low position is relative: it need not be low in comparison with the whole population, the average position in society, or even the top 5 percent; it is inferior in comparison with the position of a person emotionally significant to us.

We may envy only one aspect of another person, yet continue to consider ourselves superior in general. We may envy someone for being rich, but if we know this person to be dishonest, we consider ourselves superior. Frontline troops may envy noncombat troops in the rear but simultaneously develop a feeling of superiority to them; they wish they could replace safer troops, but nevertheless feel greatly superior to them. A person clearly superior to another person may be envious of the same person who surpassed her in a specific sphere. In such cases envy would not usually be intense. Similarly, we may desire to possess something, but if this thing does not belong to our self-defining domains, envy will not arise nor will it be intense. The lack of these things does not make us feel inferior since we either have enough other good things to which our self-esteem is linked, or we have found deeper satisfaction elsewhere.[10]

Whether we admire or envy another person is among other things determined by the relevance of that person's good fortune to our self-esteem. When the good fortune is relevant, our self-esteem and the evaluation of ourselves by others is threatened and envy arises. This is particularly true of domains in which large discrepancies exist between actual and ideal self-description. Here the threat to our self-esteem is especially strong.

The partial nature of envy is one feature distinguishing typical adult envy from the envy typical of children. For young children the value of most things comes simply from seeing others with them. General envy, nonspecific to certain people or domains, is typical only of young children who lack a well-defined sense of what is relevant or irrelevant to themselves, and consequently feel discomfort every time they fail to measure up to another's performance. Older children are more selective in this respect: failure in domains of importance elicit more envy than that in marginal domains.[11] Similarly, we may characterize children's pleasure-in-others'-misfortune as nonspecific to certain people or domains; they enjoy many types of failures.

Sometimes envy involves, in addition to the wish to eliminate inferiority, the wish to achieve superiority. The latter wish may be understood as a preventive measure against being in an inferior situation. It is said, for example, that Rise Stevens refused to sing at the San Francisco Opera House, although she had been granted the top fee she had demanded, because her other request, that no other star should be paid as highly, had been rejected. Stevens did not actually envy other people; she just wanted to state her superiority in a way that would prevent any comparison with other people and hence the threat of envy.

The importance of the inferiority concern in envy has led many people to believe that envy is characteristic of people with low self-esteem who have grown up with an inferiority complex or a similar personal problem. Accordingly, people of excellent character and background have claimed to be entirely unacquainted with envy. This claim is mistaken as it fails to take into account the relative nature of the inferiority concern in envy. Relative inferiority is typical of all people as no person is superior in all domains. Indeed, although in fiction the envious person is often depicted as having a negative and poor background, psychological research has failed to reveal a significant positive correlation between envy and jealousy and a person's low self-esteem.[12]

The foregoing discussion has indicated that envy is not concerned with inferiority in general but with specific inferiority regarding people who are emotionally significant to us. This conclusion complicates the suggestion that inferiority is the sole concern in envy and that we should therefore expect a positive correlation between the intensity of envy and the subject-object gap. Since social comparison is chiefly limited to those similar to us, envy should be more typical of small subject-object gaps. In small gaps the question of desert is quite prominent. In comparison to people similar to us, we would presumably consider our inferior situation incompatible with what we deserve. Indeed, emotional intensity is greater in unjustified than in justified circumstances. This is because the situation is considered to be more abnormal and the availability of an alternative is greater. Moreover, if a strong wish to obtain something that another person has were to persist for a long time, we would tend to feel in some degree entitled to the desired object. Desert has after all some role in the generation of envy. This may explain why when people are envious, they think of themselves as rather unlucky, whereas the person they are envious of is considered to be extremely lucky.[13] Contrary to Aristotle and many others, the envied people are typically perceived not to deserve their superiority but to be extremely lucky.

The failure to distinguish between emotional desert and moral rights and to realize that envy is concerned with the former underlies the above two approaches to explaining envy. Both approaches assume that desert is always a part of the moral domain. Accordingly, the approach considering inferiority to be the sole concern in envy realizes that in many cases the moral concern is absent and hence concludes that desert has no role in the rise of envy. The approach characterizing envy as a moral emotion identifies envy with resentment and considers both to be moral emotions.[14] Explaining envy and resolving the dispute between the two approaches require the rejection of the identification between the moral domain and the domain of desert.

The inequality associated with envy is often concerned with natural differences or with those arising from other impersonal causes. Since such inequality does not entail the immoral behavior or attitude of an agent, there is usually no occasion to blame anyone for this situation. Nevertheless, the situation may still be considered undeserved or unfair: it encapsulates some kind of injustice, since it places us in an undeserved situation. We often envy lucky people or those born with natural gifts. In being envious toward these people we do not accuse them of behaving criminally or immorally, but rather consider ourselves as occupying an undeserved inferior situation. The situations perceived to be unfair by envious people are often not perceived to be unfair by others. Although envy typically addresses unfairness belonging to the domain of desert, it may sometimes address immorally induced injustice. Envious people often describe the unfairness involved in their situation as belonging to the moral domain rather than to that of desert; they thus attempt to legitimize their envy and may even present it as resentment rather than envy. The urge to find some kind of unfairness in our inferior position may also be explained by referring to H. L. Mencken's aphorism, "Injustice is relatively easy to bear; it is justice that hurts." In any case, since the borderline between the moral domain and that of desert is not clear-cut, it is not always easy to distinguish between envy and resentment.

Although the issue of desert plays some role in the rise of envy, this is not the role suggested by the aforementioned two approaches. The first approach is right in arguing that inferiority is of concern in envy, and the second is right in assuming that desert is of concern in envy. The first is wrong in believing that this concern refers to what we consider to be deserved inferiority, and the second is wrong in claiming that the concern of desert is directed at others. Accordingly, envy is neither concerned with *our deserved inferiority* nor with the *other's undeserved good fortune*. Envy is rather concerned with *our undeserved inferiority*. The issue of desert is always accompanied by the issue of our inferiority. Our concern is not a general moral concern for justice, but a particular personal concern for what we consider as undeserved inferiority.

Sometimes envy includes the suspicion that our inferior position indeed reflects what we actually are; even in these cases we may still feel the situation to be unfair since being inferior is unfair. Here the complaint is not against the wrongdoing of people but against a divine or impersonal cause.

At first sight it may seem odd that envy is morally condemned despite its apparent moral demand of eliminating inequality. This difficulty is resolved by noticing that the perceived undeservingness in envy does not express moral injustice; hence, envy is not a moral emotion. Nevertheless, envy involves value claims concerning the situations in which we think we deserve to be. Hence, it has some normative justification.

The fact that in envy we consider our inferiority to be undeserved implies that we do not consider ourselves to be generally inferior to the envied person; we may even often consider ourselves superior in some sense. The current inferior situation is taken not to reflect our real worth adequately; this helps us to cope with the unpleasant situation. If the other person is perceived to be clearly above us, no such defense mechanism is available. In this case, admiration is more likely to emerge than envy.

The element of desert is not obvious in some cases commonly characterized as envy, for example, when I am hungry and see someone eating. The issue of desert is clearly present if I do not have the money to buy food. If I do have the money, however, but do not enter the restaurant because I am in a hurry, the issue of desert is hardly relevant. But such a case should not be regarded as envy—anyway not a typical case of envy. It concerns a momentary deprivation and not inferiority. Moreover, if I am in a hurry to do something that I like, I value this thing more; accordingly, the momentary hunger will not be of significance and it may be overcome by eating a sandwich. If I am hungry because I am obliged to attend a certain tedious meeting, I may think that there is something unfair in my situation; in this case my attitude will be closer to envy. Deprivation in satisfying our needs is not identical with envy. Envy involves our comparative inferiority and the belief that it is undeserved.

Consider another example. Rita thinks of herself as lazy but nevertheless envies Ingrid's success, which is the result of Ingrid's hard work. If Rita believes that her laziness is due to an innate disposition that she cannot overcome, she may consider her situation unfair, and envy is likely to emerge. If Rita can overcome her laziness, however, but chooses not to do so because she considers Ingrid's success to be not worth the price of not being lazy, then envy is not likely to appear, or it will at least not be intense. Rita may want the results of Ingrid's success, but since typical envy is directed at a person and not at a certain thing that the person has, this would not be typical envy in which we are ready to exchange our present position with that of the other person.[15]

Diverse classifications of the different types of envy have been suggested. One classification is between weak and strong envy. In weak envy our welfare has priority over the damage to other people: we may wish for the destruction of their assets, but only if it does not hurt us. In strong envy, we are willing to give up some of our welfare for a decrease in another's welfare. In the two kinds of envy, our attitude toward the envied person is not necessarily negative, though this is often the case; our behavior may be described as selfish rather than malicious or spiteful. In this regard envy may be distinguished from spite: while envy wishes for a situation in which the other's superiority is eliminated, spite wishes for the other's inferiority.[16] The wish to overcome the other's superiority can be achieved in two ways: we can either bring the other person down to our level, or we can raise ourselves up to the level of this person. The first way requires a malicious attitude and has received a lot of the attention in literature and popular legends. To cite just one proverb: "The envious man thinks that he will be able to walk better if his neighbor breaks a leg." The second way of overcoming the subject-object inequality requires explicit admiration—in contrast to the implicit admiration of the first type. This can be described as nonmalicious envy in which people aspire to gain their hero's position and even take pride in the hero's achievement. No wonder that most people welcome nonmalicious, but reject malicious envy.

*Jealousy*
He that is not jealous, is not in love.
—Saint Augustine


In contrast to envy, which is essentially a two-party relation, jealousy is basically a three-party relation. It concerns the mate's relationships with others, since these may threaten our favorable and exclusive relationship with the mate. The threat in jealousy may be either of completely losing our relationship with the mate, or losing qualities of that relationship, even though the relationship itself may endure. The prototypical instance of jealousy is romantic jealousy.

In light of the fact that envy is a two-party relation and jealousy is a three-party relation, envy may be part of jealousy, but jealousy is not part of envy. Situations creating jealousy inherently also create envy to some degree. Even when the rival is believed to be unattractive, incompetent, and unsuccessful, the attention the rival receives from the protagonist's romantic partner is sufficient to elicit envy.[17]

The objects of jealousy are, typically, two people: the primary emotional object is the mate (or another person close to us); the secondary object is the rival. The lesser significance of the rival is expressed by the fact that the rival can be imaginary, and even known to be so to us. The object of envy functions more as a reminder of our disadvantageous situation than as the cause of this situation (though sometimes it is also perceived as a cause), whereas the object of jealousy functions more as a cause than as a reminder of our disadvantageous situation (though it is also a reminder).

Since jealousy is typically directed at our mate, and the number of mates we can have is limited, as is the number of people with whom we have special relationships, jealousy is essentially directed at a few people. Although envy is less restricted in this respect, it is not indiscriminate either: we do not envy everyone who is superior to us. The objects of jealousy are fewer in number as a result of the more personal nature of jealousy. This is in contrast to envy, whose objects may be substituted because envy does not presuppose a previous personal relationship and is often evoked by characteristics shared by many people. If David envies Adam because he has a better car than David, David's envy will cease not only when he gets the same car as Adam's but any similar car. However, David's jealousy toward his wife who has a lover will not necessarily cease, even if he also has a lover who is as attractive as his wife. His attitude toward his wife is personal, and someone else cannot be a suitable substitute for her.

Jealousy is more personal and generates greater vulnerability than envy; it is more likely to cause profound injury to our self-esteem since it touches on far more significant aspects of our self-esteem. The threat it carries is posed by a person with intimate and reliable information about us. The severity of the threat may explain why jealousy is so intense despite the prevalence of sexual infidelity (the estimates in this regard vary considerably: most surveys indicate a 30 to 50 percent incidence of extramarital affairs, but some surveys even reach 80 percent). The intense pain generated by jealousy is not because something extraordinary has happened, but because we may lose something of crucial importance to us.

The focus of concern in jealousy is the threat to our exclusive position and in particular to some unique human relationship. We are afraid of losing our present favorable position to someone else and of ending up in an inferior position. Experiencing a loss to a rival, rather than merely losing something, is the central factor in jealousy. Accordingly, when people kill their mate out of jealousy, they do not

prevent the loss of the mate, but the loss to a rival. Preventing this loss is important to them, even if it means the loss of their own life. Hence the instances of
those who murder their partner and then commit suicide. Jealousy would not arise
if one were rejected by one's partner without the partner taking up a new relationship with someone else. Although both rejection and jealousy may lower self-
esteem, simple rejection does not necessarily mean loss to a rival and hence does
not necessarily arouse jealousy.

In the typical case of jealousy the object is a human being and we are concerned
with losing a unique relationship with that person. Jealousy is an expression of a
three-party relationship in which each party is typically a human being. In cases
of the most typical example, romantic jealousy, the human identity of each party
is obvious. In less typical cases, the role fulfilled by a human partner and a human
rival may be fulfilled by an inanimate object. For instance, the husband of a
woman who devotes most of her time to music may be said to be jealous of the
music. He loses the exclusive relationship he enjoys with his wife to the music.
We can also be jealous of an inanimate thing. Someone unwilling to share a unique
recipe with someone else is said to be jealously guarding the recipe: this person
does not wish to lose an exclusive standing. Although these situations may be
described as cases of jealousy, they are not typical. Someone refusing to share a
recipe is not an example of typical jealousy because this case does not involve an
all-or-nothing personal rivalry over preference for a third party. The case of the
musician is atypical because there is no real competition: since music is so different from a human being, the husband does not have to consider himself a loser
and, hence, as inferior in this rivalry. For similar reasons the fear of a mate's death,
which is also fear of losing one's mate, is not a type of jealousy since it does not
entail an experience of losing to someone else. Typical instances of jealousy
involve two human beings competing over a favorable chosen relationship with
a third human being.

In jealousy, maintaining self-esteem comes by proving the suspicions groundless. Improving our situation in envy greatly depends on ourselves; in jealousy,
the partner's attitude is more significant. Therefore, the motivation to improve
ourselves is more salient in envy than in jealousy.[18]

In jealousy we want to "get even" with both the mate and the rival, and to maintain the relationship. These two desires are often incompatible.

In envy we are mainly troubled by an existing inferior situation rather than, as
in jealousy, by the threat of winding up in such a situation. Envy is concerned
with a current situation in which our inferior position is already evident; jealousy
anticipates a future or possible threat. Accordingly, the envious person wants to
change the existing situation, whereas the jealous person fears a change in the
existing situation. The cognitive element is therefore usually more veridical in
envy than in jealousy as the threat in jealousy can be imaginary. Jealousy often
involves fantasy. Proust compares jealousy to a historian without documents.
Frequently, our jealousy does not die when we realize our error; any pretext

whatsoever is sufficient to revive this emotion. Indeed, the most frequent event eliciting jealousy among married people is not actual infidelity, but involves the partner paying attention, or giving time and support to, a member of the opposite sex. This situation tends to elicit extreme jealousy when the third party is the partner's ex-spouse.[19]

Exclusivity does not necessarily mean the exclusion of all people. There are various types and degrees of exclusivity. We may speak about exclusivity in the quantitative sense and the qualitative sense. Quantitative exclusivity refers to the number of people with whom our partner can have relationships without invoking our jealousy; qualitative exclusivity refers to the types of relationships that can invoke jealousy.

From a quantitative perspective, the claim to exclusivity does not have to refer to the relationship merely between two people. There can be some flexibility in this regard. A woman in a polygamous marriage may not be jealous of any of the other women married to her husband, but she may be jealous of women outside the marriage. Similarly, a woman who was divorced for a long time told a reporter: "For six years, I had an affair with a married person. I loved him very much and we had wonderful sex. Once I found out that he had affairs with other women, I terminated our relationship." It was clear that this woman did not have an exclusive relationship with her married lover, but she did expect some limited exclusivity; however, once this limited exclusivity was abrogated as well, she was jealous and could not continue the relationship. In such cases, sexual jealousy still requires exclusivity, though a more flexible variety.

There is also a quantitative aspect to jealousy which is expressed in the types of relationships which may evoke jealousy. A very strict jealousy in this respect forbids all types of social relationships between a married person—usually, a woman—and a person of the opposite sex. Thus, in some very religious communities, a married woman is not allowed to be in any type of social contact with a man other than her husband. A less strict jealousy may refer only to sexual relationships. There can even be some flexibility in the sexual context. We may allow our mate to have one short affair, say once every year, or to have an affair with people we do not know, without considering it an abrogation of our exclusive relationship, and hence without giving any cause for jealousy, at least not of an intense kind. These types of less strict exclusivity are often practical arrangements for not losing the mate, but they do not necessarily abolish jealousy. It is plausible to expect that when the more flexible types of exclusivity are abrogated, jealousy will be less intense than when typical strict exclusivity is abrogated.

There can be types of exclusivity other than those which forbid all types of social relationships or those which forbid merely sexual ones. These types may refer not merely to sexual relationships but also to going to a movie, having a meal together, working together, or spending a lot of time together. The personal and cultural differences associated with jealousy are expressed in the type of exclusivity which underlies jealousy.

Sometimes, jealousy is not concerned with actual exclusivity but merely with apparent exclusivity. A man may be indifferent to the fact that his wife is having an affair as long as this affair is kept secret and his apparent exclusive position remains intact. We may distinguish here between adultery and infidelity. Adultery has a clear definition which is not dependent upon the attitudes of the two partners; infidelity is related to their attitudes and to their explicit or implicit agreements. There are cases, such as open marriages, where adultery is not regarded as infidelity. There are also cases in which an activity is considered to involve infidelity although it is not adulterous—for instance, going to a movie with someone without the knowledge of one's partner.

Although there are various types of exclusivity, it seems that some type of exclusivity is emotionally significant. As I have argued, emotions are partial attitudes assuming unique relationships. Not only in the emotional realm, but in other realms as well, exclusivity is of significant value. To give one example, the price of a flawed coin is often literally millions of times higher than that of otherwise identical coins which were minted in large quantities.[20]

Like envy, jealousy also involves competition—not general but specific competition with a third party. Jealousy stems from the desire to be "favored" in some respect and the suspicion that one is not. The choice of someone else over us contributes to the painful nature of jealousy. The loss is no accident but a clear preference for the other. The issue of preference is of crucial importance in jealousy. This also suggests that jealous people do not treat their mate as an inanimate object, but as a free, responsible person able to make reasonable choices.[21] The crucial element in jealousy is the mate's free choice, not our own. We may be jealous of a mate whom we never chose. But our jealousy would be weaker, if not completely eliminated, were our mate's behavior to be forced upon him or her. As indicated, the lack of personal control reduces emotional intensity.

Jealousy is often interpreted as a sign of our caring and love for the mate, and many instances show a positive correlation between jealousy and romantic love. Like love, jealousy typically presupposes some type of commitment underlying the relationship, and it cannot arise if our attitude is one of utter indifference. However, jealousy does not necessarily involve love. It may arise even in the absence of love and caring. A man who despises his wife may, nevertheless, become jealous when someone else looks covetously at her. Here the central feature is losing to a rival. In this case, jealousy is more germane to selfishness than to love. La Rochefoucauld said that jealousy is always born with love, but does not always die with it. Jealousy, then, is not always indicative of love. Does romantic love always involve jealousy? Augustine claimed, "He that is not jealous, is not in love." It may be better to say that wherever there is romantic love, there is always the *possibility* of jealousy. This is because romantic love entails a favorable relationship that we value. The prospect of losing that relationship could provoke jealousy. The level of involvement in the relationship is often positively correlated with the level of jealousy.[22]

The loss associated with sexual jealousy, which is often described as a loss of attention or love, is really a loss of exclusivity, or at least of a favorable relationship. Thus, we often hear the claim that infidelity makes us jealous because, as a consequence of the mate's behavior, we lose much of the attention, time, and sexual energy of the mate. But this is not necessarily the case. There are situations in which the mate, for reasons of guilt, personal considerations, or a better emotional state in general, lavishes extra-loving attention on a partner while developing an outside attachment. Jealousy appears also in these cases. This may suggest that the value of certain activities is raised if the partners engage in these activities only with each other. Some rewards may lose much of their value if they are not exclusive. This is true even when the violation of exclusivity is only imaginary. Jealousy exists also when the partner is merely sexually interested in someone else, even when this interest is restricted to the level of fantasy. Attention is not necessarily a game of all-or-nothing, but (strict) exclusivity is. An increase in attention may be interpreted as a violation of exclusivity and may therefore not be welcomed.[23]

The competitive and comparative concern is more central to envy than to jealousy. This is because in envy, the wish is to be like others, whereas in jealousy it is to maintain a relationship regardless of others. In this sense envy has the more social character. Envy usually employs a simple consideration of what we have in comparison with others; such a consideration is not essential to jealousy. For instance, a jealous person may strongly oppose the termination of a certain relationship without necessarily valuing that relationship very much.

Jealousy also involves a competitive concern, but this is different from the one prevailing in envy. The competitive concern in jealousy does not refer to social comparison concerning a higher or lower status; rather, it presupposes personal rivalry—someone else may obtain what I have. This is a zero-sum game: the other's loss, or gain, leads to a change in my own situation. In envy, the other's loss, or gain, need not lead to a change in my objective situation but merely in my subjective one—for instance, an alteration in my relative status.[24]

The desert claim in jealousy is stronger than in envy since in jealousy we are already involved in the relationship we want to maintain, and we believe that we deserve to be so. We feel more entitled to something that we already have than to something that we have never had. The intensity of jealousy, like that of envy, is reduced if we believe our situation to be deserved; for example, when the rival is perceived to be much better than us. A loss is less humiliating in jealousy if the rival is clearly perceived as superior and hence more "deserving" of the favorable relationship. Here the loss appears inevitable; we could do nothing to prevent it.

The same holds if the mate, rather than the rival, is perceived as superior. A man of low self-esteem, who considers his wife to be superior, will be typically less jealous of her; rather than feel animosity toward her, he may feel only gratitude to her for having given him whatever attention she has. The man's self-esteem is boosted by being with this superior woman and therefore, although her infidelity hurts him, in the overall calculation his relationship with such a woman increases his self-esteem. It is obvious that in these cases jealousy may also emerge—especially if the infidelity becomes public and the blow to his self-esteem exceeds other benefits he derives from being with this woman.

I have claimed that the moral concern is not central in envy. Is this concern central in jealousy? It seems to be more central in jealousy than in envy, although in both cases it is not the major concern. Indeed, an important element in jealousy is a belief in being treated unjustly. Although the norms which the jealous person believes are violated are usually not merely the norms of fairness, as is often the case in envy, but moral norms as well, jealousy cannot be explained by merely referring to moral injustice. We can be jealous without believing our jealousy to be justified. For instance, a husband who has continual love affairs may recognize his wife's moral right to have affairs as well, but he will still be jealous when she does. John F. Kennedy, who had many love affairs, was nevertheless quite jealous of his wife Jacqueline when he suspected her of having an affair with the wealthy Greek businessman Aristotle Onassis (whom she later married).

Interestingly, psychological research has discovered that people who intended to have love affairs reported less jealousy than those who did not have such intentions, but individuals who actually had extramarital sexual experiences were not less jealous.[25] The reason for these peculiar findings may be the following: the mere intention to have an extramarital affair focuses our attention on the anticipated future pleasure; actually experiencing the affair is more complex and arouses our keen awareness of all the elements involved in having an affair. Jealousy is considerably enhanced by realizing what is going on.

I have suggested that the focus of concern in envy, namely, our undeserved inferiority, is specific in the sense that it refers to a specific person who is relevant to our self-esteem. Jealousy is similar in this respect. It obviously refers to a specific person, namely, the mate, who is very relevant to our self-esteem. Jealousy also depends on the specific characteristics of the rival. Generally, jealousy increases when the domain of the rival's achievements is also relevant to our self-esteem. Thus, a jealous reaction might be more likely with individuals who place great importance on physical attractiveness when their rival is unusually attractive. Similarly, a woman with a large real-ideal discrepancy in personal wealth, and for whom wealth is very important to her self-esteem, is likely to report great envy if her neighbor won the state lottery and great jealousy if her husband flirted with a wealthy woman at a party—more so than if her husband flirted with a woman with different attributes such as fame, attractiveness, or popularity.[26]

The significance of the rival's achievements in jealousy depends not only on their relevance to the way we desire ourselves to be but also to the way we believe our partner finds them desirable. Jealousy would also be intense if we knew that our partner liked smart people and our rival was smart. The threat to our relationship increases when the rival is compatible with our partner's desires.

These two different considerations, namely, those relevant to our self-esteem and those to the partner's desires, express two major concerns in jealousy: a concern for self-esteem and a concern for the future of the relationship. Different people may give different weights to each of these concerns. For example, women give more weight to the second concern than men do. So their jealousy is greater when it stems from a belief that the rival possesses characteristics that their partner finds desirable. Men's jealousy, from the standpoint of their own self-esteem, is greater in response to a rival who possesses enviable qualities. Women, more so than men, consider their partners' desires as constituting domains relevant to their self-esteem.[27]

A major concern in envy is a certain inequality, whereas a major concern in jealousy is a certain exclusivity. It could be argued that jealousy is concerned with maintaining inequality and envy with abolishing exclusivity. But though exclusivity often connotes inequality and inequality connotes exclusivity, the two are not identical. "Exclusivity" here is a certain social *limitation*; it refers to something that is limited to a single individual or group. In this context "inequality" refers to social *disparity*, to a situation in which someone occupies an inferior position. Exclusivity would not contradict equality if everyone had similar exclusive access. Thus, there could be equality among all people who form married couples, even though they all had exclusive relationships with their mates.

Typically, envy and jealousy involve unpleasant feelings which disturb us and which we would like to overcome. Jealousy is a more negative personal attitude, expressed in more intense desires and feelings and in being more aggressive than envy. Jealousy is usually more painful than envy (a) because of its more personal nature, and (b) because it is more difficult to bear the loss of something you have than not to gain something you never had. The first reason is self-evident: a personal offense is clearly more injurious than one which can be construed as general. The second reason, namely, the more painful nature of a loss, is clearly exemplified in everyday experience. Given the choice, people usually prefer to win $40 when the odds are certain, rather than take a 50 percent chance of winning $100. One possible explanation for this is that the displeasure associated with losing a sum of money is generally greater than the pleasure associated with winning the same or even a greater sum. For similar reasons people value goods they have acquired more highly than identical goods not in their possession. Hence workers expend more effort to avoid a 10 percent cut in pay than to win a 10 percent increase. In most instances, losses loom larger than gains. Success, if not given in too strong doses, usually makes for a less tense emotion than failure. This means that the stakes in jealousy are higher and the unpleasantness unpleasanter. By having a unique relationship one gets to know better the value of the other person and thus the size of the loss. Such an enduring relationship also has cumulative benefits referring to the building of a shared history. (This also explains the enduring nature of love.) Indeed, jealousy is experienced as a more intense emotion than envy. The more painful nature of the loss may also suggest that the damage to our self-image is greater because we bear most of the blame for the unfortunate situation.[28]

The prevalence of envy and jealousy in everyday life is expressed in their dominance in religious and literary works. Envy and jealousy are quite common in the Old and New Testament, Greek mythology, and many folk stories. The first murder reported in the Bible, namely, Abel's murder by his brother Cain, is associated with these emotions. Sibling jealousy is also found in Jacob's attitude toward Esau. Envy is also prominent in the Biblical stories of Rachel and Leah, Joseph's brothers, and Saul and David. Envy and jealousy are also central to Shakespeare's plays and many other works of art. Fairy tales, such as *Cinderella* and *Snow White*, also deal extensively with envy and jealousy. The place of these emotions in movies is crucial as well.

Jealousy is often described in fiction as a masculine attribute (e.g., in *Othello*) and envy as feminine (e.g., in *Cinderella*); empirical research is less clear in this regard. Although there are some indications that envy may also be more common in men, men and women seem to experience equal amounts of jealousy.[29]

There are gender differences concerning the typical behavioral responses of envy and jealousy and the events triggering these emotions. For example, when it comes to handling their jealousy, women are generally more willing to pretend indifference in order to patch up the relationship. An interesting claim in this regard is that for women jealousy is primarily triggered by emotional infidelity, and men's jealousy by sexual infidelity. It may be the case that men's sexual infidelity is perceived to be less emotionally loaded than women's sexual infidelity, hence the lesser weight women accord to sexual infidelity of their male mates. An evolutionary explanation for this may be that men were primarily concerned that their partner's offspring would be their own; women's major concern was that their partner would continue to invest resources in raising their offspring. Sexual infidelity endangers the first concern and emotional infidelity the second concern.[30]

*Borderline Cases*

I haven't committed a crime. What I did was fail to comply with the law.
—David Dinkins, New York City mayor, answering accusations that he failed to pay his taxes

In this section the discussion focuses on several cases whose classification as envy or jealousy is problematic because they seem to have elements of both. A discussion of these cases should lead to a better understanding of envy and jealousy. The existence of such cases is in accordance with the prototypical nature of emotional categories. The membership in prototypical categories is determined by the degree of similarity to the category's best example, and no sharply defined boundary separates members from nonmembers. Hence we are likely to find quite a few borderline cases of envy and jealousy.

An obvious complication in classifying attitudes as either envy or jealousy occurs when envy is directed at the kind of human relations which are the focus of concern in jealousy. When David envies Michael for having a beautiful wife, this is a case of envy: there is not necessarily any personal rivalry between David and Michael. Like other types of envy, this attitude is more general than that found in jealousy. It would begin to resemble jealousy if David became concerned with the attitude Michael's wife has toward him.

How should we characterize the attitude of the wife's lover toward the husband? It is complex, with features typical of both jealousy and envy, and as such it may be regarded as a borderline case. The lover may envy the husband if he regards his own position as inferior stemming from the fact the husband is able to spend more time with his wife without the need to conceal their relationship. Yet this is not a typical case of general envy because, as is characteristic of jealousy, there is personal rivalry over the favorable attitude of a particular person. The lover will usually be jealous of those aspects that are precious to him in his relationship with the wife, regarding which he wishes to have an exclusive position. The lover will envy the husband who enjoys those aspects that are missing from his own affair with the wife. If the lover and the wife have sexual relations, the lover will probably be jealous of her sexual relations with others, including the husband, and be envious of the open and intense social interaction the husband has with his wife. If the love affair is limited to an intense social association, the lover will probably be mainly jealous of the wife's social interactions with other people, including the husband, and be envious of the husband's sexual relations with the wife. Lovers, then, are often both envious and jealous—suggesting that, contrary to the common image, the lover's life is not that pleasant. It is said that Bertrand Russell, who had a long love affair with Lady Ottoline Morrell, was extremely jealous of her and demanded she cease allowing her husband, Philip, access to her bed. Russell was also jealous of Ottoline Morrell's intimate, but nonsexual, relationship with Lytton Strachey, who was a homosexual. (Just for the record, Lady Ottoline did not comply with Russell's demand.)[31] The lover's attitude is not a typical case of jealousy since the wife does not clearly choose the husband over the lover; hence, the lover does not experience a loss to someone else. The wife's original choice was made long before she knew the lover, and there are objective difficulties in the current situation—related, for instance, to the couple's children—which inhibit canceling that original decision. The lover can, therefore, believe that the wife does not really prefer the husband and his attitude may be closer to envy than to jealousy. And even though he may not feel he is losing something he possessed to someone else, he may still feel his inferior situation to be unjustified. The lover's attitude is similar to typical jealousy in the sense that it involves rivalry and the risk of losing is high.

Consider another case. Irving and Immanuel are good friends who often go to parties together. At one party, Irving leaves with Ruth, whom he met there, and Immanuel leaves alone. As a consequence, Immanuel has an unpleasant emotion. Is this envy or jealousy? I believe Immanuel's feeling is a complex attitude involving typical features of both. Immanuel may be thinking about his generally inferior position in comparison to Irving's, and so be envious of him. But Immanuel may also have approached Ruth only to find that she preferred Irving. In this case, Immanuel may feel he lost something to someone else, and thus may be jealous. The focus of concern is more particular in the latter speculation and involves three parties since Ruth is an independent party and not merely part of Irving's success. It can be argued that Immanuel cannot feel jealous because he never had a relationship with Ruth and, hence, cannot fear losing her favor. True, this is not typical jealousy. Nevertheless, an essential feature of jealousy is present: a personal rivalry over the favor of a third party, with the prospect of losing the competition. It is important to reemphasize that jealousy does not stem from every loss, but from the loss of a favorable attitude. If, at the beginning of the party, Irving and Immanuel agreed to toss a coin to decide who would approach Ruth, and Irving won, Immanuel's attitude would be that of envy rather than jealousy because this would have been a two-party situation which did not involve the preference by a third party.

Another type of borderline case is "professional jealousy." Suppose Rachel has always been known as the best ballerina in the country, but lately more and more people regard Nadia as the best. Rachel may be jealous because she is losing the public's favor. In light of the general and nonpersonal nature of the relationship between Rachel and the public, this is not typical jealousy. Rachel's attitude may also be described as envy of Nadia's success, or it may quickly turn into envy.

"Sibling rivalry" is also a borderline case. Eldest children may be jealous of a new sibling since the children may conceive of themselves as losing an exclusive relation with the parents. However, one sibling may envy another sibling for having more friends or for doing better at school. It is not clear, for example, whether Cain killed Abel out of envy or jealousy. Envy seems to be involved in Cain's attitude since it is written that he killed Abel because Abel's sacrifice was more pleasing to the Lord. However, if we remember that they were two brothers competing for a favorable attitude of a third party, we may describe Cain's attitude as involving jealousy.

Envy is more likely to be generated when sibling closeness is significant, and jealousy when their uniqueness is more obvious. Important factors of closeness are similarity in background, such as age and sex, and proximity in current situation, such as current interest, work, and status. In significant closeness, the comparison between the siblings is quite natural and their rivalry is mainly a two-party relationship typical of envy; the parents' behavior, when not discriminative, is not a significant factor in the generation of this rivalry. When siblings differ greatly, social comparison, and hence envy, are less likely to appear.

However, their significant difference forces the parents to behave differently toward each of them. Parents cannot behave similarly toward a two-year-old son and a nine-year-old daughter since their needs are different. The different behavior can be interpreted by the children as discriminative, and jealousy may arise. Like typical cases of jealousy, it consists of rivalry over the favors of a third party. The parents here are a significant factor in the generation of jealousy and they can do much to reduce it. They can explain, for example, that real equality, or nondiscriminative behavior, does not entail identical treatment but equal effort to satisfy the different needs of each child. Moreover, it can be indicated that unlike romantic love, parental love may be directed at several objects without losing its intensity with respect to each object. Accordingly, sibling jealousy is easier to overcome than sibling envy. Reducing envy among siblings can be achieved by either reducing closeness or relevance. Since reducing closeness is not always possible or desirable, decreasing relevance is a more effective means. When family members consider the success of another member as irrelevant to their self-image, they can admire rather than envy each other and family relations can remain close. Taking this attitude is hard when proximity in current situation is significant, as when family members pursue related occupations.[32]

The above examples show that envy and jealousy are complex attitudes having similar features. Even though the borderlines between them are at times unclear, the distinction between their typical cases is obvious.

*Relationships with Other Emotions*

Distance is a great promoter of admiration.
—Denis Diderot

Jealousy would be far less torturous if we understood that love is a passion entirely unrelated to our merits.
—Paul Eldridge

Like other emotions, envy and jealousy are complex attitudes consisting of various emotional strands. In this section, I analyze these strands and then compare the whole emotional attitude with other attitudes.

Both envy and jealousy involve *sorrow* expressing our negative evaluation of present or future circumstances. In jealousy, a positive situation that previously had a fair chance of enduring is suddenly interrupted. The sorrow in envy and jealousy may be associated with discontent, humiliation, shame, embarrassment, and frustration, as well as feelings of insecurity, helplessness, and of being unlucky. Insecurity and shame are generated when we believe that the current unpleasant situation is somehow related to our own flaws. If these flaws were to emanate from our own behavior, regret would probably arise as well. Like hope, our regret expresses the belief that the given situation is, by nature, alterable.

Our future situation is of great concern in envy and jealousy. Both *hope* and *despair* can be associated with envy. Despair, rather than hope, is generated when we perceive the situation to be unchangeable or when we cannot construe our inferiority as unfair. These situations are typical of cases where we are unable to give up unattainable goals.[33] In jealousy *fear* is the major attitude toward our future. The presence of hope, instead of fear, makes envy less painful than jealousy. A significant improvement in our situation is also more typical of envy than of jealousy. However, like jealousy, envy involves some degree of fear and even anxiety related to the possible decrease in our self-esteem. Hope is also present in jealousy: because jealousy entails the fear, rather than verified knowledge of loss, there is always the possibility that this will not materialize.

Jealousy is often a kind of struggle against potential loss and contains a retributive desire for revenge on the betraying partner. However, there are other kinds of jealousy. When jealousy is associated with depression, it typically discourages action and encourages fantasy. Such a situation resembles resignation, which is related to disappointment, and is more like the response to an actual loss.[34] In the same way that envy is not a species of hope, jealousy is not a species of fear. Hope and fear are emotional strands associated with the complex attitudes of envy and jealousy. Because of the transient, changeable nature of emotions, many carry some positive (such as hope) or negative (such as fear) reference to the possibility of such change. Hence, hope and fear are also associated with many other emotions.

The emotional attitude toward the object in envy is often associated with admiration and hostility. There are different types of admiration: explicit or implicit, partial or full, profound or superficial, and so on. Some type of admiration is always present in envy. Hostility is more common and intense in jealousy than in envy, but it is nevertheless also present in envy. Since hostility is a natural response to a feeling of injustice, its presence indicates that envy includes a belief in the undeserved nature of the situation, especially if the envied person is perceived as the cause of our disadvantage.

In jealousy the emotional attitude toward the object is more complex and negative: anger, hostility, resentment, and suspicion may be generated toward the mate and the rival. Anger is dominant. There are also positive strands such as love and admiration. Although this complexity has both positive and negative features, it is basically a negative attitude of distrust. The negative attitude is principally directed at the mate rather than the rival because it is the mate who has violated our trust.[35] Our attitude toward the rival varies: it may be resentment, anger, humiliation, or even indifference. If the rival succeeds, we may envy this person because she has acquired something we desire.

The presence of positive and negative emotional attitudes in both envy and jealousy make them ambiguous emotions.

Both envy and jealousy involve self-referential emotions. Sometimes envy is associated with self-pity, indicating our inability to alter the situation. Jealousy can be associated with guilt or related emotions, such as regret and embarrassment.

Guilt is associated with jealousy when we believe that we play an active role in the partner's association with a third party. But generally jealousy involves blaming another person for the unpleasant situation, whereas guilt involves blaming oneself.

Can we speak about *self-jealousy* or *self-envy*? In light of the importance of others for the generation of these emotions, this possibility seems to be implausible. This is especially true concerning jealousy, which implies a complex relationship between three human parties. It makes no sense to speak about fear that one will lose to another person a special relation one has with oneself.

The situation seems to be similar in envy. Envy involves the wish to be in a situation that is different from our current situation; again, it makes no sense to construct a self-referential wish like this. In a mental reconstruction of self-envy, we would have to create the subject-object distance by detaching ourselves from our present situation and viewing ourselves as inferior to whom we actually are, while nevertheless wishing to be in the superior position. Such a wish hardly makes sense since we are already in the superior position. It may make some sense if we considered ourselves as undeserving of our public image and would like our real self to be just like the public one. In this sense we may be described as envying our superficial or public image. Such a type of self-envy, if present at all, is not common since people usually think that their inferior situation does not reflect their real worth—thereby giving a reason for self-pity—rather than that their superior situation is undeserved.

One may suggest that self-envy exists in nostalgia where we wish to return to a past situation. Indeed David Hume considers as envy cases in which our past pleasures cause us uneasiness. He also considers as pleasure-in-others'-misfortunes cases in which our past pain gives us some pleasure.[36] If we consider ourselves to consist of the same self during the two periods, then there is a sense of self-envy in nostalgia. Indeed solipsistic preoccupation with oneself is often found in envy. But this phenomenon is different from self-envy referring to our present situation. It is exactly because we cannot go back to our past superior position that we can speak of some sort of envy in the case of nostalgia. But when there is no such time difference, we can easily lower our position, thereby removing any reason for self-envy.

It is more natural to speak about self-pleasure-in-our-misfortune than about self-envy. When we laugh at our own situation, this may be considered as a kind of self-pleasure-in-our-misfortune. It seems that self-referring emotional states are more natural when our own situation is considered as unfortunate, as is the case in pity and pleasure-in-others'-misfortune, than when it is considered fortunate, as is the case in envy.

Both envy and jealousy are unpleasant feelings for those experiencing them. What do the people at whom these emotions are directed feel? The central role of competition in modern society encourages people to be the object of envy, which is held to indicate their superiority. A major reason for conspicuous consumption is to become the object of envy.[37] It is hard otherwise to explain, for example, why William K. Vanderbilt needed to live in a house with forty-five bathrooms and a garage for one hundred cars, or why people buy gold belts for $30,000. People look to their goods not just for pleasure or convenience, but for meaning; they want their possessions to tell them and other people who they are.[38] People are typically pleased to be the object of admiration and envy. The assumed superiority of the envied is also the reason why many types of advertisements urge the purchase of a certain item, promising to make the buyer an object of envy.

Envy is not welcomed in all cases: it is welcomed in cases of nonmalicious (admiring) envy, but often not in cases of malicious envy. The trouble is that it is hard to tell in advance whether malicious or nonmalicious envy will emerge. Consequently, many people are careful not to be the object of too intense envy. However, this is not easy to achieve. Thus, should we avoid being seen as happy so as not to invoke envy among those who are miserable? And should we invite someone to our anniversary party if she has recently been divorced? Avoiding envy, as other emotions, often entails avoiding close relations.

Being the object of jealousy may also be flattering since it may be perceived as indicating love and care. However, jealousy is often expressed in attitudes and behavior which are hard for its object to cope with. Hence, people do not like to be the object of jealousy.

*Covetousness* is closely related to envy and jealousy. To "covet" has two principal meanings: (1) the desire to possess that which is another's, and (2) to have an excessive or culpable desire. Covetousness is concerned with the desired thing itself, not with other independent human parties related to it. In cases of covetousness directed at persons, the latter are treated as inanimate objects. Unlike envy, coveting does not involve a belief in our inferiority as compared with the person having the desired object. In fact, those of superior standing often covet what belongs to people in an inferior position. Covetousness is more similar to greed than to envy. Like greed, it does not cease when the desired object is obtained, and like kleptomania it is directed at something one does not really need.

To covet is to be concerned with having something; to envy is to be concerned with someone who has something. The move from coveting to envy is the move from the desired thing to its holder.[39] Unlike jealousy, covetousness does not include rivalry over the favor of a third party because there is not really any second or third human party; there is merely the subject and her desire to have something regardless of the situation. Jealousy is typically a three-party relation, envy a two-party relation, and coveting a one-party relation. While competitive comparison is essential to envy, and personal rivalry to jealousy, the essential element in covetousness is that of overcoming a challenge. Competition and rivalry presuppose overcoming a challenge, but overcoming a challenge does not necessarily presuppose competition and rivalry.

In light of the increasing complexity from covetousness to envy and then to jealousy, one may argue that envy is a particular species of covetousness, and jealousy a particular species of envy (and covetousness). But the differences in the essential features of each emotion make any attempt to reduce them to a single shared attitude pointless.

Envy is related to *admiration*. In both cases the emotional object is superior to us, but in the one case we evaluate this fact in a negative manner and in the other, in a positive one. A major difference in this regard is that only in envy does the object belong to our reference group. Admiration will not turn into envy if the person we admire does not belong to our specific reference group, namely, the person's success is not relevant to determining our worth. Here, we perceive the other's good fortune as an enhancement of our self-esteem.[40] In this state, which has been characterized as basking in reflected glory, we feel that we share in the glory of a successful person with whom we are in some way associated. Hence, the attempt to imitate this person and via such imitation, to get closer to her. This attitude appears even when the one who basks in the glory of another has done nothing to bring about the other's success. The aspect of similarity, in light of which the subject-object association is made, may vary, but its establishment creates a significant emotional relationship. Fans of championship teams gloat over their team's accomplishments and proclaim their affiliation in different ways. The fans assume that observers of these relations tend to evaluate connected objects similarly. By being associated with someone's success, our social value, as well as our self-esteem, is thought to be enhanced. No wonder that this phenomenon is more pronounced when our self-esteem is threatened.[41]

In envy the subject-object relationship is characterized by high relevance, close similarity, and proximity. In admiration one of these factors is low. In typical admiration, relevance to our self-esteem is low and therefore we can enjoy the success of another person. The low degree of relevance usually stems from a lack of proximity in current situation, while similarity in background may be high. Admiration, rather than envy, emerges where the other's superiority is perceived to be not threatening and usually unalterable. In envy we perceive the other's good fortune to demean our esteem or at least to be better than our own. In admiration the other's good fortune has no negative impact on our self-esteem as there is no comparison between us. On the contrary, although our association with the other's success is quite remote, this success may also be reflected upon us, increasing thereby our self-esteem.[42] This attitude of basking in reflected glory is a mixture of admiration, happy-for, and pride. As in admiration, the other person is superior to us but poses no threat to our self-esteem. As in happy-for, we are satisfied with the other's success. Typical cases of pride involve either our satisfaction with our own success, or with the success of those closely related to us. In pride we typically play an instrumental role in the other's success, but sometimes mere association with a successful person may lead to pride, as is the case in basking in reflected glory.

Although envy is typical of small gaps, it may also occur in large gaps. Hostile or malicious envy, which is the prototypical kind in pathological cases discussed in the clinical literature on envy, is more common in large gaps. In *Amadeus*, Salieri's envy of Mozart is an example of how painful and destructive envy involving a large gap can be. Indeed, envy of natural gifts often turns into hate since in both cases the other's basic and permanent characteristics are negatively evaluated. Salieri does not doubt Mozart's significant superior standing in music, but he doubts God's judgment in bestowing a great musical talent on such a rude and nasty person as Mozart.[43] We should not reduce envy to hostility, however, or vice versa. Envious people do not necessarily feel hostility or dislike toward the envied person; their main concern is directed at their own inferiority.

*Intensity Variables*

The way to hold a husband is to keep him a little jealous; the way to lose him is to keep him a little more jealous.
—H. L. Mencken

The major global variables affecting the intensity of emotions were discussed in chapter 5. In the chapters analyzing specific emotions, the general discussion is applied to the emotions in question. Some variables have already been discussed throughout the whole chapter while describing other characteristics of the given emotions. This is particularly true concerning the variable of the *event's strength*, which is closely related to our focus of concern. Thus, in envy the event's strength is constituted by our inferiority and this issue was discussed while analyzing the general characteristics. The event's strength in jealousy is expressed in the degree of the partner's involvement with the rival. Indeed, we are less upset if no emotional involvement accompanies the partner's affair. Accordingly, when caught having an affair, people often plead that the other person "means nothing."[44]

The relationship of the variable of the *degree of reality* to emotional intensity fits the general correlation in envy and jealousy: a higher degree of reality increases envy and jealousy. This variable has greater weight in envy where a comparison is made between our present situation and that of another person. Jealousy is also concerned with future or possible events and as such the actual reality of these events is sometimes of less concern. Someone may know that her husband is faithful to her and that in no ordinary circumstances would he have an affair. Nevertheless, even the remote possibility of such an unlikely event may make her jealous.

Analyzing the relationship of the variable of *relevance* to emotional intensity is quite complex as relevance is composed of a few factors. If relevance is taken as a single unit, then it is positively correlated with the intensity of envy and jealousy (as of other emotions): the more relevant the event is to our goals and self-esteem, the more intense these emotions are. The general positive correlation between relevance and emotional intensity was previously discussed when describing the general characteristics of envy and jealousy. Now I want to consider the components constituting relevance and in particular the elements of *closeness*. Closeness is quite crucial in determining relevance but the relationships among its elements are complex. My discussion of these elements will be quite detailed, especially concerning envy, as it illustrates their nature in other emotions as well.

Many people have observed that *envy* is directed at those who are similar or equal to us. The Greek poet Hesiod wrote that "the potter is furious with the potter and the craftsman with the craftsman, and the beggar is envious of the beggar and the singer of the singer." Aristotle argued that we envy those who are near us in time, place, age, or reputation.[45]

Kant's position on this issue is interesting. Although he argues that "Persons of the same station and occupation in life are particularly prone to be jealous of each other," he contends that people compare themselves with others in order to achieve a higher self-esteem. A favorable comparison is likely to emerge since people "choose as a rule the worst and not the best of the class with which they set up comparison; in this way their own excellence shines out."[46] Kant's position is consistent if we assume that we choose people similar to ourselves when constituting our comparative framework, but within this framework the particular individual we choose for comparison is one who occupies a somewhat inferior position. Although it is true that in order to cheer ourselves up we sometimes compare ourselves to those inferior to us, such an escape device is often not helpful; otherwise, envy would not be so common.

In envy our attention is focused on those perceived to be immediately above us, since these people occupy the first rungs we will have to climb on fortune's ladder. These are the people we are most likely to be compared with or whose accomplishments are most likely to demean us. Elster describes this as "neighborhood envy": each person within a hierarchy primarily envies the person immediately above herself. In cases of extreme inequality, especially cases of unattainability, far less envy is aroused than in cases of minimal inequality, which inevitably provokes the envious one to think, "I could easily be in her place." Where no closeness exists, comparison is less likely to arise and we are less prone to feel inferior. Those who are close to us, but still above us, emphasize our own inferiority more than do those who are distant from us. Moreover, the issue of desert is more central in greater closeness: the comparison is easier, our inferiority is not taken for granted, and its presence is more likely to be perceived as unfair. Although in typical envy we imagine ourselves in the other's place, we do not lose our identity; we maintain it while imagining an improvement in our situation. It is easier to keep our identity while imagining ourselves in the place of those similar to us.[47]

Closeness is often associated with competitiveness. Competition presupposes the presence of differences, but these should not be too large, otherwise the competition loses its significance. Competition exists when inequality among the parties is small or alterable: we envy more strongly those in whose place we can more easily perceive ourselves to be. Consequently, we envy people more strongly who are similar or equal to us, than people well above us. Our inferiority is more obvious but less emotionally significant when there is a large gap between the subject and the object. When equality is clearly not achievable, we behave as if we do not want it. When there is a small gap between subject and object, as in relationships within a reference group, our emotional sensitivity to others' privileges, and hence to our own inferiority, increases as privileges become rarer and more controllable; attaining the alternative is more possible in these circumstances. Hence, slight inequality has often greater emotional impact than great inequality. Fighting against inequality within the reference group has greater functional value.

The correlation between the intensity of envy and the subject-object gap would be simpler if envy could be defined in terms of mere inferiority or mere desert. If envy were related merely to inferiority, it would be plausible to assume that the larger the gap, the more intense envy would be. If envy were related merely to desert, it would be plausible to postulate a mainly negative correlation between the intensity of envy and the subject-object gap because questions of desert are more prominent in smaller gaps where inferiority is less evident. Since envy has been defined as concerned with undeserved inferiority, it is not immediately obvious what the relationship is between the intensity of envy and the subject-object gap. Take, for example, the case in which our colleague wins a professional prize which presumably reflects the recipient's merits. If the colleague indeed deserves the prize, then our inferiority is evident and envy is likely to arise. If the colleague does not deserve the prize, we may feel that we should have received it, once again provoking envy. The former case is more typical of envy, the latter of resentment. In both cases inferiority, as well as desert, plays a role in the generation of the negative emotional state.

Social comparison underlying envy (and other emotions) requires not only closeness, which enables us to place the two parties in the same comparative framework, but also a certain distance enabling us to see them as distinct. This may be the reason that envy is not typical of very close relationships. A Hebrew proverb states that a person is never envious of a son or a pupil. (Some of us doubt if this is even remotely true concerning one's pupil.) Achievements of those very close to us evoke pride rather than envy when these achievements are perceived to be connected to us in such a manner that we can share the credit they bestow. Moreover, very close relationships are complex and rich; hence, it is not likely that envy, which focuses upon a partial aspect, is common in these relationships. A father usually considers his son's success as part of his own success and not as something separate that threatens his own self-esteem. When those close to us have succeeded in something essential to our own self-esteem, however, or when our ties with these people are not evident, envy may replace pride. Thus envy can play a part in some close relationships such as those between parents and children, siblings, or husband and wife. A father may wish to be at his son's age, to have his son's sexual or economic opportunities, and so on. He may also perceive his own situation to be inferior to that of his son. But a father's attitude toward his son rarely becomes that of intense or malicious envy. For example, a father will usually not aspire to damage his son's position in order to nullify the inequality between them. If such intense envy does occur we can assume that the father-son relationship is not very close.

It is interesting to consider whether the mother-daughter relationship is similar to the father-son relationship with regard to envy. In tales such as *Snow White*, it is the mother, albeit a stepmother, who displays parental envy.[48] It may be the case that some features constituting the mother's self-image or mother-daughter intimacy are different from those typical of the father-son relationship and hence envy may be different in the two cases. If, for example, physical attractiveness carries greater weight for the self-image of women than it does for men (one reason given for this is that men tend respond primarily to the physical attractiveness of women, so that women's attractiveness is significant for finding a mate),[49] and if the mother's attractiveness is deteriorating while the daughter's attractiveness improves, it is plausible that this aspect will induce greater envy in the mother-daughter relationship. Men's self-image may also consist of features which deteriorate as time goes by and which are likely to induce envy. The comparative issue depends then on the relative weight of various features in determining men's and women's self-image and the manner in which these features change in the process of growing older. Although this is an empirical issue which should be determined by empirical research, I would not be surprised if such research revealed greater envy in mother-daughter relationships.

Whereas jealousy is typical within the nuclear family, envy is more rare but still present among family members. Jealousy presupposes uniqueness and envy similarity; the former is more common in very close relationships.

Sometimes envy is also present in cases of large subject-object gaps. Thus, we may envy rich or famous people with whom we can hardly compare ourselves and with whom in any case we would not think of competing. The existence of such cases does not contradict my contention that envy is typical of small subject-object gaps. Typical is not the same as universal. The tendency to compete with someone is reduced but does not completely disappear in large subject-object gaps because conditions of competition are relative and continuous, rather than a case of all-or-nothing.[50] Furthermore, the subject-object gap is not the sole factor in generating envy; other variables may sometimes be effective, even in the case of large gaps. Moreover, the sense of inferiority in large gaps is more profound, thought to be inadmissible, and cannot be ignored. Another aspect complicating the situation is that envy, like other emotions, does not appear in isolation but as part of a complex emotional state. Other components may intensify envy in the case of large gaps since they make the emotional state more painful. The less significance people attach to their immediate environment and the more significance they attach to their overall position in society, the more likely it is that envy will appear in large subject-object gaps. For these people, greater varieties of inferiority have emotional significance.

In emotions calling for comparison of our fortune with that of others, a distinction should be made between within-group and between-groups inequality. Within-(reference) group inequality concerns gaps relating to people with whom we can compare ourselves and conceive of replacing; between-groups inequality refers to gaps relating to people who are largely irrelevant to us. The suggested negative correlation between the intensity of envy and the subject-object gap refers to people belonging to different groups. Concerning within-group inequality, we may envy the person with significantly better fortune more strongly than the one with slightly better fortune. Thus, a private in the army would usually envy a corporal or a sergeant and not a general since a general is not part of his reference group.[51] However, within the group of people closely related to him, this person may envy a sergeant more than a corporal. Similarly, a worker in a big firm may envy the president of the firm less than those working with her; but within the group of people working with her, she may envy those whose yearly income is $1500 larger than hers more than those earning $100 more than she does. Big gaps in current position or salary may prevent us from considering a certain person as a candidate for our reference group despite great similarity in background. If despite the gap the person is nevertheless in our reference group, the similarity in background should be significant. Within the reference group members are quite similar to each other and hence are perceived to deserve a similar fortune. In this case the extent of inferiority is the major variable determining the intensity of envy. Outside the reference group there is not much similarity in background, the comparison is more problematic, and our inferiority is not the major factor in determining the intensity of envy. A woman may envy another woman for her beauty, but she will probably not envy a handsome man; concerning beauty, the reference group of most women includes merely women.

In describing the intensity of envy we should take into account the difference between the two major components of closeness, namely, similarity in background and proximity (or gap) in current situation. If we take proximity as constant, we should expect a generally positive correlation between similarity and the intensity of envy. This is up to a point where the similarity is so great that the two people consider the achievements of each other as their own; in these cases, typical of close emotional relationships, envy is less likely to appear.

A more complex correlation is that between the intensity of envy and the proximity (or gap) in current situation—given that similarity is more or less constant. This correlation is depicted in figure 2.

Let E be the level of envy; G, the size of the subject-object gap. G1 is the point of maximal envy. After this point an increase in the gap will reduce envy. G0 signifies the point where the gap begins to be large enough to enable significant

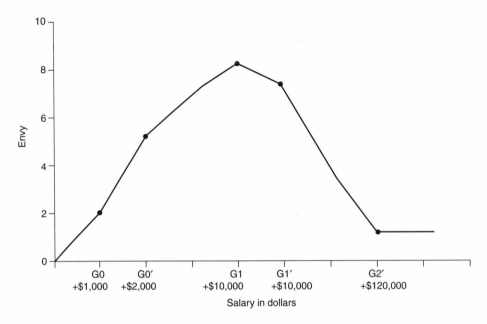

Figure 2
Levels of envy in relationship to different salaries.

emotional impact. It can be seen that immediately after this point there is a sharp increase in the intensity of envy. After G2, which signifies the presence of a great gap, the increase in the gap will not affect the intensity of envy. For most people some degree of envy still exists on any positive level of the gap. Although the locations of the reference group boundaries are not well-defined, their upper limit is located somewhere between G1 and G2; the lower limit is well below G0.

In drawing the curve it is assumed that except for the difference in the subject-object gap, all other intensity variables are constant. Though in most cases this is an unrealistic assumption, it enables us to assess the net effect that the difference in the subject-object gap has on the intensity of envy. The numbers assigned to the different levels of envy merely signify the relative positions of these levels but not the absolute level of envy. Thus, 8 degrees of envy are greater than 7 or 2, but this is not 4 times more intense than 2 degrees. The suggested scale of envy is not a ratio scale which allows us to say that 10 is twice as intense as 5. It is an ordinal scale, namely, the numbers signify a certain order, and an interval scale which allows us to say that the gap between 7 and 2 is greater than the gap between 8 and 7.[52]

As an illustration of figure 2, let us assume that it depicts the level of envy of Tom who works in a factory and earns an annual salary of $30,000. G0 signifies the salary of Adam, a fellow-worker who earns $31,000. The maximal envy, signified by G1, is directed at David, a fellow-worker who earns $40,000. G2 signifies the salary of the president of the company which is about $150,000. The exact location of the borderlines of this worker's reference group cannot be precisely determined; it is somewhere between G1 and G2. Now, suppose that Adam and David receive an increase of $1000 in their salary. What happens to Tom's envy toward them? Looking at the curve, Adam is moving to G0' and David to G1'. If, for the purpose of illustration, we quantify the intensity of Tom's envy, we may say that Tom's envy toward Adam changes from 2 to 5 degrees of envy, and the envy toward David from 8 to 7. Accordingly, the moment Tom hears about Adam's increase his envy toward him increases significantly. However after a short period, when Tom has become used to the increase and his mental system has stabilized, the relevant factor is Adam's and David's current position and not the change in their previous position. At this time Tom's envy toward David is greater as it consists of 7 degrees compared to 5 degrees of envy toward Adam. We may look at the shorter- and longer-term considerations as referring to two different events: (1) Tom's attitude toward the *increase* in Adam's and David's salaries; and (2) Tom's attitude toward Adam's and David's *higher* salaries. The curve reflects (2), while Tom's envy in the short-term is mainly determined by (1).

There are, of course, many other factors which influence the specific values of the curve. Thus, if the increase that Adam and David have received is given automatically as a function of their length of service at the factory, Tom's envy will be lower than if it is given on the basis of personal achievements. Other possible factors may include the justification for the raise and personal factors such as gender and age differences. All these, and other factors, are assumed to remain equal while the curve is drawn.

The above example illustrates once again the importance of changes and small subject-object gaps for the arousal of envy. It also stresses the need to distinguish between short- and long-term considerations. If envy arises as a result of changes in the subject-object gap, the relative size of the gap is highly significant; envy is likely to be stronger in the case of small gaps. We are less envious of an increase in the income of a rich person than of a corresponding increase in the income of a person who is richer than us but poorer than the rich man.[53] However, envy may arise as a result of other types of changes, in some of which the absolute gap is also significant.

The bell-shaped curve expressing our envy toward the good fortunes of others is similar to the curve of the utility (or happiness) derived from various commodities we consume. Thus, although the utility of food, alcoholic beverages, and most recreations rises with consumption, it rises at a decreasing rate, namely, it has decreasing marginal utility. From a certain point, an additional unit of that commodity would begin to subtract from total utility; for example, additional food would have a negative marginal utility. The structure of our sadness at the success of others is therefore similar to the structure of our happiness at our own success. It seems that the curve depicting the happiness we derive from others' failure—

namely, the curve depicting pleasure-in-others'-misfortune—is similar. Until a certain point our pleasure increases as the other's failure increases; beyond that point, even as the other's failure continues to increase, our pleasure begins to decrease until it turns into sorrow.

The above bell-shaped curve depicting the relationship between the intensity of envy and the subject-object gap is different from the general correlation between emotional intensity and relevance, as well as other intensity variables. If figure 2 merely referred to people doing the same work and the only difference were their salaries, the curve would be the same as that expressed in the general correlation between emotional intensity and the variable of relevance, that is, emotional intensity would increase with the increase in relevance up to a certain point; from this point on, emotional intensity would hardly be affected by an increase in relevance. However, this is not the case in figure 2. For example, there are other differences between the unskilled workers and the firm's president which actually put them in different reference groups. When these differences are not controlled, the general correlation cannot be kept.

In itself, the subject-object gap is not an intensity variable as it does not influence emotional intensity directly, but only through other variables, mainly that of relevance.

A positive correlation also exists between closeness and the intensity of *jealousy*. When the gap in the current situation is great, jealousy is less likely to arise and will be less intense when it does. It is said, for example, that if a Frenchman of high position chose a woman who was not his social equal as his mistress, his wife would not be jealous. If, on the other hand, he chose someone of his own rank, intense jealousy would ensue. Likewise, natives sometimes prostituted their wives to colonialists without experiencing any feelings of jealousy, yet they were extremely jealous of men of their own race. Similarly, in Japan a middle-class wife may not feel jealous of her husband's visits to geishas, or even to prostitutes.[54]

Losing a mate is more painful if the rival is a close friend. The sense of betrayal is more acute and the feeling of loss is greater—we have lost not only a mate but a close friend as well.

Unlike envy, which is basically directed at those whom we perceive to be in a superior situation, jealousy is often directed at those we consider to be inferior, but still comparable, to us. Thus, it is not immediately clear whether jealousy would be more intense if the rival were superior or inferior to us. Empirical evidence is conflicting. One research found that people felt more threatened by a physically attractive rival than by a physically unattractive rival. In other research, people stated that they would prefer their spouses to have sexual intercourse with a physically attractive rival than with an unattractive rival. This is indeed a complex situation since it encompasses different types of painful considerations. The threat is greater when the rival is more attractive (or "better" in other senses) since the rival is considered to be "objectively" better than us. However, an affair with a less attractive partner expresses the insecure foundations of our relationship because it implies that virtually anyone could ruin it. Such an affair may also have a more negative impact on our self-esteem since it places us at a disadvantage, and therefore inferior to this unattractive person. A partner's affair with an "inferior" rival may also lead to the attribution of more negative characteristics to the partner and to the partner's disregard for the mutual relationship. It is more difficult to justify or forgive such an affair.[55] In short, the threat is greater when the rival is "superior," but the pain is greater when the rival is "inferior." A somewhat analogous case in envy would be if someone who is clearly superior to another person was envious of that person because she surpassed him in a specific sphere. In such a case, the sense of pain would be mitigated by the absence of a sense of threat, so the envy would be lessened.

Another group of intensity variables is that of *background circumstances*; it consists of accountability, readiness, and deservingness. *Control* of the eliciting event, which is the major factor in *accountability*, is positively correlated with emotional intensity. The degree of control is highest when it is governed by us; it is lower when governed by other people and lowest when attributed to impersonal circumstances. In jealousy the relevant factor in this context is the mate's control. If we conceive of the mate's behavior as unintentional, or as not what initiated the relationship, then jealousy will be weaker. In such cases we can perceive the partner as not really preferring the rival sufficiently to initiate matters intentionally. When caught in adultery, it is important to people to show that the third party seduced them or that it was spontaneous and quick. In other words, people try to show that their control of the situation was minimal. Take, for example, Daniel Ducruet, the husband of Her Serene Higness Princess Stephanie of Monaco, who had an affair with the one-time Miss Bare-Breasts of Belgium, Fili Houteman. When an Italian magazine published paparazzo snaps of the couple's poolside sexual athletics, Mr. Ducruet claimed that he had been trapped and that the glass of champagne Ms. Houteman had given him to drink had been laced with Ecstasy: "If I had had all my mental capacities, I would never have done what I did." (When asked about fidelity, Mr. Ducuet agreed that this has an important value, but added that being faithful was so difficult for men since "on this earth they are outnumbered three to one by women.")[56]

A related way of reducing jealousy is to attribute the mate's preference to some flaw in the mate and not in oneself. In this way God's jealous attitude toward the people of Israel can be explained. God's jealousy does not express his inferiority, but the flaws of the people of Israel. Hence, God is described in the Bible as being jealous, but not envious. We can adopt this strategy in everyday life and remind ourselves, when our partner betrays us, that this does not necessarily express any flaw on our side but rather those of our partner who seems unable to distinguish between "good" and "bad" and chooses an inferior alternative—just as the people of Israel preferred the false gods. (I am not sure that this kind of interpretation holds any comfort for all those who are or have been betrayed, but it is one way of coping with this unpleasant situation.)

The two ways of reducing jealousy mentioned, namely, considering the mate's behavior as not due to the mate's choice or as due to the mate's mistaken choice, actually reduce the mate's control by considering the mate's behavior as either involuntary or irrational.

It might be argued that in some cases the influence of our control on the intensity of jealousy is the opposite. Thus, if the mate's preference for another person depends upon behavior we can control, then jealousy can be eliminated or significantly reduced by behaving accordingly. If we cannot prevent the mate's choice of another person, then jealousy may intensify. Similarly, the more responsible we are for the jealousy-evoking circumstances, the less intense is jealousy. Jealousy in this case is less justified and the circumstances evoking it can be changed if we wish so. Although these cases seem to be exceptions to the positive correlation between controllability and emotional intensity, they are actually not so. In cases where we are able to prevent the mate from choosing another person but do not do so, the variables of the event's impact (mainly, the event's strength and its relevance) are much weaker; these variables, rather than that of controllability, considerably weaken emotional intensity. Sadness, and probably jealousy as well, may be stronger if we could have prevented the mate's preference for another person but did not do so and now regret it. In such cases the typical relationship between controllability and emotional intensity prevails.

Envy is similar to other emotions in having a positive correlation between controllability and emotional intensity. If the envy-evoking circumstances are characterized by a low degree of our control, envy would be weaker. In this case there is nothing we can do and hence acceptance of the situation is easier. If we are somehow responsible for our current inferior position, envy would be typically stronger.

The two variables constituting our *readiness* for the eliciting event are expectation and certainty. The general negative correlation between readiness and emotional intensity is also typical of envy and jealousy: the less we expect or are certain of the eliciting events, the more envious and jealous we are. In chapter 5 an apparent exception to this rule was mentioned: the more suspicious we are of our mate (and hence the higher our expectations of infidelity), the greater our jealousy in many cases. I have explained such cases as involving significant changes in other intensity variables—mainly, the event's strength and relevance—and not as exceptions to the negative correlation between readiness and emotional intensity.

As indicated throughout this chapter, the variable of *deservingness* is of crucial importance in envy and jealousy. The relation between undeservingness and the intensity of envy is in general positive: the more we believe our inferior situation to be undeserved, the greater the intensity of envy. Indeed, the tendency to feel inferior to others and to construe our disadvantages as due to unfairness predispose us to be envious.[57] When we believe that we deserve an inferior position, the competitive concern is hardly present and usually envy does not arise. We may think the inferior situation deserved if the other person is perceived to be much better than us. In such a case the intensity of envy is reduced. The same holds for jealousy: the more we feel our possible loss to be undeserved, the stronger our jealousy is.

Describing the nature of each emotion and its intensity variables can give us clues concerning the ways this emotion can be regulated. Since I have referred to this issue throughout our discussion, I will not repeat it here. I will merely look at the issue of reducing emotional intensity by briefly referring to the comparative concern which is essential to envy and jealousy.

Envy can be reduced by making the comparative concern less central, namely, by being less sensitive to the fortunes of others. Two major means of achieving this are (1) diversifying valued domains and (2) settling for less.

We may reduce the intensity of envy by expanding the range of domains we value.[58] In this way, there will be more instances in which we enjoy superiority or at least suffer less from inferiority in a particular field. If, for example, someone considers modeling to be the only valued domain for her self-image, then she is likely to suffer envy often, as there are many models who may be better than she is. However, if this person considers other domains, for example, her social relationships or her interest in music, as important for her self-image, then these domains may provide her with a broader perspective, thus reducing the envy she experiences in the domain of modeling. Diversifying valued domains requires, then, two elements: adding new domains which satisfy an individual and the realization that each domain has its own intrinsic value. Achieving these objectives, which involves emphasizing the intrinsic value of people, increases dissimilarity among individuals and reduces the weight of the comparative concern.

Another strategy for making the comparative concern less important is adopting the attitude of settling for less. In this case another person's success will bother us less, if at all. As Robert Solomon puts it, for most of us, "the antithesis of justice is not so much injustice as greed. We are not cruel or heartless. We do not cheat or lie or steal. We just want and expect too much." Jean-Jacques Rousseau believes that people are naturally moderate; society enflames their desires.[59] The ideal of being content with little is similar to the ideal of settling for less. Both attitudes realize a similar evaluation concerning the limited value of the continuous race to win. But whereas the first ideal addresses absolute deprivation, the second concerns relative deprivation. Hence, for the purpose of reducing envy, the second ideal is more appropriate. The two suggested strategies for reducing the comparative concern in envy can be combined by adopting the attitude of settling for being different. In some cases different may be less, but in others it may just refer to a noncomparable domain. Adopting these two means represents a kind of maturity in which social comparisons are not so significant in determining our happiness, which is more intrinsic to our own activities.

It is evident that also jealousy will be considerably reduced if the comparative concern would have less weight. Imagining that other people may enjoy what is perceived to be exclusively ours is an important element in jealousy. When we stop thinking that the other's good fortune necessarily diminishes our own, jealousy may be reduced. The comparative concern in jealousy is also evident in the fact that jealousy intensifies when the mate's infidelity is publicly known.

### Envy and Social Inequality

Some men must follow, and some command, though all are made of clay.
—Henry Wadsworth Longfellow

To complete the detailed discussion of the relationship between the intensity of envy and the subject-object inequality, I now turn to discuss the sociological aspect of this relationship. This discussion may illustrate the implications of our discussion, which focuses mainly on the personal, psychological level, rather than on the sociological level, which is not the focus of this work.

It would appear that the desire to eliminate inequality, namely our inferior position, is an important component of envy. In consequence two different claims have been raised regarding the envy-inequality relation: (1) the basis for envy is a concern for equality—thus a reason for condemning this concern; (2) reducing inequality will reduce envy—thus a reason for praising the concern for equality. Both claims are erroneous. I believe that reduced inequality does not lead to less envy; on the contrary, in many cases it increases envy.

The central concern in envy is different from the egalitarian moral concern that calls for the reduction or even elimination of different inequalities. No doubt, by fulfilling the desire underlying envy, namely, gaining what someone else has, we may become equal to this person in this respect, but this is not what the egalitarian moral concern amounts to. As suggested above, envy is not a moral emotion. Envy differs from the egalitarian moral concern in at least two major ways. First, it involves a partial rather than a general concern: envious people are not concerned with equality as a general value; the claim to equality is merely a desire to improve our personal situation and thus does not appear when inequality favors us. Second, envy also surfaces in cases where the demand for equality is unrealizable and has nothing to do with egalitarian moral principles; for example, when we envy the beauty or wit of another person. The claim that egalitarianism is a central concern in envy should be rejected as egalitarianism is a general, moral stand in a way that envy is not.[60]

A more complex issue concerns the relationship between equality and the intensity of envy. I will not examine complete equality here, but rather the process of reducing inequalities and the claim that this process increases envy. I will examine the level of envy in conditions of reduced social and economic inequality, rather than complete equality, since the latter is an ideal of doubtful feasibility and shaky moral grounds. Even if we could fulfill the utopian dream of complete equality which is characterized by the absence of private possessions, envy would not be eliminated.[61] There would still be personal differences in factors such as natural talents, external appearances, luck, health, the manner in which we devote our time, availability to other people, and so on. The absence of such differences, which constitute our personal identities, may result in the elimination of all emotions, as well as the disappearance of human character. Anyway, achieving complete equality is not a goal for the foreseeable future. Reducing inequalities is a more feasible goal which to some extent has already been realized in several societies.

My main claim regarding the process of reducing inequalities is that such a process would usually lead to a rise in the intensity of envy. This claim may appear surprising and requires empirical confirmation. In light of the complexities in defining and measuring emotional intensity, this is a difficult task. Measuring the intensity of envy is especially complex, since envy is highly dependent on personality traits, self-image, and the given context. Measuring the intensity of envy in a certain society is also difficult as there are no general behavioral rules that express the presence and intensity of envy unequivocally. Nevertheless, there is some empirical evidence suggesting that the inclination toward equalization of fortunes is strongest when people are more or less on an equal footing, and that envy does not diminish with reduced inequality but often even increases. One such type of evidence concerns the degree of satisfaction of African Americans from different socioeconomic levels. It was found that as African Americans move up the economic and social ladder, they become less satisfied and more likely to take part in protests or demonstrations. Similarly, there is evidence that college-educated people are less satisfied with a good income than are less educated people who earn the same amount. There is further evidence supporting the relative deprivation theory which claims that "stratified societies can tolerate higher inequality than unstratified societies. As people become more engaged with each other, they have less tolerance for a given level of inequality."[62]

In what follows I do not present results of empirical investigations, but analyze the level of envy in one of the most egalitarian contemporary societies, the Israeli kibbutz. The Israeli kibbutz is by and large an egalitarian society whose members spend a great deal of their life together and enjoy equal standing with respect to basic necessities such as food, health, education, and housing. Inequality is minimal and is usually represented by different quantities of luxury items or in the type of work done by each member. It is instructive to find out if the significant reduction of inequality in this society has led to a reduction in the level of envy.

The characteristics of kibbutz society which increase the level of envy are related to the following intensity variables: (a) reality, (b) relevance and closeness, (c) accountability, (d) readiness, and (e) deservingness. The only global intensity variable that is absent here is the event's strength. Let us briefly describe the influence of each characteristic.

a. *Reality.* The other's superiority is quite real in the sense of being vivid. Personal encounters are frequent, making it difficult to forget prevailing envy: the dynamic of "out of sight, out of mind" does not exist. (The size of each kibbutz varies from a population of about one hundred to about fifteen hundred, small enough for frequent encounters and keeping people informed about the fortunes of the others.)

b. *Relevance.* Other people's gain is quite relevant to achieving one's goals. There is a strong (and quite justified) feeling that one's gain is very relevant to others' loss. This feeling, which is not a necessary feature of envy (it is more so of jealousy), is common in the kibbutz where the gross income is shared by all members; if one gets more than other members, these members are in a certain sense supporting this person. The significant relevance of other people to the achievement of one's goal is also evident when the agent is not the person who envies, but the one who is envied. Envy of other people can have significant practical results in the kibbutz: the society is actually capable of demoting envied people from their position. This can be done either by making them less welcome from a social viewpoint, or by not approving their special requests.

*Closeness.* There is great similarity in the members' background and current situations and there are small differences in the members' monetary resources and ways of life. When easily perceived differences are infrequent, smaller differences become easier to perceive and acquire greater emotional significance. Moreover, when a society is not large or flexible enough to permit segmentation into smaller reference groups it may not be able to maintain a variety of opinions, abilities, and fortunes, thereby increasing similarity and hence envy.

c. *Accountability.* Since the background and opportunities of each member are more or less similar, one can only blame oneself for one's inferior position. Greater personal responsibility, or controllability, typically intensifies emotions.

d. *Readiness.* Inequality is less frequent and hence its appearance is less expected. Lesser readiness increases emotional intensity.

e. *Deservingness.* Envy has more legitimacy in the kibbutz than in other places. There are two major reasons for this. (1) Egalitarian ideology justifies condemnation of inequality and thus may be perceived as implying some justification of envy. Moreover, because of the predominance of the egalitarian ideal, people are often preoccupied with equality for its own sake, thereby decreasing their readiness to be satisfied with their own situation and thus facilitating the generation of envy.[63] (2) When small differences pertain, we feel more entitled to have what the other has than we do when large differences are concerned.

Some characteristics of kibbutz society reduce envy. The major ones refer to (a) the intensity variable of the event's strength, (b) broad perspective, (c) ideology.

a. *The event's strength.* Inequality in kibbutz society does not concern the basic needs of life but rather, items of marginal importance; accordingly, its influence should be weaker. Marginal inequality may also have weaker effects on the agent's self-esteem.

b. *Broad perspective*. A person in the kibbutz has a broader perspective in two senses: (1) the knowledge of the envied person's other attributes is broader, and (2) the social group of the kibbutz is considerably different from the reference group.

An envious person is usually ignorant of many of the other's qualities, focusing attention only on what is envied. The desired qualities therefore receive disproportionate attention from the envious person. In the kibbutz this distortion is less likely to occur, because there is more intimate acquaintance with all the qualities, including the shortcomings, of the envied person. A broader perspective typically decreases emotional intensity. Of course, more intimate acquaintance may induce further envy as when the other is superior to us in these areas as well. Indeed, in classical antiquity it was assumed that whoever excels in one respect excels in all. But since no one is perfect (so at least some of us believe), it is always possible to find shortcomings and to assign them disproportionate weight.

Although the social group in the kibbutz is quite small and stable—consisting mainly of the members of that kibbutz—it is typically different from the reference group. That is, many people with whom we have social contacts are not relevant to determining our self-image. This is so since in the kibbutz we have social contacts with most members—even those who are not relevant to our self-image. Such a diversification decreases the level of envy in the kibbutz since it broadens one's perspective; it enables us to see beyond the partial and focused perspective typical of intense emotions. It should be noted that typically we try to eliminate from our social group those who are likely to be a target of our envy. However, such elimination is limited as we tend to include in our social group those who are similar to us, namely, those with whom we have more things in common. Although these people are natural candidates for our envy, they do not necessarily generate envy each time we meet them. Including in our social group more people who do not belong to our reference group is a useful means of decreasing envy.

c. *Ideology*. This factor is part of the influence that cultural and moral norms have on our emotional evaluation. The kibbutz's egalitarian ideology attaches more importance to the person herself than to her social and economic status; consequently kibbutz society is less competitive in many areas.

The above analysis indicates that even in this small and largely homogeneous society, different factors have conflicting influences on the level of envy. These conflicting factors make it hard to determine the comparative level of envy in each kibbutz with certainty. Moreover, personal and contextual factors typical of each particular kibbutz would often have to be taken into account to determine the exact level. Nevertheless, it seems safe to conclude that the weight of the factors increasing envy is greater than that of the factors reducing it. Hence, envy is likely to be stronger in this society.

The suggested negative correlation between reduced inequality and the intensity of envy seems to hold for most types of inequality; a notable exception may be equality of need satisfaction. Unlike most other kinds of equality, this kind does not express a quantitative identity but a qualitative similarity which is not associated with a continuous comparison with others. This kind of equality increases our overall satisfaction and is therefore more likely to reduce envy. The problem is that this is the hardest kind to achieve, especially under conditions of scarcity. Kibbutz ideology is aimed at equality of need satisfaction; the ideal is: "From each according to her abilities, to each according to her needs." The areas in kibbutz life that are close to fulfilling this ideal are food, health, and to a lesser extent education. In these areas, where inequality of need satisfaction is significantly reduced, the level of envy is reduced as well.

A similar analysis can be conducted with regard to modern Western society in general. Although I do not intend to carry out such an analysis here, I wish to point out that the level of envy seems to increase in this society. One major factor in this regard is the greater flexibility of social and economic strata. It is easier for people to overcome initial gaps. In this sense modern Western society is less stable than traditional societies, and instability is a major characteristic of emotional states. In the political realm, changing one's position is facilitated by the democratic structure of modern societies and the absence of legal barriers to mobility. Isocrates argues that monarchy is preferable to democracy since it involves less envy: the king is so far above his subjects as not to excite envy.[64] In the same vein, Elster claims that in a society where fortunes are constantly being made and unmade, a poor man looking at a rich man can tell himself, plausibly: it could have been me. Such mobility increase the availability of an alternative and induces both envy ("I could have had it") and hope ("I may get it").[65]

A particularly interesting development in this regard is the growing importance of what Robert Frank and Philip Coop call "winner-takes-all markets"—markets in which small differences in performance often give rise to enormous differences in economic reward. They suggest that the celebrity columnist who appears on a weekly television news panel and earns $15,000 per appearance on the corporate lecture circuit is often only slightly more talented than his peers who live on modest local newspaper salaries. The same goes for the differences between the opera singer Pavarotti and other opera singers, or between basketball superstars and other players.[66] In a winner-takes-all society, reacting emotionally to small differences is understandable, as indeed these seemingly small differences have quite significant implications. I believe that winner-takes-all situations, which increase envy, are quite common in many everyday circumstances and in many societies, but they have become particularly pronounced in modern Western society.

Other related factors contributing to a rise in the level of envy in modern Western society are the following: (a) modern Western society is much more competitive than its predecessors; (b) the communications revolution brings people closer to each other; (c) the present hierarchy is no longer accepted as a justified, natural phenomenon. There are of course conflicting factors, for example, improved living conditions and greater emphasis on personal development. I cannot compare the weight of these and other factors here, but the factors responsible for increased envy seem to be more central.

The presence of a mainly negative correlation between the level of inequality and envy does not imply that we should not strive to reduce inequalities; reducing inequalities may have positive results of a different sort. Thus, there are studies that have found an association between the degree of income inequality within a country and its incidence of disease. There is also evidence that greater income equality alleviates stress by promoting greater social cohesion. Other findings reveal a significant negative association between income inequality and growth.[67]

We should nevertheless be aware of the negative consequences concerning envy. Reducing inequalities may lead to a more just society, but this society may witness a rising level of envy. Whatever the social and moral advantages of reduced inequality, reduced envy is not part of them. If we are to witness a reduction in social and economic inequalities, we should expect the problem of envy to become more prominent. When social and economic gaps are large, the chances of rage, hate, frustration, and several types of violent reactions are greater. When these gaps narrow, a reduction in these attitudes usually follows, together with an intensification of envy.

### Moral Value

Moral indignation is, in most cases, 2 percent moral, 48 percent indignation, and 50 percent envy.
—Vittorio de Sica

Envy is often criticized on moral grounds. For Aristotle, envy is intrinsically evil—it is very near to hatred. Spinoza also considers envy to be tantamount to hate, and Thomas Reid describes it as "the most malignant passion that can lodge in the human breast."[68] Augustine considers envy to be the worst of sins—and indeed Christianity characterizes envy as one of the seven deadly sins, while Buddhism regards envy as one of the six types of poison. In light of its seemingly very negative nature, many people deny that they experience this emotion. Thus, Montaigne says, "About envy I can say virtually nothing: that passion which is portrayed as so powerful and violent has no hold on me."[69] (Although from a theoretical viewpoint, one may lack an emotion such as envy, I believe this to be a very rare occurrence associated with abnormal human circumstances.)

Unlike envy, jealousy often receives some moral justification. Several reasons may be offered to explain the difference in moral attitude toward envy and jealousy. First, because jealousy involves something belonging to us, it is presumed that we have some rights to it. Second, typical jealousy involves love and caring, which are positive attitudes. Third, the very existence of emotional relations presupposes a certain kind of exclusivity or favorable discrimination. In this sense, jealousy is a natural response underlying the wish to preserve emotional bonds. Fourth, the jealous, but not the envious person, wishes to maintain the status quo. If we merely address the generation of new negative situations and assume the preceding situation to be morally neutral, then jealousy would appear to be preferable. Retaining the status quo seems especially important in human relations because they require some stability. Fifth, because jealousy is more intense, it is more painful. Accordingly, it is more difficult to control jealousy and hence our moral responsibility is reduced. Sixth, envy is closer to hate and jealousy to anger. Anger is usually seen as more justified than hate, so jealousy is considered more justified than envy.

In light of these considerations jealousy seems to be less negative than envy; in some circumstances jealousy is even a positive normative requirement. Indeed, we are less likely to be ashamed of our jealousy than of our envy, and in educating our children we give more emphasis to the eradication of envy than of jealousy. Accordingly, people more readily confess to jealousy than envy. This is a further indication that a majority consider jealousy to be a morally more justified attitude. Some even consider jealousy in its prototypical form to be a virtue.[70]

The assumed justification of jealousy is also apparent in the fact that, as opposed to envy, jealousy is considered a mitigating circumstance. Seeing a spouse in the act of adultery has been considered among the gravest provocations, warranting reduction from murder to manslaughter.

The nature and extent of the provocation generated by adultery depends on social and personal norms. Judge Holt expressed an extreme view in this regard. He wrote in 1707 that "when a man is taken in adultery with another man's wife, if the husband shall stab the adulterer, or knock out his brains, this is bare manslaughter: for jealousy is the rage of the man, and adultery is the highest invasion of property."[71] Holt even wondered why it should be lawful to kill a thief but not the man who comes to rob a man's posterity and family. Indeed, in Texas until 1974, it was legal for a husband to kill his wife and her lover if he did so while they were engaged in the act of sexual intercourse.

It is interesting to note that a husband's infidelity was not considered an extreme provocation justifying killing. Jealousy was often connected with honor and the husband's honor was assumed to be damaged more by his wife's infidelity than vice versa. The connection of jealousy to honor may also explain why in many courts a married person who kills upon "sight of adultery" can be convicted of manslaughter, but an unmarried person killing under similar circumstances is convicted of murder.[72] From a psychological point of view this practice is hardly justified. The definition of homicide as manslaughter rather than murder is largely based on the influence of an extreme mental or emotional disturbance which makes the person less responsible for his actions. Nevertheless, it is not obvious that the "sight of adultery" arouses a more intense and disrupting emotion in a married person. It can even be argued that an unmarried person's passions are sometimes more intense because the relationship is not underpinned by factors not directly connected to the emotion; for instance, economic factors or the wish not to hurt the couple's children. Moreover, marriage may bring satiation in emotion. However, there is some evidence indicating that in comparison to dating, people conceive of marriage as reducing a partner's right to engage in outside involvements.[73] The court's practice may also be explained as assuming that personal and public insult is greater in the husband's case since the husband's honor is more vulnerable than that of an unmarried person. But in this case, it is doubtful whether jealousy is the emotion underlying the husband's behavior; humiliation may be a better description.

The role played by social norms in generating and justifying jealousy can also be deduced, for example, from the fact that an old man in a relationship with a young woman, or an old woman with a young man is unlikely to receive sympathy, let alone justification, from society, if their jealousy is provoked by a young rival. Their "right" to their partners seems to be in question and hence the intensity of their jealousy is assumed to be weaker.

It is an empirical matter to determine whether the partner's infidelity generates greater jealousy in different social groups, for example, men vs. women, married people vs. unmarried people, and people from similar age groups vs. people from different age groups. It is obvious, however, that there is no place for a simplistic generalization which draws clear differences in this regard between the various groups, and that the nature and extent of jealousy depend on many social and personal factors.

The moral advantage of jealousy over envy may be further doubted when we compare their focus of concern. Jealousy's focus of concern is exclusivity; envy's is a certain type of inequality. Our demand for an exclusive relationship with a certain person should be accompanied by that person's consent. But such consent is clearly absent in a typical case of jealousy. On the other hand, the demand of the envious for a more equal distribution of fortunes may be understood as a general moral demand. Its validity is not dependent on anyone's consent. In this sense, envy seems to be even more morally justified.[74] Moreover, jealousy tends to lead to more violent behavior than envy does. Male jealousy is a leading cause of spousal homicide in the United States today; it has been estimated that up to 20 percent of all murders involve a jealous lover. (Not only jealousy but also love motivates some of our worst behavior.) Although many crimes have been committed out of envy, envy is typically not connected to severe crimes like murder.[75] All this does not imply of course that envy is a virtue. Envy has also some harmful consequences and, as previously mentioned, the demand for equality in envy is basically not a moral demand. In addition, "the point of view of morality is not that everyone should have *the same* but that each should have *enough*."[76] Envy is not concerned with having enough, but with others who seem to have more; the moral value of this concern is questionable.

Despite the presence of some positive moral elements in envy and jealousy, they seem to be overall negative emotions from a moral point of view. Accordingly, it is difficult to say which is morally preferable. It is not at all clear that jealousy should be preferred. There are cases in which jealousy is far more condemnable than envy. We would sooner censure the housewife who jealously keeps her recipe than the friend who envies her for having the recipe. This moral preference is based on the view that the recipe should be shared. Matters become more complex in typical cases of jealousy involving exclusive human relations which are assumed to be nonshareable. Here, the moral comparison between envy and jealousy is more complicated and depends on circumstances.

Sometimes envy and jealousy are regarded as affective traits.[77] In contrast to emotions, affective traits are more general, not as dependent on circumstances, and last longer; affective traits are largely dispositional. When describing envy and jealousy as affective traits, we refer to our disposition to become envious or jealous. In light of our negative evaluation of them, together with the permanent nature of affective traits, the evaluation of envy and jealousy as affective traits is more negative than when they take the form of emotions. When envy and jealousy are provoked by special circumstances, they can be justified, and may even have a positive aspect. But when envy and jealousy are the rule rather than the exception, they are very negative and disturbing attributes.

It is difficult to avoid the common emotions of envy and jealousy, and therefore condemning them on moral grounds is problematic.[78] Condemning the underlying conditions for the generation of these emotions (say, the competitive concern), or some of the actions resulting from them (e.g., hurting the rival), makes more sense than condemning the emotions themselves. It is easier to be responsible for our actions, and for some of our values, than for our emotions. Moreover, jealousy and envy play important roles in human life: jealousy guards the exclusivity of emotional ties; envy emphasizes certain egalitarian principles in human relations and promotes individual achievement. In this sense, neither are pathological defects, but rather address genuine human concerns and have useful social functions.

It seems that although the capacity to experience envy and jealousy is inherited, the actualization of this capacity and the intensity of its expression depend upon social conventions. The influence of such conventions is not unlimited. Thus, jealousy exists even in cases where the couple agree on a nonexclusive romantic relationship, for example, in open marriages.[79] The limited role of social conventions might explain why there is no society devoid of envy and jealousy. If discovered, such a society would probably be less humane than our own.

Some degree of jealousy and envy is required for preventing attitudes of total indifference between people. In fact, quite often deliberate attempts are made to induce jealousy in mates, or envy in friends. This does not mean that a lower level of jealousy and envy is not preferable to prevailing levels. An excessive amount is harmful, like all excess. However, the most common type of jealousy and envy is the moderate and not the intensive type, in spite of what is often believed. This belief is one cause of the highly negative evaluation of the two attitudes.

We should try to moderate, rather than eliminate, the intensity and frequency of our jealousy and envy, not merely because we cannot do otherwise but also because their elimination would possibly have negative moral results.

As indicated, jealousy is an important emotional device for safeguarding unique relationships. Abolishing all forms of jealousy implies abolishing all forms of interdependence, which is the core of intimate relationships.[80] If jealousy can lead to constructive steps that improve the relationship with the mate—rather than destructive steps preventing the mate from forming other relationships—then jealousy may have positive functional and moral value.

Similar considerations apply to envy. An excessive amount of envy is harmful from a moral point of view and is an obstacle to an enjoyable and interesting life. However, complete elimination of envy is harmful too, since it may imply a complete indifference toward comparison with other people and hence toward improving the present conditions of both other agents and oneself. Envy may be valuable if it does not lead to hurting other people but only to improvement of our own situation and that of people in worse positions. As suggested in the next chapter, it seems that envy toward those who are better off may go together with compassion for those who are worse off. Moreover, it has been claimed that moderate experience of envy is valuable in the development of competence and the acquisition of skills. Moderate envy can provide growing children with a motive for further development and adaptation. The experience of envy can also be an alternative to depression; with envy, hope is not lost.[81]

Since the urge to compare ourselves with other people is fundamental to our social life, envy and jealousy are natural phenomena. Moderate types of envy and jealousy are sometimes a private vice but a social virtue. As with most other emotions, intensity rather than the nature of the given emotion is the major factor in evaluating it as harmful or beneficial.[82]

Although envy and jealousy are natural and prevalent emotions and encompass a wish to overcome a certain injustice or at least unfairness, we are ashamed of them and are often not ready to admit their presence. One reason is that these emotions are still negatively evaluated from a moral viewpoint. Their moral concern is personal and often not considered as just by other people. Another reason is the admission of inferiority inherent to these feelings, and few like to admit inferior status. Although we consider our situation to be unfair, to express it in public means to admit our inferiority and this is difficult to do. For similar reasons people like to say and to hear that they are modest. A prevalent conception of modesty is that the modest person is an exceptional character whose behavior is never boastful or vain.[83] Accordingly, envy is not associated with modesty, but with humiliation.

Like jealousy and envy, covetousness has a negative connotation. It is, in fact, more negative from a moral viewpoint because it seems to lack any justification whatsoever. Unlike envy, it is not based on our inferior position and the natural desire to change it. Unlike jealousy, it does not include the wish to sustain a certain type of personal relationship we value. In contrast to envy and jealousy, covetousness cannot be justified by citing the complexities and subtleties of human relations; it is more a kind of psychological deficiency.

In summary, envy and jealousy have an important common feature: the wish to have something. They differ in our relation toward this thing: in envy we wish to gain it and in jealousy not to lose it. This distinction, which at first appears as two aspects of the same attitude, actually encompasses numerous complications and significant differences. The fear of losing something we have is quite different from the wish to gain something we have never had. Jealousy is more distressing; it is more intense and pervasive, and less prepared to compromise. As all of us know, it is more difficult to lose than not to win.

# Chapter 11

# Why Do We Feel Bad When You Feel Bad?
—Pity, Compassion, and Mercy

For there are two kinds of feeling for another's suffering. One, feeble-hearted and sentimental truly, but the impatience of one's heart to escape as fast as possible from the embarrassing clutch of alien affliction; that compassion which is not compassion at all, just the instinctive fending-off of alien suffering from one's own soul. And the other, the only one that counts—unsentimental but creative compassion, knowing its own mind and determined to endure patiently and compassionately whatever may come, to the utmost of its strength and beyond.
—Stefan Zweig

The major emotions in the group of negative attitudes toward the bad fortunes of others are pity, compassion, sympathy, and grief. The discussion herein focuses on pity and compassion. I also discuss in some detail the attitude of mercy, which, although not an emotion, is closely related to pity and compassion.

*General Characteristics*

Always be a little kinder than necessary.
—James M. Barrie

If you think nobody cares if you're alive, try missing a couple of car payments.
—Earl Wilson

The attitude of most people toward beggars or the homeless is a typical example of pity. Typical attitudes of compassion address those near and dear who need constant help, for example, a family member seriously ill, mentally retarded, or physically disabled. Pity and compassion are not generated in every case of bad luck, but only when we believe that someone suffers from substantial misfortune. Pity and compassion are kinds of sympathetic sorrow for someone's substantial misfortune; they involve, however, more than general sorrow. A crucial difference between them is that compassion involves far greater commitment to substantial help. Compassion involves a willingness to become personally involved, while pity usually does not. Pity is more spectator-like than compassion; we can pity people while maintaining a safe emotional distance from them. While pity involves the belief in the inferiority of the object, compassion assumes equality in common humanity. Although the feeling component in pity is considerably weaker than in compassion, it is still present—otherwise it would not be an emotion at all.[1]

*Pity*
Pity costs nothing, and it ain't worth nothing.
—Josh Billings


In many cases of pity we could offer substantial help, but perceive ourselves as being unable, or not obliged, to do so. Thus, although I could help a few beggars by giving them most of my salary and time, I perceive this possibility as undesirable in light of my obligations toward my family and my wish to maintain a certain lifestyle. In such cases our limited power to help actually stems from a perceived lack of obligation associated with our unwillingness to become personally involved. There is also the possibility of taking pity on a beggar by giving him a considerable amount of money, though not nearly enough to affect adversely our own lifestyle. Even in such a case, our assistance would probably have limited effect as we could not ensure the future well-being of this beggar, nor assist him in other important aspects of his life.

A typical belief associated with pity is that many creatures in the world suffer, but a single person cannot do much to improve their situation. Quite often the best we can do—at least so many of us believe—is to help in a very limited way or to restrict the help to our intimates. The suffering of homeless people is recognized by many people, but the majority think that they cannot offer real help. At best they think they can pay their dues to the suffering of the homeless by pitying them. Accordingly, pity is often sympathy for the helpless by the powerless—or those who consider themselves to be essentially powerless. An advertisement for the Multiple Sclerosis Society states: "They do not want your pity; they want your help." Indeed, social work students are taught not to pity their clients, as such pity may prevent them from helping the clients. Because of its noninterventionary nature, we speak about pity as a luxury.

Pity is improper if we have power to alleviate suffering. Doctors who can cure their patients do not pity them. Similarly, it is improper for the President who can help the homeless to pity them. Pity is also improper if my son is homeless and I have the resources to help him. The closer the other person is to us, the more we are obliged to assist this person through hardship. When we can help, but do not want to change our priorities in doing so, guilt may be part of the complex emotional state of pity. This guilt is often repressed by either perceiving the other person as inferior—and hence as undeserving of an essential change in our priorities—or as being able to solve his own problem. There are other cases of pity, for instance, when a person is dying of cancer, in which the perceived impotence is real.

Our acceptance of the other's situation and our unwillingness to become personally involved may stem from our beliefs that (1) the other's position is unalterably inferior; (2) the other person is somehow responsible for his inferior position; or (3) we lack the required resources. These beliefs are a kind of defense mechanism which somehow justifies our passivity in pity. We do not have to hold all three beliefs; one or two of them may be sufficient for supplying the required justification. In many cases, however, all three beliefs are held, thereby enabling us to have a better defense in case one of them proves unconvincing. If we hold only one of these beliefs, pity would usually be strongest with (3) and weakest with (1); this is so since our ability to change the situation is greatest in (3) and most limited in (1). Generally, if we had no qualms about our position, one convincing belief would be enough. For similar reasons, lawyers present alternate arguments to sustain their claims. For example, they may argue that (a) the claim must be rejected because it is not convincing; and (b) if the claim is found to be convincing it nevertheless must be rejected since the police did not act properly in collecting the evidence. In pity we rationalize our passive attitude by having many "convincing" beliefs for not helping others.

Owing to the belief in the other's inferiority, pity may easily insult or humiliate the recipient. Indeed, pity is often associated with the ridiculous. That is why most people do not like to be pitied. (Some people like to be pitied mainly because of the attention they would not otherwise get. This is probably the reason why George, in the television show *Seinfeld*, proudly claims that "Nobody is sicker than me.") When others pity them, people understand that they lack something and are therefore regarded as inferior. It is disputable, however, whether indeed all those who pity conceive of the pitied as inferior.

Pity involves the belief that the object does not deserve such substantial misfortune; the stronger the belief, the more intense the emotion. Accordingly, Aristotle suggested that pity is not felt by those who believe that evil is inherent in human beings; if you think everyone is basically evil, you are likely to consider that bad fortune is deserved.[2] Belief that a person is undeserving of substantial misfortune does not necessarily involve a moral positive evaluation of this person as a whole, or of her past activities. We may pity a mass murderer and still believe this person should be executed. Although the emotional experience in such situations is contrary to what formal justice requires, it expresses our unique humane nature. Even when we think the other person deserves some kind of punishment, the presence of pity or compassion indicates that from some personal point of view the misfortune is perceived to be too severe. We may consider this point of view as marginal and hardly give it any weight in determining our actions; nevertheless, by feeling pity and compassion we implicitly testify to the presence of some emotional perspective in light of which the object's misfortune as a whole, or merely its severity, is perceived as not deserved.

It seems that the underlying assumption in judging undeservingness of the objects of pity and compassion is the belief that no human being deserves to be in such a miserable situation. From an intellectual point of view, we may justify the miserable situation of a mass murderer who faces execution, but if we disregard general background circumstances and focus only on the individual, we may generate emotions which imply that the misfortune is too severe. Such emotional evaluation may be overridden by intellectual evaluation when we come to decide upon our course of action. However, the intellectual system may override, but not eliminate, the presence of the differing emotional evaluations concerning personal desert. In this sense pity toward a mass murder is similar to other situations in which emotional evaluations clash with intellectual ones.

### Compassion

If you were arrested for kindness, would there be enough evidence to convict you?
—Unknown

People are not homeless if they're sleeping in the streets of their own hometowns.
—Dan Quayle

In compassion we are more willing to help and perceive ourselves as more obliged and able to do so. Consequently, compassion involves a greater commitment to help and is less passive. Compassion requires us to transcend different types of disparity and assume equality with regard to common humanity. Our evaluative perspective in compassion stems from basic similarity with the other. Since only pity, but not compassion, contains the belief in the other's inferiority, we can feel compassion, but not pity, for someone in circumstances no worse than our own. Both pity and compassion refer to someone who suffers. However, consideration of the other's suffering for its own sake is deeper in compassion. The other's suffering when we pity is typically considered from our own egoistic perspective; thus, the sympathetic attitude in pity stems more from our fear of sharing the other's situation.

The readiness to help is more evident in compassion. Pity typically includes a kind of acceptance of the present situation, and an unwillingness to become personally involved. This attitude is clearly absent from very close relations; accordingly, compassion, rather than pity, is typical of these relations. The father of a retarded child may be angry at his son's misfortune or feel ashamed of him, but his emotion will not be that of pity. The father's attitude would not be that of detachment from an inferior creature, but rather that which emphasizes the son's human attributes and involves helping him as much as possible. His attitude will be that of compassion. In this case both compassion and shame involve perceiving the son as having fundamental ties with the father. The presence of these ties does not merely result in the generation of shame but also in the recognition of the son's humanity.

In compassion, as in anger, we express dissatisfaction with the present situation. Yet unlike anger we conceive it as unalterable in the short run. Hence, we try to help the other person endure the painful situation rather than change it. Even this kind of acceptance is absent in anger, which involves the desire, and often the intent, to change and even destroy the situation in the short run. The difference between anger and pity is not just that pity lacks the intense feeling dimension of anger, but that it also lacks anger's orientation toward change.[3]

Like pity, compassion is associated with the belief that the other person does not deserve such substantial misfortune. In compassion this belief is more dominant and is typically concerned not only with the undeserved *severity* of the misfortune but with the presence of any misfortune. This difference in emphasis is related to different attributions of responsibility: in compassion we tend to emphasize the nonvoluntary elements of others' behavior; in pity the emphasis is on their responsibility for their current situation. In some cases compassion may also merely refer to the severity of the misfortune. We can feel compassion toward a relative of ours who lost all his money gambling despite our continual urging that he break the habit. Such compassion is also associated with the belief that our relative is not entirely responsible for his condemnable deeds. In other cases, compassion may grant that there is justification for human suffering in general, but not justify a particular person's specific misfortune.

Both pity and compassion encompass the desire for the other's relief. This desire is connected with our belief that the other person does not deserve such severe misfortune. It seems, however, that in pity we wish for the relief of the other's suffering, but not of the other's inferiority. The more profound wish of abolishing the other's inferiority is only typical of compassion.

*Mercy*
Sweet mercy is nobility's true badge.
—William Shakespeare

He was so benevolent, so merciful a man that he would have held an umbrella over a duck in a shower of rain.
—Douglas Jerrold

Mercy is often confused with pity and compassion. Understanding mercy would help us understand pity and compassion as well.

A few paradigm cases may be attributed to mercy:

1. a *judge* who does not impose a harsh sentence on the accused;
2. a *merchant* waiving the right to collect a loan given to a poor person;
3. a *gunman* capturing but not killing a hostage (an enemy soldier, or an innocent person).[4]

In all cases a person is seriously suffering, or is about to undergo such suffering, and someone intervenes and immediately alleviates the suffering without investing much time or effort. An act of mercy may then be characterized as treating a person considerably less harshly than she would have been treated, given the power of the mercy giver and the presence of an established general course of action increasing the likelihood of harsh treatment. The likely course of harsh events is prevented by a particular action (or omission) by someone.[5]

The importance of actions (or omissions) in mercy is represented by the fact that favorable attention to the other's suffering alone is not sufficient; mercy must include real help. One cannot be merciful, but one can pity, without actually doing anything. A judge who expresses sympathy with the accused's situation but nevertheless imposes severe punishment may be described as showing pity, but not as being merciful. The judge would be merciful only if the sentence were not as harsh as it would normally be.[6]

When acting mercifully, the judge, the merchant, and the gunman are treating someone considerably less harshly than they might have done given their power and the general course of action common in such cases. The departure from an established general course of events characterizes an act as merciful. In the case of the judge, the general course of events is expressed in formal general laws; the judge's personal wish cannot abolish the general laws. The general course of events in the merchant's case are rules of conduct which are often expressed in formal contracts; the merchant's personal wish can override these rules in an act of mercy. In the gunman paradigm the general course of events is not expressed in formal rules; it is rather a pattern of behavior that is common in these situations. The gunman's personal wish is of crucial importance in this case.

The relationship between mercy and justice is most problematic in the judge paradigm when the general course of events, expressed in formal laws, is considered to be justified. This issue is hardly present in the merchant paradigm: in most cases there is no doubt that the merchant has the right not to collect her loan; one can usually waive one's right without tampering with justice. The issue of a possible conflict between mercy and justice is absent in the gunman paradigm since the gunman has no right to impose hardship in the first place. The merchant's power derives from her personal wealth. The source of the gunman's power is personal strength. Unlike the merchant and the gunman, whose power depends on their own personal wealth or strength, the judge's power is an institutional power invested in the individual to serve the aims of society. Unlike the merchant, the judge has no right to use her power freely; the judge has an obligation to uphold the rule of law. Although the judge has discretion, it is limited and problematic.[7]

Mercy is defined in the *Oxford English Dictionary* as "holding oneself back from punishing, or from causing suffering to, a person whom one has the right or power to punish." This definition captures important elements of mercy. It seems, however, that holding oneself back from causing suffering is more crucial than refraining from punishment and that the element of power is more essential than that of right. The issues of punishment and right are not present in all paradigm cases.

The three paradigms reflect most cases of mercy, but borderline cases, which do not fit into a single paradigm, exist. For example, the case of a soldier who is supposed to take harsh measures against enemy soldiers during combat, but does not do so, is related to both the gunman and the judge paradigms. Another borderline case is that of mercy killing, for example, fulfilling a person's request for an earlier death when this person suffers from an incurable disease accompanied by great pain. This case may be related to the merchant paradigm in which a certain person waives her right—in this case the right to live. However, unlike the merchant situation, it is disputable whether in this case anyone, the patient or the one assisting her, has any right to the waiver. The difficulties in classifying these cases do not, of course, mean that these are not cases of mercy. Reality is not neatly divided, as our conceptual classifications are. This is one reason for the use of paradigm cases and not of clearly defined categories.

A better understanding of mercy may be achieved by comparing it with pity and compassion. I will focus on the following issues: (a) is mercy an emotion? (b) the other's inferiority; (c) the ability to help; and (d) the other's deservingness.

*IS MERCY AN EMOTION?*      Mercy is similar to pity and compassion in involving a negative evaluation of another person's substantial misfortune. However, whereas the negative evaluation in pity and compassion is expressed in an emotional state, in mercy it is expressed in a certain action. Unlike pity and compassion, mercy is essentially not an emotion but a certain attitude conveyed by action.[8]

A major difference in this context is the possible absence of intense feeling in mercy. One can be merciful without experiencing intense feeling; one cannot experience pity or compassion without intense feeling. Similarly, the motivational state of the actor is of great importance in emotions but not in mercy. Agents can act mercifully from the most deplorable motives. The nonemotional nature of mercy is also expressed in the presence of intellectual deliberations. Typical emotional evaluations, like those included in pity and compassion, are spontaneous rather than deliberative. The act of mercy is typically an intended, deliberative action. One cannot act mercifully by accident.[9]

Mercy is related to emotions by being a partial and discriminative attitude. However, mercy is partial not because it requires many resources, as emotions do, but because it is a departure from an established course of events.[10] The judge, merchant, and gunman would not be able to continue their usual activities if mercy ruled their behavior in general. Departing from an established course may be due to emotional considerations and may generate emotional reactions, but it does not have to be an emotional state.

Like mercy, forgiveness is not an emotion: it expresses the termination of emotions, often those of anger and resentment. Whereas forgiveness is connected to overcoming a negative emotion, mercy is related to overcoming power. Mercy is often associated with forgiveness. This is obvious in the merchant and gunman paradigms; in the judge paradigm forgiveness is not personal but institutional. However, the connection between mercy and forgiveness is not necessary as the emphasis in mercy is on actions and in forgiveness it is on attitudes. Avoiding harsh treatment, which is typical of mercy, can be done without a change in attitude, which is typical of forgiveness. A woman who has vowed not to be with her husband after he has been unfaithful to her, may agree, out of mercy or concern for the children, to have him back, but she need not forgive him. In most cases mercy may express at least a partial forgiveness, but it does not necessarily imply full forgiveness. It is more difficult to imagine cases of forgiveness in which mercy is denied. A change in our attitude (such as that expressed in forgiveness) is likely to result in a change in our actions (such as that expressed in mercy). However, this may not be true of all cases.

*THE OTHER'S INFERIORITY*    Pity, compassion, and mercy include a negative evaluation of someone's substantial misfortune and the belief that this person (or animal) needs our help; in this sense the person is inferior to us. Indeed, pity is often a depreciating attitude. However, in compassion we consider this inferiority to be limited to specific circumstances and the other person is perceived as basically similar to ourselves; in pity we often take this local, or partial, inferiority as essentially indicating the other's character. Hence, it is easier for us to identify with and feel closer to the object of compassion than the object of pity. In mercy we are usually superior to the object in a manner closer to pity than to compassion. Our superiority is often not limited to the specific aspect in question and we do not identify with the object. This is indeed the way we perceive God's superiority over human beings or the judge's superiority over a criminal. The typical attitude of God toward the misfortune of human beings is mercy since in mercy the subject's superiority and ability to help are most pronounced. Pity also involves the subject's superiority, but since it implies the subject's impotence, it cannot be attributed to God. God may have compassion toward human beings. Although compassion implies some fundamental similarity with the object which cannot be attributed to God, God is able to assume a human perspective and thus be compassionate toward human beings.

*THE ABILITY TO HELP*    As indicated, in compassion, but not in pity, we are willing to become personally involved. Because of the grave misfortune typical of pity and compassion, changing the other's situation usually requires many resources, including time. If the situation could be reversed immediately, there would be no room for pity or compassion. Pity includes the perception that the required resources are absent or that it is not worthwhile to invest them. In compassion there is readiness to invest resources while knowing that it is a demanding and long-term commitment which may not always be successful. Consequently, compassion is of longer temporal duration than pity. In many cases of pity and compassion the change that stems from our activity somewhat improves the other's current situation although it does not eliminate the misfortune. Mercy and grief differ from both pity and compassion in this regard: in grief our ability to help is absent while in mercy it is easily available. In mercy we are not as powerless as in pity, and unlike compassion the relief is immediate and does not require much time or effort.

Pity, compassion, and mercy differ not merely in our ability to help but also in our emotional attitude toward that ability: the pitier revels in such power, the compassionate person is proud of it, and the mercy giver is almost embarrassed by it. The feeling of superiority associated with pity is the source of the subject's satisfaction and even gloating. Satisfaction and gloating are absent from compassion where the other's situation is of greater concern. The pride that may be associated with compassion stems from the great sacrifice required to effectively help the other. Mercy may be associated with embarrassment in light of the strong considerations against the act of mercy.

THE OTHER'S DESERVINGNESS    Pity, compassion, and mercy encompass the belief that there is some perspective in light of which the other does not deserve this kind of substantial misfortune. The belief is expressed in the negative evaluation of the other's misfortune. If we approved of the situation, these attitudes would require a positive evaluation of the other's situation and hence happiness or satisfaction—as is the case with pleasure-in-others'-misfortune. Pity, compassion, and mercy differ with regard to whether the other deserves any misfortune at all. As indicated, in pity we often believe the object to deserve some, though a lesser kind of misfortune; in compassion the typical belief is that the object does not deserve any misfortune. The case of mercy is more complex. In the gunman paradigm the object obviously does not deserve the imposed hardship. In the merchant and judge paradigms the hardship imposed on the object seems to be justified from one perspective but unjustified from another. Despite the moral justification of harsh treatment, the object is perceived to deserve less harsh treatment in some personal sense of desert.

To sum up, pity, compassion, and mercy have been distinguished on the basis of the following characteristics:

1. *The emotional nature of the attitude*—only pity and compassion are emotional attitudes; unlike typical emotions, mercy often occurs without an intense feeling, it does not take time, and may be the result of intellectual deliberations.

2. *The other's inferiority*—pity and mercy, but not compassion, include the belief in the other's inferiority.

3. *The ability to help*—the ability to help is obviously present in mercy and hardly present in pity; compassion may also result in substantial help, but only after a considerable length of time.

4. *The other's deservingness of the bad fortune*—in all stances the other is conceived as not deserving such a severe misfortune; only in compassion do we often believe that no misfortune at all is deserved.

Although the difference between prototypical cases of pity and compassion is obvious, it is in degree rather than in kind. Since most of the features typical of pity can appear in different degrees, a shift in degree may turn pity into compassion. Mercy is more clearly distinguished from pity and compassion, but nevertheless borderline cases do occur. Take, for example, the case of so-called mercy sex in which a woman (or a man) is not particularly attracted to someone who is in love with her and wishes to have sex with her; she sleeps with him only because she feels sorry for him. It is unclear whether mercy sex is an example of mercy—belonging to the merchant paradigm—or of pity; it seems to have some properties of both. As with other emotional terms, the common usage of "pity," "compassion," and "mercy" is less rigorous than the one suggested here. We may hear phrases, such as "God pities his poor creatures," in which the suggested psychological distinction is not kept. Such deviations should not worry us too much in light of the prototypical nature of emotional attitudes and the fact that scientific precision is not a major concern of common sense.

*Relationships with Other Emotions*

If you want others to be happy, practice compassion. If you want to be happy, practice compassion.
—The fourteen Dalai Lama

The emotional strands associated with pity and compassion are to a large extent similar: both are associated with *sorrow* and *sympathy* for the other's suffering and a tacit *fear* that we, or some people close to us, may suffer such misfortune. The difference between pity and compassion in this respect is in degree: sorrow and sympathy are more intense in compassion, whereas fear is more dominant in pity. Like sympathy, compassion also requires empathy with the other person, namely, emotional identification. Typical cases of pity do not involve respect but rather contempt; indeed, sometimes we say "I pity you" in contempt.

Pity typically involves a feeling of *satisfaction* based upon the favorable comparison between our situation and that of the other person. Accordingly, pity sometimes arouses our awareness of, and maybe even the pleasure in, being lucky. The belief that our position reflects credit on ourselves offers satisfaction entailing pride. Our satisfaction, which is compatible with the belief in the other's inferiority, is absent in very close relations and in compassion; those require dissatisfaction with the current situation. For similar reasons grief may sometimes be pleasant—not in its own right, but owing to some elements associated with it, for example, the fact that you are at center of other people's attention and the sympathy you receive from them.

The feature of satisfaction in pity is somewhat similar to the feature of delight found in pleasure-in-others'-misfortune, but these two complex emotional states are quite different. Whereas pity is basically sorrow for the other's substantial misfortune, pleasure-in-others'-misfortune is basically delight in the other's relatively minor misfortune.

The group of negative emotions toward the bad fortune of others includes other emotions besides pity and compassion. One such emotion is sympathy. *Sympathy* is the most general emotion in this group. Compassion and pity require some sort of sympathy, but when sympathy is isolated from other emotional attitudes it usually addresses slight misfortunes. We feel sympathy, rather than compassion, pity, or grief, for someone whose car has been scratched or who coughs a lot. Since the misfortune is slight, the emotional intensity of sympathy is usually lower than that of other emotions in this group.[11]

Grief may also be regarded as belonging to the group of negative emotions which involve the bad fortune of others, since grief is concerned with something unhappy, namely, death, which has happened to another person. However, when a person we perceive to be an essential part of our life dies, our grief may be also regarded as belonging to the group of negative emotions which involve our own bad fortune. Accordingly, I discuss grief when considering sadness in chapter 15.

Pity may be directed at dead people because the element of helplessness, typical of our attitude toward dead people, is also associated with pity. Because this element is not typical of compassion, it is usually not directed at dead people. Compassion is "suffering with" another person, and it is hard to construe an attitude involving similar suffering of both the living and the dead person. Compassion can be directed at the suffering of the dead person while the person was alive or at the present conditions of the dead person if the person is considered to exist somewhere, for example, in hell. The fact that we cannot do anything about dead people does not eliminate our emotions toward them; also, regarding terminal patients, we can do nothing but still may have various emotions toward them.

Compassion is similar to a general type of *love* recommended by some moral theories. In both cases the person as a whole is positively evaluated mainly because we assume that we should respect, help, and care for other human beings. When this general love is not expressed in intense feelings, it is better described as a general attitude rather than an emotional state. The presence of such feelings turns the general moral attitude into the more specific emotion of compassion.

Compassion and pity are essentially negative attitudes: they evaluate the misfortune of others negatively. In this sense they are similar to *anger* and *hate*, which also entail a negative evaluation of the situation. However, anger and hate encompass a negative evaluation of the other's activity or personality and not necessarily of the other's situation. Compassion involves a positive evaluation of the other's activity and personality; in pity such evaluation is negative but to a lesser extent than is the case in anger and hate. Like pity, hate usually also includes the assumption that there is not much one can do to change the current situation—the only real change in hate may come by eliminating the other person. Compassion and anger entail the possibility of changing the current situation, but whereas in anger this is done by destructive means, in compassion it is accomplished by constructive and positive actions.

I would like now to turn to a more detailed comparison of pity and *envy*. At first sight they appear to be quite different; pity seems to be a basically positive attitude, highly valued in human relations, while envy seems to be a basically negative attitude we try to avoid. A closer examination of pity and envy reveals that from a psychological viewpoint, they are similar in some important aspects. Discussing this similarity is useful for understanding the nature of these emotions.

Envy, pity, and compassion are sometimes characteristic of the same person.[12] Envy toward those who are better-off may go together with pity and compassion for the worse-off. This is in accordance with the great sensitivity of emotional people to all types of circumstances; thus, those who experience intense sadness are also likely to experience intense happiness. Sensitivity to the fortunes of other people is typically evident when their fortune is different from ours: either it is better or worse. Our well-being is reduced when someone else either has more or substantially less than we do. When we feel pity for other people, we are in a superior position, which provides some compensation for our inferior position when feeling envious. Hence what in pity appears to be simple altruism may in reality be a form of self-interested envy reduction.[13]

Pity is similar to envy in being associated with the perception of inferiority. However, whereas envy typically involves our relative deprivation, pity addresses the substantial deprivation of others. We do not pity anyone who is simply unlucky, but we often envy those who are in a slightly better position than us. Both emotions are associated with small hope of changing the unfavorable situation. In pity the hope is even weaker as pity is associated with greater acceptance of the situation—the other's misfortune, no doubt, is less disturbing than our own. An obvious difference between envy and pity concerns the ways in which the subject-object inequality can be annulled. This can be accomplished either by elevating the lower or lowering the superior. The envier would often permit both; the pitier would permit only the former.

Our own situation is of greater concern in envy, and therefore the other's situation plays a far more crucial role in the generation of pity than in the generation of envy. In pity the concern for our situation is less significant and mainly refers to a possibly dangerous future situation; accordingly, fear is a component of pity. In envy we are concerned with our present inferior situation; accordingly, shame is an important component of envy. Although pity arises in cases of substantial misfortune and envy largely in cases of small differences, the element of unfairness is often more dominant in envy. Accordingly, resentment, which is a kind of moral protest, is more often associated with envy than with pity. Two major reasons for this are: (1) unlike pity, envy does not involve a kind of acceptance, and hence justification, of the given situation; (2) when we are in an inferior position, the misfortune is magnified. For similar reasons, the desire for relief is stronger in envy as it is concerned with our own relief.

Both pity and envy express some weakness in us. In envy the weakness is expressed in our inferior position, and in pity in our perceived inability to change the undesirable situation. Also envious people often believe that personally they cannot do much to alter their inferior situation. The inability to overcome the situation is often perceived as due either to differences in natural capacities or to external circumstances: in both cases an immediate change in the situation is usually beyond our power. The suggested weakness should not be understood as implying that envy and pity make people passive in these emotions. On the contrary, the unpleasant situation in both envy and pity forces us to take steps to avoid it. However, both emotions involve a perceived self-weakness, which limits our ability to change the situation. This weakness is more dominant in pity since (a) in pity the misfortune is more substantial, and thus it is objectively harder to change the situation, and (b) changing the situation in envy will benefit us and hence we tend to be more optimistic concerning its feasibility.

In pity we reduce the unpleasantness of the situation not by solving the basic problem, but by diverting our attention from it. This is often done by paying lip service to the other's misfortune or by offering token help which cannot change the basic misfortune. In envy, too, we may reduce the unpleasantness by diverting our attention from it. But envy often leads to hard work aimed in the long run at changing the basic causes of the inferior situation. This difference expresses our belief that in envy, but usually not in pity, the situation can in principle be changed. In this sense pity is more passive than envy. However, since like pity, envy also includes the belief that we are not responsible for the unpleasant situation, in envy we also perceive the given situation as beyond our *immediate* control. In short, although envy and pity cause us to embark on diverse actions, our attitude entails a perceived weakness with respect to our ability to immediately change the unpleasant situation.

Like pity and compassion, envy comprises sorrow; its intensity is often even greater since it is we who are in the unhappy situation. Whereas the sorrow in pity and compassion is a sympathetic sorrow for the misfortune of others, the sorrow in envy is a kind of self-sorrow.

In pity we are satisfied with our comparatively favorable situation, whereas in envy we are dissatisfied with our comparative unfavorably situation. If we connect the disparity in position to us—as opposed to external circumstances—envy may be accompanied with shame and pity with pridefulness. Regret may also be associated with these circumstances.

Typically, pity, compassion, and envy require mental substitution in which we place ourselves in the other's situation; hence the fear, or the hope, of being in that situation. Since the focus of concern in envy is our *inferiority* and in pity and compassion, the other's *misfortune*, the element of comparison is less dominant in pity and compassion. Accordingly, the fear of being in the other's situation in pity and compassion is not as crucial as the hope of being in the other's situation in envy. We also try, for moral reasons, to diminish the role of this fear. It would appear morally deficient to suffer sorrow over the substantial misfortune of others merely because we fear that we may meet such misfortune in the future.

Both envy and pity contain conflicting emotional strands: attraction to and repulsion from the other. In envy attraction is expressed by admiration and in pity, by sympathy. The component of repulsion is represented by hostility in envy, and by contempt in pity.

As suggested, we may envy only one aspect of a certain person while still considering ourselves on the whole as superior. Although such cases in which the emotion is directed only at a partial aspect of the object are also possible in pity, they are rarer. Since envy is concerned with small differences, we may be superior to the other person in other aspects than those at which the envy is directed. Hence, we may still consider ourselves as being in an overall superior position. Because pity is concerned with substantial misfortune, it is less likely that we will still consider the other person to be in an overall superior position. Nevertheless, we do sometimes speak of pity that refers only to some aspects of the other's life while we still regard this person as enjoying a superior position. A workman may say that he pities the royal family for having no private life. In this case the word "pity" is used largely metaphorically, not referring to pity but to the wish not to be in the other's position in this respect only. Here "It is such a pity" is like "It is such a shame." Both express a certain negative evaluation but neither really involves genuine emotions. Likewise, when rich people say that they envy the poor for having no worries, they in fact express their wish not to have worries but do not describe an actual emotion. If the rich really envied the poor, they could easily become poor by giving away all their money. The fact that they do not do so suggests that they are not really envious.

*Intensity Variables*

Kindness consists in loving people more than they deserve.
—Unknown

As in the preceding chapter, so here and in coming chapters, I will not further analyze the variable of the *event's strength* in addition to what I have already said when introducing the general characteristics of the emotion.

The variable of *degree of reality* is important in pity and compassion as it is important in envy and jealousy. Pity and compassion deal with actual situations of agents and the reality of these situations is emotionally significant.

The variable of *relevance*, which includes that of *closeness*, is quite significant in pity and compassion. People whose fate is irrelevant to our own, or who are far away from us, generate less intense emotions. Whereas in envy and jealousy relevance to self-esteem is the most crucial variable, in pity and compassion it is closeness. In envy, and to a lesser extent in jealousy, relevance to self-image often determines closeness. In pity and compassion, where the other is in an inferior situation, the relevance to self-esteem is not so significant. As indicated, emotional closeness consists of two major components: (1) similarity in background, (2) proximity in current position. In envy both components are important. In pity and compassion there is no proximity in current position since the object is in a considerably inferior position; hence, the emphasis is on similarity of background. When our situation is slightly worse than the other's, envy and self-sorrow are generated. When our situation is slightly better, pleasure-in-others'-misfortune is often the typical emotion.

Like other emotions pity and compassion often require mental substitution in which we place ourselves in the other's situation. The greater the psychological closeness, the easier this substitution becomes. Indeed, Aristotle argues that "we pity those who are like us in age, character, disposition, social standing, or birth; for in all these cases it appears more likely that the same misfortune may befall us also."[14] Hence, pity and compassion are more intense when the psychological distance is not great. Indeed, those who wish to withhold compassion and pity describe the sufferers as quite dissimilar to the rest of us. Thus, Nazi descriptions of Jews portrayed them as nonhuman: either as insects or vermin, or as inanimate objects, "cargo" to be transported.[15]

Pity and compassion differ with regard to the required closeness. Compassion comprises far greater closeness. Contrary to compassion, pity does not require genuine care or help; therefore, pity may be directed at strangers about whom we hardly know anything. Pity is not dominant in very close relations where the central concern is what happens to the other person rather than our future state. When an unjustified misfortune falls on a person very close to us, we feel compassion, or even anger, rather than pity. When we do not wish to become personally involved in the fate of someone who needs substantial help, we increase the psychological distance between us, thus making pity rather than compassion the more natural attitude. The closeness involved in envy seems to be between that of compassion and pity. Unlike pity, in envy the two components of closeness, namely, similarity in background and proximity in current situation, are important; in pity only the first component is significant. In compassion the similarity in background is so great that the weight of other factors is marginal.

There are, then, certain emotions, such as envy and pity, which are not typical of people who are very close to each other. It is interesting to note that envy and pity are more likely to emerge in the attitudes of children toward their parents than vice versa.[16] Since envy and pity are not typical of very close relations, we may conclude that parents feel closer to their children than the reverse. It should be emphasized that I am not arguing that children do not feel close to their parents, but rather that parents generally feel closer to their children than children do to their parents. The Oedipus complex, in which a son considers his father as his rival for his mother's favor, is an example of jealousy in which the son perceives great closeness to his mother, but some distance from his father.

The claim that pity is not typical of very close relations may explain an interesting story told by Herodotus about the Egyptian king Psammenitus who did not weep at the sight of his son being led to his death, nor at the sight of his daughter being humiliated, but burst into tears when he saw his friend begging. Aristotle says that this behavior indicates that he felt pity toward his friend but not toward his son (and daughter); the son was too close to him to be pitied.[17] Herodotus tells us that Cambyses, the Persian king who ordered the execution of Psammenitus's son, was so impressed by Psammenitus's behavior that he ordered the boy's life to be saved. It was, however, too late: those who were sent after the boy did not find him alive.

Why does the close relationship between Psammenitus and his son prevent Psammenitus from pitying his son? At first sight, it seems odd to say that a father does not pity his son, especially when he is being led to his death. Why should a basically positive attitude, such as pity, not arise in such a relationship? The explanation is connected with the above claim that pity is not typical of very close relations.

As in other cases of pity, Psammenitus believed his son to suffer from an undeserved misfortune with respect to which Psammenitus was impotent; Psammenitus felt sorrow for his son's suffering, and desired his son's relief. But unlike typical cases of pity, Psammenitus's attitude did not involve an acceptance and justification of the son's situation. Psammenitus held the same emotional attitude as his son, namely anger and fear typical of unjustified threatening situations. Psammenitus's dominant attitude was neither that of recognizing the inferior position of another person and wishing not to share such a position, nor that of satisfaction with his own superior position. His attitude rather involved the realization that a very important part of himself was being destroyed. Psammenitus was therefore terrified and angry. The son's inferior position was experienced as his own inferior position. Psammenitus's dominant wish was to change the current situation rather than to avoid it in the future. Psammenitus's lack of pity for his son was not due to a lack of sorrow or compassion at seeing him led to his death.

Psammenitus explained his behavior by saying "my own griefs were too great to cry out about, but the sorrow of this friend is worth tears; he had much, and much happiness, and has lost all and become a beggar when he is upon the threshold of old age."[18] Psammenitus's explanation refers to his children's misfortunes as his own; hence, he does not pity them. In the case of his friend, the distance was sufficient for pity to be generated. Since Psammenitus was very close to his son, crying while seeing him could have been interpreted as dishonorable behavior, like begging for his own sake. Such an interpretation was unlikely in the friend's case because of the distance between them. Psammenitus's behavior is unique. Most people would burst into tears in a similar situation. Nevertheless, their emotional attitude would not usually be pity. Their emotional attitude would be a complex including sorrow, but seldom pity. There may be other behavioral explanations for Psammenitus's crying in one case and its absence in another: thus, it may be argued that the friend's begging was less expected and more humiliating. Pity is more intense when the other's current misfortune follows former good fortune. The son's misfortune is more expected in light of the vulnerability of kings and their children at this period. The humiliation involved in the friend's situation is strong and this is compatible with the other's inferiority typical of pity.

After suggesting that very close relations may prevent pity, the phenomenon of self-pity should be considered since it seems to contradict this suggestion: the relation between the two factors in self-pity is the closest one can achieve because they actually consist of a single entity. In self-pity we construct the required subject-object distance by detaching ourselves from our actual situation and viewing ourselves as if we were superior to what we actually are. The given position is viewed as the consequence of arbitrary misfortune and does not reflect our "proper" position. Also in other negative emotions directed at oneself, for example, guilt, embarrassment, and regret, the global self-esteem is often higher than the specific self-esteem of our current situation or deeds. In contrast to the attitude typical of very close relations, self-pity contains many typical features of pity: perceived impotence of oneself, acceptance of the situation, and unwillingness to become personally involved. Indeed, the pronounced self-impotence is what accords this attitude its negative connotation. The agent constantly thinks or talks of his misfortune but does not do much to change it. Two features that seem to be absent from self-pity are satisfaction with our position and fear of being in the other's situation. But it may be argued that self-pity is not completely devoid of these features either. Self-pity may be viewed as a way of protecting our positive self-image by not attributing the current inferior situation to us and as involving our fear of remaining permanently in this inferior position. Although self-pity is not the typical case of pity, it is a kind of pity.[19]

The possibility of self-pity and the unlikelihood of pity in very close relations indicates once again that the relevant subject-object distance in emotions is a constructed psychological distance rather than actual physical separation.

I now turn to discuss the variables constituting background circumstances of the agents involved in the emotional state, namely, accountability, readiness, and deservingness.

The variable of *controllability*, which is dominant in constituting our accountability, is more significant in pity than in compassion. Controllability can either refer to our control of the eliciting event or to the control of others. In compassion, which is a very profound attitude, the emphasis is on the other's present situation; past circumstances, leading to this situation, are less significant. It is not of great importance for the nature of compassion if the man dying from AIDS was infected by a homosexual relationship (high object control) or by blood transmission (low object control). In pity this issue is of great importance since it justifies in our mind our passive attitude. It is as if the other person deserves his bad fortune and we are not morally obliged to intervene. In pity we perceive ourselves as not responsible for the other's misfortune and as unable to change it in the future. This helps us to reduce emotional intensity.

The greater significance attached to past circumstances in pity also explains why the variables constituting *readiness*, namely, expectation and certainty, play a greater role in pity than in compassion. In compassion, what we expected is of little emotional significance for the other's current suffering. In pity it is of greater significance since it also may serve to justify our passivity.

The variable of *deservingness* plays an important role in both compassion and pity. Generally, the negative evaluation toward the other's misfortune indicates that pity and compassion include a belief that the sufferer does not deserve such a misfortune. Extremely malignant behavior may prevent the generation of compassion and pity since the other person is perceived to deserve severe misfortune. Thomas Reid tells us that in Portugal and Spain, "a man condemned to be burned as an obstinate heretic, meets with no compassion even from the multitude. It is true, they are taught to look upon him as an enemy to God, and doomed to hellfire."[20]

Determination of the object's deservingness is sometimes complex as it may involve a conflict between the subject's and the object's points of view. The subject's point of view is typically more dominant in determining the other's deservingness. When we feel compassion or pity toward an old woman who has lost her reason and memory, we negatively evaluate her situation although she does not do so.[21] But we believe that in normal conditions of human functioning, this person would make the same evaluation. The values and wishes of the other person should have a considerable weight in determining the deservingness of this person's misfortune. I may have compassion toward a ballet dancer who broke her leg and consequently must miss the whole season, although from my own point of view breaking a leg is not so traumatic as one can read many books while recuperating. However, for this dancer, missing a whole season is a severe misfortune which she does not deserve. The weight of one's personal perspective in determining one's deservingness is not unlimited. Take, for example, the story of the Roman aristocrat who discovered that his shipment of peacock's tongues from Africa had been interrupted. Feeling that his dinner party that evening would be a total disaster in consequence, he wept bitter tears, and implored his friend Seneca to pity him. Seneca laughed, for he did not think that this person deserved to be pitied.[22] Although deservingness is to a great extent personal, it is not arbitrary.

In compassion the issue of deservingness is less problematic than in pity since we usually believe that the other person does not deserve to be in such a miserable situation, almost regardless of one's background circumstances as these are often perceived as beyond this person's control. The basic human equality associated with compassion has typically greater weight than the specific circumstances. In pity, background circumstances are more important as we believe that the other person is in some way responsible for this situation. Our perspective is often different from that of the person we pity.

The intensity of both compassion and pity decreases if the other person is perceived to deserve the misfortune. When the misfortune is justified, there is no place for a negative emotional evaluation of it.

Contrary to my claim concerning the positive correlation between accountability and emotional intensity, the correlation in pity seems to be negative: the more responsible the other person is for her current situation, the less intense our pity toward her will be. The case in anger, for example, is different. In anger, the more the other person is responsible for the eliciting event, the angrier I will be. Explaining this difference should be done by referring to the relationship between deservingness and controllability in pity and anger.

In both anger and pity the issue of deservingness is central. However, this is so for different reasons. In anger our negative attitude is toward the other's *action*; in pity the negative attitude is toward the other's *situation*. The issue of the other's controllability is part and parcel of our negative attitude toward the other's action. Knowing that the agent is not responsible for the eliciting event typically eliminates, or at least considerably reduces, anger. Overcoming anger is primarily overcoming the insult, or humiliation, caused by an action which the other is considered to be responsible for. The place of the other's controllability in pity is more complex as the main concern is not the other's *previous action* but the other's *present situation*. Unlike anger, pity can be immediately eliminated without referring to the issue of the other's controllability: improving the other's situation will suffice. Improving our situation may not eliminate anger since the insult and humiliation may not be affected by such improvement.

The issue of controllability in pity is relevant to determining the other's deservingness: if the other person is responsible for her bad situation, the agent deserves, to a certain extent, this misfortune. The influence of the controllability variable is mainly indirect—through the variable of deservingness. The correlation between the other's controllability and the other's deservingness of our pity is negative: the greater the other's controllability, the less the other deserves our pity;

consequently, the less intense pity is. Hence the impression that unlike other emotions, in pity controllability is negatively correlated with emotional intensity. However, this is so only because of the negative correlation between the other's controllability and the other's deservingness of our pity. If we are able to neutralize the influence of the deservingness variable in pity, the typical positive correlation between controllability and emotional intensity will prevail. In anger, the correlation between the other's controllability and the other's deservingness is positive: the more the agent is responsible for the eliciting event, the more justified is our anger. Hence, neutralization of the deservingness variable will not change the overall positive correlation between controllability and emotional intensity.

*Moral Value*

It is a glorious thing to be indifferent to suffering, but only to one's own suffering.
—Robert Lynd

Among the attributes of God, although they are all equal, mercy shines with even more brilliancy than justice.
—Miguel de Cervantes

There is a longstanding philosophical tradition that argues that pity is worthless from a moral viewpoint or even has a negative moral value. Spinoza, for example, argues that "Pity, in a man who lives according to the guidance of reason, is evil of itself, and useless." The main reason for criticizing pity is that it does not improve the situation. Philosophers like Kant and Nietzsche, who assume that pity is worthless from a moral viewpoint, argue that even if one is unable to overcome this emotion, one should prevent others realizing that they are the object of our pity. Among other important philosophers who criticize pity are Plato, Seneca, Epictetus, Locke, and Spinoza.[23]

The bad press received by pity concerns both what pity lacks, namely, actual assistance, and what it implies, namely, a feeling of superiority and satisfaction with our own position. Nevertheless, pity is not vicious. Pitiers may not do enough from a moral point of view, but they do no harm. Moreover, since pity involves paying attention to the suffering, rather than the success, of others, it may ultimately lead to some improvement. In pity we overcome our natural tendency to look away from people who suffer. This is no doubt socially useful and morally commendable. But mere acknowledgment is not enough; real assistance is often called for.

It is interesting to compare the moral value of pity and envy which are both considered by many to be basically negative. Pity is usually considered to have a higher moral value than envy since it involves sorrow over others' misfortune rather than over their good fortune. Like pity, envy involves paying attention to other people, but not to those who need help. It involves sorrow over others' good fortune, which is certainly not commendable from a moral point of view. Despite these obvious shortcomings, envy is not completely negative. It does address some demand for equality and forces people to pay more attention to the feelings and attitudes of their fellow humans. The assumed greater moral value of pity may also be connected with the different superior-inferior relations in pity and envy. Since the superior is often in a position to offer help, it is considered to be legitimate for the superior person in pity to pay attention to the inferior situation of the other person. In the case of envy, where we are in the inferior position, paying attention to the superior situation of another person will rarely involve help; hence, it is usually considered to have no positive function. Both pity and envy are hard to avoid, and they fulfill some basic human needs. Although it is difficult to imagine human society devoid of these emotions, we can try to foster their more suitable forms. By increasing the willingness to help, pity can acquire a greater moral value, and by decreasing its intensity and frequency, envy can become less harmful or may even be useful in certain circumstances.[24]

Compassion has far higher moral value than pity. It exceeds mere attention to the suffering of others by greater commitment to substantial help. Compassion is the recommended moral attitude toward the suffering of other agents.

Mercy incorporates a moral predicament since it is considered a virtue as well as something which tempers justice: imposing hardship when it is deserved may be just, but nevertheless the merciful act is considered morally desirable or even a sort of duty. Thus, we criticize those who fail to act mercifully. Such situations illustrate Sophocles' saying that there is a point beyond which even justice becomes unjust.

The moral predicament is absent from the gunman paradigm. In this paradigm, where someone has the power but not the right to cause suffering to another person, mercy is necessary from a moral point of view. The conflict in this case between power and right is not a moral conflict. The moral situation is less obvious when the gunman claims to be justified in punishing the other person; for example, when the gunman is a battered wife and the other person is her cruel husband. Such situations are closer to the judge paradigm where punishment is justified. However, since the wife has no institutional power to punish other people severely, her right to do so is morally doubtful.

In the merchant paradigm, where someone has both the power and the right not to alleviate the other's suffering, mercy is in most cases morally recommended. The merchant's case may be more complex when several poor people owe the merchant money but she only waives the loan of one person. Doubts concerning the moral value of mercy arise only when general considerations regarding other people enter the picture. This is even more evident in the judge paradigm.

The merchant has the *right to alleviate* the other's suffering since we are entitled to freely allocate our personal resources. The gunman has the *duty to alleviate* the other's suffering since such suffering is unjustified in the first place. The judge seems to have the *duty not to alleviate* the other's suffering since such suffering is what justice requires. In the judge paradigm, notions of punishment or retribution, which are hardly relevant to the merchant and the gunman paradigms, are crucial. The moral predicament of mercy is most acute in the judge paradigm where general considerations are most relevant. Why should a judge alleviate suffering when one of her primary tasks is to punish wrongdoers? Why should a judge spare one when others have been punished severely for the same transgression? In these cases justice requires harsh treatment, while mercy requires alleviation of suffering.

I have characterized an act of mercy as involving an intervention in, or departure from, a likely course of events. The moral difficulty associated with mercy arises when the established course of events is considered to be justified. The most acute difficulty is when the established course is that endorsed by general moral rules and the particular act of mercy deviates from them. At the heart of the moral difficulty underlying mercy is the tension between two requirements of justice: the call for individuation and the call for generality. This tension is indeed greatest in the judge paradigm where general comparative considerations are of utmost importance. We have also seen that mercy is problematic in the merchant paradigm where other people are in a similar situation to the one whose loan the merchant waives. If we want to establish the moral value of mercy we should explain why in some cases the call for individuation morally overrides the call for generality.

The demand for individuation is part of what we mean by taking each person seriously as a person and is thus a basic demand of justice. A basic demand of justice is that morally relevant differences between people should affect our treatment of those persons.[25] The problem, however, is to determine which individual differences are morally relevant. Determining moral relevance is not derived from criminal law or other general principles of justice, and no precise theory of moral relevance is possible.

General rules and categories are most useful in understanding a diverse and complex environment and in being able to manage in such environment. Taking notice of all the minute differences associated with each individual item will exhaust all our resources. In order to have a more general understanding, we must overlook many differences by regarding them as irrelevant to our given purpose. In this way we can recognize all dogs as belonging to a certain species despite the differences among various dogs. Too specific categorization requires investing many cognitive resources in very few objects; too general categorization may overlook important differences among individuals.

Not only in the cognitive domain but in the moral domain as well, we must overlook individual differences in order to establish the validity of general rules of moral behavior. Paying attention to each particular difference will prevent application of the general rules. Considering, for example, the hair color and the weight of a person to be relevant moral differences will considerably limit the value of general moral rules. General moral rules overlook such individual differences, as those are considered to be irrelevant. While hair color and weight are indeed irrelevant to almost all moral situations, there are other individual differences whose classification as morally relevant or irrelevant is less obvious. Background circumstances, such as one's childhood and education, are examples of problematic individual differences. In many cases such circumstances are morally relevant, but it is extremely difficult, if possible at all, to encapsulate them in a general set of moral rules. Accordingly, moral rules, and criminal laws in particular, often overlook these differences; this may result in treating the person unfairly. Mercy may be characterized as the attempt to prevent such injustice. The importance of individual considerations in mercy makes it impossible to tell in advance the precise circumstances in which mercy is the appropriate attitude. Understanding the whole story is the only moral way to evaluate whether mercy is apt in a particular case.[26]

A common argument against mercy is that reason should treat like cases alike, and since merciful behavior does not do so, it is irrational.[27] In light of the above discussion the weakness of this argument is evident. There is no doubt that reason should treat like cases alike, but the problem is that there are no completely like cases. Hence, in using general categories and rules, reason is forced to treat unlike cases as like cases. This treatment may be viewed as irrational because it distorts reality; nevertheless, it has great practical value and for many purposes these differences are indeed irrelevant. Treating a special case in a special manner, as is the case in mercy, is not only allowed but is even obligatory from a moral point of view. Hence, when used properly, mercy can be regarded as preventing some gross distortions committed through the need for generalization. It is not the case that in mercy we treat two identical cases differently; rather we treat differently two different cases which cannot be differentiated by prevailing general rules. Merciful behavior is not irrational behavior; it is a unique type of rational behavior. The individual discretion associated with mercy is not identical to an arbitrary decision. On the contrary, such discretion can be quite reasonable, but is not based on prevailing general rules. This discretion does not intend to exempt people from their just deserts but to give them their just deserts in situations where general rules fail to do so.

Behaving mercifully does not go against behaving equally; rather it goes against perceiving a certain specific case as equal to other cases in which a certain general rule is implemented. The moral criticism against mercy should not be directed against the possibility of giving special treatment to special cases, but rather against perceiving a certain case as a special case. It should be noted that we cannot in all cases use a partial perspective when looking at special circumstances. As suggested, individual treatment is particularly important in our relationship with those who are close to us: with regard to our intimates, partial treatment is morally required and justified. There are, however, situations in which our attitude toward strangers should also take account of partial, individual considerations. Typical situations include those involving the possibility of grave harm to strangers. Mercy is of particular moral value in such situations. Individual, partial considerations should have a limited role in determining our behavior toward strangers. Otherwise, mercy would not be an exception to basically useful and just rules, but rather would become partial and unjustified behavior; punishment would lose its value and no general justice would be available.

Being partial here does not necessarily mean being emotional. One reason for the lack of intense feelings in mercy is that contrary to emotions, mercy is directed at strangers toward whom our feelings are not intense. An interesting question in this regard is whether in making a merciful decision the judge (or other merciful people) should be guided by emotions as well. It is clear that the judge can be merciful without relying on emotions; the question is whether this is to be recommended. A prevailing approach within the legal system answers this question affirmatively: it is assumed that the judge should be impartial and nonemotional. In light of the importance of emotional sensitivity in detecting moral wrongdoing, this is a doubtful approach. I have argued that virtuous people are not merely less prone to immoral temptations, they are also more sensitive to moral wrongdoing. The emotional sensitivity of virtuous people is accompanied by more acute moral perception.

If mercy indeed represents a departure from an established, general course of events, it cannot be directed toward our intimates, as our relationship with them is based on individual considerations. The partial attitude we exhibit toward our intimates is not that of mercy but of love, compassion, and other related attitudes. Consider two examples: my son lied to me and I did not punish him for this, and I waived my right to collect a loan given to my brother. These are not genuine examples of mercy as my relationship with my son and brother are constituted by individual considerations rather than by general rules.

How should we characterize the cruelty of a parent who abuses his child? Can we describe such behavior as merciless, implying that mercy can be part of an intimate relationship with those close to us? There is no doubt that sometimes hardness of the heart is part of relationships with those near and dear to us. In such cases harsh behavior is meant to improve the other person's situation in the long run and hence is not merciless. The cases of real abuse, in which the individual needs of the other person are obviously neglected, cannot be regarded as part of intimate relationships with those close to us.

*Mercy and Punishment*    The value of imposing harsh treatment on wrongdoers, namely, punishment, is bound up with two major ideas: (1) deterrence, which has an instrumental value in preventing the same person and other people from committing similar offenses; and (2) retribution, which has an intrinsic value of giving perpetrators their due. The focus of concern in deterrence is the future behavior of the wrongdoer and other people; the focus of concern in retribution is the past behavior of the wrongdoer.

Mercy is relevant to both ideas. Deterrence and retribution are clearly associated with the judge paradigm. Deterrence is absent from the merchant paradigm but retribution is often present in this paradigm. Deterrence and retribution are often absent from the gunman paradigm.

When deterrence is the central factor in punishment, the extent of the punishment is determined not merely by specific considerations fully relevant to someone's personal deserts but also by instrumental considerations intending to prevent other people from committing similar offenses. When such a punishment is severe, it may be unfair to the particular offender. If, for example, a certain offense is currently quite prevalent and consequently, as a warning, a judge passes a heavier sentence than that received by previous offenders, then personal deserts are sacrificed to the safety of society. This is accepted as the lesser of two evils. In order to achieve deterrence, society has formal laws in which the severity of the punishment is limited within a predetermined range, regardless of individual considerations. Such general rules may be efficient and just in most circumstances. However, there may be circumstances in which individual considerations are so powerful that ignoring them is obviously wrong from a moral point of view. In these circumstances, the lesser of two evils may be to sacrifice the safety of society to personal deserts; hence, an act of mercy is required. Indeed, the idea of mitigation incorporates the belief that although severity of punishment should primarily be determined by reference to general considerations, justice requires that those facing special difficulties in keeping the law which they have broken should be punished less.[28]

If retribution is considered to be the only, or at least the essential, element of justice, individual considerations have greater weight. Retribution implies that one gets what one deserves, and if individual considerations determine that one should not be severely punished, no other external considerations should be relevant in this regard. If indeed punishment were merely based on retribution, and the judge had complete knowledge and wisdom, no general rules would be needed and mercy would be absent too, as there could be no individual decisions incompatible with general rules. This ideal situation cannot be achieved because deterrence is still an important factor in punishment and unfortunately our judges do not have complete knowledge and wisdom. Even if our judges had such knowledge and wisdom, formal general rules would be required for the purpose of deterrence. Hence, acts of mercy would be required as well.

An interesting situation which is similar in its structure to mercy is that in which individual considerations call for more severe hardship than that recommended by general considerations. For example, in Western movies the hero is sometimes in a position to kill the villain, who indeed seems to deserve death, but the hero hands him over to the sheriff. The hero believes he has the right to kill the villain although this right is incompatible with the law. The hero refrains from killing not because he thinks that the villain deserves the less severe punishment that will be imposed upon him by the legal system, but because such killing may lead to further killings, or because he feels pity or contempt, or is now completely indifferent to the villain. A similar case is that in which the prosecution refrains from requesting that harsh punishment be given to a terrorist, fearing that such punishment will escalate the political violence. In these cases there is also a conflict between individuation and generality, but here generality recommends the less harsh treatment. These are not typical cases of mercy. The reduction in harshness of treatment consequent to mercy stems from the conviction that in light of various individual considerations, the person does not deserve the harsh treatment; hence, mercy is compatible here with justice. In the above examples, the offenders are considered to deserve the harsh treatment, but only practical considerations prevent such treatment. Unlike the situation in typical mercy, in such cases justice is not done.

In comparing the moral value of pity, compassion, and mercy, we can easily determine that compassion has the highest moral value since it incorporates real help and does not clash with justice. Comparing the moral value of pity and mercy is more difficult. Unlike pity, mercy includes real help and in this sense is morally more valuable. However, the assistance accorded by mercy does not require any significant sacrifice, as is the case with compassion and even with pity. This may be one reason why mercy is more controversial than pity: in being merciful, the judge does not sacrifice any of her resources but may endanger the well-being of society. In this paradigm, mercy is morally controversial since we may be perceived to be granting too much to the other person; pity is morally controversial for the opposite reason: we may be viewed as granting too little.

# Chapter 12

# Why Do We Feel Good No Matter What You Feel?
# —Happy-for and Pleasure-in-Others'-Misfortune

---

I'm just glad it'll be Clark Gable who's falling on his face and not Gary Cooper.
—Gary Cooper, on his decision not to take the leading role in *Gone With the Wind*

Positive emotions toward the fortune of others are less complex, or at least less differentiated, than negative emotions toward the fortune of others. The basic emotions in this group are pleasure-in-others'-fortune (or, in short, happy-for) and pleasure-in-others'-misfortune (*Schadenfreude*). Although these are common emotions, some languages do not even have separate terms for them.

*Happy-For*

Is that a gun in your pocket or are you just happy to see me?
—Mae West

Happy-for and pleasure-in-others'-misfortune are types of the emotion of happiness and as such they contain a positive evaluation. However, whereas happy-for is directed at someone's good fortune, pleasure-in-others'-misfortune is directed at someone's misfortune. In happy-for the focus of concern is the person enjoying good fortune. In pleasure-in-others'-misfortune the focus of concern is our comparative position. Happy-for involves no conflict between our evaluation of the situation and that of the other person: both are positive. Pleasure-in-others'-misfortune involves this conflict: we positively evaluate what the other negatively evaluates. In this sense, happy-for is far less complex than pleasure-in-others'-misfortune.

Some people doubt whether an emotion such as happy-for is common or even exists. Thus, Rousseau argues that nobody can share the happiness of even his best friend without envy. Only the friend's neediness, which poses no threat to us, can bring out our generous emotions. Happy people are an insult to us as they seem to be superior and in no need of us; unhappy people are an affirmation of our own worth and superiority.[1]

The above argument, although valid in many circumstances as it expresses the centrality of the comparative concern in emotions, is not valid when the other person is so close to us that her success is considered to be our own and hence poses no threat to our self-esteem. An obvious example of such cases is parents who are happy for their children's success and happiness. The more we can see the other person as close enough to form part of our self-identity, the more we are able to be happy with this person's happiness without being distressed by a social comparison. Since these cases lack a competitive concern, the good fortune of the other person is not perceived as threatening our own fortune. On the contrary, it may even make us appear in a more favorable light because of our close connection with this person. In such situations we believe that we are not harmed by the other's good fortune and that the other person deserves such fortune.

The scope of happy-for is, however, limited. The two major limitations are the closeness of the other person to us and the extent of the other's good fortune. The high degree of closeness required in this emotion does not guarantee its presence even among family members. Happy-for is the least conditional, namely, the least dependent on other intensity variables, in parents' attitude toward their children; in the children's attitude toward their parents, it is much more conditional. The less close we are to the other person, the more important are the extent and nature of the other's good fortune. When the other's good fortune is better, lasts longer, and is relevant to our own fortune, negative emotions such as resentment or envy are more likely to appear even in the case of good friends. Similarly, a substantial misfortune of someone is more likely to induce pity rather than pleasure-in-others'-misfortune.

In typical cases of happy-for we like the object, and the more we do, the happier we are with the object's good fortune. Nevertheless, cases of happy-for for someone we dislike are possible though not typical. The situation in pleasure-in-others'-misfortune is the opposite: the more we like the person, the less likely we are to be pleased with their misfortune. Nevertheless, we are sometimes pleased with minor misfortunes of people we like.

*Pleasure-in-Others'-Misfortune*

It is not enough to succeed; others must fail.
—Gore Vidal


As in the case of other emotions, I am not concerned here with linguistic considerations but with psychological attitudes. However, the absence in many languages of a special term for what is called here "happy-for" and "pleasure-in-others'-misfortune" is intriguing. The absence of the first term, which is less common than the absence of the second term, may be explained in light of the less differentiated nature of positive emotions and the fact that the emotion of happy-for is quite similar to the general emotion of joy or happiness.

In the case of pleasure-in-others'-misfortune, it is not only that most languages do not have a special term for this common emotion, but that even in those having such a term, its meaning is not always clear. In this regard, Maurice Blondel attacks the Germans for having such a term, which he claims is "without equivalent in any language." It is beyond the scope of this work to analyze why many languages do not have a special term for this emotion. However, contrary to what some people suggest, I do not take the absence of an English equivalent to the German *Schadenfreude* as an indication that this emotion is less common in English-speaking societies. The explanation must be more complex.[2]

In an interesting study on *gratitude* in southern India, Appadurai points out that it is difficult to say "thank you" in a direct way in the Tamil language. To be sure, there is a word in Tamil for "thanks" and it is neither impossible nor inadvisable to *show* our gratitude in Tamil society. This difficulty may be explained by arguing that in Tamil, and in other societies where nonmarket reciprocities are critical to social relations, immediate, verbal expressions of gratitude are regarded as either inappropriate or as modest promissory notes for the substantial thanks that must take the form of the eventual return gift.[3] The absence of a special word for pleasure-in-others'-misfortune is not connected to the absence of this attitude either, but to some normative judgment concerning its inappropriateness. Unlike the issue of gratitude in Tamil society, here the inappropriateness concerns the attitude itself and not merely its verbal behavior.

Many people consider pleasure-in-others'-misfortune to be the worst emotion. This extreme negative evaluation may lead to a collective attempt to repress this attitude. There are, of course, other attitudes, such as cruelty and sadism, which are morally worse than pleasure-in-others'-misfortune, but nevertheless have a special word denoting them. These attitudes, however, do not involve a moral predicament since their negative moral evaluation is not disputed and most people are able to avoid them. The case of pleasure-in-others'-misfortune is different as it is a very common emotion which is not affected by its assumed negative character. Hence, the tendency to repress public linguistic acknowledgment of this attitude. Such collective repression cannot persist for ever, as more and more people acknowledge the prevalence of this emotion.

In describing pleasure-in-others'-misfortune, two features are not disputable: our pleasure and the other's misfortune. These features describe a significant conflict between our positive evaluation of the situation and the negative evaluation of the other person. This conflict indicates the presence of a comparative, and sometimes even a competitive, concern. A major reason for being pleased with the misfortune of another person is that this person's misfortune may somehow benefit us; it may, for example, emphasize our superiority. In calculating our comparative position, the misfortune of others appears on the credit side. In this sense, pleasure-in-others'-misfortune is close to envy: in both the comparison of our fortune with that of another person is crucial. However, contrary to envy, pleasure-in-others'-misfortune allows us to occupy the superior position. The comparative concern is significant in all emotions, but in particular in those, like envy and pleasure-in-others'-misfortune, that are concerned with the fortunes of others.

The role of the comparative concern in evoking our pleasure is evident in many everyday cases. For example, when driving north we see that the south-bound traffic is jammed and is hardly moving, we are often pleased that others and not ourselves are traveling in that direction. Kant argues that "in stormy weather, when comfortably seated in our warm, cosy parlor, we may enjoy speaking of those at sea, for it heightens our own feeling of comfort and happiness."[4]

The type of pleasure in the above two examples is quite close to pleasure-in-others'-misfortune since the other's misfortune reminds us of our better situation and this generates our pleasure. In typical pleasure-in-others'-misfortune another factor is added: the belief that the others deserve their misfortune. St. Thomas Aquinas, who claims that one of the pleasures of the saints in heaven will be to observe the torments of the damned in hell, also emphasizes the role of the comparative concern in pleasure-in-others'-misfortune. He claims that "everything is known the more for being compared with its contrary. . . . Therefore in order that the happiness of the saints may be more delightful to them and that they may render more copious thanks to God for it, they are allowed to see perfectly the suffering of the damned."[5] Aquinas's argument gives us all a special incentive to achieve sainthood.

It is not enough to characterize pleasure-in-others'-misfortune as including our pleasure and the other's misfortune. I would like to suggest three additional typical characteristics: (1) the other person is perceived to deserve the misfortune, (2) the misfortune is relatively minor, and (3) we are passive in generating the other's misfortune.

A central feature of pleasure-in-others'-misfortune is the belief that the *other person deserves her misfortune*. For example, when stuck in a traffic jam, should a driver pass us on our right by driving on the hard shoulder, our anger will be replaced by pleasure when we see a policeman giving the driver a ticket. The belief that the other person deserves her misfortune expresses our assumption that justice has been done and enables us to be pleased in a situation where we seem required to be sad. Moreover, this belief presents us as moral people who do not want to hurt other people.

The more deserved the misfortune is, the more justified is the pleasure. A study of people's attitudes toward the downfall of those in high positions shows that the fall was greeted with positive approval when the fall was seen to be deserved, but reactions were negative when the fall was seen to be undeserved. Deservingness was one of the key variables that affected reactions in these cases.[6] Indeed, we often hear people who delight in others' misfortune saying that "There is a

God in heaven," or, "There is justice in this world." Consider the following two descriptions of real cases of pleasure-in-others'-misfortune that were sent to me:

> A supervisor at my work was making me miserable and almost got me fired once. He is not a nice guy at all. So when I heard that he was not making his shift limit and was fired, I cannot describe the joy, the happiness, the little dancing and singing, Oh, what a glorious day!

> Last winter, I had a lover, who had this awful girlfriend. Some days after I had an aching throat, I heard them talking on the phone, and she was surprised to discover she did not feel well and that her throat ached. Well, the smile on my face was not easy to conceal.

Assuming that a person's misfortune is justified gives us some kind of moral confirmation for this emotion, which at first seems morally unfounded. In the same vein, when we are happy about the failure of the "bad guys" in a movie, we think that justice has been done. We identify with the "good guys" so that the failure of the "bad guys" becomes a success for our side. The assumption that justice has been done is also typical of comedies. The normal response of the audience to the happy ending typical of comedies is the normative judgment, "This is how it should be."[7] In these situations, the assumption that the object deserves her misfortune is compatible with the belief that desire confers value on its object: the very fact of being pleased with someone's misfortune implies our belief that this misfortune is somehow deserved.

Kant's description of pleasure-in-others'-misfortune is compatible with the view suggested here: "our pleasure in the misfortune of another is not direct. We may rejoice, for example, in a man's misfortunes, because he was haughty, rich and selfish; for man loves to preserve equality." Aristotle, who describes envy as "pain felt at deserved good fortune," argues that the feeling—which has no name—of the person who rejoices at misfortunes involves "rejoicing over undeserved ill fortune."[8] In this regard, my view is somewhat different from that of Aristotle. Unlike Aristotle, who characterizes envy as involving a negative evaluation of the *other's deserved good fortune*, I believe that the focus of concern in envy is *our own undeserved misfortune*. And unlike Aristotle who describes pleasure-in-others'-misfortune as involving a positive evaluation of the other's *undeserved* misfortune, I consider it to involve a positive evaluation of the other's *deserved* misfortune.

As in the case of other emotions, it is not clear at which age pleasure-in-others'-misfortune actually emerges. One way of finding this out is to examine when a child begins to refer to the issue of deservingness while laughing at something. It seems to me that at quite an early age (perhaps three or four) children are able to say that they are pleased at the misfortunes suffered by the villain in a movie because he deserves his misfortune. The issue of deservingness is what distinguishes laughing at someone who slips on a banana peel from pleasure-in-others'-misfortune.

The second element in the overall characterization of pleasure-in-others'-misfortune which needs clarification concerns the *minor nature of the misfortune*. This characteristic is associated with the comparative, and often the competitive, concern prevailing in pleasure-in-others'-misfortune. Comparison is possible when the two parties are not too far apart, when they are considered to belong to the same comparative framework. Competitiveness is most significant when the gap between the two parties is not great and the situation may still be reversed: the person in the superior position could occupy the inferior position. Accordingly, pleasure-in-others'-misfortune is concerned with small differences. When the misfortune is severe, pleasure-in-others'-misfortune often turns into pity. For example, should our noisy, inconsiderate, and snobbish neighbor have his new car scratched, we may feel some pleasure; however, if his daughter becomes seriously ill, we are more likely to feel compassion or pity, not pleasure.

In the event of a severe misfortune the element of deservingness is missing. We do not usually perceive the people around us as deserving of severe misfortune. These people may deserve to be punished because they dare to be more successful than we are, but this does not justify severe misfortune befalling them and those near and dear to them.

When the suffering is no longer a minor misfortune, but begins to involve substantial suffering, pleasure-in-others' misfortune gives way to pity. When the other person suffers a real disaster, the personal comparative concern is absent. When this person suffers a slight misfortune, which is irrelevant to our own fortune, sympathy is likely to be generated. Sympathy does not necessarily presuppose a personal comparative concern. In saying that pity and sympathy do not necessarily involve personal comparative concerns I do not imply that no comparison is made while having these emotions. All types of meaning are relational and hence involve some kind of comparison. However, the personal comparative concern discussed here refers to a more profound comparison: that in which our self-esteem is derived from the comparison. Envy, which also involves a personal comparative concern, is similar to pleasure-in-others'-misfortune in addressing small differences. When the other's superior situation is not comparable to our inferior situation, envy may turn into admiration. Admiration is close to pride and both are related to happy-for. When comparison is meaningless, pleasure-in-others'-misfortune or envy does not arise. In great differences, where we cannot conceive of a way to bridge the gap, we accept the situation and hence the differences are of little emotional significance.

Since pleasure-in-others'-misfortune concerns relatively minor misfortune to the other, we typically do not receive any substantial practical benefit from the circumstances causing our pleasure. The benefit is mainly psychological and is expressed in a positive mood that we have for a while. Sometimes the perceived benefit in pleasure-in-others'-misfortune is illusory since it is perceived to be more than merely a tentative psychological benefit. Consider, for example, the case in which someone has been elected to a position I desire and after a while it is clear he is not fulfilling his duties successfully. His failure, however, does not imply that I will be given the position. If such implication is present in my pleasure, then it is likely to be illusory. Similarly, if Tom divorces his wife and marries Rachel who then leaves him, Tom's first wife may be pleased about this, but this pleasure is no more than an imaginary benefit since her own romantic life is unlikely to be improved.

Pleasure-in-others'-misfortune is associated with the *passivity* of the agent enjoying the situation. In happy-for we are ready to be personally involved in bringing about and sustaining the other's good fortune. Such readiness is typically absent in pleasure-in-others'-misfortune. An active personal involvement is contrary to the rules of fair competition; it would present us as deliberately harming the other, and hence as not being the real winner in the ongoing competition. It may also be considered an offense; although the other person might deserve misfortune, or even punishment, we lack the authority to impose it. Typically, one of the greater contributions to the pleasure we take in others' misfortune is the feeling that the failure of our competitor is not due to our own wicked behavior, but to inexorable fate. It is as if justice has been done in the spirit of the Talmudic saying: "The tasks of the righteous get done by others." This is a kind of unsolicited gift. Because of our passivity in pleasure-in-others'-misfortune, this emotion may not be so important in conducting our life though it is quite common. Elster claims that "many who find a titillating pleasure in a friend's misfortune would be horrified at the thought of going out of their way to provoke it. Doing so by omission or abstention might be easier."[9]

Let us consider some examples illustrating that typical cases of pleasure-in-others'-misfortune indeed involve the other's minor and deserved misfortune and our passivity.

> · a. Saul and David are colleagues at a certain university; they are at a comparable academic level. David is known for his arrogance and lack of intellectual depth. Saul has just found out that David has failed to publish his paper in a major scientific journal.
> · a'. Saul and David are colleagues at a certain university; they are at a comparable academic level. David is known for his modesty and has recently suffered some unjustified failure. Saul has just found out that David has failed to publish his paper in a major scientific journal.

It is evident that pleasure-in-others'-misfortune is more likely to appear in the first case, where David deserves to fail. The rise of pleasure-in-others'-misfortune in the second case would be rare. For similar reasons the rise of envy would be less intense in the second case if David succeeded in publishing his paper.

> · b. Saul and David are colleagues at a certain university; they are at a comparable academic level. Saul has just found out that David has failed to publish his paper in a major scientific journal.

· b'. Saul and David are colleagues at a certain university; they are at a comparable academic level. Saul has just found out that David's son was killed in a car accident.

Again it is obvious that pleasure-in-others'-misfortune is typical only in the first case. Pity is typical of the second case.

· c. Saul and David are colleagues at a certain university; they are at a comparable academic level. Saul has just found out that David has failed to publish his paper in a major scientific journal.

· c'. Saul and David are colleagues at a certain university; they are at a comparable academic level. David has failed to publish his paper in a major scientific journal since Saul persuaded the editor of this journal not to publish David's paper.

Pleasure-in-others'-misfortune is more likely to be generated in the first case, where Saul has been passive. The joy in the second case would be more like joy over a victory which is different from the joy over others' deserved and minor misfortunes.

To give another example. Simon is an arrogant person who lives in a small community and frequently travels abroad, much more often than the average person in his community. This week he is supposed to attend an important meeting abroad but he suddenly breaks his leg and must cancel the trip. Many people in his community will be pleased with Simon's misfortune. These people will perceive the misfortune to be minor and deserved, and they were not involved in its occurrence. However, they would not be pleased, or at least would be less pleased, if one of these factors were different. If Simon were a modest, hard-working person, his misfortune would not be perceived as deserved and other people would not be pleased with his misfortune. The same holds if the misfortune were grave; for instance, if Simon had to cancel his trip because his wife died. Similarly, if it were the case that Michael deliberately broke Simon's leg, Michael's attitude would not be that of typical pleasure-in-others'-misfortune but rather that of joy of victory. In this example, the competitive concern is absent; there is, however, a more general comparative concern.

The suggested importance of the *comparative concern* in pleasure-in-others'-misfortune may be questioned on two major grounds: (1) the other's misfortune is often *substantial* and hence the comparative concern is not at the heart of this emotion; and (2) the other's misfortune is often *insignificant* or irrelevant to our relationship with this person and hence the comparative concern is once again not central. The first objection states that the subject-object difference is too big for a comparison to take place; the second assumes that such a difference is insignificant, preventing once again a comparison which may generate pleasure-in-others'-misfortune. When discussing these objections we should bear in mind that in characterizing typical cases some exceptions are expected; it should, however, be determined whether the above objections refer to exceptions or to common and characteristic cases.

We can admit that in some circumstances the other's misfortune may be *grave*, but it is still not significantly graver than that caused by this person—especially to ourselves and those related to us. One may be pleased by the murder of a brutal dictator, but this murder is not too grave in comparison with what the dictator did to other people. Similarly, Inga may be joyful over the infidelity of Kate's husband Richard, since Kate used to be her own husband's lover. Kate may suffer a great deal because of Richard's infidelity, and Inga may know it; nevertheless, in enjoying this event Inga thinks that justice has been done and that Kate's suffering resembles her own, thus putting them on an equal footing. In such cases the other's misfortune may be substantial, but it is not much greater than what used to be, or may still be our own misfortune. Here punishment also fits, and in no way exceeds, the crime, and we can continue to believe that justice has been done.[10]

There are also cases in which the other's misfortune is severe in light of every plausible comparison and therefore it is preferable to classify these cases as pathological cases rather than typical cases of pleasure-in-others'-misfortune. The following are two such real examples. A mother whose son was killed in the army told me that before his death they had been regarded as a very happy family which had suffered no misfortune. When people came to visit them after her son's death she felt that some of them were satisfied that finally her family had also experienced some misfortune. This is a pathological, rather than a typical, case of pleasure-in-others'-misfortune since a child's death is the most severe misfortune a parent can suffer. Another such example is a man whose wife had an affair. As a result, they divorced, the wife married her lover, and shortly afterward, gave birth to a son. A few years later when the child developed cancer, the man expressed pleasure that his ex-wife had been punished. This is also a pathological case since not only is the wife's misfortune far too severe but the misfortune is shared by an innocent child.

The second type of objection to the major role attributed to the comparative concern in pleasure-in-others'-misfortune refers to the *insignificance* or irrelevance of the other's misfortune. Examples of insignificant misfortunes are cases in which people slip on a banana peel without hurting themselves, spill tea over their companion, or lose money, but still have more than we have. Examples of irrelevant misfortunes are cases in which a corrupt leader of another country is arrested or when we see, while driving, that another person gets a ticket. Both types of cases do not contain rivalry or an improvement in our comparative position. They have, however, symbolic importance in demonstrating some failure on the part of the other person and hence our satisfaction in occupying a better situation. Such insignificant and irrelevant failures may not justify elation, but some pleasure is not to be denied. This is a pauper's joy. Joy over insignificant or irrelevant misfortune may also express humor rather than the emotion of pleasure-in-others'-misfortune (to be compared shortly).

As in other emotions, typical cases of pleasure-in-others'-misfortune consist in a *subtle equilibrium* of different characteristics. When the relative weight of one characteristic is changed, changes in the weight of other characteristics may be expected. If a cruel criminal suffers a substantive misfortune, one can still be pleased with this misfortune since the criminal deserves it, and in comparison with the crimes he committed the misfortune is not too grave. In this case, the presence of a graver misfortune is made acceptable by the overriding weight of the issue of desert. This greater weight may also make the comparative concern less important. If a stranger pushes an old lady and then falls into a mud puddle, we may be pleased at his misfortune, mainly because the issue of desert is so central. When it is less significant, other characteristics may be changed as well: for example, the misfortune would have to be less severe. When the misfortune is not severe, we may be actively involved in the other's misfortune and still be pleased with it. When the relative weight of one characteristic is too great, the nature of the emotion in question may be changed as well; as suggested, when the misfortune is too grave, pleasure-in-others'-misfortune may turn into pity or another type of joy.

### Relationships with Other Emotions

Malice is like a game of poker or tennis; you don't play it with anyone who is manifestly inferior to you.
—Hilde Spiel

The relation between happy-for and pleasure-in-others'-misfortune is somewhat similar to that between *pity* and *envy*. Happy-for is similar to pity in containing no conflict between the subject's and object's evaluations of the situation: both are positive. Pleasure-in-others'-misfortune is similar to envy in containing such a conflict. The similarity between happy-for and pity is less pronounced than that between pleasure-in-others'-misfortune and envy because of the ambivalent nature of pity. Although in pity our negative evaluation of the situation is correlated with the other's negative evaluation, pity also involves a positive evaluation, expressed in our satisfaction with our superior position. It is true that such a positive evaluation is not as central in pity as the negative evaluation of the other's position; nevertheless, its presence is still one reason why people do not like to be pitied. Since happy-for is not ambivalent in such a manner, the similarity between the two emotions is not pronounced. Happy-for is more similar to compassion: both involve positive, nonambivalent evaluations.

Happy-for is a less complex joy than pleasure-in-others'-misfortune since its underlying evaluations are more straightforward. The feeling dimension in happy-for is often less intense and less confined to specific circumstances. The emotional strands associated with happy-for are indeed quite simple. They involve *delight* in the other's good fortune and satisfaction with our own position.

When we are not satisfied with our position, bitterness, rather than delight, is our likely response to another's good fortune. Another emotional attitude is evoked by our hope that the other's better situation may somehow improve our own. A related attitude is that of admiring the other's achievement.

The emotional strands associated with pleasure-in-others'-misfortune are more complex since the comparative concern is more significant. One strand is straightforward: *delight* in the other's misfortune. As La Rochefoucauld remarks, "In the misfortunes of our best friends we always find something which is not displeasing to us." This maxim also expresses the fact that like envy, and other emotions, pleasure-in-others'-misfortune typically entails a certain closeness.

Other emotional strands which express the comparative concern are satisfaction with our situation, appreciation of the other person, and fear of sharing the other's misfortune.

The *satisfaction* with our situation refers to a limited, momentary aspect. Our overall situation is often not much better and may even be worse—otherwise no comparative concern would arise. Another emotional strand is that of *appreciating* the other person; appreciation is also compatible with the comparative concern and once again indicates that beyond this transient aspect, our position is not much better.

Consider the following case that I was told: "Among my husband's group of friends is someone who is extremely successful: he is a prominent lawyer, very tall, most attractive, and highly intelligent, too. I've always envied his wife for having such a wonderful husband. The last time I saw him, I noticed that he is beginning to go bald. This gave me great satisfaction."

*Fear* is understood in light of a possible reversal of the situation, which would result in us occupying the other's inferior position. Because pleasure-in-others'-misfortune involves minor differences, this possibility is quite real. Indeed, the Biblical exhortation against pleasure-in-others'-misfortune—"Do not rejoice when your enemy falls"—is explained by the fear that we may find ourselves in the same situation.

Sometimes what seems to be pleasure-in-others'-misfortune is actually other types of *joy*. There are cases in which we do not believe the other person deserves the misfortune, but nevertheless we continue to enjoy it. In these cases, we believe that justice has been done in the sense that we deserve to enjoy a temporarily superior position. Here the other's misfortune is not the object of our pleasure, but merely its cause. Similarly, if Don achieves his prestigious position as a result of the death of his friend Jim, this probably involves a joy that is different from pleasure-in-others'-misfortune. Don may be sincerely sad about Jim's death, but nevertheless be pleased to be given his position. Don's joy is not pleasure-in-others'-misfortune, but rather general joy stemming from the improvement in his own situation. This joy is not directed at Jim but at Don himself.

When we are victorious, this pleasure is also different from pleasure-in-others'-misfortune, although both cases involve the failure of another person. The principal difference between the two types of joy is in the more *active* role we play in the joy we derive from a personal victory. This joy represents the culmination of a planned and usually long series of activities which have been performed in order to achieve the advantageous situation. In a great victory the object may end up much inferior to us. Joy in victory is associated not only with the comparative concern but with the competitive one as well. Pleasure-in-others'-misfortune is less deliberative, our role is much more passive, and the other person does not occupy a significantly disadvantageous position. Accordingly, whereas the comparative aspect is central to pleasure-in-others'-misfortune, in victorious joy the emphasis is on personal success. Consequently, the world chess champion Garry Kasporov may derive victorious joy from defeating the computer Deep Blue, but he will not experience pleasure-in-others'-misfortune if some bug in Deep Blue makes the computer lose the game.

A few elements typical of *humor* also appear in pleasure-in-others'-misfortune. Both express joy which typically stems from the perceived misfortune of agents. In both cases the typical misfortune is minor: we usually do not enjoy hearing about substantial misfortunes. Both humor and pleasure-in-others'-misfortune require a strong element of incongruity or change. In humor we do not anticipate the particular punch line and in pleasure-in-others'-misfortune we typically do not expect the others' particular misfortune. In both cases unspecified expectations of some kind of conclusion may be present. Thus, in hearing a joke about a group of people or about a certain politician, we may expect a general type of conclusion, but we do not expect the particular one. Similarly, we may expect the downfall of a certain person for a long time, but the particular misfortune responsible for our current pleasurable experience is not usually anticipated. The events associated with pleasure-in-others'-misfortune are unexpected in the sense that most emotional events are unexpected: their particular appearance at a specific moment and in a specific form is usually unexpected.

A significant difference between humor and pleasure-in-others'-misfortune is that in the case of humor, the evaluative component, and hence the issue of deservingness, is absent or at least reduced. Humor can stem from merely cognitive incongruity; pleasure-in-others'-misfortune requires evaluative incongruity as well. Comedy gives us pleasure not because we compare the present situation with a different one and believe the present one to be more desirable. We laugh because the situation is unique or incongruent with normal situations. The feeling of superiority is typical of pleasure-in-others'-misfortune but not necessarily of humor. In light of the more complex nature of pleasure-in-others'-misfortune, which includes evaluative incongruity in addition to cognitive incongruity, I would speculate that it appears later in our personal development.

Other differences between pleasure-in-others'-misfortune and humor are related to differences between emotions in general and humor. In contrast to the practical orientation of emotions, humor represents a nonpurposeful, more abstract activity. Another difference arises from the perspective used in both experiences. Emotions usually employ a limited and partial perspective: the personal perspective of an interested agent. Humor, which seems to be related to intelligence more than to emotions, has a broader perspective. It links different, apparently unrelated items within a more general perspective, generating a disinterested experience. Pleasure-in-others'-misfortune is more practical. The pleasure gained here is closely related to our interested perspective. Whereas pleasure-in-others'-misfortune represents a less practical orientation than the joy we derive from personal victory, its orientation is more practical than that of humor.

Pleasure-in-others'-misfortune is often associated with *gossip*. Both are severely condemned on moral grounds as malicious—indeed, their practice often makes us feel uncomfortable. Do the characteristics typical of pleasure-in-others'-misfortune—namely, the subject's pleasure, the object's misfortune, the perceived minor and deserved nature of the object's misfortune, and the subject's passivity—typify gossip as well? Although the subject's pleasure is not as essential to gossip as to pleasure-in-others'-misfortune, it is certainly typical. Whereas in pleasure-in-others'-misfortune we cannot be sad, in gossip we may at times be sad, albeit rarely. The subject's passivity is typical also of gossip: we do not usually gossip about our own activities. It may be less accurate to describe the object's situation in gossip as misfortune. Like pleasure-in-others'-misfortune, gossip is often associated with envy; both are usually directed at those whose general fortune is comparable to or better than ours. Those who enjoy better fortune are of more interest to us because we would like to imitate them. In gossip the typical misfortune is more likely a social failure related to embarrassment rather than to shame. The violation of social norms presumably justifies the right of other people to talk about it, and in this sense, the object of gossip (as with pleasure-in-others'-misfortune) seems to deserve to have his intimate life be the topic of other people's conversations.

Despite the prevalence of both pleasure-in-others'-misfortune and gossip, both are subject to moral reproach. A major reason for this is the inclination to take extreme cases as typical and common of both pleasure-in-others'-misfortune and gossip. The distorted public image that results from confusing extreme with typical cases surfaces in the identification of both with a malicious attitude. I believe that such an identification is mistaken and the pleasure derived from both does not stem from someone else's suffering. As in the case of pleasure-in-others'-misfortune, in gossip the other's misfortune is usually also perceived to be minor.[11] And when gossip does inflict significant damage on other people, the gossipers themselves do not usually consider the damage to be significant. The idle nature of gossip implies not merely the absence of declared purpose but lack of concern about such a purpose.

In some important aspects pleasure-in-others'-misfortune is similar to *envy*; indeed, people tend to identify the two emotions. Thus, Plato understands envy as also involving pleasure in our friend's misfortunes and Aristotle claims that "the man who is delighted by others' misfortunes is identical with the man who envies others' prosperity." Similarly, John of Salisbury defines the envious as "one who enjoys the misfortune of others and considers as his own misfortune the fortunes of others."[12]

The two are related, no doubt, especially because both involve a significant comparative concern and both imply a conflict between the evaluation of our own fortune and that of others. Typical envy and pleasure-in-others'-misfortune involve a comparative, and sometimes even a competitive concern and accordingly the subject-object gap is minor and the issue of desert central: in envy our inferior position is considered to be undeserved, whereas in pleasure-in-others'-misfortune the other's inferior position is considered to be deserved. The sorrow or pleasure of these emotions is greater in cases of direct competition referring to domains which are highly relevant to our self-esteem. The two emotions are also common when there is no direct competition. In the same way that we can envy rich people with whom we are not competing, we can also be pleased with the fall of rich people with whom we are not competing. Although there is no direct competition in these cases, there is some sort of social comparison and even an underlying rivalry. The absence of direct competition usually results in less intense emotions. Another similarity between the two emotions is that neither can be self-referential. This again suggests the importance of the comparative, and in particular the competitive concern in these emotions. Their strong similarity also surfaces in the fact that each can easily turn into the other. This is especially true concerning the transformation of envy into pleasure-in-others'-misfortune.

Despite the similarities, envy and pleasure-in-others'-misfortune are *two distinct emotions*. The most obvious difference is that one involves an enjoyable and the other a painful experience. The focus of concern in envy is our undeserved situation, whereas the focus of pleasure-in-others'-misfortune is the other's deserved situation.

Another difference is that pleasure-in-others'-misfortune is usually more transient and specific than envy. Envy, reflecting a very profound concern of ours, namely, our inferiority, persists for a long period. Pleasure-in-others'-misfortune reflects a more accidental activity of another person which does not necessarily refer to our overall situation. It is more difficult to adjust to circumstances underlying envy: being inferior is more difficult to ignore than being superior. Moreover, it seems that our superiority in pleasure-in-others'-misfortune is often less real than our inferiority in envy. The apparent improvement in our situation in the first case is more superficial and short-lived than the decline of our situation in the second case. Our passivity in pleasure-in-others'-misfortune indicates that no real improvement has taken place. Another person's misfortune seems to be less relevant to evaluating our comparative situation than another person's success. The joy in others' misfortune may disappear the moment our attention is focused on others' superiority. It is more difficult to cancel inferiority feelings by focusing on those inferior to you. Accordingly, envy has a more profound impact on our self-esteem. The feeling dimension is usually more intense in envy since losses are emotionally more significant than gains.

An interesting item in the comparison between envy and pleasure-in-others'-misfortune concerns our readiness to admit that we are experiencing them. Which emotion are people more likely to hide? This question partly depends upon the type of society in question. To eliminate this factor, this, discussion refers to contemporary Western society. When people are asked about this, their first response is usually that we are more likely to hide pleasure-in-others'-misfortune than envy.[13] A major reason for this is the more negative public image of this emotion which stems from taking extreme cases involving cruelty, sadism, and hate as prototypical cases of pleasure-in-others'-misfortune. Moreover, it would also appear that enjoying another person's misfortune is more negative from a moral viewpoint than being sorry for one's own. It seems, therefore, plausible that people will tend to hide their pleasure-in-others'-misfortune more than their envy. This is indeed what most people would initially report about their behavior. The question is whether this initial report is compatible with their actual behavior. In examining this question we should distinguish between two issues: (1) admitting the presence of the emotion, and (2) expressing the emotion in actual behavior. In the second issue we should distinguish between hiding the emotion from (1) the object, and (2) other people.

It seems that we are *less likely to verbally admit the presence of envy* than that of pleasure-in-others'-misfortune. There are a few reasons for not publicizing our envy. The major reason is that in admitting envy we admit our inferiority and no one likes to do this. We are likely to confess to almost any other sin or emotion before confessing to our envy. Hence, in describing our emotional attitude we tend to substitute envy with other emotions, for example, resentment and hate, which involve a moral concern. We prefer to consider our emotion as stemming from a moral concern rather than from an inferior position. Substituting envy for hate is interesting since hate is often considered to be more immoral than envy. Nevertheless, people more readily admit that they are bad from a moral point of view than that they are inferior. In Eugène Sue's novel, *Frederick Bastien: Envy*, Frederick even admits his intention to murder before admitting his envy. Pleasure-in-others'-misfortune does not involve admitting our inferiority; on the contrary, for the moment we are in a better position. In publicizing our pleasure-in-others'-misfortune we publicize the others' failure; in publicizing envy, we publicize our own. There is no doubt that we are less likely to do the latter. Moreover, in light of the superior position of the other in envy, it is reasonable that we may need this person in the future; hence, hiding our envy has a functional value.

Other reasons for being ready to admit our pleasure-in-others'-misfortune are related to the fact that it is not as morally wrong as it may first appear to be. This is because it involves minor misfortunes, our belief that justice has been done, and our passivity. Furthermore, if we remember that both emotions are usually judged to be negative, the fact that pleasure-in-others'-misfortune is a more transient, specific, and superficial state than envy makes it less condemnable.

It is more complex to determine whether our actual behavior, in contrast to verbal admittance, would be more likely to express our envy or pleasure-in-others'-misfortune. Although we are less likely to admit the presence of envy than of pleasure-in-others'-misfortune, our actual behavior is more likely to reveal our envious attitude. This is so since envy is a more profound attitude that is more difficult to hide.

Turning to the distinction between hiding the emotion from the object and other people, I believe that we usually hide both envy and pleasure-in-others'-misfortune from the object, since the object may be powerful or on a level comparable to ours. Exceptions are more common in the case of envy, since by revealing that we are envious we flatter the object—we implicitly admit the object's superiority. This attitude usually prevails in cases where the object does not belong to our immediate emotional environment, or when the object does not consider us a threat, and hence would not be bothered by our negative attitude toward her superiority. Confessing real, intense envy is not easy for most people. Sometimes openly excessive praise is a way of hiding envy.

Whereas there is no significant difference between hiding envy or pleasure-in-others'-misfortune from the object, there is a difference in hiding these emotions from other people. I believe that we are more likely to hide envy from people in our social group. When a less-than-favorite acquaintance fails in something, we will quickly report it to other acquaintances without hiding our pleasure. We are less quick in spreading a rumor concerning the success of such an acquaintance and we will usually be careful to hide our sorrow over this event. If, for example, a student, who usually gets straight As, gets a C in a certain examination, other students in this class who usually get lower grades will be pleased and will not hide their pleasure from each other. They will not be so quick to report another good grade this student achieved or that they envy her. The human tendency to enjoy pleasant situations in the company of friends and to suffer from unpleasant situations alone is another consideration indicating that we are less likely to hide pleasure-in-others'-misfortune than envy.

Pleasure-in-others'-misfortune is similar to *pity* in that it refers to the misfortunes of other people. It differs from pity in its positive evaluation of the misfortune. Another difference is that pleasure-in-others'-misfortune refers to minor misfortunes, pity to major ones. Accordingly, the emphasis in pity is on the other's suffering, in pleasure-in-others'-misfortune, on the other's inferiority. In both cases we are willing to preserve the other's inferiority but usually not the suffering. These elements make the two emotions quite different. I therefore reject the claim that pleasure-in-others'-misfortune is pity reversed. The subject-object relation in these emotions is different and not reversed.

Some people identify pleasure-in-others'-misfortune with *sadism*, arguing that the difference between them is negligible and pleasure-in-others'-misfortune is a kind of sadism involving hate and cruelty.[14] It is true that pleasure-in-others'-misfortune often has such a public image, but this merely represents extreme and nontypical cases. It is a common distorting inclination to take extreme cases as representing a whole category, whereas in fact they are quite rare. The unique characteristic of pleasure-in-others'-misfortune is the pleasure over someone's misfortune. An extreme manifestation of this pleasure is the sadistic enjoyment associated with cruel activities such as torture. It is obvious that this is not the typical case of pleasure-in-others'-misfortune. Many, if not all, people have experienced pleasure-in-others'-misfortune, but merely a few have experienced sadistic pleasure associated with torture or the wish to torture someone. When we want to induce pleasure through movies we see comedies in which the other's misfortune is minor and not tragedies in which the other's misfortune is grave. An interesting study on unrequited love indicates that contrary to the stereotype of the rejecter as a sadistic heartbreaker, rejecters do not enjoy this experience and have negative emotions such as guilt and regret. In their verbal and nonverbal behavior rejecters try to minimize the hurt to the other.[15] Again, the stereotype of a rejecter is compatible with extreme cases, but not with typical and common ones.

Common cases of pleasure-in-others'-misfortune are fundamentally different from sadism, hate, or cruelty. Unlike pleasure-in-others'-misfortune, sadism is a personality trait and not an emotional state. The comparative concern, which is central to pleasure-in-others'-misfortune, has no place in sadism. The three typical characteristics of pleasure-in-others'-misfortune, namely, the dominant role of deservingness, the minor nature of the misfortune, and our passivity, are absent from sadism. In sadism the issue of deservingness is not dominant at all: the other person is typically not perceived to deserve the misfortune and if such a perception is nevertheless present, it is not a dominant element. Personal egoistic pleasure, rather than deservingness, is central to sadism. The difference between pleasure-in-others'-misfortune and sadism is also evident in regard to the nature of the misfortune: in pleasure-in-others'-misfortune it is minor while in sadism it is substantial. When the misfortune is severe, the personal comparative concern disappears and with it the pleasure-in-others'-misfortune. The availability of an alternative to the current situation is an important factor in pleasure-in-others'-misfortune, but not in sadism. Another difference concerns the subject's role: unlike typical pleasure-in-others'-misfortune, sadism involves the active role of the subject in generating the misfortune; the sadist is responsible for the suffering. The satisfaction in pleasure-in-others'-misfortune is different; it is mainly due to our momentarily superior position. This superiority does not require an active role on our part in bringing about the object's misfortune.

All these differences suggest that sadism is substantially different from pleasure-in-others'-misfortune. These differences are expressed in the fact that sadism alone involves cruelty. Cruelty is not the essential factor that makes us enjoy another person's misfortune; a sense of just desert or competitive concern matters much more.

The identification of pleasure-in-others'-misfortune with its extreme manifestation has led some people to claim that this emotion is not common. Schopenhauer was of this belief and therefore urged that those in whom pleasure-in-others'-misfortune is observed should be permanently expelled from healthy communities. Similarly, some psychologists argue that in general, pleasure-in-others'-misfortune is pure ill will; accordingly, they claim that many of us, of course, do not experience it. Kant and Nietzsche take pleasure-in-others'-misfortune to be universal.[16]

The claim that pleasure-in-others'-misfortune is rare would be correct if the identification with its extreme manifestation were correct; since it is not, the claim is also incorrect. Although being pleased with someone's misfortune is symptomatic of pleasure-in-others'-misfortune, substantial misfortune is neither typical nor common in this emotion. Prevailing circumstances are those in which we are pleased with minor misfortunes of other people. Such misfortunes are more common in everyday life than is grave adversity.

One may claim that contrary to the suggested view, people are often fascinated when observing the tragedies of others; hence the habit of following a fire engine to see where the fire is, or being unable to avert one's eyes, no matter how horrified one may feel, from looking at mutilation and even death at the scene of a road accident, or at television newscasts of disasters. I would interpret these cases as demonstrating human interest in unusual events and not as expressing sadistic enjoyment. Thus, it is hard for people to look at all the gruesome details of such disasters, and television editors usually omit such details.

Human curiosity is also one of the factors which can explain people's enjoyment of soap operas, even though they may feel inferior to the portrayed characters, who are often extremely wealthy, talented, or beautiful. Yet misfortune inevitably befalls them: their mates betray them, they lose their fortunes or their reputations, and so on. However, their misfortunes do not generally place them in a position inferior to that of the viewer and in any case their misfortunes are usually well deserved. This indicates that pleasure-in-others'-misfortune is a central factor explaining the enjoyment we derive from watching soap operas. There are also some severe misfortunes that viewers do not enjoy watching. Their presence attempts to add verisimilitude to the show; nevertheless, because such misfortunes are often justified or can be overcome, their negative impact is reduced.

It may be argued that pleasure-in-others'-misfortune is related to *hate* and *anger*. Again, it seems that if such a relation is present it is not central in typical cases. Hate usually requires a negative evaluation of another person's whole personality, and anger, the negative evaluation of another person's specific act. Pleasure-in-others'-misfortune seldom requires either. Its focus of concern is not the negation of another person's personality or activity, but confirmation of this person's bothersome situation. No doubt, if those we hate or are angry with fail, we will be glad—or at least not sad—but pleasure-in-others'-misfortune is not limited to these cases. On the contrary, it is often directed toward those we are associated with or appreciate—hence, the comparative concern. In assuming that typical cases of pleasure-in-others'-misfortune involve minor rather than substantial misfortunes, I am not claiming that some people do not enjoy the great suffering of others. However, such feelings usually reflect hate or sadism rather than pleasure-in-others'-misfortune.

In some respects, pleasure-in-others'-misfortune is opposed to *guilt* and close to *pride*. Whereas pleasure-in-others'-misfortune involves pleasure over minor and deserved misfortunes in whose generation we were passive, guilt involves sadness over major and undeserved misfortunes caused by us. The major social function of guilt is to protect and strengthen social bonds by preventing harm-doing. Pleasure-in-others'-misfortune also has the function of strengthening social bonds. However, this is done by excluding the object from a certain social group. The deserved nature of the other's misfortune indicates that this person's behavior deviates from conventional social norms. Guilt may be associated with pleasure-in-others'-misfortune when the misfortune is more severe, leading us to feel that we should help this person rather than passively feel joy over her misfortune. The similarity of pleasure-in-others'-misfortune to pride is manifested in the fact that in both states we are pleased by what we consider our deserved good fortune. However, like guilt and unlike pleasure-in-others'-misfortune, pride is concerned with significant changes caused by us.

*Intensity Variables*

People seem to enjoy things more when they know a lot of other people have been left out on the pleasure.
—Russell Baker

The significant role that changes play in the generation of emotions is indeed evident in pleasure-in-others'-misfortune, which is usually generated when unexpected changes occur. When someone encounters misfortune all the time, the pleasure of laughing at this person is considerably reduced and will usually turn into pity. It is no fun to laugh at someone who constantly suffers and who is considerably below us. It is, however, a great pleasure to watch people who are comparable to, or even above, us having some misfortune which changes their relative position and demotes them for the time being to a position below our own. As mentioned, the element of incongruity plays an important role in the emergence of pleasure-in-others'-misfortune. Changes also play a role in the generation of happy-for, though in a less significant manner. We would be happier for one who does not often experience good fortune. We would hardly be happy with the additional good fortune of a highly fortunate person.

As mentioned, in both emotions the *event's strength* is constrained by an upper limit: a significant misfortune or fortune may turn pleasure-in-others'-misfortune into pity and happy-for into envy.

The variable of *reality* is important in happy-for where we are concerned with an improvement in the other's situation. In pleasure-in-others'-misfortune this variable is of somewhat lesser importance: since the other's misfortune is minor, its reality is usually of no great concern.

The variable of *relevance* is important in generating intense emotions of happy-for and pleasure-in-others'-misfortune. We are happy over the good fortune of another person, when it is perceived to enhance or at least not to decrease our own good fortune. Similarly, when the other's misfortune is relevant to us in the sense that it improves our own situation, pleasure-in-others'-misfortune will be quite intense. Less intense instances of these emotions occur when the issue of relevance is hardly present. When the other's good fortune is not relevant to us, we may not be envious of this person but neither will we be particularly happy, since this person is of little emotional significance to us. Similarly, the misfortune of someone who is irrelevant to our well-being may make us laugh or please us in other superficial manners, but it does not typically give rise to the intense emotion of pleasure-in-others'-misfortune.

The variable of closeness is more significant in happy-for and pleasure-in-others'-misfortune. Closeness is positively correlated with the intensity of happy-for. We are more delighted with the good fortune of those close to us than that of strangers as long as the variable of relevance remains constant. The good fortune of those close to us is often quite relevant to our self-esteem and hence it often generates envy; the good fortune of those remote from us is more likely to be irrelevant and hence may generate a moderate emotion of happy-for.

The role of closeness in pleasure-in-others'-misfortune is more complex. Like other emotions, pleasure-in-others'-misfortune is directed at people in our emotional environment. Concerning strangers toward whom we are indifferent, we will neither be pleased with their misfortune, nor sad at their success. However, like envy and some other emotions, pleasure-in-others'-misfortune is not typical of *very close* relationships. Thus, we will usually not be pleased with the misfortunes of our children. We may be pleased at very minor misfortunes of our good friends. The more severe the misfortune, the greater distance is required for pleasure-in-others'-misfortune to be generated. It would appear that the rise of pleasure-in-others'-misfortune requires a greater distance than that of envy; it is less acceptable in close relationships. In such relationships it seems more selfish and morally distorted to be pleased with the other's disturbing position than to be displeased with our own. Envy exists, though in a less intense form, even toward those who are significantly above us. Pleasure-in-others'-misfortune is usually not present when we are significantly above the object; pity is more typical of such situations. As with some other emotions, such as envy and pity, the relationship between the intensity of pleasure-in-others'-misfortune and closeness (or rather emotional distance) is somewhat similar to a bell-shaped curve. With very small or very great distances these emotions are not usually generated; they are typical of an intermediate distance.

Pleasure-in-others'-misfortune is directed at those who *currently* occupy a situation comparable to ours. Accordingly, this emotion can be directed at those who were greatly superior to us, but owing to a misfortune now occupy a somewhat comparable situation. Pleasure-in-others'-misfortune can also be generated in cases where we are well above the unlucky person, but there is a good chance that this person may achieve a comparable, or even superior, position in the future.

Concerning the variable of *controllability*, happy-for fits the general correlation: the more we were in control of the circumstances generating the good fortune, the happier we are. The same goes for most other types of joy. Pleasure-in-others'-misfortune seems to constitute one exception to this general correlation. In pleasure-in-others'-misfortune we are unwilling to be personally involved in order not to be viewed as morally evil people who violate the rules of fair competition. Accordingly, pleasure-in-others'-misfortune is more enjoyable the less we are responsible for the object's misfortune. This case does not actually constitute an exception to the general positive correlation between emotional intensity and controllability since it is the issue of *deservingness*, rather than controllability, that is crucial here in determining emotional intensity. When we are responsible for the other's misfortune, this person's deservingness of the misfortune decreases and accordingly emotional intensity decreases. This issue is very important in pleasure-in-others'-misfortune, where the other's deservingness of her misfortune is a crucial element, enabling us to maintain this seemingly immoral attitude. In happy-for the issue of deservingness is also evident and is expressed in our belief that the other person deserves her good fortune.

Another group of intensity variables is *readiness*; this group expresses our past expectation of and certainty in the occurrence of the eliciting event. In happy-for, which focuses on the other's present good fortune, our past readiness is of lesser importance than in pleasure-in-others'-misfortune, where our relative past and present positions are the focus of concern. The unexpected nature of the relative improvement in our situation significantly increases the intensity of pleasure-in-others'-misfortune.

*Moral Value*

On an occasion of this kind it becomes more than a moral duty to speak one's mind. It becomes a pleasure.
—Oscar Wilde

The moral value of the two positive emotions evoked by the fortunes of other people would appear to be clear. The positive evaluation involved in happy-for is recommended from a moral point of view. No doubt, we should try to adopt this attitude as much as possible. Doing so requires overcoming the competitive concern and not viewing the good fortune, and especially the success, of others as a threat to our own good fortune. Although maintaining this stance constantly may be difficult and perhaps even impossible, we should try to make it more common.

The emotion of pleasure-in-others'-misfortune has a lower moral value than happy-for. In the former we positively evaluate the bad fortune of others, not their good fortune. There are valid moral reasons for condemning someone who is pleased with another person's misfortune. Indeed, there is hardly any dispute concerning the immoral nature of pleasure-in-others'-misfortune. The dispute merely concerns the degree of malice typical of this emotion. The general assumption is that pleasure-in-others'-misfortune is morally evil. Thus, pleasure-in-others'-misfortune is often considered to be less acceptable than envy, which is regarded as a deadly sin. It would appear to be morally more perverse to be pleased with another person's misfortune than to be displeased with another person's good fortune. The sorrow implicit in envy is perceived to be directed at someone whose situation is generally good; hence, such a sorrow can scarcely hurt the other person. The joy implicit in pleasure-in-others'-misfortune is perceived to be directed at someone who is already in a bad situation; hence, the presence of pleasure-in-others'-misfortune may only worsen the situation. Accordingly, the presence of joy in pleasure-in-others'-misfortune is seen as morally worse than the presence of sorrow in envy. Indeed, Schopenhauer argues that to feel envy is human, but to enjoy other people's misfortune is diabolical. For Schopenhauer, pleasure-in-others'-misfortune is the worst trait in human nature since it is closely related to cruelty.[17]

Such severe moral criticism can be challenged. To begin with, I have indicated that we should distinguish between pleasure-in-others'-misfortune and cruelty as expressed, for example, in sadism or when the other person experiences great suffering. Accordingly, pleasure-in-others'-misfortune does not indicate a vicious character. In contrast to sadism, the delight in pleasure-in-others'-misfortune does not stem from the suffering of another person, but from our advantageous position. Indeed, the most severe criticism of pleasure-in-others'-misfortune comes from those who fail to distinguish it from cruelty and in general fail to distinguish between the severity of various misfortunes. Thus, Schopenhauer does not acknowledge distinctions between various kinds of suffering: "intentional mutilation or mere injury to the body of another, indeed every blow, is to be regarded essentially as of the same nature as murder, and as differing therefrom only in degree." As John Portmann rightly remarks, this is a strong claim, one with which our legal system is at odds.[18]

Portmann discusses various types of moral criticisms against pleasure-in-others'-misfortune and indicates that despite such criticism, pleasure-in-others'-misfortune is a natural phenomenon which is not diabolic. The moral problem that pleasure-in-others'-misfortune poses is that taking pleasure in the suffering of another person appears to threaten the most basic ethical tenet of all, to do good and to avoid evil. In order to deal with this problem, Portmann connects pleasure-in-others'-misfortune with punishment. He claims that it is difficult to endorse punishment while condemning pleasure-in-others'-misfortune, for punishment involves the willful infliction of suffering. When we hear of a criminal being sentenced in court, we may feel a kind of pleasure which derives from the belief that justice has been served, or that the criminal will suffer, or both. In light of such considerations, the belief that the other deserves her misfortune is central to the moral vindication of pleasure-in-others'-misfortune. Pleasure whose object is undeserved misfortune must be considered morally unacceptable. It is ethically wrong to take pleasure in the undeserved misfortunes of others. However, when the misfortune is deserved, being pleased about this is not necessarily a vice.

Portmann suggests following various traditions in order to distinguish between pleasure-in-others'-misfortune that is a function of *suffering*, and pleasure-in-others'-misfortune that is a function of *deservingness*. Cruelty involves the former type and is morally condemned; typical pleasure-in-others'-misfortune is expressed in the latter type and may not be morally condemned. Aquinas makes such a distinction: A thing may be a matter of rejoicing in two ways. First, in itself, when one rejoices in a thing as such, and thus the saints will not rejoice in the punishment of the wicked. Second, accidentally, by reason namely of something joined to it; and in this way the saints will rejoice in the punishment of the wicked, considering therein the order of divine justice and their own deliverance, which will fill them with joy.[19] Portmann indicates that it is not the operative suffering in itself that will please the saints, but rather contemplation of the order to which that suffering testifies. Believers may insist that they do not feel malicious joy, but rather joy at the confirmation of divine justice.

Only when the misfortune is quite minor, and hence one can scarcely call it suffering, may the focus of concern be on the misfortune, rather than on deservingness. This attitude is related to, but not identical with pleasure-in-others'-misfortune. This is, for example, the case with humor, which is sometimes directed at undeserved misfortunes. Portmann rightly argues that we need not trouble ourselves about trivial misfortunes which are associated with pleasure-in-others'-misfortune for this lies at the heart of comedy and humor, both of which are valuable in helping us to cope with life.[20]

A somewhat similar distinction can be made in connection with envy. Aquinas indicates that we may grieve over another's good, not because the *other has it*, but because the good which the other has we do not have; if the focus of envy is virtuous goods, it is praiseworthy.[21] The focus of concern in the first case is the person enjoying the good fortune; in the second case, it is the fortune itself. Similarly, in malicious joy the focus of concern is the person who suffers and in typical pleasure-in-others'-misfortune it is the situation. If the situation is deserved, as is the case in typical pleasure-in-others'-misfortune, then our attitude can be morally approved.

The moral flaw in pleasure-in-others'-misfortune is bound up with the comparative concern and not with cruelty. Indeed, when this concern is not present, as when the other's misfortune is substantial, the emotion is absent as well. Since this concern is natural for humans, pleasure-in-others'-misfortune should also be considered as natural. Pleasure-in-others'-misfortune seems even to have some moral justification: it represents the right to be glad when our position improves, though one may condemn the way we calculate the improvement in our position, that is to say, one may condemn the comparative concern. Moreover, owing to our passivity in pleasure-in-others'-misfortune, its negative aspects are less significant. This passivity reduces the danger of actually harming the object.

Pleasure-in-others'-misfortune is not a public mocking intended to humiliate someone; it is typically a private enjoyment lacking any element of severe mocking or humiliation. Moreover, pleasure-in-others'-misfortune is not concerned with those in an inferior position to me, but rather with those who are basically similar to me. Accordingly, Rabbi Jonah of Gerona, the thirteenth-century moralist, argues that mocking the poor, which is overt blasphemy, is more grievous than pleasure-in-others'-misfortune, which causes no injury by deed or speech.[22]

The important role deservingness plays in pleasure-in-others'-misfortune implies that this emotion can be found only in people who are sensitive to moral considerations. People who are unable to distinguish deserved from undeserved situations cannot be pleased over deserved misfortune. Those who are pleased over the misfortune of others are not indifferent toward the person suffering the misfortune or toward misfortune in general; on the contrary, they may even be sensitive to misfortunes. They believe that this misfortune is deserved and in the long run may even reduce undeserved misfortunes, so making the world a more just place in which to live. As indicated, pleasure-in-others'-misfortune is similar to gossip in expressing interest in others.

To sum up, the moral evaluation of pleasure-in-others'-misfortune should be determined in light of the following major factors: (a) the extent of the other's misfortune; (b) the extent of our involvement in bringing about this misfortune; (c) the extent of the justification we attach to the other's misfortune. It has been suggested that in typical cases of pleasure-in-others'-misfortune the first two factors are marginal: the other's misfortune is minor and our involvement is minimal. Concerning the third factor, cases of pleasure-in-others'-misfortune involve our belief that justice has been done. All this implies that typical cases of pleasure-in-others'-misfortune are not strongly negative from a moral viewpoint; they are no worse than many other emotions. The greater the extent of the first two factors and the less justified the other's misfortune, the more negative is the moral evaluation that should be attached to pleasure-in-others'-misfortune. As in the case of gossip, I do not claim that pleasure-in-others'-misfortune is a virtue; however, it is also not a vice—at least not a grave one.

In light of the above considerations, doubts should be raised concerning the moral comparison of envy and pleasure-in-others'-misfortune. Although the conventional view suggests that pleasure-in-others'-misfortune is much worse than envy, it is doubtful whether this view adequately represents our moral codes and behavior. For one, envy, but not pleasure-in-others'-misfortune, is included in the traditional Christian list of the seven deadly sins (in addition to greed, sloth, wrath, lust, gluttony, and pride); some even consider envy as the worst evil. Moreover, if pleasure-in-others'-misfortune addresses minor misfortunes, if we believe that justice has been done, and if we are passive in eliciting the misfortune, then the moral justification of pleasure-in-others'-misfortune is no weaker than that associated with envy. It seems that the conventional view which condemns pleasure-in-others'-misfortune more strongly than envy stems from taking cruelty, sadism, and hate as prototypical cases of this emotion. We have seen that this view is mistaken. Moreover, since pleasure-in-others'-misfortune is usually more transient than envy, its moral damage is often less evident.

# Chapter 13

# When You Are Bad, I Am Mad—Anger, Hate, Disgust, and Contempt

Speak when you are angry and you will make the best speech you will ever regret.
—Ambrose Bierce

Hating people is like burning down your own house to get rid of a rat.
—Henry Emerson Fosdick

Previous chapters discussed the group of emotions toward the *fortune* of other agents. This chapter begins the discussion of the two other major groups: emotions toward specific *actions* of another agent and emotions toward another *agent as a whole*. The typical emotions in the first group are anger and gratitude; those of the second group are disgust, attraction, hate, and love. The basic evaluative pattern of the first group refers to the praiseworthiness of the specific action. The second group is divided into two major subgroups: the first refers merely to the evaluative pattern of appealingness and the second to both the praiseworthiness of the other's actions and to the other's appealingness. This chapter examines the negative emotions in these groups; the next chapter discusses the positive emotions.

*General Characteristics*

*Anger and Hate*
To hate someone is to feel irritated by his mere existence. The only thing that would bring satisfaction would be his total disappearance.
—José Ortega y Gasset

Once I got past my anger toward my mother, I began to excel in volleyball and modeling.
—Gabrielle Reece

Everyone who ever walked barefoot into his child's room late at night hates Legos.
—Tony Kornheiser

Hate may be characterized as involving a global negative attitude toward someone considered to possess fundamentally evil traits. Disgust is similar to hate insofar as it contains a global negative evaluation, but it is directed toward someone considered to possess fundamentally unattractive traits. Anger is similar to hate and disgust in involving a negative evaluation, but it is the evaluation of a specific action rather than a global attitude. Love is similar to hate in that it involves a global evaluation, but in this case it is a positive one. Sexual desire, like any other type of attraction, is similar to disgust in the sense that the evaluation is based upon appealingness. Gratitude is similar to love in involving a positive evaluation, but as in anger it is the evaluation of a specific action.

Anger is aroused in response to a specific, undeserved offense. We blame the other person for such an unjustified offense, whether or not the offense was deliberate or due to negligence or lack of foresight. In anger the other's action is not merely perceived as unjust but also as depreciating our position. A schoolteacher who feels angry with pupils when they talk while she is speaking believes that their behavior is unjust and depreciates her position in the sense that her authority is undermined. Similar considerations probably explain why people typically do not appreciate their guests playing with the remote control of their TV. Taking control of the remote control is seen by many people as a demeaning offense against them. Improper treatment by a blameworthy person is hurtful not only because of the damage it inflicts but also because the wrongdoer conceives of us as inferior in the sense that our position, needs, and values are worthless.[1]

People are unlikely to respond with anger if they judge the other person to be justified, nonarbitrary, or not in control. People provoking anger are most often viewed as doing something voluntarily that they had no right to do, or as doing something that they could have avoided had they been more careful. The issues of justification and controllability constitute the main discrepancy between the description of anger by those who experience it and those at whom anger is directed: people who are the target of anger consider that either they were justified in their actions or that the incident was beyond their control. The personal harm to the angry person is assumed to be inflicted by a blameworthy person. We do not become angry with inanimate objects that damage us, unless we construe these objects as agents rather than as inanimate objects. Since inanimate objects cannot treat us improperly, we cannot be angry with them.[2]

Like anger, hate is typically directed at a particular person, but rather than stemming from a specific act by this person, it usually stems from what are believed to be general traits that are not limited to specific circumstances. The negative character of those we hate is perceived to be "in their blood." Elster rightly claims that whereas in anger we believe that "because they do bad things, they are bad," in hate we assume that "because they are bad, they do bad things."[3]

Hate is a long-term attitude whose generation is frequently not triggered by a personal offense. Hate requires an evaluation of the object as possessing inherently dangerous traits; the object of anger is guilty of merely instrumental negative actions.

Anger is typically an immediate response to what we consider as unjustified harm which someone has inflicted upon us or those related to us. In anger the harm is often a kind of personal insult, and thus the wish for revenge is personal. Hate is more general: it can be related to more potential and nonpersonal circumstances. The hated person may not have harmed us at all, at least not in the present or the recent past, but the negative character of this person is thought to be capable of such harm. The object of anger is usually a person well-known to us, whereas hate is not personal in this sense. The particular details of the object of hate are often unknown to us. To a certain extent, hate involves depersonalization. As in prejudice, hate often feeds on partial or distorted information, which ignores the object's real character. The more general nature of hate is also reflected by the fact that hate is often directed at groups and not at individuals, regardless of the individual differences among group members. Aristotle distinguishes between anger and hate in a manner similar to the one suggested here: "Whereas anger is always concerned with individuals, hatred may be directed against classes, e.g., any thief, any informer. Anger may be cured by time, hatred cannot. . . . Anger is accompanied by pain, hatred is not."[4]

Although the object of hate is more general than that of anger, it has to have some degree of specificity and closeness in order to maintain a high level of emotional intensity. Thus, terrorist groups begin their activities by adopting a unifying general ideal as the basis for their hatred. However, very soon this general ideal turns into more proximate and specific matters, such as revenge for a comrade's death or fighting against the humiliation of parents. Hate does not incorporate abstract concern about the other's continued power, but rather concern that this power will harm us or those related to us. The more personal nature of anger makes it closer to a typical emotion than hate. Hate is often turned into a long-term sentiment. In light of its specific nature, the greatest remedy for anger is to take a broader perspective; for example, by delaying our response we are able to see things from a broader perspective. This remedy is less effective in hate, which is not so limited to specific circumstances and hence already has a broader perspective.

Anger is essentially directed at a person who has committed a specific, blameworthy act; in hate the person's basic traits are more crucial. Anger is typically elicited by the perception of having been treated unfairly. In hate the emphasis shifts from unfair to bad treatment. The harm involved in hate is more profound than that in anger, and it is believed to stem from more fundamental traits of the other person. Therefore, the negative character of the other person and the danger inherent in the other's continued power are more central to hate. In anger we want the person who has hurt us to suffer as a corrective measure; in hate, where corrective measures are irrelevant since we do not believe that they can succeed, we do not mind whether the other person suffers or not; we simply wish he would cease to exist.

Both anger and hate may occur not only as a result of the hurt that other people inflict upon us but may also be a consequence of the hurt that we inflict upon them. We blame them for putting us in a situation in which we do not want to be, namely, a situation in which we were forced to hurt them.[5]

The negative evaluation in hate is global, not in the sense that every aspect of the hated person is considered to be negative, but in the sense that the negative aspects are so fundamental that other traits become insignificant. The positive evaluation in love is global in a similar manner: the beloved is believed to be an essentially positive person rather than a perfect being without flaws. The basic evaluative pattern in grief is global in another sense: we are dealing with a total loss which cannot be recovered; hence, the persistence of grief. In grief we cannot change our partial perspective and take another, more cheerful perspective; from every perspective we look, the object of grief is dead. Those believing in life after death can refer to this belief as a comforting factor.

The threat in anger is more concrete and, to a certain extent, it has already materialized. This threat can stem from a number of causes. In animals it usually stems from an existential physical threat. In humans the threat is more socially induced, referring to depreciation of our worth. In light of the social nature of the threat in most cases of anger, it is usually directed at persons within our social group. The threat in hate is often perceived as directed at the foundations of the social framework in which we live rather than merely at our status within this framework. Since the threat usually comes from someone outside the framework, hate is typically directed at those who are socially more distant. Whereas in hate we wish to avoid confronting the other person, in anger we wish to correct the person's behavior in order to be able to sustain social bonds. The threat in hate may either be in the form of an intended threat by another person or of an unintended formidable obstacle to our well-being.

Hate is in some respects more complex than anger, since it often does not refer to concrete harm inflicted upon us but to a potential threat posed by some fundamental negative aspects of the other person. Moreover, anger employs only one basic evaluative pattern, namely praiseworthiness, whereas hate requires two: appealingness and praiseworthiness. The object of hate is not only a person who has done evil deeds but also a person to whom we are not attracted. In light of the more complex nature of hate, animals may experience disgust and anger (or more precisely rage), but not hate.

Describing the intensity of hate is a complex issue. On the one hand, due to its more general and less personal nature, the feeling dimension of hate is sometimes of a lesser intensity than that of anger. It is as if a given intensity is spread over a longer period of time and therefore it is weaker at each given moment. Hence, hatred can prompt actions carried out in "cold blood." In his poem, "Fire and Ice," Robert Frost compares desire to fire, but adds that:

> I think I know enough of hate
> To say that for destruction ice
> Is also great
> And would suffice.

One can kill out of hate without having intense feelings, as in the case of the Nazis. When one kills in anger, or rather rage, the feeling dimension is quite intense. On the other hand, hate can sometimes be quite intense. Because there is no hope for changing the object, the situation is viewed in extremely negative terms, thereby increasing emotional intensity. In light of such considerations, we may say that whereas anger can scarcely be conceived without having an intense feeling dimension, there are many cases of hate in which the feeling dimension is hardly noticed.[6] Cato said that "An angry man opens his mouth and shuts his eyes." We cannot say such a thing about those who hate; their eyes are often quite open. Elster reminds us that the greatest act of hatred in history, the Holocaust, was carried out in a very efficient and calculated manner.[7]

The borderline between anger and hate is not always clear: anger often involves a hostile attitude, which is central in hate, and hate involves the annoyance that is typical of anger. Moreover, anger can sometimes persist in a way that develops into hatred. This may easily occur, since people who evaluate the bad actions of another person as stemming from that person's basic character will tend to transform their anger into hate. In cases where revenge would seem sweeter if achieved later, anger will last longer than usual. Similarly, there are some cases of hate that stem from a specific and hence short-term state; here hate will be limited to the specific case and thus will usually be brief.

In light of the fuzzy borderline between anger and hate, the linguistic uses of "anger" and "hate" are not always compatible with the distinction suggested here. It seems that "hate" has a broader meaning than that described: it may denote the attitude of hate described here, as well as strong dislike or anger. The word "anger," on the other hand, usually has the more specific meaning discussed here. Hence, no wonder that in a study on love, hate, jealousy, and anger, hate was the least accurately identified. In particular, hate prototype information led a number of people to incorrectly identify it as anger, while they did not confuse the prototypical anger features with hate.[8] In everyday language, the term "hate" refers to *extreme* rather than *global* negation. It covers a continuum of attitudes beginning with simple dislike, such as "I hate soup," and ending with hate in the sense characterized here. Simple dislike is not necessarily a response to a threat, but, like hate, it involves the wish to dissociate from the object. Anger, whose place on the continuum is between dislike and hate, already involves a threat, but this is not the significant and comprehensive threat typical of hate.

In accordance with the fundamental nature of the conflict in hate, it is believed that the situation can be changed only if the other person is avoided or even eliminated. Thus, Spinoza argues that "one who hates strives to remove and destroy the thing he hates."[9] In anger the other person is assumed to deserve to be punished, rather than avoided or eliminated as is the assumption in hate. People are to be blamed for their actions inducing our anger, since they must take some responsibility for them. Those whom we hate do not have to be actively responsible for their negative traits. Since these traits are considered to be more or less permanent, they probably do not bear actual responsibility for their generation. Therefore, hate is often directed at different groups regardless of the personal differences between their individuals.

The spontaneous nature of anger itself has some influence on determining the intensity of anger. We feel comparatively little anger toward those who harm us while they are angry, since we assume that they do not wish to harm us. This also indicates the importance of the other's intention in generating our anger; the absence of intention reduces responsibility and hence emotional intensity. It should be noted, however, that responsibility is not identical with doing something deliberately. Forgetfulness also causes anger when it is perceived as being due to negligence.[10]

The issue of the blameworthiness of the agent is more dominant in anger than in hate. Like responsibility, blameworthiness presupposes the agent's ability to act otherwise. Indeed, in anger the availability of an alternative is more dominant than in hate. In hate, when the other's negative character is taken to be more or less permanent, it is more difficult to blame the agent or hold the agent responsible for negative behavior.

The motivational component, represented by the various desires, is quite different in anger and hate. Since anger entails a belief in the effectiveness of our acts, the motivational domain is strong and is often expressed in a nonstandard aggressive act. The urge to attack is essential to anger, even if it is expressed in nonaggressive behavior. In anger we want to personally punish the other person who is seen as deserving of punishment.[11] Hate also involves an intense desire, but as we usually believe that changing the other's basic faults is beyond our power, it is often associated with perceived self-impotence and is not always expressed by nonstandard aggressive behavior. Hate is often more passive than anger. The willingness to become personally involved is much weaker in hate, due to the belief that it would be difficult to change the undesired circumstances. Only in anger is there typically a strong conviction that such circumstances can indeed be altered. This may be one reason that despite the more negative nature of the object of hate, we are often more aggressive toward the object of anger. However, in extreme cases of hate, physical elimination may be the only way seen as effective in fighting the dangers associated with the hated person. Typical hate involves an extreme type of intolerance and opposition to diversity.

However, hate does not have to involve physical elimination or even the wish to hurt the other person physically; it must, however, involve the creation of some psychological distance. In marital relationships, for instance, hate is usually expressed by evading the situation and acting coldly as if the partner were no longer within the close relationship which is supposed to prevail in marriage. In one study, only 27 percent of the people who reported hate toward their partner claimed to have wanted to take revenge and physically hurt the hated party, and only 2 percent did physically hurt their partners.[12]

The above differences in the motivational component are expressed in the fact that we often hate people who no longer exist, but it is less common to feel anger at such people. Anger, but not hate, requires the belief that the object can be changed. Perceived self-impotence, which is proper for our attitude toward dead people, is associated with hate but not with anger. The availability of an alternative, which is not dominant in hate, is indeed weaker in emotions toward dead people. A general type of love may also be directed at people who no longer exist. It is less common for more specific emotions, for instance, anger, jealousy, and sexual desire, to be directed at dead people.

In extreme cases of hate, when physical elimination is not possible, emotional tension is created and various substitutes are sought. The most common form of substitution is verbal aggression. Such aggression enables us to express our negative attitudes within the limits of acceptable standard behavior. An interesting example of verbal aggression associated with hate is that of political hate letters. A writer of such letters explained his motives: "Why am I verbally aggressive? Because I cannot shoot a bullet through them. It would not be logical for me to sit in jail because of political assassination. So I shoot them with words." Political hate letters clearly express the wish to eliminate the object. The elimination can be physical, and indeed the letters may contain direct threats. However, the most typical method of punishment employed is exclusion from the collective, for example, by considering the recipient as belonging to the enemy camp. Such an exclusion enables the subject-object detachment which is desirable in hate. The letters may try to influence the recipients to change their ways, but this must be a radical change in which the recipients lose their identity.[13]

Owing to the profoundly negative evaluation of the object of hate, we wish to detach ourselves from the object, namely, to increase the subject-object distance as much as possible by avoiding or eliminating the object. If such detachment were attainable, then our attitude toward the object would be indifference, which is the typical attitude toward strangers. The problem typical of hate is that such detachment and indifference are impossible. Despite the profound negative evaluation of the object, and hence our wish to avoid or eliminate the object, we are compelled to cope and even communicate with this person. The wish to avoid or eliminate is contrary to the wish to understand; the latter is what underlies genuine communication. The need for communication is then in conflict with a basic desire involved in hate, and therefore communication is ambivalent and often negative.

Indeed, political hate letters are ambivalent in nature. Thus, they may utter calls for both exclusion from the collective or inclusion or reincorporation in it. In these letters, the political foe is both one of "us" and against "us." Accordingly, these letters are seldom directed at parties considered alien and outside the collective. In Israel, for example, most political hate letters have been sent to the Jewish, but antireligious, Zionist party of the Citizens' Rights Movement and not to the Communist Party, which is more extreme in its political views but is almost exclusively supported by Arab votes and defines itself as anti-Zionist. Despite their intense hate, the writers of hate letters feel the need to communicate with the recipients and to restore harmony to the collective by bringing stray members back to the fold.[14]

The wish to avoid or eliminate the object, together with the realization that this is impossible or at least very difficult, generates the emotional intensity typical of hate. Intense hate is usually generated when detachment and indifference toward the object of a profoundly negative evaluation are impossible. Anger is typical when positive, normal communication is possible and when modifying the object's negative deeds does not require a radical change in the object's identity.

Anger has a higher functional value than hate. The major functions of emotions, namely, mobilization of our resources and social communications, are quite evident in anger. Anger is essential as an energizer and organizer of our behavior. Anger also has an important social function. It is often perceived as a means for strengthening or readjusting a relationship, and as such both parties usually regard it as beneficial to the relationship in the long run, despite its short-term unpleasant circumstances. It often provides the basis for a reconciliation on new terms.[15] Like other emotions, anger is functional when it is in the right proportion, for example, when it is expressed in a socially constructive way without becoming highly aroused. Intense anger may be harmful, as are other types of excess. Thus, high levels of chronic anger and aggressive behavior can be harmful and are related to higher mortality and in particular to coronary heart disease.[16]

Hate may be functional in the sense of mobilizing resources, but it can hardly serve any social role insofar as it attempts to disconnect all relationships with the object.

Is hate more rational than anger (as Aristotle claims[17]) or is anger more rational than hate (as common sense often assumes)? Either position may be correct, according to the two different criteria of rationality. As mentioned, emotions can be considered rational in two basic senses: (1) their generation involves intellectual calculations; (2) they express an appropriate response in the given circumstances. Hate is more rational in the first sense, whereas anger is more rational in the second sense.

Identifying hate is more problematic than identifying anger for both the person who experiences them and for other people. Anger has more specific evaluations and distinctly public behavioral expressions than hate. Moreover, we often try to hide our hate, either because of its negative moral value or because it may hurt us in the long run if the object, who is often powerful, learns of our hate. For similar considerations, we try less to hide our contempt, which is directed at those who are inferior to us and have less opportunity to hurt us.

*Disgust*
I do not like broccoli. And I haven't liked it since I was a little kid and my mother made me eat it. And I'm President of the United States and I'm not going to eat any more broccoli.
—George Bush

Disgust is the most common emotion in the group of emotional attitudes expressing repulsion of the object. The basic evaluative pattern of this group, as well as of the opposite group expressing attraction toward the object, is the object's appealingness. Disgust constitutes one of the most primitive and immediate emotional reactions; accordingly, it is usually closely related to a perceptual mode, such as vision, smell, taste, or touch.

Disgust is a strong sense of aversion to something perceived as capable of contaminating us: either in physical terms, referring to bodily infection, or in more symbolic terms, referring to violating the boundaries of self. The original function of disgust had to do with actual, physical contamination and in particular with food contamination; hence, eating and taste are at the core of disgust. In the course of its development in human conditions, it has become a reaction not only to possible food contamination but to all kinds of contamination, including mental and moral contamination. The idea of contamination associated with disgust is quite sophisticated in that it requires the separation of appearance and reality, as well as an implicit knowledge of the history of the contact. Fear of contamination is enhanced by similarity or, more precisely, the belief that if things are superficially similar, then they resemble each other in a deeper sense as well. Accordingly, things that look like something disgusting, but are known not to be, are often treated as disgusting. Thus, many North American college students were reluctant to consume imitation dog feces which they knew was made out of chocolate fudge.[18]

The bodily type of disgust may refer to a few major categories of objects. Paul Rozin suggests the following categories:

  · Food—you see a dead cockroach in your juice (most people are not willing to drink their favorite juice if a dead cockroach has been dipped in their glass, even if the cockroach has been sterilized).
  · Body products—you see a bowel movement left unflushed in a public toilet.
  · Envelope violations—you see someone accidentally stick a fishing hook through his finger.

· Hygiene—you discover that a friend of yours changes underwear only once a week.
· Animals—you are walking barefoot on concrete, and you step on an earthworm.
· Death—Your friend's pet cat dies, and you have to pick up the dead body with your bare hands.

These domains of disgust are correlated: people who are easily disgusted by food items are also more bothered by incest, rats, and amputations. The idea of contamination, and in particular an offensive and infective entry into our body, is clearly evident in these categories. The entry can be by all sorts of means: the mouth, the nose, the skin, or the eyes. In the last category, namely, death, the contamination of the mind is significant as well. Death is of particular importance, as it may involve both bodily contamination which spreads diseases and the psychological contamination of our very existence. Only human beings know that they are destined to die and need to repress full awareness of this threat. Here, disgust functions as a rejection of thoughts or experiences that might remind us of mortality.[19]

The more symbolic type of disgust is illustrated by disgust at certain types of taboo sexual behavior, ranging from homosexuality, to pornography, to incest. We find here an extension of human disgust from protection against bodily disease to protection against more symbolic contamination of the self. Deviance from the narrow class of "normal" heterosexuality is often seen as unnatural, inhuman, and therefore disgusting. Sexual disgust is the most basic kind of disgust in a larger group, referring to moral offenses. Other examples evoking moral disgust are Nazis, people who steal from beggars, and lawyers who chase ambulances to acquire new clients. Not all immoral behavior evokes disgust—only those considered to be clearly abnormal. Thus, criminal acts with "normal" human motivations, such as robbing banks, are seen as immoral but not disgusting. Sexual disgust is the most typical example of this group, since the idea of actual contamination is most vivid here. Accordingly, the nonsexual examples evoke a less intense disgust and are associated to a lesser degree with other types of disgust; these examples are more dependent on symbolic presentation and cultural norms.

When the symbolic type of disgust is concerned with immoral deeds, such as rape, child abuse, torture, genocide, sadism, and masochism, disgust is quite similar to hate since it also involves the basic evaluative pattern of praiseworthiness. In these cases, the object is not merely repulsive but dangerous as well. It does not merely sicken us, as in disgust, but is quite harmful to our well-being, as is the case in hate. The more symbolic types of disgust express, in addition to the basic evaluative pattern of appealingness, also the basic pattern of praiseworthiness.

Ian Miller suggests that if disgust protects us from contamination, then the relaxation or suspension of the rules of disgust, in relation to a specific person, indicates the intimacy we feel toward this person. The more we are ready to relax or suspend some of these rules, the more intimate we feel toward this person. Changing diapers and caring for a sick family member are examples of such intimacy. In overcoming the disgust inherent in contaminating substances, we express our unconditional love and care for our intimates. Similarly, allowing another person to see us in a disgusting, shameful, or humiliating situation is an indication that we consider this person to be our intimate. Miller notes that disgust barriers may be thrown to the winds for reasons other than intimacy; ignoring some barriers may indicate contemptuous indifference to the other, rather than intimate care. Miller further distinguishes between overcoming disgusting situations because of intimacy and overcoming them because of familiarity. The second case is typical of doctors and nurses and is not a sign of a privileged intimacy; on the contrary, it often breeds contempt.[20]

Our negative evaluations of other people while we are in anger, hate, or fear stems from the fact that in some sense these people are dangerous to us: they may hurt us even if we remain quite passive; hence, we wish to punish them (as in anger), eliminate them (as in hate), or run away from them (as in fear). In contrast, something may disgust us even if it poses no danger to us. Accordingly, escape mechanisms for regulating the emotions, such as avoiding looking at or thinking about the object, are much more useful in disgust than in hate, anger, or fear. Escape mechanisms are less useful in the latter emotions since the object may still be dangerous even if I avoid the object. In disgust, avoiding the object significantly reduces or even eliminates the emotion since it poses no danger to me. For example, David may be disgusted upon hearing of an adult woman who has sex with her father, but because this woman poses no personal danger to him, he can eliminate his disgust by diverting his attention to something else. Similarly, looking at something that is extremely ugly may generate disgust, but it poses no real danger; again, the disgust can be eliminated by averting one's gaze. The situation is more complex in cases of moral disgust which is similar to hate since it is dangerous, so that ignoring the object is not sufficient for coping with the disagreeable situation.[21]

It seems, then, that the emotional object of disgust is perceived in the most unflattering manner because of its repulsive nature and not because it has inflicted or may inflict personal harm upon us. In this sense, the role of personal considerations can be insignificant in disgust; accordingly, the negative evaluation of the object is likely to be less based on personal considerations and more on the repulsive nature of the object itself.

In light of its great intensity and the obvious facial expressions and bodily behavior associated with it, disgust clearly communicates our aversive attitude. Such clear communication is extremely important as the stakes are very high: the risk of contamination poses serious danger to our existence. Because of the clarity of the message and the gravity of the situation, disgust is easily infectious: when seeing a person who is disgusted, we quite often experience disgust as well.

In human society, disgust seems to acquire another, somewhat surprising function: it reminds us of our basic equality. Disgust focuses our attention on those bodily secretions, such as earwax and mucus, and the waste products of metabolism which all of us must excrete. Bodily functions are a stark reminder that at baseline we are all equally disgusting. The way to overcome such disgust is not to consider ourselves or other people as superior, but to seek intimacy so that social gaps are reduced to the point where we can consider the other as belonging to an almost similar self. Contempt is an attempt to emphasize some measures of inequality, sustaining the presence of different reference and social groups.

Some of the activities which currently evoke disgust were not considered disgusting in other periods or in other societies. For example, from the prohibitions mentioned in books of etiquette dating from the fifteenth century, it can be concluded that people regularly engaged in activities we now consider disgusting. Readers were entreated not to blow their noses with the same hand that they used to hold the meat, nor to greet a person while urinating, nor to return tasted morsels to the general dish.[22]

## Contempt
Familiarity breeds contempt—and children.
—Mark Twain


The group of negative emotions toward someone's whole personality also includes *contempt*. Contempt expresses the subject's superiority over the object.

An important difference between disgust and contempt concerns their basic evaluative patterns: disgust is associated with appealingness, contempt with praiseworthiness. In contempt, the other person is evaluated as inferior to us in some basic sense; in disgust, the other person is merely displeasing but not necessarily inferior. Like disgust, contempt is more focused on the object than on the subject. The object may pose no direct threat to the subject and avoiding the negative impact of the object can essentially be done by using escape devices.

The inferiority associated with contempt does not have to be global: it can merely refer to a few aspects of the other person's characteristics. I can feel contempt for another person's accent or looks, but still realize her general superior status.

Ian Miller has suggested the existence of "upward contempt," that is, the contempt that people who occupy a conventionally lower social role harbor toward someone higher. Examples include the contempt teenagers have for adults, servants for masters, workers for bosses, blacks for whites, the uneducated for the educated, and so on. A few basic differences between downward and upward contempt can be discerned: (a) upward contempt is less likely to be coupled with disgust; (b) unlike conventional contempt, upward contempt is secure in its legitimacy; (c) unlike conventional contempt, upward contempt is often coupled with pleasure-in-others'-misfortune; and (d) upward contempt is more partial than downward contempt. Miller claims that upward contempt is present not only in cases where the lower may consider himself superior in some respect to the higher but also when the lower discerns that the higher is below the level which the higher claims for himself.[23]

I believe that in upward contempt the subject also considers the other person to be inferior in some important sense. The object is considered as inferior only in some limited aspects which are conventionally considered to be insignificant. Furthermore, cases of contempt in which the lower discerns the higher to be below the level which the higher claims may be cases in which the lower is superior to the higher in some important sense, for example, the moral sense or his ability to live without the need to deceive other people constantly.

An interesting case of upward contempt is our attitude toward lawyers and politicians. Miller terms these people "moral menials" as they perform functions in the moral order similar to those played in the system of provisioning by garbage collectors and butchers. Moral menials need to deal with moral dirt in order to do their job, but we nevertheless feel some contempt toward them, as we hold them accountable for being so attracted to moral dirt. These people—politicians more so than lawyers—often exhibit vices such as hypocrisy, betrayal, fawning, and cruelty. Despite our contempt of them, they have a high status in our society which is expressed in the hefty payments and great power we accord them. These benefits may be a sort of compensation for being moral menials.[24]

As in pity, contempt can have enjoyable aspects: when we consider not merely the inferior position of the other but also our relative superiority, this may please us. In this sense, contempt is quite different from disgust: we do not enjoy the disgusting object—by its very nature, the disgusting object is displeasing.[25]

Contempt may look like indifference as it seems to involve a certain unwillingness to elevate the object from his or her inferior situation, as the object is in some sense perceived to deserve the inferior position. Despite this similarity, contempt is an emotion and, like other emotions, differs from indifference. Contempt is not merely a theoretical knowledge concerning the inferiority of other people: it involves a negative evaluation of these people and a positive evaluation concerning our own superiority. Such evaluations are accompanied by other emotional components such as an intense disagreeable feeling and the motivation to avoid engaging in certain activities with these inferior people. Contempt may involve the wish to be completely disassociated from the people at whom the contempt is directed, but since these people are typically necessary for maintaining the lifestyle of those who feel the contempt, this wish is limited to certain activities.

When contempt is very intense, it may involve, in addition to a highly negative evaluation of the object's characteristics, a highly negative attitude toward the object. In these cases, intense contempt may involve elements similar to those found in disgust; these elements may also include the physiological markers typical of disgust. Nevertheless, the basic difference between disgust and contempt should be clear: the object of contempt is inferior to us but is still within some of our frames of reference; the disgusting object is not inferior but impure: it may contaminate us. Contempt marks social distinctions, whereas disgust marks boundaries of the self.[26] Hence, issues of equality are relevant only in the case of contempt; it is not the case that disgust works against ideas of equality—it is simply irrelevant to such ideas. Since disgust may be associated with other negative emotions, such as contempt and hate, the issue of equality may be part of the more complex emotional attitude.

Like hate, contempt is directed at the whole agent and not merely at a particular action. Contempt is also a long-term attitude, although usually less intense than hate. The difference between hate and contempt is that in contempt the emphasis is on the inferiority of the object, whereas hate stresses the object's dangerous nature. In contrast with hate, contempt allows for competitive coexistence.

The difference between hate and contempt is illustrated by the difference between the Nazis' attitude toward the Jews and the attitude of whites toward blacks during the period of American slavery. At the risk of oversimplification, the basic emotional attitude of the Nazis may be characterized as hate, and that of the whites as contempt. Accordingly, the official doctrine of Nazi Germany held Jews to be irredeemably evil, and this was incompatible with allowing them to survive under any conditions; blacks, however, were not considered as such. Consequently, during the Holocaust, the only good Jew was a dead Jew, whereas during American slavery, a good black was a properly subservient black. This difference in attitude is expressed in the fact that Jewish infants were supposed to possess the same evil traits which were held to be inherent to Jewish adults. The nature of this evil was such that it was considered incorrigible even if "treated" early. Therefore, Jewish infants and children were also executed during the Holocaust. This is in sharp contrast to slavery, where it was not at all unusual for the children of slave owners and the children of slaves to play together.[27]

The generation of the Ku Klux Klan is also interesting in this regard. Two noteworthy facts are relevant here: (1) the Ku Klux Klan emerged after blacks began to receive more equal status, and (2) the typical Klansman was poor and inferior to the upper class in almost every perceived aspect. The elevation of blacks deprived these poor whites of a target for their contempt and put them at the bottom of the social rank. Accordingly, their contempt turned into hate, a typical transformation that occurs when a prevailing superiority is threatened.

Another difference between hate and contempt is that hate is typically both symmetrical and asymmetrical, whereas contempt is typically asymmetrical.[28] Hate of the enemy is symmetrical, whereas hate of thieves is asymmetrical.

Although cases of upward contempt indicate that contempt, too, can be symmetrical, usually it is asymmetrical. Those we view as inferior may develop various negative emotional attitudes toward us, but not necessarily contempt. The global negative evaluation associated with contempt does not imply that the object of contempt is inferior to us in all respects. The object of contempt may be superior to us in certain features, but those features are perceived to be inessential. Similarly, the global evaluation in hate does not imply that the object has no positive features; it merely implies that the object is essentially evil.

### Relationships with Other Emotions

The flame of anger, bright and brief, sharpens the barb of love.
—Walter Savage Landor

A man who lives, not by what he loves but what he hates, is a sick man.
—Archibald MacLeish

Both anger and hate contain a central element of the other emotion: anger contains a *hostile* attitude, and hate involves *annoyance*. In anger the hostility is weaker than in hate; accordingly, anger is often directed at those who are closest to us. In hate the annoyance is weaker than in anger; accordingly, the feeling dimension in hate is often not intense. Moreover, hostility in anger and annoyance in hate are typical, but not necessary, components. One can imagine anger without hostility and hate without annoyance. The former case is much more frequent; hence, anger is embedded in hate more profoundly than hate in anger. The existence of common elements in anger and hate is not surprising in that they both express a negative attitude toward another person.

Although annoyance is often associated with anger, we should distinguish between the two states. Anger is more intense, predominantly interpersonal, and more likely to involve attributions of blame and the intention of revenge; it carries a greater commitment to action and is a response to a more serious and personal threat. Annoyance is more diffuse and less concrete; the issue of intention is less central in annoyance than in anger.[29]

*Sadness* is often associated with hate and anger; those who consider sadness and happiness to be the basic emotions regard hate and anger as kinds of sadness. There are, however, some important differences. Sadness is a response to a loss which does not necessarily involve external blaming. Since the loss is often considered irrevocable, sadness is more passive than anger and hate. Anger and hate, which involve external blaming, are typically not concerned with loss, but rather with damage which is not necessarily irrevocable. In anger reinstating a positive situation is possible and likely; in hate it is possible but highly unlikely in light of the object's fundamental negative traits.

In addition to sadness, or dissatisfaction, anger and hate may also be associated with *delight*. This indicates the ambivalent nature of these emotions, and is particularly true of anger, which involves delight arising from the expectation of personal revenge.[30] Delight is a component of anger itself and not merely part of a subsequent emotion, such as vengeance, which is different from anger. Anger may encompass another positive component: the hope of overcoming the undesirable situation. Hate is less ambivalent than anger, as its negative element is more dominant. Nevertheless, hate still contains some ambiguity: we say that we love to hate someone. Bertrand Russell once said that few people can be happy unless they hate some other person, nation, or creed. The delight component in hate is perhaps rooted in a type of relief in unloading our negative, unpleasant moods. The unpleasant situation of the hater, as illustrated by those writing political hate letters, is understandable in light of the great emotional stress under which they are operating. Indeed, feeling depressed is often associated with hate. Accordingly, people are often advised to overcome their hate because it is bad for them, not just for the object of their hate. The element of hope is less evident in hate, where the likelihood of changing the object's negative character is lower.[31]

Anger and hate contain a kind of *fear* regarding the continuation of the undesirable situation. The fear in anger addresses continued effects of the unjust harm, and in hate, our future existence. The threat in hate is more substantial but more remote than in anger; the threat in anger is more concrete since to a certain extent it has already materialized. Anger is distinguished from fear by the temporal dimension: anger involves past harm, whereas fear refers to future harm. The objects of anger are more personal and specific than those of fear. In this sense, hate is similar to fear. It seems, indeed, that fear is more central in hate than in anger.

Other emotional strands often associated with anger are *regret*, *frustration*, and *disappointment*. These strands express the belief that things might have been different, and that we expected the other person to behave differently. Such expectations are not typical of hate, which is bound up with more permanent circumstances.

Like hate, *envy* is often a long-term attitude directed at general characteristics that are not limited to specific circumstances; its generation is usually not based upon a personal offense, and its feeling dimension is not necessarily very intense. In *On Envy and Hate*, Plutarch presents an interesting comparison between envy and hate. As in the analysis offered here, Plutarch claims that increasing wickedness increases hate, but increasing prosperity extinguishes envy. Referring to Alexander the Great, he argues that Alexander certainly had none who envied, but many who hated him. I believe that increasing prosperity expands the subject-object gap, hence the object's fortune is of lesser significance. Since envy is mainly concerned with relative, rather than absolute, deprivation, the competitive concern is hardly present in large gaps, thereby reducing envy. Hate is not concerned with perceived small flaws, but with fundamental ones. The basic negative aspect of the object of hate is not the object's good fortune, but the object's wickedness. Hence, an increase in such a negative aspect will increase the intensity of hate.

Plutarch also claims that hate is more justified than envy by arguing that no one is ever justly envied because no one is unjust in being fortunate; on the other hand, many are justly hated. Plutarch's argument is problematic. The moral concern may indeed be more dominant in hate than in envy, but this does not make hate more justified. Although there are cases of justified hate, only in rare cases are we justified in harboring an utterly negative evaluation of a human being's very existence. Moreover, envious people typically believe that they occupy an undeserved inferior situation; sometimes this belief is indeed justified.

The comparative concern is undoubtedly far more dominant in envy, but it is still present in hate. King Saul is described in the Bible as hating David and seeking to have him killed, because of David's prowess as a warrior. David's behavior was not immoral and was not even directed at Saul, but it still threatened Saul's social status.[32] When we perceive fundamentally negative consequences in a lowering of our position, envy and resentment toward the responsible person may be augmented by hate. Hence, the sayings "we hate most those we envy most," and "people hate those who make them feel their own inferiority." Sometimes envy also turns into hate when envy is concerned with natural gifts. As in hate, the negatively evaluated qualities are basic and permanent. Contrary to envy, hate does not allow for competition, which presupposes the coexistence of the two parties. The competitive concern in hate refers to our very existence; hence, there is no place for coexistence. The conflict in hate is believed to be a zero-sum conflict. Whereas hate involves the fear of being in a dangerous position, envy involves the belief of being in an inferior position. Anger allows for coexistence, but is often motivated by a retributive, rather than a competitive concern.

Following Elster, we may claim that the action tendency in hate is to destroy the emotional object and in envy, to destroy his superiority. The destructive urge in envy is directed against a person only if I envy him for something that cannot be destroyed separately, such as his kindness.[33]

Anger is typically not associated with *pity*. Pity involves a kind of acceptance of the other's bad situation; in anger we reject the current situation which involves what is perceived to be an unjustified offense against us. Emotional acceptance or rejection of a bad situation greatly depends on whether we or others are in this situation. Hence, the importance of the moral precept: "What is hateful to you do not do to your fellow person."

The personal nature of anger makes it closer to *jealousy* than to envy. Jealousy involves a more personal attitude expressed in more intense desires and feelings than those of envy. Whereas envy mainly involves a negative evaluation of other people's good fortune, in jealousy there is a stronger emphasis on a negative evaluation of their behavior (or future behavior), as is typically the case in anger.

Hence, the moral concern, which attaches greater weight to behavior, is more central to anger and jealousy.

*Resentment* is similar to anger in many respects. Like anger, it is a negative attitude toward a particular action of a blameworthy person rather than toward the person himself. We usually say "I resent what you did" rather than "I resent you." Resentment is usually a long-term attitude, while anger is often momentary, lasting from a few minutes to at most a few hours. Resentment is usually directed at an action which repeats itself or at a general pattern of actions, whereas anger is often directed at actions which have never previously occurred. Like anger, and unlike hate, fear is not a significant factor in resentment. Yet, resentment lacks the urge to attack that is so typical of anger. The central motivational component in anger is the desire personally to punish the object. The parallel component in resentment is protest and accordingly resentment is typically more public and evident than anger; there are fewer reasons to hide or control it. Resentment may be characterized as an emotional protest against perceived injustice. Unlike anger, which refers to immediate personal harm, resentment is mainly directed at moral injustice, the consequences of which are more remote.

In comparison with anger, the feeling dimension of resentment is less intense and its intentional dimension more complex. Hence, we do not attribute resentment to infants and animals. Resentment is more general than anger, as it refers not merely to blameworthy actions, as anger does, but also expresses a negative attitude toward the fortunes of other agents, as in envy and pity. Hence, resentment is associated with both groups of emotions. However, since a moral protest is an essential component of resentment, it should be classified as anger is, with the group of emotions that refer to the blameworthy actions of agents.

In light of its moral concern, resentment probably has the most positive connotation among negative emotions toward other agents. However, if one takes into account that both are often criticized on moral grounds and that anger expires sooner than resentment, then anger may be considered as less negative from this perspective. In the continuum of states beginning with typical emotions, which are short-lived and intense, and ending with typical general attitudes, which persist longer and are less intense, resentment is farther away from a typical emotion than anger. The more personal resentment is, the more similar it is to a typical emotion.[34]

Within the group of negative emotions directed toward a particular action of an agent, we may add *frustration* to anger and resentment. One difference between anger and frustration is that while anger is typically directed at an agent responsible for harming us, frustration lacks the intent to harm and sometimes even the agent responsible for the harm. Accordingly, it is often directed at oneself or at nonagents. We may say that we are frustrated with the current situation, but we do not say that we are angry at the current situation. Anger typically refers to personal harm, whereas the negative event associated with frustration can be more general in the sense that it is often not personally associated with us. Frustration also lacks the urge, typical of anger, to personally punish the object. Like frustration, *rage* is also a less specific type of anger. The feeling dimension in rage is more intense than in anger, and accordingly, the intentional dimension is less complex.

The group of negative emotions toward the actions and traits of other agents also includes *despair*. Despair, however, is closer to moods than to emotions: it is more general than both hate and contempt and its object is not clear. Considerations of our own situation are more central in despair than in contempt.

In everyday language we find expressions referring to emotions that are similar to those discussed above, except that they are self-referential. We hear of self-hate, self-contempt, self-anger, and self-frustration. Although it is clear that there are self-referential emotions, such as shame, guilt, and pride, most attitudes referred to by these terms are different from those discussed above. It is hard to comprehend such attitudes as *self-hate* or *self-disgust*, and to a lesser extent, self-contempt. Hate, which requires global negation of the object and the wish to be dissociated from or even to eliminate the object, can hardly be perceived as self-referential. Even those who commit suicide do not do so out of self-hate, but primarily out of frustration. Shame may be the closest attitude to self-hate; however, the negative evaluation is not as comprehensive as in hate, and in any case it does not involve the wish to avoid or eliminate the object. There are several ways to explain the frequent use of "self-hate" in everyday language. Self-hate may be conceived of as (a) a metaphorical linguistic usage which does not literally explain an emotional state; (b) a pathological state involving a split personality; (c) the negative attitude of a particular person toward the group to which he belongs—the attribution of this negative attitude can be made either by the person himself or by other people perceiving the person to behave in this manner. All three usages can be found in everyday language. Since "hate" is used in everyday language in a broader sense than the one employed here, it is plausible that "self-hate" is also used in this broader sense.

It is easier to speak of *self-anger* because anger involves a more limited negation. However, since anger involves a strong desire to punish the object for an unjustified harm inflicted, self-anger is still somewhat problematic. Nevertheless, we can speak of self-anger and the wish for self-punishment. A self-referential emotion in this group that is not problematic is *self-frustration*, which involves disappointment with our achievements. Self-contempt is again problematic insofar as it involves a global self-negation.

*Intensity Variables*

The greatest remedy for anger is delay.
—Seneca

When I am right, I get angry. Churchill gets angry when he is wrong. So we were often angry at each other.
—Charles De Gaulle

Familiarity is the root of the closest friendships, as well as the intensest hatreds.
—Antoine Rivarol

The *event's strength*, namely, the level of damage in comparison with our ability to remedy it, is probably the most influential variable affecting the intensity of anger. The second most important variable is probably accountability, which is expressed in the intentions of the wrongdoers and their ability to have prevented such damage. Readiness and relevance are also important in determining the intensity of anger.[35] Equally, in hate the event's strength and relevance are important as the object may destroy us or prevent us from achieving our goals. Variables relating to the specific background circumstances, such as accountability and readiness, are less influential.

The variable of *reality* is more important in anger than in hate. In anger, which is usually concerned with present events in our immediate environment, the reality of the event has significance for its generation and intensity. In hate, which is usually concerned with more remote events, their reality carries less weight. While experiencing hate, we often know that the way in which we are perceiving the specific object is not quite real. However, this does not negate the hatred, since we think that the person is essentially similar, or will end up being similar, to the character whom we actually hate.

The variable of *relevance* is most significant in both hate and anger, but whereas in hate it mainly refers to the relevance to the achievement of our goals, in anger it refers to the relevance to our self-esteem.

The influence of the *closeness* component upon the intensity of anger seems to be straightforward: the closer the person is to us, the more we care about the person, and the angrier we are when this person hurts us. The situation, however, is more complex, as closeness has two opposing effects upon the intensity of anger. The first is that we expect more from those close to us and therefore will be angrier when they inflict unjustified harm upon us. Aristotle claims that "we are angrier with our friends than with other people, since we feel that our friends ought to treat us well and not badly."[36] This effect is in accordance with the general positive correlation between unexpectedness and emotional intensity. Indeed, the greater the degree of unexpectedness, the angrier we are. The second effect is different: we are less likely to evaluate the deeds of those close to us as a deliberate attempt to hurt us. We tend rather to interpret the situation from a more favorable and conciliatory perspective—"seeing the bright side"—and will look for extenuating circumstances. This manner of reducing the event's strength may reduce the intensity of anger toward those close to us.

The influence of closeness on hate is more complex. As an emotion, hate should also be concerned with those close to us. However, considering its content, namely, the global negative evaluation which implies the wish to avoid the object, hate should be directed at those who are distant from us. It is clear that hate is not directed at those who are complete strangers to us and who have no contact with us whatsoever. When the wish to avoid the object is fulfilled, there is no reason for hate to emerge. Hate is then directed at people whom we perceive to be too close to us. These people may be close to us, but we wish them not to be so close. While we may wish to further distance ourselves from them, this wish is not fulfilled. Hate, then, involves an unfulfilled desire to avoid, or at least to distance ourselves from, a certain person. The greater and more meaningful the actual closeness, the greater the difficulty underlying hate, and consequently the more intense the emotion. Indeed, the most difficult cases of hate are those in which it is directed at those who are very close to us, for instance, family members. The Roman historian Tacitus said that hatred toward relatives is the most violent. In these cases, we are unable to distance ourselves from the other person, and accordingly the intensity of hate cannot be diminished. On the other hand, we are less likely to evaluate the behavior of those very close to us as fundamentally evil, and accordingly hate is less likely to occur in such circumstances. One is less likely to hate one's own son who appears to have a negative character than to hate another person's son with a seemingly similar character. If, however, such a negative evaluation is obviously present, then hate is most intense, and is characterized by what we perceive to be overcloseness.

It should be noted that in many cases, the global negative evaluation typical of hate derives from a superficial acquaintance with the other person and especially from attributing excessive weight to one of this person's negative traits. Upon knowing the person more intimately, such a superficial acquaintance is replaced by a more profound one that usually provides no basis for intense hate. When people refer to their hatred of strangers, the objects are not people who are completely unknown; rather, these people were strangers but have become close. This closeness does not encompass a profound acquaintance, but it is sufficient to influence our lives.

Various fictional works, as well as everyday descriptions, refer to what is known as a love-hate relationship, that is, an emotional attitude which demonstrates simultaneous attachment and aversion and is typical of close personal relationships such as marriage. I believe that the so-called love-hate relationships do indeed involve emotional ambivalence, but that the negative component, which is often part of love, is closer to anger than to full-fledged hate. As in anger, the negative evaluation in these cases is partial and the hostility element weaker. A global positive attitude toward another's whole being, such as pertains in love, may contain negative partial perspectives, but it cannot *simultaneously* be a global negative attitude toward another's entire being, as pertains in hate.[37] When two lovers separate in anger, hatred may follow, thereby implying that the failure to preserve the mutual relation was due to some basic flaws in the other person or in the relationship.

As mentioned, the variables of background circumstances, namely, *controllability*, *readiness*, and *deservingness*, are of crucial importance in anger, but less so in hate. In anger, which is a more specific and transient emotion than hate, specific details of the background circumstances, for example, the object's control, expectations, and deservingness, are quite important. Such details are usually at our disposal since the object is in our immediate environment. In hate the profound negative evaluation does not depend on specific personal details; hence, these are less significant. Hate is more general and less personal than anger.

*Moral Value*

Anyone can become angry—that is easy, but to be angry with the right person at the right time, and for the right purpose and in the right way—that is not within everyone's power and that is not easy.
—Aristotle

I shall never permit myself to stoop so low as to hate any man.
—Booker T. Washington


Anger and hate are often criticized on moral grounds. Anger is more acceptable than hate from a moral viewpoint for several major reasons. First, in anger the negation of other people is limited to specific, unjust actions; it is not, as in hate, a comprehensive negation of one's entire personality. Accordingly, forgiveness is more often associated with anger than with hate. Moreover, the basic evaluative pattern in anger, namely, praiseworthiness, is mainly concerned with moral aspects. Hate includes another pattern, namely, appealingness, which has nothing to do with morality and hence may distort moral considerations.

Second, anger has some sort of justification: it is often conceived as a response to injustice. As such, anger sometimes seems to be an appropriate reaction which one should not surrender. By being aggressive toward one who has wronged us, we feel that justice is being done. For Aristotle, the virtuous, good-tempered person is not a calm person who feels no anger; such a person is deficient in the sense that he does not feel the pain of an insult to himself or those related to him. This person does not have a rich enough view of himself to notice a slur upon his character. Thus, Aristotle argues that one ought not "to be in such a state as never to be angry with anybody; for this character also is blameworthy, as being insensible."[38]

Third, as mentioned, anger has a higher functional value than hate. In the normative sense of being rational, hate should be considered as less rational. Hate is a less appropriate response with less effective results.

Fourth, because of its more immediate and nondeliberative nature, anger involves less intellectual calculations and is more difficult to control. Consequently, only anger, but not hate, is accepted by the law as an extenuating circumstance for criminal behavior. One is less likely to consider acts proceeding from hate as being free of malice.[39]

In light of the more negative moral value of hate, people readily admit that they are angry, but are less inclined to admit that they hate someone. In the spirit of "hate the sin, never the sinner," people often deny that their negative attitude toward someone is a case of personal hate. Even God is described as being angry with people rather than hating them. The global negation of a human being is contrary to the belief that God is responsible for the creation of all creatures.

I have indicated that hate involves a global negative evaluation of another person. Which of these elements, namely, the negative or global evaluation, is the major factor responsible for the moral criticism against hate? A negative emotional evaluation is not necessarily morally wrong, as cases of justified anger would indicate. Also, the global evaluation is not morally wrong in itself. A similar type of global, but positive evaluation is found in love, and love is not morally wrong. I believe it is the combination of global and negative evaluations that makes hate especially subject to moral criticism.

The destructive nature of global evaluations is more evident in negative evaluations since (a) it is more difficult to change them, and (b) they have graver moral consequences.

In love we wish to be as close as possible to the other person; therefore, our evaluation can take note of specific actions and traits of this person in order to modify the positive global evaluation, or at least to add some negative aspects to the original positive evaluation. In hate, when we have no real contact with the other person, a distorted global evaluation cannot be modified in light of the real activities and traits of the object; therefore, it usually remains unchanged. Moreover, it is more problematic to change a negative global evaluation than a positive one: admitting the existence of the former often involves admitting that we have done something that is morally wrong. Hate is a kind of distorted prejudice which is largely resistant to change.

The fundamental difficulty in global evaluations is that they tend to be distorted, since they do not take into account each person's unique nature; such distortion has a more destructive nature in the case of global negative evaluations. The negative global evaluation involved in hate is related to the wish to avoid or even eliminate the other person. This wish may have irreversible negative consequences. Positive global evaluations can also be harmful, for example, when they arise from blind admiration for a vicious person. The harmful nature of positive evaluations in this case is mainly indirect, that is, via the support they provide for the vicious person. No doubt, the deeds of such a person, committed out of hate, are morally more reprehensible than the support granted him by others.

Hate is similar in many respects to negative prejudice. Both involve a global negative evaluation of the object, often based upon partial and distorted information. Hate, like prejudice, can become an epidemic. One who hates or has some prejudice against a given group will hate friends of this group and then those defending the friends, and so forth. The struggle against hate is similar to that against prejudice. Education to eradicate hate primarily involves dispelling sweeping global evaluations which are blind to the individual nature of actual people. A major means of fighting both prejudice and hatred is to know the other person better. Such knowledge will force us to exchange the negative global evaluation for a more specific evaluation which incorporates both positive and negative elements. A well-known advertisement for hair shampoo asserts that "You will never have a second chance to make a good first impression." Concerning hate and prejudice, I would state the opposite: "You will always have a second chance to make a negative evaluation of another person." Accordingly, we should avoid negative global evaluations of other people and be content with specific evaluations which reflect more adequately their individual nature.

Disgust plays an important moral role in presenting intense emotional resistance to immoral deeds. Disgust expresses our unqualified opposition to the violation of fundamental norms. Since disgust expresses an intense emotional opposition to something, cultivating it in a way that it will emerge when we are witnessing immoral deeds is a powerful incentive for moral behavior and the condemnation of immoral deeds. Thus, being disgusted by cruelty, betrayal, and hypocrisy is morally virtuous as it expresses a recommendable integration between emotional and moral norms. Our emotional reactions here are in accordance with moral norms. (This is the same type of integration mentioned in chapter 9.)

Although spontaneous emotional reactions have some moral advantages, they are also associated with some moral drawbacks, mainly pertaining to the fixation of moral norms and to the excessive nature of the reaction. If, for example, disgust has been a common reaction to homosexual relationships, and if these days we become convinced that there is no moral harm in such relationships, the intense reaction of disgust may hinder our ability to change our moral norms in a manner that is more considerate of other people's moral rights. Moreover, the intensity of such a reaction may degrade people in an immoral manner. The problem is even more severe in cases where disgust is concerned with nonmoral issues; for example, when it is directed at stigmatized people: the obese, the disabled, the deformed, the mentally ill, and the grotesquely ugly. The disgust in these cases is unjustified punishment. Since disgust urges us to withdraw from any contact with its objects, it poses an extremely difficult obstacle to normal social relationships with these people and to defending their moral and civil rights. Sometimes, disgust at the stigmatized is associated with blaming them for their situation, even though we may intellectually believe that it is not within their power to change. In these cases, the disgust is even more intense, as accountability increases emotional intensity.[40]

The analysis of the moral value of contempt is somewhat similar to that of disgust: having contempt when immoral deeds are evident is an important moral guide; however, this guide may be misleading when it is concerned with non-moral aspects of other people, for example, their appearance, economic or social status, religion, gender, sexual preferences, and so forth.

Letting disgust and contempt order our moral and social lives can be quite costly from a moral point of view. We must constrain these emotions by other emotional and intellectual attitudes. I would not recommend that we abandon these emotions altogether in determining our moral behavior, but we should reserve them mainly for the moral, rather than the social domain, and for grave moral sins.

To sum up, it is easy to realize the destructive nature of hate and contempt which involve general emotional evaluations; history can teach us many lessons in this regard. The more specific emotions of anger and resentment are less destructive and, in many situations, are the appropriate attitude to adopt. In most circumstances, the moral demand is to avoid the more general negative emotions, such as hate, disgust, and contempt, and to moderate the intensity of the more specific ones, such as anger and resentment.

# Chapter 14

# The Sweetest Emotions—Romantic Love and Sexual Desire

Love is a canvas furnished by Nature and embroidered by imagination.
—Voltaire

Sex without love is an empty experience, but as empty experiences go it's one of the best.
—Woody Allen

Romantic love and sexual desire are central emotions in our life. Some equate the two and some consider them to be completely different. This chapter analyzes the basic characteristics of each emotion and describes the connections between them.

Love has been divided into many types: romantic love, parental love, sexual love, love of friends, religion, country, and so on. There is also the love of food which George Bernard Shaw thought to be the most sincere love. Not all these attitudes are emotional. Love of food or of one's country is not a typical emotion. Romantic love itself can be categorized according to its various stages: falling in love, being in love, and staying in love. My main concern here is in characterizing typical cases of romantic love and sexual desire and examining the relationships between them. (Unless otherwise indicated, "love" refers to romantic love.)

## General Characteristics

Many a man has fallen in love with a girl in a light so dim he would not have chosen a suit by it.
—Maurice Chevalier

I never miss a chance to have sex or appear on television.
—Gore Vidal

I begin the discussion of romantic love and sexual desire by examining the following general issues: (a) basic evaluative patterns, (b) the emotional object, and

(c) fundamental questions concerning romantic love. The discussion of these issues will give us an initial description of love and sexual desire.

*Basic Evaluative Patterns*
You must look into people, as well as at them.
—Lord Chesterfield

I have never liked sex. I do not think I ever will. It seems just the opposite of love.
—Marilyn Monroe

The positive emotions directed at others' actions and personality consist of three major emotions: gratitude, sexual desire, and love. The basic evaluative pattern in *gratitude* is praiseworthiness of the other's action; that in *sexual desire* is appealingness of the other; and *love* comprises both praiseworthiness and appealingness. A similar structure is found in negative emotions: *anger* concerns praiseworthiness of the other's action; *disgust* involves appealingness of the other; and *hate*, both praiseworthiness and appealingness. Regarding the specific-global issue, the relation between love and gratitude is similar to that between hate and anger. Love and hate are long-term attitudes referring to another agent as a whole entity. Romantic love, however, is more specific than hate: it requires a more specific knowledge and a more personal relationship. Gratitude and anger are short-term states, mainly referring to specific actions of another agent. In the same way that hate entails a kind of anger at the object, love encompasses some gratitude for the object. Like disgust, sexual desire is based on the object's appealingness and is also directed at the whole object.

Different kinds of love carry different weight in terms of its two basic evaluative patterns: appealingness is more dominant in romantic love, and praiseworthiness in friendship. Likewise, in different instances of romantic love, different relative weights are attached to these patterns. In Yeats's poem, "For Anne Gregory," a woman wants to be loved not for the yellow color of her hair, which stands for the element of appealingness, but for herself alone, namely, her actions and traits. An old man tells her that "only God, my dear, could love you for yourself alone and not your yellow hair." An unattractive woman may wish the contrary: she may wish that her lover's attitude would attach a greater weight to her appealingness rather than her actions or wisdom. These women realize that genuine romantic love requires the presence of both patterns and wish to make this happen despite their apparent disadvantage insofar as one of the two patterns is concerned. Their "weak" pattern is cause for greater concern to them, since the positive evaluation from the perspective of the other pattern is never in doubt. In the movie *The Truth about Cats and Dogs*, a witty but not so attractive radio talk-show host finds the man of her dreams on the air. Terrified that he will lose interest in her if they meet face to face, she asks a tall blonde friend to take her place.

At the beginning the man falls in love with the beautiful blonde friend, but gradually he comes to realize that his love is based on the wit and intelligence of the radio talk-show host. Having realized this, he begins to be attracted to her appearance as well. The muscular actor Arnold Schwarzenegger maintains that women (who are probably aware of the wish to be positively evaluated in light of both patterns) tell him that they are attracted not merely to his physical strength but to his brain as well.

Quite often we hear statements such as: "You don't love me, you just love my body (or, beauty, money, kindness, humor, wisdom, etc.)." We may notice that that this statement can be voiced not only when it is concerned with features perceived as superficial, such as beauty and money, but also with regard to more profound features, such as kindness, humor, and wisdom. We may say that beauty and money are not legitimate reasons for love, whereas kindness and wisdom are more legitimate reasons—since they express characteristics more fundamental to us.[1] Nevertheless, none of these reasons alone is perceived to be sufficient for romantic love. Such love requires the presence of the two basic evaluative features of praiseworthiness and appealingness. Someone would be offended if her partner said: "You are rather ugly and I am not sexually attracted to you, but your brilliant brain compensates for everything." But she would also be offended if he said: "You are rather stupid, but your attractive body compensates for everything."

Some people would like to change the relative weight of one of these patterns—not in the beloved's attitude toward them, but in their own attitude. Thus, some people wish that they could attach less weight to appealingness, which may be of less value in the long run. Other people may wish the opposite: that their love could be more spontaneous and less calculated; they wish to attach more weight to appealingness. The familiar unsuccessful experience of trying to love the "right" person indicates the importance of appealingness in love. The familiar experience of being attracted to a beautiful person up until the moment he opens his mouth indicates the importance of praiseworthiness in love. In any case, some weight should be given to each pattern; otherwise, the attitude will not be of romantic love, but of gratitude, sexual desire, or other types of positive emotions.[2]

The relative weight of praiseworthiness and appealingness depends, to a certain extent, on personal and social factors. For example, with age, the relative weight of the two basic patterns constituting romantic love may change, probably in the direction of increasing the relative weight of praiseworthiness. Similarly, the same person may give different relative weight to these patterns in varying situations.

Some differences between men and women may also be present in this respect. It has been said, for example, that men love the women they are attracted to, whereas women are attracted to the men they love. Indeed, physical attractiveness is more important in determining male love for females than female love for males. This claim is supported by cross-cultural studies indicating that, among the thirty-seven cultures studied, there was no culture in which women cared more about the looks of their partners than men did. Another support for this claim has been found in a study on the focus of men and women's initial gaze upon first meeting. Women tend to look at men's eyes, whereas men initially look at women's bodies. While the body is of central importance for sexual attraction, the eyes are perceived as the best indicators of one's character.[3]

In the same vein, it has been claimed that whereas vision is the most important sense underlying sexual desire in men, hearing is the most important for women. Vision is more closely related to physical attractiveness, while hearing involves a more comprehensive attraction in which the intellectual aspect is quite prominent. In the television series *Seinfeld*, Jerry is surprised that Elaine is interested in going on a blind date with a man she spoke to on the phone, while Elaine is surprised that Jerry wants to go on a "deaf date" with a woman whose picture he has seen, but to whom he has never spoken. In light of the different relative weights of appealingness (which vision quickly assesses) and praiseworthiness (which hearing can discern more easily), it is not clear which date has more chance of success. It seems that in the short run, the deaf date is more likely to succeed, as good looks are of more importance to a short-term partner, whereas in the long run the blind date may have a greater chance of success, as speaking with a person is more likely to reveal diverse characteristics. If we remember that the emotional system is more easily activated by visual than by verbal stimuli, whereas the intellect is more susceptible to verbal stimuli, we may conclude that women are more intellectual in this regard. It seems that men, who are generally less emotional than women, are more influenced by emotional aspects when falling in love.

Personal ads placed by women who are seeking to attract men are most likely to advertise their beauty; a man seeking to attract a woman is more likely to mention his sincerity, friendship, and financial security. As one dating service director said, "men just look at the pictures, women actually read the thing." Hence, no wonder that the best-looking girls in high school are more than ten times as likely to get married as the least good-looking, while the more intelligent girls have no such advantage. On the contrary, one comprehensive study indicated that the women who had never married were significantly more intelligent than the women who had married. Another study found that although both men and women preferred good-looking partners, women considered other qualities, such as status and money, to compensate for looks. This was not true when men evaluated women: unattractive women were not preferred, no matter what their status. Some studies even indicate that many men prefer a spouse who makes less money than they do and whose occupational status is lower than theirs. But this is due to men's concern for their self-esteem rather than to the issue of attractiveness.[4]

It is interesting to note that gender differences concerning the relationship between love and sex may be a function of age as well. Thus, in a sample of adults between the ages of twenty-two and fifty-seven it was found that as women get older they are more likely to report physical arousal and less likely to report love as their motivation for sexual intercourse, whereas the reverse pattern was true for men.[5] It may be the case that the initial attitudes of men and women concerning the role of each evaluative pattern (namely, appealingness and praise-worthiness) in intimate relationships are, in later life, found to be a kind of ideal-ization and hence the trend toward a more balanced attitude regarding these patterns.

Gender differences concerning falling in love may, but need not, be connected with gender differences concerning choosing a partner for marriage—as such a choice depends on other factors. A study undertaken in the mid-1960s found that men are more "romantically" and women more "realistically oriented": 64 percent of the men, but only 24 percent of the women, said that they would not marry a person possessing all other qualities they admired, but with whom they were not in love. However, when this study was revisited some twenty years later, women were found to have grown significantly more romantic and had closed the gap with men. One important explanation for this change is women's entry into the workforce: less dependent on the institution of marriage for their economic sur-vival, women could now "afford" to marry for purely romantic reasons; conse-quently, women can give more weight to appealingness.[6]

The two basic evaluative patterns involved in love are not independent: the praiseworthiness of people depends to a great extent on their appealingness, namely, attractiveness. There is much evidence suggesting that attractiveness significantly influences ratings of intelligence, sociality, and morality. We may speak here about the attractiveness halo—what is beautiful is good. Nancy Etcoff, summarizing an extensive research on this issue, claims that although most people would say they no longer believe that "what is beautiful is good," preferential treatment of beautiful people is extremely easy to demonstrate, as is discrimina-tion against the unattractive. Etcoff claims that from infancy to adulthood, beau-tiful people are treated preferentially and viewed more positively; they find sexual partners more easily and are more likely to find leniency in the court and elicit cooperation from strangers. Similarly, ugliness leads to major social disadvantages and discrimination.[7]

Attractive people are socially assigned more praiseworthy personality attrib-utes than are unattractive people. They are perceived as being more honest, more likely to hold prestigious jobs, experience happier marriages, enjoy more fulfilling social and occupational lives, be better in bed, and healthier. An important excep-tion in this regard is the attribute of being better parents: attractive people were regarded as making worse parents than middling or unattractive people. A dif-ferent study found that in comparison to mothers of less attractive newborns, mothers of more attractive newborns spent more time holding the baby close, touching and patting the baby, staring into the baby's eyes, and vocalizing to the baby. Men are more likely to volunteer for altruistic and risky acts, such as helping move furniture, donating blood or a kidney, and even risking their lives for a beau-tiful woman than for a less attractive woman. The only thing they seemed reluc-tant to do was loan her money. Apparently, we perceive beauty not to be closely connected to moral virtues. Indeed, people are less likely to ask good-looking people for help.[8]

In one experiment conducted in 1952, girls who wore lipstick were described as more frivolous, unconscientious about work, and more overtly interested in the opposite sex. The men making these judgments were not aware that the use of lipstick was probably the crucial factor in their judgments of the girls' personalities. Similarly, it was found that dark men prefer the personalities of brunettes—contrary to the saying, "gentlemen prefer blondes"—and most women prefer the personalities of dark men. Another study suggests that attractive women influence the opinion of a male audience more strongly than do unattractive women. Likewise, taller graduate students (6 ft. 2 in. and over) were found to receive a 12.4 percent higher average starting salary than those who were under 6 ft. tall. Personal ads placed by taller men receive more responses from women than those placed by shorter men. In Western cultures, tall men make more money, and receive more and earlier promotions. Few American presidents have been less than 6 ft. tall and almost all American presidents in the twentieth century were taller than the candidate from the other party. In light of such evidence, it has been claimed that unattractive people, especially women, are discriminated against when applying for jobs. Such discrimination is even evident in the judicial system: attractive criminals receive lighter jail sentences; suspects with ugly features have a more difficult time proving their innocence, and are dealt with more harshly if they are found guilty. Accordingly, there has been a cry for "equality for uglies."[9]

People will usually not admit or even be aware of the great weight they assign to the pattern of appealingness. They tend to claim that they assign greater weight to the pattern of praiseworthiness. A popular old song states that "it does not matter how you cut your hair; what counts is what's inside." This song is not entirely accurate. The fact is that appearance does matter, and even if what's inside is the most important thing, the way you cut your hair determines how people evaluate what is inside your head.

Romantic love may involve the pattern of desirability in addition to the patterns of praiseworthiness and appealingness. The rewards one gets from having an attractive partner can be compared to those one might get from owning a new car. Desirability in terms of a higher social status is crucial in judging the value of an attractive partner or a new car. Such competitive concern is typical of emotions having desirability as their central evaluative pattern. In having an attractive wife, men often feel as if they have overtaken other people in the race for a higher social status; hence, such wives are regarded as "trophy wives." Generally, acquiring an attractive mate enhances a man's status more than a woman's. Due to similar considerations, men who are discovered having sex with unattractive women suffer social humiliation; they lose status and prestige in the eyes of their peers.[10]

To further complicate the determination of the evaluative structure of romantic love, it seems that maintaining love requires something beyond the mere repetition of the variables that initiated it and something besides the mere absence of the variables associated with its failure. The variables underlying a short-term emotion are different from those underlying its corresponding long-term sentiment. As an acute emotion, love largely consists in gazing at each other, but as a sentiment, love basically consists in looking outward together in the same direction.

With regard to sexual desire, some people do not consider this to be an emotion but rather something else—for example, a biological drive like hunger and thirst.[11] I disagree. When considering all basic characteristics and components of typical emotions, sexual desire emerges as a most typical emotion. It involves instability, great intensity, brief duration, and partiality. All four basic emotional components, namely, cognition, evaluation, motivation, and feeling, are clearly present in sexual desire. Moreover, the role of change is quite important in the generation of sexual desire and it is typically directed at humans. The focus of concern in sexual desire is no doubt a personal concern, but because of its strong evolutionary function the comparative concern is of lesser importance here.

The basic evaluative pattern of sexual desire is appealingness. This does not mean that praiseworthiness is utterly absent from sexual desire, but rather that it is far less significant. The praiseworthiness of the other's character and deeds in sexual desire is often derived from the other's appealingness. The intentional capacities involved in sexual desire are more primitive than those involved in romantic love. Sexual desire is a simpler attitude based largely on feelings and nondeliberative evaluation, whereas romantic love often requires both deliberative and voluntary evaluations. Sexual desire is largely based upon various kinds of perceptions, whereas love also encompasses capacities, such as thinking and memory, that are important for praising the object. Moreover, sexual desire is focused on a few external parts of the person's body which can be instantly revealed by sense perception. Spontaneous evaluations are more dominant in sexual desire than in romantic love since appealingness, the basic evaluative pattern of sexual desire, is more spontaneous than the pattern of praiseworthiness, present in love in addition to appealingness.

The more complex nature of love requires far greater personal involvement than sexual desire. Hence, breaking up a relationship based on love is more painful than breaking up a mere sexual affair. Sexual desire is more primitive than love, since it merely involves one, basically spontaneous, evaluative pattern—appealingness. The more primitive and spontaneous nature of sexual desire may account for why it is less disturbing when we find a lover having a sexual affair with someone else than when we discover a love affair. Love cannot be dismissed as being a transient, uncontrollable feeling, since it expresses our most profound attitudes. Due to its primitive nature, it is easier to artificially induce or terminate sexual desire. Love, which is a far more profound attitude, is neither available on demand nor terminable at will.[12]

In contrast to love, sexual desire is often an effortless experience requiring no acquired characteristics. This is due to the more spontaneous nature of sexual desire. Once certain standards of attractiveness are met, sexual desire is likely to emerge. Some of these standards have been shaped by millions of years of human evolution, and are common to people all over the world; other standards are more culture-bound. The more universal standards include, for instance, full lips, clear skin, smooth skin, clear eyes, lustrous hair, and good muscle tone. Apparently, whites and blacks display similar standards for the face but different standards for the body. Yet, even concerning body shape, the situation is more complex. Female bodily attractiveness varies from culture to culture regarding light vs. dark skin, as well as a slim vs. plump body. However, the preference for a particular ratio of waist size to hip size is invariant, being about 0.70. Men find women with this waist-to-hip ratio more attractive, regardless of their being thin or fat. It has even been claimed that this ratio is an accurate indication of long-term health status.[13]

The universal nature of certain standards of attractiveness is also supported by developmental evidence. Thus, in one study, it was shown that infants of two months of age and up spent more time looking at attractive faces, suggesting that standards of attractiveness apparently emerge quite early in life. Furthermore, older infants showed increased pleasure and play involvement when interacting with strangers who wore attractive masks than with those who wore unattractive masks; likewise, this pattern was repeated with attractive dolls vs. unattractive dolls. In another experiment, people of different races showed a great consensus regarding who is and is not good-looking.[14]

Learning is more typical of love than of sexual desire, since praiseworthiness, present only in love, depends more on social standards than appealingness, which is only the basic evaluative pattern in sexual desire. Similarly, disgust which, like sexual desire, is based mainly on the object's appealingness, is a more spontaneous attitude than hate and is more difficult to change by social norms.

The spontaneous nature of sexual desire does not mean that this emotion is utterly detached from learning and social standards. In fact, there is evidence to the contrary. As a result of the global spread of American and European films and television, ideals of sexual attractiveness have become more standardized. Thus, when black and white men were asked to rate the attractiveness of women from both races based on their photographs, they all showed a clear preference for white girls. Similarly, the beauty standards in Oriental and African countries are seemingly changing in accordance with Western standards.[15] It appears that the opposite trend has now begun to prevail as well: Oriental and African standards of beauty have become more and more popular in Western countries.

Despite the spontaneous nature of sexual desire, there are institutes which successfully teach people how to be more sexually attractive to their partners. (Obviously, there is no need for an institute to instruct people on how to be attracted to another person's partner.) Other institutes specialize in reducing sexual desire, thereby enabling people to be faithful to their partner. Increasing sexual desire may be accomplished by appealing to the imagination and strengthening the element of change. It is less clear what means are used to reduce sexual desire, as it is hard to repress imagination and the opportunities for change. (The story goes that a man went to a marriage consultant in order to strengthen his sexual desire for his wife. Following the consultant's advice, his sexual appetite did indeed increase considerably. His wife, however, discovered that just before their sexual encounters, he would sit in the bathroom for a long time mumbling "she is not my wife, she is not my wife . . .")

No precise borderline between romantic love and sexual desire exists. The latter usually is an essential component of the former. Hence, elements typical of the one are often found in the other. The close relation between romantic love and sexual desire indicates that we cannot be as unromantic about sex as we are about eating, but it does not deny cases in which sexual desire has nothing to do with romantic love. Conversely, romantic love may involve other types of attraction and not necessarily sexual desire. In one study, over 90 percent of the subjects rejected the statement: "The best thing about love is sex." Similarly, 53 percent of the females and 79 percent of the males agreed with the statement: "I have been sexually attracted without feeling the slightest trace of love"; and 61 percent of the females and 35 percent of the males agreed with the statement: "I have been in love without feeling any need for sex." However, the majority of people, especially women, enjoy sex most when they are in love with their partner. Thus, most people think that love and sex can be separated, but would prefer to have them combined. The importance of sexuality in romantic love is also indicated by the fact that most people consider sexual involvement between their partner and a rival as more threatening to their love relationship than high degrees of nonsexual intimacy between partner and rival. The separation between love and sexual desire is more evident in other kinds of love.[16]

There are some gender differences in this regard: men tend to separate sex and love, whereas women tend to believe that love and sex go together. Thus, erotic pictures generate more arousal in men than in women, whereas pictures of romantic couples generate much more arousal in women than in men. Similarly, extramarital sexual involvements of women are more likely to be love-oriented and those of men to be pleasure-oriented. Accordingly, men are more likely to engage in extramarital sex with little or no emotional involvement, whereas women are more likely to engage in extramarital emotional involvement without sexual intercourse. It has been argued that a wife commits adultery generally only when her feelings are deeply involved or likely to become so.[17]

*The Emotional Object*
No woman ever falls in love with a man unless she has a better opinion of him than he deserves.
—E. W. Howe

The emotional object in romantic love is a person we see as having fundamentally *attractive* and *praiseworthy* traits and as being a suitable partner with whom to live.

Whereas the object in hate is considered essentially a *bad* agent, the object in romantic love is perceived to be both *attractive* and *good*. Whereas moral standards are essential to the generation of hate, or at least to its justification, the generation of love depends on other standards as well, including aesthetic, economic, and physical ones. We do not usually say, "He is perfect from a moral viewpoint, but I still hate him." However, we often say, "He is perfect from a moral viewpoint, but I still do not love him." In romantic love, "chemistry" is often more important than moral concerns. In hate, the emphasis is on the harmful consequences of the object's character rather than on the subject-object personal relationship. This is not to say that the object of love is not considered to have virtuous traits or the object of hate to be unattractive. However, the emphasis in the two emotions is different. The lesser weight of moral praiseworthiness in love is evidenced by the fact that we may love a vicious person. However, we usually present excuses—such as a rough childhood or hardship in the present situation—for the beloved's immoral behavior. Such excuses indicate that unfortunate external circumstances forced the person, who is essentially decent, or at least not inherently vicious, to behave immorally. They also indicate that praiseworthiness is of considerable weight even in such cases of romantic love.

The element of attractiveness is even more pronounced in sexual desire and disgust. The emotional object in sexual desire is basically one-dimensional, whereas in romantic love the object is more complex and consists of several evaluative dimensions: "In short-term sexual encounters, all that really matters is what the other person looks like and whether they are willing—both things that can be discovered fairly quickly. There is not the time nor any need to find out what the other person is 'really like.' Long-term relationships and marriage, on the other hand, mean more than 'four legs in a bed,' so partners will be chosen more carefully."[18] Similarly, the emotional object in disgust is basically one-dimensional, whereas in hate it is more complex, though not as complex as in love, since it is viewed from a distance and with a very practical concern in mind.

The concern for the object's happiness and the mutual subject-object relation are particularly important in love. Love is characterized by intrusive thinking or preoccupation with the beloved. Although romantic love encompasses genuine care for the beloved, it is not a general concern for the beloved's happiness in all circumstances. Typically, the lover desires the beloved's happiness only insofar as the lover is either a part or the cause of this happiness. In romantic love, the lover's own well-being is tied up with that of the beloved. Picasso expressed this concern in a rather extreme manner when he said, "I would prefer to see a woman dead than see her happy with another man." This is one significant difference between romantic love and parental love.

Love includes the desire to fuse with the beloved, to form a *we* with a particular person. This is clearly expressed in Edgar Allan Poe's wonderful poem, "Annabel Lee":

And neither the angels in Heaven above
Nor the demons down under the sea,
Can ever dissever my soul from the soul
Of the beautiful Annabel Lee.

In love, we wish to know the beloved and be known by the beloved, to form a unique and intimate relationship with the beloved, to improve the beloved's situation, and so on. Being with the beloved means engaging in special types of activities with this person: spending time together, having prolonged eye contact, touching and holding, caressing, kissing, and making love. The desire to be with the beloved often becomes a desire to fuse with the beloved and in a sense to lose one's identity. Lovers begin to develop similar likes to those of their partners; for example, to enjoy music to which they were previously indifferent, or even to wear similar clothes to those of the beloved. In sexual desire, the wish to be with the other person is relatively superficial in that it entails a more limited time span and type of contact.[19]

The beloved's favorable attitude toward the lover, that is, the element of reciprocity, is important in love: the lover wants to be loved in return, to be kissed as well as to kiss. The lover is ready to be committed, but expects to find similar commitment in the beloved's attitude. Accordingly, claims such as "I love (or care for) you so you don't have to love (or care for) me" are most uncharacteristic of love. Assuring reciprocity, for example, by repeatedly declaring their love for each other, is of crucial importance to lovers. Indeed, people tend to reciprocate positive emotions and evaluations directed by others toward them. The lack of reciprocity, namely, the knowledge that you are not loved by your beloved, usually leads to a decrease in love intensity, and ultimately, to humiliation. This decrease does not tend to be immediate; the one suffering from unrequited love persists in trying to win the other's heart. Indeed, many books and movies feature as their theme aspiring lovers persisting doggedly to win the hearts of their beloved. In some cases, love may even briefly intensify while one tries to win the other's heart. However, when the romantic rejection is perceived as irrevocable, it is a humiliating blow to our self-esteem, as it reflects a negative global evaluation of our worth.[20]

The reference to the object is less important in sexual desire, in which case satisfying our needs is the major, and sometimes the only, concern. Whereas lovers care about their beloved's attitude and want their beloved to prosper, in sexual desire the object's needs and attitudes are less of a priority. Nevertheless, sexual activities are not completely devoid of concern for the other person, as this person's satisfaction often increases our own. However, this is a more superficial and egoistic concern which does not focus on the fulfillment of the other's wishes. The value of the sexually desired person is for the limited purpose of sexual satisfaction. Sexual desire has a purposive nature which is not typical of love: as long as the sexual desire exists, there is a need which is not satisfied; the moment it is satisfied, attraction disappears or is significantly diminished.

The positive evaluation in romantic love is comprehensive: it refers to many aspects and not merely to a few, as does sexual desire. Yet, a comprehensive positive evaluation does not mean that every aspect of the beloved is positively evaluated. The lover is not necessarily oblivious to faults of the beloved. The positive evaluation may refer only to particular aspects, but those are viewed as so significant that they overshadow the negative aspects and cast the whole personality in a positive light. Similarly, hate may allow for a positive evaluation of some partial aspects of the object, but as a whole, the person is negatively evaluated.

Sexual desire is more partial and transient than romantic love; similarly, disgust is more partial and transient than hate. The transient nature of sexual desire is due to the fact that it is concerned with particular aspects whose impact is limited to specific circumstances. Love, on the other hand, is an enduring emotion, since it refers to global aspects. It takes time to develop and maintain lasting love, which involves an intimate and reciprocal relationship. Hence, we may characterize the enduring attitude toward one's beloved as ups and downs of the same loving attitude. In contrast, different instances of sexual desire toward the same person should be considered as separate states. Unlike the enduring nature of love, sexual desire lacks continuity: it emerges and disappears. A man can love his wife for fifty years, during part of which his love is dispositional; but a man does not have sexual desire for his wife for fifty years and not even for fifty continuous days. Similarly, hate, but not disgust, is an enduring attitude.[21]

The comprehensive positive evaluation in love indicates that the beloved is evaluated as having intrinsic worth. The comparative concern in love is less significant: we do not ordinarily criticize a man who deeply and happily loves a certain woman just because we think he could have done better.[22] The value of love is not determined, or at least not entirely determined, by its practical value as a means to achieve certain ends. Loving someone as a means, for instance, to satisfy one's sexual desire or to become rich, is partial and transient: the moment the end is achieved, or a better means found, then love disappears. Because of its intrinsic value, it has been claimed that, unlike other emotions, genuine love cannot be criticized. It has been described as involving disinterested care for the beloved, that is, care which does not contain considerations of our own benefit.[23]

Love itself, and not only the beloved, is considered to have intrinsic value. No wonder that love is one of the most important factors in determining happiness. Interestingly, although not surprisingly, the major emphasis on the importance of love comes from those who do not have it. Sex is also an important element in general happiness, but not as important as love. This is in accordance with the more partial and instrumental value of sex. The number of sexual partners one has, as well as the frequency of sex, matters very little in terms of happiness or even sexual satisfaction. Although different sexual partners evoke sexual desire more easily, they do not necessarily increase happiness; happiness is more complex, and a mere change or greater quantity cannot guarantee its presence.[24]

By characterizing love as involving a comprehensive positive evaluation, it should not be assumed that love lacks detailed perception and evaluation of the beloved. On the contrary, such a detailed picture is typical of love, since it entails a close relationship. A comprehensive evaluation is not necessarily contrary to detailed cognition. Paying attention to relatively insignificant details shows caring and personal involvement. Accordingly, it can be a means of flirting.[25] Ortega y Gasset emphasizes the role of facial details and gestures in love. He argues that whereas the indifferent man will be charmed by the broad lines of the face and figure of a beautiful woman, the lover will find beauty in separate, small, and unrelated aspects: the color of her eyes, the way her mouth turns, the sound of her voice, and the like. Whereas sexual desire involves superficial knowledge and evaluation of many objects, love involves a more profound knowledge and evaluation of very few objects. Thus, the depth of attitude in love can be achieved because of its more discriminative nature. Like other instincts, sexuality tends "to amplify indefinitely the number of objects which satisfy it, whereas love tends toward exclusivism." In love, there is "a progressive elimination of the things which formerly absorbed us. Consciousness contracts and is occupied by only one object."[26]

Moral theories often recommend general types of love in which we should love everyone. Such moral love is recommended regardless of the object's general characteristics: it should occur without any particular reason besides the trivial fact that the object is a human being, or even merely a living creature. This is an indiscriminate love of humanity, insofar as all human beings deserve to be loved. In accordance with this notion of love, Mother Teresa said that "If you judge people, you have no time to love them."

In contrast to this view, romantic love, like other types of emotions, are judgmental: the evaluative component is essential to them. Accordingly, romantic love is often idealized and described as exactly the opposite of the above general type of love: it is not based on general and repeatable characteristics of the object, but on the unique intimate history shared by the lovers. The reason is that these characteristics, for example, beauty, intelligence, wealth, or sense of humor, may also be found in other people and even in a better form. Idealized romantic love is often described as ignoring repeatable general characteristics because they are too general, as compared with the particular shared history. Moral love should ignore these characteristics because they are too particular, as compared with the general nature of human beings. In both types, love is described as not stemming from the object's general characteristics.

Actual emotional attitudes of love clearly differ from those of moral love in that they are discriminative: loving everyone means loving no one. One can try to have a favorable attitude toward all human beings, but this is different from love, especially romantic love. The difficulty in the idealized notion of romantic love is the opposite: it involves a too particular description of love in which shared history is almost the sole factor. However, a shared history is not enough for maintaining love, as the many cases of divorce clearly indicate. It is obvious that the beloved's general characteristics are important for the generation of love. As Ronald De Sousa rightly says: "If I love you, I must love you as you uniquely are . . . But *being yourself and no other* is not enough to distinguish anyone, since it is a property shared by every particular. Thus I must *know* what properties distinguish you from others."[27]

We fall in love with someone because of, among other things, this person's general characteristics, such as beauty, intelligence, wealth, humor, and so on. General characteristics are also important for maintaining love, although these are sometimes different from those responsible for its rise. If general characteristics were of no importance, then love would be arbitrary and we would constantly fall in love with every person we meet. This is obviously not the case. However, the object of love is not merely determined by general characteristics; otherwise, love would be conditional, something that would disappear if the characteristics did.

The dispute concerning the general or particular nature of romantic love seems to be based on a questionable conceptual distinction between the person as such and the person's general characteristics. The object of love is a complex entity which includes both particular and general features. The former are responsible for the uniqueness of the object, and the latter for determining its comparative worth. In loving someone, we cherish both aspects of the beloved.

*Fundamental Questions Concerning Romantic Love*
My mother-in-law broke up my marriage. My wife came home from work one day and found me in bed with her.
—Lenny Bruce

After describing the basic evaluative patterns of love and sexual desire and the typical object of each attitude, we are in a position to discuss a few fundamental questions which are at the center of heated disputes concerning the nature of romantic love. I will focus on the following issues: (1) Is there love at first sight? (2) Is love blind? (3) Is love replaceable and nonexclusive?

*IS THERE LOVE AT FIRST SIGHT?*
There is a lady sweet and kind,
Was never face so pleased my mind;
I did but see her passing by,
And yet I love her till I die.
—Barnaby Googe

Do you remember when we met? That was the date I knew you were my mate.
—Phil Phillips

We have heard many wonderful tales about "love at first sight." Many books and movies idealize this phenomenon. Some people even consider love at first sight to be the only kind of genuine love. Thus, in Shakespeare's *Twelfth Night*, it is claimed that "Whoever loves, loves at first sight." Israel Zangwill reached the same conclusion but for ironic reasons: "The only true love is love at first sight; second sight dispels it."

Despite its glamorous place in our culture, love at first sight is not easy to explain. How can we explain that in one quick glance we can fall profoundly in love? How can such a glance persuade us to believe that we want to spend the rest of our life in the arms of a stranger we have just seen for the first time? I have argued that appealingness alone cannot sustain love; praiseworthiness is needed as well. But praiseworthiness is built on characteristics such as kindness, honesty, and a sense of humor, which cannot be revealed in one glance. Knowledge of such characteristics requires familiarity and a common history, which are clearly impossible at first sight. Hence, some people deny the existence of love at first sight, arguing that what is termed "love at first sight" is a contradiction in terms.[28]

Although people often confuse love at first sight with sexual desire at first sight, there are nevertheless genuine cases of love at first sight. Many people report such cases so we should try to avoid the tendency to dispute these incidents; we should rather try to explain them. Our task is to explain how love at first sight is possible despite the virtually total absence of knowledge concerning the beloved's characteristics.

The fundamental mistake in denying the existence of love at first sight is the assumption that we cannot attribute to a person characteristics which are not present at the moment. Praiseworthiness can also be evaluated spontaneously. This is what underlies most stereotypic evaluations. When, for instance, we have a certain schema of an ideal person and we meet someone who activates this schema, then that person is spontaneously evaluated as having praiseworthy traits. Indeed, people form evaluations more quickly when their expectations are consistent with the event's value. To activate a schema, each and every aspect does not have to fit; a few aspects are often sufficient. Sometimes items of seemingly no significance, such as a business suit, a physician's white jacket, a certain smile, or a particular voice, may activate one's schema of an attractive person. These considerations are clearly consistent with the aforementioned "attractiveness halo," in which what is beautiful is evaluated as good as well. Accordingly, attractive people, who are evaluated mainly on the basis of their appealingness, are more likely to be the object of love at first sight. It is as if these people begin the struggle to be loved with the initial obstacle already behind them.[29]

The spontaneous nature of the evaluations underlying love at first sight is not an exception in the emotional realm, but rather the common situation. In fact, since emotions are immediate responses to typically novel situations, love at first sight seems to be even more natural than long-term love. As someone said, "It is easy to understand love at first sight, but how can we explain love after two people have looked at each other for years?"

In light of its stereotypic nature, love at first sight is often misleading. We may praise a property which actually does not exist. Hence, "Love at first sight is in fact only a small part 'sight' and a much larger part fantasy."[30] The deceptive aspect which may be present in love at first sight does not imply that the subject's experience is not a genuine case of love.

I do not want to adopt Shakespeare's assumption that "whoever loves, loves at first sight." Love can be developed over time. We may discover characteristics we adore and which are not evident at first sight, and we may evaluate differently those characteristics which were evident but were not positive enough to make us fall in love. Hence, we may fall in love with a person once we get to know her better. We should also avoid the other extreme which denies the existence of love at first sight. Love can emerge in diverse ways. It seems, however, that love at first sight is to be found more often in works of art than in reality.

*IS LOVE BLIND?*
Faults are thin where love is thick; faults are thick where love is thin.
—Unknown

Love is not blind—It sees more and not less, but because it sees more it is willing to see less.
—Will Moss

Love is blind and marriage is an institution for the blind.
—James Graham

Lovers in general, but particularly lovers at first sight, are often blind to the beloved's negative traits and tend to create an idealized image of the beloved. We often love the idealized object rather than the real one. Men seem to idealize women more than women idealize men. For example, a survey of love songs has found that females more often than males were described as "heavenly" or "angels."[31] One reason for idealizing the beloved is that we tend to evaluate positively that which we desire. Our inclination toward something often leads to its positive evaluation. Idealization of the beloved may also be considered a kind of defense mechanism, enabling us to justify our partly arbitrary choice. A similar defense mechanism is typical of people who have recently bought a new car and subsequently spend a lot of time reading its advertisements and avoiding reading those for other cars they might have bought instead.[32]

Idealization of the beloved is more typical of love at first sight and of the initial stages of love, when a spontaneous evaluation, made on little information, has an important role. If the person fits the schema underlying the spontaneous evaluation, then the person is evaluated positively. When more information is available, this evaluation must also take into account negative aspects. The initial ignorance of the person's characteristics, which is expressed in idealization, is later replaced with a more realistic picture based upon new and more detailed information. Many divorcées testify that they cannot understand how they could have been so blind to their partner's characteristics. The lover's blindness is not necessarily due to misperception of the beloved's traits; it may also be a matter of emphasis (or overemphasis), namely, focusing upon positive qualities only.

Most married people are able to enumerate their partner's character defects, physical defects, and bad habits. Moreover, we may love an evil person, an unintelligent person, an aesthetically unpleasant person, or an arrogant person while knowing this person to be so.[33] The epistemic change of gaining additional negative information about the object does not necessarily lead to separation. However, if love is to be sustained, this epistemic change must be accompanied by an evaluative change compensating for the new negative information. The evaluative change may be either in the content of an evaluative schema, for example, a change in what we conceive to be beautiful or kind, or in its relative weight. Evaluative changes, which are more common the younger a person is, may also lead to the termination of love. Indeed, marriages among very young couples are the least likely to succeed.[34]

In light of the complexity typical of love and the fact that lovers are often unwilling to face reality, self-deception and mistakes are likely to occur. We can be wrong in identifying the beloved's attitude, since the person can easily fake or hide it. We can also be wrong in identifying our own loving attitude, one reason being that sexual desire can be confused with romantic love. This is especially true in the first stages of romantic love when sexuality plays a dominant role. According to the troubadour tradition, the love test used to prevent such confusion is to spend a night in his mistress' arms without sexual consummation.[35]

The primitive nature of sexual desire, and in particular the presence of the evaluative pattern of appealingness alone, reduces, if not eliminates, the possibility of misidentifying our own attitude. One may argue that sexual desire could reflect self-deception in cases where, due to a shortage in available attractive people, we consider as attractive a person who in normal circumstances would not be so considered. Although these cases are common, it is doubtful whether they demonstrate self-deception; rather, they show a tentative, superficial change in our evaluative standards.

*IS LOVE REPLACEABLE AND NONEXCLUSIVE?*
When I fall in love
It will be for ever
Or I'll never fall in love.
When I give my heart
It will be completely
Or I'll never give my heart.
—The Lettermen

After all, my erstwhile dear,
My no longer cherished,
Need we say it was not love
Just because it perished?
—Edna St. Vincent Millay

An important issue in the characterization of love and sexual desire is whether their objects are (a) replaceable, and (b) nonexclusive. "Replaceable" is used in a diachronic sense, namely, replacing the object after a certain period of time; "nonexclusive" is used in a synchronic sense, namely, having different objects at the same time.

It is obvious that sexual desire is both replaceable and nonexclusive. We are sexually attracted to different people in the course of our lifetime, and we may also be attracted to several people at the same time. There are gender differences in this regard: men desire to have more sexual partners than women do. As David Buss indicates, a key male sexual fantasy is to have sexual access to dozens of fresh, beautiful women who respond eagerly. Women's sexual fantasies are half as frequent and often contain familiar partners. One study showed that college men, on average, would like to have eighteen sex partners in their lifetime, and women, only four or five. In another study the following scenario was presented: Imagine that an attractive person of the opposite sex walks up to you and says: "Hi, I've been noticing you around town lately, and I find you very attractive. Would you go to bed with me?" A full 100 percent of the women participating in the study said no, and 75 percent of the men said yes.[36]

The case of romantic love is more complex. Genuine romantic love is often described as nonreplaceable and exclusive. Take, for example, the following passage from Tolstoy's *Kreutzer Sonata*:

> "Yes, but how is one to understand what is meant by 'true love'?" said the gentleman . . .
> "Why? It's very simple," she said, but stopped to consider. "Love? Love is an exclusive preference for one above everybody else," said the lady.
> "Preference for how long? A month, two days, or half an hour?" said the gray-haired man and began to laugh.
> "Excuse me, we are evidently not speaking of the same thing" . . .
> "Yes, I know . . . you are talking about what is supposed to be, but I am speaking of what is. Every man experiences what you call love for every pretty woman."
> "Oh, what you say is awful! But the feeling that is called love does exist among people, and is given not for months or years, but for a lifetime!"
> "No, it does not!"[37]

The man, who we learn later has murdered his wife, identifies romantic love with sexual desire. Later on the lady modifies her position and the disagreement between them shifts to how long love can last.

Nonreplaceability of romantic love is hard to accept. While it is certain that we would not describe every love affair as genuine romantic love, there is no reason to suppose that one can only experience a single instance of genuine love in a lifetime. It is worth mentioning that Romeo's love for Juliet, which is often considered the ideal of romantic love, is not his first passion. While still pursuing his love for Rosaline, Romeo sees Juliet, instantly transfers his desire, and falls in love with her.[38] There is no reason to assume that one cannot find a new and more compatible partner. After all, Adam and Eve are the only couple who were truly made for each other. The replaceability of the beloved does not deny the existence of cases in which one has only one genuine love throughout one's life. The popular song arguing that "true love can never die" is not entirely wrong; however, a more precise, though less romantic, description would be "true love may never die."

The replaceable nature of love does not mean that democracy should be applied to love and that love is like linen—the more often changed, the sweeter. On the contrary, people who are rapidly replacing their partners are often inadequate in their ability to form loving relationships. Many of them are addicted to destructive love relationships, and despite huge efforts on their behalf, they cannot achieve the stability and warmth of healthy, loving relationships.

Romantic love is replaceable, though not as replaceable as sexual desire. Replacement of a partner may take place for any of the following reasons: (a) knowing our partner better and consequently realizing that the partner is not as valuable as previously considered; (b) finding someone who has higher emotional value for us; (c) changing our evaluative patterns.

The anthropologist Helen Fisher argues that love sputters out in something like four years. Thus, primitive couples stayed together just long enough to rear one child through infancy, and then each would find a new partner and start all over again. Similarly, in most cultures divorce rates peak around the fourth year of marriage. Additional children help keep couples together longer.

The brief duration of passionate love is also suggested by considering its underlying chemistry. Research suggests that in passionate romantic love, we are flooded by chemicals, in particular phenylethylamine (PEA). However, PEA highs do not last forever. The body builds up a tolerance to PEA; thus, it takes more and more of the substance to produce love's special kick. After two to three years, the body simply cannot crank up the needed amount of PEA. This being the case, then what accounts for the fact that many romances endure beyond the first years? It is the presence of another set of chemicals, endorphins, which are soothing substances; they are natural painkillers which give lovers a sense of security, peace, and calm. Accordingly, we may distinguish between the heated infatuation induced mainly by PEA and the more intimate attachment fostered and prolonged by endorphins; the former is more similar to typical emotions.[39]

The claim that romantic love is not exclusive, that is, that one can love a few objects at the same time, is less obvious than the claim that love is replaceable. Exclusivity seems to have a few important roles in love, for example, to ensure high confidence in paternity and to ensure mutual commitment. Furthermore, since romantic love requires many resources, such as time and attention, its objects should be limited. One does not have enough free time and attention, not to mention sexual energy, to love many people simultaneously. However, there is no conceptual contradiction in saying that one can be in love with more than one person. This is especially true when the few people one is in love with are considerably different from each other—hence, comparison is less significant. Thus, fewer than 5 percent of mammals form rigorously faithful pairs. The human pattern has been monogamy with clandestine adultery. Even those arguing for the exclusive nature of love are usually not immune to the experience of romantic temptations. Resistance to such temptations stems from considerations external to the emotion of love itself.[40]

As in other emotions, repetition reduces emotional intensity as it reduces the crucial element of change. It is therefore doubtful whether strict exclusivity is a necessary condition for romantic love. It is not, for example, a necessary condition for parental love. Parental love is less replaceable than romantic love—parents' love for their children is usually maintained as long as they live; and it is also less exclusive than romantic love—the number of children a parent can love is greater than the number of people a person can love romantically. It should be noted, however, that in both cases there is a limit to the number of intimate relations one can maintain at a given time without reducing the quality of each relationship.

Sexual desire, which is typically an important component in romantic love, is a major factor opposing the tendency to make romantic love exclusive and nonreplaceable. An interesting fact in this regard is that many people who have extramarital affairs still consider their marriage to be happy and are sexually satisfied with their partners (this is especially true of men).[41] Sexual desire for someone else is not necessarily a sign of some deficiency in the relation with one's partner. It is not always the case that the person one chooses to share one's life with and the person one expects to provide the greatest sexual satisfaction are one and the same.

The relationship between romantic love and sexual desire is a major factor in understanding extramarital affairs. Although the typical extramarital affair includes a sexual relationship, there are also nonsexual extramarital involvements such as spending a private evening together, going to the movies, going out to dinner at a secluded place, taking a short holiday together, dancing together, and so on. Some of these nonsexual extramarital events are considered socially acceptable, but sexual extramarital events are typically not acceptable. Indeed, acceptance of extramarital sex is often absent in psychological counseling. Stanton Peele notes that the popular and liberal media sex counselor, Dr. Ruth Westheimer, who has been married three times, has declared extramarital sex as taboo while okaying such practices as threesomes and sex with inflatable dolls. In this approach, partners may break up with each other because they love each other too much to tolerate a single infidelity of their own or their partner's. It is odd, Peele remarks, that while people today, as opposed to earlier periods, often accept divorce and desertion, they find it hard to imagine the ability to share oneself with more than one person.[42]

Peele's doubts seem to make sense. It is not clear why one should prefer having sex with inflatable dolls over sex with another human being who happens not to be one's partner. However, it is doubtful whether there is, as Peele assumes, an inverse correlation between infidelity and divorce; the correlation is often direct. Indeed, empirical evidence indicates that extramarital affairs often lead to divorce or to an overall negative atmosphere stemming from the fact that the betrayed spouses suffer significant damage to their self-image.[43]

We may distinguish between the conditions for the generation of love and love itself. These conditions tend to limit the objects of love and keep them exclusive, but love itself is not limited in such a manner. The apparent exclusive nature of romantic love may be deceptive: it may reflect the practical and social limitations of romantic love, rather than being an inherent property of it. In many cases, love remains exclusive because of considerations external to the attitude itself, for example, social norms and the wish not to hurt the partner and the children. Although many people think they can and do love more than one person at the same time, intense romantic love tends to occur with only one partner at a time. The object of romantic love may be replaceable and not necessarily exclusive, but a deliberate search for someone with "better" characteristics is not compatible with romantic love. If there is readiness for a change, it should appear in the form of an improvement in one's mate, not via replacement by someone else.[44]

*Relationships with Other Emotions*

We always love those who admire us; we do not always love those whom we admire.
—La Rochefoucauld

Shopping is better than sex. If you're not satisfied after shopping you can make an exchange for something you really like.
—Adrienne Gusoff

The confusion between loving and *liking*, like that between hating and disliking, is common. We often use "love" to describe nonemotional attitudes or emotional states that are different from typical love. Liking is more general than loving in that it involves a less intense feeling dimension and a less specific and complex intentional dimension. Whereas love is directed at the whole person, liking often involves a partial evaluation which can also refer to inanimate objects, situations, activities, and other things that are not typically objects of love. Liking is often not an emotion, but a general positive attitude involving some sort of, usually mild, enjoyment. The linguistic usage of "liking" and "loving" sometimes overlooks the differences between the two attitudes. However, this is not always the case. A woman who says to a man, "I like you" may be emphasizing that while she enjoys his company, she is not in love with him. In between we may find expressions such as "I like you a lot," and "I really like you."[45]

The linguistic distinction between loving someone and being in love with someone reflects the difference between the prototypical attitude of liking and that of loving. We may be said to love people, objects, and situations (this is the way "liking" is used here), but we can be in love only with people. Being in love expresses a more intense type of love and therefore is not part of less intense forms of love. Profound care, which is typical of romantic love and friendship, is often absent from mere liking. Whereas liking is always part of the more profound attitude of love, it may sometimes be absent from sexual desire. In one survey, most men admitted that they have had sex with a woman they actively disliked.[46]

Love often involves *respect* for and *admiration* of the beloved; sexual desire often lacks such attitudes. Admiration is different from love in implying distance and hence lack of reciprocity.

Love may express an ambivalent nature: *joy* and *hope*, stemming from being together with the beloved and from the prospects of a happy life, along with *fear* and *jealousy* associated with the fear of losing this person. In sexual desire, which is more concerned with the immediate situation, ambivalence is less central.

The emotional strands typical of romantic love are quite different when it is reciprocal and when it is not. In the former case, we are happier, more positive about life in general, more outgoing, and kinder to others. In the latter case, we are humiliated, angry, anxious, depressed, preoccupied, and unable to concentrate.[47]

Love is often described as the opposite of *hate*. Indeed, the basic evaluative patterns in the two emotions are similar, except that one is positive and the other negative. Whereas hate involves the wish to eliminate the object, love entails the opposite wish: a refusal to exist in a world from which the beloved is absent. The difficulty in claiming that love and hate are diametrically opposed is that there are many kinds of each emotion, and each kind is not the exact opposite of all kinds of the other emotion. Romantic love is not as general as hate, since it involves close contacts with the other person. Love for humanity may be as general as hate, but its feeling dimension is hardly noticed, whereas that of hate is obvious. Is there specific hate as there is specific love? Hate may indeed be directed at a particular person; in this case, it is typically mixed with anger and disgust, as romantic love is typically mixed with gratitude and sexual desire.

There are more kinds of love than of hate; this is perhaps the only pair of correlated emotions in which the positive one is more differentiated than the negative. This is due to the more essential role of the different kinds of love which are important for maintaining the various types of attachments and relations in our social life.[48] Love satisfies our need for human companionship, for an emotional support system, and for the survival of those related to us, especially our off-spring. Love has important functions in preserving social frameworks and fulfilling several biological functions. Hate is less important in this respect and is easier to avoid. Indeed, it is easier to find a person who has never experienced hate than to find a person who has never experienced love. Love also has more varieties than sexual desire, which seems to have only one basic type. The reason for this is not a low survival value of sexual desire, but its primitive nature.

Both hate and love are continuous long-term attitudes. Since the one who hates is hardly in touch with the hated person, this continuity is due to lack of a change in the hater's evaluative patterns. Love may continue despite a genuine change stemming from a more intimate acquaintance with the beloved.

*Gratitude*
Gratitude is a duty which ought to be paid, but which none have a right to expect.
—Jean Jacques Rousseau

If you pick up a starving dog and make him prosperous, he will not bite you. This is the principal difference between a dog and a man.
—Mark Twain

Gratitude is similar to love and sexual desire in that it involves positive evaluations of other people. We typically feel gratitude when we attribute our personal success, at least in part, to others rather than to ourselves alone. Pride in a specific personal success is present when the success is attributed to our own accomplishments. Gratitude is generated when we receive or are about to receive from other people a gift in the form of an action or object. The crucial role that exchanging gifts, or more simply, helping each other, plays in a moral human society can explain the importance of gratitude in such a society. Indeed, the Roman author Cicero claimed that "Gratitude is not only the greatest of virtues, but the parent of all the others."

Gratitude comprises two basic desires: the desire to reward the object personally and the desire for the object's positive evaluation of us. The first desire expresses the positive evaluation of the object; the second reflects our wish to be on an equal footing with the object. The subject-object relationship in gratitude often expresses inequality, with the receiver being in an inferior position. Hence, envy, resentment, and hostility are often associated with gratitude. Elster rightly argues that resentment and hostility may be enhanced rather than attenuated by the act of giving if the recipient suspects that the motive of the donor was in fact to make him feel inferior.[49]

The above considerations explain our desire for reciprocity. A most significant form of reciprocity is to return a gift. If one cannot return the gift immediately, then a tacit promise of future return is part of gratitude. Thus, a common way of expressing gratitude for an act of generosity is to say that one will never forget this act, that is, one will not forget to make the appropriate return at the appropriate time. The giver, who gives willingly, attempts to abolish the impression of inequality and is often uncomfortable with signs of gratitude; accordingly, the giver asks the beneficiary "don't mention it," or "forget it," or says that "it was nothing."[50] Although gratitude is quite strong when an unexpected and unusual good deed is done on our behalf, we may feel even deeper gratitude in response to long-term kindness.

Gratitude does not arise from every gift. A few conditions matter in this respect:

1. *the attitude of the benefactor*—the act of the benefactor is under volitional control (or the benefactor is at least partially responsible) and the action is intended to benefit the recipient;

2. *the attitude of the recipient*—the recipient should receive the gift favorably;

3. *the nature of the gift*—the gift should seem to be extra, that is, something beyond what we normally expect or what justice requires.

The first condition indicates the good intention and responsibility of the giver—as anger implies the ill intention and responsibility of the other. Gratitude is maximized when the gift is given deliberately rather than accidentally and it is intended to benefit only the receiver as opposed to a situation in which the gift enhances the reputation of the giver. When the giver's intention is perceived to be morally wrong, resentment rather than gratitude is likely to emerge.[51] The second condition is required, since there are situations in which we are burdened with a surfeit of gifts which formally oblige us to return the favor. Accordingly, some people generate gratitude for purposes of bribery. The third condition is needed, since social norms define many occasions on which a gift is expected. If the gift does not exceed what we normally expect on such occasions, then intense gratitude, if any, may not result. If the gift is less than what we normally expect, resentment is likely to be provoked.[52]

Characterizing the specifics of the above conditions must make reference to personal and social details. The first two conditions are typically easier to describe, as the attitudes of both parties are typically evident from the given circumstances. For example, it can be assumed that in personal, warm relationships, receiving a very special gift or an exceedingly large number of gifts will usually be appreciated and will be given with good intention. Nevertheless, an excess here may also generate a psychological burden.

Describing the third condition, namely, when a gift is perceived as extra, is sometimes difficult, as it requires determining the personal baseline against which actions or objects seem to be extra. The sociologist Arlie Hochschild describes the complexities of such baselines by examining the generation of gratitude in a two-job marriage:

> A husband does the laundry, makes the beds, washes the dishes. Relative to his father, his brother and several men on the block this husband helps more at home. He also does more than he did ten years ago. All in all he feels he has done more than his wife could reasonably expect, and with good spirit. He has given her, he feels, a gift. She should, he feels, be grateful. However, to his wife the matter seems different. In addition to her eight hours at the office, she does 80% of the housework. Relative to all she does, relative to what she wants to expect of him, what she feels she deserves, her husband's contribution seems welcome, but not extra, not a gift.[53]

The importance of the deservingness issue in gratitude implies that mere consideration of one's neediness is not enough for the generation of gratitude. If we regard our very baseline inferiority as unjust, then we may resent the gift and its giver.[54]

In light of the belief that the other's action exceeds what we formally deserve, gratitude seems to imply unpaid debt. This makes the debtor's position inferior, and it makes the inferior-superior relation a significant component of gratitude. Another possible metaphor of typical gratitude is that of a trustee: gratitude is often like having accepted a deposit rather than like having taken out a loan. Unlike taking out a loan, in receiving a deposit we are not inferior to the object; we already have some credit and do not have to prove ourselves. Whereas loans are associated with shame, deposits are a source of pride.[55] Gratitude involves both types of situations: of debtor and trustee. In cases of real friendship, the trustee metaphor is more adequate than the debtor metaphor; however, in gratitude toward people less close to us, the debtor metaphor is more adequate.

Gratitude is directed at a person who has performed a praiseworthy action which is also desirable from a personal viewpoint. This element of desirability often distinguishes the emotion of gratitude from a nonemotional attitude of mere approval.[56] Likewise, anger is directed at a person who has performed a blameworthy action that is nondesirable from a personal viewpoint. Gratitude and anger are also similar in that they both focus on specific actions for which other people are perceived as responsible, and in that they both encompass an important personal element of desert. In anger, we believe that we are the targets of an undeserved offense; in gratitude, we believe that we are the recipients of a gift we do not deserve. The feeling component is stronger in anger, indicating the greater significance of negative demeaning situations associated with anger.

*Intensity Variables*

To know him is to love him
Just to see him smile
makes my life worthwhile
—The Teddy Bears

A friend is one who knows us, but loves us anyway.
—Fr. Jerome Cummings

The basic factor underlying emotional intensity, namely, *change*, is evident in sexual desire, which is considerably more intense toward a new partner than a familiar one. As someone once said: "You don't want to eat the same vegetable every day." A survey of people after heart attacks indicates that these people should not avoid sex. Of 5559 cases of sudden death, only 18 were related to sexual activity. But of the 18 cases, 14 occurred while having extramarital sex. The excitement of extramarital sex was too much for them. The moral for heart patients, as well as for other people, seems to be quite straightforward: If you want safe sexual relations, stick to your partner; however, if you are looking for excitement, then changing your partner may provide what you need.[57]

In this context, there is an amusing story about the American president, Calvin Coolidge, who once visited a farm with his wife. Soon after their arrival, they were taken off on separate tours. When Mrs. Coolidge passed the chicken pens, she paused to ask the man in charge if the rooster copulates more than once each day. "Dozens of times," was the reply. "Please tell that to the President," Mrs. Coolidge requested. When the President passed the pens and was told about the rooster, he asked: "Same hen every time?" "Oh no, Mr. President, a different one each time." The President nodded slowly, then said, "Tell that to Mrs. Coolidge." In light of this story, the expression "the Coolidge effect" was coined for the phenomenon of male rearousal by a new female. The Coolidge effect is widespread among mammals. Thus, in one study, a cow was placed in a bullpen, and after copulation the cow was replaced with another cow. The bull's sexual response continued unabated with each new cow—even if it was the twelfth female—but diminished quickly when the same cow was left in the pen.[58] It is interesting to note that Jean Jacques Rousseau believed that in the state of nature, any female suffices for man's desire, and that she is always desired for the same old monotonous deed.[59] The presence of the Coolidge effect among mammals casts doubts on this belief.

One way to deal with the problem stemming from the Coolidge effect is to diversify encounters with the present partner, thereby restimulating interest in each other, or to create an imaginary alternative. However, these approaches are typically less effective than replacing the partner. In sexual desire, imagination, rather than knowledge, is the more important element; accordingly, a novel partner induces greater attraction. In long-term love, knowledge is more important; accordingly, marital happiness is positively associated with the length of the courtship period. Incidentally, the longest engagement on record was between a Mexican couple, Octavio Guillen and Adriana Martinez, who took sixty-seven years to make sure they were right for each other.[60]

In some cases a significant change in our situation may lead to a reduction in sexual desire. This may occur when the change is associated, for example, with some threat that frightens us. Many pathological cases of reduced sexual desire are of this nature. These cases do not contradict the general correlation between change and emotional intensity. This kind of change gives rise to other emotions, such as fear, whose presence prevents the generation of sexual desire.

The relationship between romantic love and change is more complex, as it comprises two basic evaluative patterns which may be differently influenced by significant changes. Examining this relationship requires a discussion of the relationship between *liking*, which is a general form of positive attitude found in both love and sexual desire, and *familiarity*, which seems to be the opposite of change.

Momentary liking is positively related to familiarity, at least to some extent. It has been shown, for example, that children's liking for novel food increases with the number of times they are served this food, regardless of whether they actually eat any of it. The correlation between liking and familiarity need not be linear, that is, a given increase in familiarity does not necessarily result in a similar increase in liking. Moreover, from a certain point, there is an inverse correlation between familiarity and liking. Up to a point, "the more the merrier," after which "one can have too much of a good thing." The relationship between familiarity and liking also differs in different objects. Familiarity may decrease the intensity of liking in sexual activity but may increase it in wine: the more we drink the same wine, the more we like it.[61]

There is no doubt that familiarity is an important variable in determining the intensity of liking. The question is what the basic factors constituting familiarity are. An obvious factor is frequency of exposure. Accordingly, the correlation between frequency of exposure and liking is positive. However, exposure alone cannot explain the complexity of the familiarity-liking relationship.

An interesting study concerning familiarity in music may shed some light on the role of familiarity in love and sexual desire.[62] There is evidence indicating that frequency of listening to a certain kind of music may increase the preference for this kind. William Gaver and George Mandler explain this by assuming the continuous activation of relevant evaluative schemes. We like what is closest to the central tendency, the prototype, of a relevant schema. We tend to like music that is typical of its kind. A continuous activation of an evaluative pattern increases familiarity and hence liking. However, too much familiarity produces boredom. Accordingly, we may not like music more, just by virtue of the fact that we are hearing it more. In order to explain the different effects of familiarity, the factor of complexity should be taken into account: simple music is liked less with increased exposure, while a complex piece is liked more. The interaction of familiarity and complexity causes listeners to dislike the incomprehensible, enjoy the newly understood, and be bored by music that is too well-known. The relationship between liking (music) and familiarity is not a simple, direct relationship. Familiarity is required for some understanding of the object; when such understanding is achieved, new elements have greater emotional weight.

Romantic love may be explained along similar lines. We tend to fall in love with, and be sexually attracted to, those who are the best examples of attractive persons. The claim, "gentlemen prefer blondes," reflects (if true) the basic evaluative pattern of gentlemen. Within the group of blonds, there are the better examples to whom gentlemen are more attracted. The positive evaluation in music and love is not merely a function of exposure, but is based on a certain favorite prototype. The presence of such a prototype in love can explain why so many people keep falling in love with partners who resemble each other and seem to be of a similar type, even when that type has proved disastrous several times in the past. There is a kind of return to earlier love in such a phenomenon, but one should not take this to its extreme Freudian interpretation, assuming that it can only have been the first love—an infant's love for its parents.[63] The prototype is not a rigid structure that cannot be modified or even completely changed, as is the case in music too. The prototype in sexual desire is simple; that in love is richer, more complex, and more specific. In light of the flexible nature of our evaluative patterns, there is room for change in our romantic dispositions. Accordingly, the ideal object of love or sexual desire is, to a certain extent, a constructed entity depending on changeable personal and social characteristics.

Familiarity often correlates directly with romantic love. Mere exposure, in the absence of anything else, makes people more favorably inclined to each other.[64] However, mere exposure only sets the scene for falling in love. People become lovers not just because they happen to see each other every day. Rather, frequent meetings enable them to further deepen their concern for and attachment to each other. This may be one explanation why people tend to marry someone living near them. Yet, knowing someone is a necessary, but not a sufficient, condition for developing profound love. Moreover, sometimes too much knowledge may hinder the development of a love relationship. Love, like other emotions, is associated with a significant degree of imagination, thereby enabling us to idealize the beloved. Full and detailed knowledge may block this ability as it reduces the availability of any alternative. The better we know the essential nature of things, the less emotional impact they usually have upon us. There is indeed some evidence suggesting that marriage is less common among people who grew up together into adulthood.[65]

As in the case of music, the complexity of the object is an important factor in determining whether love will be more or less intense as a result of greater familiarity: a simple psychological object is liked less with exposure, while a complex object is liked more. Romantic love refers to a complex psychological personality, with numerous aspects, whereas sexual desire refers to a few, mainly external, aspects. Accordingly, sexual desire is considerably increased by replacing the object, as too much familiarity may decrease sexual excitement and produce boredom. In contrast, increasing the intensity of love often involves increasing familiarity with the object. Replacing the object is often a temporary and elusive remedy for love. An indication of this is that very few people who leave their marriage for a lover eventually remain with that lover. Enhancing novelty and excitement in romantic love does not necessarily mean replacing the object; indeed, knowing the object better can make for heightened novelty and excitement. Hence, learning plays a greater role in romantic love than in sexual desire. Novelty has a less significant role in love than in sexual desire, since love is a longer-lasting and more profound relationship; as such, it must be related to more permanent features. The issue of novelty is even less significant in parental love.

An obvious difficulty in assuming a positive correlation between romantic love and familiarity is that sexual desire is an important component of romantic love, and in light of the Coolidge effect, there is a negative correlation between sexual desire and familiarity. Increasing familiarity has, then, two major opposing effects upon the intensity of romantic love: liking increases, but sexual desire decreases. There may be some love relationships in which sexual desire is so important that increasing familiarity reduces the intensity of love. However, since liking involves a more comprehensive attitude, the intensity of love may increase. Moreover, we should distinguish between sexual desire and sexual satisfaction. Sexual desire is a relatively simple desire and as such can be generated by many objects, whereas sexual satisfaction is a more complex emotional experience in which familiarity plays a more significant role. This explains why monogamous married couples report greater emotional satisfaction from their sexual lives than do single people or married people having affairs on the side. Ironically, married people having affairs often report better sex with their primary partners than through secondary relationships.[66] Familiarity is important for sexual satisfaction, as it makes the relationship less stressful and more comfortable, enabling a more intimate acquaintance with the partner's needs and desires.

The positive correlation between familiarity and love is also problematic with regard to the group of variables constituting our *readiness*, namely, unexpectedness and uncertainty. The variables of this group are obviously in direct opposition to familiarity. In order to deal with this difficulty, we should describe familiarity as referring to our basic evaluative framework, and unexpectedness or uncertainty as referring to specific deviation from this framework. Loving someone presupposes that the evaluation of this person is compatible with our evaluative framework. Unexpected activities of this person may increase our emotional intensity. Generally, the variables of readiness are less important in long-term emotions, such as love and hate, referring to profound characteristics. In transient emotions, such as gratitude and sexual desire, these variables take on more significance. Hence, mystery is more important in sexual desire than in love. Nevertheless, unexpectedness and uncertainty do play some role in long-term romantic love. Their role is to help us realize that despite the close relation with the beloved, this person is not part of the furniture; the beloved is an independent agent who cannot be taken for granted.

Another global variable for emotional intensity is *reality*: the more real the situation, the more intense the emotion. This variable is more important in love than in sexual desire, since love involves a more profound relationship. What are the implications of the role the reality variable plays in love and sexual desire, and what role does imagination play in both these emotions? We should distinguish in this respect between (a) imagining an alternative to our present partner, and (b) imagining our partner while he or she is away. The fact that love is a more profound attitude implies that the first instance is stronger in sexual desire and the second in love. People can be sexually attracted to their partners while fantasizing about someone else; people cannot really love their partners while constantly fantasizing about others. In this case imagination plays a stronger role in sexual fantasy than love. Imagination is stronger in love when the partner is absent. Since love involves a more profound and comprehensive relationship, it can survive the temporary absence of the beloved. Love can persist and even intensify in the temporary absence of the beloved, as expressed in the popular wisdom that "absence makes the heart grow fonder." In sexual desire, which involves a more superficial and specific relationship, sorrow over the mate's absence is shorter and less intense. Similarly, the absence of the emotional object usually decreases anger but not hate.

The variable of *relevance* for our well-being is important in love as in other emotions. As previously suggested, our wish for the beloved's well-being is not separated from considerations of our own well-being. The reciprocal nature of romantic love indicates the importance of this variable to love. In sexual desire, the well-being of the object is of lesser importance, and the relevance to our own good feeling and particularly for our self-esteem is very crucial.

The variable of closeness is another factor constituting the relevance of the event. Many findings indicate the importance of background similarity in choosing a mate; dissimilarity is often a source of dissatisfaction and conflicts. Background similarity is manifested in many aspects, including education, socioeconomic background, race, religion, cultural background, physical attractiveness, general attitudes concerning issues like desired family size, sex roles, abortion, capital punishment, and so on. Today, education is an important factor in this regard as it both provides occasions to meet other people and it often expresses the status and opportunities of the other person. It was found, for example, that college attendance is a far better predictor of marriage than religion, ethnicity, or even income.[67]

In parental love, too, the perceived similarity is important. A perception that the child is different from the parent often reduces parental love.[68] The importance of similarity in parental love is expressed in the fact that when a new baby is born, one of the first questions that is often asked is "Who does the baby look like?" Background similarity, especially genetic similarity, is probably a major factor in explaining why parental love is typically more intense than romantic love, despite the more exclusive nature of romantic love: at any given time we can love more children than romantic partners. I recently visited an old lady whose son had been killed in the army over twenty-five years ago, while her husband had died just a few months previously. She spent over fifty happy years with her husband; her son was only twenty years old when he was killed. Nevertheless, she did not cry when she spoke about her husband whom she had greatly loved, but about her son she could say no more than a few sentences before bursting into tears. Her child's death evoked much greater sorrow than her husband's, despite the fact that her husband's death was much more recent and that she had spent much more time with him than with her son. Although the more intense sorrow for her son's death was also influenced by the unnatural death of the son, by the pain of a tragically brief life, and perhaps by other factors as well, I believe that greater similarity in background, and especially genetic similarity, is a crucial factor in this regard.

Proximity in current position is another important factor influencing romantic love. For example, proximity in socioeconomic status contributes to forming romantic bonds. Similarly, people who judge themselves to be low in certain personality traits, such as intelligence, creativity, responsibility, and industriousness, express a desire for mates who are also low in them. Likewise, although initial romantic attraction depends on the partner's desirability, so that the most desirable partners elicit the strongest attraction, people eventually settle into relationships with partners whose attractiveness is about equal to their own.[69] This does not mean that Cinderella's good fortune is not possible, but the likelihood of its happening is not high.

Similarity and proximity, however, are somewhat vague properties. Thus, one can find similarities and dissimilarities between any two human beings. Love depends on many different factors, and it would undoubtedly be an oversimplification to explain it by referring merely to similarity. Nevertheless, some measure of similarity and proximity is usually helpful in maintaining love relations. Referring to the notion of a comfort zone, we may say that our partner should be within the core of our comfort zone; this requirement, which is fulfilled by the similarity factor, ensures that we will feel comfortable with the partner. However, in order to ensure excitement in the relationship, the partner should be able to expand our comfort zone; this may be fulfilled if the partner is somewhat different from ourselves. Opposites do attract, since they may enlarge our comfort zone, but significant differences can throw us out of our emotional equilibrium into discomfort.[70]

In the case of sexual desire, the relationship is more limited in nature, and the issues of background similarity and proximity are of less importance; differences and changes are more significant. The longer the sexual relationship endures, the more important the issues of similarity and proximity become, as these indicate the couple's compatibility.

The variable of *controllability* is usually of little significance to love and sexual desire. Concerning the object's control, it is usually taken for granted that the object is in full control of the situation, and hence what appears as the object's love or sexual desire is genuine. When we have doubts in this regard, as when we suspect that the object is continuing the relationship only out of pity, then love and sexual desire decrease. Our own control is also insignificant in love and sexual desire, since these emotions focus on the present situation, and retrospective considerations concerning the way the emotions were generated are usually unimportant.

Our *effort* has some role in the generation of love and sexual desire. If a person seems unattainable these emotions are stronger. As someone once suggested, "By keeping men off, you keep them on." This has become known as the Romeo and Juliet effect: if real impediments exist, such as a family feud or marriage to another person, our love or sexual desire is likely to intensify. Indeed, playing hard to get is a most effective strategy for attracting a partner. It should be noted, however, that when the required effort is too immense and the probability of its success is low, people may give up the idea and may not invest extra effort. At a certain point, an increase in the effort required decreases emotional intensity since people begin to believe that the outcome for which the effort is being invested is actually unattainable and hence unreal.

Sometimes the opposite of the Romeo and Juliet effect is true: the more available the person, the more intense the sexual desire. Indeed, accepting a person's sexual invitations is the most effective way for someone to attract a prospective partner into a casual liaison. There are many signals that women use to convey their interest to men. Such signals include darting glances, head tossing, lip-licking, hair-flicking, as well as coy smiles, and dancing alone. Signals like these can indicate availability and have a strong seductive effect. This effect is due to the general correlation between the availability of an alternative and emotional intensity. It has been argued that these signals predict who will be approached by whom 90 percent of the time and the frequency and intensity of these gestures are a better predictor of which women will be approached by men than is their physical beauty. There is also evidence suggesting that perceived opportunity is a significant factor in extramarital sexual affairs. This is in accordance with a more general tendency of ours: we tend to be drawn to those who show signs of friendliness and cooperation.[71]

In what circumstances are each of the seemingly contradictory tactics, namely, playing hard to get or playing easy to get, more effective? The tactic of playing hard to get is most effective when used in the context of long-term love or the marital context in which a person wishes to be sure of the partner's fidelity. Long-term romantic love may have significant and enduring benefits for us and hence we are ready to invest a lot of effort and other resources in order to attain it. Playing hard to get forces the other person to make significant investments and ensures that indeed this person is ready to make a commitment to an enduring relationship. The tactic of playing easy to get is most effective when used by someone in the context of casual sex, where availability is the most important commodity. In this context, people are not ready to make a significant investment since the benefits are smaller and more temporary; hence, playing hard to get here will not be effective at all.

Both tactics are less effective when used by men. The more overt the sexual advances by men, the less attractive women find them—probably because women do not want men to consider them promiscuous. Playing hard to get is also less effective in men, as they are the ones who are socially expected to initiate the relationship.[72]

The variable of *deservingness* also plays an important role in love and sexual desire. The more we believe that we do not deserve such a good partner, the more intense our love and sexual desire may become. In these cases the emotional attitude may be more ambivalent, since fear, jealousy, and envy are more dominant. When we think that our partner does not deserve us, our love and sexual desire will be reduced, and we are likely to look for other partners. Here the issue of deservingness is closely related to that of the event's strength: a partner we do not deserve is a more attractive person than the one who does not deserve us.

In this context it is relevant to mention the equity theory which postulates that those involved in an inequitable relationship feel there is something unfair or undeserved in such relationships. This is the case for the overbenefited, who feel guilty because they receive more from the relationship than their partner does, as well as for the underbenefited, who feel hurt because they receive less than their partner. Involvement in extramarital relationships can sometimes be explained as a way of restoring equity. One obvious consequence of such relationships, which has been confirmed in empirical studies, is that the more deprived persons feel in their marriage, the more concessions they expect their partners to make and the more likely they are to risk engaging in extramarital sex. A more surprising result is that the overbenefited will also be more inclined to become involved in sexual relationships outside their marriage. At least two major reasons can explain this result: (1) inequity is an adverse state that persons seek to escape, (2) overbenefited persons justify their situation by proving to themselves and their partner that they are attractive to the opposite sex. It seems then that inequity in marriage may result in extramarital relationships as a way to restore equity. Even those who have moral objections to extramarital affairs might contemplate such a relationship when their marriage is inequitable. The issue of inequity is more salient for women; this may be due to the disadvantaged position of women in our society and to double standards assuming that women should have better reasons for engaging in extramarital relationships than men.[73]

*Hurting the One You Love*

A typical feature of love is its ambivalent nature which sometimes is even manifested in hurting the beloved. This phenomenon is expressed in the unforgettable song of the Mills Brothers (written by Allan Roberts and Doris Fisher):

You always hurt the one you love, the one you should not hurt at all;
You always take the sweetest rose, and crush it till the petals fall;
You always break the kindest heart, with a hasty word you can't recall;
So if I broke your heart last night, it's because I love you most of all.

An interesting question is why the song's theme is "You always hurt the one *you love*" rather than "You always hurt the one who *loves you*"? To defend the second claim is easier. This claim is not problematic from a psychological viewpoint; it has more to do with moral difficulty than with psychological perplexity. Indeed, hurting the one who loves you is a common phenomenon. The question is whether the other claim—"You always hurt the one you love"—is plausible as well. This claim presents a puzzling psychological attitude: in addition to the very strong positive evaluation of the beloved, there also exists a strong negative evaluation expressed in harm to this person. To illustrate the problematic nature of this claim, consider a case in which you are writing a song about envy on the theme, "You always discredit the one you admire." Again we find it easier understanding the claim, "You always discredit the one who admires you."

A tendency to hurt can be interpreted either as (a) *likely to hurt* without intending to do so, or (b) *intending to hurt*. We can easily show that the lover is likely to hurt the beloved without intending to do so. Love is a close and intense relationship. The lovers spend considerable time together, and many activities of each have significant implications for the other person. Naturally in such circumstances, the lover may unwillingly hurt the beloved. For instance, you may devote a lot of time to your work, thereby neglecting, and unwillingly hurting, your beloved. In many cases a byproduct of an enjoyable activity for one person is an unpleasant situation for another. The more time two people spend together, the greater the likelihood of such situations. The great significance in our life of those we love is that these people are both a source of great happiness and deep sadness; they may benefit us as well as hurt us.[74]

The phenomenon of hurting without intending to do so can also be explained by referring to the trust and sincerity which are essential to love. Accordingly, the role of politeness or good manners, which may prevent some kinds of insult, is of less importance in such a relationship, and lovers are less careful in what they say and do. This opens the way for a lover to easily get hurt. As the song indicates: "You always break the kindest heart, with a *hasty* word you can't recall." The price of being able to behave freely without having to consider every consequence of your deeds is saying and doing hasty things that may hurt your lover. Another relevant consideration in this context is that each partner in love usually has firsthand, intimate knowledge of the other. Hasty use of this knowledge in conflicts hurts considerably. Truth is usually more painful than slander, since it is more difficult to dismiss.

Generally, the absence of disappointment means that there is nothing valuable to lose. In love, which involves much happiness and valuable moments to trea-

sure, there is much to lose. Hence, disappointment and frustration, and consequently hurt, are common. It has, therefore, been said that no joyous love exists.
Indeed, in a survey of over five hundred lovers, almost all of them took for granted
that passionate love is a bittersweet experience. Similarly, it has been found that
people low in defensiveness have more experiences of love than do highly defensive people. This link suggests that to love is to make oneself vulnerable in ways
that enhance the possibilities of pain.[75]

These considerations indicate how easily you may hurt your beloved without
intending to do so. Our everyday life is full of such occurrences. However, to
explain hurting a loved one on purpose is more complex, as it involves emotional
ambivalence, namely, the presence of two conflicting evaluations in the same attitude. Love expresses a basically positive evaluation of the beloved, whereas
intending to hurt someone reflects a negative evaluation of that person. This
ambivalence is usually absent when hurting the beloved without intending to do
so; in this case, hurting does not stem from a negative evaluation but from the
unique circumstances of love. In the case of hurting a beloved on purpose, the
presence of two conflicting evaluations of the same person is puzzling. In order
to establish the possibility of intending to hurt the beloved, the possibility of emotional ambivalence should be established first. Then it will remain to be seen how
typical this situation is in love.

Emotional ambivalence is present when the same attitude contains (at least) two
conflicting emotional evaluations. For example, envy involves both a positive
evaluation of the other's achievements and a negative evaluation of the other's
good fortune. Similarly, anger involves displeasure with an unjustified insult and
pleasure with the anticipation of revenge. Similar situations are found in cases in
which we enjoy a sad movie or sadly drink a glass of good wine and yet enjoy its
bouquet. The positive evaluation is expressed here in the enjoyment of the movie
or the wine and the negative evaluation concerns the movie's sad story or our sad
mood.

Emotional ambivalence does not merely refer to contradictory emotional evaluations occurring at different times. It also applies to situations in which
conflicting evaluations coexist at the same point in time. The negative and positive evaluations involved in envy belong to the same state. Similarly, our song
does not contain different tenses; it goes, "You always hurt the one you *love*,"
rather than, "You always hurt the one you *loved*."

At first glance, emotional ambivalence is incompatible with love. Thus, it has
been claimed that part of love's magic is the freedom it grants from the ambivalence inherent to most relationships.[76] Contrary to this contention, I will show that
emotional ambivalence is typical of romantic love too.

The most plausible way to explain emotional ambivalence is to assume the presence of diverse *perspectives* which stem from our intentional capability to know
and evaluate the object in different ways. Since not all perspectives refer to
the same aspect, they do not necessarily involve the same evaluation. Each

perspective is partial and does not have to be compatible with other perspectives. Two major conflicting perspectives typical of emotional ambivalence are those evaluating (1) diverse aspects of the emotional object, and (2) the value for the subject and for the object. In order to display the ambivalent nature of love, we should demonstrate that these two perspectives are typical of love.

A common conflict in evaluating different aspects of the same object is the conflict between a global and a partial perspective: the global perspective often refers to the agent's overall well-being, whereas the partial perspective refers to more limited benefits. This conflict surfaces in several forms, for example, in clashes between long-term and short-term considerations, or between enjoyable situations and moral or health considerations. The global-partial conflict is obvious in the love of parents for their children. This love involves deep concern for the children's overall well-being, even though the children themselves often do not share this concern, particularly when it conflicts with satisfying their immediate wishes.

The conflict between long-term and short-term considerations is also common in romantic love. The lover may evaluate the wishes of the beloved negatively because they clash with the overall well-being of the beloved. Sometimes such a deep concern is even more dominant in the lover than in the beloved. A positive global evaluation of the beloved can coexist with a negative partial evaluation of some specific traits, actions, and wishes of the beloved. Although love requires a positive general evaluation of the beloved's individuality as a whole, it does not necessarily involve a positive evaluation of each aspect and activity of this person. True, lovers consider many of the beloved's characteristics as virtues where others see faults; nevertheless, lovers are not completely blind to faults of the beloved.

The conflict between global and particular considerations may also take the form of a clash between first- and second-order considerations. This is the way we can explain cases such as enjoying a sad movie. Our sadness is directed at the events in the movie, and our enjoyment is a second-order experience referring to the movie's impact upon us. Similarly, it has been claimed that many British people are uncomfortable, or even embarrassed, while experiencing emotion. This embarrassment is again a second-order experience.

A partial perspective can not only conflict with a global one but also with another partial perspective. Since people have complex personalities, we may evaluate some of their characteristics positively and others negatively. In envy, we may evaluate the talent of a rich person positively, but negatively evaluate that person's dishonest behavior. Similarly, in love you may evaluate the beauty of the beloved positively, but negatively evaluate that person's intelligence. In light of the intimate knowledge involved in love, each partner knows many shortcomings of the other and evaluates them negatively.

Another type of conflicting emotional evaluation is that between the value for us and for others. This conflict is obvious in envy. When evaluating the success of my neighbor without taking into consideration its effect on my position, this success is evaluated positively and may please me. However, when the competitive concern is brought to bear, the neighbor's success may indicate my failure. Accordingly, envy involves both admiration for and sorrow over the other's success. This kind of conflict and emotional ambivalence is typical of love too. Since love involves a close and intimate relationship, the activities of each partner have significant implications for the situation of the other. An activity considered positive from the viewpoint of one person may not be so from the angle of the other person or from the viewpoint of their relationship. A man may evaluate his wife's dedication to her work positively, but when considering the effects of this dedication on their relationship, he may evaluate it negatively. In love, as in other emotions, a positive correlation does not always occur between the positive evaluation of the other's action as such and its evaluation from our perspective. We can conclude that emotional ambivalence is not problematic if we take it to express different perspectives of a complex emotional attitude.[77]

After explaining emotional ambivalence and showing that it is present in romantic love, we are now in a position to explain the perplexing phenomenon of hurting the beloved. It is one thing to have conflicting evaluations toward the beloved, but quite another to actually hurt the beloved. Emotional ambivalence is a necessary, but not a sufficient, condition for hurting the beloved. Let us now examine what factors are responsible for turning emotional ambivalence toward the beloved into a situation which hurts.

A major factor in this regard is connected with the central role of mutual dependency in love. Mutual dependency may exist in inappropriate proportions: lovers can consider their dependency on the partner to be too great or too little. Hurting the beloved may be one resort, usually the last one, which the lover takes to bring this dependency to its appropriate proportion. Mutual dependency has many advantages, stemming from the fact that two people are joined together in an attempt to increase each other's happiness. However, a sense of independence is also important for each person's self-esteem. Indeed, in a study of anger, the most common motive for its generation was to assert authority or independence, or to improve self image. Anger has been perceived as a useful means to strengthen or readjust a relationship.[78] This type of behavior is frequent in the child-parent relationship: children often hurt parents in order to express their independence. This behavior is also part of romantic love in which mutual dependency may threaten each partner's independence. Sometimes lovers hurt their beloved in order to show their independence. Other times, however, hurting the beloved expresses an opposite wish: the lover's wish for more dependency and attention. Indeed, a common complaint of married women, far more than of married men, is that their partners do not spend enough time with them.[79]

By hurting the beloved, the lover wishes to signal that their mutual relationship, and in particular their mutual dependency, should be modified. Hurting the beloved may be the last alarm bell that warns of the lover's difficulties; it is an extreme measure signaling urgency. If the relationship is strong enough, as the lover wishes it to be, it should sustain this measure. A less extreme and more common measure employed is that of moodiness. Moodiness, which imposes a small cost on the relationship, may function as both an alarm bell and as an assessment device to test the strength of the bond. In hurting their beloved, lovers either wish to assert their independence or to seek further dependency in the sense of receiving more attention. Love involves a dynamic process of mutual adaptation, but not all adaptive processes are smooth and enjoyable; hurting the beloved is an example in kind.[80]

Another consideration, in light of which the lover may sometimes hurt the beloved, is related to the lack of indifference in love. Since the lover greatly cares for the beloved and their mutual relationship, the lover cannot be indifferent toward anything that may harm the beloved or the lover's own position. This lack of indifference toward the beloved may lead the lover to take measures which hurt the other when viewed within a partial perspective, but which can be seen as beneficial from a global perspective. This is the painful side of care: a close connection exists between the things that help and the things that hurt. Sometimes "we regard love as a *justification* for treating people far worse than we would ever condone treating a stranger."[81] In the same way that improving the quality and happiness of our lives may demand some suffering, improving the quality and happiness of our beloved's life may require such suffering.

As for people who love us but whom we do not love, we may be indifferent, or at least would not harbor such a deep overall concern. Accordingly, we may not bother to help them by hurting them. Therefore, people in love prefer to be hurt by the beloved rather than be treated with indifference. The person in love "prefers the anguish which her beloved causes her to painless indifference."[82] Similarly, the saying goes that it is better to break someone's heart than to do nothing with it. Concerning those who are near and dear, we prefer anger to indifference.

I do not want to say, as Oscar Wilde did, that "each man kills the thing he loves"; however, hurting one's beloved is frequent. Since the beloved is a major source of happiness, this person is also a major threat to our happiness; more than anyone else, the beloved can ruin it. Similarly, the security involved in love goes together with the fear of losing that security. Feeling happy is often bound up with the fear of losing that happiness. Caring for the beloved sometimes goes together with hurting the beloved.

Cases in which we do not intend to hurt the beloved but nevertheless do so are more frequent than cases in which we hurt the beloved on purpose. Hurting the beloved deliberately should be viewed as a means of achieving a certain goal. When such hurt is frequent, it is often a goal in itself, rather than an avoidable means. Hurting the beloved without intending to do so is usually neither a means nor a goal of the lover's actions; it is an unwitting byproduct of these actions.

Love is closely connected with vulnerability: the ability to hurt and to be hurt. Although some kinds of hurt in love are intended, most of them are not. Nevertheless, someone who deliberately hurts another person can simultaneously claim to love that person. The phenomenon of emotional ambivalence, stemming from the presence of two different evaluative perspectives, can account for such a possibility. The lack of indifference and mutual dependency typical of love suggest why this frequently occurs in love.

*Moral Value*

Give me chastity and continence—but not yet.
—Saint Augustine

I love being married. It's so great to find that one special person you want to annoy for the rest of your life.
—Rita Rudner

Fidelity is possible—anything is possible, if you're stubborn and strong. But it's not that important.
—Michelle Pfeiffer

Love is morally desirable in that it increases attachment between people, and this is of utmost importance in maintaining social and personal relationships. The great importance of care and attachment in human affairs makes it obvious that we should consider those who fail to love as sinners.[83]

As in other emotions, romantic love lacks a broad perspective. For example, romantic love involves impatience, namely, a narrow temporal perspective. In light of its discriminative nature, it has been argued that it is impossible to love and be wise and that love's true opposite is justice. Hence, little wonder that Stevie Wonder claims that "all in love is fair." This is not to say that love is always compatible with moral norms, but that everything done in love is fair within that context; in this sense, considerations of fairness are irrelevant to love. It seems that Mr. Wonder's declaration pushes a basically sound insight a bit too far. If we wish to emphasize our active involvement in love, then we should argue that love's true opposite is indifference rather than fairness or justice. Although both claims reflect important aspects of love, being indifferent is less compatible with love than being just.

Moral criticism of love is often directed at some particular instances of it, mainly when love is excessive or causes damage to us and other people. This may occur, for instance, when love leads someone to concentrate exclusively on the interests of the beloved. Such criticism, however, is not directed at the emotion itself; all types of excess are harmful. It is interesting to note that moral criticism of negative emotions is mainly directed at the emotions themselves. Moral defense of these emotions is usually based on the social and personal context in which they appear. The case of positive emotions is the opposite. In and of themselves, these emotions are morally recommended. Their moral criticism concerns the particular social and personal context in which they appear.

In contrast to love, sexuality itself is widely held to be morally negative unless it is expressed within an accepted social framework such as marriage or is part of romantic love. Sexuality for its own sake as, for instance, in commercial sex or in casual, uncommitted relations, is often perceived to be morally wrong. The difficulty with such a critical attitude is that, like most other emotions, sexual desire is a transient state typical of short-term relationships; restricting it to long-term relationships is often an artificial demand which is incompatible with the major variables responsible for its generation. In the same way that anger is not restricted to hatred, sexuality should not be restricted to romantic love. In many cases, the short-term states of anger and sexual desire are not compatible with the long-term attitudes of hate and love.

Although sexual desire increases attachment between people, it is often condemned because of the moral restrictions many societies impose upon sexual relations. Because of the crucial place of sexuality in romantic love, this type of love is also sometimes criticized as being sinful. It is interesting to note the gulf between a psychological evaluation of sexual activity and a moral evaluation. From a psychological viewpoint, sexual activities are one of the most enjoyable and hence valuable of our activities; from a moral viewpoint, this activity is often criticized. The issue of an extensive sexual experience can illustrate this difference. From a psychological viewpoint, such an experience is highly valuable as it usually increases sexual satisfaction; from a moral viewpoint, such an experience is usually a negative mark—especially when referring to women. Women are often valued not for their sexual experience but for their sexual innocence. Accordingly, a woman who has intercourse with multiple sexual partners is usually referred to as a "loose woman," "slut," or "whore" and not as a "liberated woman," or "skilled sexual performer."[84]

A major moral dilemma with regard to positive emotions toward other people is whether the great attachment to the object does not imply neglecting the needs of other people or being uncritical toward the object. Because of the discriminative nature of love, an intense positive attitude toward someone may be in conflict with positive attitudes toward other people. The more intense the love is, the more discriminative it is, and hence the more acute is the problem of our attitude toward those who are not included in this particular relationship.

The moral problem of loyalty is similar: does our loyalty to someone imply immoral behavior toward someone else? The problem of loyalty is also part of the complex relationship between romantic love and sexual desire. Can one be in love with someone, but still be sexually attracted to someone else? This is a psychological question whose answer is obviously positive. The moral question in this regard is different: should one, while in love, have sexual relations with someone else? In other words, does romantic love require full-time loyalty? Whereas the moral ideals in most societies state that romantic love does in fact demand such loyalty, the moral practices of many people do not abide by this ideal. Loving someone does not necessarily preclude sexual desire for someone else. The nature of love is exclusive, even though there is no convincing evidence for total exclusivity. This explains the above-mentioned gap between moral norms and moral practices. Since changing the psychological nature of love and sexual desire is hard to achieve, reducing the gap between moral norms and actual practices in the future is more likely to be in the direction of relaxing the norms rather than changing our psychological nature.

A central problem of romantic love concerns the possibility and moral desirability of maintaining lifelong romantic commitments. This problem is particularly acute concerning whether romantic love and marriage necessarily go together. People have indicated different conditions evoked by romantic love—being in a thrilling dream, idealization of the other, interest-free emotion, considering only the present—and those necessary for a successful marriage—sharing the dullness of daily life, coping with a less-than-perfect other, the responsibilities of family and work, considering the future. This is the difference between ideal romance and the realistic maintenance of a relationship.[85] Indeed, some characteristics of marital satisfaction require nonemotional attitudes. This is true, for example, concerning the need to make compromises, the ability to handle differences, and a sense of humor. These characteristics are contrary to the partial and intense nature of emotions. Accordingly, one study has found that when a relationship begins, negative emotions are typically not discussed; when the relationship continues there is more place for expressing negative emotions, and once the relationship stabilizes (as in marriage), emotions are hardly discussed.[86] Other characteristics of marital satisfaction, such as commitment to the spouse, respect for the spouse, and trust in the spouse, are often associated with emotional attitudes and especially with love. It seems that a successful marriage requires a combination of both emotional and nonemotional attitudes.

Although love is central to choosing a mate in modern society, quite a few people marry someone with whom they are not in love. It is clear that the fact that two people are married does not indicate the presence of love, but in many cases may rather suggest the centrality of economic considerations. Thus, there is a clear correlation between women's economic independence and divorce rates.[87]

Indeed, many people have claimed that marriage and romantic love are a contradiction in terms. The following are a few examples.

- "Most marriages do not express enduring love: lasting marriages are based less upon love than upon truce." Richard Taylor
- "Love is an obsessive delusion that is cured by marriage." Karl Bowman
- "Those who want to read about love and marriage should buy two separate books." Alan King
- "Marriage is like a bank account. You put it in, you take it out, you lose interest." Irwin Corey

· "It is most unwise for people in love to marry." George Bernard Shaw
· "A husband is what is left of the lover after the nerve has been extracted."
Helen Rowland
· "If you want to sacrifice the admiration of many men for the criticism of
one, go ahead, get married." Katharine Hepburn
·    "I just want what every married woman wants, someone besides her
husband to sleep with." Peg Bundy, the character on the television show
*Married with Children*

It is obvious that the connection between love and marriage is not a necessary
logical connection; the question is whether it is a typical or prevailing connection.
This depends, among other things, on the given society. Thus, it has been claimed
that the opposition between the "dullness of marriage" and the "thrill of romance"
was a central idea in popular American culture of the eighteenth and nineteenth
centuries. Only in the first half of the twentieth century did advertising and
movies advance a new vision of love as a utopia wherein marriage should be eter-
nally exciting and romantic.[88] Obviously this is not always the case. There are quite
a few happy marriages in which the couple have decided not to have sexual relations at all.

Despite a prevailing negative attitude toward marriage, empirical research indicates that married people are happier than single people and are more satisfied
with their sex life.[89] It seems that marriage provides a good opportunity for long-
term love if other conditions are met as well.

A common attempt to overcome certain shortcomings of marriage and still
enjoy some of its benefits is that of having a lover. Although providing the sexual
excitement of a new partner, a lover still allows keeping the marriage relationship.
Having a lover encounters its own difficulties concerning the attitudes of each one
of the romantic triangle. The moral problem in this regard mainly concerns the
lies, deceptions, and exploitation which are often part of such sexual relationships.
Generally speaking, the major moral fault of adultery (namely, extramarital sex)
and promiscuity (namely, sex with a series of other adults, not directly related
through marriage, with no commitments) lies not in noncommittal sex but in the
violation of moral principles such as to keep promises, to tell the truth, and not
to deceive or exploit others. Accordingly, adultery and promiscuity themselves
may be considered to be morally neutral; however, things that are typically associated with them in our society are wrong.[90]

In acts of adultery and promiscuity in which the above moral principles are
not violated, for example, "open marriage" in which each partner is allowed to
have sexual relationships with other people provided that it is not kept secret, the
major difficulty may not be moral but rather emotional. The many sexual partners may eliminate the discriminative nature which is so important for the generation of intense emotions. Moreover, the lack of commitment may raise the

question of whether we are still speaking here about marriage in the deep sense of the term.

Benjamin Franklin, who wrote a book entitled *Advice to a Young Man on the Choice of a Mistress*, suggested a way to reduce these difficulties. Though he said that marriage is best, he added that if one does not take his advice and insists on having a mistress, one should prefer old women to young ones. Franklin listed eight reasons for preferring older mistresses:

1. Older women have greater knowledge of the world.
2. When women cease to be handsome, they study to be good: they supplement the diminution of beauty by an augmentation of utility.
3. There is no hazard of children.
4. They are more discreet in conducting an affair.
5. Although an older woman could be distinguished from a younger one by her face, regarding only what is below the girdle it is impossible to distinguish an old woman from a young one.
6. The sin is less, as the debauching of a virgin may make her unhappy for life.
7. The compunction is less: having made a young girl miserable may give you frequent bitter reflections, none of which attend making an older woman happy.
8. Older women are more grateful.[91]

Despite the deep insights provided by Franklin, it is still doubtful whether having an older woman as a mistress will solve all moral and emotional difficulties connected with having an affair.

The moral issue of marital fidelity, as expressed, for example, in traditional wedding vows, which include a commitment "to love and to cherish till death do us part," is quite complex. I suggest that from a psychological point of view, keeping such a vow is quite difficult, though not impossible. Given such a psychological difficulty, one may doubt whether lifelong romantic commitments are morally desirable. The central objection to lifetime romantic commitments is that love is an emotion and that it is incomprehensible to commit ourselves to a certain emotion. This is so since either the external circumstances or our own personal dialectics may change, thereby rendering infeasible the continuation of the initial emotional attitude.

In response to this objection, it can be claimed that a commitment to love is not aimed at creating emotions from scratch; it is aimed at sustaining an already-present dynamic. A commitment to love does not imply manipulation of emotions; it implies the intention to ignore the inevitable periods in a relationship when the emotion of love is not experienced.[92] Marriage is an act of placing trust in the relationship, rather than merely hoping or expecting it to succeed. Such a trust is essential, since it tends to be self-fulfilling. Indeed, many marriages still last for life. However, love commitments are conditional on two major factors: (1) that there is no substantial change in the persons involved as they grow older, and (2) that there is something good in the love relationship.[93] Maintaining romantic love for a long time requires effort and other activities which create circumstances conducive to its maintenance. However, if we consider this relationship to be valuable, we should attempt to maintain it. Generally, we bear far greater responsibility for our long-term than for our short-term emotions. Accordingly, moral praise or condemnation of people maintaining long-term emotions should be stronger.

# Chapter 15

# Caring about Oneself—Happiness and Sadness

---

The young man who has not wept is a savage, and the old man who will not laugh is a fool.
—George Santayana

So far I have discussed the group of emotions directed toward others; in this chapter I examine the other group of emotions, namely, those directed at oneself. The discussion of this group will be briefer since I have already addressed these emotions while describing the previous group of emotions, and many of the arguments made in connection with the first group are valid for the second group as well. Within the group of emotions directed at oneself, I first discuss emotions like happiness and sadness, which are directed at our own fortune. In chapter 16, I consider the emotions of hope and fear which are also directed at our own fortune, but which refer to the future. In chapter 17, I examine pride and regret, which are directed toward our specific actions; finally, in chapter 18, I deal with the emotions of pridefulness and shame, which are directed at our personality in general.

*Happiness*

Do not worry; eat three square meals a day; say your prayers; be courteous to your creditors; keep your digestion good; exercise; go slow and easy. Maybe there are other things your special case requires to make you happy, but my friend, these I reckon will give you a good lift.
—Abraham Lincoln

Happiness is a central concern of us. We often wonder whether we and those around us are happy; we ponder about the precise nature of happiness; we consider the pursuit of happiness to be a basic individual right; and like love, happiness is a central theme in works of art. Despite its centrality and the many philosophical and psychological discussions devoted to it, the nature of happiness is still a mystery. The following discussion is not intended to solve the mystery, but rather to reduce its extent by drawing a few related distinctions which are often overlooked.

### Types of Happiness: Emotion and Sentiment
It is not easy to find happiness in ourselves, and impossible to find it elsewhere.
—Agnes Repplier

What do you take me for, an idiot?
—General Charles de Gaulle, when a journalist asked him if he was happy

A distinction should be made between two major types of happiness: a long-term sentiment of happiness (well-being, flourishing) and a short-term emotion of happiness (joy, satisfaction).

As a sentiment, happiness is the most general positive emotion. It comprises a general evaluation of our life as a whole or at least of significant aspects of life, such as work and family. Happiness in this sense touches upon our deepest strivings and concerns. It is, therefore, not merely a pleasant feeling but also entails evaluating our situation and the things around us as basically right and good.[1] In containing a positive profound evaluation of significant aspects, happiness is similar to love, but love mainly refers to another person. The affinity between love and happiness is expressed in the fact that love is one of the most important features determining our happiness.

As an acute emotion, happiness is a short-term state of pleasure or satisfaction occurring as a result of a specific (real or imaginary) positive change. Even a person who is generally depressed can laugh from time to time and be pleased with a specific event. Senile people and infants may often be satisfied or contented with their situation. They may also be described as having a certain degree of happiness, but this is not the profound sentiment of happiness typical of healthy adults and desired by them. Happiness in the latter sense involves the optimal functioning of human beings, not the minimal functioning of mere contentment or relaxation which can be found in the life of dumb animals. Hence, most of us would rather be a dissatisfied Socrates than a satisfied pig. To be merely contented with our current state may reduce ambitions and fulfilling activities in a way that will make us miserable in the long run. This may be the reason why television viewing may help us to feel more relaxed, but does not generally help us to feel substantially happier. For similar reasons, gorging ourselves on consumer goods may please us in the short run, but may not make us substantially happier; gluttony is not the same as nourishment.[2]

The acute emotion of happiness may be regarded as the occasional foreground reaction to specific positive events; happiness as a sentiment is the background framework.[3] The relation between the background and the foreground elements of happiness is complex. There is no doubt that the background framework determines to a certain extent the foreground element of occasional happiness. The evaluations underlying the occasional emotion of happiness, like other emotional evaluations, are made in relation to a certain background baseline. Outcomes above the baseline generate happiness; below, unhappiness; and those matching the baseline are experienced as neutral. People's baselines slide up or down to match their experiences. The same event may be associated with different emotions due to differing baselines. People whose baseline is basically lower, for instance, whose living standards and expectations are lower, are more likely to be happy. Thus, it was found that people who grew up during the Great Depression tended to report higher levels of subjective well-being in their current lives compared with those who had not experienced the Depression. In addition, the more these people suffered during the Depression, the greater their current satisfaction. Similarly, survivors of cancer treatments report greater happiness three years after their treatment than do a healthy control group. Indeed, social and personal comparisons are crucial in determining happiness.[4]

The function of the background framework is more complex than merely that of a baseline ruler measuring whether a specific event is above or below a certain neutral point. This framework, which expresses our personal makeup, also determines the very nature of our emotional sensitivity. It determines, for example, whether we typically interpret the specific events around us in a positive or a negative manner. As in other emotions, individual differences are quite important in determining happiness. Many people seem to be happy or unhappy in most types of circumstances regardless of their objective situation. Some people are happy in almost all circumstances—except those of severe misfortune—regardless of their current situation. These people are predisposed to view the world in an optimistic way. On the other hand, other people are unhappy in most circumstances regardless of how well they are doing. Compared with the lives of most other people, the lives of many wealthy people are indeed easy and without substantial misfortunes; nevertheless, many wealthy people are not happy. These people are unhappy not because money makes them miserable, but because there is something in their personality which prevents them from being happy. These wealthy people would be unhappy most of the time even if their economic situation were not so good. Indeed, the different reported levels of happiness of people are reasonably stable over time.[5]

In light of the above individual differences, we may speak about a talent for happiness, or a constitutive disposition to be happy. Empirical evidence concerning the nature of this talent is hard to obtain as we need to isolate many factors. Nevertheless, there is evidence that genetic variation is quite important in determining our happiness. Some even estimate that the heritability of the stable component of our subjective well-being approaches 80 percent. No doubt, negative events may diminish our happiness, but the effects of these events appear to be transitory fluctuations of a more stable baseline (or a "set point") that is characteristic of the individual. The idea is similar to the set point concept in weight control which assumes that the brain is wired to ratchet the body's metabolic rate up or down to maintain a preset weight. Similarly, there may be a set point for happiness, a genetically determined mood level that the vagaries of life may nudge upward or downward but only for a while.[6]

In accordance with such a view, it was found that those people who are relatively the happiest now will be the happiest ten years from now, despite day-to-day fluctuations. Indeed, the reported well-being of one's identical twin, either now or ten years earlier, is a far better predictor of one's self-rated happiness than is one's own educational achievement, income, or social status. Hence, it may be that "trying to be happier is as futile as trying to be taller and therefore is counterproductive."[7]

In addition to the genetic factor influencing long-term happiness, another such important factor is the frequency with which people experience the occasional emotion of happiness and other positive emotions; this factor has been found to be the single best predictor of happiness as a sentiment.[8] In a sense, happiness as a sentiment consists of the acute emotions of happiness; so a succession of specific positive experiences will increase our long-term happiness. Combining the two factors together generates the following practical advice suggested by the psychologist David Lykken: "A steady diet of simple pleasures will keep you above your set point. Find the small things that you know give you a little high—a good meal, working in the garden, time with friends—and sprinkle your life with them. In the long run, that will leave you happier than some grand achievement that gives you a big lift for a while."[9]

The distinction between occasional factors, responsible for the generation of happiness as an emotion, and constitutive factors, responsible for the generation of the sentiment of happiness, should also be taken into account when we provide emotional support for others. In the same way that our own happiness does not depend merely on occasional factors, our emotional support of others should not depend merely on such factors. For example, in attempting to reassure students who are uneasy about a forthcoming examination, teachers should not express confidence that the students will do well. Rather, they should say that they know the students well enough to continue to hold them in high regard, no matter how this specific examination turns out.[10] The high regard we have for others should be based on their constitutive and occasional factors. In realizing that their happiness and the emotional support they receive from us do not depend only on the outcome of a specific task, they will be calmer and happier and will be able to perform the task better.

Once the distinction between the occasional emotion of happiness and the sentiment of happiness is made, we can turn to the determinants of the emotion and sentiment of happiness. The discussion will focus on the long-term sentiment of happiness (unless otherwise indicated, I use "happiness" in this sense).

*Determinants of Happiness*
It is pretty hard to tell what does bring happiness; poverty and wealth have both failed.
—Kin Hubbard

We are no longer happy as soon as we wish to be happier.
—Walter Savage Landor

Empirical evidence and commonsense observations indicate the influence of many factors in determining happiness. Let us consider some of them.

A common dispute concerning happiness is whether it depends on subjective, individual personal factors or on objective, general factors. Empirical findings support the presence of both.

Many studies have indeed found a positive correlation between income and long-term happiness. This is true both within and between countries. Richer people reported higher average levels of happiness than poorer people, and people in rich countries are on average happier than those of poor countries. The correlation within a certain country is kept even in groups of very rich people. In 1975 the Gallup organization surveyed people all over the world and found some correlation between a country's wealth and the percentage of people saying they felt generally happy. Wealthy nations like Sweden, Canada, the United States, and West Germany had about 95 percent of people saying they were happy. Countries that were relatively unsuccessful economically, like Britain, Italy, and Spain, had between 60 percent and 80 percent of the population rating themselves as happy. In poor nations, such as India and Colombia, the proportion of people describing themselves as "not too happy," the lowest point offered on the response scale, was about 80 percent. Various studies indicate that the rich report significantly higher levels of happiness (well-being, life satisfaction) than the poor. Indeed, most people believe that more money would significantly improve the quality of their lives.[11]

In light of such evidence, Keith Oatley claims that the idea that a simple life without money or possessions is a happy one is generally romantic nonsense. This does not mean that money is always crucial to happiness. It should be remembered that the effect of money on happiness is not very strong and there are other factors that are even more important to happiness than money. However, money helps people to be happier. In some situations money has a declining marginal utility in regard to happiness. Although the very poor are generally not happy, above some minimal income the amount of money you have matters less in terms of bringing happiness.[12]

A great deal of evidence also supports the presence of subjective, individual elements in happiness. Thus, the inhabitants of poorer environments are not less happy than the inhabitants of a more favored locale, and the blind, the retarded, and the malformed are not less happy than other people. There is no consistent relationship between economic improvement and increased happiness. Objective circumstances alone may not produce long-term happiness. For example, it was found that although lottery winners felt quite pleased with winning the lottery, they derived less pleasure than other people from a variety of ordinary events and were not in general happier than others. Thus, they were no happier than other ordinary people and only slightly happier than recently paralyzed accident victims. Another study found that disabled people recorded more incidents of happiness than an abled-bodied comparison group. A plausible explanation for this is that disabled people often felt happy about achieving something that would not be noticed by able-bodied people.[13]

These findings can be explained by assuming that, like other emotions, happiness is typically comparative: our relative position is usually more significant than the absolute one.[14] Thus, lottery winners experience such euphoria, in light of which all other events in their life appear insignificant. After winning 10 million dollars, you are less likely to experience a high level of satisfaction from your child's good grades, or from the tree in your garden which yields more fruit than usual. Similarly, it was found that a woman is 16 to 25 percent more likely to work outside the home if her sister's husband earns more than her own husband.[15] The comparative concern is indeed central in many circumstances.

There are, however, cases in which the comparative concern is not important. For example, the death of a child does not make the parents able to experience increased happiness from other events, although in comparison with this terrible event all other events in their life will be less distressing in the future. The grief of the parents is related to an irrevocable loss, and not to a low point of well-being from which one's happiness can only grow. The death of a child does not function as a comparative baseline, in light of which all other events are perceived as happy events. This loss does not immunize the system from further pain; it is rather an open wound which reduces, if not completely eliminates, the very possibility of being happy.

It is interesting to note in this connection that despite the aforementioned great advantages in everyday life of good-looking people, they are not significantly happier than other people. Good-looking people are more satisfied with their romantic life, but this does not lead to greater overall satisfaction with life. These surprising results may be explained by referring to two issues which were mentioned above: (1) the genetic aspect of happiness—people are born with a greater or smaller talent for happiness; (2) the comparative aspect of happiness—the good-looking compare themselves with the even better-looking.[16]

The genetic aspect of happiness is expressed in the fact that for any given person, the various self-reported measure of subjective well-being tends to be strongly positively correlated over time.[17] This is illustrated in the tragic life of famous and wealthy persons, such as Judy Garland, Marilyn Monroe, and Christine Onassis, who all apparently committed suicide at a young age. It is also vividly expressed in Edwin Arlington Robinson's poem "Richard Cory":

Whenever Richard Cory went down town,
We people on the pavement looked at him:
He was a gentleman from sole to crown,
Clean favored, and imperially slim.

And he was always quietly arrayed,
And he was always human when he talked;
But still he fluttered pulses when he said,
"Good-morning," and he glittered when he walked.

And he was rich—yes, richer than a king—
And admirably schooled in every grace:
In fine, we thought that he was everything
To make us wish that we were in his place.

So on we worked, and waited for the light,
And went without the meat, and cursed the bread;
And Richard Cory, one calm summer night,
Went home and put a bullet through his head.

The considerations I have mentioned are relevant to both the sentiment of happiness and the occasional emotion. Positive objective experiences, such as getting a raise in salary, winning a certain contest, or getting an unexpected gift, will almost always generate the acute emotion of happiness. The experience of having a little bit more than we currently have is usually a positive experience resulting in the acute emotion of happiness. However, such an experience may not change our personal affective baseline and hence may not necessarily change the long-term sentiment of happiness. This may explain why people would usually deny that money can buy happiness, but would agree that a little more money would make them a little happier. In many cases, money cannot significantly change our constitutive disposition to happiness; consequently, it cannot alter the long-term sentiment of happiness. Thus, although we may be richer now than we were forty years ago, we are not significantly happier. Money, however, may improve our situation in a way that will bring us more occasions for happiness.

The distinction between objective and subjective determinants of happiness is not always obvious. Money is an objective factor, while our attitude toward money is a subjective factor. However, when money improves our relative position, it combines both objective and subjective factors. Moreover, many factors are not clearly either objective or subjective. It has been found, for example, that social factors, such as marriage, family, friends, and children, are more significant in determining long-term happiness than economic elements, such as job, income, and standard of living.[18] These social factors are not clearly classified as either objective or subjective. These factors are objective in the sense that they do not depend on the agent's thinking; however, they depend on the agent's activities.

Another distinction which is crucial to understanding the determinants of happiness is that between intrinsically valuable activities and extrinsically valuable ends. This distinction is related to the distinction between subjective and objective determinants since activities may be considered as subjective and external ends as objective.

Aristotle distinguishes between an extrinsically valuable action and an intrinsically valuable activity. An extrinsically valuable action, for example, building a house, is a means to a certain end; its value is in achieving this end. This action is always incomplete: as long as the end has not been achieved, the action is incomplete, and the moment the end has been achieved the action is over. In an intrinsically valuable activity our interest is focused upon the activity itself, not its results. Although such an activity has results, it is not performed to achieve these; rather, its value is in the activity itself. Intellectual thinking and happiness are Aristotle's examples of this kind of activity.[19]

In suggesting the four basic types of moods, that is, calm-energy, calm-tiredness, tense-energy, and tense-tiredness, Thayer argues that calm-energy is the optimal mood for maintaining our happiness. He indicates that many people fail to distinguish between calm-energy and tense-energy since they believe that whenever they are energetic, there is a certain degree of tension in their situation. Thayer claims that the idea of calm-energy is foreign to many Westerners, but not to people from other cultures. He provides the following citation from the Zen master Shunryu Suzuki: "Calmness of mind does not mean you should stop your activity. Real calmness should be found in the activity itself. It is easy to have calmness in inactivity, but calmness in activity is true calmness."[20] It seems that the idea of calmness in activity is related to the Aristotelian idea of intrinsically valuable activity. We can find calmness in an intrinsically valuable activity since it is not an incomplete action that depends upon external factors for its fulfillment.

Happiness is then to be found in activities we value in themselves. Even in highly extrinsically valuable actions, such as hunting, prospecting, gambling, or practicing law, the ends are often not the crucial factor in the happiness of the people engaging in these activities. Giving the huntsman his prey and the gambler the chips staked on the game may make them pleased for a moment, but will not make them happy; they must get these things through their own activities. It is the activity itself which excites them. As Chris Verbiski, a once-impoverished mineral prospector who recently became a millionaire, said: "It's the hunt—not the money—that makes my blood race; after all, you can only sleep in one bed at a time, and drive one car at a time."

Happiness cannot be achieved by merely repeating good experiences. An enjoyable event is often progressively less enjoyable with repetition. A new acquisition, highly valued at first, comes to seem ordinary. Hence, it is not merely acquisitions which can provide us with enduring satisfaction. As Jonathan Freedman argues, "We cannot capture happiness and then sit still and hope to maintain it. We change, the world changes, our needs change, and our requirements for happiness change all the time."[21] Happiness is not an isolated achievement, but rather an ongoing dynamic process.

The minor and momentary significance of the ends is expressed in the fact that when the end is obtained, it no longer continues to occupy our mind: a new desire follows, and the imagination, as before, is directed at a distant goal. In accordance with the Aristotelian tradition, Ferguson argues that happiness depends on the way we act rather than on the specific results of our activities. Happiness "arises more from the pursuit than from the attainment of any end whatever." It "depends more on the degree in which our minds are properly employed, than it does on the circumstances in which we are destined to act, on the materials which are placed in our hands, or the tools with which we are furnished."[22]

Psychological research confirms the link between unhappiness and leading a life focused on attaining external goals: "The more beliefs people hold that link the attainment of goals to their long-term happiness, the more likely it is that they will ruminate about goals they want but do not have." Such rumination is aversive in nature and "adds a long-term negative pall to people's overall affective states. The end result is that linkers spend significantly more of their time *unhappy* than do non-linkers."[23]

The importance of activities to happiness is further illustrated in cases where we want something but fail to enjoy it when attained. George Bernard Shaw wrote (in *Man and Superman*) that "There are two tragedies in life. One is not to get your heart's desire. The other is to get it." Disappointment sometimes attends the nominal satisfaction of our desires. A Latin saying has it that every creature is sad after coitus. The common and intriguing phenomenon of being disappointed after getting what you want may be dismissed by claiming that either what we imagined to be desirable is different from what actually is, or that our personal and contextual circumstances have changed by the time we achieve the desired end. Although in some cases this is true, there are also situations in which we are not happy although we get exactly what we expect and the personal and contextual circumstances have not been significantly changed.

A more comprehensive explanation must distinguish between happiness as an emotion and happiness as a sentiment. Attaining a specific goal may lead to occasional emotions of happiness rather than to the long-term sentiment of happiness. Attaining a specific goal may make us feel happy at a particular moment, but it may not lead to greater long-term happiness.[24] Believing that it does, as many of us do, can lead to disappointment when the goal is attained. If the desire to have more than others is essential to our happiness, no matter how much we have, we will always want more. As we ascend the socioeconomic ladder, we aspire to greater heights. We may satisfy more needs, but we constantly need and want more. Edward Gibbon rightly argued that "I am indeed rich, since my income is superior to my expense, and my expense is equal to my wishes." Indeed, happiness depends little on the quantity of things we have attained; our attitude toward these things is of greater significance. This is why happiness is so elusive; once attained for a moment, it slips from our grasp.[25]

Advertisers make full use of this phenomenon: they know that new demands can be created constantly because people are never fully satisfied or happy for very long. As a result, we are regularly offered new and improved products that promise a better and happier life.[26]

Leibniz claimed that our world is the best of all worlds not because it lacks evil but because we manage to overcome evil. By overcoming it we are in a better position to appreciate the good we enjoy. As John Milton observed, "knowledge of good bought dear by knowing ill." Indeed, early literature associated a significant joy of a woman—bringing a new child into the world—with great pain: "In sorrow thou shalt bring forth children" says the Bible. In light of such considerations, one may say that we are happy because we overcome obstacles. In this sense, infants and senile people cannot be happy.

We have seen that happiness is indeed related to intrinsically valuable activity. However, we should distinguish between intrinsically valuable activity and overcoming obstacles. The value of an intrinsically valuable activity does not stem from overcoming obstacles and hence is not necessarily correlated with the difficulty of the obstacle. Some people may be engaged in an intrinsically valuable activity in an easy and relaxed manner without having to overcome substantial obstacles; nevertheless, their activities may make them quite happy. Others may suffer and struggle a lot while engaging in an intrinsically valuable activity and this may reduce the happiness associated with this activity.

The psychological problem of disappointment upon achieving our goals is related to a more general philosophical problem concerning the meaningfulness of a life in which the struggle is more significant and enjoyable than achievement of the end. Realizing that this is our nature may easily generate the feeling that life is meaningless.[27] However, we may draw a different implication from this tendency. We should realize that what is meaningful in life is the nature of our activity and the value we attach to it rather than the attainment of external ends. Recognizing this point would make most of us happier and greatly contribute to a more humane and kinder society.

We have seen the importance of both subjective and objective factors in happiness and hence the problematic nature of happiness. Two extreme positions have been suggested in this regard: (1) objective factors have no weight in determining happiness; (2) objective factors are crucial in determining happiness.

Aristotle discusses these positions and rejects them both. He rejects the first view, arguing that without external, objective fortunes, it is not possible to be happy. A good and happy life requires actual activity for its completion and this activity can be disrupted or decisively impeded by external conditions. Furthermore, activities which are intrinsically valuable are vulnerable to impediment as they also presuppose certain external conditions. Thus, severe chronic illness, extreme poverty, and the death of a loved one can disrupt even intrinsically valuable activity. Extreme misfortune could dislodge a good person from full happiness.[28] External fortunes are not enough to make us happy; happiness also depends on our activity which fulfills our potential. The value of these activities is intrinsic: it is to be found in the activity itself and not in an external end which is supposed to be achieved. Happy people are not those who are immune from misfortunes and their negative influence. However, they can usually cope with them in a way which does not considerably interrupt their intrinsically valuable activities. For example, despite their terminal illness they are able to "put their illness in brackets," namely, to subjectively ignore their background framework while attending to everyday events.

The two extreme positions concerning the role of objective factors in happiness can also be found in contemporary views of therapy. The position that objective factors have no role in our happiness is expressed in the "positive thinking" approach to therapy. Thus, Richard Carlson, an influential therapist, argues that "happiness is the result of a decision to be happy." Accordingly, "happiness exists independent of your circumstances; it's a feeling that you learn to live in." Whenever we attach external conditions to our happiness we will not experience it. Happiness, in this view depends merely upon our thinking and imagination and not upon external, objective factors.[29] The opposite position is that objective factors are crucial in determining our happiness. There is not much we can do about this and the best strategy is that of self-acceptance.

The above extreme positions are inadequate when formulated as the only means to happiness. However, they contain important elements of happiness: happiness consists of both objective and subjective features. As the famous prayer goes, "Grant me the courage to try to change what can be changed, the serenity to accept what can't be changed, and the wisdom to know the difference."

We can conclude that happiness depends on both objective and subjective factors and is dynamic in nature. In extreme situations, the role of objective factors is greater as they prevent normal functioning. In normal circumstances our ability to determine happiness is greater. In these circumstances the dynamic nature of happiness is more evident: our activities have greater weight in maintaining happiness.

*Maintaining Long-Term Happiness*
Happiness is not a state to arrive at, but a manner of traveling.
—Margaret Lee Runbeck

The happiness of most people we know is not ruined by great catastrophes or fatal errors, but by the repetition of slowly destructive little things.
—Ernest Dimnet

There is evidence that most people in most places report a positive level of happiness and recount their satisfaction with domains such as marriage, work, and leisure. As suggested, this is also true of the majority of disadvantaged persons, such as those who use wheelchairs, those suffering from spinal cord injuries, and those with extreme quadriplegia.[30]

As indicated, the comparative concern is crucial in emotions: we are sad when our current situation is perceived to be worse than our personal affective baseline, and we are happy when our current situation is perceived to be better than this baseline. The way our personal baseline is determined has great significance for the determination of our happiness.

The determination of our personal affective baseline depends of course on many subjective factors, but the fact that the average person perceives himself as happier than the average person, indicates that there may be some common principles in such determination.

I have suggested in chapter 4 that negative events, and hence negative emotions, are more noticeable than positive events and positive emotions. One reason for this phenomenon is that the risks of responding inappropriately to negative events are greater than the risks of responding inappropriately to positive events. If indeed negative events are more noticeable than positive ones, we may conclude that most of the time we are more sad than happy—since the world seems to be basically a negative place. However, as suggested above, empirical evidence indicates the contrary.

The explanation for this may be that our happiness depends not so much on the way we perceive the world but on the way we cope with the world. Perceiving the world in a somewhat more negative light than it is gives us greater satisfaction when we overcome these difficulties. This is similar to the case when, before a certain game, the coach of one team describes the rival team as very good—more so than they really are. In evaluating the chances of his team as somewhat more negative than they really are, the coach encourages his players to take the game more seriously and hence invest more effort in it. Moreover, the coach's perception of the opponents also contributes to more positive affective states after the game is over. If the team loses then the loss is less painful, as the alternative of winning the game was perceived to be more remote. And if the team wins the joy is greater, since the alternative of losing the game was perceived to be quite close. In overcoming tasks that are perceived to be more difficult than they are, we feel much better since our success is more significant.

The need to be happy and its connection to the more noticeable nature of negative events may be also related to the following surprising phenomenon: people tend to judge a positive outcome with a fixed probability as more surprising than a negative outcome with the same probability. For instance, a medical treatment that has a probability of 0.50 of success (and of 0.50 of failure) is clearly rated as more surprising when it succeeds than when it fails.[31] In order to be less disappointed, we typically perceive negative outcomes as more salient, and positive outcomes become more surprising.

It should be noticed that when our perception of our environment is much more negative than it is in reality, we may be less motivated to do anything, as we perceive the probability of overcoming these negative events to be very low. We should perceive our tasks as only a little bit more difficult than they actually are. Similarly, when the rival team is indeed much better than ours, we should over-rate the strength of our own team to some extent, in order to make our players more optimistic. Optimism, which is very important for our happiness, does not necessarily entail perceiving the world as less negative than it is; rather, it entails perceiving ourselves as having greater chances of overcoming our difficulties. Being happy, or at least assuming that we are above our affective baseline, is then important for optimal functioning. Maintaining or increasing happiness has much to do with the gap between our affective personal baseline and objective reality.

Dealing with the baseline-reality gap can be done by (a) eliminating the gap by changing the baseline or reality, and (b) coping with the gap by changing our atti-tude toward it. These strategies, which differ in their feasibility and the required resources, are used in different circumstances. Let us consider first the more radical strategy—attempting to eliminate the baseline-reality gap.

The baseline-reality gap can be eliminated by changing objective circumstances in reality or subjective factors of our personal baseline. Believing that our partner is well below what we deserve to have expresses a profound baseline-reality gap and is a major obstacle to happiness. We can eliminate this gap by either chang-ing our partner or changing our fundamental evaluative patterns in a way that eliminates the gap between evaluating ourselves and our partner.

Changing reality can be done by changing our social and physical environment; for example, changing our place of living, workplace, profession, mate, friends, crucial circumstances in our current environment, and so on. While taking a passive attitude we ordinarily assume that we cannot do much to change things around us. This assumption is typical of attitudes such as sadness, depression, and self-pity. Happiness is quite different as it is dynamic in nature; it is associ-ated with activity rather than passivity. An important belief in overcoming the baseline-reality gap is the belief that reality can be changed.

Changing the subjective baseline means changing some fundamental personal-ity traits. One example of such a change is taking the attitude of settling for less. With lower standards, regular accomplishments would be much more satisfying. Take the case of a woman who has in her imagination an exalted picture of an ideal man, a standard that no real-life man could meet. Because of such exalted standards, all her romantic relationships are doomed to be disappointing. If this woman lowers her standards, or changes the relative weight she is giving to the various attributes of a man, she could be happier. What now appears to her as "the best" may be a real-life man, with all the faults that previously seemed too grievous to bear.[32]

One way of coping with the adverse influence of external, objective factors is to lower our expectations. In doing so we will be less frustrated by negative and more surprised by positive external events. People who expect nothing will never be disappointed; however, their happiness will be limited as well since their emotional sensitivity will be quite low. If we can truly settle for less, that is, if we can lower our baselines, happiness is likely to increase since we are more likely to gain what we want and less likely to be envious or frustrated. Indeed, the French scholar, Fontenelle, said: "A great obstacle to happiness is to expect too much happiness."

Achieving greater adaptation to reality by merely modifying the subjective baseline is dangerous as it may lead to indifference and passivity. Happiness cannot be achieved by asking very little of life or from being passive. Settling for less is not recommendable when a higher level of happiness can be achieved. Our baseline should be compatible with our character and possible fulfilling activities. The maxim of "know yourself" is quite important also for happiness.

It is very hard, if possible at all, to change our personal makeup from essentially unhappy to essentially happy. Therapy and other means of making us happy can increase our occasional emotions of happiness, but often have marginal effects concerning our long-term sentiment of happiness. To be sure, they can be very effective for certain individuals, and can somewhat improve the situation of many people, but they cannot basically change the individual talent for happiness since it is very hard to change the basic personality of an adult. The possible changes that such means can bring about are typically related to our ability to cope with our environment given our specific personality. Accordingly, such means may increase the frequency of occasional emotions of happiness. It is plausible that the earlier these means are applied, the better the chances, as the child's personality is less crystallized than the adult's.

Although changing reality and our personal baseline are important for maintaining happiness, our ability to do so is quite limited. Accordingly, making the two compatible is not an easy task. If it were, everyone would be equally happy in the long run, and this is not the case.

Given our significant limitation in using the first strategy which deals with the baseline-reality gap (eliminating the gap), it is the second strategy (coping with the gap by changing our attitude toward it) which is a key to happiness in most daily situations. Happiness can be maintained despite this gap by using the various means of regulating emotional intensity that were discussed in chapter 6. For example, (a) *behaving* as if the gap does not exist or is not important, (b) *not recognizing* the gap or at least not to its full extent, and (c) *devaluing* the weight of the gap. The first method is basically behavioral, the second cognitive, and the third evaluative. There are, of course, other possible classifications of means for coping with the baseline-reality gap.

The *behavioral* manner of dealing with the baseline-reality gap is mainly expressed in our ability to avoid unpleasant circumstances and to approach pleasant ones. Avoiding or approaching given circumstances can be done by actual behavior or by directing our attention away or toward these circumstances. The way we behave toward or think of what is happening is of particular importance for maintaining long-term happiness. Our tendency to join the winning side is part of the behavioral means of increasing happiness. One explanation for the fact that depression is twice as common in women as in men refers to the way men and women respond to a predepressive episode: men's responses to their predepressive episode are more behavioral and thereby dampen their depressive episodes, whereas women's responses are more ruminative and thereby amplify them.[33] (Other explanations for women's greater sensitivity to depression have been suggested. One of them contends that emotional breakdowns such as depression are not predominantly due to anything wrong with people's minds, but with their lives.[34]) Women's stronger inclination to ruminate may be related to their greater concern over close interpersonal relationships. This makes women less likely to distract themselves from close relationships which are typically quite relevant to the generation of intense emotions and depression. Without getting into the dispute of whether this is indeed the major reason for women's greater sensitivity to depression, and emotions in general, it is obvious that ruminating about negative events does not foster happiness. As indicated below, intellectual curiosity is often negatively correlated with happiness.

Happiness seems to have an elusive nature; it is often the case that the more we think of how to become happy, the less happy we are. William Shenstone, the eighteenth-century English poet, indicated that "what leads to unhappiness, is making pleasure the chief aim." Happiness is a kind of a byproduct of other activities whose main goal is not achieving happiness. If dwelling on negative events is indeed instrumental in making us unhappy, then in such a situation, little needs to be added to people's lives to make them happy. Rather something needs to be subtracted—the constant preoccupation with negative events.[35] An important means for achieving happiness in certain circumstances is not to focus our attention on failures, that is, on the baseline-reality gap.

The *cognitive* method of dealing with the baseline-reality gap is observed in cases where we do not recognize this gap or its full extent. This can be done either by diverting our attention away from the gap (which is also a type of behavioral method) or by interpreting our situation in a way which does not recognize the gap. Partial or full self-deception is typical in these situations. Happiness is not necessarily correlated with detailed knowledge: on the contrary, commonsense wisdom suggests that knowledge, or excessive intellectual curiosity, is associated with unhappiness. Adam and Eve were expelled from the Garden of Eden because of their desire to gain further knowledge. In the Pandora myth, all the diseases and troubles of the world were released because of Pandora's curiosity to know what the box, given to her by the gods, contained. If someone is not clever, a precise knowledge that he is in the lowest 10 percent, will not make him happy. Accordingly, it is better for him to believe, for instance, that most people think differently from the way he does. In both the cognitive and behavioral means of maintaining happiness, we do not face reality; we ignore it or perceive it in a more convenient manner. Accordingly, the value of these means is limited—using them for a long time may be damaging. The self-deception involved in overcoming the baseline-reality gap may be compared to white lies, such as not telling a seriously ill person that her doctors do not have much hope that she will survive. In both cases the deception is not intended to hurt other people, but to help a person in need. As indicated, positive illusions are quite useful in maintaining happiness. Moreover, in light of the importance of imagination in emotions, happiness often depends on having the right imaginative attitude. Nevertheless, there are situations in which such illusory methods can be damaging beyond a limited period.

The *evaluative* method of coping with the baseline-reality gap involves not attaching much weight to the gap. Making excuses is an example of such a method. Excuses reduce the weight of a certain negative event by distancing ourselves from its cause, or by shifting the responsibility to a less important aspect of our personality. Excuse-making is similar to behavioral and cognitive means in the sense that an increase in our happiness is achieved by avoiding certain aspects of reality or interpreting them in a favorable manner.

Another useful attitude for increasing happiness through changing the values we attach to things around us is achieved when we change our reference group, thereby enabling more favorable comparisons. A similar change in attitude involves downward counterfactuals in which we bear in mind that the given situation could be worse. Another example is when we see a half-full glass rather than a half-empty one. Downward counterfactuals are particularly useful in nonextreme situations. The usefulness of such means stems from the fact that we do not ignore reality—and hence the possibility of improving it—but rather evaluate it in a more positive way.

Another profound manner for devaluating the reality-baseline gap is to adopt the above-mentioned attitude assuming that our own activities, rather than external ends, are what matter to happiness. As the popular song, "Green Fields," puts it: "You can't be happy while your heart is on the road." Attaining external ends depends upon external constraints of reality; attaching the most significant value to our own subjective activities devaluates the importance of the gap between the objective reality and our subjective baseline. The weight is shifted to our subjective circumstances and activities. In doing the activities we like, we are less constrained by objective circumstances than by trying to achieve external ends.

The cognitive and evaluative means for coping with the baseline-reality gap are comparative in nature. Such comparisons can use either an interindividual (between persons) frame of reference or an intraindividual (within the same person) frame of reference. The issue of whether our happiness is greater or less than that of others or than that we used to have is of great emotional significance. The intraindividual comparison may not be compatible with the interindividual comparison: we may consider ourselves happier than other people, but still less happy than we used to be.

Both types of comparison are important for happiness, but they are used in different circumstances. In modern Western society, where competition is quite dominant, the use of interindividual comparisons in determining our happiness prevails. Such comparisons may easily lead to envy, resentment, and disappointment since there will always be people who are in some sense superior to us. In light of our tendency to improve our situation, it is natural that we will look at those above us and accordingly our happiness will be decreased. In order to avoid this we frequently use downward counterfactual comparisons in which we compare our current situation to a worse situation for other people or ourselves.

The above methods for maintaining happiness are used by most of us with good results. Indeed, on average people rate their happiness as more than one third of the way up from the middle toward the top of the scale. As indicated, on average people report themselves to be happier than they believe the average person is. Despite the more noticeable nature of negative emotions, and contrary to a popular belief, in most issues we consider our own grass to be greener. A notable exception is sex: we tend to assume that our neighbors are having more sex with more people and are more satisfied with it than we are. However, this assumption has little effect on our sexual satisfaction and happiness.[36]

Maintaining a high level of happiness is important for adequate functioning; reporting this is important for protecting our self-image. The importance of maintaining happiness and reporting this is expressed, for example, in the constant attempt of the major mass communication medium, namely, television, to promote an optimistic, cheerful attitude about life. Most TV shows promote the assumption that things usually work out for the best; hence worry is in some sense improper. On television, everything ends happily: criminals are always caught, guilty people always break down under a good lawyer's cross-examination, and generally most problems are solved before the show is over. (In soap operas, where the plot develops over several weeks, the solution is not immediate, but also here problems are finally solved and the overall mood is optimistic.) This is even more evident in the case of commercials. In many commercials a problem is posed and through an insightful moment a happy ending is reached; the problem is resolved within thirty or sixty seconds. In accordance with this optimistic mood, the world of television is peopled by the middle and upper classes, whereas minorities and the elderly are underrepresented.[37] By depicting a clean and cheerful environment lacking long-term problems, television helps us to maintain our overall high level of happiness. Some may say that this is an artificial environment and watching it is a kind of escape device. This may be true, but such a device is in many circumstances useful for maintaining happiness. Like other useful devices, using it in excess can be harmful.

In light of the importance of intrinsically valuable activities for our happiness, it seems that intraindividual comparisons will be more conducive to our happiness. The comparison with other people usually concerns their external possessions as it is very hard to find out the intrinsic value other people attach to their activities. Intraindividual comparisons can more easily refer to intrinsically valuable activities and hence may further enhance our happiness.

Education for happiness is first of all education for optimal handling of the baseline-reality gap. We should learn to cope with the gap and not view its presence as a grave misfortune. Giving more weight to what we actually do and have may facilitate our coping potential.

## Sadness

One can endure sorrow alone, but it takes two to be glad.
—Elbert Hubbard

It is our job to make women unhappy with what they have.
—B. Earl Puckett, an advertiser

Sadness is another negative emotion toward the misfortune of agents. Whereas pity and compassion are concerned with the bad fortune of others, sadness is concerned with one's own bad fortune. In this sense, it includes a more profound negative evaluation. The sadness associated with a specific negative event concerning ourselves is often not much more than ordinary sorrow. When the event is more significant, and the sorrow more intense, we will be more inclined to characterize our emotional attitude as sadness. Sadness is deeper and longer-lasting than mere sorrow, that is, it will often be a sentiment rather than an emotion. Extreme cases of sadness can turn into the affective disorder of depression.

In light of the underlying profound negative evaluation of our situation it contains, sadness is typically not associated with putting up resistance but with passivity and resignation in the face of everyday affairs. Indeed, activities typical of a state of sadness are listening to music and taking a nap. Nevertheless, sadness may also lead to the fostering of constructive self-examination. Sadness confirms our appraisal of things as valuable; hence it may happen that we take pride in our ability to feel sadness. As someone once said, "When it gets dark enough you can see the stars." This would suggest that a major function of sadness is to help people become more aware of what they value and hence conserve it.[38]

Unlike fear, which anticipates an event to come, sadness is a response to an event that has already taken place or is perceived as inevitable and hence may be regarded as an event that has already taken place. Unlike guilt and shame, in sadness the self is not necessarily responsible for the problem. As in anger, the responsibility can belong to another person, but unlike anger it can also be impersonal. Typically, we are not angry toward an earthquake, but the damage caused by the quake may sadden us. Both sadness and anger include the belief that the situation might have been reversible, but whereas sadness typically entails acceptance of the loss, anger involves the belief that the loss can be replaced. In one study a person deliberately interfered with a child's wish. Differing proportions of children expressed anger and sadness, but much more sadness was expressed when the interferer was someone over whom the child could have little control (a teacher) and much more anger when it was a peer.[39]

*Grief*

Let us so live that when we come to die, even the undertaker will be sorry.
—Mark Twain

Grief is the most profound type of sadness. It is concerned with death, the most substantial misfortune we encounter: it expresses the irrevocable loss of someone very close and of great value to us. In situations of grief we are rendered utterly helpless. Because of the profound impact of death, grief is focused on the same issue for a long period of time. Most new information is irrelevant to the intensity of grief. Hence, grief typically develops into a sentiment and in extreme cases into depression.

Sometimes grief is also concerned with misfortunes which do not involve death but nevertheless are considered as grim as death. Grief may also be directed at people whose mental life has been considerably changed for the worse, and we are helpless in the face of this change. Thus, people sometimes grieve for an Alzheimer's victim. Some people also grieve if their son or daughter changes religion, becomes an atheist, or embarks in other ways on what the parents consider to be sacrilege. Sometimes cases of betrayal, abandonment, and separation from a beloved also generate grief.

Although grief is classified as an emotion toward the bad fortune of others, it has much to do with our own misfortune as well. If grief is indeed the most profound emotion we have, one may wonder why our most profound emotion is evoked by the misfortune of others and not our own. In truth, a great deal of concern in grief is that of our own misfortune or feeling of loss. The death of the beloved is negatively evaluated not merely because we believe this person is suffering now or missing things she would like to experience, it is also because we feel something in us has died, that our life has lost a valuable aspect. In an interview on Israeli Radio, a man whose brother had been killed in the army 23 years ago said that this event had changed him in the sense that he worries much more for those near to him and especially his children. He explained that he does not fear his own death as much as that of his children because after having once experienced the sudden death of someone young and very close to him, he cannot imagine that he could ever cope with such an experience again. In other words, while his fear is directed at others, its rationale is his own suffering.

I have suggested that the personal concern is crucial in emotions and accordingly we are much sadder when our child is hurt than when we hear about the death of a stranger in a remote country. Since we consider those who are close to us as part of us, often we would prefer to suffer hurt ourselves, and in extreme cases even sacrifice our own life to protect those who are close to us, such as our children.

In a letter to Pollot, Descartes compares the loss of a brother to the loss of a hand and asks why we are far more saddened by the former. After all, Descartes argues, reason dictates that a brother's friendship can be replaced by acquiring new friends, and religion gives us no cause to be concerned about the welfare of our dead brother.[40] I believe that Descartes is wrong concerning both our own account and that of the brother. Concerning our own account, the loss of a brother is much more than a loss of a friend. But even if we consider the death of a friend, the intimate and unique history we had with this friend is not replaceable—no matter how many other friends we have. Concerning the brother's sake, even if we believe that our brother will go to Paradise, we still grieve for the activities and experiences he will never again enjoy.

Parents' grief over the death of their child is perhaps the most intense emotion a person can experience. Because of the event's great impact, the comparative concern is of lesser significance. Thus, the general rule of "company in distress makes sorrow less" is not applicable in this case. When bereaved parents hear of a child's death in another family, rather than reduce their sorrow, it tends to bring back the memory of their own dead child, thereby increasing their grief.

The grief over a child often lasts for life: it is hard for bereaved parents to continue as usual because they are overwhelmed with thoughts and memories of the deceased. Sometimes their grief may even harm their relationship with the surviving children. This is due, among other things, to the parents' tendency to idealize the deceased and to overidentify with the dead child. An interesting issue in this regard is whether the intensity of parental grief decreases over the years. Many parents testify that the intensity of their grief remains the same throughout their lives. However, studies indicate that the impact of loss lessens with the passage of time, but nevertheless continues over the years. The impact seems to be greater on women. It may be the case that because of personal changes that the parents undergo, such as becoming more vulnerable due to old age, coping with their grief becomes more difficult, but this does not necessarily indicate that the intensity of their grief is greater. Indeed, younger parents seem better able to adapt to the loss and better able to recover from the death of a child.[41]

Happiness is parallel to sadness. But grief, which expresses the most profound loss and hence sadness, has no parallel positive emotion expressing the greatest possible gain. A major reason for the lack of such an emotion may be that whereas the loss in grief is irrevocable, our greatest gains are not irrevocable: there can always be something that abolishes or reduces the gain.

Because of its great intensity, in most cultures and religions there are recommended patterns of behavior associated with grief. These patterns are supposed to regulate the appropriate proportions of grief. Two central customs in the Jewish tradition are those of the shiva and a year of mourning. The custom of shiva (from the Hebrew, "seven") involves all family members sitting in the house of the deceased for seven days. The emotional function of this custom is to somewhat reduce the intensity of grief when it is at its peak: by sitting together with family members, having small talks, and receiving friends who come to express their condolences, the intense personal pain may be reduced. The custom of a year of mourning is required from children whose parents died. In light of this custom, the children are supposed to say a prayer for the deceased at least twice a day; they are not supposed to go to social events or to entertain guests in their home. The emotional function of this custom is the opposite of shiva: it is to keep the intensity of grief at the appropriate level at times when it tends to be reduced. It is interesting to note that the required period of mourning for a mate or a child is only three months. It seems that in these cases there is no need to increase the intensity of grief and there is an urgent need to maintain a normal schedule.

Despite the great impact of the event involved in grief, the intensity of grief is also influenced by background circumstances expressed in the variables of accountability, readiness, and deservingness. Take, for example, accountability. Grief may be somewhat reduced if the death of our beloved is attributed to impersonal circumstances. When people believe that someone's death was due to God's will, the intensity of grief is usually reduced. For similar considerations, memorial booklets for soldiers killed in combat seldom refer to fatal mistakes by friendly forces which might have been avoided. Likewise, it is most difficult for parents to cope with the death of a child who committed suicide. In this case, the child's—and sometimes also the parents'—control of the eliciting event is typically higher than in most other cases. Accordingly, a common phenomenon among these parents is their attempt to put the blame on other people or on external circumstances beyond their control. For example, I know of one father, whose son committed suicide in the army, who assaulted his son's commander, accusing him of responsibility for his son's suicide. A few days later, a letter from the son was found in which he accused the father of being responsible for his suicide. Indeed, there is some evidence suggesting that parents of children who committed suicide or who died in an accident reported more guilt than did parents of children who died of chronic illness. Deaths linked to suicide or accidents may be perceived as preventable, and thus are more likely to elicit guilt.[42]

Our readiness for the particular death of someone close to us also influences our grief. When we expect the death of someone who has been seriously ill for a long time, our grief is usually less intense than in the case of a sudden death. Similarly, when we believe that someone deserves to die—this is quite a rare belief if it is concerned with someone who is very close to us—then the intensity of our grief is somewhat reduced.

*Loneliness*

The sum of man's problems comes from his inability to be alone in a silent room.
—Blaise Pascal

It is better to wake up alone and know that you are alone, than to wake up with somebody and still feel lonely.
—Liv Ullmann

Loneliness is a type of sadness: it is sadness which stems from the absence of desired social relationships. Loneliness involves a discrepancy between a person's desired and achieved level of social interaction; it may be described as an emotional hunger for intimacy in personal and social relationships. Lonely people do not so much yearn for others to be part of their lives but even more desperately wish to be a part of the lives of others. They want more to be an emotional object than an emotional subject. Lonely people feel themselves to be nonentities, and special to no one. This may explain why quality relationships with family members do little to prevent or ameliorate the experience of loneliness. Family members are with us not out of choice but because they were born into this relationship; friends, on the other hand, choose our company and indicate by this our special value.[43]

The attitude of others toward us, rather than their actual company, is at the focus of our concern in loneliness. As Arnold Isenberg rightly claims, loneliness would not be so sad if it did not imply that nobody cares for you, that you are abandoned: "What you might want of other people when you think you would like to see them is not their company so much as the assurance that you can have their company if you want it—that somebody is willing to kill his time with you."[44]

Although the lonely are people who desire more intimate and meaningful relationships with others, they often send messages of disinterest and noninvolvement. Their fear of failure in forming relationships, which in most cases is supported by past experience, generates a negative attitude toward such relationships and toward other people as well. Lonely people also expect others to hold negative views toward them. This negative attitude of lonely people is a kind of defense mechanism against possible failure in developing rewarding relationships with others. The discrepancy between what lonely people desire and what they expect adds another unhappy dimension to their difficult situation.[45]

We should distinguish between loneliness and being alone. Being alone means that an individual is not with another person, while loneliness is a subjective phenomenon and may be experienced whether or not the individual is in the presence of others. In *The Little Prince* by Antoine de Saint-Exupéry, the little prince says that he feels lonely in the desert without human beings; the snake replies that we can also feel lonely among human beings. Lonely persons may not be alone and persons alone are not necessarily lonely; nevertheless, it is often assumed that the two are correlated.[46]

Loneliness may be considered as a type of emotion directed at desired social relationships. However, it is not a typical emotion since it is not directed at a specific object. Loneliness is often associated with shyness, shame, guilt, anxiety, and frustration; each of these emotional states indicates the problem we have with our self-esteem.

Loneliness is usually evaluated in a negative manner since it expresses involuntary separation from social relationships which are so central to human life. But being alone in a voluntary and constructive manner, namely, solitude, has many positive aspects, as it facilitates self-knowledge and a better perspective on life. We devote a lot of time to conversations with other people; we may as well devote some time to conversations with ourselves—quite often the latter will be even more intelligent and rewarding. Like other negative emotions, loneliness is valuable as long as it is temporary; when it becomes a sentiment, it is related to feelings of emptiness and is hard to bear. Fulfillment and happiness both require a supportive social environment and our ability to separate ourselves from that environment.

*Moral Value*

Happiness, it is said, is seldom found by those who seek it, and never by those who seek it for themselves.
—F. Emerson Andrews

Thousands of candles can be lighted from a single candle, and the life of the candle will not be shortened. Happiness never decreases by being shared.
—Buddha

Sorrow makes men sincere.
—Henry Ward Beecher

If a way to the better there be, it lies in taking a full look at the worst.
—Thomas Hardy

Happiness is considered to have high moral value: we expect all to strive for happiness and to make other people happy. Sadness, on the other hand, is considered to be something we all should avoid. Recommendable moral activities are those that increase happiness and reduce sadness; such activities may promote the well-being of human beings.

Although the above statements seem to be morally obvious and indisputable, the issue is more complex. To begin with, it must be clear that our aim should not be to eliminate sadness. Sadness may be unpleasant, but it is extremely important for moral behavior. Without sadness and its related negative emotional attitudes, the impact of hurting other people would be merely abstract. Sadness often provides us with the most sober perspective on life. As indicated above, happiness is often achieved through positive illusions; in sadness, reality is better known. I have proposed the survival importance of occasionally overlooking the unpleasant aspects of reality, but this does not mean ignoring them all together. By realizing our finite and limited existence, something that is often associated with sadness, we may take a more considerate attitude toward other people. Modesty, which is (as I argue below) quite crucial for moral behavior, is related to such realization.

It seems that a recommendable moral attitude is one integrating happy and sad perspectives. Sadness may be more dominant in the background framework, reminding us of some profound existential aspects of our life; happiness is a way of coping with these aspects—often, by overlooking them. A complete ignorance of the sorrowful existential perspective may prevent us from realizing the deep moral commitments we should have toward other creatures. Life that lacks any shade of sadness and merely consists of constant joy is somewhat similar to the state of senility. Senile people may be joyful all the time but this is because they have lost contact with reality; consequently, they can no longer be regarded as moral agents. Moral behavior requires distinction between the bad, which is often sad, and the good, which is often joyful. The joyful state of drugged people is also achieved by ignoring reality and hence losing the human capacity to behave morally.

Sadness is unpleasant, but it is morally valuable for committing ourselves to the more profound moral obligations. Happiness is also morally valuable but for different reasons: its main value is in helping us to perform the "small" everyday moral deeds. Sadness is more conducive to revealing the most profound moral commitments; happiness is more useful in translating these commitments into everyday activities. Sad people may be aware of the profound moral perspective, but in many circumstances it is harder for them to translate this perspective into moral action. Morality requires us to be both sad and happy; the manner of integrating them is a matter of great psychological and moral complexity.

# Chapter 16

## Caring about Our Future—Hope and Fear

It is better to be feared than loved, if you cannot be both.
—Niccolo Machiavelli

Hope springs eternal in the human breast.
—Alexander Pope

This chapter deals with the group of emotions which are concerned with our own future; here, the two fundamental emotions are hope and fear. In light of the crucial role that the future plays in shaping our present life, those emotions addressing the future are of particular importance as well.

### General Characteristics

Don't worry about what other people think of you. They're too busy worrying about what you think of them.
—Unknown

Don't worry about the world coming to an end today. It's already tomorrow in Australia.
—Charles Schultz

Like happiness and sadness, hope and fear are directed at our own fortune; the importance of these emotions stems from the importance of the personal concern in emotions. Indeed, Aquinas considers these four emotions as the principal emotions. However, whereas happiness and sadness are concerned with our present fortune, hope and fear are concerned with future fortune; in this sense, the former seem to be more crucial. Indeed, happiness and sadness tend to be more intense than hope and fear: the temporal distance existing in hope and fear between the agent and the emotional object reduces emotional intensity—as do other types of distance. At a distance, things are usually perceived to be smaller than they are.

Accordingly, if future events are to have emotional impact upon us, they need to be of considerably greater magnitude than present events, and their appearance should be perceived to be imminent.[1]

Although the temporal distance of the future typically weakens its impact, the future has another aspect which may intensify the impact of its events: the future has a longer duration than the present and hence future events may occupy us for a longer period. As Charles Kettering said: "My interest is in the future because I am going to spend the rest of my life there." If indeed a future event is the focus of our attention for a long time, the event may be perceived as stronger and more central to us.

It should be noted that although hope and fear are typically directed at the future, they may also be directed at any event unknown to us. I may hope that I did well in my written examination, or may fear that I left bad impression in my job interview.

### Hope

A man's delight in looking forward to and hoping for some particular satisfaction is a part of the pleasure flowing out of it, enjoyed in advance. But this is afterward deducted, for the more we look forward to anything, the less we enjoy it when it comes.
—Arthur Schopenhauer

Hope is the passion for the possible.
—Søren Kierkegaard

The theoretical attitudes toward hope are diverse. Some theories (predominantly, the philosophical and the religious) have considered hope to be one of the most fundamental emotions—as indicated, Aquinas considers hope to be one of the four basic emotions. Two of the British empiricists, Hume and Hartley, also classified hope among the fundamental emotions. Other theories (mainly, psychological) do not even include hope in their list of emotions. It seems that the two approaches actually refer to different phenomena: while psychological theories refer to the acute emotion, philosophical and religious theories refer to the sentiment of hope.

As an acute emotion, hope is not as intense as most other typical emotions. Consequently, some people have claimed that hope is not an emotion since it lacks an intense feeling dimension and hence does not involve any behavioral or physical symptoms. In such a view, hope is a sort of disposition. In fact, people usually conceive of hope as lasting for a relatively long period of time, which is more typical of a sentiment. Thus, in one study, the majority of subjects describe an episode of hope as having lasted from one to six months.[2] Indeed, many linguistic expressions of hope, such as "I hope you will sleep well" or "I hope for a better future," do not express an emotional state, but rather an expression of good wishes or a general expectation.

Hope is not as intense as other typical emotions because of the temporal distance between us and the emotional object. When the emotional object of hope is not so far away in the future, hope may be intense and could have all emotional characteristics, including intense feeling. It is interesting to note that although fear is also directed at a future situation, no one has claimed that fear is not an emotion; on the contrary, fear is often described as the most basic and typical emotion. This difference expresses the greater emotional impact we attach to negative events as compared with positive ones.

As a sentiment, hope is a kind of background framework that is crucial for human life: a person is someone with hope—someone "without hope" is close to the grave. In this sense, hope is a profound attitude determining our basic attitude toward life. This kind of fundamental hope is not goal-oriented hope, since it lacks a specific object or target; it may be characterized as a type of evaluative openness. Nevertheless, such hope does have an orientation, and this is toward a better and more valuable future.[3] Hope helps us overcome everyday hardships by valuing life and orienting us toward a better and more just future; a hopeful attitude like this is of great practical and moral value.

Hope and fear have two basic intentional elements: (1) a desire to be in or to avoid a certain situation, and (2) a belief that the desired or undesired situation is probable. The first element expresses the evaluative and motivational components, whereas the second expresses the cognitive component. In hope these elements relate to the desire for a certain situation, and a belief that the desired situation is probable despite indications to the contrary. These elements are necessary for the emergence of hope, but are not sufficient. We can desire a certain situation—for example, we may want peace between two remote countries, and may believe that such a peace is possible, but our attitude in this matter would not be the emotional attitude of hope since we do not care intensely about these countries. In order for the emotion of hope to be generated, the desired object must be of great importance to us. Factors which determine such importance are, for example, relevance, degree of reality, the strength of the given event, as well as various personality features.

The probability of the cognitive belief in hope should be between 0 and 1. Hope can be present even if the probability of the desired situation is low; in this case we are hoping against hope, namely, we are hoping against the odds or probabilities. When the probability we attach to the desired event is high, we say we are "hopeful that . . ." Here, we do not merely hope that the object of hope will be attained, but we also expect it. In cases where the probability is low, we may say: "I hope for the best, but expect the worst." If the probability is quite high and we see no difficulties in reaching the desired situation, hope will not be intense, if present at all. In typical cases of hope, it is difficult to attain the desired situation, but it is nevertheless possible.[4]

Changes in the probability of the emotional object often generate hope. Hope is mostly initiated when we confront events that cause a decrease in the probability of a previously certain event, or an increase in the probability of a previously unlikely event. In both cases an increase in the appraised importance of the future event will intensify hope. Similarly, hope is terminated due to reduction in the perceived probability or importance of the event, as well as when we obtain what we were hoping for or believe that obtaining it is certain.[5]

When it is certain that the desired situation either will not be achieved or will be achieved, there is no place for hope. When I know for certain that my team will not win the national championship, I cannot hope that it will win this championship. I can imagine it winning or wish it would have won, but I cannot hope for something when I know for certain that it will not be fulfilled. Similarly, when I know for certain the existence of a certain situation, I cannot hope for it. I cannot hope that my neighbor will not come to visit me this evening when I know that she is already here.

The element of probability is what distinguishes hope from fantasy. Unlike hope, in fantasy the cognitive element of believing that the desired situation is probable is not significant. Although hope involves future uncertainties, the uncertainties should not be too great. When the probability of attainment is unrealistically low, hope is usually inappropriate, and it is often not intense; in this sense, hope involves realistic imagination.

Hope is also distinguished from fantasies or other types of desires by its evaluative norms. Our hopes reflect our values and hence we do not consider a state as hope if it implies values different from our values. When in the heat of a discussion, a person desires the death of a colleague, we would not describe him as hoping for the death of that colleague, if such a desire does not reflect his actual values. This difference is expressed in the motivational component: we would not take serious actions to fulfill our fantasies or immoral desires, while we would take such actions to fulfill our hopes. In this sense, the object of hope has some kind of priority over the objects of fantasies or immoral desires.[6]

In this context, it may be indicated that the difference between "I hope that P" and "there is hope that P" concerns the nature of the probability: in the first case, it is a subjective probability and in the second, the probability is of more objective nature. This does not mean that the probability in the first case is always lower than in the second case.

The uncertainty conditions of both hope and fear should exclude deliberative uncertainty. If the only reason why I am not certain whether given circumstances will take place is that I am undecided which of several possible actions I will take, I cannot be said to fear or hope for these circumstances. Hope and fear are present when I know my own attitude toward the emotional object, but I do not know whether it will be realized.[7]

Empirical studies indicate that most episodes of hope involve achievement-related goals, for example, success in some academic, artistic, or athletic endeavor, obtaining a good job, and so forth. The hopes of the second largest group pertained to interpersonal relationships, such as romantic hopes and hopes for good relations with those close to us. The third group expressed altruistic hopes for the well-being of another person. Other objects of hope were less common.[8]

Optimism is closely related to hope: in both we anticipate possible positive events. However, optimism is not an emotion, but an attitude which may turn into a mood or an emotion. In this regard we may distinguish between expectation, optimism, and hope. I can expect X without considering X to be positive or negative. When I am optimistic concerning X, I consider X as positive, but this does not imply yet an emotional attitude toward X. I can be optimistic concerning the future development of a certain city, but I do not experience an emotional state with all its typical characteristics, such as instability, great intensity, partiality, and brief duration. (In everyday language, we do sometimes describe such states as hope, and this is one reason why some psychologists tend not to include hope within their list of emotions.) Hope implies not merely expectation toward a positive event but also personal significance which turns our experience into an emotional one. Hence, hope better expresses our personal values. Although optimism indicates our general positive attitude toward the expected event, it does not express our profound values—it often may express a general and uninvolved attitude. In this sense, optimism refers more to our assessment of the situation rather than, as in hope, to our values.

Another difference between the emotion of hope and the nonemotional attitude of optimism concerns the probability of the expected event. As with other types of emotions, hope is also present in unstable circumstances, namely, when the event's probability is neither too unlikely nor virtually assured. Optimism, by contrast, may increase linearly with the probability of attainment.

The issues of personal significance and the event's probability, which distinguish hope from optimism, are closely related in hope. If an event is sufficiently important, hope may be generated even though the probability of attainment is practically nil. By contrast, the importance of an event does not, by itself, justify optimism. Thus, a person with presumably incurable cancer might be told: "Though there is little reason for optimism, don't lose hope."[9]

We may characterize hopefulness, which expresses optimism or a hopeful disposition, as a kind of affective trait.

As indicated in chapter 7, hope and optimism in general help us in our everyday life. They make it easier for us to make certain sacrifices on behalf of others and to cope with our own negative events. They lead us to higher motivation, more effective performance, and ultimately, greater success. There is mounting empirical evidence that optimism and hope may indeed have a beneficial effect on recovery from illness, and, conversely, that pessimism may have adverse effects. It has been suggested, for example, that whereas pessimism promotes depression, optimism promotes courage.[10]

Hope and optimism thus tend to be self-fulfilling. Indeed, it was found that the level of hope was a better predictor of students' grades than their scores in intelligence tests. Students with high hopes set themselves higher goals and knew how to work hard to attain them. People who are optimistic see failure as due to something that can be changed, enabling them to anticipate success the next time around. Moreover, optimists make mental excuses to lessen the impact of current and potential failures. Pessimists take the blame for failure, ascribing it to some lasting characteristic they are helpless to change; hence, they tend to become depressed. Whereas the optimist gives external, variable, and specific reasons for failures, the pessimist makes internal, stable, and global attributions.[11] Seligman has argued that for a given level of intelligence, your actual achievement is a function not just of talent but also of the capacity to withstand defeat. Being able to take rejection with grace is essential in sales of all kinds, especially with a product like insurance, where the ratio of "noes" to "yeses" can be discouragingly high. The emotional reaction to defeat is crucial to the ability to marshal enough motivation to continue. Indeed, Seligman found that optimistic insurance agents sold 29 percent more insurance in the first year than did their more pessimistic peers, and 130 percent more in their second year.[12] As President Eisenhower said, "pessimism never won any battle."

Empirical studies concerning hope indicate that compared to low-hope people, high-hope people have a greater number of goals, have more difficult goals, have more success at achieving their goals, experience greater happiness and less distress, have superior coping skills, recover better from physical injury, and report less burnout at work. Contrary, then, to the common stereotype about useless hopes, hope has a high functional value.[13] This value of hope is not due to some mysterious quality or entity; it is rather due to the fact that a hopeful attitude puts us in a better condition to overcome everyday hardships. Hope may be the dreams of those who are awake, but often those are very realistic dreams.

*Fear*
I am not afraid of tomorrow, for I have seen yesterday and I love today.
—William Allen White

Anything I've ever done that ultimately was worthwhile . . . initially scared me to death.
—Betty Bender

Human fears are not random: some fears are very common and others extremely rare. The most commonly reported type of fear is a fear of snakes (this is true even in areas containing few snakes) and that of heights. Many fears are focused on objects that have threatened survival, such as potential predators, unfamiliar places, and the dark. However, the prevalence of these fears is not necessarily related to their present survival value. Some of our most common fears, such as fear from small, harmless spiders, have no apparent biological significance, while fears from really dangerous situations, such as driving at high speed, which may threaten survival, are oddly uncommon. The distribution of types of fear varies with many personal and social factors. One such factor is age. A predominant pattern of fears reaches peak incidence in early adulthood and declines in succeeding years. Examples of this pattern include fear of animals and of the dark. The second, less common pattern is that of a gradual increase in fear, reaching its peak in middle adulthood, and involves, for example, fear of illness, injury, and crowds.[14]

We may distinguish between acute and chronic fear. Acute fear, such as the fear of snakes or the fear of an anxious passenger as an aircraft descends, is typically brief, has a high peak of intensity, is provoked by tangible stimuli or situations, and is easy to detect. By comparison, chronic fear, such as the fear of getting old or being alone, is typically of longer duration, its peak intensity at most moments is lower, it is not necessarily connected to tangible stimuli or situations, and is harder to detect. Chronic fear is a type of sentiment.[15]

The importance of belonging to a reference group is clearly indicated also in the case of fear. There is consistent evidence that membership in a small, cohesive group can play an important part in controlling fear. With a few exceptions, most people appear to be more susceptible to fear when they are alone. Even imagining a feared situation is less distressing if people think of themselves as being accompanied rather than alone. However, sometimes when we in a group, we are open to fear by contagion.[16]

The intentional components of hope are as follows: (a) a cognitive component which attaches some probability to the desired situation, (b) an evaluative component which includes a very positive evaluation of the desired situation, and (c) a motivational component which expresses a strong desire and readiness to act. The intentional components of fear are parallel: (a) a cognitive component which attaches some probability to the undesired situation, (b) an evaluative component which includes a very negative evaluation of the undesired situation, and (c) a motivational component which expresses a strong desire and readiness to act.

Like hope, fear also consists of a desire for a certain situation—or more precisely, for the aversion of a certain situation—and a cognitive belief attaching some probability to this situation. Unlike hope, the evaluative component in the desire is negative. The presence of some probability that the undesired event will not materialize indicates the close connection between fear and hope. Fear implies hope. The belief that something can be avoided or remedied is typical of hope and this belief is absent when things are hopeless. Similarly, hope implies fear, namely, the belief that the desired event will not materialize.[17]

As in hope, fear also tends to be self-fulfilling since it tends to inhibit hope and optimism which promote the success rate. The rock climber who fears that he will fall tends thereby to increase the probability of this very same event.[18]

Fear has evolved as a response to existential threats; its adaptive value is obvious and it is no wonder that it emerges quite early in our personal development—according to most accounts around eight months—and some fear responses may even be hard-wired.[19]

What is the object of fear? It is obvious that one's self is the focus of concern in fear, but it is less obvious what the emotional object of a certain fear might be. When I am afraid of a particular person or of a storm, is the emotional object myself or someone else (such as the other person) or something else (such as the storm)? It is not problematic to say that emotions such as shame, regret, and pride are directed at oneself; the situation is less clear concerning fear.

We may discern various types of emotional objects for fear:

1. A certain situation—I am afraid of the dark.
2. Another person—I am afraid of this violent person.
3. Oneself—I am afraid of losing my reputation as the brightest person in my department.

It seems that the above order reflects the order of development of the various types of fear: fear whose object is a certain situation appeared first in our evolution, whereas fear whose object is oneself appeared last. Fear expresses the most significant warning sign of threats to the organism; hence, it is plausible that our cognitive resources will be focused upon the threat. This is especially true concerning existential threats, which have generated the development of fear. Focusing on the external threat is advantageous even if we are not clearly aware of the specific nature of the threat, as is the case with the fear experienced by primitive organisms or when our cognitive capacities cannot properly function (e.g., when we are in the dark). In these circumstances danger is sensed, but there is no awareness of the source of the danger. Being afraid of the dark is not like being afraid of an aggressive person: you do not consider the dark as an object which is possibly going to hurt you. Concerning its object, this type of fear is closer to a type of mood than to a typical emotion. Like moods, the object of such fear is diffuse and unspecific; consequently it appears to lack an object. The dark is feared because it renders us vulnerable, unable adequately to observe possible threats.[20]

Fear that is directed at a specific person (or animal) requires a more developed cognitive system which can clearly identify the specific source of the threat. An even more developed cognitive stage is that in which the cognitive resources are focused upon the effects of the threat to the self. Darkness can be threatening in certain situations, and a person who sometimes exhibits aggressive behavior poses a certain threat to me, but this does not mean that I should always feel fear whenever I am in the dark or around this person. A more sophisticated cognitive system is able to be concerned with circumstances where my own activities may induce a real threat to me, for instance, when I try to run in a dark, unfamiliar place or when I confront the aggressive person. In developed human societies fear is often concerned with social, rather than existential, issues. Here, the concern is not my very existence but my status and well-being. Hence, the cognitive focus is not upon the threat which may terminate my existence, but upon my own activities and relationships in a future social environment.

In light of its various types of emotional object, fear may be classified either in the group of emotions toward others (or toward external objects in general) or in the group of emotions toward oneself. I have chosen to classify it in the latter group, because in many everyday situations fear is not existential but social, and in most of these cases one's self is the emotional object. Moreover, hope clearly belongs to the same group of emotions as fear, and hope is directed at oneself.

The difficulties in identifying the object of fear do not characterize hope: hope is clearly an emotion toward oneself. My hopes are directed at future situations in which I, or those related to me, are in a better situation. Even when I hope for a cleaner environment in the future, I am nevertheless still considering my own desire, or the desire of others, to enjoy such an environment. Unlike fear, which is concerned with an immediate event, hope is concerned with a more remote event and hence the agent's cognitive resources do not have to be focused on that event to the exclusion of reference to the agent.

## Relationships with Other Emotions

No man in the world has more courage than the man who can stop after eating one peanut.
—Channing Pollack

I would rather be a coward than brave because people hurt you when you are brave.
—E. M. Forster

In light of the two basic intentional elements of hope and fear, that is, the desire to be in or to avoid a certain situation, and the belief that the desired or undesired situation is probable, we may describe the following family of attitudes:

1. *Hope*—A wishes that P and thinks that P is probable.
2. *Fear*—A wishes that not-P but thinks that P is probable.
3. *Despair*—A wishes that P but thinks that P is contracertain.
4. *Resignation*—A wishes that not-P but thinks that P is certain.
5. *Confidence*—A wishes that P and thinks that P is certain; and A wishes that not-P and thinks that P is contracertain.[21]

The fact that in both hope and fear P and not-P are probable indicates that there is indeed no hope without fear and no fear without hope. When P or not-P is considered as certain or contracertain, then hope and fear are not evident. I believe that whereas hope and fear are typical emotions, *despair* and *resignation* are usually affective, but not emotional, attitudes—they are closer to moods than to emotions; and *confidence* may not be an affective attitude at all.

The intensity variable of certainty may partially explain these differences. As indicated above, uncertainty is positively correlated with emotional intensity: the more we are certain of the eliciting event, the less available is its alternative and the lesser is its emotional intensity. There are indeed findings suggesting that fear and hope are associated with uncertainty.[22] Certainty is, then, not typical of emotions. This may explain why confidence is typically not an affective attitude: when we are certain that our wish will materialize or that a situation we do not desire will not take place, there is typically nothing about which to be excited. Such a situation does not involve changes which generate affective states. Despair and resignation also involve certainty but their affective impact is different since they refer to negative events; the affective impact is particularly significant when we do not know how to cope with events that are relevant to our well-being. Although despair and resignation are not emotional attitudes, they are nevertheless affective states. Unlike confidence, in despair and resignation there is tension between what we desire and the expected event and this generates affective attitudes. Those attitudes are not emotions since they are not focused on a specific object— the desired situation is not considered probable any more. Confidence is related to hope in expressing a certain harmony between the agent's wish and the expected event; despair is related to fear in expressing a certain discrepancy between the two.

*Despair* is similar to hope in its evaluative component, but the cognitive component is quite different as it involves the belief that the desired situation is contracertain. This difference is also expressed in different motivational components: although in both hope and despair there is a strong desire for a certain situation, in despair this desire is not accompanied by readiness to act. The belief that no action will be able to bring about the desired situation eliminates the value of any action. Despair is closer to a negative mood and sometimes it may turn into a nonaffective attitude of indifference. In an episode in the television series *Seinfeld*, George expresses his hope to be hopeless, namely, to be in a state of despair; he explains that he no longer cares about his failures with women. Such lack of caring is consequent upon a lack of emotional attitude.

In this context, Day suggests that we distinguish between *despair* and *desperation*. In both cases, "A wishes that P, but thinks that P is contracertain." The difference between them concerns their motivational component: When A is in despair, A will do nothing; when A is desperate, he will do anything, notwithstanding that he thinks it to be contracertain.[23] It should be noted that the actions taken by a desperate person are usually not connected with the specific desired situation, since such a situation is considered to be contracertain; these actions usually relate to other aspects of the person's life.

*Resignation* is similar to fear in its evaluative component, but the cognitive component is quite different as it involves the belief that the undesired event is certain. This difference is also expressed in different motivational components: although in both fear and resignation there is a strong desire to avert a certain situation, in resignation this desire is not accompanied by readiness to act. The belief that no action will be able to eliminate the undesired situation abolishes the value of any action. Like despair, resignation is closer to a negative mood and sometimes it may turn into a nonaffective attitude of indifference.

*Horror* is a kind of intense fear which denies flight or any other viable manner of coping with the situation. Horror is similar to resignation in wishing that something will not happen but nevertheless thinking that its occurrence is almost inevitable. However, whereas resignation may lead to a nonaffective attitude, horror is always an intense affective state—there is no such a thing as mild horror.

*Courage* is often regarded as the opposite of fear. In terms of the two above-mentioned elements of desire and belief, courage is similar to fear as it may also be described by the statement: A wishes that not-P but thinks that P is probable. The evaluative component in fear and courage seems to be similar as in both cases it consists of a negative evaluation of P. The cognitive component in both attitudes also seems to be similar since in both cases it includes the belief that P is probable; however, typically, the probability given to P in courage is considerably greater. The most significant difference between fear and courage concerns the motivational component: whereas in fear flight is the typical behavior, in courage the agent usually confronts the threat, as the agent believes that she can successfully overcome it.

Courage is often identified with fearlessness, namely, the absence of fear. This is misleading as courage seems to be a way of facing fear and not a lack of fear. Aristotle characterizes a brave person as the one "who faces and who fears the right things with the right aim, in the right way and at the right time, and who feels confidence under the corresponding conditions."[24] It is not the absence of fear, but rather the presence of confidence under fearful circumstances that is characteristic of the brave person. Indeed, people who have done courageous deeds describe their attitude while doing these deeds as that of confidence under fear. There are also a small number of people who are relatively impervious to fear; in most circumstances typical of fear, they experience no fear; for example, they experience none of the usual physical accompaniments of fear, such as palpitations or sweating. These people may be fearless, but they are not courageous—they have no fear to cope with or overcome. The presence of a genuine effort to cope with or overcome fear is what distinguishes courage from fearlessness. People are not blamed for being afraid, but merely for a lack of genuine effort to cope with and overcome the fear; doing this often expresses courage and is highly praised.[25]

An interesting study in this regard investigated the attitudes of astronauts. The study suggests that although the astronauts experienced fear during training, by the time they had finished their training they were able to complete the space journey with minimal fear: they had undergone a transition from courage to fearlessness. Apparently, the astronauts felt convinced that their intensive training had prepared them to handle any emergency and hence could adopt the attitude of fearlessness. This indicates that fearlessness can be acquired: the successful practice of courageous behavior leads to a decrease in fear and finally to a state of fearlessness.[26]

In light of the above distinction, it seems that courage is not an emotion but rather a behavioral attitude. Accordingly, the feeling component in courage is not always intense. Courage may be associated with fear, but is not the opposite of fear.

From the standpoint of the agent performing a certain act, this act can be regarded as courageous only if it involves coping with or overcoming fear. From the standpoint of the observer, a certain act by someone may be regarded as courageous if fear is typically associated with the given circumstances. However, such attribution may be mistaken, and we must take into account the agent's attitude in order to determine whether we are dealing with courage or fearlessness. Since courage is defined by referring to the way the agent deals with his particular fears, acts of courage may be performed by everyone and not merely by a few selected people.[27]

*Cowardice*, which is the opposite of courage, may be analyzed in a similar manner. Spinoza characterizes cowardice as fear of some evil which most people do not usually fear.[28] When we refer to a specific act of cowardice, then we refer to a behavioral attitude and not to an independent emotion. However, cowardice can also refer to a more enduring characteristic of the agent and hence may be described as a sentiment or an affective trait. In a similar manner, courage can also be described as a specific behavior, a sentiment, or an affective trait.

Both courage and cowardice are contagious—the courageous or cowardly behavior of one person may easily affect the behavior of other people.

Fear should be distinguished from *anxiety* and *anguish*. Fear is an emotion with a specific object; anxiety is an affective disorder which has a more general concern than fear. Anguish takes a middle position between fear and anxiety. Unlike anxiety, whose object is not always clear, the object of anguish is the self. In comparison with fear, anguish is concerned with more fundamental problems relating to our very existence; the nature of the self and its future are of primary concern in anguish.[29] Because of its general nature, anguish may not be regarded as a typical emotion, but nevertheless it is closer to a typical emotion than is anxiety.

*Intensity Variables*

We hope vaguely but dread precisely.
—Paul Valery

Blessed is the person who is too busy to worry in the daytime and too sleepy to worry at night.
—Leo Aikman

I have indicated that the intensity of hope and fear is usually not as strong as that of happiness and sadness since the former are directed at the future and the latter at the present. The temporal distance, like other types of distance, decreases emotional intensity. This is expressed in several intensity variables.

The event's strength is one intensity variable which is typically weaker in hope and fear because the event is located in the future. At a distance, things are usually perceived to be smaller. As noted, there are also circumstances in which temporal distance may amplify the event. In these cases, the time which separates us from the event is used for continual rethinking about the event and this makes the event stronger and more central for us.

The intensity variable of the degree of reality is weaker in hope and fear mainly because we are not certain whether the event will actually materialize; the hoped-for or feared events are only probable. The temporal distance further weakens the intensity variable: something far away is less real for us; its image is, so to speak, somewhat blurred.

The temporal distance typical of hope and fear also decreases the degree of relevance of the expected event. Something that is not close to us is usually less relevant to our self-image and the attainment of our goals. As in an instance of physical threat, in the case of emotional threats we try to place ourselves at a safe distance. In the emotional situation this means that we reduce the relevance of the event for ourselves.

The weakening effect of the above intensity variables is less obvious in fear than in hope. Accordingly, fear is typically stronger than hope. As indicated, there are many examples of attitudes which seem to have the intentional components of hope, but lack an intense feeling component. The weakening effect of the temporal distance makes these attitudes more similar to general nonaffective attitudes than to emotional ones. There are fewer examples of attitudes having the intentional components of fear, but lacking an intense feeling component; negative evaluations of our own fortune are typically of great concern to us.

The issue of our accountability is of much significance in hope and fear; unlike other emotions, here it is not a retrospective matter. In other emotions, our accountability for the event which triggers the emotional attitude indicates whether the current emotional situation could have been otherwise. In hope and fear the triggering event has not yet been actualized and our accountability is most significant for determining whether it will be actualized. Accordingly, the connection between our ability to control potentially threatening situations and the experience of fear appears to be the following: if a person feels unable to control the probable outcome, she is likely to feel fear, and if she feels able to control it, she is unlikely to feel fear. If controllability means that we perceive ourselves as able to reduce the likelihood of an adverse event, then fear will be reduced. Similarly, perceiving ourselves as able to increase the likelihood of a desired event will increase hope. Indeed, confidence is a major factor in decreasing fear and increasing hope.[30]

It would appear then that the general positive correlation between controllability and emotional intensity is not maintained in fear: unlike retrospective emotions, in fear greater controllability seems to decrease emotional intensity.

Nevertheless, I do not consider the condition of fear to be an instance which is counter to the above general correlation. Greater controllability in fear usually entails greater ability to avoid the adverse event, which in turn means that the threatening event has much less of a chance to become real. It is the variable of reality, rather than controllability, which is the major factor in reducing the fear. If we were able to eliminate the effect of greater accountability on the probability of the adverse event, fear would not decrease. Take, for example, a situation in which we can choose what course of events to take, but it is difficult to determine whether our choice will result in greater or lesser harm to us. In this case, greater accountability does not affect the reality variable and there is no change in the intensity of fear. We are likely to be more excited in this case, as our own role is more significant—even if this role may be an illusory one.

The ability to exert some control in a potentially dangerous situation can help to inhibit fear—again, because it reduces the degree of reality of the threatening event. Thus, being the driver of a car when road conditions are difficult is less frightening than being a passenger in the same car.[31] Since we typically overestimate our own abilities and underestimate those of others, our own driving is perceived to be safer. (In this regard someone said: "When I die, I want to go like my grandfather did, peacefully in his sleep. Not yelling and screaming, like all the passengers in his car.")

In hope, as well, the general correlation between controllability and emotional intensity is maintained as long as greater controllability does not change the likelihood of the desired event.

It is interesting to mention in this connection that there are indications that anger can act as a potent inhibitor of fear, and fear may inhibit anger.[32] One possible explanation for such a relationship has to do with the issue of controllability. In anger, our sense of controllability is greater and this is a factor which reduces fear, as it decreases the degree of reality of the threatening event; and when we are fearful, we tend not to experience aggressive attitudes such as anger, as they might further worsen our situation if we lack the strength to support them.

I have already discussed above some of the relationships between the emotions of hope and fear and the intensity variables expressing our readiness, namely, expectedness and certainty. Here, I would merely like to mention that the general negative correlation between these variables and emotional intensity is maintained in fear and hope. Fear is less intense in the case of predictable adverse events if we perceive ourselves as able to cope with these events. If we perceive ourselves as unable to cope with the expected events, then we become helpless and our fear increases.

Hope may indeed be more intense in the case of predictable desired events since the degree of reality of such events increases. Nevertheless, when there is growing certainty concerning the lack of future changes, hope will decrease. In research on happiness, people from rural areas were found to be, not less happy than people in big cities, but less hopeful about their future happiness.[33] Since rural life is relatively static and unchanging, one knows the type of life one is going to have; hopes of becoming rich and famous are not merely unrealistic, but cannot even be sustained as sweet illusions. Hence, rural life is harder to bear for youngsters who hope to fulfill these dreams.

The issue of desert seems to be of lesser significance in fear.[34] This may be explained by taking into account the great existential value of fear. The issue of desert is dominant when social concerns are central; it is less important when threats to one's life are evident. However, even in the latter case there is a sense in which the issue of deservingness is present: we assume that we deserve to live. Moreover, I have suggested that in light of the evolution of our social environment, all basic emotions, including fear, have become more and more occupied with social concerns. Hence, the issue of desert becomes central in those common cases where social concerns are central to fear—for example, when there is a threat to our status.

I believe that the issue of desert is even more central in hope since hope, more than fear, is concerned with social issues. A prominent element of hope is our belief that we deserve to be in the state we desire.

*Moral Value*

Hope is a good breakfast, but a bad supper.
—Francis Bacon

Who is more foolish, the child afraid of the dark or the man afraid of the light?
—Maurice Freehill

According to Greek mythology, when Prometheus stole fire from the gods and gave it to mankind, Zeus in fury sent Pandora to earth with a box which the gods warned her never to open. Unable to resist the temptation, she opened the box and out flew the cloud of evils which infest the earth. When Pandora closed the lid of the box, only hope remained inside. Prometheus's brother, Epimetheus (whose name may be translated as "second thought") married Pandora, although she brought with her no gift but hope. Epimetheus was wise enough to recognize the value of the gift of hope.[35]

In many personal, political, psychological, and religious contexts, hope is considered to be a blessing. Thus, hope is one of the three theological or Christian virtues, the others being faith and charity or love. Hope is often considered a virtue given by God and connecting directly to God. In philosophy, it is worth mentioning the work of Ernst Bloch who points out the importance of hope in achieving a more moral and fulfilling life. As indicated, hope helps us to overcome everyday difficulties by looking beyond them to a better future. Hope is a soft cushion to lean on in adversity. In many cases, hope is the best medicine available to us. In light of its high functional value, hope is often considered an obligation, part of our duty to improve our own life and the lives of others, in moral and other qualitative aspects.[36]

Hope has also been regarded negatively. Such a perspective is found, in for instance, Plato, Kant, and Nietzsche. Nietzsche claimed that hope is the worst of evils for it prolongs the torments of man. From the depths of Auschwitz, Tadeusz Borowski judged hope as useless and even harmful: "We were never taught to rid ourselves of hope, and that is why we are dying in the gas-chambers."[37] Hope may have a negative moral value if the hope for a better future makes us ignore present evils. In this sense, hope has a deceptive character; hence, we have the saying that hope is a poor guide, but very good company along the way. Moreover, when people hope for immoral objects, hope ceases to be morally valuable.

Spinoza argued that hope and fear cannot be good in themselves, since they are always accompanied by sadness; fear is a type of sadness and there is no hope without fear. Hope and fear can be good in themselves only insofar as they can restrain an excess of joy. According to Spinoza, the free man who is guided by reason is not led by fear; fear arises from weakness of mind. A more critical approach to the functional value of fear is expressed by the Italian physiologist, Angelo Mosso, who considered fear to be one of the main evils of human existence and argued that "fear is a disease to be cured; the brave man may fail sometimes, but the coward fails always." In a similar vein, Anwar el-Sadat, the assassinated Egyptian president, said: "Fear is, I believe, a most effective tool in destroying the soul of an individual—and the soul of a people."[38]

Contrary to the above views, I believe that fear has a crucial functional role in increasing our chances of survival; no wonder that it is prevalent among animals and human beings. The functional value of fear is not merely existential but social as well: it keeps us aware of our norms and prevents some of the activities which may violate them. The emergence of fear points out the dangers related to what we cherish. Like many other emotions, the value of fear depends upon the specific circumstances. Generally, when fear relates to events with negative implications for us, it has a positive value, and when it prevents us from doing things with positive implications, it has a negative value.

Consider, for example, fear regarding the possible loss of a mate to a rival, which is expressed in jealousy. If this fear is excessive, it may be harmful since it may be a self-fulfilling prophecy. When we are indifferent to the fate of this relationship, fear does not arise even if there is a real threat to the relationship. Indifference entails our evaluation of the relationship as insignificant. A low degree of fear, and hence a low degree of jealousy, may be the optimal attitude. Similarly, an excessive amount of fear may be harmful in the sense that it prevents us from functioning properly. However, a total absence of fear is also harmful; fear is an important biological mechanism enabling us to avoid unnecessary dangers. As indicated, courage is a virtue not because it abolishes all types of fear, but rather because it enables us to take the optimal action while being in danger and afraid.

The fear underlying jealousy has, then, some adaptive value: it helps to maintain and improve a certain type of relationship. Accordingly, our aim should not be to abolish jealousy but to reduce it to a reasonable degree which will not prevent us from behaving in an optimal manner.

Hope may function as a dream or an ideal which helps us cope with the hardships of our life. We know, for example, that the beautiful song, "Home, Sweet Home," was composed by a longing, homeless wayfarer in a corner of a New York cafe. Like our other dreams, no one can steal our hopes and when reality is hard, we can indulge in the pleasure of hopes. In this sense, hope is fundamental to our life. It seems that children are more hopeful than adults and this may be one reason why children are so attractive.[39]

I have suggested that emotions are mainly concerned with events within our immediate environment, while intellectual considerations are more general and typically refer to circumstances beyond our immediate environment. Accordingly, future events are more central in intellectual considerations. The diminished emotional impact of the future and the importance of emotions in determining our conduct may severely distort our proper conduct concerning future events. One way to cope with this problem is to use both intellectual considerations together with an emotional attitude when determining our conduct. Another way is to take account of our hopes and fears. Accordingly, one function of hope and fear may be to give objects which are far away from us their due importance. Thomas Reid clearly expresses this point: "Imagination, like the eye, diminisheth its objects in proportion to their distance. The passions of hope and fear must be raised, in order to give such objects their due magnitude in the imagination, and their due influence upon our conduct."[40]

Chapter 17

Taking Account of Our Specific Deeds—Pride, Regret, Guilt, and Embarrassment

The one regret I have in life is that I'm not someone else.
—Woody Allen

In this chapter, I describe emotions directed at our own specific deeds. These deeds can either be in the past or in the present. When we negatively evaluate our past deeds we may experience the emotions of regret or fear; when we positively evaluate them, the emotion of pride may emerge. Our present deeds may evoke in us the emotions of embarrassment, guilt, and pride. We can see that "pride" is used to denote our positive attitude toward both past and present activities. In the negative realm, the terms are more differentiated and whereas regret is clearly directed at past activities, embarrassment is concerned with present ones; guilt may arise from reflections upon both our past and present actions.

Pride and regret are emotional attitudes directed at our particular actions; pridefulness and shame are emotional attitudes directed at our more general characteristics. Pride and regret are then correlated with gratitude and anger, while pridefulness and shame are similar to love and hate. The first group of emotions are directed at ourselves and the second group at others. (In everyday language, we sometimes use shame to refer also to specific deeds; thus, we say that we are ashamed of what we did. In everyday language, we also use pride, rather than pridefulness, to express our positive attitude toward our general characteristics.)

*General Characteristics*

*Pride*
I learned to put the toilet seat down . . . it makes you look like a warm, caring, sensitive human being.
—Ralph Noble

Two major elements are essential to pride: (1) evaluating something as positive, (2) considering oneself as somehow connected to that positive thing. Pride is a function of both elements and an increase in one can compensate for a lower degree of the other. The absence of one of them usually eliminates pride.

The connection to oneself can be of various types: I may be responsible for the generation of a certain event, I may own a certain thing, I may be associated with a person who is responsible for the event or who owns a certain thing, and so forth.

As in other emotions, the comparative concern is important in pride. The comparative value, rather than the absolute one, is of greatest concern in pride. Winning a competition, or being first in other respects, is a source of great pride. Pride does not necessarily presuppose exclusivity, but it presupposes some sense of a comparatively high value and often also superiority. We may be proud of something many people have, for example, our health or the fact that we belong to a certain nation. Although we share the object of our pride with many people, we are still in a better position than others with whom we can compare ourselves. Similarly, a disabled person may be proud of managing to perform a simple action which many nondisabled people can easily do. In this case, the pride comes not so much from performing the action per se, but from overcoming a personal handicap.[1]

The more exclusive a certain quality is, the more proud we are of having it. But if we compare two achievements of different magnitudes and of different degrees of exclusivity, it is not clear which will generate greater pride: the one with the greater achievement but lesser exclusivity or the one with lesser achievement but greater exclusivity. Such determination depends, of course, on the unique context and the type of achievement and exclusivity.

The importance of the comparative concern in pride indicates that although pride is directed at ourselves, the opinion of others is of crucial importance as well. Accordingly, if we perform in a manner which we believe is inferior to our past performance, but nevertheless people around us praise our performance highly, we may still feel pride. The importance of the people around us for the generation of pride may even cause us to feel pride toward actions we find morally questionable. Such types of pride, however, will not be as profound as pride that is compatible with our values and beliefs.

Pride is not only the consequence of achievements but of "gifts" as well. We are proud not only of something we have purposefully achieved by investing effort and talent, such as winning a certain competition, but also of something we have inherited, such as good looks. Distinguishing achievements from gifts is hard since achievements are also based on natural gifts such as talent. It might be argued that in the end everything is a gift. Talent or kindness of heart, the capacity for self-discipline and self-development, and the aptitude for learning are all various kinds of gifts.[2]

Whether an attribute is considered a gift or an achievement has bearing on the issue of responsibility. We are not responsible for a gift in the same manner that we are responsible for our actions or achievements. The inability to distinguish gifts from achievements could endanger the whole notion of personal responsibility. Without entering into a discussion concerning personal responsibility, I will just note that in everyday life and in moral discussions, we distinguish between different degrees of personal and moral responsibility. This enables us to speak about different degrees of credit that we and others can ascribe to us and which gives rise to different degrees of pride. Indeed, I have suggested that accountability is an important intensity variable: a greater degree of controllability, effort, and intent increases emotional intensity and this is true of pride as well. I am more proud of a successful event for which I was responsible, at which I aimed, and in which I invested effort, than of a successful event which occurred through pure luck.

It is interesting to note that whereas we are often proud of our health, we are less frequently ashamed or feel guilty about our illness. We tend to believe that we are healthy due to our effort or unique way of living, whereas our illness is attributed to factors external to us. This is in accordance with our tendency to attribute our success to ourselves, whereas our failure is often attributed to others or to external factors.

Since pride is a type of pleasure taken in the possession of some quality that one deems valuable, there is a tendency to increase this pleasure either by imputing to ourselves qualities which we do not in fact possess, or by valuing too much the good qualities which happen to belong to us.[3] This tendency to self-ascribe gifts has an important function in maintaining our self-esteem. It is also of great importance in maintaining social bonds. We can consider ourselves as belonging to a certain group only if we see ourselves as part of the group and hence we take pride in, or regret, what other people in the group have done—even those who had nothing to do with us, or who died long before we lived. In the next chapter I discuss further the issue of collective pride.

*Regret*
You miss 100 percent of the shots you don't take.
—Michael Jordan

Regrets, I had a few, but then again, too few to mention . . . I did it my way.
—Frank Sinatra

Regret is basically a sorrow over a past alternative which was available to us, but which we missed. The more available the alternative was, the more intense is the regret. Thus, we more regret missing our bus by one minute than by twenty minutes.

There are many expressions indicating our negative attitude toward taking the past into consideration: "No use crying over spilt milk," "You can't turn back the clock," and "The past is gone." In a goal-oriented society, such as Western society, the past is of little concern: our eyes are directed at the future, where our goals are located. Indeed, avoiding the past is a common tendency for many of us. Such a negative attitude toward the past implies that it is not rational to invest resources in past events and we rather focus our limited resources on future goals. Accordingly, repudiation of the past is a prevalent criterion of rational decision making.

Although the past seems to be unchangeable and irremediable, our attitudes toward past events, and hence the impact of the past upon us, is constantly changing. Faulkner put it nicely when he asserted that "The past isn't dead. It's not even past."[4] Sometimes we should cry over spilt milk, otherwise how can we value milk and how can we avoid spilling it once again? One of the best ways to take account of the past is to take account of our emotions, as emotions are shaped by, among other things, past events. It is rational to care about the past even if only out of consideration for present and future circumstances.

Regret is an emotion which bridges the past and present with an eye to the future. In typical regret, we presently evaluate in a negative manner something we did, or refrained from doing; we do so in light of present and future considerations. As in emotions directed at our future, in emotions directed at our past the temporal distance between our present time and the time of the emotional event reduces emotional intensity. Time does heal many wounds. To give one example, we tend to show more leniency toward crimes committed in the past. In certain crimes there is a time limit after which we cannot prosecute the person who committed the crime. Our negative emotional attitudes toward this person also become less intense as time goes by. One reason may be that this person may have changed considerably; another reason may be that distance blurs our sight and emotional reactions. One function of emotions toward the past, such as regret, is to give the past its due significance. Also, we hope that we, and therefore others, are able to learn from the past, and thus will not be forever haunted by, or punished because of, past errors.

Regret affects people's behavior not only after a decision is made but also before the decision is made, when they anticipate the regret they may feel later. Therefore, most people tend to make regret-minimizing choices, that is, they make choices to minimize their possible future regret. These choices are typically risk-avoiding. Thus, people are ready to sacrifice monetary gain to ensure that they will not experience subsequent regret. An apt illustration of the tendency to minimize regret is provided in a study indicating that people are reluctant to exchange their lottery tickets. In this study, students were given lottery tickets and then were asked to exchange their ticket for another one, together with a small monetary incentive. Fewer than 50 percent agreed. In contrast, when given pens and the same exchange offer, over 90 percent agreed. The possibility for regret that exists when exchanging lottery tickets, but not pens, underlies this reluctance. The two lottery tickets, but not the pens, have the potential to result in different outcomes, and this suffices to induce an anticipation of regret. The reluctance to exchange the tickets is a regret-minimizing choice which involves risk-avoiding.[5]

Although regret-minimizing choices are typically risk-avoiding, some of them are risk-seeking. For example, if someone owns risky stocks and is confronted with the decision whether to sell these stocks in order to buy safer stocks, she may not sell her stocks in order to avoid regret. Although not selling is a more of a risk, it is associated with a lesser degree of possible regret, since we generally feel more personally responsible for our actions than our inactions. It seems that most people are more averse to regret than to risk; hence, they may sometimes make risk-seeking choices in order to minimize their regret.[6]

The tendency to minimize regret prevails among most people but not among all; some people are motivated to maximize joy. The tendency to minimize regret may have negative consequences as it may paralyze us and prevent us from undergoing experiences from which we may learn. Moreover, we may distinguish between two types of regret—short- and long-term regret—and reducing one of them may increase the other.

As a short-term emotion, regret is concerned with a loss caused by a specific change; it is associated with instability, great intensity, a partial perspective, and brief duration. The long-term sentiment of regret, which may be termed "wistful regret," is concerned with loss in the past, which has repercussions on the general course of life; as such, it is associated with more stability, less intensity, a more general perspective, and longer duration.[7]

The different types of regret are expressed in different determinants of each type. Thus, in the short term, people regret their actions more than their inactions, but when people look back on their lives, those things that they have not done are the ones that produce the most regret. For example, in the short term, people often regret their brief sexual affairs—this is "the morning-after effect"; in the long term, people typically regret sexual affairs they did not have. Regrettable inactions loom larger in the long run than they do in the short term. Long-term considerations are mainly concerned with lost opportunities, whereas short-term considerations are concerned more with actual gains.[8]

People are often tormented by what they imagine to be the consequences of the road not taken. Indeed, one survey of forty-eight women found that only one regretted having pursued a life dream, while almost all the women who had not pursued their life dream regretted it. Likewise, a *Glamour* article titled "The Road Not Taken" declared that "most of us don't regret what we have done so much as what we haven't. . . . I'm sorry there aren't more of me to marry some of the men I've cared about. And there are cities I wanted to live in but haven't, and babies I didn't have, and careers I would have liked to explore."[9]

Why do we regret more in the short term our failed actions and in the long term, our failures to act? Thomas Gilovich and Victoria H. Medvec, in their excellent analysis of regret, have suggested three types of mechanisms that give rise to this tendency: (1) elements that reduce the pain of regrettable actions, (2) elements that bolster the pain of regrettable inactions, and (3) elements that influence availability.[10]

Our tendency to take steps to ameliorate regrettable action more than regrettable inaction is one factor reducing the pain of regrettable actions. As Gilovich and Medvec put it, a woman who regrets marrying Mr. Wrong is likely to get divorced; a woman who regrets passing up Mr. Right typically must cope with the fact that he is no longer available. Regrettable actions tend to be further diminished by the identification of "silver linings" that offset the pain they cause. The woman who married Mr. Wrong will often say, "I can't stand my ex-husband, but without him I never would have had these two wonderful kids"; the woman who passes up Mr. Right typically finds less consolation. Moreover, regrettable actions tend to prompt more vigorous effort to reduce dissonance than do regrettable failures to act. Thus, one of the most common ways people cope with negative events is by noting how much they have learned from the experience: they acknowledge that the outcome is regrettable, but they offset the regret by indicating how much they profited from the experience itself. Gilovich and Medvec argue that such a silver lining—"But I learned so much"—is much more likely to apply to regrettable actions than regrettable inactions: people typically learn more by doing new things than by sticking to old patterns. The pain of regrettable action may be reduced in the short run by reversing some of its consequences; in the long run it is reduced by noticing some of its positive outcomes.

There are several factors that tend to bolster the pain of regrettable inaction. Gilovich and Medvec indicate that the consequences of regrettable actions are often finite: they are bounded by what actually happened. In contrast, what is troublesome about a regrettable inaction is the set of good things that could have happened had one acted. The consequences of inactions are therefore potentially infinite: they are bounded only by one's imagination. Moreover, the passage of time often brings with it increased confidence that one could have performed an earlier task successfully. A woman who passes up Mr. Right often has trouble in retrospect thinking of a truly compelling reason why such a choice was ever made. In contrast, someone who mistakenly marries Mr. Wrong can nonetheless recall how much fun he was at one time, how responsible he seemed back then, or how much everyone liked him.

Regrets of inaction occupy the mind more often than regrettable actions as people typically are more preoccupied with incomplete tasks than completed ones. The story of regrettable actions tends to be closed; the story of failures to act is usually open. Many regrets of inaction involve unrealized ambitions and unfulfilled intentions that are more available in memory and hence experienced more often than those actions which have been completed.[11]

Gilovich and Medvec indicate that one implication of their research is that people should be encouraged to act on their impulses more often; people should focus less on the short-term consequences of their action and more often "just do it." However, acting on this advice may be dangerous as the status quo is usually safer than trying something new. Giving a greater significance to unwise actions may promote risky behavior and decrease chances of surviving—and if being haunted by imagined lost opportunities is the cost of preventing such behavior, so be it. These opposing considerations suggest that there is no simple overall answer to the normative question of how we should behave in this regard.[12]

The conflict between short-term regrets concerning negative outcomes of action and long-term regrets concerning negative outcomes of inaction is not a conflict between being emotional and being nonemotional, but rather between positive and negative emotional states; to avoid negative emotional states we are quite often ready to give up positive ones. In order to avoid short-term negative emotional states, such as shame, fear, anger, and humiliation, we refrain from doing what may bring us positive emotional states, such as happiness, love, and pride. In this sense, we behave in a risk-avoiding manner: risk-avoiding behavior in the short run is preferred over maximizing joy in the long run. The cost of this strategy, which reduces our short-term risks and typically increases the overall probability of our survival, is mainly concerned with positive emotional states: it overrides short-term positive emotional states and increases long-term negative emotional states.

Various surveys of regret have found that people's single most common regret centered on their education. This is true of all types of people, including the relatively well-educated. The other common categories are work-related regrets and family-related regrets; the latter are mainly concerned with marriage and parenthood. Regrets concerning not having continued one's education, and concerning marriage, or having children too early are prominent because they prematurely close off a world of alternatives.[13]

The above groups of common regrets express our major emotional concerns. The wish to have continued our education expresses our belief that our personal capacities are by far greater than their present realization and with better education we could have been better and happier people. Work-related regrets are related to the execution of our capacities: our potential capacities have not fully materialized because of insufficient work opportunities. In the family-related regrets, the concerns are directed toward those near and dear to us and the major agency concerned is ourselves. We regret that we did not provide those close to us with the optimal opportunities for their own development. These opportunities could typically have been provided had we invested more care and attention and money; the first two are more within our control. In this case, regret is not concerned with the fact that we missed certain attractive alternatives, but that we did not provide such alternatives to those close to us.

Although regret is typically concerned with missed opportunities which we could have had if we had taken a different road, sometimes regret is concerned with missed opportunities that have nothing to do with our behavior or choices. Thus, when Eleanor Roosevelt was asked if she had any regrets, her response was that she wished she had been prettier.[14] Her regret is concerned with long-term missed opportunities, which she considered to be consequent upon her lack of beauty, but not with a road she failed to take.

Regret is fundamentally a counterfactual emotion; it is concerned with missed opportunities. Since no matter who we are, there are more things we cannot do than we can, so that all our lives are full of missed opportunities. Failed actions and roads not taken are part and parcel of human existence. We are condemned to feel regret, and future progress will not ease the problem. On the contrary, since modern life is characterized by a significant increase in possible alternatives, it is safe to predict that regret will even be more dominant in the future.

*Guilt*
Our misdeeds are easily forgotten when they are known only to ourselves.
—La Rochefoucauld


Guilt is similar to regret in referring to a specific deed (or omission), but the focus of concern is different: regret is concerned with a deed which was harmful and guilt is concerned with a deed which has violated certain norms. The violated norms involved in guilt are often, but not always, moral. Thus, breaking a diet may generate nonmoral guilt. We feel guilty after doing something which is forbidden; we feel regret after doing something which was basically a failure. The forbidden thing typically involves some harm to another agent, but it may also refer to a specific act which has violated a certain norm without hurting someone. Like other emotions that are typically concerned with those close to us, in guilt the relationship to our intimates is also of central importance. Indeed, people's descriptions of guilt-inducing situations often highlight the neglect of a partner or of other intimates, or failure to live up to interpersonal relationships.[15]

The relationship between shame and guilt is similar to that between hate and anger. Like anger, guilt is concerned with a specific action and like hate, shame is concerned with the agent as a whole. As in hate, in shame we believe that the agent is bad, and as in anger, in guilt we believe that the agent has done something wrong. An obvious difference is that hate and anger are directed at others, whereas shame and guilt are directed at oneself. Because of the more global nature of the negative evaluation associated with shame, forgiveness is less effective in the case of shame than in the case of guilt. Similarly, forgiveness, as well as punishment, is less effective in the case of hate than in the case of anger.[16]

Guilt and shame often stem from similar situations. Thus, lying to another person and hurting another person are common eliciting situations in both shame and guilt. Shame would be induced if the negative behavior is perceived to express our global personality, and guilt if it is perceived to express an isolated activity which hurts the other person. The specific actions associated with guilt are of a more voluntary nature; the traits associated with shame are more permanent and less voluntary. Hence, guilt is often associated with being morally wrong, whereas shame is associated with being in a disadvantaged situation. While both guilt and shame are concerned with oneself, shame is more about fundamental traits of the self, whereas guilt is more about the impact of one's actions—typically, but not necessarily, upon the other. In shame considerations of actual damage to the other person are less important than the reflection on our own personality. When faced with negative events caused by themselves, shame-prone persons are more likely to focus on their personal qualities, and guilt-prone persons on specific aspects of their behavior.[17]

In the same vein, we may say that when faced with negative events caused by others, hate-prone persons are more likely to focus on the others' personal qualities, and anger-prone persons on specific aspects of the others' behavior. A tendency to feel shame and a tendency toward hate are less adaptive than proneness to guilt and proneness to anger; the main reason is that shame and hate are concerned with traits which can seldom be changed; guilt and anger may be more useful as they are directed at behavior which can be altered in future similar situations.

Guilt is connected with fear—fear that if no corrective action is taken, the other agent may be angry with us and may even hurt us. With shame, there is no necessity that the other agent be angry or hostile; the possibility of contempt or scorn is sufficient. One can also be ashamed of being admired by the wrong people. In this case, the agent's fear of contempt is concerned with other people who do not value those who admire her.[18]

Shame, which involves a global negative evaluation of the self, is a more powerfully negative emotion than guilt, which involves a partial negative evaluation of specific actions. This is so because guilt provides a sense that one can rectify the situation through corrective action, whereas shame does not. Repayment and punishment are appropriate to guilt—as we believe that we can undo the wrong we have caused—but not to shame, which expresses more fundamental flaws. Accordingly, when people feel guilty, they try to repair what they have done by apologizing, explaining themselves, offering excuses, confessing, and making amends. These activities are not typical of shame.[19]

The action of another person—for instance, my child or compatriot—may make me feel shame but not guilt. Guilt refers to a specific deed over which I had a certain causal responsibility and as such it cannot arise from the deeds of others. I can feel guilty that the way I brought up my child was deficient and hence is somehow related to the misdeed of my child, but this is not guilt over the specific deed of my child. Shame is more appropriate in this regard as such a deed may express my profound deficiency as a parent or a lack in myself which includes those related to me.[20]

People may nevertheless feel guilt for something they did not do and for which they are not perceived by others as being responsible. A woman may feel guilty when she learns that a friend has died in a car accident and realizes that she could have prevented it by phoning him and so delaying his departure. Another example of guilt without apparent personal responsibility is the guilt I feel when it rains during the visit of friends from out of town. Children who are sexually abused often feel guilty even though they are clearly victims, not transgressors. A prevalent type of guilt without apparent responsibility is that of survivor guilt. Some people suffer ongoing guilt for outliving loved ones or for feeling ambivalent toward those who died. Family members of suicides, or of those who died in airplane or car accidents, or of murder victims, as well as war veterans and Holocaust survivors, feel guilt over the fact that their intimates were killed; they somehow hold themselves responsible for the deaths of these people although no one else holds them responsible. Survivor guilt was also found among those who keep their jobs when others in their company are fired, and among people who transcend the experience of growing up in a problematic family environment and begin to flourish while their siblings are unable to deal successfully with the transgressions that occurred in their family.[21]

The situation of bereaved parents is especially conducive for the generation of guilt as these parents are confronted with the most adverse emotional event. Such parents suffer a range of guilt feelings including those associated with beliefs that they contributed to the death (death causation guilt), that they should not outlive their child (survivor guilt), that they are being punished for a prior act (moral guilt), or that they are not grieving properly (grief guilt). Such types of guilt were also found in other kinds of close relationships—for instance, in the case of grown children caring for an elderly parent, family members dealing with the serious illness of a loved one, and parents raising a child with disabilities.[22]

The above examples of guilt without apparent personal responsibility may be perceived to be irrational.[23] However, a closer examination of the nature of personal responsibility and guilt may indicate that these are rational, though not typical kinds of guilt.

In discussing emotional responsibility, I have described two major aspects of responsibility: causality and praiseworthiness. Tom may be causally responsible for the death of George even if Tom is not to be blamed for this death, since Tom was unaware that the glass he gave to George contained poison. In many of the above cases of guilt, people consider the causal responsibility—which is usually a very partial responsibility—to be also the responsibility of blameworthiness. Consider, for example, the case in which Tom persuades his wife to visit her family abroad; her plane crashes and she is killed. At most, Tom's responsibility may be considered as a partial causal responsibility; nevertheless, Tom considers his responsibility to be also that of blameworthiness and hence blames himself and feels guilty about his wife's death. The example of the person who feels guilty because she did not call her friend, thereby delaying his departure and preventing the fatal car accident, clearly illustrates the switch we are making from partial (or even accidental) causal responsibility to blameworthiness responsibility. This switch is also evident in the example of my guilt at the rain during my friends' visit. I attribute to myself partial causal responsibility since I recommended the visit; this partial responsibility is sufficient for considering myself to be in one sense responsible for the visit's failure and hence to feel guilty about it.

Through counterfactual imagination, attributing an accidental, causal responsibility, which may turn into blameworthiness responsibility, is possible in almost all types of accidents and disasters. Hence, guilt is likely to emerge in these circumstances. Although the reasoning underlying this type of guilt may be disputable—especially the switch from causal responsibility to blameworthiness responsibility—I would not consider these cases to express irrational guilt. From an external, detached perspective, this kind of guilt may be a source of pointless suffering. But from the agent's perspective the suffering is not pointless: it refers to a loss of something dear to him which could have been prevented by him—although he could not know in advance how to prevent it, and it is highly improbable that it could have been prevented at all. These are not typical cases of guilt since they are not necessarily connected with a specific act which has an available alternative; hence, the possibility of avoiding the problem hardly exists, if it exists at all. In these cases, the emotion of guilt is turned into a sentiment of guilt and sometimes even into depression, which is typical of helpless situations.

The importance of imagination in inducing guilt is also evident in the types of actions one takes to prevent guilt. We try to avoid situations which we believe are likely to induce guilt. Elster notes that even if I do not have any money with me, I may cross the street to avoid coming face to face with a beggar whose visible misery would induce the unpleasant feeling of guilt.[24] Even if I can do nothing at the moment to help the beggar, it is not hard to imagine actual or counterfactual situations in which such help may nevertheless be possible.

Sometimes intended actions may lead to less intense guilt than that elicited by accidental actions. Indeed, it was found that people felt more guilty when the harm they did was accidental than when it was purposeful.[25] These results are surprising as intention is typically correlated with responsibility and greater responsibility is associated with more intense emotions—including guilt. I believe that these results can be explained by realizing that intention is not always perceived to be correlated with greater personal responsibility. When I intend to take a certain action, I consider all its possible ramifications and take the best available option. If despite these careful considerations, my action has harmful consequences, I will usually consider those to be the result of external factors beyond my knowledge and control. However, when the harm I do is accidental, I may perceive myself as someone who has not seriously considered all possible consequences and has taken an option that turned out to be wrong; had I considered all consequences, I would have realized that better alternatives are available. Although it seems paradoxical, my responsibility in the latter case is greater: I could have prevented the harm merely by considering the alternatives to my action. In the former case, I did everything I could do and hence I was bound to act the way I did in those given circumstances.

It is interesting to note that when we blame other people for harm done to us, intended actions are associated with greater responsibility and hence with more intense blame. Thus, people who felt their romantic partner intentionally engaged in negative behavior tended to report less satisfaction and more negative emotional attitudes toward their partner. The partner's transgressions, when viewed as intentionally hurtful, had a greater negative impact on the relationship than did those seen as unintended.[26] Concerning others, we do not perceive their intended actions as stemming from cognitive miscalculations of its consequences, but as stemming from immoral purposes; hence the other's blameworthiness is greater and our negative emotional attitudes toward this person are more intense. The same holds true for our own guilt: if we considered our intended harmful deed as stemming from immoral purposes and not from cognitive miscalculations, our guilt will seem greater than if the action is accidental. The difference between the two situations is that we tend to attribute our misdeeds to innocent mistakes and the misdeeds of others to immoral intentions.

*Embarrassment*
If you ever need anything, please don't hesitate to ask someone else first.
—Nirvana

I'm too shy to express my sexual needs except over the phone to people I don't know.
—Garry Shandling

Embarrassment is similar to regret, guilt, and shame in involving a negative evaluation of ourselves. It is similar to anger and guilt in terms of being specific; however, it is associated more with social, rather than moral, circumstances. Because embarrassment, guilt, and anger are related to specific circumstances, they are more transient than shame and hate.

Embarrassment is generated when, in the presence of another person, we become aware that we are the center of attention and are being judged. The judgment can be positive or negative, but it is perceived to express a certain social discrepancy.[27] The embarrassing situation can be incompatible with different states: for example, the accepted behavior in such circumstances, the ideal behavior, our past or future behavior, our expectations, and the expectations of significant others. In any case, acute self-awareness is a dominant feature of embarrassment.

A typical belief associated with embarrassment is that we have responded inappropriately to the requirements of the given social situation or that our privacy has been violated. The social nature of embarrassment is expressed in the fact that, unlike the situation in shame and guilt, we cannot be embarrassed if we are alone: embarrassment always requires an audience—typically, an actual audience but sometimes an imaginary one. This audience is perceived to impose on us certain social requirements we wish to meet but fail to do so.[28]

The specific nature of embarrassment is expressed in the fact that we do not consider the embarrassing situation to create a demand to which we are unable in principle to respond, but that we merely failed to do so in the present circumstances. The fact that we could do otherwise, and we might be expected to do so, increases our embarrassment. Consider the following real case which I witnessed. During a security check of an airline passenger, the security person heard a ticking noise coming from her suitcase; when asked whether she had a clock in her suitcase, she said no. Everyone was promptly evacuated from the terminal, the suitcase was placed in the center of the hall, and the security person carefully opened it. Out of the suitcase fell a vibrator. The lady, of course, was extremely embarrassed. Her embarrassment was due not only to the fact that she masturbates but to the fact that this had been publicly exposed in peculiar and highly unlikely circumstances which could easily have been prevented.

Unlike shame, which involves self-awareness of our profound values, embarrassment is not focused on our own profound values but rather on more superficial conventions and customs concerning our interactions with others. Hence, whereas shame is associated with failure of character, embarrassment is typically associated with a violation of convention or breach of manners. Because of the superficial nature of this failure, the failure can be removed; in shame the failure indicates a much more profound flaw which cannot be easily overcome. Indeed, the strategies used for coping with embarrassment are mainly behavioral escape devices, such as crying, laughing, changing the topic, denying failure, scapegoating, excuses, and withdrawal.[29]

Sometimes embarrassment is generated not from a negative self-evaluation of one's own actions but simply from public exposure of a deed which may in itself be quite positive. Shame, on the other hand, is concerned with significant personal misdeeds. Whereas embarrassment may merely be connected with unwelcome attention from others, shame is concerned with a perceived serious personal flaw. Embarrassment may also be associated with positive events since it is not the gravity of the misdeed which gives rise to embarrassment, but its social context; this context may also be violated in cases of success—for example, the person may be perceived as breaching the conventions of modesty.[30]

The less weight we attach to the nature of the deed in embarrassment as compared with that of shame may also be connected to the fact that whereas we may be embarrassed at being embarrassed, we are not ashamed of our shame. As indicated below, shame is often positively evaluated since it expresses the fact that although we did something wrong, we care about the norm we violated. Hence, there is nothing to be ashamed of in our shame; on the contrary, we are often proud of it. As George Bernard Shaw said: "The more things a man is ashamed of, the more respectable he is." Since embarrassment is not connected with profound norms which we care about, but may merely be connected to unwelcome attention by others, our embarrassed response may attract further unwelcome attention which will generate embarrassment at our embarrassment.

More than many other emotions, embarrassment is characterized by a fairly well-defined behavioral display: eye contact is reduced, blushing is present, and there is an increase in body motion, speech disturbances, and smiling. Some of these behaviors, such as reducing eye contact, may be explained as our wish to decrease contact with others; some, such as blushing and increase in body motion and speech disturbances, can be regarded as nervous responses, while smiling may, in some cases, be an attempt to protect one's image following a disruption of social routine. The dominance of behavioral displays in embarrassment facilitates its identification in others. This is particularly important as embarrassment expresses a social failure which we can typically help others to cope with and even eliminate—provided that we are aware of it.[31]

Embarrassment is experienced by people in all cultures and in almost all age groups with particular frequency during adolescence. Empirical studies suggest that embarrassment is absent in very young children, perhaps appearing at about three years of age. Before that age we may speak about shyness, rather than embarrassment. At a young age, namely, between the age of four and seven years, embarrassment is more likely to be concerned with the child's view of what appears to be right to her, rather than by what appears to be right to other people; from about the age of eight years, children are more likely to be concerned with conveying to others a particular self-impression and this will be the main discrepancy generating embarrassment. It seems that embarrassment is most dominant in adolescents.[32]

Since the focus of concern in embarrassment is not as profound as that in shame, it is typically of lesser intensity than shame. The intensity of embarrassment depends among other things on the number of observers present when the embarrassing situation takes place and their relative status; people embarrassed in front of many observers experience more intense embarrassment, as do people embarrassed in front of higher-status observers.[33]

Like some other emotions, embarrassment is infectious. People who observe embarrassment may be affected, and in some cases experience embarrassment themselves even though the person's actions do not reflect on the observers and the observers' self-esteem is not threatened.[34] Although this type of empathic embarrassment may sometimes involve complete strangers, it is more accurate to explain it not as emotion directed at someone completely unrelated to us, but as a situation in which people who are remote from us become closer. Because of the social nature of embarrassment and the fact that we personally witness the embarrassing situation, it is easier for us to identify ourselves with the embarrassed person and become ourselves embarrassed. It is clear, however, that the closer the embarrassed person is to us, the more intense our own embarrassment. Thus, an Englishwoman will feel more embarrassment if she sees a drunken Englishman behaving badly in Paris than if she sees a drunken Frenchman do so. When in London she may not feel embarrassed by the English drunkard. In Beijing she may feel embarrassed by both the drunken Englishman and Frenchman, as the relevant reference group in this case may be European.[35]

Despite its seemingly minor social nature, embarrassment is a quite unpleasant experience and people take precautions to prevent themselves from becoming embarrassed, sometimes avoiding particular social interactions altogether. However, in some cases, as when we attend our own birthday parties or wedding showers, we expect to be embarrassed by others but we do not avoid such a situation, since we consider the unpleasantness to be minor.

When it comes to other people we do not consider embarrassment to be such a negative experience, at least not one which may have long-term negative consequences. Accordingly, we sometimes intentionally create embarrassing situations for others. Intentional embarrassment is one of the few circumstances where initiating an unpleasant emotional state is often viewed as acceptable or even expected in social interactions.[36]

Intentional embarrassment appears in various forms and is done for different purposes. A common purpose is to indicate our negative attitude toward a certain behavior of someone related to us. We may embarrass partners, associates, or rivals in order to highlight behaviors they dislike. In this case, although we create a negative emotional state in others, this state is a means of correcting their behavior. The acceptability of such intentional embarrassment stems from the positive value of our goal.

Sometimes the purpose of intentional embarrassment is not to express our negative attitude but to immunize, so to speak, other people from a larger embarrassment which may prevent them from doing things beneficial to them. Consider the following case. David is interested in Debra but is too shy to introduce himself to her; David's friend James intentionally embarrasses David by pushing him toward Debra as they pass in the hallway so that he bumps into her. In this case, intentional embarrassment is like an immunization shot: it introduces a small dose of the negative stuff to prepare the system to cope with a larger dose of embarrassment. A significant risk of intentional embarrassment is the same as that of immunization: what is considered to be a small dose may produce harmful consequences typical of larger doses, and what was planned to be a minor misfortune may turn into quite a substantial one. Moreover, if the intentional embarrassment becomes a continual practice, its value as a one-time immunization shot disappears. The targets of such embarrassment may consider us to be constantly and deliberately causing them distress and violating their privacy, giving rise to resentment and humiliation.

Intentional embarrassment is somewhat similar to pleasure-in-others'-misfortune. Both emotions are concerned with minor misfortunes; because the misfortunes are minor they cannot substantially hurt the other person and this justifies our enjoyment. One difference between the two situations is that only in intentional embarrassment do we plan how to bring about the (minor) misfortune of the other person. But since in the long run this misfortune is going to benefit the other person, we do not feel too bad about our behavior.

### Relationships with Other Emotions

Men who are unhappy, like men who sleep badly, are always proud of the fact.
—Bertrand Russell

The distinction between regret and *remorse* is disputable. I accept in this regard the view considering regret to be the broader notion: personal responsibility for moral wrongdoing is a defining feature of remorse, but only a characteristic feature of regret. I may regret events over which I have no control and which are morally innocuous, such as the passing of summer. Janet Landman summarizes the differences between remorse and regret in the following manner: remorse applies with respect to one's own past, to voluntary, overt, and morally wrong acts or to failures to act. Regret applies to all of these circumstances but also to others—for example, one's unexecuted intentions; one's own future; involuntary, morally innocuous, or virtuous acts; and circumstances of others that share the foregoing characteristics.[37]

Like regret, and unlike guilt and shame, remorse is focused on the deed and not on the self. Remorse is similar to *guilt* in the importance it attributes to the moral aspect. The difference here is that while remorse is similar to regret in focusing on the deed, guilt is similar to shame in focusing on the self. The different focuses of guilt and remorse are the reason why they both may be directed at the very same deed. However, someone may feel remorse about something she has done and yet feel no guilt. In this case, she negatively evaluates her deed, but does not perceive herself as burdened or stained by her wrongdoing. Not all actions we consider to be morally wrong and would like to undo are also perceived as making us guilty. It seems that guilt often implies remorse: we consider as morally wrong and would like to undo those actions which leave a stain on us. There are, however, cases of guilt which are concerned more with violating norms than with doing harm to other people; here, remorse may not be associated with the guilt.[38]

Since remorse is focused on the deed, it is typically more constructive than guilt: we are more likely to see an agent who suffers from remorse taking corrective actions, than an agent who suffers from guilt. However, guilt is not merely destructive: focusing on the self may result in changing those patterns of behavior which gave rise to the immoral behavior. No doubt, this is harder to achieve than the repair work that is required in instances of remorse, but it is still possible.[39]

Regret may imply acceptance which remorse does not. I may regret something I have done, but accept the fact that given the circumstances in which it was done,

I had no plausible alternative, or that it was the best thing to do considering the information available to me at that time. Remorse never implies acceptance. I cannot feel remorse and yet believe that this was the best choice of action given the specific circumstances. If at that time it was the best thing to do, then my action will not be perceived to be morally reprehensible.[40]

The relation between regret and remorse is somewhat similar to that between envy and resentment, except that the latter are directed at other people. Like resentment, remorse is usually directed at perceived moral wrongdoing; as in envy, the main concern in regret is undesirability or dissatisfaction and not necessarily immorality. Furthermore, resentment and remorse presuppose some responsibility on the part of an agent—others in resentment and ourselves in remorse—for the immoral behavior; in some cases, such responsibility may be absent from envy and regret.[41]

Like regret, *disappointment* involves negative evaluation of our own actions and sometimes of the actions of others. It is also similar to regret in referring to the presence of negative consequences and violation of norms. However, whereas disappointment is concerned with the difference between actual vs. expected outcomes, regret refers to the difference between the outcomes of a chosen vs. an unchosen option. I regret that I did not choose the right way; I am disappointed when unexpected negative outcomes occur.[42]

In *joy* we gain something we desire and in *sadness* we lose something we desire. The connection to the self is more profound in pride or blame than in joy or sadness: the object in pride or blame, but not necessarily in joy or sadness, is something that belongs to me or for whose generation I am responsible.

Regret is a type of sadness; sadness need not entail regret, but regret entails sadness. Unlike sadness in general, regret typically implies having made a mistake. Striking employees may be saddened by their loss of income, yet not regret the act of striking. Similarly, one may be saddened at the dismissal of an employee because of his kindness, but recognize that he had to be sacked because of his inefficiency.[43]

## Moral Value

A person will be called to account on Judgment Day for every permissible thing he might have enjoyed but did not.
—Talmud

The reference to the past has been a main issue in diminishing the value given to regret. I have already argued for the importance, and rationality, of taking the past into account. Regret is important for properly evaluating our present deeds and improving our future behavior. Regret prevents repetition of immoral deeds and encourages us to undo the damaging consequences of these deeds.

Guilt has a similar function to regret, but since it is more concerned with moral issues, its importance as an impediment to immoral deeds is more pronounced. People with no regret, guilt, embarrassment, or shame are very dangerous from a social and moral point of view. They have no built-in obstacles to immoral behavior. The undesirable emotional states associated with guilt can encourage people to avoid some immoral behaviors and engage in moral ones. For instance, the emotional state of indebtedness, which is often associated with guilt, has been linked to increased altruistic behavior. Similarly, reminding people of their debts or obligations tends to increase their willingness to help others. This function of guilt reduces the need of those keeping the moral standards to control or punish wrongdoers.[44]

Guilt often tends to lose its original function as a negative evaluation of a specific action, and becomes a general negative evaluation of oneself. In such cases, guilt is typically an obstacle to normal healthy behavior. Guilt is valuable if it remains specific, namely, if it refers to a specific action of ours; in this case, it should bring about a specific change in our behavior and last for a short time.

Embarrassment also serves an important social function. It expresses the presence of certain norms which we value and wish to keep. Although these are typically more superficial norms, they are socially important.

Pride is morally valuable in enforcing our values. Pride is a kind of emotional encouragement of our values—this kind of encouragement is crucial if we want our values to be more than abstract beliefs. Our values can be rooted deep in our mental system only if we continue to get positive emotional feedback when we maintain them and negative emotional feedback when we violate them. Pride, guilt, and regret are instrumental in this regard.

# Chapter 18

# Caring about the Self—Pridefulness and Shame

Whatever is begun in anger ends in shame.
—Benjamin Franklin

Our own heart, and not other men's opinion, forms our true honor.
—Samuel Coleridge

In this chapter, I discuss pridefulness and shame, which are global emotional attitudes toward oneself; these attitudes are correlated with love and hate, which are global emotional attitudes toward others. As mentioned, the term "pridefulness" is not as common as other emotional terms referring to global attitudes; nevertheless, pridefulness seems to capture the meaning of a global positive attitude toward oneself.[1]

*General Characteristics*

*Pridefulness*
Pridefulness always finds compensations.
—La Rochefoucauld

Here lies Jan Smith, wife of Thomas Smith, marble Cutter. This monument was erected by her husband as a tribute to her memory and a specimen of his work. Monuments of this same style are two hundred and fifty dollars.
—Gravestone inscription

Pridefulness is directed at one's whole personality and pride in one's actions. Pridefulness is related to hate, and pride to anger. In Aristotle's view, the good-tempered person, appropriately angered by an insult, and the proud person, appropriately proud of an accomplishment, can expect to command respect; and both have a rich enough sense of self to demand it.[2] Hate is associated with the global type of pride, namely, with pridefulness. Unlike anger and the specific type of pride, hate is not concerned with maintaining a certain level of respect, but with our very existence.

Pridefulness is the emotion resulting from the belief that one is a good person and pride is the emotion arising from the belief that one has done a good thing. This is parallel to the distinction between shame and regret, and hate and anger. Shame is similar to hate in that it involves a global negative evaluation of the agent's personality. Regret is similar to anger in that it involves a specific negative evaluation of the agent's actions. In the same way that the hated person is perceived to be a bad person and the person at whom anger is directed is perceived to have done a bad thing, in shame we perceive ourselves to be bad and in regret to have done a bad thing. Whereas shame involves global self-condemnation in which the self is seen as the root of some failure, regret involves a more specific condemnation of unacceptable behavior, seen as somewhat apart from the self.

There is not doubt that a reference to the self is central to pridefulness and shame. Two problematic issues in this regard are (1) what kind of relations to the self are constitutive of these emotions? and (2) are relations to others constitutive of these emotions?

Pridefulness and shame refer to some fundamental properties of the self. Something that has nothing to do with us generates neither pridefulness nor shame. Thus, it would be peculiar to be proud of a beautiful fish in the ocean or to be ashamed of the behavior of an animal in the desert because they are not related to us. A reference to the self is required for the generation of pridefulness and shame. However, not every positive reference to the self is a source of pride and not every negative reference is a source of shame. In order for these emotions to appear, that which is related to us must enhance or detract from our self-esteem to a considerable extent. Being pleased about something indicates some positive evaluation, but it may not be the profound evaluation of approval or disapproval that is required for pridefulness and shame. Hence, we may take pleasure in some attribute of ours and feel ashamed rather than proud of it; thus, we may enjoy our house but not be proud of it since material possessions are of little relevance to our self-esteem. Similarly, we may suffer from something, say, our hard work, but still be proud of it as this work supports our family.

Does the global positive evaluation typical of pridefulness imply a negative evaluations of others? Does the global negative evaluation typical of shame imply a positive evaluations of others? Are other people constitutive to these emotions?

Spinoza, for example, considers pridefulness to involve overestimation: pridefulness is "thinking more highly of oneself than is just." Accordingly, pridefulness is considered negative in Spinoza's view. Elster also argues that full-blown pridefulness stems from one's belief that one is, and is thought by all to be, superior to all. The reference to others is also part of a common characterization of shame. Spinoza defines shame as a sadness, accompanied by the idea of some action of ours which we imagine that others blame. In Spinoza's view, and in the view of many others, the reference to others is constitutive of shame as it is constitutive of pridefulness.[3]

I believe that pridefulness does not have to involve overestimation of one's value and underestimation of others' value. Similarly, shame does not have to involve underestimation of one's value and overestimation of others' value. As I argue below, it also seems to me that modesty does not have to involve underestimation of one's value and overestimation of others' value. Pridefulness, shame, and modesty may involve accurate knowledge of oneself when pridefulness is focused on one's merits, shame on one's flaws, and modesty on one's limitations.[4]

The global evaluation involved in pridefulness and shame may not rest on a comparison with others, but on a comparison of standards. As Gabriele Taylor rightly indicates, "A person may be proud in that, for instance, he will not accept help from others who are better off than he is. He does not necessarily think of himself as being superior to others at all; he merely accepts certain standards the lowering of which he would regard as a threat to his self-respect."[5] A person may be proud without thinking himself superior to others.

The same, I believe, holds for shame. A person may be ashamed without thinking himself inferior to others. Consider the following example. A manager has, for personal reasons, dismissed a devoted and successful employee. Aaron, who also works under this manager, considers this act to be unjustified; he condemns the manager's action and tries to reverse the decision. Other people in the organization, although convinced that firing this employee is clearly unjustified, do not join in Aaron's struggle and the decision stands. Although Aaron has done more than any other person in the organization to overturn the unjustified deed, he nevertheless feels shame since he thinks that in light of his moral ideals, he should have done more than he did. Aaron's shame is not associated with considering himself to be inferior to other people—on the contrary, he considers his behavior to be morally superior to that of others; the shame is associated with the belief that he failed to meet important moral standards. Similarly, artists or writers may feel shame not because they compare their work to that of others, but because their work fails to meet their own high standards.

The comparative concern in pridefulness and shame refers to some fundamental norms. The degree of compatibility of our personality and behavior to these norms is a crucial factor in determining pridefulness and shame. Exceeding these norms in a systematic manner generates pridefulness; failing to comply with them gives rise to shame. Quite often the behavior and achievement of others constitute these norms and hence the comparison to others is constitutive of pride and shame in these cases. In other cases, the personality and behavior of others are the stimulus, or the immediate cause, of pridefulness or shame, but not the constitutive elements. One can have these emotions without referring to others but merely to moral, religious, aesthetic, or other normative values. I claim below that in the cases of humiliation, arrogance, and modesty, the reference to others is a constitutive and not merely a causal element.

Pride and regret, which express partial evaluations, may be directed at the same object at the same time as they may also refer to different aspects of the same object. We may be proud of something we have done, but regret doing it. Thus, someone may be proud of his cleverness in a financial transaction, but regret doing it as it involved cheating other people. Pridefulness and shame cannot be directed at the same object at the same time, as they express contradictory global evaluations which cannot refer to different partial aspects.

*Shame*
"For a long time I was ashamed of the way I lived."
"Did you reform?"
"No, I'm not ashamed anymore."
—Mae West

In comparison to the specific nature of guilt and regret, shame is more global. In shame one thinks of oneself as a bad person, not simply as someone who did a bad thing. When shame is due to a certain action, this action is taken as indisputable proof of one's own character rather than as an isolated action that may be ascribed to negligence or weakness of will.[6]

In light of the global negative evaluation of the self in shame, there is a need to hide or cover oneself—to avoid others seeing us; by contrast, the action tendency in guilt is to make atonement or to confess. Indeed, hiding is a very typical behavior in shame which is often expressed in a shrinking of the body, as though to disappear from the eye of the self or the other.[7] When there is no way of avoiding others seeing us, the ultimate solution for some people is suicide. Hate is similar to shame in involving a global negative evaluation and the wish to avoid any contact with the emotional object—in hate, this means the other. When there seems no way to escape the presence of the other, the only solution for some is to kill this person. At their extreme, shame and hate can sometimes express the belief that coexistence is no longer possible.

Shame involves viewing one's self in light of certain norms, especially those which are also adopted by others. Shame is mainly derived from an interest in how others regard us; sympathy and envy are derived from an interest in how we regard others.

Shame seems to presuppose an audience, or others who are watching us, in a way that guilt and pridefulness do not. In guilt, what we feel is related to what we imagine others would feel if they knew what we did. In pridefulness what we feel is related to what we imagine others would feel if they knew who we are. In shame there is typically a causal connection between what others actually feel and what we feel.[8]

The notion of an audience is, however, problematic. Although in many cases of shame, there is an actual audience with certain norms and points of view, this is not necessarily the case. Certainly, an actual audience is not necessary, as we may feel ashamed when we are alone. But shame may arise even when there is no imagined audience and the comparison is focused upon the agent's own high standards. Accordingly, it has been suggested that the audience can be oneself and hence shame involves a type of self-perception—a sophisticated type of self-consciousness—which is often absent from pridefulness.[9] This is so since shame refers to an incompatibility of norms, whereas pridefulness refer to a compatibility of norms. The former requires a more elaborate view of such norms. I agree that awareness of an incompatibility of norms typically requires a more sophisticated comparative system, but I believe that this is essentially a difference in degree. Both shame and pridefulness require a type of self-perception which typically, but not necessarily, involves a direct reference to other people.

The extreme measure of committing suicide in order to avoid shame illustrates the powerful impact of this emotion. Indeed, shame is a highly painful experience which also results in the disruption of ongoing behavior, confusion in thought, and inability to speak. In shame, more is at stake than a specific act of ours (as in guilt) or how a person presents herself in a social context (as in embarrassment); accordingly, shame is a more intense emotional experience than guilt or embarrassment. When people commit suicide because of shame, they usually overrate the impact of shame. These people may know that the feeling of shame is unlikely to last, but their shame is too intense to bear. Sometimes people are unable to imagine that such feelings will not last forever. The intense nature of shameful experiences also explains why these experiences often become pathological. However, the very existence of shame is not pathological—on the contrary, the absence of the capacity to feel shame is a pathological condition.[10]

The need to hide, or even disappear, which is so typical of shame, explains why shame is often connected with sight and being seen. In the biblical story of the Creation we are told that before Eve gave the apple to Adam, there was no shame. Shame emerged only after they ate the apple and "the eyes of both of them were opened, and they felt that they were naked." When God called to them, they hid from him in shame. Indeed, hiding and attempting to disappear—or at least wanting to do so—is a prevailing manner of coping with shame (and embarrassment).

This tendency may explain why a typical behavior of shame, as well as of embarrassment, is that of breaking off eye contact. (It is interesting to note that gaze aversion in embarrassment, which expresses a less profound flaw in us, is found to be briefer.) Gaze aversion is typical also of situations in which we shun unwanted intimacy, as when people move closer to us than we wish them to, or when the topic of conversation takes too intimate a turn. A sustained meeting of eyes between the sexes may be perceived as being excessively intimate or intrusive. Animals often respond aggressively or take fright when they are stared at; consequently, some animals gaze at enemies to threaten them or assert their dominance. One possible functional explanation for breaking off eye contact, then, is that by looking away from the object, the subject, who is in an inferior position, expresses an attitude of surrender. It may also be the case that we cannot bear the sight of others' judgment or are trying to keep our emotions from overwhelming us. Another explanation suggests that in breaking off eye contact, we can prevent our present mental state from being discovered—or at least make it more difficult to identify. Indeed, St. Augustine wrote that the eyes are the windows to the soul. Along these lines, Descartes argued that there is no passion which some particular expression of the eyes does not reveal. Consistent with this belief are findings indicating that larger eye size increases the perceived honesty in adult faces. (This may lead to a favorable bias toward people who have baby faces or attractive faces—both of which are characterized by large eyes.) The eyes are also important components of our physical appearance to the extent that if we wish to conceal our identity in a picture, we often do so merely by covering the eyes. The emotional significance of gazing is also expressed in the belief that an "evil eye" can hurt us, and in the custom of the veil. For similar considerations, souk vendors wear dark glasses to conceal their interest.[11]

In situations opposite to shame and embarrassment, when we want to reveal our basic attitudes and values, retaining eye contact is the typical behavior. Indeed, couples who love each other a great deal spend more time making intimate eye contact than couples who love each other to a lesser degree. (For some reason, women spend more time looking at men than vice versa.) It is not merely that love is expressed in spending more time looking at each other, but looking may also lead to loving.[12] Accordingly, Susan Anthony claims that in life, actions speak louder than words, but in love, the eyes do. Hence, the eyes, rather than the genitals or the heart, are perhaps the prime organ of love. The eyes then are quite important in communicating our emotions. No wonder that the eyes are the organs that release tears—these are typical of intense emotional states.

More than other emotions, shame expresses our deepest values and commitments; freeing ourselves from shame implies unloading these values and commitments. Freedom, Janis Joplin reminds us in a popular song, is when you have nothing more to lose. Shame is, then, a constitutive element in normative life.

The situations that are likely to elicit shame are diverse, as the significant factors constituting our own global evaluation differ. Nevertheless, there are some situations which are more common in this regard. The two basic types of situations which most often elicit shame among men are failure over a task deemed important and sexual impotence. The basic situations eliciting shame among women are those related to physical attractiveness and failure in interpersonal relationships. The different types of situations reflect the differences in the way men and women conceive the important factors constituting their self-esteem.[13]

Aristotle believes that shame is not typical of every age but only of youth. This is because Aristotle considers shame to be concerned with specific voluntary actions, and young people commit errors in such actions which may lead to shame.[14] It seems to me that both shame and guilt (which is of a more specific and voluntary nature) are present in all ages, as the self-evaluations underlying these emotions are typical of all ages.

A more interesting question is whether these emotions are more frequent and intense at a certain age. This is basically an empirical question which should be answered by empirical studies; nevertheless, a few general considerations are relevant here. As indicated above, emotions in general are more intense among young people. I suggested that a major reason for this is that during youth more events are considered to be significant changes. I believe that concerning pride-fulness and shame there are also more events in youth which may induce these emotions, and those events are experienced more intensely. In older age, we are more ready to accept our shortcomings and not to consider them as indicative of essential flaws. Similarly, we are more ready to accept the basically similar nature of human beings and hence to consider our advantages as expressing local, and to a certain extent insignificant, successes rather than significant overall superi-ority. However, retrospective emotions, such as long-term regret, are more domi-nant in older age since there are more events to regret and fewer opportunities to undo the damage.

Coping with shame essentially involves removing ourselves from the shaming situation. This can be done in various manners: (a) behavioral—humor and confession; (b) cognitive—denial and forgetting, and attributing the failure to an external source; (c) evaluative—reducing the weight of one's flaw.[15]

Behavioral means for reducing or eliminating shame contain mechanisms such as humor and confession. As indicated, in *humor* we take a new perspective which is incongruent with the present one. Taking another perspective is contrary to the partial nature of emotions and hence it is incompatible with an intense emotional state. Consequently, laughing at ourselves serves to distance us from the shaming situation as we join others in taking a fresh perspective on the situ-ation. The new humorous perspective also helps to reduce the significance of the shaming situation. Like humor, *confession* also involves distancing oneself from the event. By telling others about an event that has shamed us, we join others in a distanced observation of the event and in a way share with them some of the responsibility. Moreover, confession also involves an explicit negative evaluation of the deed—something that also distances ourselves from the event. By nega-tively evaluating our deed, we consider it as a specific isolated failure, thus keeping our global evaluation of ourselves intact.

Cognitive measures for coping with shame consist of both a mechanism for diverting attention, such as forgetting, and a mechanism for interpreting the shaming situation differently. Mechanisms for diverting our attention from the shaming situation are common. In not paying much attention to a certain situa-tion we reduce its significance and hence its relevance to our global self-evaluation. Forgetting is an extreme measure of diverting attention, and if successful it may completely eliminate shame. The problem is that forgetting does not solve the basic problems underlying the shaming situation and shame may appear later on.

Another group of cognitive means for coping with shame are those in which we interpret the shaming situation differently. One such means is that of attributing responsibility to external factors, thereby reducing or even eliminating the agent's responsibility. Generally speaking, people who do not often blame themselves for failure and do not often credit themselves for success, are less likely to experience emotions such as shame, pridefulness, guilt, regret, and pride.[16] Similarly, people who do not often blame others for failure and do not often credit others for success are less likely to experience emotions such as hate, love, anger, and gratitude.

Denial is another cognitive means of coping with shame. In denial, we usually do not deny the occurrence of the shaming situation—something which is very difficult to do—but rather that our activity in that situation violated any norm and hence there is no reason to feel shame. The denial mechanism typically operates after the fact, but in some cases it can take place prior to the event.

A central evaluative measure for coping with shame is that of reducing the weight of the relevant flaw in our global self-evaluation. Consider, for example, impotence in men, which is a typical state inducing shame, as sexual ability is important to men's self-esteem. To avoid shame, a man may rationalize that although his body doesn't function perfectly, his mental capacity is above average. A similar type of coping mechanism is used by women concerning their attractiveness. Although this kind of measure is indeed useful, it usually reduces, rather than eliminates, shame.[17]

Elster points out that since shame is an intensely painful experience, we would expect people (a) to be very careful not to get caught engaging in shameful activities, and (b) to avoid engaging in them altogether if there is even a small chance of getting caught. He indicates that whereas the first prediction seems to be borne out, the second is not.[18] If we were people whose behavior was merely determined by careful, intellectual calculations, the second prediction would be borne out as well. But the powerful role emotions play in our life prevents us from exclusively focusing our attention on distant, future possibilities. The short-term emotional gratification we experience while engaging in activities looms larger than the long-term negative consequences of what may be considered in the future to be shameful activities.

I have indicated that in emotions we are concerned not only with our own private fortune but also with that of those related to us and who in a sense constitute our extended self. As suggested, we are, for example, embarrassed not only by our own deeds but also by the deeds of those who are related to us. This type of extended self is also expressed in collective pride (or pridefulness) and shame— that is, pride and shame which relate to the achievement of a certain group to which we belong. Pride or shame at the achievement of our country or our favorite sports team are examples of such collective emotions. Sometimes we are even proud or ashamed of the activities of our ancestors who lived many years ago.

In these cases we take pride in, or feel shame about, things which are in no sense our personal doing. Nevertheless, the very presence of these emotions may indicate that we do consider ourselves to be in some sense responsible—or at least worthy of praise or blame—for these things. Thus, we see criticism of our forebears as reflecting in some way on ourselves. Somehow, the special relationship we have with these people makes us connected to them in a unit covering more generations than one. In this case, it is not our actions which generate pride and shame, but what we are—our heritage and social groups are important constituents of what we are. We are what we are by virtue of, among other things, membership in some larger group. Moreover, many of our attitudes and doings are influenced by the group to which we belong. Such types of collective pride and shame are important for strengthening social bonds—and this may be their prime evolutionary function.[19]

It might be said that there is no point in being proud or ashamed of things that happened long ago and which we cannot change. In response, we should remember that shame and pridefulness are essentially concerned with basic properties which are very hard to alter. Although rationally we may be persuaded that what cannot be altered should not be condemned or shameful, we are still ashamed of it—probably even more than those properties which we can change. Thus, we can be ashamed of our ugliness. We are what we are by virtue of some things for which we are not responsible, and hence pride and shame can also be generated by some things for which we are not responsible.

Shame and guilt typically involve responsibility for which we may be blamed; hence they are usually concerned with something we have done or have some significant connection with. However, these emotions can be also induced by something that is done to us or something we are not actually involved in. An illustration of this is the tendency of rape victims to feel shame ("I am the kind of person who attracts trouble") or guilt ("I should not have let someone I did not know into the house"). Here, guilt and shame are generated since the agent conceives of herself as somehow responsible for the rape. Shame, and to a lesser extent guilt, may occur even if such responsibility is inconceivable, as when one is ashamed of having poor parents, growing old, or becoming bald.[20]

I believe that the notion of an extended self, which explains collective pride and shame, may also explain this type of shame. As indicated, we do not perceive ourselves in isolation, but our heritage and social bonds are also important for our self-evaluation. As we are proud to belong to a successful group—since the others' glory is reflected upon us—so are we ashamed to belong to a poor group—since being poor is conceived to be a failure, and we may be regarded as failures as well. Unless we can explain our parents' poverty as due to external factors, their poverty may indicate some basic flaws in them which may also be characteristics in us. Similarly, since growing old is associated with the inability to do many things, our self-evaluation, and others' evaluation of us, may locate us in an inferior position. In this case, we are associated less with our past achievements and more with our present limitations and hence we are perceived to belong to an inferior group. In the same vein, becoming bald places us in a group of people who are sometimes considered to be inferior from an aesthetic point of view.

### Relationships with Other Emotions

When you're as great as I am, it's hard to be humble.
—Muhammad Ali

I begin this section with a detailed discussion of modesty which is often perceived to be the opposite of pridefulness; defining what is meant by modesty will be useful for understanding the related attitudes of humiliation and arrogance and the differences between them and pridefulness and shame.

### Modesty

It is time I stepped aside for a less experienced and less able man.
—Professor Scott Elledge on his retirement from Cornell

My husband gave me a necklace. It's fake. I requested fake. Maybe I'm paranoid, but in this day and age, I don't want something around my neck that's worth more than my head.
—Rita Rudner

Modesty is often taken to be the opposite of pridefulness and to be similar to shame. I consider the opposite of pridefulness to be shame, rather than modesty. Understanding the nature of modesty is crucial for understanding pridefulness and shame and for determining their moral value.[21]

The term "modest" has various senses; the most relevant to our discussion is the sense of a limited and not exaggerated estimate of one's abilities or worth, free of vanity, egotism, boastfulness, or great pretensions. This sense includes two related features: being limited and not exaggerated. The two features are not identical: an accurate estimate is not exaggerated and is not limited; and too limited an estimation is an exaggerated estimate. In my view, modesty should be characterized as connected to an unexaggerated evaluation rather than to a limited one.

We may think of three major cognitive accounts of modesty: (1) The agent *knows* her superior worth but does not reveal it in speech or behavior (and sometimes even offers misleading information); in this sense she is *insincere*. (2) The agent *underestimates* her worth; in this sense she is *ignorant*. (3) The agent *does not overestimate* her worth; in this sense she is *realistic*. I believe that the first two accounts are false. The basic assumption of the third account is correct, but is insufficient for characterizing modesty since genuine modesty is an evaluative, and not a cognitive virtue. Accordingly, a fourth account of modesty is (4) the agent *evaluates* her fundamental human worth as similar to that of other people; in this sense she is a type of *egalitarian*.

In the *insincerity* perspective the agent knows her superior worth, but since she believes that modesty is an important virtue she acts as if her worth is no higher than that of other people. Here the agent prefers the virtue of modesty to that of sincerity. A major difficulty with this view is that modesty and sincerity are fundamental virtues, and that two such virtues could be contradictory *by definition* is not plausible. Moreover, in this view one can be modest and sincere only as long as one has no significant accomplishments. Yet there are empirical examples in which someone is both sincere and modest. Clearly, if all people knew that modesty involved insincerity, it would no longer be regarded as a virtue.

In the *underestimation* account, modesty arises from the cognitive defect of not knowing our own worth: a truly modest person would never believe that she is that good.[22] This account is similar to the insincerity account in that it involves an inaccurate manifestation of our worth; but here the inaccuracy is not voluntary, and so does not involve insincerity. Accordingly, there is no inherent conflict between the two virtues (but there is a conflict between modesty and knowledge). However, the underestimation account presents other difficulties. A major one is the existence of cases in which we cannot ignore the excellence of our results; for example, in areas where the worth of results is primarily determined by quantitative methods. Since according to this view modesty involves some involuntary deficiency, we must conclude that a truly modest person cannot arrive at such results; on the other hand, the agent who arrives at such results cannot (by definition) be modest. Empirical cases falsify these implausible conclusions.

A common feature of the above two accounts is that self-knowledge is a crucial obstacle to achieving modesty. In the third account, namely, the *non-overestimation* one, the modest person may have an accurate sense of her worth but does not overestimate it.[23] Although this account rightly describes the cognitive aspect of modesty, it does not pinpoint the essential aspect of modesty, which is evaluative. Modesty and realism in self-appraisal are not identical, but are compatible. We may estimate our worth accurately but still be immodest in the sense that we consider other people to be inferior to us. There are many people who know their accomplishments accurately, but who are immodest. Similarly, there may be people who are not fully aware of the worth of their accomplishments, but are modest.

In the fourth account, which I suggest, modesty is essentially an *evaluative* attitude rather than a cognitive state. The basic evaluative belief involved in modesty concerns the fundamental similar worth of all human beings. This evaluation rests on a belief in the common nature and fate of human beings and on a belief that this commonality dwarfs other differences. Modest people believe that (a) with regard to the fundamental aspects of human life, their worth as a human being is similar to that of other human beings, and (b) all human beings have a positive worth which should be respected.

Modesty does not oblige one to deny a superior position within a given evaluative framework—hence it is compatible with realism in self-appraisal—but it requires one not to exaggerate the value of this framework in comparison with other possible evaluative frameworks. Einstein, for example, was a modest man who no doubt recognized his exceptional accomplishments in physics. His modesty was indeed based upon an evaluative attitude: our personal talents and accomplishments are of less importance when related to the role and place in the universe. Considering each human being's marginal place in the universe, or for some people, considering the greatness of God, the differences between individual human beings become insignificant. Modesty thus requires a realization of the fundamentally similar worth of all human beings, and the evaluation of this similarity as more significant than the differences resulting from the accomplishments of different human beings.

Modesty does not require us to hide our accomplishments, but rather not to display them in contexts that may promote uncomfortable feelings in our listeners. In contexts involving people (often strangers) who may be made uncomfortable by the description of our accomplishments, such description should be avoided. However, the description should not be denied to our intimates who are aware of our modesty and want to be involved in our life. It does not make sense to share only our misfortunes with those who are dear to us. Cases of what may be termed "local, professional immodesty" are not necessarily contrary to the profound human modesty described here. No doubt, if we keep telling our friends how good we are, we are not modest. (This is also true if we continually think how good we are.) Modesty consists of not overrating the significance of our accomplishments. Incessant descriptions or thoughts of our accomplishments involve boastfulness and suggest that we overrate the significance of our accomplishments; hence we are not modest. There is no formula for the degree to which it is permissible to speak about our accomplishments or the frequency with which such a story can be told. Modest people are seldom in doubt concerning this issue, since to be on the safe side they usually refrain from describing many of their accomplishments. It is clear, however, that modest people are deeply concerned with the needs of other people and are not preoccupied with themselves.

Unlike profound human modesty, which is concerned with not overrating one's human worth, professional modesty is often associated with humility, namely, with underrating oneself. There are many cases in which professional modesty is uncalled for but human modesty is still appropriate. Thus, in discussions on professional matters, professional modesty is often out of place. We should insist upon our view if we believe in its merits.

Professional modesty is related to human modesty, where despite one's proven accomplishments one is aware of how much one does not know. Socrates and Einstein would probably exemplify this well. Modest persons are often inclined to underestimate their professional accomplishments slightly, perhaps as a corrective to the prevalent inclination to overrate them. But this should not blur the distinction between esteem for our professional accomplishments and respect for our existence as human beings. The latter is at the heart of modesty. There is therefore no contradiction in being modest and being proud of one's superior standing from a social or professional angle. While acknowledging this type of superiority, the modest person will deny that it has any implication whatsoever concerning the profound similarity of all human beings.

Is modesty compatible with being competitive or with the attempt to be the best in one's field? Being modest does not mean being average. Having an egalitarian evaluation does not imply that all human beings are equal in their capacities and accomplishments. Modesty involves the realization of similar human worth despite these obvious differences. No contradiction exists in being modest and in being the best (and knowing this). In their professional work, modest people are probably not motivated by the desire to be the best in the world (since they attach less significance than others to social comparison), but by the desire to do their work better and to derive greater satisfaction from it. These people may be accomplishment-oriented but they are less likely to be competitive. Modest people usually conceive of their work as an end in itself and not as a means of arriving at material or social benefits. These benefits, no doubt, may be quite useful and they may enjoy them, but in light of their overall values they will probably not overrate their significance.

Being modest should be distinguished from being humble. Although in everyday language and in the philosophical literature "modesty" and "humility" are often identified, I relate these terms to two distinct attitudes. The crucial difference is that modest people do not overrate themselves, whereas humble people underrate themselves. Being humble may be a virtue in those circumstances where it promotes social harmony. Its value, however, is instrumental and limited to specific circumstances; this is in contrast to the more profound virtue of modesty.

Modest people are not necessarily modest in the sense of having a humble way of life (e.g., in their dress, house, or car). But since modest people usually attach more significance to a deeper sense of human worth, they will pay less attention to external features associated with their way of living. Modesty should also be distinguished from asceticism. Both attitudes may involve a certain evaluation of the limitations of human beings and hence the insignificance of social and professional status. However, whereas asceticism involves withdrawal from active everyday life, the modest person continues such activity while remaining sensitive to others' needs and inherent worth.

Kant's account of humility is close to the account of modesty offered here.[24] Kant clearly sees the need to distinguish between having a low opinion of oneself and considering oneself to be as valuable as another. The former is not a virtue: "it is a sign of little spirit and of a servile character." In the case of the monk, it may even involve a form of pride. There is no reason, Kant argues, that "I should humiliate myself and value myself less than others; but we all have the right to demand of a man that he should not think himself superior." Accordingly, "we do no harm to another if we consider ourselves equal to him in our estimation." Realizing the basic weakness of human beings should not result in denying humans any positive disposition. Such a denial would prevent us from distinguishing good people from evildoers. Proper self-respect in Kant's view involves both the elements of modesty and noble pride; shamelessness is its opposite. Recognizing our limitations and others' right to equal human esteem does not mean abolishing all differences.

I turn now to compare modesty with what seems to be its opposite, namely, pridefulness. The comparison is focused on Richard Taylor's most interesting and provocative account of pridefulness (or "pride" in his terms).[25] As modesty is a central virtue in the account offered here, so pridefulness is a central virtue in Taylor's conception of ethics, termed "the ethics of aspiration." In both cases the centrality of these virtues stems from their being the summation of most other virtues. On the face of it, the two virtues are incompatible. Thus, Taylor argues that pridefulness is incompatible with egalitarianism and the virtue of humility. A closer look at Taylor's analysis may reveal some affinity between the two virtues.

Taylor defines pridefulness as "the justified love for oneself." Pridefulness is to be distinguished from conceit, which is "the simpleton's unwarranted sense of self-importance" and from arrogance, which implies belittling another person "in an effort to draw attention to one's own presumed superiority." Pridefulness should also be distinguished from vanity and egoism. Vanity is the delight people derive from receiving flattering comments about themselves. Egoism is characterized by excessive absorption in oneself, to the extent that one's awareness of others is clouded. By these plausible distinctions, Taylor eliminates most negative connotations from pridefulness, thereby evading its characterization as a "sin."

In terms of Taylor's unique definition of pridefulness, some similarities exist between pridefulness and modesty. Pridefulness and modesty are based on correct self-perception rather than on a cognitive defect. Accordingly, both the modest and the proud person are less sensitive to the way others evaluate them. Taylor argues that proud people have little interest in the admiration of others except for what they are, but not for what they have. It can be said that modest people have little interest in the admiration of others, except for the love and respect of others. Accordingly, the comparative concern is of little significance to proud and modest people. However, the comparative concern is more significant for proud people. Both modesty and pride encompass positive self-evaluation, but whereas in modesty this positive self-evaluation does not generate negative evaluations of others, in pridefulness it often does. Because of their positive self-evaluation, modest and proud people alike are characterized by fundamental self-confidence. They do not broadcast their achievements because they do not feel the need to impress others.

Another important common feature of the two accounts is the distinction between two kinds of evaluative framework: the first is superficial to the evaluation of one's worth and the second is essential. The identification of these frameworks differs somewhat in the two accounts. The superficial framework in Taylor's account refers to externals such as dress, reputation, and standing in the popular view, and the praise or honors received from small-minded people. Proud people deem externals to be worth very little, however much they may delight others. The more profound framework refers to what one is and not to what one possesses. In the account suggested here, the superficial framework also refers to externals and the profound framework to what one is; however, the scope of the superficial framework is broader than that depicted by Taylor. In the account of modesty given here, when our common nature and fate are considered, reputation and standing in general (not merely in the popular mind) are of less importance. The two accounts stress the importance of the agent's correct self-perception and self-evaluation. It is of interest to note that Taylor takes Einstein, who is characterized here as profoundly modest, to be "one of the proudest persons of our century."

A major difference between Taylor's account and mine is that Taylor divides other agents into those inferior to and those equal to or above the subject. The proud person cares only about the latter. Therefore, proud people delight only in the company of other proud and worthwhile people. Proud people are oblivious to flattering comments only from inferior people. Contrary to modest people, proud people are hardly in touch with inferior people since on matters which are of interest to inferior people, such as the weather, minor political issues, or local trivia, proud people "normally say nothing at all." Proud people "perceive themselves as better than others, and their pride is justified because their perception is correct."[26]

Taylor's distinction between inferior and superior people is problematic since there will always be people superior to us in some respects and hence pridefulness cannot be a central moral virtue because it is relevant only to very few. Taylor is right in arguing that pridefulness is not a vice and that it has some positive aspects. Without pridefulness, one's unique individuality is in danger. Accordingly, people should be proud of what they are or have achieved in a certain domain. However, this should not make them think that they are better individuals or have higher value as human beings. One should always remember the limited scope of one's evaluative perspective: there are other possible evaluative perspectives and in particular there is the profound perspective in light of which we do not differ much from each other in respect of our fate and basic nature. Modesty does not involve placing oneself on a higher plane than other people. Whereas modesty represents a positive evaluation of others, pridefulness may entail a negative evaluation of many of them.

Although pridefulness may be compatible with modesty, modesty is by far a more profound virtue. Pridefulness is by no means a vice, but it is not a central virtue as is modesty. Modesty is more closely connected to basic moral tenets and it has more significant implications for the moral domain.

In light of the above considerations, we may say that one can be proud and modest—as many great people are—but one cannot be proud and ashamed at the same time. We may even take pride in our modesty.[27]

Modesty is closer to shyness than to embarrassment and shame, but nevertheless it differs from all of them. In contrast to these attitudes, modesty does not involve a negative evaluation, and therefore it is not accompanied by unpleasant feelings. Modesty is similar to a character trait in being general and not highly sensitive to contextual circumstances. In arguing that modesty is a type of character trait, I am not assuming that it is an innate trait which cannot be acquired. Perhaps some natural dispositions, such as shyness, facilitate the acquisition of modesty, but there is no necessary connection between them. We can be modest but not shy.

*Humiliation and Arrogance*
A sure route to humiliation is to admit you paid what the car dealer was asking.
—Unknown

I am returning this otherwise good typing paper to you because someone has printed gibberish all over it and put your name at the top.
—An English professor at Ohio University

In feeling humiliated, we conceive of our position to be inferior—typically, undeservedly inferior; in arrogance, we perceive our position to be deserved superiority. In modesty, we perceive ourselves as essentially similar to other people. Whereas the comparison with others is at the center of humiliation and arrogance, the complement of norms is at the center of pridefulness and shame. Such norms can be the achievements of others, and in this case the comparison with others will be central also to pridefulness and shame, but these norms can also refer to moral or religious norms, which one should fulfill no matter what other people do.

Humiliation, arrogance, and modesty are not emotions, but rather general evaluative attitudes which may or may not be associated with certain emotions. Like emotions, these attitudes are basically evaluative attitudes which involve both cognitive and motivational components; however, unlike emotions they do not necessarily involve an intense feeling component. When they do, they are associated with emotions. Humiliation and arrogance are more likely to have an intense feeling component as the comparative concern is more significant in them: it indicates differences which may not last for ever.

Feeling humiliated is often associated with envy and anger, since all of these attitudes are concerned with some undeserved hurt being done to us: in envy, it is undeserved inferiority and in anger, undeserved offense. Sometimes humiliation is associated with the belief that our inferior situation is deserved; in this case, humiliation may generate shame. Arrogance is often associated with pridefulness and contempt. Modesty may be associated with love and compassion: underlying the latter attitudes is the belief that human beings are essentially equal. This equality mainly concerns our profound limitations and our common susceptibility to misfortune.

Pridefulness and shame are connected with other emotions as well. Thus, envy is often associated with pridefulness and shame. Envy often generates shame, and pridefulness is an attitude which may prevent envy.

Shame is typically generated when we are the targets of the actual or anticipated contempt of others.[28] Both emotions involve a global negative evaluation of an agent; whereas in contempt the evaluation is done by other agents, in shame it is done by the agent herself. From another perspective, contempt is the opposite of admiration, which also involves a global positive evaluation of another person.

Shame is often associated with fear and in extreme cases also with anxiety. Aristotle even defines shame as a type of fear.[29] The global negative self-evaluation raises the danger of a similar evaluation from others or the fear of losing one's integrity and ability to function properly. Hence, sadness and even depression are also associated with shame.

## Moral Value

Pridefulness conceals our faults from others and often from ourselves.
—La Rochefoucauld

Writing is not necessarily something to be ashamed of, but do it in private and wash your hands afterwards.
—Robert Heinlein

In the group of emotions focused on others, positive emotions toward others' actions and personality in general, for instance, gratitude and love, are typically considered as positive from a moral perspective, and negative emotions toward others' actions and personality in general, for instance, anger and hate, are typically regarded as negative from a moral perspective. In the group of emotions toward oneself the situation is the opposite: negative emotions toward oneself, such as guilt and shame, are typically positively evaluated from a moral perspective, and positive emotions toward oneself, such as pride and pridefulness, are often negatively evaluated. These differences are particularly evident in the case of sentiments or personality traits. Someone who tends to love other people, be grateful to them, and is able to regret or be ashamed of her deeds is usually taken to be morally superior to someone who tends to hate other people, be angry with them, and often feels pride.

In discussing the moral evaluations of hate and love, I indicated that the global negative evaluation (underlying hate) is morally wrong in a way that the global positive evaluation (underlying love) is not. I suggested that a global evaluation is not morally wrong in itself; it is the combination of global and negative evaluations that makes hate especially wrong. I claimed that the destructive nature of global evaluations is more evident in negative evaluations since (a) it is more difficult to change them, and (b) they have graver moral consequences. Can we make similar claims concerning pridefulness and shame? Is the global negative evaluation involved in shame morally worse than that involved in pridefulness?

Moral values are perceived to be more pronounced when we have positive emotional attitudes toward others and negative emotional attitudes toward ourselves than when we have negative emotional attitudes toward others and positive emotional attitudes toward ourselves. The former are more related to helping others and less related to self-interest.

The above difference is less evident when we speak about specific rather than global emotions. We have seen that pride, regret, and guilt are often justified emotional attitudes. These emotions express our positive or negative evaluations of our specific activities and this is important for improving our behavior. Pridefulness and shame, which express global evaluations of ourselves, are more problematic as they seem either to overlook human limitations or to overrate them. Thus, from a moral point of view, pride appears to be better than pridefulness as it is less likely to involve arrogance and a belief in one's overall superiority. And guilt and regret seem to be morally better than shame as they induce corrective actions and do not make us wish to hide and withdraw as shame often does.

Despite the above observations, I would like to argue that there are many circumstances in which emotions involving global self-evaluations are morally valuable and this is true of positive self-evaluations as well.

There are circumstances in our life when specific self-evaluations are not enough for a critical evaluation of ourselves; more global evaluations are required as the challenges are more profound. In these circumstances we may have to consider changing some of our basic attitudes and values. Pridefulness and shame are important for these circumstances. There is, then, nothing inherently wrong with these emotions, but we should consider what the circumstances are which indeed justify them. Many moral theories that are focused on actions rather than attitudes consider specific emotions, such as guilt, regret, and pride, to be morally superior to the more global emotions, such as pridefulness and shame, which often express our attitudes and traits. In virtue theory, which is focused on one's global attitudes and character traits, the global emotions are important as well.

There is a widespread belief that the broader the focus of my pridefulness (or pride) the less morally objectionable it is. For example, taking pride in the achievement of my country is less objectionable than taking pride in my own achievements. On the other hand, shame has higher value when its focus is narrower. Personal shame has higher moral value than shame of a certain group.[30] This belief is due, among other things, to the assumption that morality is essentially egalitarian and concerned with our attitude toward others. Hence personal pride, which expresses one's belief in one's superiority over others, is wrong, whereas personal shame or humility, which may express a more egalitarian and considerate attitude toward others, is right. By broadening the focus of our pridefulness, individual differences level out and superiority is less warranted. Similarly, by narrowing the focus of our shame, we evaluate other people more positively.

Taking into account these considerations, which are indeed valid in many circumstances, we nevertheless must realize the functional and moral value of global self-evaluation in reference to merely one person. It is, after all, a particular person who is the prime moral agent. Moreover, it seems that such collective pride or shame is often undeserved as the individual has done nothing to merit the pridefulness or shame.

I will now show that pridefulness and shame are indeed valuable in many moral circumstances.

*Pridefulness* occupies an ambivalent position between two sets of concepts—one of which is clearly positive and contains attitudes such as honor, dignity, self-respect, and self-confidence, and the other which is clearly negative and includes attitudes like vanity, conceit, arrogance, and boastfulness. Indeed, conflicting moral evaluations have been directed at pridefulness; for example, Aristotle regards it as an important virtue, while Judaism and Christianity take pridefulness to be the worst of sins because it is seen as essentially a rejection of God.[31]

The divergence of attitudes toward this emotion is partially due to the fact that the positive self-evaluation underlying pride can be further subdivided into various types: for instance, global or specific (pridefulness or pride), genuine or false (appropriate pride or vanity), excessive or nonexcessive. Some of these attitudes are morally wrong almost by definition; others are more neutral.

To evaluate in a positive manner a specific action of ours or ourselves in general is not morally wrong. We do not have to make merely negative evaluations about ourselves or to be neutral in this regard. In this sense, neither pride nor pridefulness is inherently morally wrong. Nevertheless, pride and pridefulness are often evaluated negatively from a moral viewpoint. I believe that this negative moral evaluation is due to the danger of excess which may lead to vanity and arrogance; it is the excess, rather than pride and pridefulness themselves, which is morally wrong. When the positive evaluation of oneself is limited to a specific action done, as in the case of pride, the danger of excess is less than when the positive evaluation is more comprehensive, as in the case of pridefulness. The excess, leading to vanity and arrogance, indicates that pride or pridefulness is not merely concerned with self-evaluation but with a negative evaluation of others.

*Shame* is probably one of the most powerful emotions for moral behavior. Shame is closely connected with self-esteem and self-respect. Its emergence indicates that some of our most profound values are violated. When a person loses self-respect, and hence shame, this person becomes very dangerous. Shame prevents many people from behaving immorally and from losing their own self-respect. A preventative type of morality would be, therefore, to educate people to realize their value as human beings and hence to enhance their self-respect; in this case, shame is likely to emerge when immoral deeds are even merely contemplated.[32]

People will never be ashamed of anything they have done unless they accept a certain standard of rectitude. The feeling of shame, therefore, can bear witness to an uncorrupted conscience; and such a person is better than one who is both wicked and shameless. As Arnold Isenberg rightly argues, a positive morality does not forget the past, but recalls it in order to reconsider. However, we cannot reflect upon our errors without exposing ourselves to an attack of shame. Shame is seen as a price we may have to pay for our weaknesses and the attempt to cope with them.[33]

The importance of shame to moral behavior indicates the double moral aspect of shame: shame indicates that we violated a certain profound norm, and in this sense we are morally bad, but it also expresses the fact that we care about this norm and this caring is commendable from a moral point of view. Indeed, we often praise people who are ashamed. In a somewhat similar vein, although we usually perceive self-confidence as a morally positive property, it is sometimes criticized on moral grounds since it may be taken to imply the absence of caring.[34]

As noted, Aristotle says that we should praise only young ones for being ashamed since they are prone to many mistakes; older people should not make the mistakes that give rise to shame.[35] Although I agree that lack of experience makes young ones more prone to shameful mistakes, I do not consider older people to be immune from mistakes and hence from shame. Shame is commendable for older people, too—although it is preferable to avoid, or at least to reduce significantly, those situations in which our behavior gives rise to shame. It may be the case that more virtuous people are ashamed at less profound misdeeds than are less virtuous people. They believe that they should and could prevent misdeeds which, although considered minor by others, are enough in their own minds to generate shame rather than mere embarrassment. The relative perception of the severity of our misdeeds is another indication that shame may appear at all ages and in all types of moral agents.

I have indicated that shame involves an audience. It seems that the larger the audience is—other things being equal—the more intense is the shame. It is plausible to assume that if more people are aware of our bad behavior, then our shame is likely to be more intense—hence, the wish to hide or disappear from as many people as possible. In modern times we are witnessing a perplexing phenomenon in this regard: public confessions of shameful deeds. Many daytime television talk shows have in common a confessional format, which encourages participants to make public what in earlier times would have been subject to the sanction of shame.[36] The same holds true for the prevalence of pornography. Pornography is largely the conveyance of the idea that sex is pleasurable. This idea itself is not as threatening as the portrayal in public of people enjoying sex devoid of shame and guilt, although their sexual activity is in conflict with moral constraints of genital modesty and heterosexual monogamy.[37]

Do these phenomena indicate the decline in shame in modern society? Not necessarily—they may rather indicate a change in fundamental values constituting our self-image. There are certain deeds that were once regarded as fundamentally negative and now are more acceptable; consequently, these deeds no longer generate shame. Some of the above cases do indeed express loss of shame and not merely a change of values. It should be remembered that participants in these television programs or in pornography shows are rewarded with publicity or financial incentives. Participants' willingness to abandon shame in return for such rewards has threatening implications from a moral point of view. The presence of shame, which expresses our basic values, is helpful in maintaining human dignity and integrity.

# Chapter 19

# Epilogue

Why should I be bitter
About someone who was
A complete stranger
Until a certain moment
In a day that has passed.
—Saigyo

I once participated in a public debate which dealt with the question: "What is Love?" In the few minutes I had, I described what is meant by a typical emotion and then what distinguishes love from other emotions. A famous author, who also participated in the symposium, severely criticized my research on emotions in general and on love in particular, claiming that such research is not merely unable to provide a better understanding of emotions but also that it ruins the very nature of the emotional experience. He believes that we cannot explain the nature of love, but can only describe specific cases of love. For example, he can describe his intense love for his wife or how his mother fell in love with his father, but he maintains that no one can provide interesting insights on the nature of love.

We find this criticism of the very possibility of doing research on emotions among various philosophers. Thus, Anthony Kenny argued that empirical psychology can tell us nothing about emotion. In a similar vein, Paul Griffiths claims that emotions "do not have something specially in common that distinguishes them from other arbitrary collections of objects. . . . There is no rich collection of generalizations about this range of phenomena that distinguishes them from other psychological phenomena." Accordingly, "the general concept of emotion has no role in any future psychology." Like the concept of "spirituality," he holds that the concept of "emotion" may be useful in everyday life, but as far as understanding ourselves is concerned, it can only be a hindrance.[1]

The above criticism actually consists of two separate claims; the first is descriptive and the second normative: (1) in light of the complexity of emotions, there is no general regularity typical of emotions and we must settle for descriptions of specific cases; (2) knowing the nature of our emotions will ruin emotional experiences. I believe that both claims are basically mistaken.

I agree that the description of specific cases is of utmost importance in various forms of art. Such a description is valuable, too, for understanding emotions. As indicated in the introduction, I believe that the best descriptions of emotions have so far been provided by artists rather than by psychologists or philosophers. The artistic point of view is, however, only one possible perspective on emotions; its success should not undermine the value of other, more general perspectives. The artist's perspective is highly personal, but if we limit ourselves to this perspective our understanding will remain partial and narrow. As the poet Rachel wrote: "Only about myself I could speak, my world is as narrow as the ant's world." The artist may be able to speak only about herself, but it would be pretentious to assume that only artists can speak about emotions. Philosophers, psychologists, and other scientists can also shed useful light on the mechanisms which generate emotions. Despite the generality and diversity inherent in the concept of emotions, we nevertheless can provide plausible generalizations. There are many studies on the emotions—including this book—where this is exemplified.

Without entering into a discussion concerning the nature of art, it seems that the ability of art to describe emotions stems, among other things, from the fact that the specific cases described by artists have implications for other cases, especially those with which the reader can identify. The artists do not explain the general characteristics underlying the particular cases they describe, but such characteristics are present in their descriptions. A specific case having no implications for and similarity to other cases, or which has no special relevance to me, will have no emotional significance for me. As suggested, meaning is relational; emotional meaning, and any other type of meaning, presupposes certain relations. Meaningful understanding implies some understanding of those relations. Artists refer to these general relations through the description of a specific case; the philosophers and scientists refer to them more explicitly, in an attempt to elucidate their nature.

Assuming that the descriptive claim (i.e., we are unable to describe general regularities typical of emotions) is false, then the normative claim criticizing such a description carries more weight. Although I believe that the normative claim is more interesting than the descriptive claim, it is nevertheless mistaken as well—even if less obviously.

There is a long tradition which considers knowledge to be an obstacle to happiness. Adam and Eve were expelled from paradise because they wanted to know more about the world. And the myth of Pandora implies that all troubles were released in the world because she wanted to know what was inside the box given to her by the gods. Also relevant to this tradition is the story about a man who has a long beard; the man is asked whether he puts his beard above or beneath the blanket at night. From this time on, the man is unable to fall asleep.

The tradition which considers knowledge to be an obstacle to happiness is expressed in the emotional context by the claim that knowledge of how our emotions are regulated will make us less happy since it will ruin the uniqueness of the emotional experience. Thus, a character in Oscar Wilde's short story, "The Remarkable Rocket," says "love is not fashionable any more, the poets have killed it. They wrote so much about it that nobody believed them, and I am not surprised. True love suffers, and is silent."[2] Such criticism is even more forceful once it is directed at scientific investigations of the emotions.

Contrary to this tradition, I believe that scientific progress enables us to better know our environment and ourselves, thereby increasing our adaptivity and more fully realizing our capacities. Although scientific progress is not a unitary and direct march toward greater happiness, neither is it a constant downward spiral into misery. The life of our ancestors was not better than ours and they were not happier than we are. There are, of course, many cases in which knowing more will make us sadder—hence the great value of positive illusions. But such cases should not be taken as recommendations for ignorance. Ignorance is a local value in specific circumstances; it cannot be recommended as a way of living. Coping with the complexity of life is not simple: sometimes we need to open our eyes and sometimes close them. Constant sleep is not a solution—it is, rather, a complete surrender.

Knowing our emotions and the circumstances in which they are generated may also have positive as well as negative implications, but ignorance, which is often associated with stupidity, is not the remedy for coping with the negative implications. Starving to death is not the optimal solution for weight problems. Emotional knowledge, and even labeling the emotions, usually increase our ability to regulate them. Such an increase is not essentially negative—on the contrary, it usually enhances our well-being. This knowledge enables us to reduce the frequency and intensity of negative emotions and intensify positive emotions. Thus, knowing the reason for the generation of a certain negative emotion, such as anger, hate, or fear, will usually reduce its intensity; in other negative emotions, such as embarrassment, focusing on our own experience can make that experience more intense. Knowing the emotional circumstances associated with positive emotions, such as love or admiration, typically increases their intensity. In any case, knowing the chemical activities underlying love should not reduce its intensity. On the contrary, such knowledge may enable us to provide better circumstances for the emergence of love.

I have tried in this book to reduce somewhat the mystery surrounding the emotions. Although this work is merely a small step toward understanding the emotions, it may indicate some initial directions and the importance of emotions to everyday life. Emotions are, and should be, central to human life. In the wonderful words of the English author John Lubbock:

> Do not be afraid of showing your affection. Be warm and tender, thoughtful and affectionate. Men are more helped by sympathy than by service; love is more than money, and a kind word will give more pleasure than a present.

# Notes

## Introduction

1. Horton 1957; Wilkinson 1976; Shaver et al. 1992.
2. De Sousa 1990:434; Elster 1989:61; C. A. Smith and Lazarus 1990:609.
3. Descartes 1649:art.1.
4. Stumpf 1899:67; cited in Reisenzein and Schonpflug 1992:38.

## Chapter 1

1. This example was suggested by Scheller—see G. Taylor 1985:61.
2. Weiner 1985:559.
3. See, for example, Griffiths 1997; Kenny 1963.
4. See also Ben-Ze'ev 1993a; Lakoff 1987; Rosch 1977, 1978; Smith and Lazarus 1990.
5. See, for example, Alston 1967; Fehr 1988; Fehr and Russell 1984; Fitness and Fletcher 1993; Kovecses 1990; J. A. Russell 1991; Shaver et al. 1992; Smith and Lazarus 1990.
6. Lyons (1980:146–149), for instance, distinguishes a few senses of "typical": (a) natural concomitant; (b) commonly or frequently found; (c) appropriate, sensible, or rational; and (d) conventional concomitant.
7. Tversky and Kahneman 1982:86.
8. Tversky and Kahneman 1983.
9. Hupka 1991:258–259.
10. Fitness and Fletcher 1993; Shaver et al. 1987.
11. Lyons (1980), for example, notes that "Freud's clinical interests were clearly bound to be centered on the emotions of disturbed persons, so it is no surprise that he most frequently refers to emotions such as anxiety and fear, and often to these in their extreme manifestation" (26).
12. See also A. Smith 1759:243.
13. The prototype approach to emotion has also been criticized on the following counts: (a) the presence of good and poor exemplars is not decisive, because such exemplars also occur with concepts that have necessary and sufficient conditions; (b) the argument that prototypicality is established where there is no clear boundary between what are and what are not instances of the concept tends to confuse meaning with verification (see Oatley 1992:84–85). Although I accept (a), it is not clear that the presence of good and poor exemplars entails the presence of graded membership, which is the decisive element for the prototypical analysis. Concerning (b), the prototype approach does not assume that it is hard to *verify* the clear boundaries of emotion categories, but rather that emotion categories *do not have* clear boundaries. The claim refers to both the ontological and epistemological levels of discussion, and not merely to the latter. It is worth noting that no one has presented a precise definition of the necessary and sufficient conditions underlying emotion categories. Accordingly, all researchers actually use prototypical characterizations. I believe that this

is not merely due to our current primitive stage of understanding emotions, but also to their intrinsic nature.

14. Aristotle, *On the Soul* 412b19.

15. De Sousa (1990:434) argues that an important aspect of emotions is their level ubiquity: "emotions affect our experience and our performance at virtually every level of analysis." Accordingly, "no single level of analysis can do justice to the emotions." Similarly, Parkinson and Manstead (1992:123) claim that "emotions are multilevel syndromes that develop over time rather than unitary responses to delimited interpretations of significant stimuli."

## Chapter 2

1. Frijda 1988:353–354; see also Oatley 1992:50; Ozick 1983:201. My characterization is closely related to Oatley's (1992) view that "emotions occur when a psychological tendency is arrested or when smoothly flowing action is interrupted" (46). Likewise, Batson et al. (1992) argue that "the shift from a less valued state to a more valued state is accompanied by positive affect; a shift in the opposite direction is accompanied by negative affect" (302). Similarly, Lazarus (1991) claims that an emotional state is "always in flux, changing from one context or moment to another." An emotional state serves "as a compelling signal that something of significance is occurring." Accordingly, an emotion involves a provocation, which is an event that signifies a change in the person-environment relationship for better or worse" (175, 47, 107). See also Aristotle, *Rhetoric*, 1378a21; Izard 1991; Lyons 1980. Nico Frijda (1988:353) suggests that "pleasure is always contingent upon change and disappears with continuous satisfaction. Pain may persist under persisting adverse conditions." This difference may indicate that painful feelings have stronger connections to objective circumstances than pleasant feelings. Since objective, negative circumstances can destroy us, paying closer attention to them is adaptive.

2. Kagan 1992:99; Freedman 1978:228.

3. Buss 1994; Metts et al. 1998.

4. Spinoza 1677:IIIp6; IIIdef.aff.; Vp39s. The above characterization refers merely to what Spinoza terms "passive emotions"; it does not refer, for example, to the intellectual love of God.

5. See Ben-Ze'ev 1993a:175–176; C. I. Lewis 1929:129.

6. Minsky 1985:68.

7. See Nussbaum 1986, forthcoming. Nussbaum emphasizes the role of profound change in determining emotional sensitivity; we should, however, also see the connection between the two types of changes.

8. Spinoza 1677:IVp67.

9. Ibid.:IIIp6.

10. Frijda and Mesquita 1994:54.

11. C. I. Lewis 1929:82, 128; see also Ben-Ze'ev 1993a:17.

12. Collingwood 1923:59.

13. Hume 1739–1740:73.

14. C. I. Lewis 1946:19–20.

15. Festinger 1954; Higgins 1987; Kant 1924.

16. Strack et al. 1990; cited in R. H. Frank 1999:132; see also Medvec et al. 1995.

17. Gleicher et al. 1990; Landman 1995.

18. Kahneman and Tversky 1982; Kahneman and Miller 1986.

19. Gladue and Delaney 1990.

20. Baron et al. 1992:3. Thibaut and Kelley (1959) argued that our dependency on a relationship is primarily a function of what our other options are, that is, the profit we can anticipate in our "next best deal"; they refer to this value as the comparison level for alternative. See also Baron et al. 1992:2–3.

21. Gilovich and Medvec 1995a:380.

22. Graham et al. 1993:1000; Heider 1958:141–144; Kahneman and Varey 1990; Ortony et al. 1988:74–75.

23. Hansen 1991.

24. Kahneman and Miller 1986; Lazarus and Lazarus 1994:chap.8. The importance of the alternative availability in determining the nature and intensity of emotions has been shown repeatedly in empirical studies concerning many emotions, for example, happiness, sympathy, regret, envy, and gratitude; for some references, see Gleicher et al. 1990; Teigen 1997.

25. See Kahneman and Miller 1986. They suggest several factors determining the availability of an alternative. Some of these are (a) exceptional features are more mutable than routine ones and hence more likely to evoke available alternatives; (b) when an alternative to an event could be produced either by introducing an improvement in some antecedent or by introducing a deterioration, the former will be more available; (c) attributes about which little is known appear to be relatively mutable and hence more likely to evoke alternatives; (d) when people consider a cause-effect pair, alternatives to the effect will be more available than alternatives to the cause; (e) the mutability of any aspect of a situation increases when attention is directed to it.

26. Teigen 1997.

27. Kraut et al. 1998:1018.

28. Baron et al. 1992:chap.2. An interesting claim in this regard is that the human brain evolved to handle the complexities of social life; see Cummins 1997.

29. Brennan 2000; Hatfield et al. 1994.

30. Tannen 1990:chap.1.

31. Cartwright and Zander 1968:46–47; Lewin 1948:184; Sherif and Sherif 1964:53.

32. Lewin 1948:146.

33. Sherif and Sherif 1964:54–55, 272.

34. Forgas and Fiedler 1996; Harnad 1987.

35. Spinoza 1677:IVp18s.; Reid 1788:558; see also Izard 1991:128; Oatley 1992:179; Parkinson 1995:186. Hume claimed that "the object of hatred or anger is a person or creature endow'd with thought and consciousness" (1739–1740:411). Hume points out that in the case of animals, the objects of their love and hate extend beyond animals of their own species and "comprehends almost every sensible and thinking being" (397). In this sense human emotions are more confined; see also P. Russell 1995:68.

36. Reid 1788:559,569.

37. Nissenbaum 1985.

38. Reid 1788:571; see also James 1997:13. Dictionary definitions of *emotion* emphasize the element of change and instability. For example, the four suggested meanings in the *Oxford English Dictionary* are (1) a moving out, migration, transference from one place to another; (2) a moving, stirring, agitation, perturbation; (3) a political or social agitation; a tumult, popular disturbance; (4) any agitation or disturbance of mind, feeling, or passion; any vehement or excited mental state. Although some of these meanings are obsolete, they indicate the origin as well as the core element of "emotion."

39. Cited in De Sousa 1987:50; see also Sherman 1997:54.

40. Larsen and Diener 1987:27.

41. McGill 1989:198; Roese and Olson 1995:33.

42. Lazarus 1991; Oatley and Jenkins 1992:78.

43. Arnold 1960:171; B. Stein 1987:220. The hammer metaphor should be credited to Abraham Massalo.

44. Diener, Sandvik, and Larsen 1985.

45. Spinoza argues that "the affects are excessive, and occupy the mind in the consideration of only one object so much that it cannot think of others." For example, "a greedy man thinks of nothing else but profit, or money, and an ambitious man of esteem" (1677:IVp44s.). See also Beck 1976:91–92; Larsen et al. 1987; McCosh 1880:42–47; Z. Rubin 1970:272; R. C. Solomon 1990. For a review of empirical findings indicating that emotions—especially negative ones—serve to narrow people's attentional focus, see Derryberry and Tucker 1994.

46. Pavelchak et al. 1988.
47. Parnas 1996.
48. Tulloch 1990:196.
49. Indeed, people often describe their emotionality as a state in which they are unable to think clearly and in particular to appreciate others' points of view (Parrott 1995:76–77).
50. Horder 1992:75.
51. Ekman 1984, 1992b.
52. Frijda 1986:101; Frijda et al. 1991; Oatley and Jenkins 1996; Scherer et al. 1986.
53. Gilboa and Revelle 1994:145; Oatley 1992:23.
54. Lyons (1980, 1992) holds this view. He argues that a person is in an emotional state if and only if he is in an abnormal physiological state caused by his evaluation of the context in relation to himself. And "abnormal" in relation to physiological changes is defined as departing significantly from normal human physiological states. Therefore, "the emotional person is literally exhibiting a set of physiological changes which would not be listed in a medical textbook under the description of the normal stable state" (1980:60). As De Sousa (1987:55) rightly remarks, the notion of "normal condition" cannot be defined by strictly physiological criteria; we should also refer to the functional or mental levels.
55. Devlin 1987; Tulloch 1990:65.
56. De Sousa (1987) argues that "Much of what matters to us emotionally does so because it recalls or repeats some past experience (though generally we like our repetitions spiced with difference). In any case, neither excitement nor boredom makes sense except against a background of salient memories and expectations" (207).
57. Drever 1952; see also Alston 1967; Lazarus 1991:36; Lyons 1980:53–57.
58. Thus, Schachtel writes that "I believe there is no action without affect, to be sure not always an intense, dramatic affect as in an action of impulsive rage, but more usually a total, sometimes quite marked, sometimes very subtle and hardly noticeable mood, which nevertheless constitutes an essential background of every action" (1959:20; see also Tomkins 1981).
59. M. D. Lewis 1995.
60. McIntosh and Martin 1992.
61. For systematic discussions of different philosophical views of emotions and their various characteristics, see, for example, Calhoun and Solomon 1984:3–40; Lyons 1980:chaps.1–3; 1992.

## Chapter 3

1. See also Ben-Ze'ev 1993a.
2. Damasio 1994:233; Ferguson 1767:45; Melzack 1973:29–31.
3. Wundet seems to hold this view; see, for example, Reisenzein 1992:145.
4. For a more detailed discussion of my view, see Ben-Ze'ev 1993a.
5. See also Lyons 1980:chap.7. My intellectual debt to Lyons' excellent book *Emotion* is evident throughout this book. Lyons terms his view "the causal-evaluative theory of emotions." I share Lyons's contention that evaluation is a crucial component of emotions in distinguishing one emotion from another. My major disagreement with Lyons concerns the causal part of his theory. Thus, I disagree that "X is to be deemed an emotional state if and only if it is a physiologically abnormal state caused by the subject of that state's evaluation of his or her situation" (Lyons 1980:57–58). I do not consider the causal relationship to be crucial for the definition of an emotion, and in general I do not think it is adequate to consider the mental and physiological components as successively located on a single causal line. In typical emotions all components are present at the same time. Our disagreements on this issue may stem from a somewhat different approach to the mind-body problem. In any case, these disagreements are not crucial for understanding my own view since the issue of mental causality is not discussed here. Moreover, Lyons himself admits that he does not and cannot give an account of how an evaluation can cause physiological changes (1980:62).

6. In the same vein, Lazarus distinguishes between knowledge, that is, accurate or inaccurate beliefs about the way things are and work, and appraisal, which consists of a continuing evaluation of the significance of what is happening for one's personal well-being. Lazarus (1991) notes (and I concur) that knowledge and appraisal are "different aspects of one instantaneous process" (147). See also Lazarus and Smith 1988; Smith and Lazarus 1990. Since in philosophy and elsewhere, knowledge involves true belief, it is better to use the term "cognition" (or "information") instead of "knowledge." Lazarus and Smith consider knowledge and appraisal to be part of the cognitive component. I restrict the term "cognition" to descriptive beliefs, including those which are mistaken. In this way a confusion between descriptive and evaluative components is less likely to occur.

7. Aristotle, *Nicomachean Ethics*:1149a26–29; Malebranche 1675:314; see also James 1997:chap.7. Aristotle claims that in intense emotions the senses are easily deceived because perceivers project their own emotions onto the environment. Slight resemblance may deceive the coward into thinking that he sees his enemy, or the lover into believing that he sees his beloved. Generally, in emotions "all men become easily deceived, and more so the more their emotions are excited" (*On Dreams*:460b). Similarly, Aristotle claims that "when people are feeling friendly and agreeable, they think one sort of thing; when they are feeling angry or hostile, they think either something totally different or the same thing with a different intensity" (*Rhetoric*:1377b31–78a1).

8. In accordance with such considerations, Aristotle argues that hate is more reasonable than anger since only anger is accompanied by pain, which is an impediment to reason (*Politics*:1312b34).

9. Cited in Jauregui 1995:19.

10. Hastorf and Cantril 1954; Hochschild 1983:30; Kahneman 1973; Lazarus 1991:chap.10; Reid 1788:574. On the effects of emotions upon cognition see, for example, Ellsworth 1991:150–152; Forgas 1995; Forgas and Fiedler 1996; Scheffler 1991:3–17; Wilson and Klaaren 1992.

11. Even Freud (1915:78) claimed that strictly speaking "unconscious affect" is a contradiction in terms. This claim is astonishing when we take into account other claims made by Freud. Rorty (1988b) explains this claim by arguing that here Freud means that the feeling dimension of emotion could not be unconscious but that other components could. See also De Sousa 1987:37; Lazarus 1991:chap.4.

12. Ryle 1949; chap.4.

13. Bedford 1957; Ortony et al. 1988. See also Gordon 1987:29–30; Lazarus 1991:147; Lazarus and Smith 1988; C. A. Smith and Lazarus 1990.

14. This distinction is often overlooked. Thus, Reid (1788) claims that benevolent affections are accompanied by agreeable feelings; hence, they are pleasant in their nature. Nevertheless he includes pity among benevolent affections and considers it an agreeable feeling (559, 570).

15. Damasio 1994:132.

16. Elster (1999a:57) rightly argues that whereas modern writers tend to think of an emotion as associated with pleasure *or* pain, Aristotle believed that a specific emotion is typically associated with pleasure *and* pain. Elster himself holds that although many emotions are indeed mixed, not all emotions are mixed emotions as Aristotle seems to believe.

17. This distinction has been suggested in various forms concerning different phenomena; see, for example, Ben-Ze'ev 1993a:chap.4; Clore and Ortony 1999; Ekman 1992b:187–189; Lazarus 1991:151; Leventhal and Scherer 1987; Lyons 1980:86–89; Sloman 1996; C. A. Smith et al. 1993; C. A. Smith and Kirby forthcoming; Van Reekum and Scherer 1997. Physiological evidence for the presence of such a schematic emotional system is presented in LeDoux 1996. Further analysis of the neurophysiological basis of emotions can be found in Panksepp 1998.

18. Thayer 1996:chap.4.

19. C. A. Smith and Lazarus 1990:629.

20. Oakley 1991.

21. Attempts to present a computational model of emotions can be found, for example, in Dyer 1987; Elliott 1992; Ortony et al. 1988; Picard 1997. My criticism of the computational approach is presented in Ben-Ze'ev 1993a:chap.4; see also Ben-Ze'ev 1990.

22. For a more detailed discussion, see Ben-Ze'ev 1993a:chap.4.
23. Batson et al. 1992:308.
24. Cited in Etcoff 1999:8.
25. For empirical evidence see Clore and Ortony 1999.
26. Frijda 1986; Gaus 1990:65; Lyons 1980:chap.9.
27. Scherer 1984; see also Clore and Ortony 1999.
28. Devlin 1987; Van Evra 1990:102.
29. Fiske 1988:104; Oatley and Jenkins 1996:chap.9; Van Evra 1990:chap.7.
30. This claim was made by Wallace Chafe and is cited in Tannen 1990:140.
31. Morreall 1983; De Sousa 1987:chap.11; Frijda 1986:sec.2.5.
32. In this matter I follow Sully who claims that the term "feeling," when applied in its strict sense, "is confined to those modes of consciousness which are in a peculiar sense affections of the subject, and which do not, in the same direct way as our thoughts and volitions, involve a clear reference to objects" (1892:sec.2.4.3).
33. R. C. Solomon 1993:10.
34. There is indeed evidence for the independence of the pleasure-displeasure continuum (the hedonic level) and the degree of arousal; see Larsen and Diener 1985; see also Diener and Larsen 1993:405; Reisenzein 1994. Some people have claimed that each distinguishable emotion has a distinct, non-analyzable feeling quality (McDougall 1935:149–151; see also Lazarus 1991:60). Although the precise number of feeling continua is not clear, the position assuming a single feeling continuum ranging between pain and pleasure and the position claiming that each emotional experience has a distinctive quality should be rejected.
35. Perhaps the term "enjoyment" is the best term to describe the raw feeling associated with positive emotions. The difference between enjoyment and the more general type of pleasure is expressed in their grammatical objects: pleasure is defined in terms of statements taking "that" clauses as their grammatical objects, for instance, "I am pleased that she succeeds in her task"; enjoyment cannot, grammatically, take such objects (Sircello 1989:7–11).
36. Gaus 1990:41–44.
37. Olds and Milner 1954.
38. Wittgenstein 1967:#504; Dewey 1894–1895.
39. Abramson and Pinkerton 1995:37.
40. This emphasis is found, for example, in Aristotle, the Stoics, and Spinoza. For contemporary exposition of this view among philosophers, see, for instance, Brown 1987; De Sousa 1987; Gaus 1990; Greenspan 1988; Helm 1994; Lyons 1980; Nussbaum forthcoming; Solomon 1976; and among psychologists, see, for example, Arnold 1960; Ellsworth 1991; Lazarus 1991; Lazarus and Lazarus 1994; Ortony et al. 1988; Parkinson 1995; Roseman 1991; Scherer 1982; C. A. Smith and Pope 1992.
41. Descartes 1649:art.52. Contrary to the view suggested here, Reisenzein and Schonpflug (1992:38) argue that in Carl Stumpf's view cognitions, rather than evaluations, are the primary discriminating features of the emotions.
42. Reisenzein 1994. Reisenzein, who advocates this view, responds to this criticism by suggesting we distinguish the emotions in light of their different appraisal causes. In this suggestion, it is doubtful whether emotions are still distinguished in light of their feeling dimension. However, this suggestion suffers from other flaws. The main one is that the causal history is not always relevant to the present emotional situation. In defining the nature of an emotion, the reference to its causes is often redundant since different emotions can be caused by the same event and the same emotion can be caused by different events.
43. Lyons (1980) argues that the evaluative aspect is "the linchpin of the different parts which make up an emotional state, and the differentiator of the different emotions. In separating off one emotion from another, then, one need make reference only to the evaluation . . . though in defining certain emotions, it may be the case that one has also to refer to the appetitive aspect" (81). See also Greenspan 1988:54. For a different interpretation of the above example, see Brown 1987:6.
44. See also Nussbaum forthcoming.

45. Carson 1986; Day 1969:91; Neu 1996.
46. Oatley (1992) argues that "We can call emotions positive if the probability of attaining a goal is increased and negative if such a probability decreases." He urges us not to confuse this claim with the view that "each emotion has a fixed primary valency of pleasantness or unpleasantness." He considers the latter view to be incorrect since "it makes it difficult to understand why, for instance, anyone should ever watch a thriller, the object of which is to induce anxiety" (49). Oatley is right in denying that each emotion has a fixed valency of pleasantness or unpleasantness. He seems to be wrong in denying such a primary valency. Love has a primary positive valency and hate a negative one. This does not mean that we should always pursue love and avoid hate; however, this is typically the case. We enjoy watching a thriller since the pleasant aspects of such an experience are dominant. This, however, is not the case concerning all dangerous situations, especially those which are real. I discuss this issue further in chapter 14 while addressing the phenomenon of hurting the one we love.
47. A prominent representative of the causal view is Lazarus (e.g., 1991); some form of the constitutive view can be found in Parkinson 1995 (e.g., pp. 39–40). A discussion on related issues is found in Clore and Ortony 1999.
48. Ekman et al. 1983; Levenson et al. 1990; Zajonc 1980.
49. In his radical criticism of appraisal theories (or for that matter, any propositional attitude approach), Paul Griffiths (1997:2.3) presents six major problems which he considers fundamental to appraisal theories and which, in his opinion, make such theories of little explanatory value. I will briefly mention these problems and possible responses to them.

> 1. *Objectless emotions—states such as depression, elation, and anxiety seem to have no object and hence to involve no propositional attitudes.* I deal with this problem in the next chapter. I argue that these affective states, which are termed "emotional disorders," differ from typical emotions: although they lack the specific objects which emotions have, they do exhibit some type of intentionality and hence are some sort of propositional attitudes.
> 2. *Reflex emotions—in emotions such as the fear exhibited by earthworms, there is no evaluation.* This problem may be connected only with a causal version of appraisal theories, not with a constitutive version: in the latter version, the evaluative component is a necessary component of the emotional state only and not of the process generating it. If we were unable to ascribe an evaluative component to any state experienced by an earthworm, we could not ascribe emotions to them—at least not the type we find in humans.
> 3. *Unemotional evaluations—identifying emotions with evaluative judgments gives us far too many emotions.* I have already discussed this issue in this chapter. Although evaluations constitute a necessary condition for the presence of emotions, they do not constitute a sufficient condition. Hence, emotions should not be identified with evaluations.
> 4. *Judgments underdetermine emotions—a certain evaluation can generate different emotions.* Unlike the previous objection which refers to the possibility of distinguishing emotions from nonemotions on the basis of the evaluative component alone (a possibility which, I believe, does not prevail in all circumstances), this objection refers to the possibility of distinguishing one emotion from another on the basis of the evaluative component alone. As indicated, I believe that sufficient specification of the evaluative component may distinguish each emotion from another; the specification should include, of course, the agent's own attitude. It is true, as Griffiths indicates, that the judgment "Ashkenazy is a fine pianist" cannot distinguish between envy and admiration; but the judgment "I positively evaluate the fact that Ashkenazy is a fine pianist" can distinguish between the two.
> 5. *Emotional responses to imagination—people can experience emotions by imagining suitable objects.* I cannot see why the fact that imagination plays a major role in emotions should pose any particular problem to a propositional attitude approach; after all, imagination itself is a propositional attitude (see chapters 5 and 7).
> 6. *Physiological responses—the propositional attitude school neglects the physiological aspect of emotion.* There is nothing in the propositional attitude approach which implies that we

should neglect the physiological aspects of emotion. This approach happens to deal with another aspect of emotions. Both aspects are legitimate, and in my opinion even complementary; there is nothing wrong with analyzing one aspect as long as we remember that there are other legitimate perspectives. Similarly, I would not consider the fact that physiologists do not discuss the philosophical aspects of emotions to be a flaw in their theory. In this context, I would warn against confusing the two levels of description. Such a confusion is evident in many discussions of emotions and may be implied in this objection.

I am not claiming that there are no problems implicit in appraisal theories of emotions—there certainly are. But these are not the problems suggested above, and in any case they are not the kind that eliminate, or even considerably reduce, the explanatory power of appraisal theories.

50. On this issue see also Parkinson and Manstead 1992; Reisenzein 1995. Parkinson and Manstead agree with the above position, arguing that appraisals are intimately involved in several of the many stages and aspects of the causal process generating emotions but are never the exclusive determinant of emotion (1992:123).

51. This view can be traced to theories emphasizing the importance of impulse in explaining emotions (Aquinas and the psychologists Shand and McDougall exemplify scholars holding this view) and to the behaviorist theory of emotions (as expressed, e.g., by Watson and Skinner). For discussion and criticism of this tradition, see Lyons 1980:17–25; 35–44. More recently, Oatley (1992) argues that "the core of an emotion is . . . a mental state of readiness for action" (19–20; see also Frijda 1986). Oatley does not assume a complete reduction to the motivational component. For example, he suggests that the state of readiness for action "is normally based on an evaluation of something happening that affects important concerns," and it has a specific phenomenological tone (1992:22). For criticism of the attempts to reduce emotions to one component, whether it be feeling, cognition, or sometimes even motivation, see Lyons 1980:chaps.1 and 2; Oakley 1991:chap.1.

52. Lyons 1980:37, 96. For the complex role of the motivational component in emotions see also Reisenzein 1996; Sherman 1995.

53. See, for example, Elster 1999b:40. Elster accepts Hume's claim that "pride and humility are pure emotions in the soul, unattended with any desire, and not immediately exciting us to action" (1739–1740:367).

54. Contrary to the view presented here, some philosophers consider desire to be an independent emotion (see, e.g., Descartes 1649:art.57; Spinoza 1677:IIIdef.aff.; Hume 1739–1740:438–439). Such a contention is often fed by the philosopher's metaphysical assumptions rather than by psychological descriptions. See also Allen 1991:16.

55. See, for example, Laird and Bresler 1992.

56. The view which reduces emotions to feelings can already be found in Descartes' writings; nevertheless, Descartes mentions all four basic emotional components. Hume's view can also be considered as a form of the feeling theory of emotions. Hume (1739–1740) believes that the distinct sensations of the various passions "constitute their very being and essence" (286). Hence, passions can be distinguished by feeling alone (1739–1740:277, 329, 472, 590, 606–607); see also P. Russell 1995:chap.6. The psychological manifestation of this view appears in James-Lange's theory. For a discussion and rejection of this view, see, for example, Alston 1967; Gaus 1990:26–32; Kenny 1963:chap.3; Lyons 1980:chap.1; 1992; Oakley 1991:16–22; Reid 1788:651, 670–671; Ryle 1949:chap.4. For the view denying that feelings are essential to emotions, see Oakley 1991:8.

57. I am grateful to Nico Frijda for helpful remarks in this regard. For the difference between a substantial and a functional explanation, see, for example, Cassirer 1923; see also Ben-Ze'ev 1993a:2.1.

## Chapter 4

1. See Ben-Ze'ev 1993a:chap. 6.
2. Rosenberg 1998.

3. Frijda 1994.

4. Ibid.; Frijda et al. 1991.

5. For the first view, see Lyons 1980; R. C. Solomon 1976; for the second view, see Gaus 1990:63; Leighton 1985; Ryle 1949.

6. For a distinction between moods and emotions similar to the one presented here, see Oatley and Jenkins 1996:124–127; Parkinson 1995:9.

7. Thayer 1996.

8. See also Elster 1999b:210. Elster describes indifference as the absence of net pleasure or pain, but there are situations in which there is no preference concerning pleasure or pain, but nevertheless the agent is not indifferent because of other reasons. Moreover, there are situations which are pleasurable but nevertheless we are not indifferent since we prefer one alternative over the other because of reasons not connected to net pleasure or pain.

9. Ekman 1984, 1992b; Lazarus 1991:49.

10. Davidson 1994:53; Thayer 1996:5.

11. Bloom 1993:24, 45, 47; Aristotle, *Nicomachean Ethics* 1118a24–b8; Gaus 1990:64.

12. Babcock 1988.

13. Lormand 1985; Oatley 1992:24, 64–65.

14. Morris 1992:265.

15. See also Oatley 1992:64.

16. Lormand 1985.

17. See also Armon-Jones 1991; Oatley and Jenkins 1996:chap.4.

18. Spinoza 1677; Hume 1739–1740; Reisenzein 1994.

19. These classifications are used, for example, by James McCosh (1880).

20. This classification is suggested by Robert Gordon (1987). Gordon's formulation of the distinction between factive and epistemic emotions is too strong. Thus, he writes that in factive emotions "S emotes (e.g., is angry) that P" is true only if it is *true* that P and, further, that S *knows* that P (1987:43). The two conditions for the factive emotions, namely, knowledge and factivity, are too strong. One can be angry that P (someone did X) without knowing for certain that this person actually did X or without X being done at all. Factive emotions should rather be described as merely involving our belief that P.

21. See Elster 1999b:20–25.

22. As Gaus (1990:62) indicates, "liking" (or "disliking") here is a generic notion that applies to positive (or negative) emotional states. "Liking" is used in the sense of "having a favorable attitude toward" rather than in the sense of "enjoying or being pleased by"; see also MacLean 1980:12. The emotional component of cognition, which provides information about the given situation, does not contain positive or negative aspects although it can generate such aspects.

23. See, for example, Spinoza 1677:IIIp11s.; III,p13,s.; Brentano 1874:199. I owe this observation, and many other insights in this book, to Michael Strauss; see Strauss 1999.

24. Gaus 1990:56–57; see also Wilson 1972.

25. This division is suggested by Ortony et al. 1988. My classification of emotions is greatly in debted to this important work, see Ben-Ze'ev 1990.

26. Beck 1976:60–61.

27. For a similar use, see Elster 1999a:207; M. Lewis 1992:75.

28. Nussbaum 1999a:263.

29. Ellsworth and Smith 1988; Fredrickson 1998.

30. Gilboa and Revelle 1994; D. L. Thomas and Diener 1990.

31. Damasio 1994:267; Ellsworth and Smith 1988; Fredrickson 1998:p.301; Gilboa and Revelle 1994.

32. Alloy et al. 1990; Kinder 1995:143; Snyder 1994:16–18.

33. Frijda 1994:63; Lazarus and Lazarus 1994:96.

34. Diener and Diener 1996.

35. Descartes 1649:art.137; Ferguson 1767:41,36; Spinoza 1677:IVp18.

36. Fredrickson 1998.
37. Ibid. 1998; S. E. Taylor 1989:chap.2.
38. Batson et al. 1992:315–318; Oatley 1992:363.
39. Pavelchak et al. 1988.
40. Batson et al. 1992.
41. See, for example, Ekman 1992b; Ekman and Davidson 1994; Ortony et al. 1988; Ortony and Turner 1990.
42. Goodall 1986.
43. M. Lewis 1993.
44. Abramson and Pinkerton 1995:12.
45. Weisfeld 1980.
46. Bridges 1930; Graham and Weiner 1986.
47. Oatley and Johnson-Laird 1987.
48. Fridlund 1994.
49. Barresi and Moore 1996.
50. Batson et al. 1997.
51. Oatley, 1992.
52. See, for example, Barresi and Moore 1996; de Waal 1989; Goodall 1986; Masson and McCarthy 1995.
53. Smuts 1985.
54. Masson and McCarthy 1995:29–30.
55. Barresi and Moore 1996; Chismar 1988:260.
56. Weisfeld 1980.
57. Clark and Watson 1988; Oatley and Duncan 1992.
58. Averill 1982; Oatley and Duncan 1992.
59. Aristotle, *Rhetoric* II, 2–3; see also Nussbaum forthcoming.
60. Chazin 1994; Freedman 1978.
61. Chapman and Wright 1976; Parkinson 1995:185.
62. Rozin et al. 1993.
63. Coyne and Downey 1991; Parkinson 1995:186–188.
64. In the study of Oatley and Duncan (1992) such cases constituted about 6.5 percent of all episodes.

## Chapter 5

1. Gilboa and Revelle 1994.
2. M. Lewis 1992:88, cited in Elster (1999a:280) who also further discusses various difficulties in comparing different aspects of emotional intensity.
3. De Sousa (1987:75) suggests distinctions between a few dimensions in analyzing a motive: (a) its power to attract attention; (b) its power to be selected for action and to override alternative motives; (c) its priority in a temporal dimension. He argues that the first dimension refers to the motive's intensity, the second to its importance or strength, and the third to its urgency. A significant emotional event is usually expressed by all dimensions.
4. Frijda et al. 1992; Sonnemans and Frijda 1994.
5. Parkinson and Manstead 1992.
6. Diener and Larsen 1993:408; Wintre and Vallance 1994.
7. In his analysis of "incommensurable," Griffin (1986) points out that this concept covers a fair amount of ground: "In a strong sense it can mean that two items cannot be compared quantitatively at all; the one is neither greater than, nor less than, and not equal to the other." In a weaker sense, "incommensurable" can mean that "no amount of one sort of item can equal, in respect of some quantity, a certain amount of another" (77). It is obvious that in everyday life emotional intensity is not incommensurable in the strong sense. Even if it is incommensurable in the weaker

sense (which is not at all obvious), this does not mean that different degrees of emotional intensity are incomparable. Neither incommensurablity nor nonequivalence imply incomparability (Griffin 1986). See also Day 1970.

8. See also Green 1992:136–138; Sonnemans and Frijda 1994.

9. Various psychologists have suggested lists of intensity variables, or basic appraisals, which have some similarity to my list. The list most similar to my own is discussed by Ortony et al. 1988; see also Frijda 1987; Frijda et al. 1989; Lazarus 1991; McCornack and Levine 1990; Roseman 1991; Roseman et al. 1990; Scherer 1988; C. A. Smith and Ellsworth 1985, 1987.

10. D. T. Miller and Gunasegaram 1990.

11. Ira Roseman has a different approach: he attempts to define the nature of emotions in light of their intensity variables; see, for example, Roseman et al. 1996. I believe that distinguishing between the various emotions should take into account other types of evaluation besides those implied in the intensity variables.

12. Clare 1986:13.

13. Coats and Feldman 1995; Tulloch 1990:55–157; Van Evra 1990:79.

14. Michael et al. 1994.

15. Day 1970.

16. Frijda 1988:352; 1986:206.

17. C. I. Lewis (1929) considers the second criterion to be the only criterion of reality. In doing so, he attributes a similar ontological status to all types of realities in the second, epistemological sense. Such an ontological implication is absent from the view presented here which is merely concerned with the perceived impact of different types of reality upon us. See also Quine 1964.

18. Koriat et al. 1972.

19. Devlin 1987.

20. Frijda 1988:352; A. Smith 1759:9; Spinoza 1677:IVp9.

21. Schelling 1984:328. It may be argued that even if a fictional movie provokes our tears more than does news of fatalities in a place remote from us, this does not mean that we are necessarily more saddened by the movie. Although this may be true in some cases, I still maintain that there are instances in which a movie evokes greater sorrow in the viewer.

22. Frijda 1989.

23. Van Evra 1990:85–88.

24. Degenhardt 1978; McCosh 1880:53–61; Neill 1993; Tulloch 1990:235. Yanal (1994) formulates a few possible philosophical positions concerning the relationship between emotion and fiction: (a) *factualism*—our emotions only apparently take fictional characters as their objects; their objects are really something actual; (b) *counterfactualism*—in fiction our emotions are directed at a possible, counterfactual world; (c) *fictionalism*—our seemingly emotional responses toward fiction are not really emotions; (d) *realism*—we feel emotions toward fictional characters while believing them to be fictional and not real. The first three positions deny that we feel emotions toward characters known to us to be fictional. This denial is problematic, as it is contrary to common sense. The fourth position seems to be the most plausible, but we need to explain how something fictional can induce emotions. Yanal explains this by arguing that in relationships with real people, our role is that of a participant, and with fictional characters, that of a spectator. Although it is true that we are more passive in emotions toward fictional characters, the distinction between participant and spectator cannot explain the wide variety of emotions toward fictional and imaginary characters. I have suggested that in some sense, we believe in the reality of fictional characters while suspending for the moment our belief in their fictional nature. The difference here is between a first-level, specific belief in the possible reality of certain characters and events and a second-level, general belief concerning the imaginary nature of the whole setup.

25. Ortony et al. 1988:61–62.

26. Buss 1994:118.

27. *Webster's New Collegiate Dictionary.*

28. Many philosophers and psychologists emphasize the importance of the closeness variable in emotions. Spinoza (1677) claims that "men are by nature envious, *or* are glad by their equals' weakness and saddened by their equals' virtue" (IIIp55s). Hence, one "cannot be saddened because he considers a virtue in someone unlike himself. Consequently he also cannot envy him. But he can, indeed, envy his equal, who is supposed to be of the same nature as he" (IIIp55c2d). Hume (1739–1740) says that "the great disproportion cuts off the relation, and either keeps us from comparing ourselves with what is remote from us, or diminishes the effects of the comparison" (377–378). Adam Smith (1759) argues that "we should be but little interested . . . in the fortune of those whom we can neither serve nor hurt, and who are in every respect so remote from us" (140). In the same vein, Festinger (1954) claims that "the tendency to compare oneself with some other specific person decreases as the difference between his opinion or ability and one's own increases" (120).

29. Rushton 1989; Jaffee and Fanshel 1970; Etcoff 1999:39; see also Spinoza 1677:IIIp16, p27.

30. Festinger 1954; Lewin et al. 1944.

31. R. H. Frank 1999:73–74; Freedman 1978:139–141.

32. Spinoza 1677:IVp9c.; on Pascal's view, see James 1997:167–168.

33. Stein 1987; Tuchman 1987.

34. Elster 1999a:III.3; Plutarch *On Envy And Hate*; Tesser and Campbell 1980; Tesser et al. 1988.

35. Folger 1984; Phares 1976:chap.3; C. A. Smith and Ellsworth 1985; Thibaut and Kelley 1959. Spinoza (1677) realizes the importance of controllability in emotions and claims that sadness "is more and more encouraged if we imagine ourselves to be blamed by others" (III55c). He further argues that the doctrine assuming the absence of free will teaches us how we must bear ourselves concerning matters of fortune and that "we must expect and bear calmly both good fortune and bad." It teaches us "to hate no one, to disesteem no one, to mock no one, to be angry at no one, to envy no one"; it also teaches us "that each of us should be content with his own things" (II49s).

36. McMullen et al. 1995.

37. Langer 1989; see also Picard 1997:77.

38. Karasawa 1995; Teigen 1995; Whitley and Frieze 1986.

39. Oatley and Larocque 1995; Sigmon and Snyder 1993.

40. See also Kahneman and Miller 1986.

41. Hill et al. 1976:159.

42. Sigmon and Snyder 1993:152.

43. Snyder and Higgins 1988.

44. S. E. Taylor 1989:75–76.

45. Weiner et al. 1982.

46. Ortony et al. 1988:71–73.

47. Graham et al. 1993.

48. Weiner 1985; Weiner et al. 1979.

49. See also Smith and Pope 1992.

50. Weiner 1985:554.

51. Aristotle, *Rhetoric*:1379a22; Frijda 1986:273, 291–295; Lyons 1980:chap.7; Ortony et al. 1988:64–65. Spinoza (1677) defines *remorse* as sorrow "accompanied by the idea of a past thing that has turned out worse than we had hoped." The remedy for this sorrow is to realize that there was no available alternative: sorrow "over some good which has perished is lessened as soon as the man who has lost it realizes that this good could not, in any way, have been kept" (IIIdef.aff.; Vp6s).

   Descartes (1649) considers wonder as "the first of all the passions. It has no opposite, for, if the object before us has no characteristics that surprise us, we are not moved by it at all and we consider it without passion" (art.53). The prominence given to wonder is probably influenced by Descartes' general philosophy in which the mind is basically an intellectual entity: wonder is a kind of intellectual emotion—if it is an emotion at all. Wonder differs from other emotions in being based merely upon a cognitive and not an evaluative component (art.71). In my view, wonder, or rather surprise, is also basically a cognitive element, but as such it is better to consider it (even in light of Descartes' own psychological analysis—see art.52) as a factor that intensifies emotions rather than as an isolated emotion in itself.

52. Frijda 1986:299.
53. McCornack and Levine 1990.
54. Frijda 1986:295–298; Law et al. 1994; Seligman 1975.
55. Spinoza 1677:IVp50s.
56. Smith and Ellsworth 1985.
57. Seneca, *Epistulae Morales*:IV,5,9. Spinoza, taking a similar stand, claims that the more the mind understands things adequately, "the less it is acted on by affects which are evil, and the less it fears death" (1677:V38). See also Rorty 1983.
58. Roseman 1991.
59. Aristotle, *Nicomachean Ethics*:1136b6; Janoff-Bulman and Frieze 1983; Ortony et al. 1988:77; Spinoza 1677:IVapp.XV. Aristotle indicates that his claim that no one wishes to be unjustly treated does not imply that one may not be voluntarily harmed and voluntarily suffer what is unjust. This implication is different from the logical impossibility of wishing to have what is contrary to one's wish (Curzer 1995).
60. Jackson and Huston 1975; cited in Etcoff 1999:47.
61. Frankfurt 1998:6. The claim that desires confer value on their objects is clearly expressed by Spinoza: "we neither strive for, nor will, neither want, nor desire anything because we judge it to be good; on the contrary, we judge something to be good because we strive for it, will it, want it, and desire it" (1677:IIIp9s). Similarly, Sher (1987:58) claims that if "persons themselves matter, then what matters to persons should matter as well." My discussion of desert is heavily indebted to Sher's excellent analysis. For further discussion of this matter, see De Sousa's (1987) discussion of bootstrapping, which is a process in which we bestow real value on some prospect just by choosing it; see Prentice and Crosby 1987.
62. Sher 1987.
63. Feinberg 1970; Sverdlik 1983; see also Pojman and McLeod 1999.
64. As Adam Smith (1759) rightly argues, "The most sincere praise can give little pleasure when it cannot be considered as some sort of proof of praise-worthiness. . . . An ignorant and groundless praise can give no solid joy" (114–115).
65. Frijda and Mesquita 1994; see also Ellsworth 1994.
66. Elster 1985:382–383; 390–395; Hatfield 1988:201–205; Larsen and Diener 1987; R. L. Solomon and Corbit 1974.
67. Bentham (1789:chap.6) made a list of thirty-two types of circumstances influencing our sensibility to pleasure and pain; most of them are also relevant to emotional sensitivity. Among these are health, knowledge, moral and religious sensibility, sympathetic sensibility, insanity, age, rank, education, and climate. I have tried to organize the long list of personal variables into a few major categories; otherwise their usefulness in understanding emotional intensity would be limited.
68. Diener and Larsen 1993; Larsen and Diener 1987; Pervin 1993; Rorty 1978.
69. Gilboa and Revelle 1994.
70. Kinder 1995.
71. Brody and Hall 1993; Fujita et al. 1991; Hoffman 1975; Josephs et al. 1992; Larsen and Diener 1987; Oately and Jenkins 1996:chap.11; Robins and Tanck 1991.
72. Fabes and Martin 1991:532; LaFrance and Banaji 1992:178; Cancian and Gordon 1988.
73. Brody and Hall 1993; Fischer and Manstead 1998; Hull 1998.
74. For the former view see, for example, Larsen and Diener 1987; the latter view is expressed in LaFrance and Banaji 1992.
75. Shimanoff 1985; see also Landman 1993:162–164.
76. Diener, Sandvik, and Larsen 1985; Landman 1993: 157–162; Tulloch 1990:chap.1.
77. S. E. Taylor 1989:193.

78. Alvarado et al. 1995; Genia 1993; Park et al. 1990.
79. Buss 1994:69.
80. R. E. Thayer 1996.
81. Fisher 1992:48.
82. See, for example, Dyer 1987; Elliott 1992; Ortony et al. 1988:82–83; Picard 1997.

*Chapter 6*

1. Ben-Ze'ev 1993a:chap.4.
2. Further discussions on the rationality of emotions can be found, for example, in De Sousa 1987; Elster 1985, 1999a:IV.3; Greenspan 1988; Lyons 1980; Oatley 1992a:chap.3; Pugmire 1998; Turski 1994.
3. Ryle 1949:28.
4. See also Aristotle, *Nicomachean Ethics*:1102b28.
5. Ben-Ze'ev 1993a:chap.4.
6. Elster 1999a:91.
7. See Allen 1991; Engel 1964; James 1997:13; Leeper 1948; Salovey and Mayer 1990; Kemp Smith 1957:5.
8. Kinder 1995:43–44.
9. This is essentially Marx's and Engels' view, as well as that of Weber and Simmel, to mention just a few; see, on this issue, Barbalet 1998:105–110.
10. In a somewhat similar manner, Elster distinguishes between rationality and reason. By rationality he means the instrumentally efficient pursuit of given ends; by reason he means any kind of impartial motivation or concern for the common good (1999a:101–102, IV.3, V.1). Elster's notion of rationality is parallel to the normative sense of rationality I am suggesting, and his notion of reason is parallel to the descriptive sense. However, my characterization of the two notions is broader. When describing the normative sense (rationality, in Elster's terminology), I speak about an appropriate response, whereas Elster speaks about "instrumentally efficient pursuit of given ends." Although in many cases the two descriptions overlap, there are cases in which an appropriate response is not an instrumentally efficient pursuit of a given end, but acting in a nonpurposive manner. This is, for example, the case of achieving happiness (see chapter 12). Concerning Elster's notion of reason, I agree that intellectual reasoning is characterized by its impartiality: intellectual calculations should take into account all possible alternatives. However, I do not think that such impartiality is always concerned with the common good. I also believe that we should speak about "emotional reasoning."
11. Oatley (1992) claims that emotions may be viewed as biological adaptations to situations that "have no fully rational solutions." He argues that "Mechanisms that cope with limited and imperfect resources are not to be regarded as failures of rationality. They are among our most highly sophisticated cognitive features" (165,175). See also De Sousa 1987; R. H. Frank 1988; R. C. Solomon 1990:47.
12. R. H. Frank 1988.
13. Elster 1999a.
14. Descartes, for example, argues that the passions are intrinsically excessive in that they usually cause the goods and evils they represent to appear greater and more important than they actually are (1649:138); see also James 1997:168.
15. Jauregui 1995:5.
16. My view concerning the functionality of emotions is heavily indebted to Keith Oatley. Oatley (1992) argues that an emotion is not necessarily disorganized but only discontinued: it is "part of an arrangement by which new plans can be generated to meet conditions that change in an unpredictable way" (175). See also Oatley and Jenkins 1992, 1996; Johnson-Laird and Oatley 1992; Lazarus 1991; Lazarus and Lazarus 1994:179–180; Plutchik 1991; Scherer 1982.

17. Elster 1999a:284; 1996:144, 159; see also De Sousa 1987:194–196.
18. Damasio 1994.
19. Gibson 1979; see also Ben-Ze'ev 1993a.
20. Aristotle, *Nicomachean Ethics*:1119a6–10; Jauregui 1995:30; Masson and McCarthy 1995.
21. See also Picard 1997.
22. Margaret Kemeny, "Emotions and the immune system," in Moyers 1993; Lazarus and Lazarus 1994:chap.12; see also Goleman 1995:chap.11.
23. Scheler 1974:156–7; see also Allen 1991.
24. Ross 1984; cited in De Sousa 1987:66. This story is also interesting because it indicates the importance of perceived changes (in this case, changes in intonation) for attributing emotions to other people; see also Hochschild 1983:30.
25. Berenson 1991.
26. Goleman 1995:50–52.
27. Arnold 1969.
28. Aristotle, *Nicomachean Ethics*: 1154a15; Lyons 1980:chap.12.
29. My comparison is based on C. A. Smith and Lazarus 1990:612–615.
30. Bergson 1907:155; Hume 1739:40:415.
31. The integration between the schematic and deliberative systems can refer to the cognitive or evaluative realms. Since Spinoza speaks about different levels of knowledge, I exemplify my position by referring to the cognitive realm, but the same is true of the evaluative one as well.
32. See, for example, Spinoza 1677:IIp40s1,2; IIp47; V5p33. On the importance, in seventeenth-century philosophy, of emotions to knowledge, see James 1997:chaps.9 and 10.
33. Ambady and Rosental 1992; Goleman 1998:53.
34. I have discussed this issue in more detail in Ben-Ze'ev 1993a:4.4.
35. Goleman 1998:7, part 4.
36. James 1997:234–242; Wainwright 1995:3, 148–154.
37. Picard 1997.
38. See, for example, Goleman 1995, 1998; Mayer and Salovey 1995, 1997.
39. Goleman 1998:31.
40. Goleman 1995:80–83; Shoda et al. 1990.
41. Goleman 1998.
42. For an interesting discussion of this issue, see Elster 1999a:96–98.
43. Indeed, Paul Ekman (1992a) has shown that it is hard to fake emotions. Accordingly, I disagree with La Rochefoucauld's claim that "It is harder to disguise feelings we have, than to put on those we have not" (*Maxims posthumes*:56). However, I agree with him that "Where love is, no disguise can hide it for long; where it is not, none can simulate it" (*Maxims:70*; cited and discussed in Elster 1999a:96).
44. Malamuth and Brown 1994.
45. For a more detailed discussion, see Ben-Ze'ev 1994; Heilman 1973:153.
46. Tannen 1990:104; for the gender difference, see Hochschild 1983:165; Levin and Arluke 1987.
47. Millar and Millar 1988.
48. Fine 1977.
49. Levin and Arluke 1987; Tannen 1990:chap.4; see also other articles in Goodman and Ben-Ze'ev 1994.
50. Spacks 1985.

## Chapter 7

1. Medvec et al. 1995.
2. Ibid.

3. Kubey and Csikszentmihalyi 1990:176; Hofeldt 1987; Gerbner et al. 1987.
4. Kubey and Csikszentmihalyi 1990: 171.
5. *Cosmopolitan*, December 1994:200.
6. St. Clair 1996:145.
7. Roese and Olson 1995b.
8. *Glamour,* January 1995.
9. S. E. Taylor and Lobel 1989; Kasimatis and Wells 1995; S. E. Taylor 1989:170–174.
10. Roese and Olson 1995b; Kasimatis and Wells 1995.
11. Seelau et al. 1995.
12. Ibid.:60–61.
13. Ibid.:62.
14. Ibid. 1995.
15. Kahneman 1995.
16. Spinoza 1677:Vp6s; see also Kvart 1986.
17. Roese and Olson 1995b:5, 12.
18. Spinoza 1677:Vp9d.
19. Ogden 1994; St. Claire 1996:140, 58.
20. This passage is based on the excellent discussion of this issue in Lazarus and Lazarus 1994:chap.8; see, in particular, pp. 169–170.
21. Jauregui 1995:31.
22. Buss 1994:64–65; Kenrick et al. 1989.
23. See Abramson and Pinkerton 1995:169.
24. S. E. Taylor 1989:4.
25. My discussion on these biases is based on S. E. Taylor, 1989:chap.1.
26. M. Lewis 1992:103–107; S. E. Taylor 1989:chap.1. Various people have claimed that vanity stems from our disposition to overestimate our value and underestimate the value of others; on this issue, see James 1997:177–179.
27. S. E. Taylor 1989:49.
28. Ibid.:chaps.2, 5.
29. Ibid.:chap.3. Elster (1999a:IV.3) indicates the duality in assessing the value of optimism: on the one hand, to achieve much, one has to believe one can achieve more than one can; on the other hand, those who are capable of taking an unbiased view of the world are the depressed—they are sadder but wiser.
30. Isen et al. 1978.
31. S. E. Taylor 1989:126–127; 134–136, 144–151, 159.
32. Achenbach and Howell 1989; Goleman 1998:11; Kraut et al. 1998.
33. Kraut et al. 1998.
34. Stoddard 1929:4–5, 28, 57.
35. See also Nagel 1979; Nussbaum 1986; Statman 1993:introduction; Williams 1981:chap.2.
36. Rescher 1993:147–152; for criticism on the move from describable regularities to personified agency in perception, see Ben-Ze'ev 1993a:112–113; Heil 1981.
37. S. E. Taylor 1989:166–170.
38. Teigen 1995, 1996, 1997, 1998.
39. Teigen 1996.
40. Ibid.
41. Teigen 1998.
42. Teigen 1997.
43. Teigen 1996.
44. Stoddard 1929:306–307.
45. Rescher 1993:147–152.
46. Teigen 1996.

## Chapter 8

1. Gross 1998.
2. Campos et al. 1989; Gross 1998; Lyons 1980:196–202; Masters 1991.
3. Beck 1976:73.
4. Hankinson 1993:200; Laird and Bresler 1992.
5. Kinder 1995:118; Lazarus and Lazarus 1994:chap.8.
6. Hoffmann 1980:chaps.5, 6.
7. Thayer 1996:126, 128.
8. Folkes 1982; see also Kulik and Brown 1979.
9. Kant 1798:120; cited in Sherman 1997:170.
10. Kubey and Csikszentmihalyi 1990:xiii; Thayer 1996.
11. Eisenberg and Fabes 1992.
12. Goleman 1995:106–107; Hochschild 1983.
13. Frijda 1988:356; Lyons 1980:chap.13.
14. S. E. Taylor 1989:171–172.
15. Hochschild 1983:113.
16. Elster 1999a; Etcoff 1999:50–51.
17. Walcot 1978:35.
18. See Gross 1998.
19. Snow 1995; see also Ben-Ze'ev 1993b.
20. Hochschild 1983:33,35.
21. Rorty 1980b:482; Brown 1987:chap.2.
22. Heider (1958:291) cites Scheler's book *Vom Umsturz der Werte* as including a similar analysis of the story of the fox and the grapes; see also Day 1970:379; Reid 1788:567. On the means for preventing envy, see Salovey and Rothman 1991:274; the means for preventing jealousy are discussed in Hansen 1991:220–226.
23. Higgins 1987.
24. These individual differences are discussed in Thayer 1996:chap.10.
25. Scitovsky 1976:61; cited in Illouz 1997:172.
26. Kinder 1995:chap.9.
27. Gross and Munoz 1995.
28. Hochschild 1983:chap.8; see also Oakley 1991:135–144. Further studies on regulating emotions at work can be found, for example, in Illouz 1997; Jackall 1988; Kunda 1992.
29. As an example of the difficulties in this regard, consider La Rochefoucauld's hesitations concerning the effects of the awareness of the cause of jealousy upon its intensity. Elster (1999a:82) provides the following formulations of La Rochefoucauld's position. In the first edition of *Maxims*, La Rochefoucauld claims that "one ceases to be jealous when one is illuminated about the cause of the jealousy." In the second edition the claim is that jealousy "becomes a frenzy as soon as one goes from doubt to certainty." In later editions the formulation is the following: "Jealousy feeds on doubts, and as soon as doubt turns into certainty it becomes a frenzy, or ceases to exist." I accept the later formulation which takes into account the complexity of emotional situations.
30. Elster 1999a:101.
31. De Sousa 1987:243.

## Chapter 9

1. Oakley 1991:chap.4.
2. Horder 1992:1–2.
3. See also Alston 1967:482–483; Bedford 1957:91; Elster 1999b:chap.5; Lyons 1980:6–8; Pitcher 1965:329. Kant, who refers to emotions as simple feelings for which we are not responsible, indeed

considers them to be irrelevant or even obstacles to responsible moral behavior. For criticism of Kant's view, see Lauritzen 1991; Oakley 1991:chap.3. Various comments in Kant's writings may suggest that his view on the role of emotions in morality is more complex than a simple rejection of such a role; see Sherman 1997.

4. See also Hochschild 1983:chap.4; Lyons 1980:chap.13.

5. Sherman 1997:75–93. For further discussion of this matter see Elster 1999a:IV.3. Elster examines and rejects the claim that emotional dispositions as well as occurrent emotions can be the result of rational choice.

6. Aristotle, *Nicomachean Ethics*:1106b16–23; Horder 1992:44; Sherman 1997. The indirect nature of emotional regulation has been indicated by other philosophers as well. For example, Descartes (1649) argues that our passions "cannot be directly aroused or suppressed by the action of our will, but only indirectly through the representation of things which are usually joined with the passions we wish to have and opposed to the passions we wish to reject" (art.45). Similarly, Spinoza (1677) claims that "An affect cannot be restrained or taken away except by an affect opposite to, and stronger than, the affect to be restrained" (IVp7).

7. Scruton 1980:525.

8. See also Elster 1999a; P. S. Greenspan 1988:10, 155; Oakley 1991:chap. 4; Sankowski 1977.

9. For the first claim, see Dancy 1983; for the second, De Sousa 1987.

10. For an excellent discussion of this matter, see De Sousa 1987.

11. LaFollette 1996:4.

12. Sidgwick 1966:434; Jeske 1997:51. Diane Jeske argues that the two dominant contemporary moral theories, Kantianism and utilitarianism, have difficulty accommodating our commonsense understanding of friendship because of their underlying commitment to impartiality, that is, to the claim that all persons are equally worthy of concern. Aristotelian accounts of friendship are partialist insofar as they assume that some persons are more worthy of concern than others (51). Jeske's own view attempts to take account of both partial and impartial elements. In the view which I suggest below there is also a place for both elements—as there is a place for both emotions and intellectual reasoning.

13. Toulmin 1981.

14. Ibid.

15. LaFollette 1996:199.

16. Blum 1994; Nussbaum 1993, and forthcoming; R. C. Solomon 1990; see also Cottingham 1983, 1986; LaFollette 1996:chap. 13; Williams 1981. It is interesting to note that sensitivity to the particular person is also part of Kant's morality which requires that we respect individuals in their own right as ends having intrinsic value; see also Sherman 1997.

17. See, for example, Dillon 1992; Gilligan 1982. The feminist struggle carries some of its supporters to the extreme position of denying any real gender differences. Such a position, which denies one type of individual difference, seems to be incongruent with the care morality which emphasizes the emotional and moral significance of all types of individual differences. Radical egalitarianism cannot be integrated into the emotional domain, as it neglects individual differences which are so essential in emotions. Such differences should not harm any individual, but they may give rise to different emotional attitudes toward various individuals.

18. Higgins 1997. Higgins uses this distinction mainly to discern two types of behavior of different individuals. Thus, some parents are more inclined to use the prevention mode as a major principle of behavior toward their children, and some the promotion mode. In my discussion this distinction refers to different types of moral objects: our intimates and strangers. In both cases, we are not speaking about a clear-cut distinction but about two prototypical modes of behavior.

19. Grunebaum 1993:52.

20. Nathanson 1989; Railton 1984; Walsh 1970:2. The opposite view is expressed, for instance, by Rachels: "Universal love is a higher ideal than family loyalty, and . . . the obligation within families can be properly understood only as particular instances of obligations to all mankind" (1998:46; cited in LaFollette 1996:198).

21. LaFollette 1996:208–209.
22. Cited in Nussbaum forthcoming.
23. Ferguson 1767:53.
24. Ibid.:36.
25. Sherman 1994:32–33, 1997; see also Nussbaum 1986:chap.12.
26. Tannen 1990:chap.4.
27. On the issue of avoiding empathy in order to resist the desire to help, see Shaw et al. 1994.
28. Kant 1797: 35. This statement indicates that Kant attributes some role to emotions in morality; see also Hesman 1993; Nussbaum forthcoming; Sherman 1997.
29. Hartz 1990; Nussbaum forthcoming; Oakley 1991; R. C. Solomon 1976; Stocker 1996. The claim that from a moral viewpoint, we also care how people feel and not merely how they act is contrary to Cicero's position that we can be generous without compassion "for our obligation is not to take upon ourselves bitterness and pain for the sake of others; it is simply, where possible, to relieve others of their pain" (quoted in Hands 1968:82; see also Statman 1994). Having a certain emotional attitude may not constitute a moral obligation, but it certainly constitutes a proper moral attitude.
30. J. Martin 1990:65.
31. Hume (1758) claims that if a person is unaffected with the images of human happiness or misery, he must be equally indifferent to the images of vice and virtue.
32. Landman 1993:18–19. Hitler was also described as a thoroughly rational person: "Hitler never said anything, even when he appeared to have lost his temper, without calculating the effect both on those present and on those to whom they would recount it" (Bullock 1991:571; cited in Elster 1999a:386).
33. Jauregui 1995:232. Similarly, Weber claims that the institutionalization of confession in the Catholic Church went hand in hand with "weakening the demands of morality upon the individual" (1968:561); cited in Elster 1999a:247.
34. M. W. Martin 1986:8.
35. Sherman 1990:152–153.
36. See, for example, Clark 1997.
37. Frijda 1996.
38. See also Sherman 1997.
39. Adams 1985:10–11.
40. Ewin 1992; Railton 1984.
41. On this issue see, for example, D. H. Frank 1990.
42. Hume 1739–1740:415; Plato, *The Republic*, IV,440; see also Landman 1993: 5–6.
43. Aristotle, *Nicomachean Ethics* I, 13; Kant 1785:I. My discussion here is based on Rosalind Hursthouse's excellent analysis (Hursthouse 1997). Hursthouse indicates that Aristotle's and Kant's positions may not be as simple as they appear, and in any case they are much closer than is usually supposed.
44. Aristotle, *Nicomachean Ethics* 1103b12–20; Elster 1999a:303; Ewin 1990:142; Waley 1938:2.4; see also Averill et al. 1990:87; D. H. Frank 1990; Sherman 1997.
45. Smilansky 1996.
46. Blum 1994:chap. 3.
47. Sher 1997.
48. Some integration between the two perspectives may be implied in Hume's view. Chazan (1992:60) suggests that according to Hume "we must correct our own perspectives and sentiments so that they are in line with everybody else's." To speak the language of morality, "we must go beyond our own private point of view and take account of the interests of all." However, unlike the view suggested in Chazan's interpretation, I would not say that the moral sentiment is felt from the point of view of humanity, or that pride, or any other emotion, must be felt after having taken general perspectives.
49. Chazan 1992:63.
50. See also Nussbaum forthcoming.

51. Averill et al. 1990:34.
52. Nicholson 1985.
53. Ibid.: 167.
54. Ibid. 1985.

## Chapter 10

1. In the nineteenth century George Crabb, in his *English Synonyms*, made a similar distinction between envy and jealousy: "We are jealous of what is our own; we are envious of what is another's. Jealousy fears to lose what it has; envy is pained at seeing another have that which it wants for itself" (cited in Walcot 1978:1).
2. Parrott and Smith 1993; R.H. Smith et al. 1988.
3. Smith 1759:244. In the *Eudemian Ethics*, Aristotle argues that "envy is pain felt at deserved good fortune"; he further speaks about proper indignation which includes pain felt at undeserved good fortune (1233b19–25). Rawls (1971:533) takes a similar stand and distinguishes between envy that arises because "the better situation of others catches our attention," and resentment, which addresses injustice and wrongful conduct. Only resentment is a moral emotion.
4. Descartes 1649:art.62; Ortony et al. 1988:101–102. Descartes compares envy with pity, arguing that "if we judge the others unworthy of the good or evil, in the former case envy is aroused and in the latter case pity" (art.62). Descartes justifies envy only when the benefits coming to those we think unworthy are due to fortune. Regarding the advantages we possess from birth, "the fact that we received them from God before we were capable of doing any evil suffices to make us worthy of them" (art.182). The psychological fact that there is no significant difference between these kinds of envy undermines the usefulness of the distinction and the import Descartes attaches to the moral element in envy.
5. Kohn 1986:14.
6. Montaldi 1991.
7. Crosby 1976:85; see also Kohn 1986; Neu 1980. The relative deprivation typical of envy may, however, be connected with what we perceive as nonrelative deprivation of respect or attention which we would like to gain. Indeed, the quest for respect or fame is a crucial element of envy.
8. Descartes 1649:art.183.
9. Aristotle, *Rhetoric*:II,10.
10. Montaldi 1991.
11. Bers and Rodin 1984; Salovey and Rodin 1989; Tesser and Campbell 1980.
12. Salovey and Rodin 1989. The Danish sociologist Svend Ranulf (1938) argues that moral indignation, which in his opinion is a kind of envy, is typical of the middle class and is entirely lacking in some classes (such as the aristocrats) and societies (such as those found in India and China). It is interesting to note that in the appendix to his study on indignation, Ranulf (1938) severely criticizes Max Scheler's (1912) work on resentment for not providing systematic, empirical evidence to support his basic thesis (which Ranulf admits is identical with his own). He criticizes Scheler's references to everyday life experiences which might possibly "prove to be nothing but a system of generally accepted prejudices." He argues that the "methodological standpoint like that of Max Scheler should be met with general and absolute condemnation in the scientific world" (200, 204). The scientific method of Ranulf did not prevent him from presenting unfounded claims such as that envy is basically limited to the middle class. No wonder that Ranulf's work is almost entirely forgotten, whereas Scheler's work is quite influential even today. By mentioning this I do not intend to imply the inferiority of scientific methods, but just to indicate that empirical research alone is far from providing comprehensive understanding of emotions.
13. Teigen 1997.
14. The assumption that desert is part of the moral domain is explicitly stated by a few philosophers. Thus, Aristotle, who sees inferiority as the principal concern in envy, argues that "whatever is

undeserved is unjust" (*Rhetoric*:II,9). Similarly, Hospers claims that "justice is (simply) getting what one deserves" (1972:361).

15. My view here is similar to that suggested by Richard Smith. Smith (1991) speaks about "the subjective, unsanctioned nature of the sense of injustice in envy." He rightly argues that "In an unconventional but arguable sense, people on the short end of the distribution have been unfairly treated by fate." Accordingly, "the envied person's advantage is, to some degree and on some subjective level, unfair" (85,92–93). Smith clearly distinguishes the sense of injustice typical of envy from that typical of resentment.

16. Elster 1991, 1999a:III.3; see also G. Taylor 1988.

17. Parrott and Smith 1993.

18. Parrott 1991.

19. Fitness and Fletcher 1993.

20. Koford and Tshoegl 1998; cited in R. H. Frank 1999:119.

21. Farrell 1980; Van Sommers 1988:19.

22. Neu 1980; Bringle 1991:124–125.

23. Buunk 1991:155, 162; Van Sommers 1988.

24. See also Foster 1965:26; 1972; Friday 1985:105–106.

25. Salovey and Rodin 1989:235; see also Buunk 1991:159.

26. Salovey and Rodin 1989:229; see also DeSteno and Salovey 1996a; Salovey and Rothman 1991.

27. DeSteno and Salovey 1996a.

28. Elster 1985:389; Kahneman and Tversky 1979; Lewin et al. 1944:373; see also Salovey and Rodin 1989; Tversky and Kahneman 1981; Thaler 1980.

29. Buss 1994:127–129; Gold 1996.

30. Buss et al. 1992; Buss 1994; for a different interpretation of these results, see DeSteno and Salovey 1996b.

31. Van Sommers 1988:32–33.

32. Tesser 1980; 1988.

33. R. H. Smith 1991:93.

34. Neu 1980.

35. Mathes 1991:72–74; R. H. Smith 1991; White and Mullen 1989:219.

36. Hume 1739–1740:376.

37. Elster 1999a:177–178; Veblen 1899.

38. Shames 1989:146.

39. Montaldi 1991.

40. Spinoza (1677) argues that we envy those people having a similar nature to us; hence, their success is highly relevant to our self-esteem. On the other hand, we venerate a man because we imagine his virtues "to be peculiarly in him, and not as common to our nature. Therefore, we shall not envy him these virtues any more than we envy trees their height, or lions their strength" (IIIp55c2s).

41. Cialdini et al. 1976.

42. Ibid.; Lyons 1980:82–83; Tesser 1988.

43. R. H. Smith 1991.

44. Buss 1994:155.

45. Walcot 1978:9; Aristotle, *Rhetoric*:II,10; see also Bacon 1625:sec.9; Gay 1731:sec.IV.

46. Kant 1924:215–217.

47. Elster 1991, 1999a:III.3; Heyd 1991:187; Schoeck 1970:62, 237; Silver and Sabini 1978a,b.

48. Ulanov and Ulanov 1983. Although in most such tales, the mother is a stepmother, it is known that in some of the original versions of such tales, for example, in *Snow White*, the mother is not a stepmother. Making the parent a stepparent reduces the very problematic emotional situation of parental envy.

49. Gold 1996; Lerner and Brackney 1978.

50. Hoffman et al. 1954; Dakin and Arrowood 1981.

51. Hume 1739–1740:377. Similarly, Tocqueville argues that "Men are much more struck by inequalities within the same class than by inequalities between classes" (1848:355); cited and discussed in Elster 1999a:199–200.
52. See Griffin 1986:VI.
53. Paul 1991.
54. Davis 1936; Oatley and Jenkins 1996.
55. Buunk 1991:163–164; Mathes 1991.
56. *The Daily Telegraph*, 7 July, 1997.
57. Parrott 1991.
58. Nozick 1974; R. H. Smith et al. 1990.
59. R. C. Solomon 1990:79; Bloom 1993:44.
60. See De La Mora 1987; Schoeck 1970:chaps.14–15, 17; Young 1987.
61. Schoeck 1970:chap.17.
62. Yitzhaki and Lerman 1991; see also Crosby 1976; Freedman 1978; Heider 1958:288–289; Schoeck 1970. The relevant sociological literature may be that referring to class conflict and, in particular, class resentment (see, e.g., Barbalet 1998:chap.3). We should, however, distinguish between class conflict and class resentment (or class envy). In the case of decreased inequalities, class conflict may be reduced whereas class envy may be increased.
63. Frankfurt 1988:135.
64. Walcot 1978:30. Similarly, Tocqueville (1848:310) characterizes envy as "the democratic sentiment"; see also Elster 1999a:III.3.
65. Elster 1999a:200; Tocqueville 1848:531.
66. Frank and Cook 1995; see also R. H. Frank 1999:chap.3.
67. Wilkinson 1996; Glyn and Miliband 1994:3; cited and discussed in R. H. Frank 1999:142–145, 243–244.
68. Aristotle, *Rhetoric to Alexander*:1445a19; Spinoza 1677:IIIdef.aff.xxiii; Reid 1788:567.
69. Montaigne 1991:975; cited in Elster 1999b:13.
70. Kristjansson 1996; forthcoming.
71. Cited in Horder 1992:39.
72. Buss 1994:129; Dressler 1982:440; Salovey and Rodin 1989.
73. Margolin 1989.
74. Descartes (1649), who also considers envy to be a vice, sees some justification for the emotion that arises when the less worthy possess a good that we seek. Similarly, Joseph Butler (1726) argues that "to do mischief is not the end of envy, but merely the means it makes use of to attain its end" (ser.I).
75. Fisher 1992:168; Schoeck 1970:chap.8; White and Mullen 1989:chap.8.
76. Frankfurt 1988:134.
77. Gold 1996.
78. Rawls 1971:534.
79. Buunk 1991:160; Hupka 1991. Mathes (1991) presents some evidence suggesting that jealousy is "an inevitable and universal emotion found even in dogs and cats. Jealousy appears to be a universal distress response to the possibility of losing a loved one to a rival" (63). See also Clanton and Kosins 1991.
80. Buunk 1991:172.
81. Bers and Rodin 1984:778; Frijda et al. 1992.
82. For further defense of envy, see Greenspan 1988:115–128; for further criticism of envy and jealousy, see Silver and Sabini 1978b; G. Taylor 1988.
83. Ben-Ze'ev 1993b; see also chap. 18, this volume.

## Chapter 11

1. Blum 1994: chap. 8; Snow 1991:197.
2. Aristote, *Rhetoric*, 1386a; see also Nussbaum 1986:384.

3. Greenspan 1988:66.

4. See also Statman 1994.

5. Brien 1991, 1995. My discussion on mercy has benefited from detailed comments by Andrew Brien.

6. The importance of actions in mercy does not mean that mercy can be merely defined in terms of actions. As Andrew Brien (1995) rightly indicates, intentions, though not motives, are important in determining whether the given action is merciful.

7. Twambley (1976) considers the merchant paradigm to be the only paradigm of mercy. Hence he argues that there is no essential relationship between mercy and punishment and that when one has no right, one cannot be merciful. Murphy (in Murphy and Hampton 1988) also consider the merchant paradigm to be central to mercy, but leave room for the judge paradigm as well. They term the first paradigm "the criminal law paradigm," and the second "the private law paradigm." I think that the major psychological characteristics of mercy appear in all three paradigm cases and indeed in everyday language we refer to all of them as cases of mercy. Accordingly, there is no reason to drop any from the list.

8. See also Spinoza 1677:IIIdef.aff.xxxviii.

9. Brien 1991, 1995.

10. Brien 1995.

11. For a good comparison between compassion, pity, grief, and sympathy, to which I am indebted, see Snow 1991.

12. Spinoza, *Ethics*:III32s.

13. Elster 1991, 1999a:III.3; see also Scott 1972:16.

14. Aristotle, *Rhetoric*:II,8.

15. Nussbaum, forthcoming.

16. Tesser 1980.

17. Herodotus, *The History*:III,14; Aristotle, *Rhetoric*:II,8. For some unknown reason Aristotle's version of the story gives the father's name as Amasis who, according to Herodotus, was the father of Psammenitus. This substitution may be explained either as a slip of memory by Aristotle, or as a different version of the same story. In his interpretation of the story, Aristotle follows the Greek tradition, assuming that pity is manifested by weeping and groaning (Belfiore 1992:186). Although weeping is typical of intense pity, it is not a necessary feature. For example, in the eighteenth century collective tears were considered in France to express the virtue of compassion, but in the nineteenth century tears showed an absence of self-mastery and were better suppressed (Vincent-Buffault 1991).

18. Herodotus, *The History*:3.14.

19. See also Higgins 1987. The problematic nature of self-pity is illustrated in Aristotle's view, which leaves no room for such an emotion. Aristotle's definition of pity contains two major features: (1) a feeling of pain at an apparent evil that befalls one who does not deserve it, and (2) expectation that this evil will befall ourselves (or our friends). Self-pity contains the first, but not the second feature. Accordingly, Aristotle does not speak about self-pity (*Rhetoric*:II,8; Stocker 1983). I believe that typical pity contains more features than those suggested by Aristotle; however, not all of them have to be present in each instance of pity.

20. Reid 1788:563.

21. This is Adam Smith's example; see 1759:12. My discussion of the whole issue is heavily indebted to Nussbaum, forthcoming.

22. Nussbaum, forthcoming.

23. Callan 1988; Cartwright 1984; Nussbaum, forthcoming; Spinoza 1677:IVp.50.

24. For further discussion on the moral value of pity and envy, see Callan 1988; Cartwright 1984; Statman 1994; G. Taylor 1988; Greenspan 1988:115–28.

25. Murphy and Hampton 1988:171.

26. Aristotle, *Nicomachean Ethics*:1137b8ff.; *Rhetoric*:1374b2ff.; Nussbaum 1999b; Rainbolt 1990; Walker 1995.

27. See Harrison 1992.
28. Hart 1973:24–5.

## Chapter 12

1. Rousseau 1762:221; Bloom 1993:68-9.
2. Blondel 1947:7. I thank Robert Ginsberg for bringing to my attention Blondel's claim, which is, incidentally, mistaken, as some languages such as Arabic have a special term for this emotion. One translation of the German term *Schadenfreude* is pleasure-in-others'-suffering. I choose the expression pleasure-in-others'-misfortune which conveys the minor nature of the damage more clearly. Indeed the German term *Schaden*, means injury, harm, and damage, but not suffering. In Hebrew the term describing the other's situation is closer to disaster. Some psychologists suggest the term "gloating" for this emotion. However, gloating seems to encompass only the kind of pleasure-in-others'-misfortune which is expected or anticipated ("I told you so"); see also Portmann 1999. *Webster's New Collegiate Dictionary* defines *gloating* as "to observe or think about something with great and often greedy or malicious satisfaction, gratification, or delight." Here, the malicious nature of gloating is emphasized. In the discussion that follows, I argue that pleasure-in-others'-misfortune is not malicious in nature.
3. Appadurai 1985:240.
4. Kant 1924:218; see also Reid 1788:567.
5. Aquinas, *The Summa Theologica*: supplement to question XCIV: art. 1; cited in Portmann 1999.
6. Feather 1996. Similarly, Rabbi Meir Loeb Malbim, the nineteenth-century exegete, would seem to hold that the person who experiences pleasure-in-others'-misfortune is motivated by a desire for what he perceives to be retributive justice; see Harvey 1992.
7. Frye 1957:167.
8. Kant 1924:220; Aristotle, *Eudemian Ethics*, 1233b20.
9. Elster 1995:256; see also Portmann 1999.
10. Ortony et al. 1988:104.
11. Kant observes that "We feel pleasure in gossiping about the minor misadventures of other people; we are not averse . . ." (1963:218); see also Jaeger et al. 1994; Levin and Arluke 1987.
12. Plato, *Philebus*:48b7, 50a1; Aristotle, *Rhetoric*:II,9; the claim of John of Salisbury is cited in de la Mora 1987:28.
13. In an informal survey of over one hundred students of mine, the majority claimed that people are more likely to hide pleasure-in-others'-misfortune.
14. See R. Stein 1992; Whitman and Alexander 1968.
15. Baumeister et al. 1993.
16. The psychologist's claim is found in Ortony et al. 1988:105,76. On the attitude of Kant, Nietzsche, and Schopenhauer, see Portmann 1999.
17. Schopenhauer 1840; see also Portmann 1999 for an extensive discussion of Schopenhauer's view, as well as the view of other scholars criticizing pleasure-in-others'-misfortune. In his excellent discussion, Portmann presents a view similar to the one suggested here concerning both the nature of this emotion and its moral evaluation.
18. Schopenhauer 1844:vol. 1, 335; Portmann 1999.
19. Aquinas, *The Summa Theologica*: supplement to question XCIV: art. 3; cited in Portmann 1999.
20. Portmann 1999.
21. Aquinas, *The Summa Theologica*:II-2, question 36, art.2; cited and discussed in Portmann 1999.
22. Harvey 1992.

## Chapter 13

1. Averill 1983:1150; Lazarus and Lazarus 1994:13–27; Murphy and Hampton 1988:72–75.
2. Averill 1982; Oatley 1992:209–210; see also Beck 1976; Lazarus 1991:chap.6; Ortony et al. 1988.

3. Elster 1999a:64–67; see also Yanay 1996.

4. Aristotle, *Rhetoric*:II,4; see also Elster 1999a:64–67. For a discussion of the attitudes toward anger in the Middle Ages, see Rosenwein 1998.

5. Fitness and Fletcher 1993; Neu 1996.

6. As cited above, Aristotle (*Rhetoric*:II,4) claims that hate is unaccompanied by pain. These considerations suggest that Aristotle is only partly right. It is true that pain is more characteristic of anger than hate, but there are many situations in which hate is accompanied by pain. See also Elster 1999a:64–67.

7. Elster 199b:158.

8. Fitness and Fletcher 1993.

9. Spinoza 1677:IIIp13s; see also Gaylin 1984.

10. Aristotle, *Rhetoric*:II,2.

11. Greenspan 1988.

12. Fitness and Fletcher 1993.

13. Temkin and Yanay 1988.

14. Ibid.:481–482.

15. Averill 1982; Oatley and Jenkins 1996.

16. Barefoot et al. 1989; Lemerise and Dodge 1993.

17. Aristotle claims that "Hatred is more reasonable, for anger is accompanied by pain, which is an impediment to reason, whereas hatred is painless" (*Politics*:1312b34); see also Elster 1999a:65.

18. Rozin et al. 1993.

19. Ibid.:584.

20. W. I. Miller 1997:132–142.

21. In his interesting book, *The anatomy of disgust*, W. I. Miller (1997) considers all types of disgust to be dangerous and not merely repulsive. I disagree as I consider appealingness, rather than praiseworthiness, to be the basic evaluative pattern of disgust.

22. Elias 1939; Rozin et al. 1993:587–588.

23. W. I. Miller 1997:220–222; the fourth difference is added by me.

24. Ibid.:184–186. Miller considers our attitude toward the "moral menials" as disgust rather than contempt. Since I consider praiseworthiness to be the basic evaluative pattern of contempt rather than of disgust, these cases are closer to contempt than to disgust.

25. Ibid.:32–33.

26. The formulation of the differences between these attitudes is close to the one suggested by W. I. Miller (1997:218–220). However, Miller believes that disgust also is contrary to the idea of equality (251).

27. Thomas 1991a. In a similar manner Netanyahu (1995:990) explains the genocidal tendencies of the Spanish Inquisition by claiming that "the extreme, irreparable evil which allegedly inhered in the Jewish nature had to be treated in an extreme manner: since it was incorrigible, it had to be annihilated—for the good of Christianity and mankind as a whole." Cited and further discussed in Elster 1999a:67.

28. Elster 1999a:73–74.

29. Averill 1982; Oatley 1992:211.

30. Aristotle explains this feature thus: "it is pleasant to think that you will attain what you aim at" (*Rhetoric*:II,2); see also Elster 1999a:chap.2.

31. Fitness and Fletcher 1993; Neu 1996.

32. Murphy and Hampton 1988:69.

33. Elster 1999a:194–195.

34. In her excellent discussion of resentment, Hampton suggests distinguishing between resentment, which is a personally defensive protest, and indignation, which is an impersonal protest (Murphy and Hampton 1988:54–60).

35. Ben-Zur and Breznitz 1991.

36. Aristotle, *Rhetoric*:II,2.

37. See also Greenspan 1988:128–136.
38. Aristotle, *Magna Moralia*:1191b33. Aristotle's view is in contrast to the Christian perspective, which considers anger to be a vice, and to Maimonides' view, which assumes that the virtuous person should feel no anger; see D. H. Frank 1990.
39. As Aristotle indicates, "acts proceeding from anger are rightly judged not to be done of malice aforethought" (*Nicomachean Ethics*:1135b26).
40. W. I. Miller 1997:202, chapter 8.

## Chapter 14

1. Lafollette 1996:51–52.
2. Somewhat similarly, Descartes distinguishes between two kinds of love and hate. Love may be directed at something good and at something beautiful (the latter is termed "attraction"). Likewise, one kind of hate is directed at something evil and another kind ("repulsion") at something ugly. Descartes notes that attraction and repulsion are usually more violent than other kinds of love and hate (1649:art.85). In my view, the two basic evaluative patterns underlying attitudes toward good and evil and beautiful and ugly can be present in the same emotion.
3. Buss 1994; Crouse and Mehrabian 1977; Etcoff 1999:chap.3. The study on the initial gaze was done by Monika M. Moore.
4. Etcoff 1999:chap.3; Marks 1996; Townsend and Levy 1990.
5. Sprague and Quadagno 1989; see also Metts et al. 1998.
6. Kephart 1967; Simpson et al. 1986; cited and discussed in Illouz 1997:209.
7. Etcoff 1999:chap.1.
8. Ibld.:chap.2; Langlois et al. 1995.
9. Ackerman 1994:188–189; Buss 1994:38–40, 57–58; Cook and McHenry 1978:chap.2; Etcoff 1999; E.D. Lawson 1971; McKeachie 1952; Zebrowitz et al. 1996.
10. Buss 1994:59–60, 112; see also Cook and McHenry 1978:33.
11. For example, Elster (199b:3) believes that sexual desire is more similar to thirst than to emotions and argues that both thirst and sexual desire are typically "not triggered or shaped by beliefs"; on this issue see also Metts et al. 1998:356–357.
12. Brown 1987:50–59.
13. Buss 1994:55–57; Cunningham et al. 1995; Singh 1993.
14. Buss 1994:52–55; Etcoff 1999; Langlois et al. 1990.
15. Cook and McHenry 1978:chap.2.
16. Freedman 1978:chap.4; Hunter 1983:17; Mathes 1991:56–58; Tennov 1979:73–79.
17. Bradley 1998; Glass and Wright 1992; Lawson 1988:39.
18. Cook and McHenry 1978:132–133.
19. De Sousa 1991:477; Fehr 1988; Frijda 1998; Nozick 1991.
20. Baumeister et al. 1993:379.
21. See also Ortega y Gasset 1941:14; R. Solomon 1991.
22. Frankfurt 1988:155.
23. Brown 1987:24–30; Pitcher 1965.
24. Freedman 1978.
25. Tannen 1990:chap.4.
26. Ortega y Gasset 1941:43,76–77.
27. De Sousa 1991:481.
28. See, for example, De Sousa 1990.
29. Cook and McHenry 1978:chap.3; Wilson and Klaaren 1992.
30. R. C. Solomon 1988:146.
31. Wilkinson 1976.
32. Cook and McHenry 1978:99; Hendrick and Hendrick 1988.

33. Tennov 1979:31; Thomas 1991b:471–472.
34. Byrne and Murnen 1988:198.
35. De Sousa 1991:480.
36. Buss 1994:chap.4.
37. Tolstoy 1967:361–362; cited and discussed in M. W. Martin 1996:chap.3.
38. Shakespeare 1984; cited and discussed in Illouz 1997.
39. Fisher 1992; Toufexis 1993.
40. Fisher 1992; see also De Sousa 1991:484.
41. Buss 1994:90.
42. Peele 1988:177–178.
43. Charny and Parnass 1995.
44. Nozick 1991; on the replaceability of the objects of love, see also Brown 1987; De Sousa 1987; Rorty 1986; Shaver et al. 1988; R. Taylor 1982.
45. Brown 1987.
46. *Glamour*, January 1995; see also Brown 1987:17–20,70–71. Brown further distinguishes between liking and cherishing, claiming that what is being cherished, like the object of love, but unlike that of liking, is valued for itself.
47. Baumeister et al. 1993; Shaver et al. 1988:74.
48. Descartes (1649) explains that "the evils from which we are separated willingly do not differ so noticeably from one another as do the goods to which we are joined willingly" (art.84).
49. Elster 1999a:105.
50. Appadurai 1985.
51. Elster 1999a:262; W. L. Miller 1993:chap.1; Weiner 1985:563.
52. Hochschild 1989; Reid 1788:562.
53. Hochschild 1989:95–96.
54. Lazarus and Lazarus 1994:119.
55. Card 1988.
56. Ortony et al. 1988:146–154.
57. It may be claimed that the large number of sudden deaths while having extramarital sex is due not to the greater excitement while having sex but to other emotions—such as fear and guilt—which are also typical in these circumstances. Although such emotions may also contribute to the greater excitement, I believe that the greater excitement from the sex itself is an important factor in this regard.
58. Bermant 1976; Buss 1994:80.
59. See Bloom 1993:51.
60. Ackerman 1994:268; Byrne and Murnen 1988.
61. Birch and Marlin 1982; W. I. Miller 1997:125–127; Ortony et al. 1988:163–166.
62. Gaver and Mandler 1987.
63. R. C. Solomon 1988:140–147.
64. Cook and McHenry 1978:132–135.
65. Shepher 1971.
66. Michael et al. 1994.
67. Baumeister et al. 1993:378; Buss 1994:35–38; Byrne and Murnen 1988:296–297; Illouz 1997:209–210; Kalmijn 1991; Michael et al. 1994.
68. Rushton 1989.
69. Buss 1994; Michael et al. 1994.
70. Kinder 1995:68, 246.
71. Etcoff 1999:234–235; Goleman 1998:200; Moore and Butler 1989; Thompson 1983:12.
72. Buss 1994:116–118; Fisher 1992:48.
73. Prins et al. 1993.
74. Nussbaum forthcoming; Spinoza 1677:IIIp13, 14.

75. Dion and Dion 1975; Neu 1996; Tennov 1979.
76. Person 1990:65.
77. Greenspan 1980, 1988:chap.5; Koch 1987; Scheler 1967:21.
78. Averill 1982.
79. Buss 1994:150–151.
80. Buss 1994:150. Nozick (1991) argues that each person in a romantic relation "wants to possess the other completely; yet each also needs the other to be an independent and non-subservient person" (421). Neu (1996) emphasizes this point, arguing that "love brings with it dependence, and so vulnerability and risk; we naturally come to resent those we love *because* we love them, because it makes us dependent" (68).
81. De Sousa 1991:477.
82. Ortega y Gasset 1941:12.
83. Galeano 1992:91.
84. Shrage 1989:76.
85. Illouz 1997:196–198.
86. Hess 1998.
87. Buss 1994:42–44; Fisher 1992:104–107.
88. Illouz 1997:chap.1.
89. Freedman 1978:chap.5; Michael et al. 1994.
90. Elliston 1975; Wasserstrom 1985.
91. Quoted by Abramson and Pinkerton 1995:197–198; see also R. W. Clark 1983:57.
92. Lazarus and Lazarus 1994:111.
93. See M. W. Martin 1996.

## Chapter 15

1. Averill and More 1993.
2. Kubey and Csikszentmihalyi 1990:204; Shames 1989:148.
3. See also Lazarus and Lazarus 1994:86–96.
4. Brickman et al. 1978; McIntosh and Martin 1992.
5. Averill and More 1993; McIntosh and Martin 1992.
6. Diener and Diener 1996; Daniel Goleman, "Happiness May Lie in Your Stars," *International Herald Tribune*, July 18, 1996.
7. Lykken and Tellegen 1996; Goleman, "Happiness May Lie in Your Stars," op. cit.
8. Diener et al. 1991.
9. Cited in Goleman, "Happiness may lie in your stars," op. cit.
10. Lazarus and Lazarus 1994:121.
11. Diener, Horwitz, and Emmons 1985; Diener et al. 1993; R. H. Frank 1999:4, 72–73, chap.8; Freedman 1978:chap.9; Veenhoven 1984. In psychological studies happiness is often expressed by the terms "subjective well-being" or "life satisfaction."
12. Diener, Horwitz, and Emmons 1985; Diener et al. 1993; R. H. Frank 1999:chap.5; Oatley 1992:361.
13. Brickman et al. 1978; Emmons and Diener 1985:157; Freedman 1978; McIntosh and Martin 1992; Oatley and Duncan 1992:267; Parducci 1984; R. H. Smith et al. 1989.
14. See, for example, R. H. Frank 1999:chap.8; Parducci 1984.
15. Neumark and Postlewaite 1998; cited in R. H. Frank 1999:116.
16. Etcoff 1999:85–88; Diener et al. 1995; Lykken and Tellegen 1996.
17. Diener and Lucas 1988; cited and discussed in R. H. Frank 1999:70–71.
18. Freedman 1978.
19. See, for example, Aristotle, *Metaphysics* 1048b18, 1050a23; *Nicomachean Ethics* 1174a14.
20. Thayer 1996:14; Suzuki 1970:46.
21. Freedman 1978:235; see also Parducci 1984:16.

22. Ferguson 1767:41.
23. McIntosh and Martin 1992:242.
24. Ibid.:230.
25. Freedman 1978:230–231; see also De Sousa 1987:207–208.
26. Ferguson 1767:sec.7; Kubey and Csikszentmihalyi 1990:197.
27. Landau 1995.
28. Nussbaum 1986:322–333.
29. Carlson 1993:10–12; see also Peale 1952.
30. Diener and Diener 1996.
31. Karl Teigen (personal communication, 1999) and Gideon Keren uncovered this phenomenon. These may be other interpretations for this phenomenon; thus, Teigen rejects my interpretation.
32. Parducci 1984:14–15.
33. Nolen-Hoeksema 1987; see also Lyubomirsky and Nolen-Hoeksema 1993; McIntosh and Martin 1992; Nolen-Hoeksema and Morrow 1993; Thayer 1996:137–140.
34. See, for example, Oatley and Jenkins 1996:chap.11.
35. McIntosh and Martin 1992:244.
36. Diener and Larsen 1993; Freedman 1978:38, 62–63; Lazarus and Lazarus 1994:94–95; Parducci 1984:17–19.
37. Stein 1987; Van Evra 1990. Ben Stein describes in a witty manner the artificial nature of the environment depicted on TV. However, whereas he explains it by referring to the nature of the Los Angeles TV community, I believe the reason is more profound and related to such things as the nature of human happiness and the way emotions influence us.
38. Cunningham 1988; Stearns 1993. The above saying is attributed to Lee Salk.
39. Stearns 1993; Stein and Jewett 1986.
40. Letter to Pollot, Jan. 1641; cited in James 1997:263.
41. See, for example, S. Rubin 1993.
42. Miles and Demi 1991–1992; Vangelisti and Sprague 1998:144. For further discussions on grief, see Gustafson 1989.
43. McGraw, 1995:44; Segrin 1998:227–228. Segrin even suggests that people who are too close to family members, particularly parents, appear to be at heightened risk for loneliness (231). However, it is not clear whether such family ties are the cause or the result of their loneliness.
44. Isenberg 1949:10.
45. Segrin 1998:230.
46. Burnley and Kurth 1992.

## Chapter 16

1. Aristotle, *Rhetoric*:II, 5.
2. Averill et al. 1990:14; Day 1969.
3. Godfrey 1987:64.
4. Day 1969:96–97, 1970; Downie 1963–1964.
5. Averill et al. 1990:18–19, 25–26.
6. Ibid.:33–34.
7. Gordon 1980:572–573.
8. Averill et al. 1990:15.
9. Ibid.:95–96; my discussion on the difference between optimism and hope, as other discussions in this chapter, are heavily indebted to Averill et al. 1990.
10. Ibid.:100; Rachman 1990:313–316.
11. Snyder 1994:16–18.
12. On this issue see Goleman 1995:86–89; 1998; Schulman 1995.
13. Snyder 1994:24.

14. Rachman 1990:69–73.

15. Ibid.:3.

16. Ibid.:59–61.

17. Spinoza 1677:IIIdef. aff.xiii.

18. Day 1969:99.

19. M. Lewis 1992: chap. 3.

20. Gosling 1962:300–301.

21. This division is based on Day 1969. Descartes was already thinking along these lines when he argued that when hope is extreme (namely, its object is certain), it changes its nature and is called confidence; and when fear is extreme, it becomes despair (1649:58).

22. Roseman 1991.

23. Day 1969:98–99.

24. Aristotle, *Nichomachean Ethics* 1115b18.

25. Rachman 1990:297–299.

26. Ibid.:300–301; 311–312, 317.

27. Ibid.:317.

28. Spinoza 1677:IIIdef. aff.xli. Contrary to the view suggested here, Spinoza considers courage (or daring) to be an emotion (1677:IV, p69d).

29. See, for example, Sartre 1956:628.

30. Rachman 1990:13–15, 49; Seligman 1975.

31. Rachman 1990:61.

32. Ibid.:56–57.

33. Freedman 1978:chap.11.

34. Elster 1999a:69. Elster indicates that indeed in Aristotle's definition of fear there is no reference to desert. Elster believes that the issue of desert is also of lesser significance in hope.

35. See also Godfrey 1987:1–2; Snyder 1994:2.

36. Averill et al. 1990:3, 102–104; Bloch 1959; Godfrey 1987:1.

37. Godfrey 1987:1.

38. Spinoza 1677:IVp47; IVp73d; IVapp.xvi.; Mosso's claim is taken from his book *Fear* and is cited in Kemp Smith 1957:5.

39. Wu 1972.

40. Reid 1788:574.

## Chapter 17

1. Hume suggests that "goods, which are common to all mankind, and have become familiar to us by custom, give us little satisfaction" (1739–1740:291). In his excellent analysis of pride, Isenberg (1949) disagrees, arguing that we can be proud of absolute and not merely comparative qualities. The above passage indicates that both are right: we can take pride in both types of qualities, but when the comparative element is also added, pride is more intense.

2. Isenberg 1949:4–5.

3. Ibid.:4.

4. Cited in Landman 1993:17. Landman's *Regret* is the best book on the subject and was instrumental in the writing of this chapter. For a discussion of the relation between past and present in regret, see Landman 1993:6–7, 16–18.

5. Bar-Hillel and Neter 1996.

6. See, for example, Zeelenberg et al. 1996.

7. Kahneman 1995.

8. Gilovich and Medvec 1995a,b.

9. Cited in Landman 1993:107–108.

10. Gilovich and Medvec 1995a.

11. Ibid.
12. Ibid.:393–394.
13. Gilovich and Medvec 1995a; Landman 1993:93–99, 110.
14. Etcoff 1999:6. Nancy Etcoff introduces Eleanor Roosevelt's response to illustrate the great impact of beauty on our life; she indicates that this statement is of particular interest as it is made by one of the most revered and beloved of women, one who led a life filled with many satisfactions.
15. Vangelisti and Sprague 1998:135.
16. See also Elster 1999a:149–153; Williams 1993:90–91.
17. Lewis 1992:71; Niedenthal et al. 1994; Williams 1993:220.
18. Williams 1993:219–223.
19. Tangney 1990; G. Taylor 1985:90; Vangelisti and Sprague 1998:143.
20. G. Taylor 1985:91–92.
21. Elster 1999a:151; Vangelisti and Sprague 1998:129, 147.
22. Miles and Demi 1983–1984; Vangelisti and Sprague 1998:144.
23. See, for example, Elster 1999a:151–159, 313–314.
24. Ibid.:302.
25. McGraw 1987; see also Vangelisti and Sprague 1998:133.
26. Vangelisti and Sprague 1998:134.
27. Bradford and Petronio 1998; Edelmann 1987:6; Sattler 1965.
28. G. Taylor 1985:69–76.
29. Bradford and Petronio 1998:113; M. Lewis 1992:82; G. Taylor 1985:75–76.
30. Harre 1990:188–189.
31. Edelmann 1987:197.
32. Ibid.:118–119.
33. Bradford and Petronio 1998:100, 102.
34. Miller 1986:1062; cited in Bradford and Petronio 1998.
35. Harre 1990:186.
36. My discussion on intentional embarrassment is based on Bradford and Petronio 1998.
37. Landman 1993:52–53; for a similar view, see Thalberg 1963.
38. G. Taylor 1985:99–107.
39. Ibid.:99.
40. Ibid.:98–99.
41. Folger 1984; Parrott 1991:8–9; G. Taylor 1985:98.
42. Landman 1993:47.
43. Ibid.:48, 51.
44. Vangelisti and Sprague 1998:134–136; on the moral significance of guilt, see also Greenspan 1995:chap. 4.

## Chapter 18

1. The Greek term *hubris* is also used in this regard (see, e.g., Lewis 1992:75, 78, 234). However, this term includes the negative connotation of exaggeration and something which should be avoided; hence it is less suitable for a neutral psychological description.
2. D. H. Frank 1990:272.
3. Spinoza 1677:IIIdef.aff.xxviii, xxxi; Elster 1999a:207; see also Hume 1739–1740:292.
4. Indeed Spinoza speaks about self-esteem which is "a joy born of the fact that a man considers himself and his own power of acting to be worthy." Self-esteem "is really the highest thing we can hope for" (1677:IIIdef.aff.xxv; IV52s); see also Isenberg 1949:6–8.
5. G. Taylor 1985:45.
6. Elster 1999a:III.2.

7. Elster 1999a:282; M. Lewis 1992:75.

8. Elster 1999a:150.

9. G. Taylor 1985:67; Taylor presents this claim as an alternative to the more simplistic claim that shame requires an audience.

10. Elster 1999a:156; M. Lewis 1992:75, 140.

11. Buss 1994:149; Descartes 1649:art.113; Fisher 1992:21–24.

12. Z. Rubin 1970; Zebrowitz et al. 1996.

13. M. Lewis 1992:178–179.

14. Aristotle, *Nicomachean Ethics* 1128b10–35.

15. For a more detailed discussion of these manners, see M. Lewis 1992:127–137.

16. M. Lewis 1992:103.

17. Ibid.:117–118.

18. Elster 1999a:156.

19. Walsh 1970.

20. On this issue, see Elster 1999a:150–151.

21. For a more detailed discussion, see Ben-Ze'ev 1993b.

22. Driver 1989.

23. Flanagan 1990; for further discussion of modesty and related attitudes, see, for example, Statman 1992; Richards 1992.

24. See "Proper Self-Respect" in Kant 1963.

25. R. Taylor 1989.

26. Ibid.:229.

27. Isenberg 1949:7–8.

28. Elster 1999a:149; Williams 1993:90.

29. Aristotle, *Nicomachean Ethics* 1128b12.

30. For a criticism of this view, see Chakrabarti 1992.

31. Chakrabarti 1992; Shklar 1984:241.

32. See, for example, Plato, *Laws*:671c; Aristotle, *Rhetoric*:1367a10; G. Taylor 1985:80–84.

33. Isenberg 1949:18–20.

34. Harre 1990.

35. Aristotle, *Nicomachean Ethics* 1128b17ff.

36. Barbalet 1998:117–120.

37. Abramson and Pinkerton 1995: 167.

## Epilogue

1. Kenny 1963; Griffiths 1997:14, 247.

2. Wilde 1966:311.

# References

Abramson, P. R., and Pinkerton, S. D. (1995). *With pleasure: Thoughts on the nature of human sexuality.* New York: Oxford University Press.

Achenbach, T., and Howell, C. (1989). Are America's children's problems getting worse? A 13-year comparison. *Journal of the American Academy of Child and Adolescent Psychiatry, 32,* 1145–1154.

Ackerman, D. (1994). *A natural history of love.* New York: Random House.

Adams, R. M. (1985). Involuntary sins. *Philosophical Review, 94,* 3–31.

Allen, R. T. (1991). Governance by emotion. *Journal of the British Society for Phenomenology, 22,* 15–29.

Alloy, L. B., Albright, J. S., Abramson, L. Y., and Dykman, B. M. (1990). Depressive realism and non-depressive optimistic illusions: The role of the self. In R. E. Ingram (Ed.), *Contemporary psychological approaches to depression.* New York: Plenum.

Alston, W. P. (1967). Emotion and feeling. In P. Edwards (Ed.), *Encyclopedia of philosophy* (Vol. 2, pp. 479–486). New York: Macmillan.

Alvarado, K. A., Templer, D. I., Bresler, C., and Thomas-Dobson, S. (1995). The relationship of religious variables to death depression and death anxiety. *Journal of Clinical Psychology, 51,* 202–204.

Ambady, N., and Rosenthal, R. (1992). Thin slices of expressive behavior as predictors of interpersonal consequences: A meta-analysis. *Psychological Bulletin, 111,* 256–274.

Appadurai, A. (1985). Gratitude as a social mode in south India. *Ethos, 13,* 235–245.

Aristotle, *The complete works of Aristotle: The revised Oxford translation.* Edited by J. Barnes. Princeton, NJ: Princeton University Press (1984).

Armon-Jones, C. (1991). *Varieties of affect.* Hertfordshire, England: Harvester.

Arnold, M. (1960). *Emotion and personality.* New York: Academic Press.

Arnold, M. (1969). Human emotion and action. In T. Mischel (Ed.), *Human action.* New York: Academic Press.

Averill, J. R. (1982). *Anger and aggression: An essay on emotion.* New York: Springer-Verlag.

Averill, J. R. (1983). Studies on anger and aggression. *American Psychologist, 38,* 1145–1160.

Averill, J. R., Catlin, G., and Chon, K. K. (1990). *Rules of hope.* New York: Springer-Verlag.

Averill, J. R., and More, T. A. (1993). Happiness. In M. Lewis and J. M. Haviland (Eds.), *Handbook of emotions,* New York: Guilford Press.

Babcock, M. K. (1988). Embarrassment: A window on the self. *Journal for the Theory of Social Behaviour, 18,* 459–483.

Bacon, F. (1625). *Essays.* In *Selected writings.* New York: Modern Library (1955).

Bar-Hillel, M., and Neter, E. (1996). Why are people reluctant to exchange lottery tickets? *Journal of Personality and Social Psychology, 70,* 17–27.

Barbalet, J. M. (1998). *Emotion, social theory, and social structure: A macrosociological approach.* Cambridge: Cambridge University Press.

Barefoot, J. C., Dodge, K. A., Peterson, B. L., Dahlstrom, W. G., and Williams, R. B. (1989). The Cook-Medley hostility scale: Item content and ability to predict survival. *Psychosomatic Medicine, 51,* 46–57.

Baron, R. S., Kerr, N. L., and Miller, N. (1992). *Group process, group decision, group action.* Buckingham, UK: Open University Press.

Barresi, J., and Moore, C. (1996). Intentional relations and social understanding. *Behavioral and Brain Sciences, 19,* 107–154.

Batson, C. D., Shaw, L., and Oleson, K. C. (1992). Differentiating affect, mood, and emotion: Toward functionally based conceptual distinctions. *Review of Personality and Social Psychology, 13,* 294–326.

Batson, C. D., Shannon, E., and Salvarani, G. (1997). Perspective taking: Imagining how another feels versus imagining how you would feel. *Personality and Social Psychology Bulletin, 23,* 751–758.

Baumeister, R. F., Wotman, S. R., and Stillwell, A. M. (1993). Unrequited love: On heartbreak, anger, guilt, scriptlessness, and humiliation. *Journal of Personality and Social Psychology, 64,* 377–394.

Beck, A. T. (1976). *Cognitive therapy and the emotional disorders.* New York: International Universities Press.

Bedford, E. (1957). Emotions. *Proceedings of the Aristotelian Society, 57,* 281–304.

Belfiore, E. S. (1992). *Tragic pleasures: Aristotle on plot and emotion.* Princeton, NJ: Princeton University Press.

Bentham, J. (1789). *An introduction to the principles of morals and legislation.* London: Methuen (1982).

Ben-Ze'ev, A. (1990). Describing the emotions. *Philosophical Psychology, 3,* 305–317.

Ben-Ze'ev, A. (1993a). *The perceptual system: A philosophical and psychological perspective.* New York: Peter Lang.

Ben-Ze'ev, A. (1993b). The virtue of modesty. *American Philosophical Quarterly, 30,* 235–246.

Ben-Ze'ev, A. (1994). The vindication of gossip. In R. Goodman and A. Ben-Ze'ev (Eds.), *Good gossip,* Lawrence: University Press of Kansas.

Ben-Zur, H., and Breznitz, S. (1991). What makes people angry: Dimensions of anger-evoking events. *Journal of Research in Personality, 25,* 1–22.

Berenson, F. M. (1991). Emotions and rationality. *International Journal of Moral and Social Studies, 6,* 33–46.

Bergson, H. (1907). *Creative evolution.* New York: Holt (1911).

Bermant, G. (1976). Sexual behavior: Hard times with the Coolidge effect. In M. H. Siegel and H. P. Zeigler (Eds.), *Psychological research: The inside story.* New York: Harper & Row.

Bers, S. A., and Rodin, J. (1984). Social-comparison jealousy: A developmental and motivational study. *Journal of Personality and Social Psychology, 47,* 766–779.

Birch, L. L., and Marlin, D. W. (1982). I don't like it; I never tried it: Effects of exposure to food on two-year-old children's food preferences. *Appetite, 4,* 353–360.

Bloch, E. (1959). *The principle of hope.* Cambridge, MA.: MIT Press (1986).

Blondel, M. (1947). *Lutte pour la civilisation et philosophie de la paix* (2nd Ed.). Paris: Flammarion.

Bloom, A. (1993). *Love and friendship.* New York: Simon & Schuster.

Blum, L. A. (1994). *Moral perception and particularity.* New York: Cambridge University Press.

Bradford, L., and Petronio, S. (1998). Strategic embarrassment: The culprit of emotion. In P. A. Andersen and L. K. Guerrero (Eds.), *Handbook of communication and emotion.* San Diego: Academic Press.

Bradley, M. (1998). Emotion and memory. Presented at the workshop on Emotions, Qualia and Consciousness, Ischia, Italy.

Brennan, T. (2000). *The transmission of affect.* Oxford: Oxford University Press.

Brentano, F. (1874). *Psychology from an empirical standpoint.* London: Routledge & Kegan Paul (1973).

Brickman, P., Coates, D., and Janoff-Bulman, R. (1978). Lottery winners and accident victims: Is happiness relative? *Journal of Personality and Social Psychology, 36,* 917–927.

Bridges, K. M. B. (1930). A genetic theory of emotions. *Journal of Genetic Psychology, 37,* 514–527.

Brien, A. (1991). Mercy and desert. *Philosophical Papers, 20,* 193–201.

Brien, A. (1995). Mercy, utilitarianism and retributivism. *Philosophia, 24,* 493–521.

Bringle, R. G. (1991). Psychological aspects of jealousy: A transactional model. In P. Salovey (Ed.), *The psychology of jealousy and envy.* New York: Guilford Press.

Brody, L. R., and Hall, J. A. (1993). Gender and emotion. In M. Lewis and J. M. Haviland (Eds.), *Handbook of emotions.* New York: Guilford Press.

Brown, R. (1987). *Analyzing love.* Cambridge: Cambridge University Press.

Bullock, A. (1991). *Hitler and Stalin*. New York: Vintage Books.

Burnley, C. S., and Kurth, S. B. (1992). Never married women: Alone and lonely? *Humboldt Journal of Social Relations, 18,* 57–83.

Buss, D. M. (1994). *The evolution of desire: Strategies of human mating*. New York: Basic Books.

Buss, D. M., Larsen, R. J., Westen, D., and Semmelroth, J. (1992). Sex differences in jealousy: Evolution, physiology, and psychology. *Psychological Science, 3,* 251–255.

Butler, J. (1726). *Five Sermons*. Indianapolis: Hackett (1983).

Buunk, B. P. (1991). Jealousy in close relationships: An exchange-theoretical perspective. In P. Salovey (Ed.), *The psychology of jealousy and envy*. New York: Guilford Press.

Byrne, D., and Murnen, S. K. (1988). Maintaining loving relationships. In R. J. Sternberg and M. L. Barnes (Eds.), *The psychology of love*. New Haven, CT: Yale University Press.

Calhoun, C., and Solomon, R. C. (1984). *What is an emotion? Classic readings in philosophical psychology*. New York: Oxford University Press.

Callan, E. (1988). The moral status of pity. *Canadian Journal of Philosophy, 18,* 1–12.

Campos, J. J., Campos, R. G., and Barrett, K. C. (1989). Emergence themes in the study of emotional development and emotion regulation. *Developmental Psychology, 25,* 394–402.

Cancian, F. M., and Gordon, S. L. (1988). Changing emotion norms in marriage: Love and anger in U.S. women's magazines since 1900. *Gender and Society, 2,* 308–342.

Card, C. (1988). Gratitude and obligation. *American Philosophical Quarterly, 25,* 115–127.

Carlson, R. (1993). *You can feel good again*. New York: Penguin.

Carson, A. (1986). *Eros the bittersweet*. Princeton, NJ: Princeton University Press.

Cartwright, D. (1984). Kant, Schopenhauer, and Nietzsche on the morality of pity. *Journal of the History of Ideas, 45,* 83–98.

Cartwright, D., and Zander, A. (Eds.), (1968). *Group dynamics*. London: Tavistock.

Cassirer, E. (1923). *Substance and function*. New York: Dover (1953).

Chapman, A. J., and Wright, D. S. (1976). Social enhancement of laughter: An experimental analysis of some companion variables. *Journal of Experimental Child Psychology, 21,* 201–218.

Chakrabarti, A. (1992). Individual and collective pride. *American Philosophical Quarterly, 29,* 35–43.

Charny, I. S., and Parnass, S. (1995). The impact of extramarital relationships on the continuation of marriages. *Journal of Sex and Marital Therapy, 21,* 100–115.

Chazan, P. (1992). Pride, virtue, and self-hood: A reconstruction of Hume. *Canadian Journal of Philosophy, 22,* 45–64.

Chazin, S. (1994). What you didn't know about money and happiness. *Reader's Digest* (large-type edition), August, 264–278.

Chismar, D. (1988). Empathy and sympathy: The important difference. *Journal of Value Inquiry, 22,* 257–266.

Cialdini, R. B., Borden, R. J., Thorne, A., and Sloan, L. R. (1976). Basking in reflected glory: Three (football) field studies. *Journal of Personality and Social Psychology, 34,* 366–375.

Clanton, G., and Kosins, D. J. (1991). Developmental correlates of jealousy. In P. Salovey (Ed.), *The psychology of jealousy and envy*. New York: Guilford Press.

Clare, A. (1986). *Lovelaw: Love, sex, and marriage around the world*. London: BBC Publications.

Clark, C. (1997). *Misery and company: Sympathy in everyday life*. Chicago: University of Chicago Press.

Clark, L. A., and Watson, D. (1988). Mood and the mundane: Relations between daily life events and self-reported mood. *Journal of Personality and Social Psychology, 54,* 296–308.

Clark, R. W. (1983). *Benjamin Franklin: A biography*. New York: Random House.

Clore, G. L., and Ortony, A. (1999). Cognition in emotion: Always, sometimes, or never? In L. Nadel and R. Lane (Eds.), *The cognitive neuroscience of emotion*. New York: Oxford University Press.

Coats, E. J., and Feldman, R. S. (1995). The role of television in the socialization of nonverbal behavioral skills. *Basic and Applied Psychology, 17,* 327–341.

Collingwood, R. G. (1923). Sensation and thought. *Proceedings of the Aristotelian Society, 24,* 55–76.

Cook, M., and McHenry, R. (1978). *Sexual attraction*. London: Pergamon.

Cottingham, J. (1983). Ethics and impartiality. *Philosophical Studies, 43*, 83–99.

Cottingham, J. (1986). Partiality, favouritism and morality. *Philosophical Quarterly, 36*, 357–373.

Coyne, J. C., and Downey, G. (1991). Social factors and psychopathology: Stress, social support, and coping processes. *Annual Review of Psychology, 42*, 401–425.

Crosby, F. (1976). A model of egoistical relative deprivation. *Psychological Review, 83*, 85–113.

Crouse, B. B., and Mehrabian, A. (1977). Affiliation of opposite-sexed strangers. *Journal of Research in Personality, 11*, 38–47.

Cunningham, M. R. (1988). What do you do when you're happy or blue? Mood, expectancies, and behavioral interest. *Motivation and Emotion, 12*, 309–331.

Cunningham, M. R., Roberts, A. R., Wu, C. H., Barbee, A. P., and Druen, P. B. (1995). "Their ideas of beauty are, on the whole, the same as ours": Consistency and variability in the cross-cultural perception of female physical attractiveness. *Journal of Personality and Social Psychology, 68*, 261–279.

Cummins, D. (1997). *Human reasoning: An evolutionary perspective.* Cambridge, MA.: MIT Press.

Curzer, H. J. (1995). Aristotle's account of the virtue of justice. *Apeiron, 28*, 207–238.

Dakin, S., and Arrowood, A. J. (1981). The social comparison of ability. *Human Relations, 34*, 89–109.

Damasio, A. R. (1994). *Descartes' error: Emotion, reason, and the human brain.* New York: Putnam.

Dancy, J. (1983). Ethical particularism and morally relevant properties. *Mind, 92*, 530–547.

Davidson, R. J. (1994). On emotion, mood, and related affective constructs. In P. Ekman and R. J. Davidson (Eds.), *The nature of emotion: Fundamental Questions.* New York: Oxford University Press.

Davis, K. (1936). Jealousy and sexual property. *Social Forces, 14*, 395–405.

Day, J. P. (1969). Hope. *American Philosophical Quarterly, 6*, 89–102.

Day, J. P. (1970). The anatomy of hope and fear. *Mind, 79*, 369–384.

Degenhardt, M. A. B. (1978). Learning from the imaginary. *Journal of Moral Education, 8*, 92–98.

De La Mora, G. F. (1987). *Egalitarian envy.* New York: Paragon.

Derryberry, D., and Tucker, D. M. (1994). Motivating the focus of attention. In P. M. Neidenthal and S. Kitayama (Eds.), *The heart's eye: Emotional influences in perception and attention.* San Diego: Academic Press.

Descartes, R. (1649). *The passions of the soul.* In J. Cottingham, R. Stoothoff, and D. Murdoch (Trans.), *The philosophical writings of Descartes.* Cambridge: Cambridge University Press (1984).

De Sousa, R. (1987). *The rationality of emotions.* Cambridge, MA.: MIT Press.

De Sousa, R. (1990). Emotions, education and time. *Metaphilosophy, 21*, 434–446.

De Sousa, R. (1991). Love as theater. In R. C. Solomon and K. M. Higgins (Eds.), *The philosophy of (erotic) love.* Lawrence: University Press of Kansas.

DeSteno, D. A., and Salovey, P. (1996a). Jealousy and the characteristics of one's rival: A self-evaluation maintenance perspective. *Personality and Social Psychology Bulletin, 22*, 920–932.

DeSteno, D. A., and Salovey, P. (1996b). Evolutionary origins of sex differences in jealousy? Questioning the "fitness" of the model. *Psychological Science, 7*, 367–372.

Devlin, L. P. (1987). Campaign commercials. In A. A. Berger (Ed.), *Television in society.* New Brunswick, NJ: Transaction Books.

De Waal, F. B. M. (1989). *Peacemaking among primates.* Cambridge, MA: Harvard University Press.

Dewey, J. (1894–1895). The theory of emotion. *Psychological Review, 1*, 553–569; *2*, 13–22.

Diener, E., and Diener, C. (1996). Most people are happy. *Psychological Science, 7*, 181–185.

Diener, E., and Larsen R. J. (1993). The experience of emotional well-being. In M. Lewis and J. M. Haviland (Eds.), *Handbook of emotions.* New York: Guilford Press.

Diener, E., and Lucas, R. E. (1998). Personality and subjective well-being. In D. Kahneman, E. Diener and N. Schwartz (Eds.), *Understanding well-being: Scientific perspectives on enjoyment and suffering.* New York: Russell Sage.

Diener, E., Horwitz, J., and Emmons, R. A. (1985). Happiness of the very wealthy. *Social Indicators Research, 16*, 263–274.

Diener, E., Sandvik, E., and Larsen, R. J. (1985). Age and sex effects for emotional intensity. *Developmental Psychology, 21*, 542–546.

Diener, E., Sandvik, E., and Pavot, W. (1991). Happiness is the frequency, not the intensity of positive versus negative affect. In F. Strack, M. Argyle and N. Schwarz (Eds.), *Subjective well-being*. New York: Pergamon.

Diener, E., Sandvik, E., Seidlitz, L., and Diener, M. (1993). The relationship between income and subjective well-being: Relative or absolute? *Social Indicators Research, 28*, 195–223.

Diener, E., Wolsic, B., and Fujita, F. (1995). Physical attractiveness and subjective well-being. *Journal of Personality and Social Psychology, 69*, 120–129.

Dillon, R. S. (1992). Care and respect: Toward moral integration. *Canadian Journal of Philosophy, 22*, 105–132.

Dion, K. K., and Dion, K. L. (1975). Self-esteem and romantic love. *Journal of Personality, 43*, 39–57.

Downie, R. S. (1963–1964). Hope. *Philosophy and Phenomenological Research, 24*, 248–251.

Dressler, J. (1982). Rethinking the heat of passion: A defense in search of a rationale. *Journal of Criminal Law and Criminology, 73*, 421–470.

Drever, J. (1952). *A dictionary of psychology*. London: Penguin.

Driver, J. (1989). The virtues of ignorance. *Journal of Philosophy, 86*, 373–384.

Dyer, M. G. (1987). Emotions and their computations: Three computer models. *Cognition and Emotions, 1*, 323–347.

Edelmann, R. J. (1987). *The psychology of embarrassment*. Chichester, England: Wiley.

Eisenberg, N., and Fabes, R. A. (1992). Emotion, regulation, and the development of social competence. *Review of Personality and Social Psychology, 14*, 119–150.

Ekman, P. (1984). Expression and the nature of emotion. In K. Scherer and P. Ekman (Eds.), *Approaches to emotion*. Hillsdale, NJ: Erlbaum.

Ekman, P. (1992a). *Telling lies*. New York: Norton.

Ekman, P. (1992b). An argument for basic emotions. *Cognition and Emotion, 6*, 169–200.

Ekman, P., and Davidson, R. J. (Eds.), (1994). *The nature of emotion: Fundamental questions*. New York: Oxford University Press.

Ekman, P., Levenson, R. W., and Friesen, W. V. (1983). Autonomic nervous system activity distinguishes between emotions. *Science, 221*, 1208–1210.

Elias, N. (1939). *The history of manners*: Vol. 1. *The civilizing process*. New York: Pantheon Books (1978).

Elliott, C. (1992*). The affective reasoner: A process model of emotions in a multi-agent system*. Doctoral dissertation, Northwestern University, Evanston, IL.

Elliston, F. (1975). In defense of promiscuity. In R. M. Stewart (Ed.), *Philosophical perspectives on sex and love*. New York: Oxford University Press (1995).

Ellsworth, P. C. (1991). Some implications of cognitive appraisal theories of emotions. *International Review of Studies on Emotion, 1*, 143–161.

Ellsworth, P. C. (1994). Sense, culture, and sensibility. In S. Kitayama and H. R. Markus (Eds.), *Emotion and culture*. Washington, DC: American Psychological Association.

Ellsworth, P. C., and Smith, C. A. (1988). Shades of joy: Appraisals differentiating among positive emotions. *Emotion and Cognition, 2*, 301–331.

Elster, J. (1985). Sadder but wiser? Rationality and the emotions. *Social Science Information, 24*, 375–406.

Elster, J. (1989). *Nuts and bolts for the social sciences*. Cambridge: Cambridge University Press.

Elster, J. (1991). Envy in social life. In R. Seckhauser (Ed.), *Strategy and choices*. Cambridge, MA: MIT Press.

Elster, J. (1995). *The cement of society: A study of social order*. Cambridge: Cambridge University Press.

Elster, J. (1999a). *Alchemies of the mind: Rationality and the emotions*. Cambridge: Cambridge University Press.

Elster, J. (1999b). *Strong feelings: Emotion, addiction, and human behavior*. Cambridge, MA: MIT Press.

Emmons, R. A., and Diener, E. (1985). Factors predicting satisfaction judgments: A comparative examination. *Social Indicators Research, 16*, 157–167.

Engel, G. (1964). Is grief a disease? *Psychosomotic Medicine, 23*, 18–22.

Etcoff, N. (1999). *Survival of the prettiest: The science of beauty*. New York: Doubleday.

Ewin, R. E. (1990). Pride, prejudice and shyness. *Philosophy, 65,* 137–154.

Ewin, R. E. (1992). Loyalty and virtues. *Philosophical Quarterly, 42,* 403–419.

Fabes, R. A., and Martin, C. L. (1991). Gender and age stereotypes of emotionality. *Personality and Social Psychology Bulletin, 17,* 532–540.

Farrell, D. M. (1980). Jealousy. *Philosophical Review, 89,* 527–559.

Feather, N. T. (1996). Values, deservingness, and attitudes toward high achievers: Reseach on tall poppies. In C. Seligman, J. M. Olson, and M. P. Zanna (Eds.), *The psychology of values: The Ontario symposium.* Hillsdale, NJ: Erlbaum.

Fehr, B. (1988). Prototype analysis of the concepts of love and commitment. *Journal of Personality and Social Psychology, 55,* 557–579.

Fehr, B., and Russell, J. A. (1984). Concept of emotion viewed from a prototype perspective. *Journal of Experimental Psychology: General, 113,* 464–486.

Feinberg, J. (1970). Justice and personal desert. In *Doing and deserving.* Princeton, NJ: Princeton University Press.

Ferguson, A. (1767). *An essay on the history of civil society.* New Brunswick, NJ: Transaction Publishers (1980).

Festinger, L. (1954). A theory of social comparison processes. *Human Relations, 7,* 117–140.

Fine, G. A. (1977). Social components of children's gossip. *Journal of Communication, 27,* 181–185.

Fischer, A., and Manstead, A. S. R. (1998). Gender, powerlessness, and crying. Presented at the Tenth Meeting of the International Society for Research on Emotions. Würzburg, Germany.

Fisher, H. (1992). *Anatomy of love.* New York: Norton.

Fiske, J. (1988). *Television culture: Popular pleasures and politics.* London: Methuen.

Fitness, J., and Fletcher, G. J. O. (1993). Love, hate, anger and jealousy in close relationships: A prototype and cognitive appraisal analysis. *Journal of Personality and Social Psychology, 65,* 942–958.

Flanagan, O. (1990). Virtue and ignorance. *Journal of Philosophy, 87,* 420–428.

Folger, R. (1984). Perceived injustice, referent cognitions, and the concept of comparison level. *Representative Research in Social Psychology, 14,* 88–108.

Folkes, V. S. (1982). Communicating the reasons for social rejection. *Journal of Experimental Social Psychology, 18,* 235–252.

Forgas, J. P. (1995). Mood and judgment: The affect infusion model (AIM). *Psychological Bulletin, 117,* 39–66.

Forgas, J. P., and Fiedler, K. (1996). Us and them: Mood effects on intergroup discrimination. *Journal of Personality and Social Psychology, 70,* 28–40.

Foster, G. M. (1965). Cultural responses to expressions of envy in Tzintzuntzan. *Southwestern Journal of Anthropology, 21,* 24–35.

Foster, G. M. (1972). The anatomy of envy: A study in symbolic behavior. *Current Anthropology, 13,* 165–186.

Frank, D. H. (1990). Anger as a vice: A Maimonidean critique of Aristotle's ethics. *History of Philosophy Quarterly, 7,* 269–281.

Frank, R. H. (1988). *Passions within reason: The strategic role of the emotions.* New York: Norton.

Frank, R. H. (1999). *Luxury fever: Why money fails to satisfy in an era of excess.* New York: The Free Press.

Frank, R. H., and Cook, P. J. (1995). *The Winner-Take-All Society.* New York: The Free Press.

Frankfurt, H. G. (1988). Equality as a moral ideal. In *The importance of what we care about.* Cambridge: Cambridge University Press.

Frankfurt, H. G. (1998). Duty and love. *Philosophical Explorations, 1,* 4–9.

Fredrickson, B. L. (1998). What good are positive emotions? *Review of General Psychology, 2,* 1–20.

Freedman, J. L. (1978). *Happy people.* New York: Harcourt Brace Jovanovich.

Freud, S. (1915). The unconscious. In *The standard edition of the complete psychological works* (Vol. 14). London: Hogarth Press (1971).

Friday, N. (1985). *Jealousy.* New York: Perigord Press.

Fridlund, A. J. (1994). *Human facial expression: An evolutionary view.* San Diego: Academic Press.

Frijda, N. H. (1986). *The emotions*. Cambridge: Cambridge University Press.

Frijda, N. H. (1987). Emotion, cognitive structure, and action tendency. *Cognition and Emotion, 1*, 115–143.

Frijda, N. H. (1988). The laws of emotion. *American Psychologist, 43*, 349–358.

Frijda, N. H. (1989). Aesthetic emotions and reality. *American Psychologist, 44*, 1546–1547.

Frijda, N. H. (1994). Varieties of affect: Emotions and episodes, moods, and sentiments. In P. Ekman and R. J. Davidson (Eds.), *The nature of emotion: Fundamental questions*. New York: Oxford University Press.

Frijda, N. H. (1996). Sympathy and moral behavior. Presented at the Ninth Meeting of the International Society for Research on Emotions. Toronto, Canada.

Frijda, N. H. (1998). Sexual emotions. Presented at the Tenth Meeting of the International Society for Research on Emotions. Würzburg, Germany.

Frijda, N. H., Mesquita, B. (1994). The social roles and functions of emotions. In S. Kitayama and H. R. Markus (Eds.), *Emotion and culture*. Washington, DC: American Psychological Association.

Frijda, N. H., Kuipers, P., and ter Schure, E. (1989). Relations among emotion, appraisal, and emotional action readiness. *Journal of Personality and Social Psychology, 57*, 212–228.

Frijda, N. H., Mesquita, B., Sonnemans, J., and Van Goozen, S. (1991). The duration of affective phenomena or emotions, sentiments and passions. *International Review of Studies on Emotion, 1*, 187–225.

Frijda, N. H., Ortony, A., Sonnemans, J., and Clore, G. (1992). The complexity of intensity: Issues concerning the structure of emotion intensity. *Review of Personality and Social Psychology, 13*, 60–89.

Frye, N. (1957). *Anatomy of criticism*. Princeton, NJ: Princeton University Press.

Fujita, F., Diener, E., and Sandvik, E. (1991). Gender differences in negative affect and well-being: The case for emotional intensity. *Journal of Personality and Social Psychology, 61*, 427–434.

Galeano, E. (1992). *The book of embraces*. New York: Norton.

Gaus, G. F. (1990). *Value and justification*. Cambridge: Cambridge University Press.

Gaver, W. W., and Mandler, G. (1987). Play it again, Sam: On liking music. *Cognition and Emotion, 3*, 259–282.

Gay, J. (1731). *Concerning the fundamental principle of virtue or morality*.

Gaylin, W. (1984). *The rage within: Anger in modern life*. New York: Simon, and Schuster.

Genia, V. (1993). A psychometric evaluation of the Allport-Ross I/E scales in a religiously heterogeneous sample. *Journal for the Scientific Study of Religion, 32*, 284–290.

Gerbner, G., Gross, L., Morgan, M., and Signorielli, N. (1987). Facts, fantasies and schools. In A. A. Berger (Ed.), *Television in society*. New Brunswick, NJ: Transaction Books.

Gilboa, E., and Revelle, W. (1994). Personality and the structure of affective responses. In S. H. M. van Goozen, N. E. van de Poll and J. A. Sergeant (Eds.), *Emotions: Essays on emotion theory*. Hillsdale, NJ: Erlbaum.

Gibson, J. J. (1979). *The ecological approach to visual perception*. Boston: Houghton Mifflin.

Gilligan, C. (1982). *In a different voice*. Cambridge, MA: Harvard University Press.

Gilovich, T., and Medvec, V. H. (1995a). The experience of regret: What, when, and why. *Psychological Review, 102*, 379–395.

Gilovich, T., and Medvec, V. H. (1995b). Some counterfactual determinants of satisfaction and regret. In N. J. Roese and J. M. Olson (Eds.), *What might have been: The social psychology of counterfactual thinking*. Mahwah, NJ: Erlbaum.

Gladue, B. A., and Delaney, J. J. (1990). Gender differences in perception of attractiveness of men and women in bars. *Personality and Social Psychology Bulletin, 16*, 378–391.

Glass, S. P., and Wright, T. L. (1992). Justifications for extramarital relationships: The association between attitudes, behaviors, and gender. *Journal of Sex Research, 29*, 361–387.

Gleicher, F., Kost, K. A., Baker, S. M., Strathman, A. J., Richman, S. A., and Sherman, S. J. (1990). The role of counterfactual thinking in judgments of affect. *Personality and Social Psychology Bulletin, 16*, 284–295.

Godfrey, J. J. (1987). *A philosophy of hope*. Dordrecht, Netherlands: Nijhoff.

Gold, B. T. (1996). Enviousness and its relationship to maladjustment and psychopathology. *Personality and Individual Differences, 21*, 311–321.

Goleman, D. (1995). *Emotional intelligence.* New York: Bantam.

Goleman, D. (1998). *Working with emotional intelligence.* New York: Bantam.

Goodall, J. (1986). *The chimpanzees of Gombe: Patterns of behavior.* Cambridge, MA: Harvard University Press.

Goodman, R., and Ben-Ze'ev, A. (Eds.) (1994). *Good gossip.* Lawrence: University Press of Kansas.

Gordon, R. (1980). Fear. *Philosophical Review, 89*, 560–578.

Gordon, R. (1987). *The structure of emotions.* Cambridge: Cambridge University Press.

Gosling, J. (1962). Mental causes and fear. *Mind, 71*, 289–306.

Graham, S., and Weiner, B. (1986). From an attributional theory of emotion to developmental psychology: A round-trip ticket? *Social Cognition, 4*, 152–179.

Graham, S., Weiner, B., Giuliano, T., and Williams, E. (1993). An attributional analysis of reactions to Magic Johnson. *Journal of Applied Social Psychology, 23*, 996–1010.

Green, O. H. (1992). *The emotions.* Dordrecht, Netherlands: Kluwer.

Greenspan, P. S. (1980). A case of mixed feelings: Ambivalence and the logic of emotion. In A. O. Rorty (Ed.), *Explaining emotions.* Berkeley: University of California Press.

Greenspan, P. S. (1988). *Emotions and reasons.* New York: Routledge.

Greenspan, P. S. (1995). *Practical guilt: Moral dilemmas, emotions, and social norms.* Oxford: Oxford University Press.

Griffin, J. (1986). *Well-being.* Oxford: Clarendon Press.

Griffiths, P. E. (1997). *What emotions really are: The problem of psychological categories.* Chicago: University of Chicago Press.

Gross, J. J. (1998). The emerging field of emotion regulation: An integrative review. *Review of General Psychology, 2*, 271–299.

Gross, J. J., and Munoz, R. F. (1995). Emotional regulation and mental health. *Clinical Psychology: Science and Practice, 2*, 151–164.

Grunebaum, J. O. (1993). Friendship, morality, and special obligation. *American Philosophical Quarterly, 30*, 51–61.

Gustafson, D. (1989). Grief. *Nous, 23*, 457–479.

Hands, A. R. (1968). *Charities and social aid in Greece and Rome.* London: Thames & Hudson.

Hankinson, J. (1993). Action and passions: Affection, emotion, and moral self-management in Galen's philosophical psychology. In J. Brunschwig and M. C. Nussbaum (Eds.), *Passions and perceptions: Studies in Hellenistic philosophy of mind.* Cambridge: Cambridge University Press.

Hansen, G. L. (1991). Jealousy: Its conceptualization, measurement, and integration with family stress theory. In P. Salovey (Ed.), *The psychology of jealousy and envy.* New York: Guilford Press.

Harnad, S. (1987). *Categorical perception.* Cambridge: Cambridge University Press.

Harre, R. (1990). Embarrassment: A conceptual analysis. In R. Crozier (Ed.), *Shyness and embarrassment: Perspectives from social psychology.* Cambridge: Cambridge University Press.

Harrison, R. (1992). The quality of mercy. In H. Groos and R. Harrison (Eds.), *Jurisprudence: Cambridge essays.* Oxford: Clarendon Press.

Hart, H. L. A. (1973). *Punishment and responsibility.* Oxford: Clarendon Press.

Hartz, G. A. (1990). Desire and emotion in the virtue tradition. *Philosophia, 20*, 145–165.

Harvey, W. Z. (1992). A note on Schadenfreude and Proverbs 17:5. *Iyyun, 41*, 357–359.

Hastorf, A. H., and Cantril, H. (1954). They saw a game: A case study. *Journal of Abnormal and Social Psychology, 49*, 129–134.

Hatfield, E. (1988). Passionate and compassionate love. In R. S. Sternberg and M. L. Barnes (Eds.), *The psychology of love.* New Haven, CT: Yale University Press.

Hatfield, E., Cacioppo, J. T., and Rapson, R. L. (1994). *Emotional contagion.* New York: Cambridge University Press.

Heider, F. (1958). *The psychology of interpersonal relations.* New York: Wiley.

Heil, J. (1981). Does cognitive psychology rest on a mistake? *Mind, 90*, 321–342.

Heilman, S. C. (1973). *Synagogue life*. Chicago: University of Chicago.

Helm, B. W. (1994). The significance of emotions. *American Philosophical Quarterly, 31*, 319–331.

Hendrick, C., and Hendrick, S. S. (1988). Lovers wear rose-colored glasses. *Journal of Social and Personal Relationships, 5*, 161–183.

Herodotus, *The history*. Chicago: University of Chicago Press (1987).

Hess, U. (1998). The communication of emotion. Presented at the workshop on Emotions, Qualia and Consciousness, Ischia, Italy.

Heyd, D. (1991). *Genethics: Moral issues in the creation of people*. Berkeley: University of California Press.

Higgins, E. T. (1987). Self-discrepancy: A theory relating self and affect. *Psychological Review, 94*, 319–340.

Higgins, E. T. (1997). Beyond pleasure and pain. *American Psychologist, 52*, 1280–1300.

Hill, C. T., Rubin, Z., and Peplau, L. A. (1976). Breakups before marriage: The end of 103 affairs. *Journal of Social Issues, 32*, 147–168.

Hochschild, A. R. (1983). *The managed heart: Commercialization of human feeling*. Berkeley: University of California Press.

Hochschild, A. R. (1989). The economy of gratitude. In D. D. Franks. and E. D. McCarthy (Eds.), *The sociology of emotions*. New York: JAI Press.

Hofeldt, R. L. (1987). Cultural bias in "MASH." In A. A. Berger (Ed.), *Television in society*. New Brunswick, NJ: Transaction Books.

Hoffman, M. L. (1975). Sex differences in moral internalization and values. *Journal of Personality and Social Psychology, 32*, 720–729.

Hoffman, P. J., Festinger, L., and Lawrence, D. H. (1954). Tendencies toward group comparability in competitive bargaining. *Human Relations, 7*, 141–159.

Hoffmann, Y. (1980). *The idea of self—East and West*. Calcutta: Firma Klm Private.

Horder, J. (1992). *Provocation and responsibility*. Oxford: Clarendon Press.

Horton D. (1957). The dialogue of courtship in popular songs. *American Journal of Sociology, 62*, 569–578.

Hospers, J. (1972). *Human conduct: Problems of ethics*. New York: Harcourt Brace Jovanovich.

Hull, J. A. (1998). The puzzle of gender and smiling. Presented at the Tenth Meeting of the International Society for Research on Emotions. Würzburg, Germany.

Hume, D. (1739–1740). *A treatise of human nature*. Oxford: Clarendon (1978).

Hume, D. (1758). *An enquiry concerning human understanding*. Oxford: Clarendon (1975).

Hunter, J. F. M. (1983). *Thinking about sex and love*. New York: St. Martin's Press.

Hupka, R. B. (1991). The motive for the arousal of romantic jealousy: Its cultural origin. In P. Salovey (Ed.), *The psychology of jealousy and envy*. New York: Guilford Press.

Hursthouse, R. (1997). Virtue ethics and the emotions. In D. Statman (Ed.), *Virtue ethics*. Washington, DC: Georgetown University Press.

Illouz, E. (1997). *Consuming the romantic utopia: Love and the cultural contradictions of capitalism*. Berkeley: University of California Press.

Isen, A. M., Shalker, T. E., Clark, M., and Karp, L. (1978). Affect, accessibility of material in memory, and behavior: A cognitive loop? *Journal of Personality and Social Psychology, 36*, 1–12.

Izard, C. E. (1991). *The psychology of emotions*. New York: Plenum Press.

Isenberg, A. (1949). Natural pride and natural shame. *Philosophy and Phenomenological Research, 10*, 1–24.

Jackall, R. (1988). *Moral mazes*. New York: Oxford University Press.

Jackson, D. J., and Huston, T. L. (1975). Physical attractiveness and assertiveness. *Journal of Social Psychology, 96*, 79–84.

Jaeger, M. E., Skleder, A. A., Rind, B., and Rosnow, R. L. (1994). Gossip, gossipers, gossipees. In R. Goodman and A. Ben-Ze'ev (Eds), *Good gossip*. Lawrence: University Press of Kansas.

Jaffee, B., and Fanshel, D. (1970). *How they fared in adoption: A follow-up study*. New York: Columbia University Press.

James, S. (1997). *Passion and action: The emotions in seventeenth-century philosophy*. Oxford: Clarendon Press.

Janoff-Bulman, R., and Frieze, I. H. (1983). A theoretical perspective for understanding reactions to victimization. *Journal of Social Issues, 39*, 1–17.

Jauregui, J. A. (1995). *The emotional computer.* Oxford: Blackwell.

Jeske, D. (1997). Friendship, virtue, and impartiality. *Philosophy and Phenomenological Research, 57*, 51–72.

Johnson-Laird, P. N., and Oatley, K. (1992). Basic emotions, rationality, and folk theory. *Cognition and Emotion, 6*, 201–223.

Josephs, R. A., Markus, H. R., and Tafarodi, R. W. (1992). Gender and self-esteem. *Journal of Personality and Social Psychology, 63*, 391–402.

Kagan, J. (1992). Temperamental contributions to emotion and social behavior. *Review of Personality and Social Psychology, 14*, 99–118.

Kahneman, D. (1973). *Attention and effort.* Englewood Cliffs, NJ: Prentice-Hall.

Kahneman, D. (1995). Varieties of counterfactual thinking. In N. J. Roese and J. M. Olson (Eds.), *What might have been: The social psychology of counterfactual thinking.* Mahwah, NJ: Erlbaum.

Kahneman, D., and Miller, D. T. (1986). Norm theory: Comparing reality to its alternatives. *Psychological Review, 93*, 136–153.

Kahneman, D., and Tversky, A. (1979). Prospect theory: An analysis of decision under risk. *Econometrica, 47*, 263–291.

Kahneman, D., and Tversky, A. (1982). The simulation heuristic. In D. Kahneman, P. Slovic and A. Tversky (Eds.), *Judgment under uncertainty: Heuristics and biases.* Cambridge: Cambridge University Press.

Kahneman, D., and Varey, C.A. (1990). Propensities and counterfactuals: The loser that almost won. *Journal of Personality and Social Psychology, 59*, 1101–1110.

Kalmijn, M. (1991). Status homogamy in the United States. *American Journal of Sociology, 97*, 496–523.

Kant, I. (1785). *Groundwork of the metaphysics of morals.* Cambridge: Cambridge University Press (1998).

Kant, I. (1797). The doctrine of virtue. In *Metaphysics of morals.* Philadelphia: University of Pennsylvania Press (1964).

Kant, I. (1924). *Lectures on ethics.* New York: Harper (1963).

Kant, I. (1798). *Anthropology from a pragmatic point of view.* The Hague: Nijoff (1974).

Karasawa, K. (1995). An attributional analysis of reactions to negative emotions. *Personality and Social Psychology Bulletin, 21*, 456–467.

Kasimatis, M., and Wells, G. L. (1995). Individual differences in counterfactual thinking. In N. J. Roese and J. M. Olson (Eds.), *What might have been: The social psychology of counterfactual thinking.* Mahwah, NJ: Erlbaum.

Kemp Smith, N. (1957). Fear: Its nature and diverse uses. *Philosophy, 32*, 3–20.

Kenny, A. (1963). *Action, emotion and will.* London: Routledge & Kegan Paul.

Kenrick, D. T., Gutierres, S. E., and Goldberg, L. (1989). Influence of erotica on ratings of strangers and mates. *Journal of Experimental Social Psychology, 25*, 159–167.

Kephart, W. (1967). Some correlates of romantic love. *Journal of Marriage and the Family, 29*, 470–474.

Kinder, M. (1995). *Mastering your moods.* New York: Simon & Schuster.

Koch, P. J. (1987). Emotional ambivalence. *Philosophy and Phenomenological Research, 48*, 257–279.

Kohn, A. (1986). *No contest: The case against competition.* Boston: Houghton Mifflin.

Koriat, A., Melkman, R., Averill, J. R., and Lazarus, R. S. (1972). The self-control of emotional reactions to a stressful film. *Journal of Personality, 40*, 601–619.

Kovecses, Z. (1990). *Emotion concepts.* New York: Springer-Verlag.

Kraut, R., Patterson, M., Lundmark, V., Kiesler, S., Mukopadhyay, T., and Scherlies, W. (1998). Internet paradox: A social technology that reduces social involvement and psychological well-being? *American Psychologist, 53*, 1017–1031.

Kristjansson, K. (1996). Why persons need jealousy. *Personalist Forum, 12*, 163–181.

Kristjansson, K. (forthcoming). *Justifying emotions: Pridefulness and jealousy.*

Kubey, R., and Csikszentmihalyi, M. (1990). *Television and the quality of life: How viewing shapes everyday experience.* Hillsdale, NJ: Erlbaum.

Kulik, J. A., and Brown, R. (1979). Frustration, attribution of blame, and aggression. *Journal of Experimental Social Psychology*, *15*, 183–194.

Kunda, G. (1992). *Engineering culture*. Philadelphia: Temple University Press.

Kvart, I. (1986). *A theory of counterfactuals*. Indianapolis: Hackett.

LaFollette, H. (1996). *Personal relationships: Love, identity, and morality*. Oxford: Blackwell.

LaFrance, M., and Banaji, M. (1992). Toward a reconsideration of the gender-emotion relationship. *Review of Personality and Social Psychology*, *14*, 178–201.

Laird, J. D., and Bresler, C. (1992). The process of emotional experience: A self-perception theory. *Review of Personality and Social Psychology*, *13*, 213–234.

Lakoff, G. (1987). *Women, fire, and dangerous things*. Chicago: University of Chicago Press.

Landau, I. (1995). The paradox of the end. *Philosophy*, *70*: 555–565.

Landman, J. (1993). *Regret: The persistence of the possible*. New York: Oxford University Press.

Landman, J. (1995). Through a glass darkly: Worldviews, counterfactual thought, and emotion. In N. J. Roese and J. M. Olson (Eds.), *What might have been: The social psychology of counterfactual thinking*. Mahwah, NJ: Erlbaum.

Langer, E. J. (1989). *Mindfulness*. Reading, MA: Addison-Wesley.

Langlois, J. H., Roggman, L. A., and Reiser-Danner, L. A. (1990). Infants' differential social responses to attractive and unattractive faces. *Developmental Psychology*, *26*, 153–159.

Langlois, J. H., Ritter, J. M., Casey, R. J., and Sawin, D. B. (1995). Infant attractiveness predicts maternal behaviors and attitudes. *Developmental Psychology*, *31*, 464–472.

Larsen, R. J. (1987). The stability of mood variability: A spectral analytic approach to daily mood assessments. *Journal of Personality and Social Psychology*, *52*, 1195–1204.

Larsen, R. J., and Diener, E. (1985). A multitrait-multimethod examination of affect structure: Hedonic level and emotional intensity. *Personality and Individual Differences*, *6*, 631–636.

Larsen, R. J., and Diener, E. (1987). Affect intensity as an individual difference characteristic: A review. *Journal of Research in Personality*, *21*, 1–39.

Larsen, R. J., Diener, E., and Cropanzano, R. S. (1987). Cognitive operations associated with individual differences in affect intensity. *Journal of Personality and Social Psychology*, *53*, 767–774.

Lauritzen, P. (1991). Errors of an ill-reasoning reason: The disparagement of emotions in the moral life. *Journal of Value Inquiry*, *25*, 5–21.

Law, A., Logan, H., and Baron, R. S. (1994). Desire for control, felt control, and stress inoculation training during dental treatment. *Journal of Personality and Social Psychology*, *67*, 926–936.

Lawson, A. (1988). *Adultery: An analysis of love and betrayal*. New York: Basic Books.

Lawson, E. D. (1971). Hair colour, personality and the observer. *Psychological Report*, *28*, 311–322.

Lazarus, R. S. (1991). *Emotion and adaptation*. New York: Oxford University Press.

Lazarus, R. S., and Lazarus, B. N. (1994). *Passion and reason: Making sense of our emotions*. New York: Oxford University Press.

Lazarus, R. S., and Smith, C. A. (1988). Knowledge and appraisal in the cognition-emotion relationship. *Cognition and Emotion*, *2*, 281–300.

LeDoux, J. (1996). *The emotional brain*. New York: Simon & Schuster.

Leeper, R. W. (1948). A motivational theory of emotion to replace "emotion as disorganized response." In M. B. Arnold (Ed.), *The nature of emotion*. Harmondsworth: Penguin (1968).

Leighton, S. R. (1985). *The concept of emotion*. Doctoral dissertation. Ann Arbor, MI: University Microfilms International.

Lemerise, E. A., and Dodge, K. A. (1993). The development of anger and hostile interactions. In M. Lewis and J. M. Haviland (Eds.), *Handbook of emotions*. New York: Guilford Press.

Lerner, R. M., and Brackney, B. E. (1978). The importance of inner and outer body parts attitudes in the self-concept of late adolescents. *Sex Role*, *4*, 225–238.

Levenson, R. W., Ekman, P., and Friesen, W. V. (1990). Voluntary facial expression generates emotion-specific nervous system activity. *Psychophysiology*, *27*, 363–384.

Leventhal, H., and Scherer, K. R. (1987). The relationship of emotion to cognition: A functional approach to a semantic controversy. *Cognition and Emotion, 1*, 3–28.

Levin, J., and Arluke, A. (1987). *Gossip: The inside scoop*. New York: Plenum.

Lewin, K. (1948). *Resolving social conflicts*. New York: Harper.

Lewin, K., Dembo, T., Festinger, L., and Sears, P. S. (1944). Level of aspiration. In J. M. Hunt (Ed.), *Personality and the behavior disorders* (Vol. 1, pp. 333–378). New York: Ronald.

Lewis, C. I. (1929). *Mind and the world order*. New York: Dover (1956).

Lewis, C. I. (1946). *An analysis of knowledge and valuation*. La Salle IL: Open Court (1971).

Lewis, M. (1992). *Shame*. New York: Free Press.

Lewis, M. (1993). The emergence of human emotions. In M. Lewis and J. M. Haviland (Eds.), *Handbook of emotions*. New York: Guilford Press.

Lewis, M. D. (1995). Cognition-emotion feedback and the self-organization of developmental paths. *Human Development, 38*, 71–102.

Lormand, E. (1985). Toward a theory of moods. *Philosophical Studies, 47*, 385–407.

Lykken, D., and Tellegen, A. (1996). Happiness is a stochastic phenomenon. *Psychological Science, 7*, 186–189.

Lyons, W. (1980). *Emotion*. Cambridge: Cambridge University Press.

Lyons, W. (1992). An introduction to the philosophy of the emotions. *International Review of Studies on Emotion, 2*, 295–313.

Lyubomirsky, S., and Nolen-Hoeksema, S. (1993). Self-perpetuating properties of dysphoric rumination. *Journal of Personality and Social Psychology, 65*, 339–349.

MacLean, P. D. (1980). Sensory and perceptive factors in emotional functions of the triune brain. In A. O. Rorty (Ed.), *Explaining emotions*. Berkeley: University of California Press.

Malamuth, N. M., and Brown, L. M. (1994). Sexually aggressive men's perceptions of women's communications: Testing three explanations. *Journal of Personality and Social Psychology, 67*, 669–712.

Malebranche, N. (1675). *The search after truth*. Columbus: Ohio State University Press (1980).

Margolin, L. (1989). Gender and the prerogatives of dating and marriage. *Sex Role, 20*, 91–102.

Marks, N. F. (1996). Flying solo at midlife: Gender, marital status, and psychological well-being. *Journal of Marriage and the Family, 58*, 917–932.

Martin, J. (1990). *Miss Manners' guide for the turn-of-the-millennium*. New York: Fireside.

Martin, M. W. (1986). *Self-deception and morality*. Lawrence: University Press of Kansas.

Martin, M. W. (1996). *Love's virtues*. Lawrence: University Press of Kansas.

Masson, J. M., and McCarthy, S. (1995). *When elephants weep*. New York: Delacorte.

Masters, J. C. (1991). Strategies and mechanisms for the personal and social control of emotion. In J. Garber and K. A. Dodge (Eds.), *The development of emotion regulation and disregulation*. Cambridge: Cambridge University Press.

Mathes, E. W. (1991). A cognitive theory of jealousy. In P. Salovey (Ed.), *The psychology of jealousy and envy*. New York: Guilford Press.

Mayer, J. D., and Salovey, P. (1995). Emotional intelligence and the construction and regulation of feelings. *Applied and Preventive Psychology, 4*, 197–208.

Mayer, J. D., and Salovey, P. (1997). What is emotional intelligence? In P. Salovey and D. Sluyter (Eds.), *Emotional development and emotional intelligence: Implications for educators*. New York: Basic Books.

McCornack, S. A., and Levine, T. R. (1990). When lies are uncovered: Emotional and relational outcomes of discovered deception. *Communication Monographs, 57*, 119–138.

McCosh, J. (1880). *The emotions*. New York: Charles Scribner's Sons.

McDougall, W. (1935). *The energies of men*. London: Methuen.

McGill, A. L. (1989). Context effects in judgments of causation. *Journal of Personality and Social Psychology, 57*, 189–200.

McGraw, J. G. (1995). Loneliness, its nature and forms: An existential perspective. *Man and World, 28*, 43–64.

McGraw, K. M. (1987). Guilt following transgression: An attribution of responsibility approach. *Journal of Personality and Social Psychology, 53*, 247–256.

McIntosh, W. D., and Martin, L. L. (1992). The cybernetics of happiness: The relation of goal attainment, rumination, and affect. *Review of Personality and Social Psychology, 14*, 222–246.

McKeachie, W. J. (1952). Lipstick as a determiner of first impressions of personality. *Journal of Social Psychology, 36*, 241–244.

McMullen, M. N., Markman, K., and Gavanski, I. (1995). Living in neither the best nor worst of all possible worlds: Antecedents and consequences of upward and downward counterfactual thinking. In N. J. Roese and J. M. Olson (Eds.), *What might have been: The social psychology of counterfactual thinking*. Mahwah. NJ: Erlbaum.

Medvec, V. H., Madey, S. F., and Gilovich, T. (1995). When less is more: Counterfactual thinking and satisfaction among Olympic medalists. *Journal of Personality and Social Psychology, 69*, 603–610.

Melzack, R. (1973). *The puzzle of pain*. New York: Basic Books.

Metts, S., Sprecher, S., and Regan, P. C. (1998). Communication and sexual drive. In P. A. Andersen and L. K. Guerrero (Eds.), *Handbook of communication and emotion*. San Diego: Academic Press.

Michael, R. T., Gagnon, J. H., Laumann, E. D., and Kolata, G. (1994). *Sex in America*. Boston: Little, Brown.

Miles, M. S., and Demi, S. A. (1983–1984). Toward the development of a theory of bereavement guilt: Sources of guilt in bereaved parents. *Omega, 14*, 299–314.

Miles, M. S., and Demi, S. A. (1991–1992). A comparison of guilt in bereaved parents whose children died by suicide, accident, or chronic disease. *Omega, 24*, 201–215.

Millar, K. U., and Millar, M. G. (1988). Sex differences in perceived self- and other-disclosure: A case where inequity increases satisfaction. *Social Behavior and Personality, 16*, 59–64.

Miller, D. T., and Gunasegaram, S. (1990). Temporal order and the perceived mutability of events: Implications for blame assignment. *Journal of Personality and Social Psychology, 59*, 1111–1118.

Miller, R. S. (1986). Embarrassment: Causes and consequences. In W. H. Jones, J. M. Cheek and S. R. Briggs (Eds.), *Shyness: Perspectives on research and treatment*. New York: Plenum.

Miller, W. I. (1993). *Humiliation*. Ithaca, NY: Cornell University Press.

Miller, W. I. (1997). *The anatomy of disgust*. Cambridge, MA: Harvard University Press.

Minsky, M. (1985). *The society of mind*. New York: Simon & Schuster.

Montaigne, M. de (1991). *The complete essays*. Harmondsworth: Penguin.

Montaldi, D. (1991). *Envy*. Unpublished manuscript.

Moore, M. M., and Butler, D. L. (1989). Predictive aspects of nonverbal courtship behavior in women. *Semiotica, 76*, 205–215.

Morreall, J. (1983). Humor and emotion. *American Philosophical Quarterly, 20*, 297–304.

Morris, W. N. (1992). A functional analysis of the role of mood in affective systems. *Review of Personality and Social Psychology, 13*, 256–293.

Moyers, B. (1993). *Healing and the mind*. New York: Doubleday.

Murphy, J. G., and Hampton, J. (1988). *Forgiveness and mercy*. Cambridge: Cambridge University Press.

Nagel, T. (1979). Moral luck. In *Mortal questions*. New York: Cambridge University Press.

Nathanson, S. (1989). In defense of "moderate patriotism." *Ethics, 99*, 535–552.

Neill, A. (1993). Fiction and the emotions. *American Philosophical Quarterly, 30*, 1–13.

Netanyahu, B. (1995). *The origins of the Inquisition*. New York: Random House.

Neu, J. (1980). Jealous thoughts. In A. O. Rorty (Ed.), *Explaining emotions*. Berkeley: University of California Press.

Neu, J. (1996). Odi et amo: On hating the ones we love. In J. O'Neill (Ed.), *Freud and the passions*. University Park: Pennsylvania State University Press.

Neumark, D., and Postlewaite, A. (1998). Relative income concerns and the rise in married women's employment. *Journal of Public Economics, 70*, 153–183.

Nicholson, P. P. (1985). Toleration as a moral ideal. In J. Horton and S. Mendus (Eds.), *Aspects of toleration*. London: Methuen.

Niedenthal, P. M., Tangney, J. P., and Gavanski, I. (1994). "If only I weren't" versus "If only I hadn't": Distinguishing shame and guilt in counterfactual thinking. *Journal of Personality and Social Psychology, 67,* 585–595.

Nissenbaum, H. F. (1985). *Emotion and focus.* Stanford, CA: Center for the Study of Language and Information.

Nolen-Hoeksema, S. (1987). Sex differences in unipolar depression: Evidence and theory. *Psychological Bulletin, 101,* 259–282.

Nolen-Hoeksema, S., and Morrow, J. (1993). Effects of rumination and distraction on naturally occurring depressed mood. *Cognition and Emotion, 7,* 561–570.

Nozick, R. (1974). *Anarchy, state, and utopia.* New York: Basic Books.

Nozick, R. (1991). Love's bond. In R. C. Solomon and K. M. Higgins (Eds.), *The philosophy of (erotic) love.* Lawrence: University Press of Kansas.

Nussbaum, M. C. (1986). *The fragility of goodness: Luck and ethics in Greek tragedy and philosophy.* Cambridge: Cambridge University Press.

Nussbaum, M. C. (1993). Poetry and the passions: Two Stoic views. In J. Brunschwig and M. C. Nussbaum (Eds.), *Passions and perceptions: Studies in Hellenistic philosophy of mind.* Cambridge: Cambridge University Press.

Nussbaum, M. C. (1999a). Constructing love, desire, and care. In M. C. Nussbaum, *Sex and social justice.* New York: Oxford University Press.

Nussbaum, M. C. (1999b). Equity and mercy. In M. C. Nussbaum, *Sex and social justice.* New York: Oxford University Press.

Nussbaum, M. C. (forthcoming). *Upheavals of thought: A theory of the emotions.* Cambridge: Cambridge University Press.

Oakley, J. (1991). *Morality and the emotions.* London: Routledge.

Oatley, K. (1992). *Best laid schemes: The psychology of emotions.* Cambridge: Cambridge University Press.

Oatley, K., and Duncan, E. (1992). Incidents of emotion in daily life. *International Review of Studies on Emotion, 2,* 249–293.

Oatley, K., and Jenkins, J. M. (1992). Human emotions: Function and dysfunction. *Annual Review of Psychology, 43,* 55–85.

Oatley, K., and Jenkins, J. M. (1996). *Understanding emotions.* Cambridge, MA: Blackwell.

Oatley, K., and Johnson-Laird, P. N. (1987). Towards a cognitive theory of emotions. *Cognition and Emotions, 1,* 29–50.

Oatley, K., and Larocque, L. (1995). Everyday concepts of emotions following every-other-day errors in joint plans. In J. Russell and J. Fernandez-Dols (Eds.), *Everyday conceptions of emotions.* Dordrecht, Netherlands: Kluwer.

Ogden, G. (1994). *Women who love sex.* New York: Pocket Books.

Olds, J., and Milner, P. (1954). Positive reinforcement produced by electrical stimulation of the septal area and other regions of the rat brain. *Journal of Comparative and Physiological Psychology, 47,* 419–428.

Ortony, A., and Turner, T. J. (1990). What's basic about basic emotions? *Psychological Review, 74,* 431–461.

Ortony, A., Clore, G. L., and Collings, A. (1988). *The cognitive structure of emotions.* Cambridge: Cambridge University Press.

Ortega y Gasset, J. (1941). *On love . . . Aspects of a single theme.* London: Jonathan Cape (1967).

Ozick, C. (1983). *Art and order.* New York: Knopf.

Panksepp, J. (1998). *Affective neuroscience: The foundations of human and animal emotions.* New York: Oxford University Press.

Parducci, A. (1984). Value judgments: Toward a relational theory of happiness. In J. R. Eiser (Ed.), *Attitudinal judgment.* New York: Springer-Verlag.

Park, C., Cohen, L. H., and Herb, L. (1990). Intrinsic religiousness and religious coping as life stress moderators for Catholics versus Protestants. *Journal of Personality and Social Psychology, 59,* 562–574.

Parkinson, B. (1995). *Ideas and realities of emotion.* London: Routledge.

Parkinson, B., and Manstead, A. S. R. (1992). Appraisal as a cause of emotion. *Review of Personality and Social Psychology, 13,* 122–149.

Parnas, J. (1996). Phenomenology of self-experience in early schizophrenia. Presented at the Fifth Conference of the European Society for Philosophy and Psychology, Barcelona, Spain, 1996.

Parrott, W. G. (1991). The emotional experience of envy and jealousy. In P. Salovey (Ed.), *The psychology of jealousy and envy*. New York: Guilford Press.

Parrott, W. G. (1995). The heart and the head. In J. A. Russell, J.M. Fernandez-Dols, A. S. R. Manstead, and J. C. Wellenkamp (Eds.), *Everyday conceptions of emotion*. Dordrecht, Netherlands: Kluwer.

Parrott, W. G., and Smith, R. H. (1993). Distinguishing the experience of envy and jealousy. *Journal of Personality and Social Psychology, 64*, 906–920.

Paul, S. (1991). An index of relative deprivation. *Economics Letters, 3*, 337–341.

Pavelchak, M. A., Antil, J. H., and Munch, J. M. (1988). The Super Bowl: An investigation into the relationship among program context, emotional experience, and ad recall. *Journal of Consumer Research, 15*, 360–367.

Peale, N. V. (1952). *The power of positive thinking*. New York: Prentice-Hall.

Peele, S. (1988). Fools for love: The romantic ideal, psychological theory, and addictive love. In R. J. Sternberg and M. L. Barnes (Eds.), *The psychology of love*. New Haven, CT: Yale University Press.

Person, E. S. (1990). *Love and fateful encounters*. London: Bloomsbury.

Pervin, L. A. (1993). Affect and personality. In M. Lewis and J. M. Haviland (Eds.), *Handbook of emotions*. New York: Guilford Press.

Phares, E. J. (1976). *Locus of control in personality*. Morristown, NJ: General Learning Press.

Picard, R. W. (1997). *Affective computing*. Cambridge, MA: MIT Press.

Pitcher, G. (1965). Emotion. *Mind, 74*, 326–345.

Plato, *The collected dialogues of Plato*. Edited by E. Hamilton and H. Cairns. Princeton, NJ: Princeton University Press (1963).

Plutarch, On envy and hate. In *Plutarch's Moralia, VII*. Cambridge, MA: Harvard University Press (1959).

Plutchik, R. (1991). Emotions and evolution. *International Review of Studies on Emotion, 1*, 37–58.

Pojman, L. P., and McLeod, O. (1999). *What do we deserve? A reader on justice and desert*. New York: Oxford University Press.

Portmann, J. (1999). *When bad things happen to other people*. London: Routledge.

Prentice, D. A., and Crosby, F. (1987). The importance of context for assessing deservingness. In J. C. Masters and W. P. Smith (Eds.), *Social comparison, social justice, and relative deprivation*. Hillsdale, NJ: Erlbaum.

Prins, K. S., Buunk, B. P., and VanYperen, N. W. (1993). Equity, normative disapproval and extramarital relationships. *Journal of Social and Personal Relationships, 10*, 39–53.

Pugmire, D. (1998). *Rediscovering emotion*. Edinburgh: Edinburgh University Press.

Quine, W. V. O. (1964). On what there is. In *From a logical point of view*. Cambridge, MA: Harvard University Press.

Rachels, J. (1989). Morality, parents, and children. In G. Graham and H. LaFollette (Eds.), *Person to person*. Philadelphia: Temple University Press.

Rachman, S. (1990). *Fear and courage*. New York: Freeman.

Railton, I. P. (1984). Alienation, consequentialism and the demands of morality. *Philosophy and Public Affairs, 13*, 134–171.

Rainbolt, G. W. (1990). Mercy: An independent, imperfect virtue. *American Philosophical Quarterly, 27*, 169–173.

Ranulf, S. (1938). *Moral indignation and middle class psychology*. Copenhagen: Levin & Munksgaard.

Rawls, J. (1971). *A theory of justice*. Oxford: Oxford University Press.

Reid, T. (1788). *Essays on the active powers of man*. In *Philosophical Works*. Edited by W. Hamilton. Hildesheim, Germany: Georg Olms (1967).

Reisenzein, R. (1992). A structuralist reconstruction of Wundt's three-dimensional theory of emotion. In H. Westmeyer (Ed.), *The structuralist program in psychology: Foundations and applications*. Toronto: Hogrefe & Huber.

Reisenzein, R. (1994). Pleasure-arousal theory and the intensity of emotions. *Journal of Personality and Social Psychology, 67*, 525–539.

Reisenzein, R. (1995). On appraisals as causes of emotions. *Psychological Inquiry, 6*, 233–237.

Reisenzein, R. (1996). Emotional action generation. In W. Battmann and S. Dutke (Eds.), *Processes of the molar regulation of behavior*. Lengerich, Germany: Pabst Science.

Reisenzein, R., and Schonpflug, W. (1992). Stumpf's cognitive evaluative theory of emotion. *American Psychologist, 47*, 34–45.

Rescher, N. (1993). Moral luck. In D. Statman (Ed.), *Moral luck*. Albany, NY: SUNY Press.

Richards, N. (1992). *Humility*. Philadelphia: Temple University Press.

Robins, P. R., and Tanck, R. H. (1991). Gender differences in the attribution of causes for depressed feeling. *Psychological Report, 68*, 1209–1210.

Roese, N. J., and Olson, J. M. (1995b). Counterfactual thinking: A critical overview. In N. J. Roese and J. M. Olson (Eds.), *What might have been: The social psychology of counterfactual thinking*. Mahwah, NJ: Erlbaum.

Rolls, E. T. (1999). *The brain and emotion*. Oxford: Oxford University Press.

Rorty, A. O. (1978). Explaining emotions. In A. O. Rorty (Ed.), *Explaining emotions*. Berkeley: University of California Press (1980); and in A. O. Rorty, *Mind in action: Essays in the philosophy of mind*. Boston: Beacon Press (1988).

Rorty, A. O. (Tov-Rauch, L.) (1980). Jealousy, attention and loss. In A. O. Rorty (Ed.), *Explaining emotions*. Berkeley: University of California Press (1980); and in A. O. Rorty, *Mind in action: Essays in the philosophy of love* (1988). Boston: Beacon Press.

Rorty, A. O. (1983). Fearing death. In A. O. Rorty, *Mind in action: Essays in the philosophy of mind*. Boston: Beacon Press (1988).

Rorty, A. O. (1986). The historicity of psychological attitudes: Love is not love which alters when it alteration finds. In A. O. Rorty, *Mind in action: Essays in the philosophy of love*. Boston: Beacon Press (1988).

Rorty, A. O. (1988). Unconscious affects, mourning, and the erotic mind. In A. O. Rorty, *Mind in action: Essays in the philosophy of mind*. Boston: Beacon Press (1988).

Rosch, E. (1977). Human categorization. In N. Warren (Ed.), *Advance in cross-cultural psychology*. London: Academic Press.

Rosch, E. (1978). Principles of categorization. In E. Rosch and B. B. Lloyd (Eds.), *Cognition and categorization*. Hillsdale, NJ: Erlbaum.

Roseman, I. J. (1991). Appraisal determinants of discrete emotions. *Cognition and Emotion, 5*, 161–200.

Roseman, I. J., Spindel, M. S., and Jose, P. E. (1990). Appraisals of emotion-eliciting events: Testing a theory of discrete emotions. *Journal of Personality and Social Psychology, 39*, 899–915.

Roseman, I. J., Antoniou, A. A., and Jose, P. E. (1996). Appraisal determinants of emotions: Constructing a more accurate and comprehensive theory. *Cognition and Emotion, 10*, 241–277.

Rosenberg, E. L. (1998). Levels of analysis and the organization of affect. *Review of General Psychology, 2*, 247–270.

Rosenwein, B. H. (1998). *Anger's past: The social uses of an emotion in the Middle Ages*. Ithaca: Cornell University Press.

Ross, E. D. (1984). The right hemisphere's role in language, affective behavior and emotion. *Trends in Neuroscience, 7*, 342–346.

Rousseau, J. J. (1762). *Emile: or, On education*. New York: Basic Books (1979).

Rozin, P., Haidt, J., and McCauley, C. R. (1993). Disgust. In M. Lewis and J. M. Haviland (Eds.), *Handbook of emotions*. New York: Guilford Press.

Rubin, S. (1993). The death of a child is forever: The life course impact of child loss. In M. S. Stroebe, W. Stroebe and R. O. Hansson (Eds.), *Handbook of bereavement*. Cambridge: Cambridge University Press.

Rubin, Z. (1970). Measurement of romantic love. *Journal of Personality and Social Psychology, 16*, 265–273.

Rushton, J. P. (1989). Genetic similarity, human altruism, and group selection. *Behavioral and Brain Sciences, 12,* 503–559.

Russell, J. A. (1991). In defense of a prototype approach to emotion concepts. *Journal of Personality and Social Psychology, 60,* 37–47.

Russell, P. (1995). *Freedom and moral sentiment.* New York: Oxford University Press.

Ryle, G. (1949). *The concept of mind.* London: Hutchinson.

Salovey, P., and Mayer, J. D. (1990). Emotional intelligence. *Imagination, Cognition and Personality, 9,* 185–211.

Salovey, P., and Rodin, J. (1989). Envy and jealousy in close relationships. In C. Hendrick (Ed.), *Close relationships.* Newbury Park, California: Sage.

Salovey, P., and Rothman, A. J. (1991). Envy and jealousy: Self and society. In P. Salovey (Ed.), *The psychology of jealousy and envy.* New York: Guilford Press.

Sankowski, E. (1977). Responsibility of persons for their emotions. *Canadian Journal of Philosophy, 7,* 829–840.

Sartre, J. P. (1956). *Being and nothingness.* New York: Philosophical Library.

Sattler, J. M. (1965). A theoretical, developmental, and clinical investigation of embarrassment. *Genetic Psychology Monographs, 71,* 19–59.

Schachtel, E. (1959). *Metamorphosis.* New York: Basic Books.

Scheffler, I. (1991). *In praise of the cognitive emotions.* New York: Routledge.

Scheler, M. (1912). *Ressentiment.* New York: Schocken Books (1972).

Scheler, M. (1967). Towards a stratification of the emotional life. In N. Lawrence and D. O'Connor (Eds.), *Readings in existential phenomenology.* Englewood Cliffs, NJ: Prentice-Hall.

Scheler, M. (1974). On the meaning of suffering. In M. S. Frings (Ed.), *Max Scheler: Centennial essays.* The Hague: Nijhoff.

Schelling, T. C. (1984). *Choice and consequence.* Cambridge, MA.: Harvard University Press.

Scherer, K. R. (1982). Emotion as process: Function, origin and regulation. *Social Science Information, 21,* 555–570.

Scherer, K. R. (1984). On the nature and function of emotion: A component process approach. In K. R. Scherer and P. Ekman (Eds.), *Approaches to emotion.* Hillsdale, NJ: Erlbaum.

Scherer, K. R. (1988). Criteria for emotion-antecedent appraisal: A review. In V. Hamilton, G. H. Bower, and N. H. Frijda (Eds.), *Cognitive perspectives on emotion and motivation.* Dordrecht: Kluwer.

Scherer, K. R., Walbott, H. G., and Summerfield, A. B. (1986). *Experiencing emotions: A cross-cultural study.* Cambridge: Cambridge University Press.

Schoeck, H. (1970). *Envy.* New York: Harcourt.

Schopenhauer, A. (1840). *On the basis of morality.* Indianapolis: Bobbs-Merrill (1965).

Schopenhauer, A. (1844). *The world as will and representation.* New York: Dover (1969).

Schulman, P. (1995). Explanatory style and achievement in school and work. In G. Buchanan and M. Seligman (Eds.), *Explanatory style.* Hillsdale, NJ: Erlbaum.

Scitovsky, T. (1976). *The joyless economy.* New York: Oxford University Press.

Scott, R. (1972). Avarice, altruism and second party preferences. *Quarterly Journal of Economics, 86,* 1–18.

Scruton, R. (1980). Emotion, practical knowledge and common culture. In A. O. Rorty (Ed.), *Explaining emotions.* Berkeley: University of California Press.

Seelau, E. P., Seelau, S. M., Wells, G. L., and Windschitl, P. D. (1995). Counterfactual constraints. In N. J. Roese and J. M. Olson (Eds.), *What might have been: The social psychology of counterfactual thinking.* Mahwah, NJ: Erlbaum.

Segrin, C. (1998). Interpersonal communication problems associated with depression and loneliness. In P. A. Andersen and L. K. Guerrero (Eds.), *Handbook of communication and emotion.* San Diego: Academic Press.

Seligman, M. E. (1975). *Helplessness.* New York: Freeman.

Shakespeare, W. (1984). *Romeo and Juliet.* London: Cambridge University Press.

Shames, L. (1989). *The hunger for more: Searching for values in an age of greed.* New York: Times Books.

584    References

Shaver, P., Schwartz, J. C., Kirson, D., and O'Connor, C. (1987). Emotion knowledge: Further exploration of a prototype approach. *Journal of Personality and Social Psychology, 52*, 1061–1086.

Shaver, P., Hazan, C., and Bradshaw, D. (1988). Love as attachment: The integration of three behavior systems. In R. J. Sternberg and M. L. Barnes (Eds.), *The psychology of love*. New Haven, CT: Yale University Press.

Shaver, P., Wu, S., and Schwartz, J. C. (1992). Cross-cultural similarities and differences in emotion and its representation. *Review of Personality and Social Psychology, 13*, 175–212.

Shaw, L. L., Batson, C. D., and Todd, R. M. (1994). Empathy avoidance: Forestalling feeling for another in order to escape the motivational consequences. *Journal of Personality and Social Psychology, 67*, 879–887.

Shepher, J. (1971). Mate selection among second generation Kibbutz adolescents and adults: Incest avoidance and negative imprinting. *Archives of Sexual Behavior, 1*, 293–307.

Sher, G. (1987). *Desert*. Princeton, NJ: Princeton University Press.

Sher, G. (1997). *Beyond neutrality: Perfectionism and politics*. Cambridge: Cambridge University Press.

Sherif, M., and Sherif, C. W. (1964). *Reference groups*. New York: Harper & Row.

Sherman, N. (1990). The place of emotions in Kantian morality. In O. Flanagan and A. O. Rorty (Eds.), *Identity, character, and morality*. Cambridge, MA.: MIT Press.

Sherman, N. (1994). The role of emotions in Aristotelian virtue. *Proceedings of the Boston Area Colloquium in Ancient Philosophy, 9*, 1–33.

Sherman, N. (1995). The emotions. In W. Reich (Ed.), *Encyclopedia of bioethics* (pp. 664–671). New York: Macmillan.

Sherman, N. (1997). *Making a necessity of virtue: Aristotle and Kant on virtue*. Cambridge: Cambridge University Press.

Shimanoff, S. B. (1985). Rules governing the verbal expression of emotions between married couples. *Western Journal of Speech Communication, 49*, 147–165.

Shklar, J. (1984). *Ordinary vices*. Cambridge, MA.: Harvard University Press.

Shoda, Y., Mischel, W., and Peake, P. K. (1990). Predicting adolescent cognitive and self-regulatory competencies from preschool delay of gratification. *Developmental Psychology, 26*, 978–986.

Shrage, L. (1989). Should feminists oppose prostitution? In R. M. Stewart (Ed.), *Philosophical perspectives on sex and love*. New York: Oxford University Press (1995).

Sidgwick, H. (1966). *Methods of ethics*. New York: Dover.

Sigmon, S. T., and Snyder, C. R. (1993). Looking at oneself in a rose-colored mirror: The role of excuses in the negotiation of a personal reality. In M. Lewis and C. Saarni (Eds.), *Lying and deception in everyday life*. New York: Guilford.

Silver, M., and Sabini, J. (1978a). The perception of envy. *Social Psychology, 41*, 105–117.

Silver, M., and Sabini, J. (1978b). The social construction of envy. *Journal for the Theory of Social Behaviour, 8*, 313–331.

Simpson, J., Campbell, B., and Berscheid, E. (1986). The association between romantic love and marriage: Kephart (1967) twice revisited. *Personality and Social Psychology Bulletin, 12*, 363–372.

Singh, D. (1993). Adaptive significance of waist-to-hip ratio and female physical attractiveness. *Journal of Personality and Social Psychology, 65*, 293–307.

Sircello, G. (1989). *Love and beauty*. Princeton, NJ: Princeton University Press.

Sloman, S. A. (1996). The empirical case for two systems of reasoning. *Psychological Bulletin, 119*, 3–22.

Smilansky, S. (1996). The ethical dangers of ethical sensitivity. *Journal of Applied Philosophy, 13*, 13–20.

Smith, A. (1759). *The theory of moral sentiments*. Indianapolis: Liberty Classics (1982).

Smith, C. A., and Ellsworth, P. C. (1985). Patterns of cognitive appraisal in emotion. *Journal of Personality and Social Psychology, 48*, 813–838.

Smith, C. A., and Ellsworth, P. C. (1987). Patterns of appraisal and emotion related to taking an exam. *Personality and Social Psychology Bulletin, 16*, 210–223.

Smith, C. A., and Kirby, L. D. (forthcoming). Consequences require antecedents: Toward a process model of emotion elicitation. In J. Forgas (Ed.), *Feeling and thinking: The role of affect in social cognition*. New York: Cambridge University Press.

Smith, C. A., and Lazarus, R. S. (1990). Emotion and adaptation. In L. A. Pervin (Ed.), *Handbook of personality: Theory and research*. New York: Guilford.

Smith C. A., and Pope, L. K. (1992). Appraisal and emotion. *Review of Personality and Social Psychology, 13*, 32–62.

Smith C. A., Haynes, K. N., Lazarus, R. S., and Pope, L. K. (1993). In search of the "hot" cognitions: Attributions, appraisals, and their relationship to emotion. *Journal of Personality and Social Psychology, 65*, 916–929.

Smith, R. H. (1991). Envy and the sense of injustice. In P. Salovey (Ed.), *The psychology of jealousy and envy*. New York: Guilford Press.

Smith, R. H., Kim, S. H., and Parrott, W. G. (1988). Envy and jealousy: Semantic problems and experiential distinctions. *Personality and Social Psychology Bulletin, 14*, 401–409.

Smith, R. H., Diener, E., and Wedell, D. H. (1989). Interpersonal and social comparison determinants of happiness: A range-frequency analysis. *Journal of Personality and Social Psychology, 56*, 317–325.

Smith, R. H., Diener, E., and Garonzik, R. (1990). The roles of outcome satisfaction and comparison alternatives in envy. *British Journal of Social Psychology, 29*, 247–255.

Smuts, B. B. (1985). *Sex and friendship in baboons*. New York: Aldine.

Snow, N. E. (1991). Compassion. *American Philosophical Quarterly, 28*, 195–205.

Snow, N. E. (1995). Humility. *Journal of Value Inquiry, 29*, 203–216.

Snyder, C. R. (1994). *The psychology of hope*. New York: Free Press.

Snyder, C. R., and Higgins, R. L. (1988). Excuses: Their effective role in the negotiation of reality. *Psychological Bulletin, 104*, 23–35.

Solomon, R. (1991). The virtue of (erotic) love. In R. C. Solomon and K. M. Higgins (Eds.), *The philosophy of (erotic) love*. Lawrence: University Press of Kansas.

Solomon, R. C. (1976). *The passions*. New York: Doubleday.

Solomon, R. C. (1988). *About love*. New York: Simon & Schuster.

Solomon, R. C. (1990). *A passion for justice: Emotions and the origins of the social contract*. Reading, MA: Addison-Wesley.

Solomon, R. C. (1993). The philosophy of emotions. In M. Lewis and J. M. Haviland (Eds.), *Handbook of emotions*. New York: Guilford Press.

Solomon, R. L., and Corbit, J. D. (1974). An opponent-process theory of motivation. *Psychological Review, 81*, 119–145.

Sonnemans, J., and Frijda, N. H. (1994). The structure of subjective emotional intensity. *Cognition and Emotion, 8*, 329–350.

Spacks, P. M. (1985). *Gossip*. New York: Knopf.

Sprague, J., and Quadagno, D. (1989). Gender and sexual motivation: An exploration of two assumptions. *Journal of Psychology and Human Sexuality, 2*, 57–76.

Spinoza, B. (1677). *Ethics*. In E. Curley (Ed.), *The collected works of Spinoza*. Princeton, NJ: Princeton University Press (1985).

St. Claire, O. (1996). *Unleashing the sex goddess in every woman*. New York: Harmony Books.

Statman, D. (1992). Modesty, pride and realistic self-assessment. *Philosophical Quarterly, 42*, 420–438.

Statman, D. (Ed.) (1993). *Moral luck*. Albany, NY: SUNY Press.

Statman, D. (1994). Doing without mercy. *Southern Journal of Philosophy, 32*, 331–354.

Stearns, C. Z. (1993). Sadness. In M. Lewis and J. M. Haviland (Eds.), *Handbook of emotions*. New York: Guilford Press.

Stein, B. (1987). Fantasy and culture on television. In A. A. Berger (Ed.), *Television in society*. New Brunswick, NJ: Transaction Books.

Stein, N. L., and Jewett, J. L. (1986). A conceptual analysis of the meaning of negative emotions: Implications for a theory of development. In C. Izard and P. B. Read (Eds.), *Measuring emotions in infants and children* (Vol. 2). Cambridge: Cambridge University Press.

Stein, R. (1992). Schadenfreude: A reply to Ben-Ze'ev. *Iyyun, 41*, 83–92.

Stocker, M. (1983). Affectivity and self-concern: The assumed psychology in Aristotle's ethics. *Pacific Philosophical Quarterly, 64*, 211–229.

Stocker, M. (1996). *Valuing emotions.* New York: Cambridge University Press.

Stoddard, L. (1929). *Luck: Your silent partner.* New York: Horace Liveright.

Strauss, M. (1999). *Volition and valuation: A phenomenology of sensational, emotional and conceptual values.* Lanham, Md.: University Press of America.

Stumpf, C. (1899). Über den Begriff der Gemüthsbewegung. *Zeitschrift für Psychologie und Physiologie der Sinnesorgane, 21*, 47–99.

Sully, J. (1892). *The human mind.* London: Longmans, Green.

Suzuki, S. (1970). *Zen mind, Beginner's mind.* New York: Weatherhill.

Sverdlik, S. (1983). The nature of desert. *Southern Journal of Philosophy, 21*, 585–594.

Tangney, J. P. (1990). Assessing individual differences in proneness to shame and guilt. *Journal of Personality and Social Psychology, 59*, 102–111.

Tannen, D. (1990). *You just don't understand.* New York: Ballantine Books.

Taylor, G. (1985). *Pride, shame and guilt.* Oxford: Clarendon.

Taylor, G. (1988). Envy and jealousy: Emotions and vices. *Midwest Studies in Philosophy, 13*, 233–249.

Taylor, R. (1982). *Having love affairs.* Buffalo: Prometheus.

Taylor, R. (1989). The virtue of pride. In J. Donnelly (Ed.), *Reflective wisdom: Richard Taylor on issues that matter.* Buffalo: Prometheus.

Taylor, S. E. (1989). *Positive illusions: Creative self-deception and the healthy mind.* New York: Basic Books.

Taylor, S. E., and Lobel, M. (1989). Social comparison activity under threat: Downward evaluation and upward contacts. *Psychological Review, 96*, 569–575.

Teigen, K. H. (1995). How good is good luck? The role of counterfactual thinking in the perception of lucky and unlucky events. *European Journal of Social Psychology, 25*, 281–302.

Teigen, K. H. (1996). Luck: The art of a near miss. *Scandinavian Journal of Psychology, 37*, 156–171.

Teigen, K. H. (1997). Luck, envy, and gratitude: It could have been different. *Scandinavian Journal of Psychology, 38*, 313–323.

Teigen, K. H. (1998). Hazards mean luck: Counterfactual thinking in reports of dangerous situations and careless behavior. *Scandinavian Journal of Psychology, 39*, 235–248.

Temkin, B., and Yanay, N. (1988). "I shot them with words": An analysis of political hate-letters. *British Journal of Political Science, 18*, 467–483.

Tennov, D. (1979). *Love and limerence.* New York: Stein & Day.

Tesser, A. (1980). Self-esteem maintenance in family dynamics. *Journal of Personality and Social Psychology, 39*, 77–91.

Tesser, A. (1988). Toward a self-evaluation maintenance model of social behavior. In L. Berkowitz (Ed.), *Advances in experimental social psychology.* New York: Academic Press.

Tesser, A., and Campbell, J. (1980). Self-definition: The impact of the relative performance and similarity of others. *Social Psychology Quarterly, 43*, 341–347.

Tesser, A., Millar, M., and Moore, J. (1988). Some affective consequences of social comparison and reflection processes: The pain and pleasure of being close. *Journal of Personality and Social Psychology, 54*, 49–61.

Thalberg, I. (1963). Remorse. *Mind, 72*, 545–555.

Thaler, R. (1980). Towards a positive theory of consumer behavior. *Journal of Economic Behavior and Organization, 1*, 39–60.

Thayer, R. E. (1996). *The origin of everyday moods.* New York: Oxford University Press.

Thibaut, J. W., and Kelley, H. H. (1959). *The social psychology of groups.* New York: Wiley.

Thomas, D. L., and Diener, E. (1990). Memory accuracy in the recall of emotions. *Journal of Personality and Social Psychology, 59*, 291–297.

Thomas, L. (1991a). American slavery and the Holocaust: Their ideologies compared. *Public Affairs Quarterly, 5*, 191–210.

Thomas, L. (1991b). Reasons for loving. In R. C. Solomon and K. M. Higgins (Eds.), *The Philosophy of (erotic) love*. Lawrence: University Press of Kansas.

Thompson, A. P. (1983). Extramarital sex: A review of the research literature. *Journal of Sex Research, 19*, 1–22.

Tocqueville, A. de (1848). *Democracy in America*. New York: Anchor Books (1969).

Tolstoy, L. (1967). *Great short works of Leo Tolstoy*. New York: Harper & Row.

Tomkins, S. (1981). The quest for primary motives: Biography and autobiography of an idea. *Journal of Personality and Social Psychology, 41*, 306–329.

Toufexis, A. (1993). The right chemistry. *Time*, February 15.

Toulmin, S. (1981). The tyranny of principles. *Hastings Center Report 11*, 31–39.

Townsend, J. M., and Levy, G. D. (1990). Effect of potential partners' physical attractiveness and socioeconomic status on sexuality and partner selection. *Archives of Sexual Behavior, 19*, 149–164.

Tuchman, G. (1987). Mass media values. In A. A. Berger (Ed.), *Television in society*. New Brunswick, NJ: Transaction Books.

Tulloch, J. (1990). *Television drama: Agency, audience and myth*. London: Routledge.

Turski, W. G. (1994). *Toward a rationality of emotions*. Athens: Ohio University Press.

Tversky, A., and Kahneman, D. (1981). The framing of decisions and the psychology of choice. *Science, 211*, 453–458.

Tversky, A., and Kahneman, D. (1982). Judgments of and by representativeness. In D. Kahneman, P. Slovic and A. Tversky (Eds.), *Judgment under uncertainty: Heuristics and biases*. Cambridge: Cambridge University Press.

Tversky, A., and Kahneman, D. (1983). Extensional versus intuitive reasoning: The conjunction fallacy in probability judgment. *Psychological Review, 90*, 293–315.

Twambley, P. (1976). Mercy and forgiveness. *Analysis, 36*, 84–90.

Ulanov, A., and Ulanov, B. (1983). *Cinderella and her sisters: The envied and the envying*. Philadelphia: Westminster Press.

Van Evra, J. (1990). *Television and child development*. Hillsdale, NJ: Erlbaum.

Van Reekum, C. M., and Scherer, K. R. (1997). Levels of processing in emotion-antecedent appraisal. In G. Matthews (Ed.), *Cognitive science perspectives on personality and emotion*. Amsterdam: Elsevier.

Van Sommers, P. (1988). *Jealousy*. London: Penguin.

Vangelisti, A. L., and Sprague, R. J. (1998). Guilt and hurt: Similarities, distinctions, and conversational strategies. In P. A. Andersen and L. K. Guerrero (Eds.), *Handbook of communication and emotions*. San Diego: Academic Press.

Veblen, T. (1899). *The theory of the leisure class*. New York: Augustus Kelley (1965).

Veenhoven, R. (1984). *Conditions of happiness*. Dordrecht, Netherlands: Reidel.

Vincent-Buffault, A. (1991). *The history of tears: Sensibility and sentimentality in France*. New York: St. Martin's Press.

Wainwright, W. (1995). *Reason and the heart: A prolegomenon to a critique of passional reason*. Ithaca, NY: Cornell University Press.

Walcot, P. (1978). *Envy and the Greeks*. Warminster, England: Aris & Phillips.

Waley, A. (1938). *The analects of Confucius*. New York: Vintage Books.

Walker, N. (1995). The quiddity of mercy. *Philosophy, 70*, 27–37.

Walsh, W. H. (1970). Pride, shame and responsibility. *Philosophical Quarterly, 20*, 1–13.

Wasserstrom, R. A. (1985). Is adultery immoral? In R. M. Stewart (Ed.), *Philosophical perspectives on sex and love*. New York: Oxford University Press (1995).

Weber, M. (1968). *Economy and society*. New York: Bedminster Press.

Weiner, B. (1985). An attributional theory of achievement motivation and emotion. *Psychological Review, 92*, 548–573.

Weiner, B., Russell, D., and Lerman, D. (1979). The cognitive-emotion process in achievement-related contexts. *Journal of Personality and Social Psychology, 37*, 1211–1220.

Weiner, B., Graham, S., and Chandler, C. C. (1982). Pity, anger, and guilt: An attributional analysis. *Personality and Social Psychological Bulletin, 8*, 226–232.

Weisfeld, G. E. (1980). Social dominance and human motivation. In D. R. Omark, F. F. Strayer and D. G. Freedman (Eds.), *Dominance relations: An ethological view of human conflict and social interaction.* New York: Garland.

White, G. L., and Mullen, P. E. (1989). *Jealousy: Theory, research, and clinical strategies.* New York: Guilford Press.

Whitley, B. E., and Frieze, I. H. (1986). Measuring causal attributions for success and failure: A meta-analysis of the effects of question-wording style. *Basic and Applied Social Psychology, 7,* 35–51.

Whitman, R., and Alexander, J. (1968). On gloating. In C. W. Socarides (Ed.), *The world of emotions.* New York: International University Press (1977).

Wilde, O. (1966). *Complete works of Oscar Wilde.* London: Collins.

Wilkinson, M. (1976). Romantic love: The great equalizer? Sexism in popular music. *Family Coordinator, 25,* 161–166.

Williams, B. (1981). *Moral luck.* Cambridge: Cambridge University Press.

Williams, B. (1993). *Shame and necessity.* Berkeley: University of California Press.

Wilson, J. R. S. (1972). *Emotion and object.* Cambridge: Cambridge University Press.

Wilson, T. D., and Klaaren, K. J. (1992). "Expectation whirls me round": The role of affective expectation in affective experience. *Review of Personality and Social Psychology, 14,* 1–31.

Wintre, M. G., and Vallance, D. D. (1994). A developmental sequence in the comprehension of emotions: Intensity, multiple emotions, and valence. *Developmental Psychology, 30,* 509–514.

Wittgenstein, L. (1967). *Zettel.* Oxford: Basil Blackwell.

Wu, K. M. (1972). Hope and world survival. *Philosophy Forum, 12,* 131–148.

Yanal, R. J. (1994). The paradox of emotion and fiction. *Pacific Philosophical Quarterly, 75,* 54–75.

Yanay, N. (1996). National hatred, female subjectivity, and the boundaries of cultural discourse. *Symbolic Interaction, 19,* 21–36.

Yitzhaki, S., and Lerman, R. I. (1991). Income stratification and income inequality. *Review of Income and Wealth, 37,* 313–329.

Young, R. (1987). Egalitarianism and envy. *Philosophical Studies, 52,* 261–276.

Zajonc, R. B. (1980). Feeling and thinking: Preferences need no inferences. *American Psychologist, 35,* 151–175.

Zebrowitz, L. A., Voinescu, L., and Collins, M. A. (1996). "Wide eyed" and "crooked faced": Determinants of perceived and real honesty across the lifespan. *Personality and Social Psychology Bulletin, 22,* 1258–1269.

Zeelenberg, M., Beattie, J., van der Plight, J., and de Vries, N. K. (1996). Consequences of regret aversion: Effects of expected feedback on risky decision making. *Organizational Behavior and Human Decision Processes, 65,* 148–158.

Zweig, S. (1980). *Ungeduld des Herzens.* Frankfurt: Fischer Taschenbuch.

# Index